The Constitutional Systems of East Asia

Comparative Public Law Treatise

Founded by Giuseppe Franco Ferrari

The Constitutional Systems of East Asia

Mauro Mazza (Ed.)

eleven
international publishing

Published, sold and distributed by Eleven International Publishing
P.O. Box 85576
2508 CG The Hague
The Netherlands
Tel.: +31 70 33 070 33
Fax: +31 70 33 070 30
email: sales@elevenpub.nl
www.elevenpub.com

Sold and distributed in USA and Canada
Independent Publishers Group
814 N. Franklin Street
Chicago, IL 60610, USA
Order Placement: +1 800 888 4741
Fax: +1 312 337 5985
orders@ipgbook.com
www.ipgbook.com

Eleven International Publishing is an imprint of Boom uitgevers Den Haag.

This volume has been published with the contribution of Fondazione Cariplo.
This volume was reviewed through a double-blind peer review procedure.

ISBN 978-94-6236-898-9
ISBN 978-94-6274-985-6 (e-book)

Printed in The Netherlands

Preface

The Comparative Public Law Treatise results from a desire to publish one single study providing a full panorama of comparative public law. Its aim is in fact to offer the reader – including scholars and students as well as the general reader – an overview, a summary and an original presentation of comparative knowledge in the area of public law, including both an account and summary of the various schools of thought as well as also, where possible, the development of original lines of thinking.

Considering the objective of the Treatise it has been decided that it will extend to more than 50 volumes, in order to ensure a detailed analysis of the issues of greatest interest from a comparative perspective. Whilst the project as a whole will be characterised by a cross-systemic approach, it will include particular monographic studies of the most significant legal systems around the world. In doing so, the aim is to give a voice to the two focuses of comparative study, first the science of comparison *stricto sensu*, and secondly the study of foreign legal systems.

In any case, the unifying characteristic of the study is its broad approach. This is not so much, or in any case not only, due to the number of volumes but rather to the choice that, within a globalised world, comparative law must open itself up to the greatest possible number of legal systems. Starting from this premise the monographic studies will seek to analyse many of the legal systems that have traditionally remained on the margins of comparative law studies.

Finally, the choice to use three languages (Italian, English and Spanish) offers a further demonstration of the broad approach of the Treatise. This is the first time that a study of comparative public law has been conveyed at the same time in three languages. The objective is not only to ensure the wide circulation of the study within the international academic community, but above all to promote and favour a more ample dialogue between different legal cultures.

Milan 2018

Giuseppe Franco Ferrari

Table of Contents

Foreword

This volume of the *Comparative Public Law Treatise,* in the main foreign languages, as well as in Italian, aims at presenting to its readers the result of a reflection on the characteristics of the public law systems of East Asia, which have been examined from the perspective of jurists who operate in different university contexts both in Italy and in Asia. In the course of the work, as well as a detailed analysis of the foreign laws studied, investigations were also carried out in relation to both an internal comparison, i.e. among the systems of the East Asia area, as well as an external comparison, that is to say with respect to the public law systems belonging to other legal traditions, mainly the Western legal tradition. The sectors of the systems that have been examined regard the constitutional system, with a separate analysis of the legislative, executive and jurisdictional bodies, and also the forms of political and administrative decentralization, as well as the catalogue of fundamental rights; some references to the relationship between language, law and culture are not missing. In accordance with the broadly prevalent guidelines in international literature in relation to comparative legal methodology (as far as it matters here, of a public law area), both the diachronic and synchronic profiles of the studied national rights have been examined.[1] The overall intent pursued by the authors, with the precious and constant support of prof. Giuseppe Franco Ferrari as director and promoter of the *Treatise of Comparative Public Law,* was that of offering to the international academic community the most up-to-date and in-depth work for the scientific analysis of the systems of constitutional and public law in East Asia.

Although the work is a collective endeavour, Mauro Mazza is the author of the Foreword, Sections 1 and 5 of the Introduction and Chapter 1, except for Section 9 written by Manuel E. Delmestro. Giorgio Fabio Colombo and Andrea Ortolani are the authors of Section 2 of the Introduction and moreover Giorgio Fabio Colombo is the author of Sections 1-4, and 8 of Chapter 2 and Andrea Ortolani is the author of Sections 5-7, and 9 of Chapter 2. Ignazio Castellucci is the author of Section 3 of the Introduction and Chapter 3, except for Sections 2.2, 2.3, 2.7, 2.8 and 4.1 written in collaboration with Andrea Serafino, who is also the author of Section 4 of the Introduction. Laura Sempi is the author of Chapter 4.

---

1 *Cf.* G.F. Ferrari, *Law and History: Some Introductory Remarks*, in *Un giurista di successo. Studi in onore di A. Gambaro*, I, Milano, Giuffrè, 2017, 143 ff.

The editorial coordination and the supervision of the translations of the work into English and Spanish are by Mauro Mazza.

Bergamo-Lecce-Hanoi-Macao-Nagoya-Taipei-Tokyo, June 2019.
Mauro Mazza (coordinator)
Ignazio Castellucci
Giorgio Fabio Colombo
Manuel E. Delmestro
Andrea Ortolani
Laura Sempi
Andrea Serafino

List of Contributors

Introduction	
1	Mauro Mazza
2	Giorgio F. Colombo and Andrea Ortolani
3	Ignazio Castellucci
4	Andrea Serafino
5	Mauro Mazza
Chapter 1	
1.1-1.8	Mauro Mazza
1.9	Manuel E. Delmestro
Chapter 2	
2.1-2.4, 2.8	Giorgio F. Colombo
2.5-2.7, 2.9	Andrea Ortolani
Chapter 3	Ignazio Castellucci
3.2.2, 3.2.3, 3.2.7, 3.2.8, and 3.4.1	Ignazio Castellucci and Andrea Serafino
Chapter 4	Laura Sempi
Translation	Antonietta Luongo

Introduction

1 East Asian Law and the Public Law Institutions of the People's Republic of China

For a long time, the study of East Asia was constructed around widespread stereotypes, according to which, on a substantial level, juridical positions (rights and interests) of a collective rather than individual nature[1] prevail in the legal systems of East Asia. Instead, with regards to the resolution of disputes, conciliatory solutions are favoured, with a worst correlative treatment that is usually reserved for judicial disputes.[2] Hence, it is from this, that a tendential disvalue derives, with respect to literary culture, of the same practice of law, be it exercised by judges or by lawyers or, in any case, by the defending technicians (variously denominated) of private parties.[3]

The cultural – rather than juridical[4] – dividing line between the Western and the Eastern conception of law, both private and public, would therefore be unbridgeable, insofar as, on the one hand, the government of men[5] is favoured in the East, while on the other hand, this latter is not compatible with the Western legal tradition of the *rule of law*.

---

1 Although awareness on individual rights is growing in the People's Republic of China: *see* P. Lorentzen, S. Scoggins, *Understanding China's Rising Rights Consciousness*, in *The China Quarterly*, 2015, 638 ff.

2 On pre-established schemes and Eurocentric prejudices still widespread today in the representations of the East in general and of China in particular, *cf.* A. Crisma, *Come si pensa la Cina? La dimensione storica contro i comparatismi astratti*, in *Inchiesta*, a. XXXXIV, n. 185, July-September 2014, 36 ff., and furthermore, the preceding essay entitled *Fra miti e stereotipi: la costruzione del'immagine occidentale del pensiero cinese*, G. Tamburello (Ed.), in *L'invenzione della Cina* (proceedings of the VIII Conference of the Italian Association of Chinese Studies-AISC, held at the University of Lecce from 26 to 28 April 2001), Galatina, Congedo, 2004, 101 ff. *See also* M. Castelnovi, *La Cina come sogno e come incubo per gli Occidentali*, in *Sulla via del Catai. Riv. sem. sulle relazioni culturali tra Europa e Cina*, VII, n. 9, May 2014 (thematic number *La Cina come sogno e come incubo. Uno sguardo sull'immaginario onirico occidentale*, M. Castelnovi Ed.) 11 ff. For the peculiarities of the comparative public law (applied to Far-East systems), *see* D. Amirante, *Al di là dell'Occidente. Sfide epistemologiche e spunti euristici nella comparazione "verso Oriente"*, in *Dir, pubbl. comp. eur.*, 2015, 1 ff.

3 *See* for all, on the atlas of juridical traditions, H.P. Glenn, *Tradizioni giuridiche nel mondo. La sostenibilità della differenza*, (2010), Italian translation with presentation by S. Ferlito, Bologna, il Mulino, 2011. For the legal professions, there are new interesting openings in China: *see* W.P Alford, K. Winston, W.C. Kirby (Eds.), *Prospects for the Professions in China*, London/New York, Routledge, 2013, where an examination of the (actually rather singular) aspects of liberal professions in an illiberal state. On the Chinese legal profession, *see* J. Chneg, X. Li, *Structural Constraints on Legal Change: Chinese Lawyers in the Interaction Between the State, the Market and Society*, in *Social Sciences in China*, 2013, n. 1, 58 ff.

4 *Cf.* M. Mathien (Ed.), *L'expression de la diversité culturelle. Un enjeu mondial*, preface by J.-C. Mignon, Bruxelles, Bruylant, 2013.

5 From which follows that, in East Asia, there are traditionally "weak law" countries. For Chinese law (and civilization), *see* L. Moccia, *Sguardo storico-comparativo sul 'diritto' in Cina*, in P. Cerami, M. Serio (Eds.), *Scritti di comparazione e storia giuridica*, Torino, Giappichelli, 2011, 28 ff.

In the East Asian societies, the Confucian ideal of harmony[6] is pursued, and even the recent theories,[7] elaborated in the East-Asian context, of the so-called Asian values,[8] indirectly end up confirming the traditional approach by which duties prevail over rights and are more important. As a consequence, collective rights rather than individual rights and personal liberties, are protected as a priority.[9]

This resulting approach (which has connection traits with the study in Western culture of "Orientalism" and "Japanonism"[10]) has been partly modified by recent investigations, which have also highlighted the existence of the not to be overlooked differences between the normative systems of East Asia,[11] especially from a historical perspective. This is due to the fact that, today, the general tendency is that not only of the convergence between the juridical experiences of the East Asia, but also of their progressive approach towards the Western juridical tradition itself,[12] that is to say, to the westernization[13] of East Asian

6 The philosophical and religious traditions of the East Asia have been somewhat "politicized" by the Chinese Communist Party; *see* M. Scarpari, *Ritorno a Confucio. La Cina di oggi fra tradizione e mercato*, Bologna, Il Mulino, 2015.

7 Including, in China, the so-called neoconfucianism: *see* J. Solé-Farràs, *New Confucianism in Twenty-First Century China. The Construction of a Discourse*, London/New York, Routledge, 2014; A. Crisma, *Celebrazioni della memoria e reticenze dell'oblio nella Cina d'oggi: ambivalenze del rapporto con il passato e reinvenzioni creative della tradizione*, in *Inchiesta*, n. 181, July-September 2013, 66 ff.

8 The relative debate developed especially in the nineties of the last century.

9 *See*, however, on the right to life, health, reputation, privacy, etc., in the Chinese-popular system, K. Oliphant, P. Zhang, L. Chen (Eds.), *The Legal Protection of Personality Rights. Chinese and European Perspectives*, Leiden, Brill, 2018.

10 *See*, for (stimulating and) extensive references, C. Goto-Jones, *Magic, Modernity, and Orientalism: Conjuring representations of Asia*, in *Modern Asian Studies*, 2014, 1451 ff.; M.D. Gu, Sinologim. *An Alternative to Orientalism and Postcolonialism*, London/New York, Routledge, 2013.

11 Thus R. Cavalieri did (brilliantly), for example, moving from the consideration of Korean law in *Il diritto coreano ed estremo-orientale in una prospettiva comparativista*, paper presented at the conference *Incontriamo la Corea. Giornate di studio su cultura e società della Corea di ieri e di oggi*, held from 18 to 20 November 2013 at the Cà Foscari University of Venice.

12 Which, however, still appears to be characterized by a (considerable) differentiation between the Anglo-Saxon or *common law* legal tradition and the Euro-continental or *civil law* tradition, as noted by P.G. Monateri, in *Geopolitica del diritto. Genesi, governo e dissoluzione dei corpi politici*, Roma-Bari, Laterza, 2013; therein the author notes that "two forms of the law still stand out in the world and in the West: Anglo-American law, the 'oral law', and continental law, the 'written law'", adding immediately after that: "They are two antithetical forms, which highlight a profound duality of the West" (*see* Preface, especially V).

13 On the "normative weaknesses" of the (current) language of *westernization, see* however, the (well-founded) observations by H. Lau, *The Language of Westernization in Legal Commentary*, in *American Journal of Comparative Law*, 2013, 507 ff., which illustrates "how the language of westernization fails to describe change in Asia", stating that the language of *westernization* "harms the dignity of non-western actors and undermines the global marketplace of ideas" (*cf.* 508). Further on, regarding the so-called *western-centrism*, the author states that: "Colonial ideology considered to be the dynamic center of the world. In this view, the West actively generates new ideas, while the rest of the world waits and receives those ideas passively. This wester-centric understanding of international relations provides alleged justifications for colonial ambitions. Colonists sought to justify Western imperialism by presenting the West as a modernization to the rest of the world. The language of westernization perpetuates this wester-centrism, albeit in milder form than in the colonial era. Recall that the language of westernization emphasizes Western causal factors of

rights as a sign of their unstoppable inclusion in the phenomenon universally known as globalization (economic, political and also juridical).[14]

New horizons, thus, open up to scholars of East Asian law, both with regards to civil,[15] commercial, penal, and procedural law, and in relation to public law institutions, especially with regard to constitutional law.[16] This renewed interest in the juridical dimension of social and political life, on the other hand, has intensely characterized the experience of the People's Republic of China, after the definitive abandonment of the (not so short)

change while obscuring the local. In doing so, it entrenches the notion of the West. Recall also that the language of westernization This again elevates the significance of the West above all else" (*see* 528). With regard to *westernization* and the role of globalization in the Chinese legal system, *see* M. Tomášek, G. Mühlemann (Eds), *Interpretation of Law in China – Roots and Perspectives*, Prague, Charles University in Prague/Karolinum Press, 2011.

14 *See* the scrupulous treatises by G. Ajani, A. Serafino, M. Timoteo (with the collaboration of H. Chen, A. Ortolani, P. Rossi), *Diritto dell'Asia orientale*, Torino, Utet, 2007; R. Cavalieri (Ed.), *Diritto dell'Asia Orientale*, Venezia, Cafoscarina, 2008 (2nd edn., 2019); T. Ruskola, *The East Asian legal tradition*, in M. Bussani, U. Mattei (Eds.), *Comparative Law*, Cambridge, Cambridge University Press, 2012, 257 ff. For recent comparative overviews on the constitutional and administrative law of East Asian countries, *see* A.H.Y. Chen, T. Ginsburg (Eds.), *Public Law in East Asia*, Farnham/Burlington (VT), Ashgate, 2013, and there especially A.H.Y. *Introduction* Chen, *Constitutionalism and Constitutional Change in East and Southeast Asia: A Historical and Comparative Overview*, XV ff.; R. Dixon, T. Ginsburg (Eds), *Comparative Constitutional Law in Asia*, Cheltenham/Northampton (MA), Elgar, 2014. On the legal family of East Asia (China, Japan, Korea and Taiwan) *see* in addition, Wen-Yeu Wang, Yen-Lin Agnes Chiu, *The Defining Characteristics of the Legal Family in East Asia*, in Comparative Law annual, 2013, 205 ff. which highlight the common substratum represented by Confucian philosophy.

15 *Cf.* M. Timothy, *Fare cose con gli emblemi. Termini e categorie del nuovo diritto civile cinese*, in M. Graziadei, B. Pozzo (Eds.), *Categorie e terminologie del diritto nella prospettiva della comparazione*, Milano, Giuffrè, 2015 249 ff.

16 Contemporary China is carefully studied in Italy from the multiple points of view of the social sciences, *i.e.* with regard to the legal, economic, political, demographic and media profiles, as demonstrated for example by the excellent collective work of S. Beretta, L Zhang (eds), *Contemporary China through the Eyes of Italian Experts*, Peking/Beijing, China University of Political Science and Law-CUPL/Zhongguo Zhengfa daxue chubanshe, 2012 (the editors are professors, respectively, at the University's Political Faculty of Pavia and the *East China University of Political Science and Law-ECUPL of Shanghai*). Sinology is now moving away from exoticism and investigations into *chinoiserie* to quickly approach economics and management studies: *cf.* M. Sportelli, *Le nuove frontiere della sinologia*, in *Quaderni asiatici. Riv. di cultura e studi sull'Asia* (published by the Italian-Asian Cultural Centre/CCIA "Guglielmo Scalise" of Milan), n. 100, December 2012, 131 ff.

parenthesis of Maoism, culminating in the excesses[17] of the Cultural Revolution[18] and the so-called juridical nihilism during the decade from 1966 to 1976.

At that time, Chinese law was completely informal and almost completely devoid of written sources; the authorities bitterly fought against the very idea of law in the technical sense. The current situation has, however, radically changed. The formants of the system are in effervescence. Chinese doctrine is today undoubtedly vast, and now also deals with comparative law profiles. Laws and subordinate sources make up the complex mosaic of the Chinese regulatory system. Jurisprudential law is abundant, and the Supreme People's Court, at the top of the judicial system, periodically issues important directive clarifications with the function of a paranormative orientating and guiding of the judges of the lower courts.[19] The teaching of legal subjects is regularly given in numerous Chinese universities,[20] while the number of legal operators is constantly growing: judges and prosecutors number

---

17 There is no lack of those, like the Slovenian philosopher Slavoj Žižek, who still move "in a stubborn and contrary direction", insofar as they believe they have individuated a "kernel of truth" in the Chinese experience of the Cultural Revolution; *cf.* S. Žižek, *In difesa delle cause perse. Materiali per la rivoluzione globale* (2008), Italian translation, Milan, Ponte alle Grazie, 2009, 197 ff., sub 4, *Il terrore rivoluzionario da Robespierre a Mao*. Therein we reads, at 263, that "Mao stepped back from draw all the consequences of the Cultural Revolution, thus the space for the capitalist explosion was opened by this compromise, by Mao's unwillingness to go all the way, from the fact that he did not remain completely faithful to the idea of the Cultural Revolution"; in short, according to the (controversial) philosopher of Ljubljana – the Cultural Revolution failed not because it was "too much", but because it stopped at the level of "too little", and in fact the final lesson that Žižek (paradoxically) gives is the following: "Try again. Fail again. Fail better".

18 At that time it remained somewhat opaque in the West (even among "Pekingologists"): *cf.* C. Boullenois, *La révolution culturelle chinoise sous le regard des français* (1966-1971), Forewod. by M. Bastid-Bruguière, Paris, L'Harmattan, 2013 (which speaks of a "repressive and doctrinal dictatorship"). Previously, *see, e.g.*, F. Ji, *Language and Violence During the Chinese Cultural Revolution*, in the *American Journal of Chinese Studies*, 2004, 93 ff., In the Italian doctrine, *see* the study by G. Crespi Reghizzi, *Diritto cinese e rivoluzione culturale*, in *Riv. dir. civ.*, 1967, II, 300 ff. Among the most significant mottoes of the Cultural Revolution there was "To rebel is justified" (in Chinese *Caofan you li*), a slogan that appeared in the first edition (of 1966) of the Little Red Book (*Mao zhuxi yulu*, in Italian the "Massime del Presidente Mao") from the "*Grande Timoniere*" (*recte*, compiled by the "dolphin" of Mao, Lin Biao, better known in Italy as Lin Piao); remembers it G. Ajani, Caofan you li. *Ribellarsi è giusto*, in R. Cavalieri, G.F. Colombo (Eds.), *Il Massimario. Proverbi annotati di diritto comparato. Liber Amicorum in honour of G. Crespi Reghizzi*, Milano, Giuffrè, 2013, 11 ff., who adds that "Oggi lo slogan conosce una nuova giovinezza, affermandosi su altri, storici, slogans di ribellione prodotti nella Cina maoista (quali 'bombardare il quartier generale', 'non c'è costruzione senza distruzione', 'il rivoluzionario è insieme freccia e bersaglio') e percorre le banlieues parigine in rivolta, i quartieri periferici di Londra; in Italia ha dato voce ai cortei di cittadini ostili all'insediamento delle basi Nato a Vicenza e alla rabbia di Napoli sommersa dai rifiuti e poi, nel mondo, ai movimenti di contrasto alla crisi finanziaria che si ispirano agli 'indignados' spagnoli" (*see* 15).

19 *Cf.* B. Ahl, *Retaining Judicial Professionalism: the New Case Guiding Mechanism of the Supreme People's Court*, on the website of the *Ostasiatisches Seminar – China Studien* of the University of Cologne (chinastudien.phil-fak.uni-koeln.de), on the "*Guiding cases*" (Chinese: *Zhidaoxing anli*) published by the Supreme People's Court in 2011 and 2012, to be used by the lower courts as *decision-making models* in the resolution of similar cases.

20 There are 634 Law Schools; *cf.* A.H.Y. Chen, *China's Long March towards the Rule of Law or China's Turn Against Law ?*, in *Chinese Journal of Comparative Law*, 2016, especially 25 ff.

approximately two hundred thousand and lawyers over two hundred thousand.[21] Within the Chinese Communist Party (CCP) itself, and therefore among its cadres and executives, the percentage of exponents who have attended university law courses is constantly increasing.

If, on the one hand, in private law the tendency towards westernization[22] is spreading uncontested, with partial and limited exceptions for matrimonial, family and succession laws, where the emergence of ancient customary Chinese law can be found, the situation is different with regards public law. Legalization is slower in public law and, above all, it is largely removed from globalization, due to the fact that the People's Republic of China has so far remained a socialist state, or in any case an authoritarian state,[23] which inevitably reflects on the overall structure of constitutional law, administrative institutions, the administration of justice and the protection and, even before, the (restrictive) conception of human rights.[24]

There is no doubt, in any case, that the model implemented in the People's Republic of China is largely that of *civil law*, that is to say of a Roman-Germanic matrix, since the influence of *common law* is essentially confined to certain areas of financial law[25] (as well

21 *See* the data reported in G. Crespi Reghizzi, *Editoriale*, in *Mondo cinese*, n. 145, 2011, 7 ff. In particular, for the magistrates *see* W. Gu, *The Judiciary in Economic and Political Transformation: Quo Vadis Chinese Courts ?*, in *Chinese Journal of Comparative Law*, 2013, 303 ff.

22 And indeed, as G. Ajani observes in *Sistemi giuridici comparati. Lezioni e materiali*, Torino, Giappichelli, 2006, 2nd edn, 15, the People's Republic of China "which maintains the reference to the communist model in its Constitution, can no longer be considered, if one observes the transformation in favour of the market realized in last twenty years within civil and business law, as a 'socialist' model".

23 *See* the classification proposed by M. Mazza, *Stati autoritari*, in G.F. Ferrari (Ed.), *Atlante di diritto pubblico comparato*, Torino, Utet, 2010, 102 ff. The taxonomic scheme has found authoritative confirmation in the thinking of the private law-compartive law scholars: *see* in this regard, G. Crespi Reghizzi, *Introduzione: diritto privato comparato in Italia ieri e oggi*, in the annual of comparative law, 2010, 3 ff., which examines the "double principle of relativity by matter and by historical epoch that governs any classification" (*see* 7 ff., text and nt. 16)

24 There has been talk of a new form of a Chinese socialist-liberal state; *cf.* A. Rinella in L. Pegoraro, A. Rinella, *Sistemi costituzionali comparati*, Torino, Giappichelli, 2017, 76 ff.

25 *See* in this sense, lastly, L. Chen, *Contextualizing legal transplant: China and Hong Kong*, in P.G. Monateri (Ed.), *Methods of Comparative Law*, Cheltenham/Northampton (MA), Elgar, 2012, 192 ff., and before, E.A. Black, G. Bell (Eds.), *Law and Legal Institutions of Asia. Traditions, Adaptations and Innovations*, Cambridge, Cambridge University Press, 2011, where the influences of the three mentalities that make up contemporary Chinese law, namely Confucian tradition, socialist ideology and Westernization, are revealed; H. Piquet, *La Chine au Carrefour des traditions juridiques*, Brussels, Bruylant, 2005; E. Ponti, *La recezione della cultura giuridica occidentale in Cina fra Ottocento e Novecento: il diritto cinese fra continuità e cesura*, in G. De Biasio, A. Foglia, R. Garré, S. Manetti (Eds.), *Un inquieto ricercare. Scritti offerti a P. Caroni*, Bellinzona, Casagrande, 2004, 407 ff. The "*vis attractiva*" of the legal tradition of *civil law* is particularly evident in the codification projects of Chinese civil law; *cf.* M. Huang, *Discussioni e tendenze nel processo di codificazione del diritto civile cinese*, in *Index. Quaderni camerti di studi romanistici – International Survey of Roman Law*, n. 41, 2013, 585 ff.; S. Comeau-Gallimore, *Towards a trans-systemic approach to observing Chinese civil law development*, in *China-EU Law Journal*, 2013, 161 ff.; S. Han, *Civil Law Codification in China: Its Characteristics, Social Functions and Future*, in Wen-Yeu Wang (Ed.), *Codification in East Asia*, Berlin, Springer, 2014 (*Ius Comparatum – Global Studies in Comparative Law*, n. 2), 201 ff.; X. Zhang, *The*

as part of contract law, consumer protection and civil liability[26]). However, the characteristics of the socialist organization of the public authorities remain unchanged (at least in

---

New Round of Civil Law Codification in China, in *University of Bologna Law Review*, 2016, 106 ff.; H. Piquet, *Le droit à la dignité dans le futur Code civil chinois: un critique lucide de problèmes passés et présents*, in *Les Annales du Droit*, 2010, 247 ff.; L. Wang, *The Modernization of Chinese Civil Law over Four Decades*, in *Frontiers of Law in China*, 2019, 39 ff.; Y. Bu (hrsg.), *Die Kodifikation des Zivilgesetzbuches der VR China*, Berlin-Münster, LIT Verlag, 2017; Y. Bu, *Die Kodifikation des chinesischen Zivilgesetzbuches – ausgewählte Fragen, in Zeitschrift für chinesisches Recht*, 2017, 183 ff.; X. Sun, *Die Kodifikation eines Zivilgesetzbuches in China: Einige Probleme mit Blick auf die Systematisiserung und Verwissenschaftlichung der Gesetzgebung, in Zeitschrift für chinesisches Recht*, 2017, 86 ff.; Y. Bu (hrsg.), *Der Besondere Teil der chinesischen Zivilrechtskodifikation. Berichte zum ersten und zweiten offiziellen Entwurf*, Tübingen, Mohr Siebeck, 2019. In recent decades, studies and research into comparative law have intensified in China, also with the aim of promoting the reform of the law of the PRC through the *legal transplant* (without prejudice to the necessary checks on the *transplantability of law*, the latter representing an essential condition for the survival of transplanted laws, in China as elsewhere); *cf.* Z. Liu, J. Su, *Comparative law in China: over 30 years' development and paradigm shift in research*, in *the Chinese Journal of Comparative Law*, 2013, 158 ff.; L. Wang, *Comparative Law Scholarship in China in 2012*, therein, 2013, 365 ff. (The author states that "Comparative legal studies should not merely introduce different legal systems, but it should also pay more attention to the exploration of the underlying elements of different legal systems and the possibilities of legal transplant and conduct in-depth research on the development of the Chinese legal system on the basis of Chinese realities"; thus at 380); *Id.*, *Comparative Law Scholarship in China in 2014, ibid.*, 2015, 390 ff. (according to which, in the period considered, Chinese comparatists examined above all the *rule of law* and globalization); X. Gao, H. Jiang, *Comparative Law Research in China: Facing the Challenges of the 21st Century*, in H. von Senger, L. Heckendorn Urscheler (hrsg.), *Das Recht der Volksrepublik China vor den Herausforderungen des 21. Jahrhunderts*, Zürich, Schulthess, 2016, 47 ff.; S. Wanzhong, *Comparative Law in China: History and Development*, in O. Moréteau, J. Vanderlinden (Eds.), *La structure des systèmes juridiques*, Brussels, Bruylant, 2003, 231 ff.; I. Castellucci, *Comparative Law in Asia*, in Tong Io Cheng, S. Mancuso (Eds.), *New Frontiers of Comparative Law*, Hong Kong, LexisNexis, 2013, 73 ff.; M. Timoteo, L. Wang, *Le classificazioni dei sistemi giuridici dalla prospettiva del nuovo diritto cinese*, in the Annual of comparative law, 2013, 223 ff. The focus in China on Italian law, and even more on Roman law, is significant: *see* L. Zhang, *La diffusione della cultura giuridica italiana in Cina: l'aspetto del modello scientifico italiano*, in S. Lanni, P. Sirena (Eds.), *Il modello giuridico – scientifico e legislativo – italiano fuori dell'Europa*, introduction by R. Sacco, Napoli, Edizioni Scientifiche italiane, 2013, 379 ff.; M. Timoteo, *La circolazione del modello legislativo italiano in Cina*, therein, 393 ff.; A. Fei, *On Promoting the Influence of the Roman Law on the Construction of the Legal System in Contemporary China*, in *China Legal Science*, 2013, 55 ff.; C. Lei, *The revival of Roman Law in China - centered on the formulation of the Chinese Civil Code*, report presented at the conference *Sistema giuridico romanistico e codificazione civile cinese*, held at the State University of Milan on 6 May 2019; L. Zhang, *Estudio del Derecho Romano en China*, in L. Vacca (Ed.), *Nel mondo del diritto romano*, ARISTEC conference (Rome, 10-11 October 2014), Napoli, Jovene, 2017, 311 ff.

26 *See*, in detail, Yun-chien Chang, Wei Shen, Wen-yeu Wang (Eds.), *Private Law in China and Taiwan. Legal and Economic Analyses*, Cambridge, Cambridge University Press, 2018; Y. Bu (Ed.), *Chinese Civil Law*, Baden-Baden, Nomos, 2013; J.S. Mo, *Legal culture and legal transplants – Law of Civil Law and Common Law in Chinese Private Law*, in *ISAIDAT Law Review (Special Issue 1: Legal Culture and Legal Transplants, Reports to the XVIIIth International Congress of Comparative Law*, Washington, DC, 2010, J.A Sánchez Cordero Ed.), 2011, 163 ff.,, especially. 177 ff. (*sub* IV.2, *Common Law Features in Chinese Private Law*); I. Castellucci (Ed,), J. Hao, *Enlarged State Power to Declare Nullity: The Hidden State Interest in the Chinese Contract Law*, in *Journal of Civil Law Studies*, 2014, 147 ff.; C. Eberl-Borges, Y. Su, *Freedom of Contract in Modern Chinese Legal Practice*, in *The George Washington International Law Review*, 2014, 341 ff.; L.A. DiMatteo, L. Chen (Eds.), *Chinese Contract Law. Civil and Common Law Perspectives*, Cambridge, Cambridge University Press, 2018; C. Eberl-Borges, Y. Su, *12 Jahre chinesisches Vertragsgesetz, in Zeitschrift für vergleichende Rechtswissenschaft*, 2012, 125 ff., commenting on the *Contract Law* which came into force

the *law in the books*[27]), with the corollaries of the principle of the unity of state power, the distinction only of functions within the framework of the unified state power, and the clear denial of the opposite principle of separation of powers. Above all, the CCP's central role in the society's development remains,[28] including naturally the tumultuous growth of the so called socialist market economy, whose exact contours escape rigorous classification attempts from the viewpoint of the ordering categories of comparative economic systems. The socialist approach of public law[29] naturally also reverberates in the field of private law,

---

on 1 October 1999, with the clarification that contractual freedom/autonomy is guaranteed in the PRC only by ordinary law (Art. 4 of the *Contract Law*), not by the Constitution, and therefore *contractual freedom* does not represent a fundamental right (for the ancient Chinese law, *see* G. MacCormak, *'Agreement', 'Contract' and 'Debt' in Early Chinese Law*, in *Comparative Legal History*, 2014, 1 ff.); *Consumer Protection. Supervision should be enhanced and customer associations at all levels should play their role*, in *Beijing Review*, 6 May 2019 (www.bjreview.com), on the *E-Commerce Law* (*PRC Electronic Commerce Law*) of 31 August 2018, entered into force on January 1, 2019; S. Sarkar, *Return Rule on E-Commerce Platforms: a Legal Right or a Loophole? Loopholes in e-commerce platforms' return rules are exploited*, in *Beijing Review*, 30 May 2019;; Z. Liao, *The Recent Amendment to China's Consumer Law: An Imperfect Improvement and Proposal for Future Changes*, in *Beijing Law Review*, 2014, 163 ff.; J. Binding, L. Jiang, *Mehr Schutz für Konsumenten – Das revidierte chinesische Verbraucherschutzgesetz tritt in Kraft*, in *Zeitschrift für chinesisches Recht*, 2014, 63 ff.; J. Shi, *La révision de la loi chinoise relative à la protection des intérêts du consommateur*, in *Rev. intern. dr. comp.*, 2015, 225 ff.; F. Panza, J. Hu, *Il nuovo diritto dei consumatori in Cina*, presentation by L. Rossi Carleo, Napoli, Edizioni Scientifiche Italiane, 2016, on the amendments to the *Consumer Protection Act* of 1993 (approved in October 2013 and which entered into force 15 March 2014); J. Hao, *Chinese tort law: Between tradition and transplants*, in M. Bussani, A.J. Sebok (Eds.), *Comparative Tort Law. Global Perspectives*, Cheltenham (UK)-Northampton (MA, USA), Elgar, 2017, 385 ff.; X. Zhang, *Legislation of Tort Liability Law in China*, Berlin, Springer, 2018. N. Thomas, *The Product Liability System in China: Recent Changes and Prospects*, in *Int'l & Comp. L.Q.*, 2014, 775 ff., on the *Tort Liability Law* of 12 December 2009, in force since 1 July 2010; X. Zheng, Z. Liao, *Consumer Law and Practice in China: A Critique on the 20-Year Experience and the Recent Amendment Bill*, in *the International Journal on Consumer Law and Practice*, 2013, 1 ff.; J. Binding, *Consumer Protection Law in the People's Republic of China*, in *the China-EU Law Journal*, 2014, 223 ff. Z. Liao, *The Recent Amendment to China's Consumer Law: An Imperfect Improvement and Proposal for Future Changes*, in the *Beijing Law Review*, 2014, 163 ff.; J. Binding, L. Jiang, *Mehr Schutz für Konsumenten – Das revidierte chinesische Verbraucherschutzgesetz tritt in Kraft*, in *Zeitschrift für chinesisches Recht*, 2014, 63 ff.; J. Shi, *La révision de la loi chinoise relative à la protection des intérêts du consommateur*, in *Rev. intern. dr. comp.*, 2015, 225 ff.; F. Panza, J. Hu, *Il nuovo diritto dei consumatori in Cina*, presentation by L. Rossi Carleo, Napoli, Edizioni Scientifiche Italiane, 2016, on the changes to the *Consumer Protection Act* of 1993 (approved in October 2013 and that entered into force on 15 March 2014); J. Hao, *Chinese Tort Law: Between Tradition and Transplants*, in M. Bussani, A.J. Sebok (Eds.), *Comparative Tort Law. Global Perspectives*, Cheltenham/Northampton (MA), Elgar, 2017, 385 ff.; X. Zhang, *Legislation of Tort Liability Law in China*, Berlin, Springer, 2018.

27 To whose study one should add that of the study of *law in action*, if one wishes to understand the *paper rules*, but also search for *the real rules*, as opportunely recalls S. Cassese, *L'educazione del giurista*, in *Nuova Antologia, Journal of Letters, Sciences and Arts*, January-March 2013, 36 ff.

28 *See* last, on the Chinese People's experience of pro-growth authoritarianism, H. Lai, China's Governance Model. Improvement without Democracy and the Durability of the Party-State, London/New York, Routledge, 2014.

29 On the circulation of public relations models in China, *see* G. Mühlemann, *Chinas Experimente mit westlichen Staatsideen. Eine rechtshistorische und zeitgeschichtliche Untersuchung zur chinesischen Rezeption europäischer Staatsideen*, Zürich, Schulthess, 2006. A complete examination of Chinese public law institutions is now in J.-P. Cabestan, *Le systeme politique chinois. A nouvel équilibre autoritaire*, Paris, Presses de Sciences

paradigmatically demonstrated in the case of land ownership, which is still a public monopoly (of the State or of the territorial communities corresponding to administrative subdivisions).

Ultimately, the Chinese legal system seems to be in a continuous phase of transition, which began in 1978 with the reform policy desired by Deng Xiaoping[30] and China's progressive opening towards the outer world (*the Open Door Policy*[31]). However, it seems difficult to believe that the "forced" coexistence between a socialist model of public law and the juridical private law institutions modelled on the civil law countries (and, in some cases, even the Anglo-Saxon countries) can really resist indefinitely over time. One must however, bear in mind the fact that the CCP is increasingly and insistently presenting itself as the effective guarantor of China's prosperity, in the sense that it is the Party itself that ensures the internal stability of the PRC and its continued rise as power (primarily, economic) worldwide.[32] In a certain sense, it could be argued that the CCP's political legitimacy is no longer based on the dogmas of Marxism-Leninism, albeit with a Chinese coloration, but directly on the impetuous economic growth of China, in accordance with the so-called model of pragmatic authoritarianism.[33] From the point of view of a comparative public law scholar, the real challenge lies in verifying the (possible) compatibility of constitutionalism (understood as the practice of a limited government) with a single-party regime as currently implemented in the People's Republic of China.[34]

Po, 2014 (a work consisting of 710 pages). For an swift introduction to the legal system of the PRC, *see* R. Cavalieri, *Letture di diritto cinese*, Venezia, Cafoscarina, 2015.

30 This was the so-called four modernizations. The era of Reformation and Opening (in Chinese *gaige kaifang*), inaugurated by Deng, can be considered not yet completed. *Cf.* M. Miranda, *La democrazia in Cina: le diverse formulazioni dagli anni '80 a oggi*, Roma, Editrice Orientalia, 2012; *Id., Una via cinese alla democrazia e il 'modello Deng Xiaoping'*, in M. Miranda, A. Spalletta (Eds.), *Il "modello Cina": quadro politico e sviluppo economico*, Roma, L'Asino d'Oro Edizioni, 2011, 54 ff. On the comparative level, *see* K.X. Zhou, S. Rigger, L.T. White III (Eds.), *Democratization in China, Korea and Southeast Asia? Local and National Perspectives,* London/New York, Routledge, 2014.

31 On the historical profiles of the *Open Door Policy, see* B.A. Elleman, *International Competition in China, 1899-1991. The Rise, Fall, and Restoration of the Open Door Policy,* London/New York, Routledge, 2015.

32 *Cf.*, Extensively, S. Trevaskes, E. Nesossi, S. Biddulph, F. Sapio (Eds.), *The Politics of Law and Stability in China*, Cheltenham/Northampton (MA), Elgar, 2014.

33 On Chinese-People's *pro-growth authoritarianism, see* H. Lai, *China's Governance Model. Flexibility and Durability of Pragmatic Authoritarianism*, London/New York, Routledge, 2016; L. Tang, *China's Authoritarian Path to Development. Is Democratization Possible?*, London/New York, Routledge, 2017. Re the relationships between *deregulation, privatization and globalization*, in China, on the one hand, and on the other hand, the enduring *Chinese Communist Party (CCP) rule, see* D. Bray, E. Jeffreys (Eds.), *New Mentalities of Government in China*, London/New York, Routledge, 2016.

34 In this sense, P. Pasquino discusses, *The Enigma of Post-Maoist China*, in *Il Mulino*, a bimonthly journal of culture and politics, 2012, 1085 ff. *See also*, on the most recent trajectories of constitutionalism in China, H. Patapan, *Towards a Cosmopolitan Constitutionalism: On Universalism and Particularism in Chinese Constitutionalism*, in *Chinese Journal of Comparative Law*, 2015, 78 ff.

2 Japanese Constitutional Law: Systemological Considerations

This volume includes a chapter on Japan as one of the systems of East Asia: those encompass, according to a widespread taxonomy, systems such as the People's Republic of China, Korea, Vietnam and, indeed, Japan. This is not incorrect, as this partition is based on common historical features of these countries: the hegemony of the Sino-imperial model, the use or the influence of the Chinese writing, the practice of the Buddhist religion and the adoption of Confucian ideology. However, it is essential to stress some important points to avoid inaccuracies and stereotypes, so frequent in the description of systems defined - in a Eurocentric way - as being "exotic", or "extraordinary".[35]

In this sense, Japan (as will be seen below) is often the "victim" of a very simplistic representation, which unravels via a series of approximations. From a diachronic perspective, in relation to the ancient period, the originality of the Japanese model (compared to the affiliate Chinese model) and the refinement of the medieval and shogunal judicial systems tend to be underestimated. With regard to the modern period, many subscribe to the thesis of a slavish adherence to the European-continental models of the nineteenth century; finally, and more interestingly for the constitutional law scholar, it is believed that the current Constitution is substantially a post-war US imposition, with few or no Japanese features. All these images obviously contain a more or less valid foundation of truth: however, one wishes to offer the reader a more complex and varied framework, aimed at presenting the most up-to-date visions on Japan's constitutional system, in the hope of going beyond an arid "legal orientalism".[36]

It was therefore considered appropriate to start from the protohistory of the Japanese legal system, since the word *kenpo* (Constitution) has been used since the beginning of the seventh century. It is true that the first Japanese codifications, which have shaped the institutional infrastructure of the country since the sixth century, are closely inspired by the Sino-imperial model. Yet some distinctive elements, such as the holiness of the figure of the sovereign, are a distinctive feature which influences can be found even in the modern era. It is also true that in the shogunal period, the rulers did not explicitly focus on private law and on dispute resolution, and yet those components were indispensable for the functioning of the whole legal system.

The first Constitution, in the modern sense of the term, was enacted in 1889, based on the Prussian model, in a period known as the Meiji Restoration. In relation to this era, it is again necessary to address taxonomical issues about Japan as a system of the Far East legal family. In this period Japan assumed the leading role for the entire area in the process

35 E. Örücü, *Comparatists and Extraordinary Places*, in P. Legrand and R. Munday (Eds.), *Comparative Legal Studies: Traditions and Transitions*, Cambridge, Cambridge University Press, 2011.

36 V. Taylor, *Beyond Legal Orientalism*, in V. Taylor (Ed.), *Asian Laws Through Australian Eyes*, Sydney, LBC Information Services, 1997.

of modernization of the law: in a period of about twenty years (1880-1899), Japan in fact equipped itself with a constitution and codes substantially in line with those of Western European countries. In doing this, the country made an enormous effort to translate foreign legal texts into Japanese and create a lexicon that could express in the local language the concepts imported from Western jurisprudence. This lexicon became, in turn, an essential part of the language of scholars and legislators of other nations in the area: the transposition of Western legal concepts into Sino-Japanese characters was in fact an extraordinary achievement, and served as an example to neighbouring countries using a writing system based on Chinese characters.

The rise of nationalism and the Second World War threw the country into a dark age, even from the point of view of institutional development. At the end of the conflict, the Allied occupation led by the United States gave birth to the new Constitution, the most important legal product of this period. The Constitution of Japan has been in force in its original form since 1947. This document, originally drafted by experts appointed by the occupation forces, is the object of great interest by constitutionalists throughout the world, first of all, due to its evident nature of legal transplant (on the success of which the debate is still open today), and for a series of unique features, among which an Emperor who is not sovereign (as sovereignty belongs to the people) but exists as a constitutional organ; or the famous principle of constitutional pacifism, according to which Japan would be prohibited not only to wage war, but also to simply possess an army.

The adoption (or imposition, according to critics) of a Constitutional charter based on the US model, centred on equality and individual rights, helped drastically to remove from the Japanese system the "traditional" elements of Japan's legal culture that prevented the modernization, in the liberal sense, of society. An example of a completely reformed area of law was family law, once based on the patriarchal family, where the protagonist and undisputed *arbiter* of family life was the head of the household, a role that was tipically handed down to the first-born male, to the detriment of the female members of the family and the younger siblings. The American influence should not be underestimated, but it should also be noted that several aspects of the legal system, depicted as authentically Japanese had often been misrepresented or even deliberately distorted or invented for political purposes.[37] For example, in family law, the Meiji codification had operated only a partial and ideologically-oriented recovery of certain previous legislation and customs, presented as authentically Japanese. The rhetoric of a Western constitution aimed at eradicating the local tradition should therefore be read with greater attention and critical sense. Moreover, the reference to the "virtuous ways"[38] of Japanese law prior to its contam-

37 S. Vlastos (Ed.), *Mirror of Modernity: Invented Traditions of Modern Japan*, Berkeley, University of California Press, 1998.

38 A.M. Pardieck, *Virtuous Ways and Beautiful Customs: the Role of Alternative Dispute Resolution in Japan*, in 11 *Temple International & Comparative Law Journal* 31–56 (1997)

ination by European models had been instrumentally used to suppress any possibility of judicial protection of rights during the darker years of nationalism and war.[39] With this, one obviously does not want to argue that the 1947 Constitution fits harmoniously onto the pre-existing substrate. On the contrary: elements of friction are abundant. And yet on the one hand one must be sceptical of explanations based on the myth of the uniqueness of the Japanese people (*nihonjinron*) – and by extension its law, at least *in action* – that has been used to support innumerable stereotypes over the years. On the other hand, another significant datum should be noted, a point which distinguishes Japan from other East Asian countries: unlike recently democratized or post-socialist systems, the Archipelago has had more than a century to "digest" and absorb European concepts of law, far from the neo-Confucian model. Today's Japan is, from the point of view of the legal system, more similar to Germany than to China or Vietnam.[40]

Let us turn to the present day. The drafting of these pages on the constitutional law of Japan comes at a time when the government of Prime Minister Shinzo Abe, in power since December 2012, declares among its priority objectives the reform of the fundamental Charter, to be developed on two levels: a) a reform of Article 9, symbol of a submission that some in Japan never accepted and b) a reform of citizens' rights, seen by some political fringes as an individualistic dystonia in Japanese culture. The political cunning of party leaders resulted in the message concerning constitutional reform as being affirmed in an ambiguous way, and modulated according to the public: constitutional revision, and in particular the modification of Article 9 is a subject on which the majority of Japanese public opinion is still very sensitive. Thus, the ambitions of a part of the political spectrum oriented to a greater international relevance, in particular from the military point of view, were kept, until a few years ago, under control by what was considered an insurmountable obstacle: the principle of the so-called constitutional pacifism. This principle, under attack by proposals for modification and semi-authentic reinterpretations (*see below*), is now more hanging in the balance than ever. The clash on Article 9 however risks distracting attention from the other objectives of reform. A part of the political spectrum (more than of public opinion) is not insensitive to the rhetoric of *Asian values.* Faced with a westernization deemed incompatible with Japanese civilization, one can find in the Japan of the past more or less remote models and values on which to re-found the country. With this in mind, the Liberal Democratic Party has recently made public its intention to revise the part of the Constitution on the rights and duties of citizens, placing an emphasis on duties towards the State and on mutual obligations rather than, as envisaged in the Charter currently in force, on the human rights and individual freedoms distinctive of liberal-demo-

---

39 J.O. Haley, *The Politics of Informal Justice: The Japanese Experience, 1922-1942*, in R.L. Abel (Ed.), *The Politics of Informal Justice*, New York, Academic Press, 1982

40 F.K. Upham, *The Place of Japanese Legal Studies in American Comparative Law*, in 1 *Utah Law Review* 639–656 (1997).

cratic systems. The Constitution resulting from the proposal would change from being a document focusing on the protection of citizens and the limits to the powers of the State, to a text that defines the limits of the rights and freedoms of individuals in order to guarantee the greater well-being of the community. It would therefore be a significant change of perspective. The Japanese Constitution has never undergone changes since its entry into force in 1947 and it is still to be seen whether these attempts will succeed in reshaping it. Nonetheless, to appreciate the current debate, a full understanding of the constitutional system of the Archipelago, its roots and its doctrinal and jurisprudential evolution, is required.

To conclude, on the basis of what is presented in these introductory pages, one might be tempted to ask: does "Far East law" even exist? As stated at the beginning, it is understandable that students and scholars approach the countries featured in this volume together. For educational purposes and as a first approximation, grouping legal systems on the basis of geography is in many respects still the best choice, or simply an unavoidable one. However, we think that after reading this and the other contributions in this volume, the attentive reader might be inclined to answer that question: "Probably not".[41]

3 The Peculiarities of the Institutions of Korean Public Law

The general and also the institutional/juridical history of Korea is heavily marked by its particular geopolitical conditions: the Korean peninsula is located between China and Japan, and is indeed one of the "bridges" between these two Asian powers, through which, for example, Chinese culture and Buddhism transited from the first to the second. The political events in the peninsula and the very survival of the Korean kingdoms have always been linked to their relationships with the Chinese Empire.

Korea is a very ancient nation, historically tending towards isolation, if one excludes the relationship with its Chinese "big brother" (in Confucian terms), which has allowed the relatively undisturbed development of its own national experience, which is characterized by a solid, very homogeneous, distinctly nationalist culture, relatively little known in the West. The traditional Korean social, institutional and legal model combines the Chinese model with local cultural elements; in particular, with Buddhist thinking and with more ancient native traditions, producing a local declination of the Confucianism government that the Koreans characterize as "*daoist law*" – in which, for example, the juridical norm is held in different and probably greater consideration than that which occurs in China, also due to the influence of Buddhist thinking: an only apparent paradox.

41 R. Cavalieri, *Introduzione*, in *Id.* (Ed.), *Diritto dell'Asia Orientale*, Venezia, Cafoscarina, 2008.

In addition to being geographically narrow and often contested between the two largest empires of Asia for its entire history as a unified nation, since the second half of the twentieth century, Korea has also been positioned at the centre of a very delicate geopolitical area, where the areas of influence of four global powers, China, Japan, USSR (subsequently Russia), and United States of America, cross.

Korea is still one of the focal points, and the only still very "hot" and unsolved focal point, of the meeting-clash in the twentieth century between Western liberal-capitalist societies and those of Chinese-type and Asiatic communism/socialism. These focal points are arranged as pearls of a necklace to identify the strategic space of China around its national borders: Korea, Taiwan, Hong Kong and Macao, Indochina and in particular Vietnam, Tibet.

The peninsula is today divided between two states, with the Democratic People's Republic of Korea to the north, and the Republic of Korea to the south of the 38th parallel.

The first is a country almost totally closed to the outside world, which maintains privileged relations with China, and which expresses an authoritarian political model of a socialist, nationalist type, marked by ancestral cultural elements, self-sufficient within the limits of what is possible, founded on Juche ideology (literally: pride, self-confidence) dictated by its founder Kim Il Sung. The country has a political-administrative organization that recalls the Chinese situation in the second half of the 1970s of the twentieth century, with hypothetical trajectories of internal reform and moderate economic opening not unlike that observed in China in the immediate aftermath at the beginning of the era of Deng Xiaoping.

The Republic of Korea of the south on the other hand, is a country that has fully entered into the western orbit after the Second World War, under the wing of the North American military. The first four decades of the country's life were marked by military governments and an economic constitution founded on indigenous and Japanese models – of a type that one can define as corporative, with the phenomenon of *chaebol*, homologous political-economic conglomerations, with some important variations, of Nipponese *zaibatsu*. The last thirty years have witnessed a transition to a country governed by more liberal models, influenced by Western models, characterized by an economy that is certainly still linked to some traditional dynamics but which is also very dynamic and globalized.

In many respects, the opposite of what has been said for Southeast Asia applies to Korea: it is a country characterized, due to its history and its geopolitical location, by various institutions which have not changed much, since its origins to 1910; a compact historical layer, on which only one layer has been recently superimposed, produced by the geopolitical events of greater external powers.

The result is always original and in some sense "extreme": one of the oldest nations in the world, and one of the most stable and isolated kingdoms of the last fifteen centuries, after the end of the Second World War, Korea gave rise to two states, still at war and mutually disowning each other: one country is one of the most "connected" to the world, while the other country is most certainly the most closed in the world.

Even in the very great differences between the two countries, the impression of heterogeneous differences remains clear. Some elements of the long tradition that characterizes the entire peninsula remain perceptible: Korean society is an ethnically homogeneous society, animated by a strong national conscience. It tends to legitimize dynastic forms of government – also via transcendent elements that can be linked both to Buddhism and to the most ancient animist and shamanic traditions – and to consider the military element as a constitutional element and government force of the nation (especially in the north).

The reunification of the peninsula, by peaceful means or not, remains an *issue* in the agenda of the two countries – both equipped with a special Ministry, for example. However, the priority assigned to this reunification at the beginning of the Cold War and maintained until a few years ago seems to have waned for both countries, in this particular historical moment. The political and military stability of the peninsula, with its reflections on the global chessboard, seems to be the main problem to be solved today. After a spike in tension in the second half of 2017, the climate suddenly changed at the beginning of 2018, with the start of a new phase of dialogue between the Koreas, and between the North Country and the United States of America, which it could lead to the end of the Korean war (formally not yet finished) and to the improvement/normalization of the relations between regional and global powers in that area.

Certainly the natural tendency to reunification, in the medium or long term, for an ancient nation, which has been divided in a relatively short time following military activities by foreign powers, cannot be underestimated. The example of Germany in the twentieth century springs to mind, with the reunification led and dominated by the economically stronger part of the country that reabsorbed the weaker part. Among the more Asian examples, but perhaps among the least probable, Vietnam springs to mind, with the communist part of the country that militarily reconquered the part that had fled to the west. There are also examples of Chinese reunification, with the peaceful return of Hong Kong and Macao (and sooner or later of Taiwan, in a Chinese perspective) to the motherland, according to the all-Chinese model of *One Country, Two Systems*.

Unless, of course, something unexpected happens.

4 Public Law of the Countries of Southeast Asia Between Complexity and Pluralism

Southeast Asia, the area located *roughly* east of India, south of China and northwest of Australia, is a vast geographic and geopolitical area, corresponding to a very populous region, ethnically, culturally and politically varied, as well as being economically dynamic:

over an area of roughly half the size of Western Europe, over 600 million people live, with hundreds of languages, cultures, ethnic groups and religions.

The region has always been critical to the world economy, due to its demographic importance, its own riches, and for its position of great transit on the roads of global trade. All of this has also meant that in this area of the world, in addition to the indigenous peoples, there was a more or less stable presence, over the centuries, of merchants, missionaries, pilgrims, soldiers and officials of foreign powers in political expansion.

From this synthesis of well-known, almost banal data, one can immediately guess what the characteristic style of the experiences, organizations and legal systems of the region is: complexity and pluralism[42] – it is also one of the first regions in which both the Arab world and the West has experimented with forms of "legal pluralism *in action*", so to speak, for the purposes of colonial *governance*. And it is also the region in which refined studies have been conducted from an expert-anthropological point of view.

The current societies and political communities of the region are represented by States strongly characterized by the results of their local history, as is obvious.

Alongside the brilliant performance of the economic models of some "tigers", hooked onto the global markets, economic cultural and political structures survive linked to the rich and diverse history of these countries as well as government structures influenced by such a history.

At a macro-descriptive level, one can individuate some great "epochs" and models of law and the institutional organization of Southeast Asia. An appropriate method for our needs is that developed by Rodolfo Sacco and successively used by Marco Guadagni for the study of African law.[43] Africa is a continent that has a lot in common with this region, from a legal point of view – which permits a description of the socio-juridical conceptions and institutions via the metaphor of geological stratifications: stratifications that produce a surface that is often apparently homogeneous but which reveal, by proceeding to the corollaries, a very complex history. The data in our possession depicts Southeast Asia as a region populated since bygone epochs by indigenous peoples, who developed their forms of social organization and chthonic rights, discovered and studied by Arab colonizers – who attributed to these customary rights the Arabic name of *adat* (use), a terminology

42 The literature on pluralism is vast. *See, e.g.*, J. Griffiths, *What is Legal Pluralism?*, in 24 *Journal of Legal Pluralism and Unofficial Law* 1 (1986); S.E. Merry, *Legal Pluralism*, in 22 *Law & Society Review* 869 (1988); S.F. Moore, *Law and Social Change: The Semi-Autonomous Social Field as an Appropriate Subject of Study*, in 7 *Law & Society Review*, 4 (Summer, 1973), 719; M. Chiba, *Legal Pluralism: Towards General Theory through Japanese Legal Culture*, Tokyo, Tokai University Press, 1989; M. Guadagni, *Legal Pluralism*, op cit. For a more recent description of the concept *see* B.Z. Tamanaha, *Understanding Legal Pluralism: Past to Present, Local to Global*, in 30 (2008) Sydney L. Rev. 375 ff.

43 R. Sacco, M. Guadagni, *Il diritto africano*, Torino, Utet, 1996, *passim*; M. Guadagni, *il modello pluralista*, Torino, Giappichelli, *passim*.

still in use today – and once again studied in the last two centuries by Western anthropologists.

Over the centuries, this fundamental juridical layer became overlapped by more complex social and juridical institutions, starting from kingdoms and empires organized according to Hindu (Cambodia and Indochina Islands) or Buddhist (especially in Continental Indochina) models, followed by the arrival probably of colonies of missionaries, starting from the period corresponding more or less to the early Middle Ages. Subsequently, starting from the XIII-fourteenth century, this was followed by the layer of Arab colonial dominions, obviously endowed with law and government apparatus belonging to the Islamic tradition, which the Muslim colonizers coordinated with the traditions found in loco creating a *governance* apparatus based on institutional pluralism, as they had already done in India.

The colonization of the Modern Age (a historical phenomenon from which Thailand alone has been exempted) added further layers to the legal complexity of those countries, linked to Western laws; the geopolitical events of the twentieth century added a socialist legal and institutional layer (Vietnam, Laos) to some countries.

Post-colonial law, produced by the new independent States of the region starting from the twentieth century, often, but not in all cases, in the wake of the law of the last colonial power or hegemon in order of time, adds a further layer of complexity, combining local elements and/or elements transplanted from third-party experiences to the "classical" legal structures of the colonial powers or hegemonic countries. Last in order of time, and very important, is the layer of the so-called. "Global law", increasingly present in economic fields even in countries historically more closed to external experiences (e.g. Myanmar).

In this stratification there is also the very ubiquitous presence in localized areas of lumps or layers of Chinese tradition, associated with the historical and current presence of Chinese communities throughout the region (e.g. in Malaysia and Singapore), which are always prone to implement specific forms of social organization, or the historical influence of the imperial model on the forms of national government (Vietnam).

The Sacco stratigraphic model permits, with simplicity and effectiveness, to account for the complexities that govern environments characterized by a strong legal pluralism. Provided that however, one does not read the stratification as being petrified and immutable, more than a geological formation, the law of this region (in a similar way to that of Africa) resembles, in our opinion,[44] a trifle: an overlap of layers that with time soften, producing mixed layers, between one another, of the original layers, combinations within the layers, surfacing at the surface of the lower layers.

---

44 *See* I. Castellucci, in I. Castellucci – M. Guadagni, *Comparando il diritto africano*, in *Ann. dir. comp.*, 2013, 261.

The juridical pluralism of Southeast Asia is often an "extreme" pluralism, a game and a negotiation between various coexistent and mutually independent normative systems – far beyond the mechanisms of an "institutional pluralism" envisaged by all the state legal systems of the region to include in the system of the state, and within the limits set by it, areas of applicability of different rules of religious or customary origin.

At the base of the societies of South-East Asia, there is a set of cultural values that vary from place to place, as is obvious, but which are based on *core values* of a community matrix; cultural archetypes that embed their roots through all the described layers and up to the chthonic level and often indicated in the sociological, political, juridical debate of the last twenty years or so, altogether, as *Asian values* – differentiating them from the set of fundamental values of Western societies.

ASEAN itself, a regional organization that includes all the states of the region, in various ways, is equipped with "Asian" community and totally consensual functioning mechanisms, different from those of most international organizations, which are normally indicated, not by chance, with the word play "*the Asean way*".

In the current *governance* models of the countries of South-East Asia, one can note the presence of Western and the so-called global models, especially in economic fields, as mentioned; but the presence of the variegated and very rich cultural and religious traditions of the region, both in private law, as well as constitutional and public law and in the forms of institutional organization, is also noticeable: the separation of powers, all linked up at the top, to a single legitimating element normally coinciding with the subject expressing sovereignty, is, at times, incomplete. The religious factor is often an element of unity, even at the constitutional level; a normally legitimizing and co-essential factor with the forms of expression of sovereignty (Thailand, Burma, Laos, Malaysia, Brunei).

At the level of apparatuses, one can also often note the central-social, constitutive and constitutional, almost cosmogonic one could say, role, linked to Hindu or Buddhist traditions – both in relation to religious orders and the army (not so, for example, in the West, where Military apparatus is thought and constitutionalized simply as one of the departments of the government).

At the same time, the political and juridical recognition of the multicultural and multi-religious nature of the respective societies is widespread in the institutions and rules that they produce.

With regards to the "modern" and "technical" law layer, almost always introduced by the colonial powers (with the exception of Thailand), areas of influence of Islamic law can be identified (Malaysia, Singapore, Indonesia, Brunei Darussalaam, and the Philippines); English law (Myanmar, Malaysia, Singapore Brunei), Dutch law (Indonesia), Portuguese law (East Timor), briefly also German and subsequently Australian law in Papua New

Guinea,[45] Spanish and subsequently North American law in the Philippines, in addition to the "global" aspects of law of a North American origin, detectable everywhere.

The legal-institutional experience of Vietnam, Laos and Cambodia, while encountering some of the general characteristics outlined above, is also characterized by the long phase of French colonization, which lasted for almost a century. While French colonial law, or the direct application of French law in some areas of Indochina (such as Cochinchina), have represented a normative and institutional grid in some ways common to the three countries, the influence of the French model has, in fact, been inserted mainly into the regulating of legal relationships between French residents and between the French and the native peoples, permitting the continuance of the normative, traditional, customary and religious rules in the relationships among native people.

The subsequent socialist experience in Laos and Vietnam instead led to a generalized application of the principles of Marxist – Leninist ideology, albeit mediated and interpreted according to the characteristics of the respective societies, so that over time, the concept of socialist legality progressively adapted to local social and cultural circumstances.

The history of post-colonial Cambodia, instead, proves to be different: after the institutional experiences of the Kingdom of Cambodia (from 1947 to 1970) and the Khmer Republic (from 1970 to 1976) the political – institutional and normative system was almost entirely dissolved between 1976 and 1979 following the Khmer Rouge's rise to power and the establishment of the new government of Democratic Cambodia, which ended following the invasion and liberation of the country by Vietnam in 1979. This led to a subsequent prevailing influence of juridical models which were not referable to the local tradition, but which were offered by the numerous international economic organizations that markedly characterized the phase of reconstruction of the institutional and juridical system of Cambodia, especially from 1989 to today, creating a significant discontinuity between the law before 1976 and the current law.

Contributing to further increasing the complexity of the systems of these three countries, is the existence of a significant number of ethnic minorities (54 for Vietnam alone, equal to 15% of the national population) that still today practice their own habits. These habits have been rarely integrated into the national regulatory context, due to also the manifestation, in some cases, of a predominantly oral culture and in any case expressed, even when

45 A country traditionally "assigned" to the Oceánic continent, more than anything else for its recent history connected to that of Australia. From a geographical as well as an anthropic (but long-term) perspective, it seems more sensible to include Papua New Guinea, for our purposes, among the states of Southeast Asia. Doing so, avoids a geographical inconsistency: the island of Papua is divided in half by an artificial border that divides the state of PNG – which would be oceanic – from the province of West Papua, part of Indonesia and certainly thus "assigned to South – East Asia". In fact, the generally available cartography complies with this curious aporia. But often PNG is simply "forgotten" in the classifications, ending up not belonging to any continent.

transcribed, in languages other than the national language (as in the case of Hmong in Vietnam).

The customary element, common to all the countries of Southeast Asia, in some cases has been the object of an attempt at incorporation into the national legislative data; such attempts however do not take into account the natural fluidity of customary law, which is difficult to crystallize into norms within a code, and render such experiments barely incisive with regard to the actual effectiveness and application of the law.

The various legal systems of Southeast Asia, in their complexity and diversity, express some common openness towards law and institutional organization. This openness permits an overall analysis and contributes to guiding the external observer along interpretive lines of the manifestations of law that culminate in the identification of traits, if not exactly common, at least are compatible and non-antagonistic.[46]

5 General Framework and Methodology

As has been observed by authoritative doctrine,[47] the constitutional law of Eastern Asia has common traits and elements of internal differentiation. It is sufficient to think, in this regard, of the different role of judicial power, depending on whether there is a so-called dominant-party or that it is a matter of "dynamic" or "fluid" democracies.[48] The exchange of informations, the dialogue between the constitutionalists of East Asia is, moreover, ever more intense, as well as aimed at the search for similarities and differences between the legal systems.[49]

In the following chapters this methodological indication, that is the study of foreign law in the search for consonance and dissonance between the systems according to the methodological approaches of both intracultural and intercultural comparison,[50] will be taken into account. The chapters are devoted to the examination of national experiences, with the integration of some comparisons.[51] Different relevance will be given to the various national experiences, according to the usual treatment of the constitutional systems of

46 *See* G. Ajani, A. Serafino, M. Timoteo, *Il Diritto dell'Asia Orientale*, in *Trattato di Diritto Comparato*, directed by R. Sacco, Torino, Utet, 2007.

47 *See* R. Dixon, T. Ginsburg (Eds), *Comparative Constitutional Law in Asia*, op. cit. With regard, in particular, to China and Vietnam, *see* H. Fu, J. Gillespie, P. Nicholson, W.E. Partlett (Eds.), *Socialist Law in Socialist East Asia*, Cambridge, Cambridge University Press, 2018.

48 *See* P.J. Yap, *Courts and Democracies in Asia*, Cambridge, Cambridge University Press, 2017.

49 As demonstrated for example by the recent institution, which took place in Bangkok in 2017, of the Association for asian constitutional studies (AACS).

50 *Cf.* R. Scarciglia, *Metodi e comparazione giuridica*, Milanofiori Assago, Wolters Kluwer, 2016, 58 ff.

51 Recently, on the different national approaches and related issues concerning fundamental rights, *see* the *Special Issue on Asian constitutional Law*, in *International Journal of Constitutional Law*, 2018, No. 2.

East Asia and aiming to give a fresh contribution to the scholarship on Asian constitutional comparative law, as well as providing useful materials for the inquiry into this area.

1 China

1.1 Evolutionary Lines of Public Law Institutions in the People's Republic of China

1.1.1 *The Historical Events of Constitutionalism in China: The Joint Program of the Chinese People's Political – Consultative Conference*

With the proclamation of the People's Republic of China (PRC) in 1949,[1] the Chinese Communist Party (CCP[2]) won a definitive victory over the Nationalist Party, with the latter abandoning mainland China to take refuge on the island of Taiwan.[3] And indeed,

1 Most recently, authoritatively, G. Samarani, *La svolta del 1949: continuità e discontinuità storiche e storiografiche, La svolta del 1949 in Cina. Radici storiche e sviluppi politici tra continuità e discontinuità*, in M. Abbiati, F. Greselin (Eds.), *Il liuto e i libri. Studi in onore di M. Sabattini*, Venezia, Edizioni Cà Foscari, 2014 (*Sinica venetiana*, collection editied by T. Lippiello and Y. Chen, n. 1), 777 ff.

2 The hegemonic position of the CCP is crucial in configuring the unique form of state of the PRC, which has recently been defined as a *'hard' neo-communist regime*: *cf.* T. Tudoroiu, *The Neo-Communist Regime of Present-Day China*, in *Journal of Chinese Political Science*, 2011, 407 ff. On the role of the CCP (ie the Chinese "party-state") and, in particular, its central committee, *see*, in addition to R. McGregor, *The Party: The Secret World of China's Communist Rulers*, London, Allen Lane, 2010, which is probably the most penetrating and illuminating portrait of the post-Mao Communist Party, Z. Bo, *China's Elite Politics: Governance and Democratization*, Singapore, World Scientific, 2010; L.C.s Backer, *Party, People, Government and State: On Constitutional Values and the Legitimacy of the Chinese State-Party Rule of Law System*, in *Boston University International Law Journal*, 2012, 331 ff.; X. He, *The Party's Leadership as a Living Constitution in China*, in the *Hong Kong Law Journal*, 2012, 73 ff., and in T. Ginsburg, A. Simpser (Eds.), *Constitutions in the Authoritarian Regimes*, New York, Cambridge University Press, 2014, 245 ff.; E.X. Li, *The Life of the Party. The Post-Democratic Future Begins in China*, in *Foreign Affairs*, January-February 2013, 34 ff.; Y. Zheng, *China in 2012. Troubled Elite, Frustrated Society*, in the *Asian Survey*, 2013, 162 ff.

3 The following discussion does not deal with the legal-constitutional system of nationalist China, currently in force in the Presidential Republic of Formosa, that is to say in the territory of the other China represented by the "rebel sister Taiwan", as defined by R. Cavalieri, *La legge e il rito. Lineamenti di storia del diritto cinese*, Milano, Angeli, 1999 (Centro studi per i popoli extraeuropei «Cesare Bonacossa» of the University of Pavia, *Coll. storica*, n. 15), 215. On the Legal Institutions of *Guomindang* (GMD), the name of the Nationalist Party that created a single party dictatorship in the part of China controlled by the Government of Nanjing (1927-1937) and then transmigrated under the Chiang Kai-shek leadership beyond the Strait of Formosa, *see* G. Crespi Reghizzi, *Il periodo nazionalista nella storia del diritto cinese*, in *Quad. fiorent.*, 1986, 551 ff., and moreover, I. González Inchaurraga, *Derecho chino*. Cizur Menor (Navarra), 2015, 113 ff.; S. Graziani, *Alcune riflessioni sulla nascita e sull'evoluzione del nazionalismo cinese moderno*, in *Nuova Secondaria*, a. XXXV, 2017, n. 1, 29 ff. (from a political point of view). For a comparison between the constitutional law of the People's Republic of China and that of Taiwan (as well as Hong Kong), *see* A.H.Y. Chen, *Constitutions and Values in Three Chinese Societies*, D. Davis, A. Richter, C. Saunders (Eds.), *An Inquiry into the Existence of Global Values, Through the Lens of Comparative Constitutional Law*, Oxford, Hart, 2015, 119 ff. On Taiwan's legal and political status in international law *see* more recently, F. Chiang, *The One-China Policy. State, Sovereignty, and Taiwan's International Legal Status*, Amsterdam, Elsevier, 2017.

as was stated in the Chinese legal-philosophical literature[4] (just before the eighteenth Congress of the Party, mentioned above), "In China, Marxism is considered not only a historical science, but also the practical ideology of the proletariat, or rather, the theoretical basis of the Chinese Communist Party",[5] which appears to be one of the few surviving "party-states" in the (now) post-communist world.[6]

The year 1949 also saw the adoption of the provisional Constitution, denominated Joint (or Common) Program (in Chinese: *Gangling*), that was approved by the People's Political-Consultative Conference (or Assembly) of the Chinese people (CPPCC).[7]

---

4 *Cf.* Hu Daping, *Il dibattito cinese su Marx*, R. Fineschi, T. Redolfi Riva, G. Sgrò (Eds.), *Karl Marx 2013*, Special number of *Il Ponte, May-June* 2013, 52 ff. (*see* the quoted passage at 52, the author is a member of the CCP and a professor of "History of Marxist Philosophy" at Nanjing University-NJU/NU, cin. 南京大学).

5 The Western reflection on the CCP's ideology is expressed, for example, in the interesting project entitled *Ideologischer Wandel und Regimelegitimität in China*, whose implementation was entrusted by the *Bundesministerium für Bildung und Forschung* (BMBF), for the period 2010-2016, to the researchers of the *Institut für Asien-Studien* (IAS) of the *German Institute of Global and Area Studies Leibniz-Institut für Global und Regional Studien* (GIGA) of Hamburg.

6 Highlights it, in the perspective of the Sino-Vietnamese comparison, B. Womack, *Moderniser le parti-Etat en Chine et au Vietnam*, in *Rev. internationale de politique comparée*, 2011, n. 1, 69 ff.

7 On the historical development of Chinese constitutionalism, *see* L. Lanciotti, *Storia ed istituzioni politiche della Cina: 1644-1949/appunti dalle lezioni tenute dal prof. L. Lanciotti nell'anno accademico 1970-71*, Venezia, Cafoscarina, 1971; P. Corradini, *L'evoluzione politica della Cina moderna: dall'Impero alla Repubblica popolare*, in *Cina*, n. 11, 1974, 7 ff.; M. Sabattini, *La rivoluzione del 1911 e la questione costituzionale: alcune note introduttive*, *ivi*, n. 11, 1974, 17 ff.; F. de Napoli, *I tentativi di riforme costituzionali alla fine dell'Impero cinese*, *ibidem*, n. 14, 1978, 53 ff.; E. Esposito Martino, *Teorie dello Stato in Cina e in Germania all'inizio del secolo*, in *Mondo cinese*, n. 86, 1994, 31 ff.; R. Cavalieri, *La legge e il rito. Lineamenti di storia del diritto cinese*, op cit.; Id., *Il diritto nella Cina socialista e postsocialista*, in M. Scarpari (Ed.), *La Cina*, III, *Verso la modernità* (G. Samarani and M. Scarpari Eds.), Torino, Einaudi, 2009, 443 ff.; L. Moccia (Ed.), *Profili emergenti del sistema giuridico cinese*, Roma, Philos, 1999, 87 ff.; Lin Feng, *La storia moderna del diritto costituzionale cinese*, in P. Costa, D. Zolo (Ed.), *Lo Stato di diritto. Storia, teoria, critica*, Milano, Feltrinelli, 2002, 776 ff.; Ding Mei, *Introduzione al diritto cinese contemporaneo*, in L. Formichella, G. Terracina, E. Toti (Ed.), *Diritto cinese e sistema giuridico romanistico. Contributi*, Torino, Giappichelli, 2005, 101 ff.; F. Ferlanti, *Rivoluzione e amministrazione: la genesi dello stato comunista (1927-1934)*, in M. Scarpari, T. Lippiello (Eds.), *Caro Maestro... Scritti in onore di L. Lanciotti per l'ottantesimo compleanno*, Venezia, Cafoscarina, 2005, 519 ff.; F.R. Antonelli, *Il contributo dei* Taiping *alla modernizzazione del sistema giuridico cinese*, *ivi*, 97 ff.; M. Mazza, *Lineamenti di diritto costituzionale cinese*, Milano, Giuffrè, 2006; J. Luther, *Percezioni europee della storia costituzionale cinese*, in G. Ajani, J. Luther (Eds.), *Modelli giuridici europei nella Cina contemporanea*, Napoli, Jovene, 2009, 69 ff.; G. Taiani, *Legittimazione e limiti degli ordinamenti giuridici: l'ordinamento giuridico in Cina tra tradizione e riforme*, in G.L. Falchi, A. Iaccarino (Eds.), *Legittimazione e limiti degli ordinamenti giuridici*, Città del Vaticano, Lateran University Press, 2012, 749 ff.; R. Heuser, *Gegenwärtige Lage und Entwicklungsrichtung des chinesischen Rechtssystems. Eine Skizze*, in *Verfassung und Recht in Übersee. Law and Politics in Africa, Asia and Latin America*, 2005, 137 ff.; H.A. Steiner, *Constitutionalism in Communist China*, in *Am. Pol. Sci. Rev.*, 1955, 1 ff.; A. Blaustein, *Fundamental Legal Documents of Communist China*, South Hackensack (New Jersey), Rothman, 1962; D.N. Rowe, *RPC's Constitutions and the Philosophy of Constitutionalism*, in *Issues and Studies* (journal edit. by Institute of International Relations-IIR della National Chengchi University-NCCU of Taipei), 1975, 2 ff.; W.T. de Bary, *The "Constitutional Tradition" in China*, in *Journal of Chinese Law*, 1995, 7 ff.; Zhu Guobin, *Constitutional Law*, in Wang Chenguang, Zhang Xianchu (Eds.), *Introduction to Chinese Law*, Hong Kong, Sweet and Maxwell Asia, 1997, 31 ff.; Id., *Constitutional Law and State Structure*, in Wang Guiguo, J. Mo (Eds.),

The special conditions of the country, in which the supremacy of the Communists led by Mao Zedong had just been established, discouraged, in the initial phase, the calling for general political elections for the formation of a National People's Congress (Parliament). Instead, a political and advisory Conference was set up, an expression of the single democratic Front of the Chinese people, whose 662 members[8] were directly designated by the CCP, from among the representatives of the democratic parties,[9] the popular, trade union and mass organizations, progressive associations,[10] as well as representatives of national ethnic minorities and the delegates of the Chinese communities abroad, supplemented by various democratic and intellectual personalities, free from rigid political party affiliations, all of which, coordinated and placed under the supervision of the Communist Party. Mao affirmed, at the opening of the work of the Political-Consultative Conference on 21 September 1949, that it was destined to manifest and implement the common, unified and indivisible will of the Chinese people. On 30 September, the Conference adopted the Joint Program as a normative document of constitutional rank. Thus, the constitutional

---

Chinese Law, London, Kluwer Law International, 1999, 23 ff.; X. Ma, *A reflection on the history of Chinese constitutionalism of last century*, in *Frontiers of Law in China*, 2007, 44 ff.; Q. Zhang, *The Constitution of China. A Contextual Analysis*, Oxford, Hart, 2012; Siao King-Fang, *Les Conceptions Fondamentales du Droit Public dans la Chine antique*, Paris, Sirey, 1940; Kong Chin Tsong, *La Constitution des Cinq Pouvoirs. Théorie-Application. Etude sur une doctrine nouvelle du Droit public chinois et les Institutions politiques de la Chine moderne*, Paris, Librairie des sciences politiques et sociales M. Rivière, 1932; S. Tcheng, *Le mouvement constitutionnel en Chine. Étude de droit comparé*, Paris, Sirey, 1925; L. Paltemaa, J.A. Vuori, *Kiinan kansantasavallan historia* [*History of the People's Republic of China*], Helsinki, Gaudeamus (Helsinki University Press), 2012 (text in Finnish). For Chinese comparative (constitutional) law studies, *see* Sun Wanzhong, *Comparative Law in China: History and Development*, in O. Moréteau. J. Vanderlinden (law), *La structure des systèmes juridiques. XVI Congrès de l'Académie internationale de droit comparé* (Brisbane, 14/20-7-2002). *Collection des rapports*, Brussels, Bruylant, 2003, 231 ff.; A. W. Conner, *The Comparative Law School of China*, in C.S. Hsu (Ed.), *Understanding China's Legal System. Essays in Honor of J.A. Cohen*, New York, New York University Press, 2003, 210 ff.

8 As recalled by F. Coccia, *L'ordinamento costituzionale della Cina popolare* (1965) in Id., *Sulla Cina (1958-1997)*, G. Mantici, P. Paderni, V. Varriano (Eds.), Napoli, Istituto Universitario Orientale, 1998 (Dipartimento di studi asiatici, *Series Minor*, LV), 67 ff.

9 In particular, the Revolutionary Democratic League and the *Guomindang* (the latter originated from a split in the Nationalist Party – *Guomindang*); *cf.* P. Corradini, *Riforme costituzionali*, in *Mondo cinese*, n. 100, 1999, 13 ff. For a historical profile of the Chinese democratic parties (*minzhu dangpai*), subordinated in full to the CCP of which they constitute non-antagonist satellites with respect to the hegemonic party, v. M. Siddivò, *Il rapporto tra il Partito Comunista e i Partiti Democratici nella Rpc*, in *Mondo cinese*, n. 61, 1988, 31 ff. In the perspective of an (albeit cautious but) progressive reinforcement of the role of these minor political formations, for over fifty years simple accessories of the political system with aesthetic functions (the Chinese refer to them with the expression *hua bing*, which literally means "flower vase"), *cf.* A. Lavagnino, *I partiti democratici fanno sentire la propria voce*, in *Mondo cinese*, n. 118, 2004, 66 ff. However, according to C. Bianchi, *Continente Cina*, Como-Pavia, Ibis, 2014, 40, the eight small legal democratic parties (*i.e.* the "flower vases"), whose leaders are sometimes important academics, "do not produce new ideas in the political field".

10 For the regulation of freedom of association in the PRC, *see* S. Woodman, *Quelle liberté d'association en Chine? La promotion des organisations à but non lucratif est concomitante d'une restriction de la liberté d'association*, in *Perspectives chinoises*, n. 51, 1999, 17 ff.

law of the People's Republic was born, with prudence baptized of the "new democracy",[11] anticipating the truly socialist phase of the Chinese experience.

The Joint Program, approved as stated by the Political-Consultative Conference and, therefore, by an institutional subject different from the People's Congress which, on the basis of the Marxist theory of public law, is placed at the top of the pyramidal system of the organs of state power, can be considered as a provisional Constitution only in fact, in the sense that it had the function of a Constitutional Charter despite not having the corresponding legal-formal value.

In terms of content, the Joint Program included references and principles of both a political-ideological and a constitutional nature. It was structured in seventy articles, collected in seven chapters, preceded by a Preamble.

The purpose of the document of constitutional importance was to affirm and legitimize the creation of the People's Republic of China, founded on the democratic dictatorship of the people.[12] The rights connected to the exercise of state power were recognized only to the people as a political entity, not to individual citizens. In order to exercise state power, Assemblies and People's Governments were constituted at various territorial levels, without any clarification regarding either the allocation of duties, functions and competences between the assembly and governing bodies or the relations between them, with an evident and radical non-recognition of the Western doctrine of the separation (*id est*, tri-partition) of powers.

In detail, the first section proclaimed the general principles on the organization and functioning of the state, contemplating the fundamental rights and duties of citizens, the constitutional position of the armed forces, the condition of national ethnic minorities and the directives of foreign policy.

---

11 On the concept of China's new democracy, posed by Mao Zedong Thinking as an ideological support of the Joint Program, *see* P. Corradini, *I Tre Principi del Popolo di Sun Yat-sen e la nuova democrazia di Mao Zedong*, in *Mondo cinese*, n. 57, 1987, 7 ff. With regards to the historical and political thought of Sun Yat-sen (Sun Yixian Cantonese pronunciation of Sun Yixian, more known in China as Sun Zhongshan), a leading member of revolutionary democratic nationalism in China, *see* Sun Yat-sen, *I Tre principî del popolo*, Introduction by E. Collotti Pischel, Torino, Einaudi, 1976. For an original interpretation of the Sunism in terms of quasi-political federalism, *cf.* G. de Cure, F. Patrikeeff, *Sun Yat-sen and a United States of China?*, in *Asian Profile*, 2005, 319 ff. On the political action of Sun and on the political theory of the "Three Principles of the People" (*San min chu-i*), *see* also, extensively, L. Lanciotti, P. Corradini (Eds.), *Atti del Convegno Nazionale commemorativo del 50° Anniversario della morte del Dr. Sun Yat-sen* (Rome, 12 and 13 December 1975) in *China*, n. 12, 1975, 7-295, and Tung Pi-wu, *Il ruolo di Sun Yat-sen nella rivoluzione del 1911*, in *La Cina d'oggi* (journal editied by *Centro per lo sviluppo delle relazioni con la Cina* in Rome), December 1961, 11 ff.; B. Zoratto, *Sun Yat-sen il rivoluzionario. Vita ed opera del fondatore della Cina libera*, pref. by A.J. Gregor, Palermo, Thule-Romano Editore Books, 1987; A.J. Gregor, M. Hsia Chang, *Marxism, Sun Yat-sen, and the Concept of "Imperialism"*, in *Pacific Affairs (An International Review of Asia and the Pacific)*, 1982, 54 ff.

12 For a Western evaluation of the Chinese demoproletary constitutional model, *cf.* F. Münzel, *Eine Verfassung der Proletarischen Diktatur*, in *WGO-Monatshefte für Osteuropäisches Recht*, 1974, 243 ff.

The second chapter concerned the institutional set-up of the organs of supreme and local state power. In correspondence with each of the territorial levels, an elective Assembly and popular government units were envisaged, up to reaching the superior organs of state power represented by the National People's Congress (NPC), the single-chamber parliament of the PRC, and by the Central People's Government. In the intervals between the sessions of the NPC, legislative functions were carried out by its Standing Committee, called the Central People's Government. The tasks assigned by the Joint Program to the People's Political-Consultative Conference, and specifically to its *plenum*, included the approval in general of legislative norms up to the convocation of the first National Congress following general elections and in particular the issue of the special law on the People's Government, having also to provide for the appointment of the members of the Council of the Central People's Government. Even the functions of the local popular Assemblies, up to the carrying out of the related popular consultations, were temporarily transferred to special organs formed in such a way as to ensure adequate representation to the various sectors of Chinese society.

The third section governed the *status* of the armed forces and the public safety force, establishing that the latter constituted a militia placed alongside the People's Liberation Army, and both being under the leadership of the People's Revolutionary Military Council.

The fourth section was dedicated to economic relations. It provided for rules on the nationalization of private companies, the promotion and consolidation of the cooperative sector, land redistribution and land reform.

Education, culture, information and press freedom were dealt with in Section 5, where measures were also taken in favour of scientific research, social sciences, art and literature and, more generally, to raise the "moral level" of society.

The Sixth and Seventh sections concluded the Joint Program, respectively: a) the protection and enhancement of national ethnic communities, divided into fifty-six different ethno-cultural and linguistic groups,[13] which were placed on an equal level, to be realized also via the creation of forms of regional autonomy; and b) the fundamental principles of foreign policy, with rules on the legal protection of both Chinese citizens abroad and foreigners in China, ensuring in the PRC, also the right of political asylum for non-citizens who are persecuted abroad due to their carrying out actions of a revolutionary nature.

13 Among them a place of absolute numerical prevalence was represented by the *Han* ethnic group, with 93% of the total population.

1.1.2 The 1954 Constitution, a Superprimary Regulatory Act Based on the Institutional Set Up of the People's Republic of China

The construction of the new Chinese democracy on the basis of the 1949 Joint Program prompted the Chinese leaders to lay the legal foundations for the transition to socialism, via the creation of the Constitutional Commission on 13 January 1953, followed by the adoption of the Constitution (Chinese: *Xianfa*) of the PRC, 20 September 1954.[14] The obvious model of this constitutional text was represented by the "Stalinist" Soviet Constitution of 1936,[15] both being aimed at creating a socialist society prodromal to the advent of communism, according to the Marx-Engelsian theory of law and the State, as well as Leninist political practices, reinterpreted with Chinese characteristics.[16]

14 *Cf.* H. Jensen, *Die Verfassung der Volksrepublik China mit besonderer Berücksichtigung der Verfassungsgrundsätze und ihrer Anwendung in der Verfassungswirklichkeit*, Marburg, Rechts- und Staatswissenschaftlichen Fakultät der Philipps-Universität zu Marburg, 1964; F.W. Houn, *Communist China's New Constitution*, in *The Western Political Quarterly*, 1955, 199 ff.; Hsia Tao-tai, *The Constitution of Red China*, in *American Journal of Comparative Law*, 1955, 425 ff.; Tsien Tche-hao, *La République populaire de Chine. Droit Constitutionnel et Institutions*, Foreword by A. Tunc e M. Lesage, Paris, LGDJ, 1970.

15 The difference is remarkable, however, between the form of state, federal in the case of the former Soviet Union and unitary for the People's Republic of China. It should also be noted that in the Soviet model the Supreme Soviet (Federal Parliament) was bicameral, whereas the People's National Assembly of China had a unicameral structure, and that the Soviet Constitution of 1936 did not include the figure of the Head of State, while the Charter Constitutionalism of 1954 placed at the top of the state apparatus the President of the Republic elected by the NPC. With regards to the observation that "it is out of the question that the 1954 constitution was intended to be a copy of the Stalinist constitution of 1936", *see* G. Crespi Reghizzi, *Lo studio del sistema giuridico cinese contemporaneo*, in *L'Est. Riv. trim. di studi sui Paesi dell'Est*, 1967, n. 3, especially 193, where the author adds that "the Chinese constitution was a" socialist type "constitution; citizens' freedoms are equivalent to those of the Soviet citizen; the constitutional bodies follow the Soviet model; the structure and form of constitution is practically identical".

16 On the peculiarities of Chinese Marxism, that is, on the signification of Marxism, *cf.* F. Avanzini, *La ricezione del marxismo in Cina*, in *Mondo cinese*, n. 47, 1984, 9 ff.; M. Sabattini, *L'introduzione del marxismo in Cina*, in *Cina*, n. 16, 1980, 9 ff.; D. Coccopalmerio, *Lineamenti del marxismo-leninismo in Cina*, in *Mondo cinese*, n. 1, 1973, 66 ff.; U. Spirito, *Comunismo cinese e libertà*, in *La Cina d'oggi*, gennaio 1961, 4 ff. *Amplius*, E. Collotti Pischel, *Le origini ideologiche della rivoluzione cinese*, Torino, Einaudi, 1979, 2ª edn; R. Pisu, *Le cause della rivoluzione cinese*, Milano, ISEDI, 1977; F. Schurmann, *Ideologia, organizzazione e società in Cina. Dalla Liberazione alla Rivoluzione culturale*, (1968, 2ª Ed.), Italian translation, Milano, il Saggiatore, 1972; B. Brugger, D. Kelly, *Chinese Marxism in the Post-Mao Era*, Stanford, Stanford University Press, 1990. Re the foundations of the Maoist theory of transition to socialism, *see* also D. Mamo Tchou, *Alle radici del maoismo*, in *Mondo cinese*, n. 21, 1978, 39 ff.; F. Fejstö, *Il pensiero di Mao e la rivoluzione culturale*, in *L'Est (Riv. trim. di studi sui Paesi dell'Est)*, 1972, n. 1, 33 ff.; A. Arndt, *Recht und revolutionäre Politik – Überlegungen zur systematischen Einheit der politischen Theorie Mao Zedongs*, in K. Wegmann, E. Franke, M. Klein (hrsg.), *Studien zum chinesischen Recht*, II, Bochum, Brockmeyer, 1980, 37 ff. On Chinese Marxist moralism, *see* S.R. Schram, *Ideology and Policy in China Since the Third Plenum, 1978-84*, London, Contemporary China Institute of the School of Oriental and African Studies (SOAS) at the University of London, 1984 (*Research Notes and Studies*, n. 6), especially 30 ff.; a thorough examination of the political-ideological data of national-communism in China, considered as the essence of Maoism, is found in Masset, *L'Empereur Mao. Essai sur le maoïsme*, Paris, Lethielleux, 1979. For a comparison with the Russian-Soviet experience *cf.* D. Losurdo, *La dialettica della rivoluzione in Russia e in Cina. Un'analisi comparata*, in *Marxismo oggi (Riv. quad. di cultura e politica)*, 2002, n. 1, 35 ff.; U. Spirito, *Comunismo russo e comunismo cinese*, Firenze,

A commission was established in 1953, presided by Mao Zedong, with the task of preparing the new Constitution project. In March of that year, the Commission approved the text of the project, acknowledging the text previously approved by the CCP Central Committee. This was followed by an extensive popular consultation on the project authorized by the Commission, with the sending of proposals and opinions by both citizens and local people's congresses (LPCs), this latter as peripheral institutions of the State, and bodies exercising power political at every level.[17] The first session of the first NPC finally adopted in Beijing, by unanimous vote,[18] the Constitutional Charter on 20 September 1954, in the resulting text following the amendments approved on 9 September, after the phases of the afore-mentioned public discussion, by the Central People's Government Committee (denomination at that time of the national government, and today's State Council, or rather the Council of Ministers) and forwarded to the national parliament.

The Constitution was structured in four chapters preceded by a Preamble, for a total of one hundred and six articles. It resumed and developed the content of the Joint Program, acknowledging and legitimizing in the constitutional text, the predominant political and ideological objective represented by the creation of the Social-Democratic State.

According to the Preamble, the transition to socialism required the socialist industrialization of the country, as well as the transformation, in the sense of socialization and collectivization, of agriculture, cottage industries, entrepreneurship and commerce.

From the point of view of electoral rules, the Constitutional Charter confirmed the exceptions to the general principles of popular and socialist democracy already contemplated by the electoral law of 11 February 1950, insofar as they provided, on the one hand, an unequal representation for the rural areas compared to urban areas, and on the other hand, the temporary deprivation of active and passive electoral rights for certain categories of citizens. Above all, the 1954 Constitution upheld both direct and indirect mechanisms of election, due to the fact that only representatives of the basic territorial communities,

---

Sansoni, 1962; F. Fischer, *Entwicklung der marxistischen Staats- und Rechtstheorie in der Sowietunion bis Stalin und in der Volksrepublik China*, in K. Wegmann, E. Franke, M. Klein (hrsg.), *Studien zum chinesischen Recht*, II, op cit., 7 ff. With reference to recent developments in Chinese theoretical reflection, *see* Zou Shipeng, *Localization of Marxism in China and the Construction of China's Modernity*, in *Social Sciences in China* (publication published in Chinese and English by the Chinese Academy of Social Sciences) 2005, n. 2, 12 ff. In the comparative perspective of today's change, *cf.* G. Iannini (Ed.), *Cina e Russia. Due transizioni a confronto*, Milano, Angeli, 2005 (Research Centre for non-European peoples «Cesare Bonacossa» of the Università of Pavia, *Coll. storica*, n. 19), and for further considerations, L. Vasconi, *La Cina oggi: ambizioni imperialistiche o urgenze democratiche?*, in *MondOperaio*, July-October 2005, 37 ff., where the author recalls the attempt, made by Zhao Ziyang in the eighties of the last century, to "remove the Marxist armor from Chinese socialism to cover it with social democratic cloths". For reflections on normative production, *see* H. von Senger, *Ideology and Law-Making*, in J.M. Otto, M.V. Polak, J. Chen, Y. Li (Eds.), *Law-Making in the People's Republic of China*, The Hague, Kluwer Law International, 2000, 41 ff.

17 The Local People's Congresses were regulated in Arts. 12 and 14, para. 2, of the common program.

18 Following the report presented on 15 September 1954 by Liu Shaoqi, *Rapport sur le projet de Constitution de la République Populaire de Chine*, Pékin, Editions en Langues étrangères, 1954.

i.e. the villages of the countryside, as well as the minor neighbourhoods and cities, were elected directly by the people, while the members of the Local People's Congresses of the various higher administrative levels (district and provincial)[19] were designated by the LPCs immediately below, up to reaching the summit of the pyramidal system of People's Congresses, the NPC. The members of the latter were elected by the LPC constituted at the levels of the provinces (the largest Chinese local authorities), supplemented by representatives of the armed forces, and held office for four years.

Moreover, since the Constitution of 1954 was to mark the transition from the phase of the new democracy to that of socialism, or at least the initial stage of socialism, on the assumption that China was not yet a complete socialist state, an articulated system of properties was maintained for the transitory period. If the primary role was attributed to socialist public property, destined for a continuous development, it, for the moment, coexisted with three other forms of property, represented by collective ownership, personal or individual property and capitalist property. In relation to the last-mentioned proprietary form, it should be noted that the Chinese constituents considered it useful at the time for the strengthening of the economic system of the PRC to recognize and guarantee the ownership of the means of production for the so called national capitalists, that is to say, entrepreneurs who were ideologically immune to compromises with the past and pragmatically available to collaborate with the people's revolutionary regime,[20] as such, differentiated and deserving of protection, compared to the poor treatment reserved for the so called bureaucratic capitalists, among other things deprived of the right to vote, in a similar way to the old descendant landowners and heirs of the feudal lords.

Reasons of interest in the Constitution of 1954 are also found at the level of the method, with regards to the complex constituent legislative process that involved a very wide public discussion in the country on the draft of the Constitutional Charter, via consultations with the various segments of the population that continued for circa twenty months with the intervention of over one hundred and fifty million citizens. The constitutional experience of the young PRC was characterized, therefore, by the close institutional collaboration between the masses of the people, the ruling class, the rulers and the national legislator.

1.1.3 The 1975 Constitution, Epiphenomenon of Legal Nihilism and the Cultural Revolution

With the progressive establishment of the component of the ultra-left within the CCP, according to a trend that began in 1956 and culminated in the decade of the "Great Prole-

19 For a diachronic look at the administrative divisions in China, *see* G. Melis, *Province e distretti cinesi. Attualità e note storiche*, in *Mondo cinese*, n. 23, 1978, 55 ff.

20 Thus becoming a member of the People's Democratic Front.

tarian Cultural Revolution" from 1966 to 1976,[21] extremist and anti-legalist political tendencies took over, to the point that the law was considered an obstacle to the realization of a communist society. In this climate of an open eulogy of illegality as a revolutionary sentiment,[22] accompanied by proposals aimed at adopting as a fundamental legal text in the Chinese Law Faculties, the works of Mao Zedong,[23] the 1975 Constitution[24] took care to incorporate the thinking and practices of the Cultural Revolution, with its theoretical kit of the so called mass line,[25] the class struggle and the Maoist doctrine of contradictions, the people's war against all forms of bourgeoisie and rebirth of bureaucratism, the campaign

21 *See* F. Coccia, *Il partito nella grande Rivoluzione culturale proletaria* (1970), in Id., *Sulla Cina (1958-1997)*, op cit., 121 ff. For a retrospective evaluation, *cf.* G. Samarani, *La Rivoluzione Culturale trent'anni dopo. Problemi storici e storiografici*, in A. Cadonna, F. Gatti (Eds.), *Cina: miti e realtà* (proceedings of the Venice convention, organized by the Institute «*Venezia e l'Oriente*» of the *Fondazione G. Cini*, of the *Associazione italiana studi cinesi-AISC*, of the Department of East Asia Studies and the Marco Polo Centre for Asian Studies of the Università «Cà Foscari» of Venice, 21, 22 e 23 May 1998), Venezia, Cafoscarina, 2001, 181 ff.; G. Samarani, *Anni difficili: la Cina dalla fine della rivoluzione culturale alla morte di Mao (1969-1976)*, in S. Dossi, E. Giunchi, F. Montessoro (Eds.), *L'Asia tra passato e futuro. Scritti in ricordo di E. Collotti Pischel*, Milano, Giuffrè, 2014, 35 ff. Regarding Chinese ideological controversies, *see* A. Russo, *How Did the Cultural Revolution End? The Last Dispute between Mao Zedong and Deng Xiaoping, 1975*, in *Modern China. An International Journal of History and Social Sciences*, 2013, 239 ff.

22 The official organ of the CCP, the *People's Daily* (Chinese: *Renmin ribao, RMRB*), in an editorial dated 31 January 1967, cited by R. Cavalieri, *La legge e il rito. Lineamenti di storia del diritto cinese*, op. cit., 153, nt. 39, stated that "destroying bourgeois law and the capitalist world is precisely the revolutionary task of any proletarian revolutionary. Just as the Monkey King, who overturned the heavenly palace, we will destroy your law, we will bring down your world, we will rebel against you and take your power."

23 *See* G. Crespi Reghizzi, Diritto cinese e rivoluzione culturale, op. cit., with regard to the revision of the teachings in the Juridical Faculty of the University of Beijing. By means of the Cultural Revolution, there was the desire to oppose the "dominion of the bourgeois scientific aristocracy", accused of having a revisionist and counter-revolutionary nature.

24 On the topic *see*: M. Brunetti, *La quarta Assemblea del popolo cinese e la nuova Costituzione*, in *Mondo cinese*, n. 10, 1975, 3 ff.; P. Biscaretti di Ruffia, *La Repubblica Popolare Cinese. Un "modello" nuovo di ordinamento statale socialista (Costituzione del 17 gennaio 1975)*, Milano, Giuffrè, 1977; Id., *Costituzioni straniere contemporanee*, II, *Gli Stati socialisti*, Milano, Giuffrè, 1987, 4th edn, *sub Cina*, especially 301 ff.; F. D'Onofrio, *La nuova costituzione cinese vista da un occidentale*, in L. Lanciotti (Ed.), *Il diritto in Cina. Teoria e applicazioni durante le dinastie imperiali e problematica del diritto cinese contemporaneo*, Firenze, Olschki, 1978, 171 ff.; L. Focsaneanu, *Révision constitutionnelle en République populaire de Chine – La nouvelle Constitution "révisée" du 17 janvier 1975*, in *Politique Étrangère*, 1975, 241 ff.; Tsien Tche-hao, *Les traits particuliers de la nouvelle Constitution chinoise*, in *Rev. intern. dr. comp.*, 1975, 349 ff.; Id., *Analyse de la Constitution de la République populaire de Chine (17 janvier 1975)*, Paris, Éditions du Centre Nationale de la Recherche Scientifique, 1976; P. Ardant, *La Constitution de la République populaire de Chine du 17 janvier 1975*, in *Rev. dr. pub. sc. pol.*, 1976, 477 ff.; M. Lindsay (Ed.), *The New Constitution of Communist China. Comparative Analyses*, Taipei, Institute of International Relations-IIR della National Chengchi University-NCCU, 1976; Kim Chin, *The 1975 Constitution of the People's Republic of China*, in Id. (Ed.), *Selected Writings on Asian Law*, Littleton (Col.), Rothman, 1982, 359 ff. An analysis with an intense ideological "colour" is also found in, in C. Donati, F. Marrone, F. Misiani, *Stato e Costituzione in Cina*, Milano, Mazzotta, 1977, and in F. Marrone, F. Misiani, *L'ordinamento costituzionale cinese dopo la rivoluzione culturale*, in *Quale giust.*, 1975, 322 ff.

25 For the notes characterizing the Maoist mass-line method, *see* D. Mamo Tchou, *L'ideologia della leadership politica in Cina: Confucianesimo e Maoismo nella loro concezione della classe politica*, in *Mondo cinese*, n. 8, 1974, 61 ff.

against the "right-wing deviationist wind" and the "anti-party gang", as well as the violence by the Red Guards[26] "inspired" by the Great Helmsman Mao. On the basis of these premises, the first session of the IV legislature of the National People's Congress approved the second Constitution of the PRC on 17 January 1975, comprising only thirty articles, which declared the construction of the socialist state in the People's China. The work of radical simplification of the constitutional text had been such that the rules on the fundamental rights and duties of citizens were gathered in four articles, while a single provision was dedicated to the administration of justice. It seems difficult to disagree with the view that "the only lesson that the Chinese people learned from the 1975 Constitution is that a constitutional document can be used to deny and block the implementation of constitutionalism".[27]

Analysing in more detail the content of the 1975 Constitution, one can note that fundamental rights were taken into consideration after the duties of citizens, and the principle of equality of citizens was also abolished before the law which was proclaimed by the 1954 Constitution. On the other hand, not only was the clear denial of the principle of separation of powers confirmed in favour of the acceptance of the opposing organizational formula (and operational rule) of the unity of state power (or non-separation of powers), albeit with Chinese characteristics,[28] but any distinction between administrative and jurisdictional functions in the sphere of the unified power of the State, was also eliminated, bearing in mind that the control of the central people's government extended on the basis of the 1975 constitutional text to both the administrative and judicial organs. This latter however, were more and more weakened by the elimination of the State Procuratorate with the devolution of the related tasks to the police forces.[29] On the other hand, the second Constitution of the PRC did not provide for, contrary to the first Constitution, the office of President of the Republic.

The peculiarity of the 1975 Constitution was, however, represented by the incorporation and exaltation of principles and revolutionary proclamations, as a reference to the dictatorship of the proletariat[30] to be understood as an "absolute dictatorship over the bour-

---

26 On the red terror in the People's Republic, during the phase of the so-called integral maoism, *see* K.A. Wittfogel, *Le Guardie Rosse cinesi e la «linea Lin Piao»*, in *L'Est. Riv. trim. di studi sui Paesi dell'Est*, 1967, n. 2, 189 ff.; A. Russo, *The conclusive scene: Mao and the Red Guards in July 1968*, in *Positions: East-Asia Cultures Critique*, 2005, 535 ff. For the connotation of the linbiaoist ideology as Asian fascism, *see* F. Coccia, *Ideologia e cultura nell'esperienza maoista* (1988), in Id., *Sulla Cina (1958-1997)*, op. cit., especially 461.

27 *Cf.* Lin Feng, *La storia moderna del diritto costituzionale cinese*, op. cit., 781.

28 On the topic, *see* M.-H. Fabre, *Variations chinoises sur l'unité marxiste du pouvoir d'État*, in *Rev. dr. pub. sc. pol.*, 1957, 45 ff. But see also J.-P. Bja, *La Chine de Xi Jinping: en marche vers un fascisme la chinoise?*, in *Pouvoirs* n. 169, April 2019, 117 ff.

29 On this innovation established by the 1975 Constitution, *see* P. Corradini, *I poteri di controllo nella Repubblica Popolare Cinese*, in *Mondo cinese*, n. 17, 1977, 3 ff.

30 *Cf.* M. Brunetti, *La dittatura del proletariato nel momento politico cinese*, in *Mondo cinese*, n. 11, 1975, 65 ff. For the Chinese point of view *see* Chang Chun-chiao, *Esercitiamo dovunque la dittatura del proletariato sulla borghesia*, in *Mondo cinese*, n. 9, 1975, 75 ff. (the author was Deputy Prime Minister of the PRC).

geoisie" to be exercised in every sector of social and cultural life, as well as the constitutionalization of the so-called "Four great democratic practices",[31] namely the manifestation of opinions, points of view, public debates and mural newspapers (*dazibao*[32]) as a means of expression of the masses.

1.1.4 The 1978 Constitution, During the Transition Phase from the Maoist Model to the Restoration of the State and the Law

The death of President Mao Zedong, in September 1976, accelerated the process underway since the beginning of the seventies to weaken the positions of the ultra-left in the CCP, in the overall picture of a cautious de-ideologization of the party. During the month of October 1976, the leaders of the ultramaoist current, represented by Mao's widow, Jiang Qing, and the leaders of the Shanghai branch of the CCP, Yao Wen-yuan, Wang Hongwen and Zhang Chun-qiao, namely the components of the so called "Gang of four", were arrested and tried.[33] Thus, the radical and extremist line was overcome by the moderate and pragmatic line,[34] led in the Party by Deng Xiaoping,[35] who in 1978, on becoming the leader of the People's Republic, started or rather continued the policy of reforms, especially in relation to the economy but also with regards to the institutional rearrangement/reorganization, in accordance with the design already prefigured at the time of the Mao Presidency by the Prime Minister, as well as Vice-President of the CCP, Zhou Enlai and known as the objective of the so-called "Four modernizations", with reference to the need to restructure the sectors of agriculture, industry, science and technology and national defence.[36]

---

31 Also indicated, by Chinese doctrine, as the "four great laws"; *see* Lin Feng, *La storia moderna del diritto costituzionale cinese*, op. cit., 789, nt. 43.

32 These are large manuscript mural posters, on which *see* S. Ticozzi, *Il «Muro della Democrazia» nel 1978-1979*, in *Mondo cinese*, n. 29, 1980, 27 ff. The *dazibao* were distinguished from the *xiaozibao*, posters (similarly affixed to the walls but) of smaller size and written in small characters.

33 *See* the contributions collected under J.C. Hsiung (Ed.), *Symposium: The Trial of the "Gang of Four" and Its Implication in China*, Baltimore, School of Law of the University of Maryland (*Occasional Papers/Reprints Series in Contemporary Asian Studies*, n. 3), 1981. On the history of the internal conflicts in the CCP, *see* the fresco in gloomy colors by F. Mezzetti, *Dietro la grande muraglia. Segreti e lotte di potere dal furore maoista al capitalismo rosso*, Milano, Valentina, 2004, where he examines the political clashes in what he defines as the "nest of vipers of the Maoist court" (at 133). *Adde* R. Rastrelli, *Ipotesi per uno studio della lotta politica in Cina*, in *Mondo cinese*, n. 26, 1979, 55 ff.

34 *See, e.g.*, the writings of X.-Y. *Li-Kotovtchikhine, Pragmatisme juridique et maintien de la stabilité en Chine post-Mao*, in *Rev. intern. dr. comp.*, 2012, 115 ff.; Id., *Pragmatisme juridique et développement économique dans la Chine post-Mao*, ivi, 2010, 931 ff.; Id., *Le pragmatisme juridique dans la Chine post-Mao*, *ibidem*, 2009, 715 ff.

35 On the Chinese *leader*, *see* E.F. Vogel, *Deng Xiaoping and the Transformation of China*, Cambridge (MA)–London, (The Belknap Press of) Harvard University Press, 2011.

36 *Cf.* S. Orviati, *Le prospettive di sviluppo economico aperte dalle quattro modernizzazioni da oggi al Duemila*, in *Mondo cinese*, n. 28, 1979, 25 ff.; G. Melis, *La modernizzazione politica nella Repubblica Popolare cinese*,

The new demands of the evolutionary phase of the economic, social and political system in post-Mao China demanded, in legal terms, the adoption of the third Constitution of the PRC, approved by the first session of the V National People's Congress on 5 March 1978.[37] It was a Transitional Constitution, in the sense that it was still marked by the visible influence of the Cultural Revolution, but at the same time laid the normative foundations for its definitive overcoming.

From the visual angle of the declamations, the Constitutional Charter adhered to the principles of the dictatorship of the proletariat, emphasized the class struggle, spoke of the "triumphant conclusion" of the Great Proletarian Cultural Revolution, and confirmed the lasting validity of the "four great democratic practices".

These aspects, so to speak, "cosmetic", were confined in the Preamble and in the first chapter, dedicated to the general principles. The overall structure of the 1978 Constitution presented four chapters, for a total of sixty articles.

The provisions of the second chapter, relating to the state organization, were linked to the provisions contained in the 1954 Constitution and reinforced the judiciary apparatus, reintroducing the organs of the State Procuratorate that had been suppressed by the "revolutionary" Maoist Constitution of 1975.[38] The 1978 Constitutional Charter, however, manifested its compromising character also in the choice not to cancel, at least in the

---

ivi, n. 28, 1979, 41 ss.; S. De Simone, *La modernizzazione militare nella R. cinese, ibidem*, n. 28, 1979, 103 ff.; A. Piazza, *La Cina di Deng Xiaoping: un lungo cammino verso la modernizzazione, ibid.*, n. 94, 1997, 21 ff.; B.L. McCormick, *Political Reform in Post-Mao China. Democracy and Bureaucracy in a Leninist State*, Berkeley, University of California Press, 1990. For specific contours of the legal reform, *see* H. Chin, *Socialist Legalism: Reform and Continuity in Post-Mao People's Republic of China*, Baltimore, School of Law, University of Maryland (*Occasional Papers/Reprints Series in Contemporary Asian Studies*, n. 1), 1982; A. Mayer, *The Rocky Road to Democracy: A Few Comments on Legal Developments in China Since the Cultural Revolution*, in *China Law Reporter*, 1989, 1 ff.; C.W. Lo, *Socialist Legal Theory in Deng Xiaoping's China*, in *Columbia Journal of Asian Law*, 1997, 469 ff.; G. Koi, *The First Three Decades of Legal Reforms in the People's Republic of China (1978/1979-2008/2009)*, in *Acta Juridica Hungarica. Hungarian Journal of Legal Studies*, 2011, 348 ff. With regard to the renewal of the ideological and party approach, *see* Hsia Tao-tai, C.A. Johnson, *The Chinese Communist Party Constitution of 1982: Deng Xiaoping's Program for Modernization*, Washington (DC), Library of Congress (Law Library), 1984. On the theoretical legacy of Denghist pragmatism, *see* A. Lavagnino, *XV Congresso del PCC: piccolo lessico 'politico' del dopo-Deng*, in A. Cadonna, F. Gatti (Eds.), *Cina: miti e realtà*, op. cit., 199 ff.; G. Samarani, *La Cina dopo Deng Xiaping (1997-2006)*, in *Il Politico*, 2006, 40 ff.

37 *Cf.* J.A. Cohen, *China's Changing Constitution*, in *The China Quarterly*, 1978, 794 ff.; Wang Hsiao-t'ang, *An Evaluation and Analysis of China's Revised Constitution*, in *Chinese Law and Government*, 1978, n. 2-3, 34 ff.; Kim Chin, *The 1978 Constitution of the People's Republic of China*, in Id. (Ed.), *Selected Writings on Asian Law*, op. cit., 395 ff.; Tsien Tche-hao, *Les institutions chinoises et la Constitution de 1978*, Paris, La Documentation française, 1979.

38 *Cf.* Hsia Tao-tai, K.A. Huan, *The Re-emergence of the Procuratorial System in the People's Republic of China*, in R.H. Folsom, J.H. Minan (Eds.), *Law in the People's Republic of China. Commentary, Readings and Materials*, Dordrecht, Nijhoff, 1989, 242 ff.

original draft, the revolutionary committees[39] created during the period of the Cultural Revolution and which had supplanted the administrative organs of local government.

With regards to the catalogue of the fundamental rights and duties of citizens, regulated in the third chapter of the 1978 Constitution, it is important to point out that it was possible to present administrative appeals (in order to obtain the so-called administrative reconsideration) against the acts and behaviour of public officials, belonging to both state and local bodies, as well as to companies.

The hybrid nature, the result of the mixing of old Maoist dogmas and new developments of the Chinese socio-political system, led, in the short space of the two years following the adoption of the 1978 Constitution, to the inclusion, in the constitutional fabric, of some amendments, by the second session of the V National People's Congress in July 1979 and subsequently by the third session of the same NPC in September 1980. The constitutional revisions led, among other things, to the elimination of the revolutionary committees that were replaced by and local governing bodies, in order to reinforce the principle of socialist legality and restore functionality to the administrative units of the various levels. In terms of constitutional declamations, the reference to the "four great democratic practices" of the Cultural Revolution was also deleted.

1.1.5 The 1982 Constitution in Force, Reforms and the New Chinese Course

The study, documentation and elaboration of the Commission created by the National Parliament began in September 1980, and took shape in the preparation of a draft of the new Constitution of People's Republic, completed in February 1982 and transmitted to the Standing Committee of the NPC, which adopted a favourable resolution on the project[40] in April of that year. The extensive public consultation procedure, which was successfully tested at the time of the approval of the first Constitution of the PRC in 1954, was thus launched. Citizen participation was decidedly remarkable, between 80% and 90% of the total population took part in fact in the popular discussion; in addition, the opinion of the Chinese citizens residing in foreign countries, as well as Hong Kong and Macao, was also acquired. Opinions and proposals were sent by the State Council, the armed forces, and the democratic parties. In view of all of this, the Constitutional Review Commission made some changes to the original project, which was presented at the fifth session of the V National People's Congress. Finally, the Parliament adopted the Constitution on 4 December 1982.[41]

39 On which *see* G. Melis, *I nuovi Comitati rivoluzionari provinciali*, in *Mondo cinese*, n. 21, 1978, 85 ff.

40 *Cf.* Peng Zhen, *Considerazioni sul progetto di revisione della Costituzione della Rpc*, in *Mondo cinese*, n. 38, 1982, 71 ff. (the author was Vice-President of the Commission charged with the constitutional review).

41 *See* P. Biscaretti di Ruffia, *La Costituzione della Repubblica Popolare Cinese del 1982: principî generali e ordinamento dello Stato*, in *Mondo cinese*, n. 43, 1983, 3 ff., now in *Mondo cinese*, n. 153, 2014, 100 ff. (n.

The new fundamental Charter concluded the long period of Maoist extremism, reconnecting to the normative system of the 1954 Constitution, overlooking, instead, the system set-ups drawn up by the Constitutions of 1975 and 1978, with the aim of establishing the general development lines of for the socialist modernization of the socio-economic system and the political-juridical institutions of the country.

The fourth constitution of the People's Republic of China has been repeatedly subjected to amendments: the constitutional revisions of 12 April 1988, 29 March 1993, 15 March 1999, 14 March 2004 and 11 March 2018,[42] respectively by the VII, VIII, IX, X and XIII

---

thematic *Un filo rosso lungo 40 anni*, R. Cavalieri, A. Luini e T. Rosenthal cur.); Id., *Costituzioni straniere contemporanee*, II, *Gli Stati socialisti*, op cit., 313 ff.; M. Siddivò, *Gli assetti istituzionali e politici nella Cina degli anni '80*, Napoli, *Dipartimento di studi asiatici dell'Istituto universitario orientale di Napoli*, 1994; Tsien Tche-hao, *La Constitution de 1982 et les réformes institutionnelles en République populaire de Chine*, in *Rev. intern. dr. comp.*, 1983, 385 ff.; Chiu Hungdah, *The 1982 Chinese Constitution and the Rule of Law*, in *Rev. of Socialist Law*, 1985, 143 ff.; W.C. Jones, *The Constitution of the People's Republic of China*, in *Washington University Law Quarterly*, 1985, 707 ff.; Kuan Hsin-chi, *New Developments in China's Constitution*, in *Studies in Comparative Communism*, 1984, 54 ff.; J. Barrett, *What's New in China's New Constitution?*, in *Rev. of Socialist Law*, 1983, 305 ff.; Hsieh Jiann (Xie Jian), *The 1982 Constitution and the Policy Toward Nationalities*, in *Chinese Law and Government*, 1983, n. 2-3, 67 ff. (n. thematic *Studies on the Constitutional Law of the People's Republic of China*, B.S.J. Weng Ed.); T. Saich, *The Fourth Constitution of the People's Republic of China*, in *Rev. of Socialist Law*, 1983, 113 ff. *See also* the annotated translation of the 1982 constitutional text by G. Melis, *Costituzione della Repubblica Popolare Cinese*, in *Mondo cinese*, n. 43, 1983, 55 ff. For an analytical comparison of the Constitutions of the PRC of 1954, 1975, 1978 and 1982, together with that of the 1949 Joint Program, *cf.* G. Melis, *Costituzioni cinesi comparate*, in *Mondo cinese*, n. 44, 1983, 61 ff.; n. 45, 1984, 55 ff.; n. 46, 1984, 39 ff.; n. 47, 1984, 71 ff. In a comparative key a) with the Constitutions of Yugoslavia and the Soviet Union, *see* Kuan Hsin-chi (Guan Xinji), *Socialist Constitutions in Comparative Perspective*, in *Chinese Law and Government*, 1983, n. 2-3, 12 ff.; b) with the US constitutional system, *see* O.M. Fiss, *Two Constitutions*, in R.H. Folsom, J.H. Minan (Eds.), *Law in the People's Republic of China. Commentary, Readings and Materials*, Dordrecht, Nijhoff, 1989, 61 ff. Some useful outlines on the Chinese constitutional system are found in E. Esposito Martino, *Struttura costituzionale cinese tra tradizione e innovazione. Sogniamo il sogno cinese 梦中国梦 mèng Zhōngguó mèng*, in *Osservatorio costituzionale* (Associazione italiana dei costituzionalisti-AIC), on the website www.osservatorioaic.it. *Ivi* the author recalls that the current constitutional text of the PRC is engraved on the "wall of the Constitution", a 23 meters long construction, circa 2 meters high, in white marble, a splendid monument set in the palace of the National People's Congress»; the marble monument was realized in 2012, on the occasion of the commemoration of the thirtieth anniversary of the 1982 Constitution. Since 2014, by decision of the fourth plenum of the CC of the CCP adopted in October of the same year, Constitution Day is celebrated in China (every 4 December, anniversary of the Chinese Constitution).

42 The innovations of the 1982 Constitution are commented by P. Biscaretti di Ruffia (with the collaboration of M. Ganino), *Costituzioni straniere contemporanee*, II, *Le Costituzioni di sette Stati di recente ristrutturazione*, Milano, Giuffrè, 1996, 6ª edn., *sub* 3, *Un superstite «Stato socialista» asiatico in corso di progressiva trasformazione economica*, 151 ff.; R. Cavalieri, *Cina: rallentano le riforme politiche e cresce la tensione internazionale*, in G. Borsa, M. Torri (Eds.), *L'incerta vigilia del nuovo secolo in Asia. Asia Major 1999*, Bologna, il Mulino, 1999, 51 ff.; G. Crespi Reghizzi, *Verso il mercato e lo Stato di diritto: recenti riforme costituzionali in Cina*, in *Dir. pubbl. com eur.*, 1999, 485 ff.; Id., M.E. Delmestro, *La Costituzione della Repubblica popolare cinese si aggiorna*, *ivi*, 2004, 575 ff.; M. Miranda, *Stabilità e riforme "con caratteristiche cinesi". La 2° Sessione della IX Assemblea Nazionale del Popolo*, in *Mondo cinese*, n. 100, 1999, 3 ff.; Id., *"Sviluppo scientifico" ed emendamenti costituzionali – I lavori della 2° Sessione della X Assemblea nazionale del popolo*, *ivi*, n. 118, 2004, 8 ff.; R. Cavalieri, *La revisione della Costituzione della Repubblica Popolare Cinese e l'istituzionalizzazione del "socialismo dalle caratteristiche cinesi per una nuova era"*, in *Dir. pubbl.*

National People's Congress, in accordance with the binding directives issued by the CCP.[43] The normative architecture of the fundamental Charter that governs the PRC today, as it results from the aforementioned constitutional changes, will be examined in the following chapters, dedicated to a study of the current Chinese constitutional law.

1.2 The Constitutional Structure of the People's Republic of China, in the Peculiar Dimension of an Ideological Formant

1.2.1 *The Categories of Fundamental Principles That Underlie the Chinese System of Constitutional Law*

The current Constitution of the People's Republic of China sets out in the Preamble and the first chapter, the fundamental principles of the upmost importance. They can be grouped into two general categories.[44]

On the one hand, one can find the cardinal principles of the constitutional system that assume unequivocal and exclusive Chinese characteristics.

On the other hand, there is the need to take into consideration the principles also accepted in the Preamble and in the articles of the first chapter of the Constitution of the PRC, which are also recurrent in the fundamental Charters of other countries.

Under the first profile, the four cardinal principles of the hegemonic role attributed to the CCP are highlighted: the supreme guiding function of Marxist–Leninist doctrine and the thinking of Mao Zedong, the strict adherence to the organizational model represented by the democratic dictatorship of the people, and the adherence to socialism.

---

comp. eur., online, 2018, 275 ff.; F. Spagnoli, *La riforma della Costituzione cinese: un'analisi della revisione costituzionale del 2018 e dei suoi caratteri principali, ivi*, 2019, 129 ff.; Li Li, *China's Constitutional Amendments and Their Implications*, in *China Report (A Journal of East Asian Studies)*, 2005, 75 ff.; Chen Jianfu, *La dernière révision de la Constitution chinoise. Grand bond en avant ou simple geste symbolique?*, in *Perspectives chinoises*, n. 82, 2004, 15 ff. For evaluations in the literature of the PRC, *see People To Get More Rights*, in *Beijing Review*, 2004, n. 3, 11 ff.; Xia Yong, *Several Basic Theoretical Issues Concerning the Chinese Constitution Reform*, in *Social Sciences in China*, 2004, n. 1, 3 ff. From the special Hong Kong observatory, *see* A. Subrahmanyan, *Constitutionalism in China: Changing Dynamics in Legal and Political Debates*, in *China Law & Practice*, 2004, n. 4, 17 ff.

43 *Cf.*, for example, J.-P. Cabestan, *La nouvelle Assemblée populaire national et l'après-XVI Congrès en Chine. Vers un autoritarisme élitiste et consultatif?*, in *Perspectives chinoises*, n. 76, 2003, 4 ff.

44 On the classification criteria of the fundamental principles constituting the basis of Chinese constitutional law, *see* Lin Feng, *Constitutional Law in China*, Hong Kong, Sweet and Maxwell Asia, 2000, 21 ff.; M. Mazza, *Diritto pubblico cinese. Appunti e riflessioni per uno studio su storia politico-istituzionale della Cina popolare, ruolo del PCC ed elementi della struttura costituzionale della RPC*, Bergamo, Bergamo University Press, 2013 (Coll. *Cooperazione Internazionale* of the UNESCO Chair: Human Rights and Ethics of International Cooperation of the University of Bergamo, n. 10), 45 ff.

Under the second of the aforementioned profiles, emerge the constitutional principles of sovereignty that belongs to the people, the *rule of law*, equality between the national ethnic groups recognized by the PRC and the protection of fundamental human rights.

Moreover, it is hardly necessary to recall that knowledge of the fundamental principles of the Chinese Constitutional Charter represents, as is the case in the constitutional legal system, the interpretive key both to grasp the overall curvature of the constitutional system as well as to evaluate the content and effectiveness of the individual super-primary provisions.

1.2.2 The Function of the Chinese Communist Party in the Constitutional Framework

The absolute pre-eminence of the CCP in the history of China's public institutions and in the current constitutional set-up is clearly highlighted and emphasized in the Preamble of the 1982 Fundamental Charter,[45] as well as in Article 1, Paragraph 2 of the same Constitution, following the amendments approved by the XIII National People's Congress on 11 March 2018,[46] The main stages of Chinese constitutional history after the end of the system of imperial dynasties,[47] are outlined in the Preamble, where they are closely linked to the activity carried out by the CCP. Indeed, apart from the reference to the revolutionary events of 1911 that led to the birth of the Republic of China under the leadership of Sun Yat-sen, the following fundamental steps, represented by the foundation of the PRC in

45 With regard to the Communist Party in the Chinese political-constitutional and legislative system, *see* K.C. Walker, *The Brittle Strength of the Chinese Communist Party*, in *Asian Affairs*, 2012, 280 ff.; D. Shambaugh, *China's Communist Party. Atrophy and Adaptation*, Washington (DC), Woodrow Wilson Center Press, 2008; S. Uhalley jr., *A History of the Chinese Communist Party*, Stanford, Stanford University-Hoover Institution Press, 1988; A.J. Nathan, *Chinese Democracy*, London, Tauris, 1986; H. von Senger, *Recent Developments in the Relations between State and Party Norms in the People's Republic of China*, in S.R. Schram (Ed.), *The Scope of State Power in China*, London-Hong Kong-New York, School of Oriental and African Studies (University of London) – Chinese University Press (Chinese University of Hong Kong) – St. Martin's Press, 1985; S. Balme, *Entre soi. L'élite du pouvoir dans la Chine contemporaine*, Paris, Fayard, 2004; J.-P. Cabestan, *Le système politique de la Chine populaire*, Paris, Presses Universitaires de France, 1994; M. Miranda, *Il Partito Comunista Cinese da "Partito rivoluzionario" a "Partito di governo"*, in *Mondo cinese*, n. 113, 2002, 15 ff.; G. Samarani, *La Cina verso il 2000. Potere politico e trasformazioni economico-sociali*, Venezia, Cafoscarina, 1994, particularly *sub Il Partito*, 13 ff.

46 *See* X. Lan, *Amending the Fundamental Law. Modernization, socialism and the people's will at the core of constitutional revision*, in *Beijing Review*, 2018, n. 12, www.bjreview.com; R. Cavalieri, *La revisione della Costituzione della Repubblica Popolare Cinese e l'istituzionalizzazione del "socialismo dalle caratteristiche cinesi per una nuova era"*, in *Dir. pubbl. comp. eur. online*, op. cit., 276; F. Spagnoli, *La riforma della Costituzione cinese: un'analisi della revisione costituzionale del 2018 e dei suoi caratteri principali*, op. cit., especially 147-150,.

47 On the Chinese legal Historiograpic methodology, *see* L. Zang, *Evolution of Research Methodologies of Chinese Legal Historiography*, in B. Sordi (Ed.), *Storia e diritto. Esperienze a confronto* (acts of the conference of Florence, held, 18 and 19 October 2012), Milano, Giuffrè, 2014, 253 ff.

1949 by Mao Zedong, from the realization of the new form of democracy, the transition to the socialist phase and the achievement of important objectives during this last phase still under way, were characterized by the dominant presence and the propulsive drive of the Chinese Communist Party. The position taken by the CCP regarding these historical events and the evolutionary process that led to the level of socio-economic development as well as the institutional configuration that can be found today in the People's Republic, undoubtedly appears to be essential. Of equal importance, is the fact that the Constitutional Preamble omits every reference to the ultramodern period of the Cultural Revolution, which also saw the Communist Party engaged in the front line in the implementation of the extremist policies of the twenty years from 1956 to 1976. From this, it emerges that the Preamble of the 1982 Constitution dwells at length on the role of the CCP, with exclusive reference, however, to the historical phases deemed worthy of mention in virtue of the lasting positive judgment expressed on these phases by the political-party leadership. The constitutional text, instead, focuses its attention elsewhere with respect to the anti-legalism of China's Cultural Revolution.

Moreover, the constitutional position of the CCP translates into a clear disregard for the principles of liberal classical democracy, since it is the fundamental Charter itself that establishes in the Preamble the leading role of the Communist Party, called to direct society and the State as the avant-garde of the Chinese people, regardless of any legitimacy through the democratic vote and by virtue of the will expressed by the Constituents in the drafting of the same Preamble.

It is worth noting that the political system of the People's Republic of China has witnessed, since its foundation in 1949, the presence of some minor political parties alongside the CCP.[48] These are the eight so-called Democratic parties (*id est*, non-communist[49]), which were even more numerous at the time of the creation of the PRC, when there were eleven. The space of concrete political action reserved for these parties is very limited, so much so, that one could say that their function is predominantly (if not exclusively) "cosmetic" or "for show", aimed at creating the appearance of a multi-party political system. In a future perspective too, the role of democratic parties as potential CCP competitors in the country's leadership is impeded, on the legal-constitutional level, by the recognition of the primary role of the Communist Party contained in the Preamble. Thus, an eventual (and, at the moment, totally unlikely) electoral success of one of these "accessory" parties, which could prevail over the CCP, would result in a violation of the constitutional text, which establishes the dominant position of the Communists in China. Political-institutional

48 *See* above, in section 1.1.1.

49 They are: a) Revolutionary Committee of the Chinese *Guomindang*; b) Chinese Democratic League; c) China Democratic National Construction Association; d) Chinese Association for promoting democracy; e) Chinese peasants' and workers' democratic party; f) *Zhigong* Party of China (or China Party of Public Interest); g) *Jiusan* Society (or Society of 3 September); h) Taiwan democratic self-government league.

democracy with Chinese characteristics is, therefore, constitutionally bound to the hegemonic role of the Communist Party.

This last (indeed drastic) conclusion could perhaps be avoided, regardless of the dominant role practiced by the CCP in China and limiting the analysis to the strictly normative level of constitutional law, should the theory for which the statements contained in the Preamble to the Constitutional Charter are to be deemed only programmatic and declaratory, since they lack legal effects and legal force, be acknowledged. Although some observations made in this sense are not lacking in Chinese doctrine, supported by the comparative analysis of foreign laws with particular regard to Japanese constitutional law,[50] the clear prevalence granted by Chinese public law experts to the perceptive value of the 1982 Preamble of the Constitution of the PRC, also in relation to the statements that, as happens with the principle of the absolute pre-eminence of the CCP, are not open to the jurisdictional bodies, exempts the scholar from carrying out further research on the point and confirms the one-party nature, according to the fundamental Charter, of the function of political, party and parliamentary leadership, assigned in China to the Communist Party. This conclusion is definitively confirmed by the constitutional revision of 11 March 2018, through the express declaration contained in Article 1 of the Constitution, that the leadership of the CCP represents a "distinctive feature of socialism with Chinese characteristics".[51]

1.2.3 *The Ideological Component of the (Economic) Theory of Law and the State in the Version, Several Times Amended, of the 1982 Chinese Constitution*

The Preamble of the current Fundamental Charter places the Marxist theory of law and the State among the bases, or cardinal principles, of the Chinese constitutional system, with the well-known underlying ideology according to which economic relations represent the systemic structure (or infrastructure), while the political-institutional, juridical and ethical-religious structures are nothing but super-structural aspects.[52] Marx's theory is integrated, in the Constitutional Preamble's statements, with the reference to Lenin's political practices, that envisages the working class organized in the Communist Party.

---

50 *Cf.* Lin Feng, *Constitutional Law in China*, cit. 25 ff., text and nt. 22, 24-25.

51 *See supra*, in this paragraph, and *see also* J. Hui, *Significato mondiale del socialismo con caratteristiche cinesi nel XXI secolo*, in *World Socialism Studies*, 2017, n. 4, 4 ss.

52 From the perspective of a legal-constitutional analysis, *see* S. Chin (Jin Sikai), *The Constitution of China and the Economic Base*, in *Chinese Law and Government*, 1983, n. 2-3, 45 ff. (in the dossier *Studies on the Constitutional Law of the People's Republic of China*, B.S.J. Weng Ed.); G. Melis, *L'economia socialista dettata nelle Costituzioni cinesi*, in *Mondo cinese*, n. 56, 1986, 3 ff. *Adde* C. Volpi, *Pianificazione e modernizzazione nelle Costituzioni dei Paesi socialisti. L'esperienza della Repubblica Popolare Cinese*, Degree thesis discussed in the academic year 2002/2003 at the Faculty of Political Sciences of the University of Pavia (supervisor Prof. G. Cordini).

The intense Chinese "colouring" of Marxism–Leninism embraced in the Preamble manifests itself, successively, in the fact that the latter expressly mentions as fundamental constitutional principles, and not solely as political-ideological statements, both Maozedong thinking and the Deng Xiaoping theory as well as the important thinking of the three representations (or three representativenesses).

Political doctrine of constitutional relevance has been progressively enriched via the introduction of the amendments to the 1982 Fundamental Charter.

The constitutional reform of 15 March 1999, incorporated within the Preamble of the Constitution, a reference to the theory of Deng Xiaoping, summarized in the formula of the socialist market economy, which, in truth, would seem not easily harmonizable with the principles of Marxist–Leninist–Maoist thought, to the extent that it constituted the basis for a profound restructuring of the Chinese economic and juridical system, directed towards radical macro-system transformations and the transition from the Plan to the Market.[53]

In turn, the so-called thinking of the three representations, incorporated in the Preamble with the constitutional revision of 14 March 2004, was elaborated by Jiang Zemin, former Secretary General of the CCP and President of the PRC, whose name was not expressly mentioned in the Fundamental Charter, alongside those of Mao Zedong and Deng Xiaoping.[54] This particular doctrine, of explicit Chinese origin and which has become one of the official ideologies of the PRC on a par with Marxism, Leninism, Maoism and Denghism, has soft edges, but has however, the aim of fully legitimizing the category of entrepreneurs and professionals, recognizing the fundamental contribution they give, albeit together with the traditional historical classes of peasants and workers, to the development of the contemporary Chinese economic system.[55]

---

53 On the aspects concerning law, *see* R. Cavalieri, *Il virus della legalità. Caratteristiche e implicazioni della riforma giuridica cinese*, Milano, Istituto di Studi Economico-Sociali per l'Asia Orientale (ISESAO) Università Bocconi, 1996. The overall modernization of the Chinese legal system was also encouraged by the fact that the PRC became part of the World Trade Organization on 11 December 2001; in this regard, *see* R. Cavalieri, *L'adesione della Cina alla WTO. Implicazioni giuridiche*, Lecce, Argo, 2003 (Istituto superiore universitario di formazione interdisciplinare, University of Lecce, Euromediterranean School of Law and Politics, *Quaderni*, n. 1); L. Wang (Ed.), *China's WTO Accession Reassessed*, London/New York, Routledge, 2015.

54 For a comparison of the politics of the three leaders, *cf.* the paper by F.C. Teiwes, *Politics at the "Core": The Political Circumstances of Mao Zedong, Deng Xiaoping and Jiang Zemin*, in *China Information (A Journal on Contemporary China Studies)*, 2001, n. 1, 1 ff.

55 The thought of the "three representatives" was acknowledged, even before the constitutional reform of 14 March 2004, in the general program of the CCP Statute, through a modification of the same, adopted on 14 November 2002 during the XVI Party Congress. *Cf.* M. Miranda, *Il Partito Comunista Cinese da "Partito rivoluzionario" a "Partito di governo"*, op cit.; Id., *Le nuove prospettive di sviluppo del settore privato nella RPC. La politica del partito*, in *Mondo cinese*, n. 108, 2001, 11 ff.; G. Samarani, *Governare la Cina: problemi e prospettive dopo il XVI Congresso del PCC*, *ivi*, n. 113, 2002, 3 ff.; L. Tamburrino, *Il Partito Comunista a congresso tra crisi di fiducia, nuove teorie e appelli al cambiamento*, *ibidem*, n. 112, 2002, 3 ff. One can note that the policy of intense economic reforms pursued by Jiang Zemin seems somewhat muffled by the fourth generation at the vertex of the CCP. In particular, the successor of Jiang Zemin, Hu Jintao,

More recently, as a result of the constitutional amendment approved by the XIII National People's Congress on 11 March 2018, President Xi Jinping's thinking about "socialism with Chinese characteristics for a new era" has been constitutionalized in the Preamble.[56]

Regarding the constitutional analysis, the inclusion of the recalled official ideologies as fundamental principles of the legal system re-proposes the theme, already taken into consideration with regards to the constitutionalization of the hegemonic role of the CCP, concerning the value to be attributed to the statements contained in the Preamble of the Constitution. If they are to be considered for all purposes binding legal rules, according to the opinion that as seen above is prevalent among Chinese constitutionalists, thus there is a further foreclosure to the articulation of an authentic multi-party system in the People's

who also placed himself in line with the ideological continuity of his predecessor, also became spokesperson and interpreter at the institutional level of the disadvantaged social strata, desiring programmatically (and pragmatically) to favour the harmonious and balanced development of Chinese society. *See* G. Crespi Reghizzi, M.E. Delmestro, *La Costituzione della Repubblica popolare cinese si aggiorna*, op cit., 580, text and nt. 27; M. Miranda, *"Società armoniosa" e riunificazione "non pacifica" – I lavori della 3° Sessione della X Legislatura dell'Assemblea nazionale del popolo*, in *Mondo cinese*, n. 122, 2005, especially 18 ff.; Id., *"Sviluppo scientifico" ed emendamenti costituzionali*, op cit., 15; Id., *La "quarta generazione" al potere – I lavori della 1ª sessione della X Assemblea nazionale del popolo*, in *Mondo cinese*, n. 114, 2003, 3 ff.; L. Tamburrino, *Cina: la quarta generazione al potere*, in E. Giunchi, C. Molteni, M. Torri (Eds.), *L'Asia prima e dopo l'11 settembre. Asia Major 2002*, Bologna, il Mulino, 2003, 241 ff. For an interpretation of the theory of the three representations as a tool for modulating Chinese authoritarianism, *cf.* J.-P. Cabestan, *La Chine évoluerait-elle vers un autoritarisme «éclairé» mais ploutocratique?*, in *Perspectives chinoises*, n. 84, 2004, 21 ff., *sub Un autoritarisme consultatif mais élitiste*, 25 ff.

56 Cfr. *Xi's Thought Enshrined in China's Constitution*, in *Beijing Review*, 11 March 2018, www.bjreview.com; The Editors, *China in Xi's "New Era"*, in *Journal of Democracy*, 2018, n, 2, 20 s.; H. Holbig, *Making China Great Again – Xi Jinpings Abschied von der Reformära*, Hamburg, *GIGA Focus/Asien*, n. 2, aprile 2018 (*sub Kanonisierung der "Xi-Jinping-Ideen"*, 2-3). For preparatory work and party documents, *see* X. Li, *The Significance of Writing Xi Jinping Thought on Socialism with Chinese Characteristics for a New Era into the Constitution: The Development of the Party and Country Calls for a New Guiding Ideology*, in *China Today*, 1 March 2018, www.chinatoday.com.cn; L.C. Backer, *Chinese Constitutionalism in the New Era: The Emerging Idea and Practice of Constitution in the 19th CPC Congress Report, Working Papers Coalition for Peace & Ethics, No. 11/1 (November 2017)*; Id., *The Ideal and Practice of Chinese Comprehensive Constitutionalism in the 'New Era', Penn State Law Research Paper No. 2-2018*; P. Sun, *The Key to Understand the "New Era". The Reform of the Party-State Institutions*, paper presented at the conference *Rule of Law and Governance in China at Home and Abroad*, held on 15 March 2018 at the *Pennsylvania State University* (PSU); S. Li, *Il significato globale del pensiero di Xi Jinping sul socialismo con caratteristiche cinesi per una nuova era*, in *World Socialism Studies*, 2018, n. 1, 9 ff.; Id., *Comprendere correttamente e scientificamente la contraddizione principale nella nuova era del socialismo con caratteristiche cinesi. Riflessioni sul rapporto al 19° Congresso Nazionale del PCC*, *ivi*, 2018, n. 2, 4 ff.; F. Chi, *Fondazione pratica, origine teorica ed essenza spirituale del pensiero di Xi Jinping sullo Stato di diritto nel socialismo con caratteristiche cinesi per una nuova era*, *ivi*, 2018, n. 1, 27 ff.; D. Liu, B. Wu, H. Zhong, *Accelerare lo sviluppo della filosofia e delle scienze sociali con caratteristiche cinesi sotto la guida del pensiero di Xi Jinping sul socialismo con caratteristiche cinesi per una nuova era*, *ibidem*, 2018, n. 2, 60 ff. In Italy, *see* R. Cavalieri, *La revisione della Costituzione della Repubblica Popolare Cinese e l'istituzionalizzazione del "socialismo dalle caratteristiche cinesi per una nuova era"*, op. cit.; M. Miranda, *Le ambizioni del pensiero di Xi Jinping per una "nuova era"*, in *OrizzonteCina*, 2017, n. 5, 13 ff.; F. Spagnoli, *La riforma della Costituzione cinese: un'analisi della revisione costituzionale del 2018 e dei suoi caratteri principali*, op. cit., 143-144.

Republic. To legitimately compete, in accordance with the requirements of the fundamental constitutional principles, in a future possible multi-party electoral consultation, the political formations must adapt to a very temperate competition, since the latter must respect the constitutional text that envisages both the CCP's supremacy and the necessary adherence to the ideologies, theories and thoughts of the Marx-Leninist and Maoist tradition, as well as those more recently of Denghism, the three representatives and the thought of Xi Jinping.[57]

1.2.4 *The Fundamental Constitutional Principle of the People's Democratic Dictatorship*

The Chinese version of the dictatorship of the proletariat, or proletarian dictatorship, evoked by Marx, is represented by the formula of the democratic dictatorship of the people, embraced in the current Chinese Constitution in both the Preamble as well as Paragraph 1 of Article 1. Maozedong Thinking and the Dengist theory have spawned a notion of the proletarian dictatorship with Chinese characteristics, such as to include in the concept of the people's democratic dictatorship, not only the workers, but also the peasants (who constitute the majority of the Chinese population, with a much more accentuated numerical prevalence in the time of Mao), intellectuals, members of the national bourgeoisie and in a broad sense, of the productive classes.

The class nature of the Chinese Constitution determines the form of the State (Chinese: *guoti*).[58] The semantic differences that can be found in the history of constitutional law in popular China do not alter the fundamental class structure of the Chinese constitutionalist architecture. If, in fact, the 1954 Constitution defined, in Article 1, the PRC as being a democratic state of the people, reproducing the analogous expression contained in Article 2 of the Soviet Constitution of 1936, Article 1 of the Chinese Constitution of 1975 and Article 1 of the subsequent Constitutional Charter of 1978, referred to the proletarian dictatorship, while the current 1982 Constitution changed the denomination of the dictatorship of Article 1 from proletarian to democratic, with a return to the term used by the Constituent of 1954.

The combination of democracy and dictatorship, in the form of the Chinese state, can appear bizarre. Democratic methods are applied, based on the intentions of the constitutional legislator and without being prejudice to the problems of effectiveness, to the gener-

57 *See* the historical reconstruction of I. Castellucci, *Kǒng Fūzǐ (孔夫子), Shāng jūn (商君), Mao Zedong, Xi Jinping: Elements of Continuity in Chinese Political-Legal Doctrines*, paper presented at the 2018 Annual General Conference of the European China Law Studies Association, held at the University of Turin from 12 to 14 September 2018; C. Sorace, I. Franceschini, N. Loubere (Eds.), *Afterlives of Chinese Communism. Political Concepts from Mao to Xi*, Canberra, ANU (Australian National University) Press, 2019.

58 The concept of form of government is rendered in Mandarin Chinese by the expression *zhengti*.

ality of Chinese citizens as well as foreigners present in the territory of the PRC. The instruments of the popular dictatorship are reserved only for the enemies of the people, that is to say, the people and hostile forces that work for the destruction of the Chinese socialist system, the employer class having now disappeared with the abolition of every form of exploitation of man by man. Much depends, as is obvious, on the interpretation given to the undeviating notion of hostile forces.

On the other hand, the "Chinese style" people's democratic dictatorship places severe limits on the exercise of the democratic principle, which is also a fundamental component of modern constitutionalism, due to the fact that desiring also to access the thesis of the application of the democratic method to the people in normal and general way and that of the dictatorial method to the enemies of the people in an exceptional and residual way, the fact remains that the binding adhesion of the political actors to the two cardinal principles, previously examined of the supremacy of the CCP and that of the Marxist–Leninist–Maoist political doctrine, prevents a comparison on the basis of equality and in free elections, of a plurality of political parties or movements, including those with a non-communist orientation that are to be considered unconstitutional, according to the provisions of the Preamble to the Fundamental Charter. If, on the other hand, one wishes to consider the first two cardinal principles as having a declamatory or programmatic significance, and thus devoid of a perceptive value, then the same fundamental principle of the popular democratic dictatorship, where it applies to members of the Chinese people who are not classified as people hostile to the socialist system of the country, should involve the constitutionalization of the "pure" democratic principle (who obtains the majority of votes is legitimized to govern) in the political-party competition. However, if the two evoked fundamental constitutional principles are to be considered, in agreement with the majoritarian Chinese doctrine, of necessary and immediate application, it would seem possible to recognize a contrast between the founding elements of the constitutional organization in the People's Republic, to the extent in which the free expression of democratic rights and freedoms, and therefore also of political rights, among those who are not enemies of the people, would find obstacles in the need to adhere to the Marxism–Leninism–Maoism dictates.

1.2.5 The (Long) Path of Socialism with Chinese Characteristics

The fourth cardinal principle of the Chinese constitutional system is expressed in the Preamble of the Fundamental Charter and reaffirmed in Article 1, Paragraph 2, of the Constitution itself. It consists in the adhesion to the socialist doctrine, be it however in *Chinese-style*. The base or economic structure is, therefore, of a socialist type, with direct influence – in conformity with the Marxist theory – on the conformation of the juridical superstructure. Moreover, due to the fact that China is still in the first phase of socialism, a phase in which it is destined to remain for a long time – as explicitly stated in the Constitutional Preamble – the maintenance of a plurality of proprietary forms is fully compatible with the official Chinese ideologies, which recognizes and guarantees both socialist public ownership and private property. Hence, therefore, the formula of socialism of the market, or socialist market economy, which in itself appears to be shared by numerous jurisdictions with a so-called mixed economy, in the political-institutional context of the People's Republic acquires particular characteristics.

On the one hand, China has progressively experimented and introduced since 1978 and, with increasing intensity since 1993, the mechanisms and dynamics of a market economy in a system for a long time dominated by state welfarism, collectivization of the means of production (so-called totalitarian collectivism), rigid centralized planning and the absolute supremacy of public property,[59] although in the current Chinese model, the market and the plan stimulate one another, and together (wish) to promote the economic development of China, according to the paradigm of the transition from the *Economic Plan* to the *Public Affairs Governance Plan*.[60] In countries of a Western juridical and economic tradition, the passage was instead in the opposite direction, that is to say, from forms of unconditional economic liberalism to the provision of increasing temperaments via instruments of social *welfare*.

On the other hand, it should be noted that it is certainly not less important that the choice for the model of socialist development, which however seems suitable to cohabit with the rules of democratic development, does not derive from the free will manifested by the Chinese electoral body, but it is definitively established by the constitutional legislator, in order that the voters are not given the possibility to express different preferences regarding the determination of the fundamental principles of the country's economic system. In this regard, the same Chinese constitutional doctrine has questioned the compatibility of adhesion to socialism, understood as a fundamental constitutional principle with respect to the concrete possibilities of development of democracy in the People's Republic of China.[61]

---

59 On the reforms and economic, political and juridical transformations of the eighties and nineties of the last century *see, extensively*, R. Cavalieri, *La legge e il rito. Lineamenti di storia del diritto cinese*, op cit., 158 ff.

60 Highlighted recently by S. Heilmann, O. Melton, *The Reinvention of Development Planning in China, 1993-2012*, in *Modern China. An International Journal of History and Social Sciences*, 2013, 580 ff.; A. Hu, *The Distinctive Transition of China's Five-Year Plans, ivi*, 2013, 629 ff.

61 *Cf.* the reflections in this sense of Lin Feng, *Constitutional Law in China*, op cit., 35.

1.2.6 State Powers and Popular Sovereignty

After the enunciation of the four so-called cardinal principles, which ultimately represent the fundamental constitutional bases for the CCP's exercise of leadership and general orientation on the evolution of the social, political and economic system of the PRC, the 1982 Chinese Constitution dealt with tracing at least another four fundamental principles, this time however very similar to those that are usually contained in the Constitutional Charters of countries of a Western legal tradition, both of *civil law* as well as *common law*.

In this sense, Article 2 of the current Constitution proclaims in Paragraph 1, the devolution to the people of all the power of the State, specifying in Paragraph 2 that the institutional bodies through which the people exercise their sovereign power are the National People's Congress at the central level and the local people's congresses at the various levels of the subordinate political-administrative divisions. As the Chinese constitutional-comparatist doctrine notes,[62] it is a fundamental principle recognized by the Constitutional Charters of many countries, both with a liberal democracy or a socialist democracy, be they developed or developing.

In the Chinese constitutional system, therefore, the source of state power is the people, to which sovereignty belongs as a unitary and indivisible concept, while the power of the state is functionally divided between the higher organs of central power and the organs of local power.

The sovereign authority of the people is expressed in China via the system of central and local popular congresses; this model outlines a form of parliamentary government. A peculiarity is, however, the penetrating control exercised by the people not only on the representative bodies (congresses) of the various levels, but also on organs, organisms and officials created by the elected congresses and controlled by them. Thus, a sophisticated system of popular controls is created, to which the national parliamentarians and all the members of the representative congresses are subjected, who are constantly accountable before the people even after the elections have been held. The same applies also to all public officials. From this point of view, the presence of a parliamentary majority free from direct popular control during the parliamentary term and until the next electoral consultation, as in states of a classic liberal democracy, is not configurable under Chinese public law.

62 For example, Wang Shijie, Qian Duansheng, *Bijiao Xianfa* [*Comparative Constitutional Law*], Beijing, China University of Politics and Law Press, 1997.

1.2.7 The "Rule of Law" v. "The Rule of Man"

The regulations of the rule of law are referred to in the Chinese Constitution of 1982 in Article 5, where the objective of the construction of the socialist rule of law is stated.[63] The "socialist" adjectivization of the *rule of law*[64] would seem to be a symptom of the still

---

63 In a predominantly historical (and comparative) key, *see* the paper by Wu Shu-chen, *La tradizione giuridica cinese e l'idea europea del* rule of law, in P. Costa, D. Zolo (Eds.), *Lo Stato di diritto. Storia, teoria, critica*, op cit., 758 ff. For a complete examination, *cf.* R.C. Keith, *China's Struggle for the Rule of Law*, London/New York, Macmillan-St. Martin's Press, 1994; Zou Keyuan, *Towards Rule of Law in China: Experiences in the Last Two Decades*, in *China Report. A Journal of East Asian Studies*, 2000, 491 ff.; R. Peerenboom, *Ruling the Country in Accordance with Law. Reflections on the Rule and Role of Law in Contemporary China*, in P. Keller (Ed.), *Chinese Law and Legal Theory*, Aldershot (UK)/Burlington (VT, USA), Ashgate-Dartmouth, 2001, 178 ff.; Id., *China's Long March toward Rule of Law*, Cambridge, Cambridge University Press, 2002; R. Heuser, *What "Rule of Law"? The Traditional Chinese Concept of Good Government and Challenges of the 21st Century*, in *Zeitschrift für ausländisches öffentliches Recht und Völkerrecht*, 2004, 723 ff.; Q. Zhang, *From Administrative Rule of Law to Constitutionalism? The Changing Perspectives of the Chinese Public Law*, in *Asia Law Review*, 2006, 47 ff.; C. Wendehorst, *Rechtsstaatsdialog mit der VR China – Fortschritt oder Feigenblatt?*, in H. Casper-Hehne, I. Schweiger (hrsg.), *Vom Verstehen zur Verständigung. Beiträge zum europäischen Jahr des Interkulturellen Dialogs*, Göttingen, Universitätsverlag, 2009, 23 ff. From the Chinese point of view, *see* Liang Zhiping, *An Intrinsic Perspective on the Rule of Law: Observations on the Movement to Modernize Chinese Law*, in *Social Science in China*, 2004, n. 3, 128 ff.; Li Zi, *NPC: the rule of law*, in *Beijing Review*, 2004, n. 9, 10 ff.; He Weifang, *In the Name of Justice: Striving for the Rule of Law in China*, Washington (DC), The Brookings Institution, 2012 (the author is a lecturer at the Law School of Peking University; in the vol., a series of writings previously published in China) Ji Weidong, *Definite Uncertainties and the Grand Design of the Legal System in China*, in S. Muller, S. Zouridis, M. Frishman, L. Kistemaker (Eds.), *The Law of the Future and the Future of Law*, II, The Hague, Torkel Opsahl Academic Epublisher, 2012, 233 ff. (The author is Headmaster of the Shanghai Jiao Tong University-SJTU Koguan Law School); Q. Gao, W. Zhang, F. Tian, *The Road to the Rule of Law in Modern China*, Beijing-Berlin, Social Science Academic Press-Springer, 2015; L. Lin, *The Chinese Model of the Rule of Law*, in *Frontiers of Law in China*, 2015, 657 ff.; T.E. Kellogg, *Rule of law in Asia: The case of China*, in C. May, A. Winchester (Eds.), *Handbook on the Rule of Law*, Cheltenham (UK)/Northampton (MA, USA), 2018, 490 ff.; for a glance at the special Hong Kong observatory, *cf.* Li Buyun, *Ideal and Reality of Rule of Law in China*, in *Journal of Chinese and Comparative Law*, 1997, 40.; from Macao, *see* the opinion of Zhang Haiting, *Chinese Culture and "the Rule of Law" in China*, in *Chinese Cross Currents* (journal edited by *Istituto Ricci*, based in the former Portuguese colony of Macao), 2005, n. 1, 58 ff. (text in English and Chinese). With reference to the law of imperial China, *cf.* K. Turner, *Rule of Law Ideals in Early China?*, in *Journal of Chinese Law*, 1992, 1 ff. For the intra-Chinese comparison with the Taiwanese system, *see* W. Chen, *Twins of Different Colors. The Destiny of Rule of Law without Democracy Model in China and Taiwan, paper* presented at the *World Congress of Constitutional Law* held at the Law Faculty of the University of Oslo from 16 to 20 June 2014; for a comparison re the extra-European area, *see* J.K. Ocko, D. Gilmartin, *State, Sovereignty, and the People: A Comparison of the "Rule of Law" in China and India*, in *Journal of Asian Studies*, 2009, 55 ff.; for the comparison with *western civilization, see* K. Blaser, *Rule of Law in China. A Comparative Approach*, Berlin, Springer, 2015.

64 Accurate translation of the Chinese expression *fa-chih* (or *fazhi*) it is, moreover, *rule by law*, rather than *rule of law*. On the communicative aspects of Chinese law, with particular regard to the notion of *rule of/by law, see* D. Cao, *Fazhi vs/and/or Rule of Law?: A Semiotic Venture into Chinese Law*, in *International Journal for the Semiotics of Law*, 2001, 223 ff.; Id., *Chinese Law. A Language Perspective*, Aldershot (UK), Ashgate, 2004; Id., *Chinese Language in Law: Code Red*, Lanham (MD, USA), Lexington Books, 2018; M. Timoteo, *Il diritto per immagini. Aspetti del linguaggio giuridico cinese contemporaneo*, in B. Pozzo (Ed.), *Lingua e diritto: oltre l'Europa*, Milano, Giuffrè, 2014, 73 ff. The historical problems and profiles of the legal translation

instrumental conception in China of normative dispositions,[65] and in particular of the regulations of the rule of law; in other words, the principle of the *rule of law* would constitute the dynamic aspect that permits and favours the effectiveness of the legal system as a (supra)structural element, with a view to the socialist functionalization of the implementation of the legal system, without however impeding the ultimate goal of the realization of a communist society, as such deprived not only of antagonistic social classes but also of the law and the State. As has been effectively stated, the Chinese tradition prefers the *rule of governance*, over the mere reference to the *rule of law*.[66]

In the transition phase, of an indefinite duration and taking into account that, after the elapsing of the not so short period of time, from 1949 to today, that the People's Republic is still in the initial stage of socialism, the way to understand, at least formally, the regulations of the rule of law in the PRC appear to be not divergent from that followed in countries of an established Western legal tradition. It thus includes, among other things, the principle of the supremacy of the law, the impartiality of public administrations and the independence of the courts.[67] On the other hand, one of the objectives of the new

---

of the Chinese language have been examined by G. Terracina, *Lo studio del diritto cinese: problemi linguistici*, paper presented at the conference "*Italia – Cina: il ponte della comparazione giuridica*", held on 2 December 2005 at the Faculty of Law and the Faculty of Political Sciences at the University of Roma Tre. As regards the *rule of law* and *rule by law* in China *see also infra*, para. 7, on the constitutional regulation of fundamental rights.

65 Even in imperial China, the law was considered an administrative tool used by the state to protect its real and political interests (as well as for the implementation of moral "instructions"): *cf.* P.R. Goldin, *Han Law and the Regulation of Interpersonal Relations: "The Confucianization of the Law" Revisited*, in *Asia Major* (biannual publication edited by *Institute of History and Philology* of the *Academia Sinica*, Taiwan), III series, Vol. XXV, part I, 2012, 1 ff., as well as *amplius* T'ung-tsu Ch'ü, *Law and Society in Traditional China*, Paris-The Hague, Mouton, 1961 (*Le Monde d'Outre-Mer Passé et Présent*, Prmiére Série, *Études*, n. 4).

66 Thus, I. Castellucci, *Law and Governance in Chinese Tradition until Now*, paper presented at the *workshop Ming Qing Studies and Late Imperial China*, held from 16 to 17 May 2014 at the Università Cattolica del Sacro Cuore in Milan (and organized by the Istituto Confucio of the UCSC).

67 More generally, on the circulation of Western legal models in the national law of contemporary China, with particular reference to Germanic, Swiss and French law, and the importance that these models of codified continental law, often the source of inspiration of legal reform and legalization (also in the sense of the professionalization of the law) of the Chinese system through the filters represented by Japanese or Taiwanese law, *cf.* G. Crespi Reghizzi, *La lunga marcia del diritto. Da società senza giuristi a Paese ricco di esperti d'impresa e avvocati*, in *Il Sole 24 ore*, 18 November 2003, *Dossier – Cina, la grande sfida*, 6; Id., *Cina 2003: l'osservatorio del giurista*, in *Mondo cinese*, n. 117, 2003, 13 ff. With regard to the prospects of the gradual westernization, internationalization, technicization, partial liberalization and codification of Chinese-popular law, *see also* G. Crespi Reghizzi, *Il diritto cinese fra tradizione e riforma*, in *Rel. internaz.*, September 1994, 38 ff. For the Chinese point of view, *see* the collected works *sub* Jiang Shigong (Ed.), *Legal Transplantation in Contemporary China, Special Issue* di *Social Science in China*, 2004, n. 3, 108 ff. In particular on the influence of German models, *see* Y. Bu (hrsg.), *Deutsche und europäische Elemente des chinesischen Rechts. Untersuchungen aus zivilrechtlicher und öffentlich-rechtlicher Perspektive*, Berlin-Münster, LIT Verlag, 2012. Note that, in Chinese history, there have been attempts to overthrow positions, in the sense that it would be the same "western" knowledge that originated in China (according to an approach, therefore, that subverts the traditional approach for which it is non-Western thinking to be typically marginalized); *see* L.K. Jenko, *Histories of Thought and Comparative Political Theory: The Curious Thesis of "Chinese Origins*

Chinese leadership (the so-called the fifth generation in power[68]), under the impulse of the President of the PRC, Xi Jinping (习近平[69]), is to encourage *rule of law-consciousness* (Chinese: *fazhi siwei* 法治思维),[70] as was also recently confirmed during the work of the annual CCP Congress (*recte:* fourth *plenum – plenary session* of the XVIII Party Central Committee, made up of three hundred and seventy members) held in Beijing from 20 to 23 October 2014, which established the date of 2020 for the full realization in China of the principle of *rule of law.*[71] In this regard, it has opportunely been observed[72] that this was the first time that a meeting of the CCP, convened at the level of a plenary session, planned as its main subject for discussion, the realization and implementation of the *rule of law*.

The fundamental problem in China, at the present time, is precisely that of the concrete implementation of the methods and principles (also declaimed at a constitutional level)

---

for Western Knowledge", 1860-1895, in *Political Theory. An International Journal of Political Philosophy*, 2014, 658 ff.

68 *Cf.* M. Dillon, *China's Rulers: The Fifth Generation Takes Power (2012-13)*, London, Europe China Research and Advice Network (ECRAN), 2012. Extensively *see*, A. Amighini, A. Berkofski (Eds.), *Xi's policy gambles: the bumpy road ahead*, introduction by P. Magri, Milano-Novi Ligure, ISPI-Edizioni Epoké, 2015.

69 Xi has haeld the office of Head of State since March 2013. According to R. Orlandi, *La Cina di Xi Jinping*, in *Italianieuropei*, 2015, n. 2, www.italianieuropei.it, "Xi Jinping was chosen to lead China because he was considered the most suitable to find a synthesis between the country's traditional strategic objectives and the interests of the nomenclature who had appointed him."

70 Noted by I. Belkin, *Law, Justice and Rights in Xi Jinping's China: Dreaming of Resolving the Contradictions*, a report presented at the seminar on *Law, Justice and Rights in Xi Jinping's China*, held on the 9 July 2014 in Australia at the *Griffith University* (*Griffith Asia Institute*). On Xi's reformist approach, *see extensively* Y. Zheng, L.L.P. Gore (Eds.), *China Entering the Xi Jinping Era*, London/New York, Routledge, 2015; J. Garrick, Y. Chang Bennet (Eds.), *China's Socialist Rule of Law Reforms Under Xi Jinping*, London/New York, Routledge, 2016. However: "what should be made of 'rule the country in accordance with law' (依法治国)? According to Xi, rule the country in accordance with law should 'safeguard the rights of people' and 'maintain social justice.' But since taken power, Xi has made it clear that this 'safeguarding' and 'maintaining' is to come from the Party itself, not from the people" (thus E.M. Lynch, *Xi Jinping's New Year's Resolutions: Rule of Law and Join Facebook?*, in *China Law & Policy*, available at the website https://chinalawandpolicy.com, doc. dated 1 January 2015, a commentary on the annual new year message given by President Xi and transmitted by the Chinese media). On the problematic aspects, *see also*, A.H.Y. Chen, *China's Long March towards Rule of Law or China's Turn Against Law?*, in *Chinese Journal of Comparative Law*, 2016, 1 ff.

71 *Cf.* R. Cai, *Accelerazione sullo Stato di diritto*, in *Cina in Italia*, n. 113, 2014, 8 ff.; *Rule of law in China*, in *The Economist*, November 2014, 14; *China. Rules of the party, ibidem*, November 2014, 55 f.; B.B. Subba, *18th CPC Central Committee Fourth Plenum: Rule of Law with Chinese Characteristics*, Institute of Chinese Studies (Delhi, India), *Analysys*, n. 22, November 2014. The full text of the Decision (entitled *CCP Central Committee Decision concerning Some Major Questions in Comprehensively Moving Governing the Country According to the law Forward*) adopted by the *plenum* of the CCP, is available, in English at the website www.leggicinesi.it. A collection (with editorial commentary notes) of the writings, speeches, statements (both public and informal) of President Xi (relating to the years 2012-2014) is now deposited in the State Council Information Office, *Xi Jinping: The Governance of China*, Beijing, Foreign Languages Press, 2014; the aforementioned book was published, in addition to Chinese, also in the following languages: English, French, Russian, Arabic, Spanish, Portuguese, German, Japanese and Italian (*Xi Jinping. Governare la Cina*, Firenze, Giunti, 2016).

72 *Cf.* P. Gewirtz, *What China Means by 'Rule of Law'*, in *The New York Times*, 19 October 2014.

of the *rule of law*,[73] also in consideration of the fact that, as is well known, the disfavour for the instrument of the juridical regulation presents, in the Chinese context, a thousand-year tradition,[74] manifested not only at the time of the "Great Proletarian Cultural Revolution" of Mao, but well before, during the imperial dynasties, when Confucian philosophy, based on rituals (*li*), that is to say social, moral and ceremonial norms, rather than on the law (*fa*), intended primarily as a penal law/code equipped with punishments – and the theory of legists (or legalists, or statesmen), who instead advocated the need for laws and positive law to regulate social life,[75] according to formulations now once again in vogue in the PRC, so much so as to speak of, drawing inspiration from ancient Chinese law,[76] the aspiration to the model of the "government of the law" (*fazhi*), which implies the

---

73 Hence, one asks: "Will China succeed in establishing the rule of law as it is understood and practiced in the West and in other parts of Asia?" (*see* A. Sheng, X. Geng, *Creare uno stato di diritto cinese*, in *Il Sole 24 Ore*, 15 February 2013).

74 G. Crespi Reghizzi, *Il diritto cinese fra tradizione e riforma*, op cit., 39. Speaks of "the country's traditional aversion to laws and the right to legal training".

75 *See, ex multis*: L. Lanciotti, Li versus Fa: *confuciani e legalisti*, in *Annali di Cà Foscari*, XIV 3 (*Serie Orientale* 6), 1975, 177 ff.; M. Sabattini, *La mistificazione «legalista»: note su un recente dibattito politico-storiografico*, in *Cina*, n 15, 1979, 75 ff.; E. Dell'Aquila, *Il diritto cinese. Introduzione e principi generali*, Padova, Cedam, 1981; Han Yanlong, Xu Lizhi, *L'influenza della tradizione confuciana sul sistema giuridico cinese moderno*, in *Soc. dir.*, 1995, n. 1, 77 ff.; R. Cavalieri, *La legge e il rito. Lineamenti di storia del diritto cinese*, op cit.; L. Moccia, *Il sistema giuridico cinese: caratteri tradizionali e lineamenti attuali*, in *Riv. trim. dir. proc. civ.*, 2000, 1251 ff. and in L. Lanciotti (Ed.), *Conoscere la Cina* (proceedings of the Turin conference of Associazione Italia-Cina, 4 and 5 April 2000), Torino, Edizioni Fondazione G. Agnelli, 2000, 23 ff.; Id., *Prologo breve sulla «originalità» del diritto (tradizionale) cinese e sull'importanza del suo studio in prospettiva storico-comparativa*, in *Riv. trim. dir. proc. civ.*, 2004, 991 ff. and in M. Scarpari, T. Lippiello (Eds.), *Caro Maestro… Scritti in onore di L. Lanciotti per l'ottantesimo compleanno*, Venezia, Cafoscarina, 2005, 813 ff.; Id. (edit.), *Profili emergenti del sistema giuridico cinese*, op cit., *sub* I, *Uno sguardo alla storia del diritto in Cina. Tradizione e Modernizzazione*, 31 ff.; Id., *Il diritto cinese nella teoria dei sistemi giuridici: dalla tradizione alla commistione*, paper presented at the conference "*Italia – Cina: il ponte della comparazione giuridica*", op cit.; Cao Pei, *La dottrina confuciana e il "governo dell'uomo": l'umanesimo cinese originario*, in P. Costa, D. Zolo (Eds.), *Lo Stato di diritto. Storia, teoria, critica*, op cit., 739 ff.; Liang Zhiping, *Explicating "Law": A Comparative Perspective of Chinese and Western Legal Culture*, in *Journal of Chinese Law*, 1989, 55 ff.; H.H. Ma, *The Chinese Concept of the Individual and the Reception of Foreign Law, ivi*, 1995, 207 ff.; Fu Zhengyuan, *China's Legalists. The Earliest Totalitarians and Their Art of Ruling*, Armonk (NY), Sharpe, 1996; P.C.C. Huang, *Morality and Law in China, Past and Present*, in *Modern China. An International Journal of History and Social Sciences*, 2015, 3 ff. For an anthropological approach, *cf.* J. Thoraval, *L'anthropologue et la question de la visibilité du confucianisme dans la société chinoise contemporaine*, in *Perspectives chinoises*, n. 52, 1999, 71 ff. On the law, custom and morals in East Asian countries, *see also* the penetrating observations of L. Abegg, *In Asia si pensa diversamente. Antitesi e complementarietà dell'Estremo Oriente e dell'Occidente*, (1949), Italian translation, Roma, Astrolabio, 1952.

76 P. Santangelo, *L'impero del Mandato Celeste. La Cina nei secoli XIV-XIX*, Roma-Bari, Laterza, 2014 (*sub* III, *Le forme del potere: l'impero e le sue articolazioni*, 40 ff., on the functions of the institutional system, and XII; *Ideologie e religioni*, 264 ff., re the art of good governance) that in China, the past resurfaces continuously in the present, so that to understand current China one cannot ignore the knowledge of the bimillennial period of imperial China.

overcoming of the opposed model of the "government of man" (*renzhi*), as a modern expression of neolegalist tendencies.[77]

And indeed, as has been noted:

> A growing number of senior PRC leaders come from a legal studies background. The importance of legal education in China is growing. The ability to translate into law political and justice needs thus contributes to shaping the "rule of law" that grows accompanied by the formation of a professional group of tens of thousands of young jurists who are trained in the multiple universities of China.[78]

1.2.8 *The Principle of Equality Among National Ethnic Communities, with a View to the (Constitutional and Legislative) Protection of Regional/Local and Linguistic Autonomy*

Article 4 of the 1982 Constitution establishes the fundamental principles of the regulations inherent to the national ethnic groups, among which harmonious relations must be established[79] and that are recognized by the PRC on the basis of meticulous ethnographic, socio-anthropological, religious and linguistic classifications[80] via which the total number

77 The legislative evolutionary dynamic restarted in the post-Maoist era, after the end of the juridical nihilism (so-called nihilistic rule) of the years of the Cultural Revolution; *cf.* G. Melis, *Il dominio della legge*, in *Mondo cinese*, n. 31, 1980, 3 ff.; G. Crespi Reghizzi, *Ricerca giuridica e continuità del diritto in Cina*, *ivi*, n. 29, 1980, 73 ff. On the manifestation "of the cyclical commuting and the indestructible interlacement, in the history of the country, between Confucianism and legalism, the government of man and the rule of law", *see* G. Crespi Reghizzi, *Cina 2003: l'osservatorio del giurista*, op cit., 13. For the Chinese point of view on the concept of administration through the law, *cf.* Fan Ren, *Governing by Law*, in *Beijing Review*, 2004, n. 22, 28 f.

78 *Cf.* S. Schipani, *Un tempo dei giuristi*, in *Cinitalia*, 2014, n. 4/12, 58 f.

79 As stated by the Art. 4 of the Constitution, after the revision of March 2018.

80 The study with taxonomic purposes of the ethnic groups of China began after the fall of the last imperial dynasty, at the time of the so-called Republic of the Five nationalities, represented by the *Han* and Mongolian, Manchu, Tibetan and Tatar national minorities. Systematic surveys on the ethnic composition and linguistic identification of the population, carried out in the first phase with the assistance of Soviet ethnographers, were launched in 1950. In addition to sociologists, anthropologists and linguists, historians and literary, music and art experts, participated too. These are ongoing investigations in the PRC, as has been recently highlighted Y. Wang, *Gli studi recenti sulle politiche etniche cinesi*, a paper presented at the First Italian Congress of Anthropology of China (dedicated to the anthropological study of Chinese cultures) held at the Bicocca University, Milan on 12 December 2013(the author is the director of *Institute of Ethnology and Anthropology* of the *Chinese Academy of Social Sciences*). *See also*, extensively, H. Hu, J. Wang, H. Zhang, *Storia dell'antropologia cinese*, (2006), Italian edition edited by A. Pia, Firenze, Seid Editori, 2014 (a work published with the contribution of *State Council Information Office of the People's Republic of China*), especially *sub* VI, *La classificazione delle minoranze e le ricerche di storia sociale*, 151 ff., and VIII, *La rinascita dell'antropologia*, 205 ff. (for the period following the conclusion of the Cultural Revolution in October 1976), and furthermore L. Xie (Ed.), *De-Politicization of Ethnic Questions in China*, Hackensack (NJ), World

has been fixed at fifty-six.[81] In addition, the PRC voted in the UN General Assembly to support the *United Nations Declaration on the Rights of Indigenous Peoples*, UNDRIP (2007), but this has not yet had any influence within China in terms of minority policies, based on the assumption, proclaimed by the Chino-popular authorities, that in the PRC there are no ethnic groups classified as being "indigenous",[82] according to international human rights law.

The most prevalent community is that of the *Han* Chinese people, that is to say, Chinese in the strict sense, with 91.59% of the total population according to the data of the fifth national census carried out in 2000, equal to 1,159,000,000 individuals (during the congressional work of the *International Union of Anthropological and Ethnological Sciences*, IUAES, held at the Faculty of Sociology and Anthropology of the *Thammasat University* in Bangkok from 15 to 17 July 2015. More specifically, in the *panel* entitled, *China Forum: Development in Indigenous Areas and Development of Minorities*, coordinated by Prof. Wang Yanzhong of the *Institute of Ethnology and Anthropology of the Chinese Academy of Social Sciences*, the demographic data was updated, in the sense that the majority ethnic group of the *Han* currently comprises 91.9% of the total population of the PRC). The members of the remaining national ethnic minorities, or "other" identities, are Chinese in terms of citizen-

---

Scientific, 2014 (*Peking University Series on Sociology and Anthropology*, vol. 2); R. Malighetti, *Antropologie dalla Cina*, preface by Herzfeld, Firenze, Seid Editori, 2014.

81 On the kaleidoscope of ethnic groups in China, with particular regard to the relative taxonomic thinking and juridical problems, *see* M. Mazza, *La tutela delle minoranze nazionali e delle autonomie*, in *Mondo cinese*, n. 147, 2011, 68 ff.; C. Turini, *Società multietnica e pluralismo culturale: considerazioni su problemi delle minoranze etniche nella Repubblica Popolare Cinese, ivi*, n. 101, 1999, 37 ff.; M. Cigliano, *La legge sull'autonomia delle minoranze e la sua attuazione, ivi*, n. 63, 1988, 13 ff.; G. Melis, *Le autonomie regionali nella Cina contemporanea, ibidem*, n. 60, 1987, 3 ff.; F. Cosentino, *Problemi e caratteristiche dello sviluppo economico nelle aree periferiche della Cina abitate dalle minoranze nazionali, ibidem*, n. 36, 1981, 59 ff.; P. Corradini, *Problemi delle minoranze nazionali in Cina, ibid.*, n. 18, 1977, 3 ff.; Wang Ke, *L'autonomia regionale per le minoranze nazionali*, in *La Cina d'oggi*, September 1958, 8 ff.; G. Casu, *Le etnie nella Cina degli Han, ibid.*, n. 18, 1977, 15 ff.; R. Toniatti, J. Woelk (Eds.), *Regional Autonomy, Cultural Diversity and Differentiated Territorial Government The Case of Tibet - Chinese and Comparative Perspectives*, London/New York, *Routledge*, 2017; R. Ma, Z. Jian, *Ethnic Relations and Minority Policies in Contemporary China*, London/New York, Routledge, 2016; Y. Zhou, M. Lundburg (Eds.), *Minorities, Autonomy and Development: Studies on Regional National Autonomy in China Contents*, Beijing, Law Press China, 2007; D.C. Gladney, *Dislocating China: Muslims, Minorities, and Other Subaltern Subjects*, London, Hurst, 2004; C. Mackerras, *China's Ethnic Minorities and Globalisation*, London/New York, Routledge, 2003; C. Keyes, *Presidential Address: "The Peoples of Asia" - Science and Politics in the Classification of Ethnic Groups in Thailand, China, and Vietnam*, in *The Journal of Asian Studies*, 2002, 1163 ff.; D. Yen-ho Wu, *The Construction of Chinese and Non-Chinese Identities*, in *Daedalus (Journal of the American Academy of Arts and Sciences)*, 1991, n. 2, 159 ff.; T. Heberer, *China and its national minorities. Autonomy or Assimilation?*, Armonk (NY)/London, Sharpe, 1989; Id., *Neue Aspekte der Autonomiegesetzgebung in der Volksrepublik China*, in *Zeitschrift für Vergleichende Rechtswissenschaft*, 1983, 152 ff.

82 On the question *cf.*, M.C. Davis, China and the UN Declaration on the Rights of Indigenous Peoples: The Tibetan Case, *University of Hong Kong Faculty of Law Research Paper No. 2014/044*, and in M. Woons (Ed.), *Restoring Indigenous Self-Determination. Theoretical and Practical Approaches*, Bristol, E-International Relations, 2014, 96 ff.; L. Wang, *The Definition of Indigenous Peoples and its Applicability in China*, in *International Journal on Minority and Group Rights*, 2015, 232 ff.

ship, not in terms of ethnic and linguistic characteristics. These still number 104.49 million people, constituting 8.41% of the entire population of China, who occupy vast areas of the country, approximately two-thirds of the total territory.

A specification of what is stated in the Preamble of the current Constitution, which defines the PRC as a unitary multinational state, Paragraph 1 of Article 4 of the fundamental law prohibits any discrimination or form of oppression to the detriment of national minorities, who are placed on an equal footing both among themselves as well as with regards to the numerically large majority ethnic community of the *Han*. The following paragraph of the same constitutional provision guarantees regional autonomy for the areas of the country where "concentrated communities" of members of national ethnic minorities live, including the establishment of local self-governing bodies in these local areas, but excluding the right of secession. The third and final paragraph of the Article 4 contemplates the protection and promotion of practices, customs and traditions of ethnic groups, as well as the protection and development of minority languages that the so-called non-Han people have the right to use freely in both in written and oral communication.

The cultural, linguistic[83] and socio-economic rights of ethnic minorities in China, the relative political-institutional *status*, as well as the composition and functions of local self-governing bodies created in the 155 independent ethnic areas[84] currently existing in the country, are regulated, in detail, by the law of 31 May 1984, dedicated to regional ethnic autonomy. This legislative provision, approved by the second session of the VI National People's Congress and that entered into force on 1 October of the same year, was subsequently amended on 28 February 2001 by the Standing Committee of the NPC.

1.2.9 The Acknowledgment of Constitutional Status to Human Rights

In terms of constitutional theory, at least three ways can be imagined for the protection of fundamental rights and freedoms. Firstly, the Constitution can provide a more or less analytical catalogue of individual fundamental rights, without declarations regarding the protection of the general category of human rights. Secondly, it is possible to have a Constitution which proclaims to protect human rights by not following the specific list of fundamental rights and freedoms, or by contemplating only brief provisions in this regard. As a third hypothesis, one has a Constitution containing statements on the protection of human rights and, moreover, norms concerning a plurality of fundamental rights and freedoms of man and of the citizen.

83 On which *see* in particular M. Zinzi, *Diritti linguistici ed istruzione bilingue in Cina*, in *Dir. pubbl. comp. eur.*, 2016, 1027 ff.

84 To be precise, these are five autonomous regions, thirty autonomous prefectures and one hundred and twenty autonomous districts.

The constitutional revision of 14 March 2004 determined the passage of the PRC from the first to the third of the aforementioned architecture of regulations. The new formulation given in Article 33 of the Constitution, placed in Chapter II dedicated to the fundamental rights and duties of citizens, now contains the declamation for which the State respects and protects human rights.

The prevailing Chinese public law doctrine believed, even before the constitutional amendment of 2004, that the protection of fundamental human rights represented a fundamental constitutional principle, even in the absence of an explicit super-primary regulatory provision, even though there were advocates of an only legal and non-constitutional *status* of "socialist" human rights.[85]

---

85 On the debate among Chinese constitutionalists, *cf.* Lin Feng, *Constitutional Law in China*, op cit., 42 ff. *See also* G. Ajani, *EU-China Relations and Fundamental Human Rights: A View from Europe*, in S. Beretta, L. Zhang (Eds.), *Contemporary China through the Eyes of Italian Experts*, op cit., 38 ff. (text in Chinese); E. Asciutti, *Diritti umani in Cina. Evoluzione storica di un concetto: 1899-1998*, in *Diritti umani e diritto internazionale*, 2009, n. 3, 282 ff.; A. Crisma, *Il problema dei diritti umani in Cina in un orizzonte di universalismo contestuale*, in S. Mattarelli (Ed.), *Il senso della Repubblica. Doveri*, Milano, Angeli, 2007, 179 ff.; Li Zhenghui, Wang Zhenmin, *Diritti dell'uomo e Stato di diritto nella teoria e nella pratica della Cina contemporanea*, in P. Costa, D. Zolo (Eds.), *Lo Stato di diritto. Storia, teoria, critica*, op cit., 791 ff.; M. Marinelli, *Modernizzazione e diritti umani in Cina*, Bologna, Pàtron, 2000; P. Corradini, *Cina e diritti umani*, in *Mondo cinese*, n. 76, 1991, 3 ff.; Id., *I diritti umani nella Costituzione cinese*, *ivi*, n. 46, 1984, 3 ff.; E. Pils, *Human Rights in China. A Social Practice in the Shadows of Authoritarianism*, Cambridge, Pllity, 2017; G.H. Nielsen, *Walking a Tightrope. Defending Human Rights in China*, Copenhagen, NIAS (Nordic Institut of Asian Studies) Press, 2014; P. Sun, *Human Rights Protection System in China*, Berlin, Springer, 2014; G. Wacker, *Norms Without Borders? Human Rights in China*, in R. Foot (Ed.), *China Across the Divide. The Domestic and Global in Politics and Society*, Oxford, Oxford University Press, 2013, 175 ff.; S. Ding, *Is Human Rights the Achilles' Heel of Chinese Soft Power? A New Perspective on Its Appeal*, in *Asian Perspective*, 2012, n. 4, *Special Issue: China and Soft Power*, 641 ff.; Li Jianguo, *The Rule of Law and Human Rights*, in *Beijing Review*, 2005, n. 44, 3; Dong Yunhu, *China's Human Rights Breakthrough*, *ivi*, 2004, n. 17, 22 f. (the author is Vice-President and Secretary-General of the Chinese Society for Human Rights Studies); S.C. Angle, *Human Rights and Chinese Thought. A Cross-Cultural Inquiry*, Cambridge, Cambridge University Press, 2002; M. Svensson, *Debating Human Rights in China. A Conceptual and Political History*, Lanham (Maryland), Rowman and Littlefield, 2002. Re the fact that in China there is a significant divergence of the human rights situation on paper and in reality, *see, e.g.*, S. Deva, *The Constitution of China: What Purpose Does it (Not) Serve?*, in *Jindal Global Law Review*, 2011, 55 ff. Sulla *human rights advocacy* in Cina, *see* E. Pils, *China's Human Rights Lawyers. Advocacy and Resistance*, London/New York, Routledge, 2014; H. Fu, *What Future is there for Human Rights Lawyering in China?*, in *Made in China. A Quarterly on Chinese Labour, Civil Society, and Rights*, 2017, n. 2, 12 ff. (in addition *see infra*, in para. 7.1). On the dialogue launched by the European Union with the authorities of the PRC aimed at promoting human rights in China, *see also* K. Kinzelbach, *The EU's Human Rights Dialogue with China. Quiet Diplomacy and its Limits*, London/New York, Routledge, 2015; with regard to German initiatives, *see* X. Gao, B. Gao, *The German-Chinese 'Rule of Law Dialogue': Influence and Outlook*, in *Verfassung und Recht in Übersee. Law and Politics in Africa, Asia, Latin America*, 2014, 392 ff. For a comparison, *see also* L. Li, Z. Xie, K. Nuotio (Eds.), *Safeguarding Human Rights and Constructing the Rule of Law. A Comparison between China and Finland*, Beijing, China Forum on the Rule of Law – Social Sciences Academis Press, 2014. Finally, on the convergence between Confucian thinking and human rights, *see* R. Cavalieri, *Diritti soggettivi e diritti umani nel contesto confuciano*, in V. Possenti, M. Nordio (Eds.), *Governance globale e diritti dell'uomo*, Reggio Emilia, Diabasis, 2007, 133 ff.

The innovations of the Constitution intervened to clarify that the protection of the rights of citizens, established in the Constitution, is a reflection of the basic constitutional principle (or guiding principle) of respect for and protection of human rights. Naturally now, there is the need to guarantee the effective implementation of the constitutional provisions, taking into account Chinese peculiarities in the approach to human rights issues. In particular, the criterion of the minimum *standard* in the protection of fundamental human rights is accepted, but with the clarification that the exact content of human rights may vary according to the socio-political and economic conditions of the different States. Moreover, on one hand, it is accepted that collective rights do not have a constitutional status higher than that of individual rights. However, on the other hand, it is added that individual and collective rights are not absolute, as they must be carefully balanced with constitutional duties. Furthermore, for the Chinese, state sovereignty is a concept that is superior to that of human rights, with the consequent rejection of any interference in the internal affairs of the PRC motivated by alleged requirements for the protection of fundamental human rights. Finally, the path towards the realization of an authentic democratic constitutionalism in China still appears not easy nor short. This is due to the fact that the primary objectives of the Chinese political-party leadership are addressed to the solution of problems typical of developing countries, which are substantiated in the effort to create the material conditions for the effective protection of the right to food and survival, rather than the purpose, currently considered secondary, of the protection of democratic rights and fundamental freedoms.

The predominantly symbolic, semantic and programmatic value of the constitutional amendment on the protection of human rights can, on the other hand, has the practical implication of offering constitutional status protection for any new rights not expressly contemplated in the catalogue of rights, liberties and fundamental duties of Chapter II of the Constitution, such as for example, one cannot rule out that this will occur in perspective for the rights of the so-called fourth generation.[86]

For the implementation of human rights in China, however, profound structural changes of the legal and institutional system, are still today on the waiting list, starting from the substantive and criminal procedural codes, the introduction of the judicial review of the constitutionality of laws and sub-legal normative sources,[87] as well as a different

86 In this sense follows the reflection of G. Crespi Reghizzi, M.E. Delmestro, *La Costituzione della Repubblica popolare cinese si aggiorna*, op cit., 589 ff.

87 The "*judicialization of the constitution*" (Chinese: *xianfa sifahua), although subject to debate in the People's Republic of China, it is not currently considered a sine qua non condition for the realization of an authentic constitutionalist State. See*, in this sense, N.S. Bui, *Beyond Judicial Review: the Proposal of the Constitutional Academy*, in *Chinese Journal of Comparative Law*, 2014, 43 ff., with extensive references to "Confucian constitutionalism", based on the discovery and enhancement of constitutional ideas in classical Confucianism (as highlighted in an efficacious manner by N.S. Bui, *Confucian Constitutionalism: Classical Foundations*, in *Australian Journal of Legal Philosophy*, 2012, 61 ff.; for a detailed examination of the *East Asian Model*

sensibility of the operators of the law that are capable of avoiding the frequent violations of the fundamental rights of the man, of remarkable entity among other things, with regard to the rights of the prisoners and persons subjected to the application of administrative measures of a sanctioning nature that provide for re-education through work (that is to say, forced labour).[88]

1.3 The Pyramidal System of the (National and Territorial/Local) People's Congresses

1.3.1 The National Parliament and the Local Parliaments, the Exclusive Holders of Public Functions and State Power

The traditional principles of public and parliamentary law of socialist states, that have almost disappeared from the juridical globe after the "revolutionary" events of 1989 in Eastern Europe and the dissolution of the Soviet Union itself in 1991, persistently survive (at least for now[89]) in the structuring of the Chinese People's Congresses.[90]

---

of Constitutionalism, as well as the notions of Confucian classic, imperial and modern constitutionalism, *see* N.S. Bui, *Confucian Constitutionalism in East Asia*, London/New York, Routledge, 2016). *Cf.*, additionally, J. Chen, *Constitutional Judicialization and Popular Constitutionalism in China: are we there yet?*, in G. Yu (Ed.), *The Development of the Chinese Legal System. Change and Challenges, London/New York,* Routeledge 2011, 3 ff., for an examination of three proposals on the control of constitutionality, namely: a) establishment of a constitutional commission within the National People's Congress; b) creation of a Constitutional Court; c) attribution to the Supreme People's Court of the judicial review of the constitutionality of the laws.

88 Regarding the "dehumanised" penalties, both judicial and administrative, and the "brutalization" of prison law in China, so as to be able to speak not only of a "cruel criminal law" but also of a "cruel administrative law" in the PRC, *see* the eloquent pages of U. Fragola, *Rudimenti di diritto amministrativo cinese*, Napoli, Edizioni Scientifiche Italiane, 2005, 97 ff. As regards, in particular, the fields for re-education through work, it was announced, during the third *plenum* of the XVIII Congress of the CCP held in November 2013, their closure by the end of the same year, but the risk is that it is a 'façade' change, which hides the maintenance of special detention facilities, as happens for example for rehabilitation centres for drug addicts, or for "classes for legal education" (known as "centres for brainwashing", where practitioners of certain religions and/or spiritual disciplines – including *Falun Gong* – are forcibly induced to renounce their faith); *cf.* Amnesty International, *Changing the soup but not the medecine? Abolishing re-education through labour in China*, London, Amnesty International Publications, 2013.

89 As observed by P. Biscaretti di Ruffia, *Costituzioni straniere contemporanee*, II, 6th edn, op cit., 3, *Un superstite «Stato socialista» asiatico in corso di progressiva trasformazione economica*, 153.

90 On the political-parliamentary assemblies of the PRC, *see* Bai Gang, *L'esperienza parlamentare nella Cina contemporanea*, in *Storia d'Italia. Annali*, 17, *Il Parlamento*, Torino, Einaudi, 2001, 1349 ff.; A. Lavagnino, *Le istituzioni "parlamentari" della Repubblica Popolare Cinese*, in *Mondo cinese*, n. 106, 2001, 13 ff.; M. Mazza, *Decentramento e governo locale nella Repubblica popolare cinese*, Milano, Giuffrè, 2009; R. Peerenboom, *China's Long March toward Rule of Law*, op cit., 6, *The legislative system: battling chaos*, 239 ff.; M. Xia, *The People's Congresses and Governance in China. Toward a network mode of governance*, London/New York, Routledge, 2008; A. Lahtinen, *Governance Matters. China's Developing Western Region with a Focus on Qinghai Province*, Helsinki, University of Helsinki, 2010 (*Publications of the Institute for Asian and African*

Therefore, the organizational criteria of public institutions in socialist or popular democracies are applied, with the powers of the State centralized in the representative Congresses created at the various territorial levels, bearing in mind that the amplitude of such powers progressively increases as one goes up to the higher levels, according to the principle of the so-called dimension of power. Furthermore, on the basis of the principle of democratic centralism proclaimed by Article 3 of the current Constitution of the PRC as a general category valid for each state body (and also, based on the statutory provisions, for the internal organization of the CCP), the resolutions adopted by the regional representative Congresses are binding for the General Congresses (Parliaments[91]) of a lower level, in accordance with the so-called vertical dependence rule, to be understood as a subcategory of the afore-mentioned principle of democratic centralism, or rather, as a centralizing component of this principle.[92]

In the public law system of China, in implementation of the aforementioned principles and criteria derived from the Marx-Engelsian theory,[93] the State form envisages the dominant role of the working class that acts under the guidance of its avant-garde represented by the CCP,[94] while the form of government is republican and based on the system of popular Congresses (Parliaments).[95] All the other organs, bodies, organizations and insti-

Studies, n. 11); Y. Sun, *Development of Chinese Local People's Congresses in the Reform Era: Dynamics and Limits*, in *American Journal of Chinese Studies*, 2010, 131 ff.; G. Zhu, *The composite state of China under "One Country, Multiple Systems": Theoretical construction and methodological considerations*, in *International Journal of Constitutional Law*, 2012, 272 ff. (also in the French translation, *L'état composite de Chine dans le prisme de la doctrine «un pays, systèmes multiples»: construction théorique et considérations méthodologiques*, in *Mélanges en l'honneur du Professeur C. Louit*, Bruxelles, Bruylant, 2016, 463 ff.); M. Manion, *Authoritarian Parochialism: Local Congressional Representation in China*, in *The China Quarterly*, 2014, 311 ff.

91 In the former USSR called Soviets.

92 On the set up of the organs of state power in the legal systems of the (ex) legal family of the countries of socialist law *see*, with reference to the Soviet system, P. Biscaretti di Ruffia, G. Crespi Reghizzi, *La Costituzione sovietica del 1977. Un sessantennio di evoluzione costituzionale nell'URSS*, Milano, Giuffrè, 1979. For an analysis also extended to the People's Republic of China, *cf.* G. Crespi Reghizzi, *Centralismo democratico*, in *Dig. (IV), disc. priv. sez. civ.*, II, 1988, 268 ff.; on the PRC, *see* Tsien Tche-hao, *Politica e diritto in Cina*, in *Quale giust.*, 1973, 539 ff. The so-called rule of horizontal dependence, for which the national and local Executives depend on the Legislatures of the same territorial level, combining on the one hand with the further vertical dependence of each Executive from the homologous higher level organ so as to originate the institutional mechanism of double dependency (or double subordination), and on the other hand with the principle described in the text of democratic centralism, determine the banning in the Chinese political-constitutional system of the principle of the separation of powers, a fundamental constitutional basis of the systems that acknowledge *western legal tradition*, and thus the remarkable differentiation between the form of (or method of training of) the Chinese government of the People's Assemblies (Parliaments) and the form of contemporary parliamentary government in the liberal-democratic states of the West.

93 As well as the historical experiences of the Paris Commune and Soviet Russia.

94 *See* what was stated *retro* Chap. II, on the ideological foundations of Chinese constitutional law.

95 *Cf.* C.B. Simonsen, *Development and Organization of the Govermental and Legal Systems of the People's Republic of China*, in *China Law Reports*, 1991, 239 ff.; nella prospettiva delle riforme costituzionali, *see* J. Tan, *Presidential, Parliamentary, or Combined System of Government: Comparison and Choice for China*, in *Columbia Journal of Asian Law*, 1997, 219 ff. On political democracy in China, *see*, Fang Ning, *Democracy*

tutions of the State, constitute a simple functional emanation and operative structure of the People's Congresses, and are created by the latter and remain always accountable to them.

According to Chinese constitutional doctrine, which uses a conceptual instrument that is partially different from that of the countries of Western law, it is appropriate to distinguish between the form of government and the method of formation of the government. The first notion concerns the nature of government, and in particular the fundamental distinction between Monarchy and the Republic. The second concept refers to the possible and different methods for forming, that is to say structuring, the government of the country. In the case of the republican form of government, Chinese public law doctrine distinguishes the fundamental methods of the parliamentary system, the presidential system and the system of popular congresses. The latter, therefore, constitutes the specific method of the formation of the government in the context of the republican nature of the form of government of the People's Republic of China. This is an alternative method to both the parliamentary and the presidential system; these three methods, which from the Chinese perspective are inspired by, the first, socialist legal thinking and the remaining two by capitalist juridical thinking. All however share a belonging to the category of the republican form of government.[96]

Given this, in terms of the general theory of constitutional law and the (macro)comparison between public law systems, one can begin by observing that the supreme body of state power, in accordance with Article 57 of the 1982 Constitution, is the National People's Congress, which can be considered the Chinese National Parliament. According to the writings and practice of Marx, Engels, Lenin and Mao, all the powers of the state are attributed to the superior representative body of the people.

The pre-eminent position of the Legislative Congress placed at the top of the parliamentary system of contemporary China is reproduced at various levels, so that each local Parliament possesses, in a similar way to the national Parliament, the unified state power, capable of division only on a functional level. The difference between the parliamentary and presidential systems of the countries of Western law is therefore distinct, since in the PRC, the representative body of the people holds the three traditional legislative, executive and judicial powers. The administrative and judicial bodies depend on those parliamentary; the delegates of the people, members of the parliamentary Congresses, appoint and dismiss from office, the members of central and local Governments as well as the higher-level jurisdictional bodies, control their activities and configure with them a so-called single-track relationship,[97] i.e. without reciprocal brakes, balances or limitations between the

With Chinese Characteristics, in *Beijing Review*, 2005, n. 45, 18 ff. (The author is the deputy director of the Institute of Political Science at the Chinese Academy of Social Sciences).

96 *Cf.* Lin Feng, *Constitutional Law in China*, op cit., 56.

97 In this sense, *see* Bai Gang, *L'esperienza parlamentare nella Cina contemporanea*, op cit., 1350.

powers of the State as occurs in the systems of consolidated Western legal tradition or even in the post-Soviet systems of the East European.

1.3.2 *The Structure of the National People's Congress*

The 1982 Constitution expanded the role of the national single-chamber Parliament, called the National People's Congress (NPC, Chinese: *quanguo renmin daibiao dahui*[98]), specifying the division of functions between the management People's Congress, formed by all representatives (*daibiao*) of the people at the national level, and the Standing Committee (*changwu weiyuanhui*) of the NPC, which includes members appointed by Parliament and revoked by it. The Standing Committee has legislative powers, which it exercises in the intervals between the sessions of the National People's Congress. According to the basic law of the NPC adopted in 1982, two parliamentary procedure regulations were issued, respectively for the National People's Congress in 1989 and for the Standing Committee of the National Parliament in 1987. The position of member of the Standing Committee, which is the real driving force of the Chinese legislative apparatus, is incompatible with the carrying out of activities or the obtaining of positions within the administrative-executive or jurisdictional bodies. Instead, the same does not apply to the "ordinary" members of the NPC. Hence, there results a tendency towards the professionalization of only the members of the Standing Committee of the National Parliamentary Congress.

According to the changes introduced in 1986, the representative electoral law of the National People's Congress established that the total number of Members of the National Parliament could not exceed three thousand. The seat of the National People's Congress

98 Expression whose literal meaning is, as recall Crespi Reghizzi, M.E. Delmestro, *La Costituzione della Repubblica popolare cinese si aggiorna*, op cit., 575, nt. 2, "Pan-Chinese Assembly of People's Representatives". On the National People's Congress, *see* J.Y.S. Cheng (Zheng Yushuo), *How to Strengthen the National People's Congress and Implement Constitutionalism*, in *Chinese Law and Government*, 1983, n. 2-3, 88 ff. (in *Studies on the Constitutional Law of the People's Republic of China*, B.S.J. Weng Ed.); M.W. Dowdle, *The Constitutional Development and Operations of the National People's Congress*, in *Columbia Journal of Asian Law*, 1997, 1 ff.; P. Keller, *The National People's Congress and the Making of National Law*, in J.M. Otto, M.V. Polak, J. Chen, Y. Li (Eds.), *Law-Making in the People's Republic of China*, op cit. 75 ff.; Jiang Jinsong, *The National People's Congress of China*, Beijing, Foreign Languages Press, 2003; A. Rinella, *Cina*, in R. Dickmann, A. Rinella (Eds.), *Il processo legislativo negli ordinamenti costituzionali contemporanei*, Roma, Carocci, 2011, 387 ff. For the observation that the importance of the Constitution is expressed in the law of the PRC, not through the courts (and the Supreme Court itself), but through the legislative process, *see* Y. Lin, T. Ginsburg, *Constitutional Interpretation in Lawmaking: China's Invisible Constitutional Enforcement Mechanism*, in *American Journal of Comparative Law*, 2015, 467 ff., according to which in this consists one of the internal constitutional mechanisms of authoritarian systems; *adde* Y. Lin, *Constitutional evolution through legislation: The quiet transformation of China's Constitution*, in *International Journal of Constitutional Law*, 2015, 61 ff.; A. Rinella, *Le costituzioni dei regimi autoritari*, in S. Bagni, G.A. Figueroa Mejía, G. Pavan (coord.), *La Ciencia del Derecho Constitucional Comparado. Estudios en Homenaje a L. Pegoraro*, I, Valencia, 2017, 1265 ff.

was set in the capital, Beijing. The NPC's parliamentary work takes place during a single annual plenary session, usually lasting two or three weeks. The election of the members of the National Parliament takes place via indirect suffrage, through designations carried out by the lower-level parliamentary bodies in accordance with the peculiar principles, as previously mentioned,[99] on political representation and the exercise of popular sovereignty in the PRC. The mandate of the members of the NPC lasts five years.[100]

The deputies of the Chinese national parliament are grouped into delegations, according to a declination of the electoral origin that follows lines of geographical and professional affinity, and so on.[101] The delegations are in turn divided into groups. Each delegation designates its own representative, or head, independently. The delegations have the power of legislative initiative, being able to present bills; they are also entitled to make proposals for investigations. Furthermore, revocation or dismissal from state and public offices may be requested by at least three national parliamentary delegations.

Among the institutional bodies that make up the structure of the National People's Congress, there is the Presidium of the NPC, usually formed by circa one hundred and fifty members, appointed during the preparatory meeting immediately before the opening of the session of the NPC's parliamentary works. Members of the Presidium are usually the heads of the national parliamentary delegations, the leaders of the CCP Central Committees and the eight non-communist democratic parties, the members of the standing committee of the PNA, the Head of State, party leaders, the heads of the administrative bodies, as well as people representing the various segments of Chinese society, such as workers, peasants, teachers, scientists and artists, together with the emerging layers of entrepreneurs and operators of the so-called *new economy*. The Presidium oversees the orderly conduct of parliamentary sessions, but also has autonomous powers of impulse, especially on the subject of proposals for investigation and dismissal from public offices. One very important power attributed to the Presidium of the National Parliament is that of proposing the names of candidates for the office of President of the Republic and to become a member of the Standing Committee of the NPC.

The National People's Congress and its Standing Committee make use of the contribution of special (or specialized) parliamentary committees. These committees have been increasing over time, in parallel with the greater breadth and increasing complexity of the sectors of economic, social and cultural life governed by the legislative provisions adopted by the national Parliament. Thus, there was a move from the four Special Commissions

99 *See* Para. 2 of this chapter.

100 Until 1975, the representatives of the people in the national parliament remained in office for four years.

101 For example – as recalled by Bai Gang, *L'esperienza parlamentare nella Cina contemporanea*, op cit., 1352 – we have the delegation from Beijing, the Tibetan Autonomous Region and the People's Liberation Army (that is, the Chinese armed forces).

established by the first session of the 1st National People's Congress in 1954[102] to the ten established by IX NPC in 1998, in relation to the following sectors: a) Education and Science; b) Environment and the protection of resources; c) Economics and Finance; d) Foreign affairs; e) Internal and judicial affairs; f) Legal affairs; g) Ethnic Affairs; h) Culture and Health; i) the Chinese Overseas; and j) Agriculture and rural affairs. As a consequence of subsequent institutional mergers, the permanent special Commissions now operating[103] concern the following issues: a) Nationality; b) Legal affairs; c) Economics and Finance; d) Education, Science, Culture and Public Health; e) Foreign affairs; and f) the Chinese Overseas.

It is interesting to note that, precisely due to the frequent need for in-depth theoretical and practical knowledge in the work of the Special Parliamentary Commissions, not only are they formed by representatives of the people whose professional experience is significant and consistent with the tasks to be performed in the various commissions, but these commissions also have the right to consult external subjects with particular expertize.

The activity of the permanent Special Commissions of the Parliament of Beijing consists in carrying out studies and research, in the preparation of reports and proposals, for the benefit of both the Legislative Congress in its plenary composition and the Standing Committee of the NPC.

It should also be noted that, in addition to the special(ized) permanent parliamentary committees, the National People's Congress and its Standing Committee have the power to set up parliamentary investigative committees (*ad hoc* committees) to examine issues and specific problems.

With regards to the Standing Committee of the National Parliament, it is the body that exercises legislative functions on an ongoing basis. It is the executive nucleus and the executive body of the NPC. Its members, who meet in ordinary session every two months, are elected by the members of the Plenary parliamentary Congress, on the proposal of the NPC Presidium. They remain in office for the same duration as the deputies of the National Legislative Congress, that is to say for five years.

As for the members of the Standing Committee of the National People's Congress, the relevant provisions of the 1982 Constitution appear to be rather laconic, to the extent that they establish that the Standing Committee is formed by the Chairman,[104] a non-pre-established number of Vice-chairmen, the Secretary General and by unspecified members.[105]

---

102 The specialized parliamentary committees were created in 1954 for the following subjects: a) Nationality; b) Bills; c) Budget; and d) Examination of members.

103 In accordance with Art. 70, para. 1, of the Constitution.

104 Placed on the protocol level in third place of the hierarchy of institutional offices in the PRC, being preceded by the President of the Republic and the Prime Minister.

105 *Cf.* Para. 1 of Art. 65 of the Constitution.

There are no limitations on the possibility of being re-elected to the position of member of the Standing Committee, except for the functions of Chairman and Vice-Chairman who are not attributable to the same person for more than two terms.

With regards to the incompatibility regime, due to the fact that Paragraph 4 of Article 65 of the Constitutional Charter expressly prohibits members of the Standing Committee of the NPC from performing functions and assuming institutional roles in administrative bodies and the judicial system (including the Procuratorate), it must be inferred that the members themselves remain free to simultaneously devote their intellectual and work energies in other fields. Thus, for example, they can perform management tasks in political parties and social and people's organizations, hold conferences and courses at universities or institutes of education, culture, art and scientific research, or even start or continue activities of an entrepreneurial nature.

Another body that performs functions both for the National People's Congress and its Standing Committee is the Presidency Council, whose structure includes the figures of Chairman, Vice-chairman and Secretary-General. In particular, the scheduling of parliamentary work and the setting of the agenda for the NPC and Standing Committee meetings, are the responsibility of the Presidency Council.

Finally, it should be noted, in relation to the structural and organizational profiles of the National Parliament, that: a) the aforementioned Special Parliamentary Commissions coordinate their activities with the Standing Committee of the NPC, during the long intervals between the sessions of the Plenary Legislative Congress; b) the two established additional Special(ized) parliamentary Commissions directly dependent on the Standing Committee of the NPC are the special commission for the examination of members, created in 1954, and until 1982, under the direction of the National People's Congress in plenary composition, as well as the Special Legal Commission, whose constitution dates back to 1979, and which in 1983, was renamed as a special parliamentary commission for legal work; and c) the Standing Committee of the NPC has the power to create administrative organs to support the work of parliamentarians; this happened with the establishment of the General Office of the Standing Committee.

1.3.3 Follows: The Powers, Responsibilities and Functioning of the National People's Congress and Its Standing Committee

The 1982 Constitution, innovating with respect to the previous texts and documents of Chinese constitutional history, outlined a division of legislative functions between the National People's Congress in plenary and the Standing Committee of the NPC. As results from a reading of Articles 62 and 67 of the current Fundamental Charter, a catalogue of functions and powers is assigned to the NPC and its Standing Committee respectively.

The new constitutional set-up assigned the task of exercising state powers to a prevalent extent, to the Standing Committee of the National Parliament.

The powers of the Legislative Congress in plenary composition, established by Article 62 of the Constitution, include:

- revision of the Constitution, and control over its application;
- the enactment and amendment (not of all laws, but) of the fundamental organic laws in criminal, civil and public law matters, the latter with regard to the organs of the State;
- the election or designation (and the possible revocation or removal, as provided for by Article 63 of the Constitution) of the highest offices of the State, and in particular of the President and Vice-President of the PRC, the Prime Minister (Premier) of the State Council, on a proposal and in agreement with the President of the Republic, the Deputy-Prime Minister (Deputy-Premiers) and the Ministers who make up the State Council, on a proposal and in agreement with the Prime Minister; of the President of the Central Military Commission and, upon his indication, all the other members of the Commission itself; of the President of the Supreme People's Court and the Attorney General of the Supreme People's Procuratorate;
- the adoption of fundamental decisions in economic and financial matters, with regard to the examination and approval of national plans for economic and social development, as well as the examination and approval of the state budget and balance sheet;
- the approval of the establishment of new administrative subdivisions placed under the direct control of the central government, with regard to provinces, autonomous regions and municipalities;
- the creation of special administrative regions, as well as the approval of the system and the rules (derogating from the common municipal law) which must be applied in these areas;
- the declaration of the state of war.[106]

Furthermore, it should be noted that in accordance with Number 11 of Article 62 of the Constitution, the Plenary Legislative Congress retains the power of control and general supervision over the legislative production activity of the Standing Committee of the NPC, due to the fact that the National Parliament has the power to modify or invalidate decisions adopted by the Standing Committee, if they are deemed "improper".

106 The enumeration contained in Art. 62 of the Constitution is not, however, exhaustive, as the provision in question establishes, *sub* n. 15, that the National People's Congress can exercise further functions and powers that it considers necessary.

The competences attributed to the Standing Committee of the National People's Congress are analytically described in Article 67 of the Constitution, that can be grouped as follows.

Firstly, the Standing Committee collaborates with the Plenary Legislative Congress in overseeing the implementation of the Constitution, having also the power to provide an authentic interpretation of the Constitutional Charter.

Secondly, as afore-mentioned, the Standing Committee has the power to adopt legislative provisions when the National Parliament is not in session, except with regards to fundamental organic laws, that is the exclusive competence of the Parliamentary Congress in plenary composition, as stated in Article 62 of the Constitution. In the intervals between the parliamentary sessions, the Standing Committee has also the power to amend and modify the legislative provisions approved by the NPC, as well as interpret the laws.

Thirdly, competence in economic and financial matters should be mentioned. The Standing Committee, when Parliament is not convened, may adopt partial adjustments to both the national plan for socio-economic development and the state budget.

Fourthly, with reference to administrative activity, the Standing Committee of the NPC supervises the work of the State Council and the local organs of state power in the provinces, autonomous regions and municipalities directly subordinated to the central government, with the power to cancel administrative decisions and regulatory rules deemed not compliant with the Constitution, laws, or other administrative and regulatory requirements.

Fifthly, there is the need to analyse the broad powers of intervention on the assignment of high offices of the State. From this point of view, the Standing Committee may, when Parliament is not in plenary session, proceed to designate and shuffle ministers, on the proposal of the Premier, and appoint members of the Central Military Commission (or Central Commission for military affairs), following a proposal by the President of the Military Commission itself. Furthermore, the Standing Committee of the NPC is responsible for appointing and revoking the Vice-Presidents and judges of the Supreme People's Court, as well as the President of the Military Court (or Court for Military Affairs) on the recommendation of the President of the Supreme People's Court. Furthermore, the Standing Committee of the National Parliament is also responsible for the designation (and possible removal from office) of the Deputy Attorney Generals and State Attorneys of the Supreme People's Procuratorate, as well as the Chief Prosecutor of the Military Prosecutor's Office, based on an indication from the Attorney General of the Supreme People's Procuratorate. To this, one must add the power of the Standing Committee of the NPC to approve the appointments and revocations concerning the management of the public prosecutor's offices established in the provinces, autonomous regions and municipalities directly subordinate to the central government.

Sixthly, one can find functions inherent to the sphere of relations with foreign states and supranational organizations, with the nomination and removal from office of plenipotentiary ambassadors abroad pertaining to the Standing Committee of the NPC on the one hand and, on the other, the ratification of treaties and international agreements.[107]

In seventh place, the deliberations of the Standing Committee of the Legislative Congress which in various ways concern order and public safety in the PRC can be considered within the scope of a unitary category. Thus, the Committee has the competence to grant pardons (while amnesty provisions are not envisaged[108]), proclaim a state of war when Parliament is not in plenary session, decide on general or partial mobilizations, decree a state of emergency in the whole country, that is to say in the individual provinces, autonomous regions or municipalities subject to the direct control by the central government.

In eighth place, of less importance, there are powers of a ceremonial nature attributed to the Standing Committee, which can institute and decree the conferment of honorary titles and medals of the State.

Finally, that which was previously stated for the National Parliamentary Congress in plenary with regards to the non-exhaustive nature of the catalogue of the functions and powers constitutionally envisaged, also applies to the Standing Committee of the NPC. Number 21 of Article 67 of the Constitution states, in fact, that further functions and powers with respect to those expressly stated in the same constitutional provision can be attributed by the NPC to its Standing Committee.

In addition to the ordinary sessions of the National People's Congress, extraordinary sessions are scheduled if deemed necessary by the Standing Committee of the NPC or following a request made by more than one-fifth of the Members of the National Parliament. The parliamentary sessions are valid if there is at least one half plus one of the members of the NPC (constitutive *quorum*), while the laws and other resolutions of the Parliament are adopted by a simple or relative majority (deliberative quorum). With regards to constitutional changes, which may be proposed by the Standing Committee of the NPC or by more than one fifth of the people's deputies, an in favour vote of the absolute majority is necessary, provided that more than two thirds of the members of the National Parliament are present. The importance of the prescribed majorities should not however be exaggerated in the peculiar Chinese context, with its large prevalence of CCP deputies in the National Legislative Congress, usually supported by the representatives elected by the armed forces as well as by the parliamentarians of the eight Democratic parties. Hence, the unanimity of the consent is easily reached, also taking into account the strong inclination of the

107 On the topic, *see* G. Conetti, *Le norme costituzionali che disciplinano le relazioni internazionali*, in *Mondo cinese*, n. 46, 1984, 15 ff., where the author notes that external relations in the Chinese constitutional system are the sole responsibility of central state bodies, without any attribution conferred on the matter to local autonomous bodies.

108 As they are not considered necessary in China; *cf.* Bai Gang, *L'esperienza parlamentare nella Cina contemporanea*, op cit., 1356.

Chinese deputies who may be dissenting or otherwise critical to the approval of legislative measures, not to vote against, but rather favouring abstention.[109]

The procedural rules of the National People's Congress stipulates that an ordinary session of parliamentary plenary work should be held in the first quarter of each year, that is to say before the fiscal year begins, in order to permit members to take informed and effective decisions in terms of the budget (planned and final balance) of the State. The practice, consolidated during the nineties of the twentieth century, stabilized the convening of an ordinary session of the NPC in the first two (maximum three) weeks of the month of March.

Public sessions are distinguished from those defined as "secret". The latter are arranged by decision of the *Presidium* of the National People's Congress, or by the conference of the heads of the parliamentary delegations. The decisions that are taken during the "secret" sessions of the national parliament are, moreover, public in a similar way to all the other parliamentary deliberations. Radio and television operators, and mass media operators in general, can assist in the sessions of the Legislative Congress.

There are also some categories of subjects that can participate in the parliamentary sessions, albeit without voting rights. A first group includes the Ministers of the State Council, the members of the Central Military Commission, the President of the Supreme People's Court and the Attorney General of the Supreme People's Procuratorate. Their participation in the work of the National People's Congress constitutes a right sanctioned by the law. Another group includes the leaders of associations, institutions and organizations who are entitled to participate in the sessions of the Parliament only with the approval of the Standing Committee of the NPC. A final group concerns those invited to take part in parliamentary work, as is the case in particular for members of the CCP who are not elected members of the NPC.

The regulation of parliamentary procedure of the National People's Congress articulates the modalities and timing of the work of the plenary sessions of the NPC. The first meeting of the national deputies is of a preparatory nature. This preliminary meeting envisages the participation of all the members of the outgoing Standing Committee of the NPC, and has the purpose of electing the members of the *Presidium* of the Legislative Congress. Subsequently, the first meeting of the *Presidium* of the NPC is convened, with the task of planning the calendar of the parliamentary work to be held in plenary composition. The session of parliamentarians that follows the convening of the *Presidium* constitutes the first official meeting of the national parliament.

109 On the voting and abstention behavior of Chinese national parliamentarians, *see* A. Lavagnino, *Le istituzioni "parlamentari" della Repubblica Popolare Cinese*, cit., 13. *See also*, Lin Feng, *Constitutional Law in China*, op cit., 63, where it is noted that "the main task of the people's congress is to turn the will of the CPC [Chinese Communist Party] into legislation".

From this point onwards the discussions and voting in the parliament follow a threefold phase, which includes the presentation of the legislative proposal or resolution, its examination by the *Presidium* of the NPC, which assesses whether it is appropriate to send the proposal to the permanent special Commissions before deciding whether to include it in the agenda of parliamentary sessions, and finally the vote of the plenary congress.

On the temporal level, the topics dealt with in the meetings or official sessions of the National People's Congress concern five successive examination areas: a) the assessment of what has been done, above all via the acquisition of the reports prepared for the NPC by the outgoing Standing Committee, the State Council, the Supreme People's Court and the Supreme People's Procuratorate; b) the discussion and adoption of decisions concerning the economic and social development sectors, as well as the state budget; c) the provision of appointments, elections and removal from state offices under the responsibility of the NPC; d) the approval of laws; and e) to examine, evaluate and decide other issues (we would say, "various").

Regarding the functioning of the Standing Committee of the NPC, one should refer to the provisions contained in the Fundamental Law of the National People's Congress, 1982, and to the regulations on the procedure of the Standing Committee of the NPC, 1987. This *corpus* of legislation shows that, alongside the ordinary sessions of the Standing Committee held, as stated earlier, every two months (with a duration of no more than seven days), the Commission can also meet in extraordinary session, following the convocation of its President. The sessions of the Standing Committee of the NPC are valid if more than half of its members participate; decisions are approved by a simple majority. The work of the Standing Committee takes place under the direction of the Chairman of the Committee, with the possibility of delegating the function to the Vice-President.

A large group of personalities are entitled to take part, without the right to vote in the meetings of the Standing Committee. This includes: the Prime Minister, the Presidents of the Central Military Commission, the Supreme People's Court and the Supreme People's Procuratorate, the Presidents and Vice-Presidents of the Standing Special Commissions of the National Parliament, as well as the members of these Commissions and also the external consultants and experts of these commissions, the Presidents and Vice-Presidents of the Standing Committees of the provinces, autonomous regions and municipalities directly under the control of the central Government. Even those taking part in the sessions of the NPC without the right to vote may be invited to take part, obviously without the right to vote, in the work of the Standing Committee of the Legislative Congress.

Three typologies of meetings are envisaged for the members of the Standing Committee of the NPC. First, the plenary meetings, attended by the members of the Standing Committee with the presence, also, of all the subjects without the right to vote, during which deliberations are taken by the Commission. There are also group and joint meetings of the groups, whose purpose is to analyse and discuss, among a smaller number of participants and with the possible presence of subjects without voting rights, the individual issues that will then be decided by the plenary meeting of the Standing Committee.

Finally, as regards the temporal succession of the work of the Standing Committee of the NPC, there are usually five stages. The main stage concerns the adoption of legislative measures. This is followed by the acts of appointment and dismissal of senior managers of the State, the examination of reports on the activities carried out by administrative and judicial bodies, the fulfilment of activities relevant to relations with foreign States and international conventions, and the exercise of additional functions possibly conferred to the Standing Committee by the National People's Congress in plenary composition.

1.3.4 The Structure of the Local People's Congresses

The local (or sub-national) parliaments of the PRC were established for the first time under the Organic Law of Local People's Congresses at all levels and local Governments at all levels of 1954. Their activity was suspended during the Cultural Revolution, when the Revolutionary Committees wanted by the ultra-Maoist left began to function in the administrative subdivisions. The Congresses and sub-national Governments were restored in 1979, with the introduction of some modifications in the organic law concerning them. Further amendments to the law on Parliaments and Local Governments of contemporary China were adopted in 1982, 1986 and 1995. The reference regulatory framework was gradually completed by the approval of local procedural regulations that governed the exercise of the powers and functions of sub-national parliaments.

There are four current levels of the People's Congresses. At the vertex, as previously stated, there is the NPC, while at the lower levels one can find, in increasing order of importance (in the sense given by socialist legal doctrine to the size of state power), the people's congresses that represent the inhabitants of: a) counties, urban districts and county-level municipalities; b) ordinary and autonomous prefectures, as well as municipalities at a prefecture level; and c) provinces, autonomous regions and autonomous municipalities, the latter placed under the control of central power (these are the municipalities of Beijing, Shanghai, Tianjin and Chongqing).[110] The People's deputies from local parliaments are elected directly by the resident population in the corresponding political-administrative division, by means of a secret ballot, only for the lower levels. In this regard, it is worth highlighting that up until the amendment approved in 1995 of the Organic Law on the Local People's Congresses, the members designated via direct elections were only

110 In the People's Republic of China there are currently thirty-three sub-national administrative units or districts, namely twenty-two provinces, four municipalities directly employed by the central government, five autonomous national regions and two special administrative regions. *Cf.* G. Zu, *The composite state of China under "One Country, Multiple Systems": Theoretical construction and methodological considerations*, in *International Journal of Constitutional Law*, 2012, 272 ff.

those of village congresses and smaller cities; currently, on the strength of the aforementioned legislative innovation, the members of both the first and second level people's congresses are elected by direct election.[111]

In relation to the term of office of the people's deputies, the members of the first-level people's congresses were expected to be elected for two years and those of the second-level local parliaments for three years. However, with the constitutional review of 14 March 2004, Article 98 of the Basic Charter was amended, which now prescribes the term of five years of a People's Deputy at every level, thus including the first and second level Local Congresses.[112] The parliamentarians of the provincial and national people's congresses are still chosen by indirect elections, being elected by the deputies of lower level Congresses.

The number of members of the local people's congresses of the levels is established taking into account various criteria and parameters, such as population density, as well as the presence and consistency of national minorities. The relative decision belongs to the Standing Committees of the local Parliaments established at the level immediately below that of the National People's Congress, that is to say in the provinces, autonomous regions and autonomous municipalities. According to the local parliamentary practice, the people's congresses of the basic level are composed of a number that varies between 35 and 55 members, the local parliaments of the upper level (or equivalent) are composed of 150-250 deputies and the third level of people's congresses of 800-1000 parliamentarians.

Unlike that which happens for the NPC, in the provincial people's Congresses (i.e. the autonomous regions and municipalities), the deputies are not grouped into real delegations, but in less structured groups of delegates. People's deputies, of the level immediately below the national level, form groups, established before the opening of local parliamentary work, taking into account above all geographical origins. Such groups of delegates elect a President and some Vice-Presidents from within their ranks. However, it must be emphasized that the groups of delegates from the provinces (and the assimilated administrative subdivisions) do not play a role similar to that of the parliamentary delegations of the National People's Congress, due to the fact that the groups of provincial delegates are not entitled to submit proposals for deliberation, and essentially represent the intra-parliamentary discussion units, aimed at deciding which voting conduct to adopt in relation to the proposals for deliberative acts examined by the Congress. The operative groups of delegates constituted at the first two levels (starting from the basic level) of the local People's Congresses are even less formalized.

111 In this regard, one is speaking about the progressive realization of a *grass roots democracy*; *cf.* A. Lavagnino, *Le istituzioni "parlamentari" della Repubblica Popolare Cinese*, op cit., 14.

112 The standardization of the parliamentary term at the various levels is aimed at encouraging, according to the intentions declared by the Chinese, the simplification of the sustainable development planning operations in the local area; *see* G. Crespi Reghizzi, M.E. Delmestro, *La Costituzione della Repubblica popolare cinese si aggiorna*, op cit., 594, text and n. 79.

As is the case with the NPC, the local People's Congresses also have their own *Presidium*, whose members are chosen from the delegates of the corresponding level during the preliminary meetings of the local Parliaments' working sessions. The members designated to be part of the *Presidium* can elect a President and some Vice-Presidents of the same body.[113] The main task of the *Presidium* of the local Parliament is the presentation of proposals for deliberation to the People's Congress of which it is an expression. Other functions include the management of the congresses' work, with decisions on the agenda and the procedures for dealing with local affairs at the parliamentary level, as well as the identification of the subjects who can participate without voting rights at the meetings of the local people's congress.

With regards to the Special Commissions of the local Parliaments, there is the need to make a distinction. The people's congresses at a provincial level (or equivalent) have special standing commissions, which collaborate both with the local parliament in plenary session and with its Standing Committee, during the intervals between the local parliamentary sessions. The congress bodies of a lower level to that of the province do not envisage, however, an articulation that includes special Standing parliamentary Commissions, but only special commissions created and which operate during the work of the Congress in plenary composition. In addition, the provincial people's Congresses (or regional and autonomous municipalities) may set up special commissions for legal, financial and economic affairs, education, science, culture and health, for bills and the budget plan, where the local Parliaments of the two lower levels have the right to use a narrower range of Special Commissions, which are usually established for the examination of proposed resolutions, the budget and the balance sheet.

Furthermore, it should be noted that the local parliaments of the two intermediate levels between the NPC and the grassroots level, envisage a Standing Committee, which performs the functions of the Congress when this latter is not in session (which occurs for a few days a year). On the first level of the political-parliamentary institutional representation, the corresponding functions are exercised by the *Presidium* of the local People's Congress, which has no Standing Committee. In cases where it is envisaged, the Standing Committee of Local Parliaments is made up of members chosen by the People's Congress of the corresponding level. Their number is variable, ranging from thirty-five to sixty-five, and in any case no more than eighty-five, in relation to the provincial level (and equivalent), and from eleven to nineteen, but without exceeding twenty-nine, with regards to the district level. These members remain in office, as stated previously, for five years. The exercise of the functions of the members of the Standing Committees of the local People's Congresses

113 However, these are possible institutional figures, which the people delegates of the levels subordinated to the PA are entitled to appoint.

is incompatible with the conferment or retention of positions of an administrative or judicial nature.

The structural articulation of the standing Committees of local Parliaments, where foreseen, includes the offices of general manager and some deputy general managers. At the provincial level only, the figure of a general secretary exists for the standing organ of the People's Congress.

1.3.5 *Follows: The Powers, Responsibilities and Functioning of the Local People's Congresses and Their Relative Standing Committees*

From the functional point of view, the local parliaments (and their Standing Committees, where established) of the People's Republic of China are endowed with a multiplicity of powers, which for convenience can be grouped into two macro-categories.

First, it is worth highlighting the functions regarding decisions related to important local affairs, adopted by way of resolution. The local people's congresses are also required to monitor the application of constitutional and legislative rules, as well as that of deliberative acts issued at their level as well as at a higher level. Local parliaments must also approve plans for economic and social development and budgets.

Second, one can find the tasks inherent in the indirect election of people's deputies of the provincial (or equivalent) and national levels, plus the powers of appointing and removing a large number of public officials, including the Governor and the Deputy-Local governor at the corresponding level, the heads at the same level of the People's Courts and the People's Procuratorate, in the latter case provided that there has been prior information sent to the People's General Procuratorate. The corollary of these powers of appointment are the functions of control over the actions of administrative and judicial bodies, as well as the power to annul the deliberations, orders and ordinances adopted by local Governments and judged "improper"[114] by popular Congresses or Standing Committees of the same level.

The Standing Committees of the provincial, autonomous and autonomous municipal Congresses perform, in the intervals between the sessions of the respective Parliaments, the corresponding functions, albeit with some limitations, such as that concerning the power to introduce only modifications to economic development plans. and social and budget plans adopted by the plenary session of the same level.

Article 100 of the 1982 Constitution attributed the power to regulate to local parliaments and their Standing committees at the provincial level (and assimilated). They were also attributed jurisdiction regarding the adoption of local statutes (the so-called local statutory autonomy), the text of which must conform to constitutional and legislative requirements.

114 *See* Art. 104 of the 1982 Constitution.

In addition to this regulatory and statutory power recognized only at the third level of the local people's congresses, all the peripheral parliamentary bodies of the PRC have the power to approve deliberations and resolutions of an administrative nature.

The functioning of the local people's congresses includes ordinary and extraordinary sessions. The first have an annual cadence, and based on a well-established tradition they take place within the month of March. The latter can be convened at the request of more than one-fifth of all the popular deputies of the corresponding level.

The *constituent quorum* is established by local statutes and regulations, which usually require a qualified majority of more than two thirds of the total number of members of the local Parliament.

The Standing Committee of the local People's Congresses, or the *Presidium* of the local Parliament, where envisaged, have the task of convening the meetings of the local People's Congresses. However, the conduct of the meeting is directed and chaired by the *Presidium*.

Parliamentary procedure at a local level includes three phases and four powers (or spheres). With regards to the phases, they refer, in a similar way to that which occurs for the NPC, to the preliminary meeting, the first meeting of the *Presidium* of the Congress and to the formal meetings of the Congress in plenary session. As for the powers, they regard: the presentation and deliberation of proposals; resolutions on business relationships, economic and social development plans and budgets plans; the appointment and removal of public officials; and the initiation of cognitive investigations.

1.3.6 The Regulation of Normative Production and the Hierarchy of the Sources, in Accordance with the Law on Legislation of 2000 (Amended in 2015)

The objective of the rationalization of the Chinese legislative process was pursued via the approval, by the third session of the IX National People's Congress on 15 March 2000, of the law on legislation (*lifa fa*).[115] It is a normative provision definable as a fundamental

115 On which *see* F.R. Antonelli, *La "Legge sulla legislazione" ed il problema delle fonti nel diritto cinese*, in *Mondo cinese*, n. 119, 2004, 23 ff.; L. Paler, *China's Legislation Law and the Making of a More Orderly and Representative Legislative System*, in *The China Quarterly*, 2005, 301 ff.; Li Yahong, *The Law-making Law: a solution to the problems in the Chinese legislative system?*, in *Hong Kong Law Journal*, 2000, 120 ff.; Zou Keyuan, *La difficile harmonisation des législations locale et nationale. Une étape majeure dans la longue marche de la Chine vers l'Etat de droit*, in *Perspectives chinoises*, n. 81, 2004, 44 ff. The law on legislation, aimed at the scientification and democratization of the legislative procedures (cfr. L. Paler, *op. cit.*, 314, nt. 57), includes six chapters and ninety-four articles. Re the preparatory work *see* Li Buyun, *Explanations on the Proposed Law on Law-Making of the People's Republic of China*, in J.M. Otto, M.V. Polak, J. Chen, Y. Li (Eds.), *Law-Making in the People's Republic of China*, op cit., 157 ff. On the sources of the production of law, *see also* Y. Zhai, *Quadro generale sulle fonti del diritto privato in Cina*, in *Diritto e società*, 2014, 805 ff. A diachronic study on the legislative tradition in imperial, nationalist and popular China is found inTsien Tche-hao, *Le modèle du législateur et la science de la législation en Chine (Des origins à nos jours)*, in

law (*jiben fa*), based on the provisions of Article 62 of the Constitution, having been adopted in a matter attributed to the competence of the National Congress in plenary composition; it is, therefore, superordinate to ordinary laws (*fa*), which can be enacted (and modified) both by the *plenum* of the NPC as well as by its Standing Committee.[116]

The division of tasks between the National People's Congress and its Standing Committee, outlined in Articles 62 and 67 of the Constitution and already examined above,[117] is further specified in Article 7 of the law on legislation. This norm implements and completes Number 3 of Article 62 of the Constitution, stating that the legislative competence for the enactment of fundamental laws belongs exclusively to the Plenary National Congress. In particular, the NPC issues and amends the criminal code, the civil code, the organic laws and other fundamental laws (Article 7, first part). Instead, the Standing Committee issues and amends laws that do not fall into the sphere of the competence of the NPC (Article 7, second part). However, the Standing Committee has the power to partially amend normative legislative provisions falling within the exclusive competence of the National Congress in plenary session, provided that the latter is not in session and that the changes introduced by the standing body do not conflict with the fundamental principles of the law approved by the *plenum* of the national Parliament.

The law on legislation also clarifies that specific questions are liable to be governed exclusively by provisions of primary legislative status, whether they are adopted, according to the aforementioned criterion of competence division, by the NPC or by its Standing Committee. The reserve of legislative competence extends to three sectors, indicated in Article 8 of the law now under examination and represented by: a) organization of functions and state powers, with regards also to the judicial system; b) protection of the fundamental rights of citizens; and c) provisions relating to tax law and the economy, such as the norms addressing special administrative areas (SARs), which can be created for the recognition of forms of autonomy on an ethnic basis or to test new and more dynamic growth modules of the economic system and the productive system (special economic zones, SEZs). The subjects included in Article 8 may, however, also be governed by norms issued by the State Council, that is to say, the national government, subject to the adoption of a delegated special law by the national parliament; the exception of the exception is constituted by the fact that the mechanism of delegation to the national executive body is not permitted for the issuance of norms concerning, on the one hand, the fundamental rights of the citizen and, on the other, the judicial institutions and the legal system.

A. Giuliani, N. Picardi (Eds.), *L'educazione giuridica*, V, *Modelli di legislatore e scienza della legislazione*, t. II, *Modelli storici e comparativi*, Napoli, Edizioni Scientifiche Italiane, 1988, 489 ff.

116 Re the characteristics of basic laws and ordinary laws in the Chinese system, *cf.* R. Cavalieri, *La legge e il rito. Lineamenti di storia del diritto cinese*, op cit., 171, text and nt. 21.

117 *See supra* in para. 3 of this same chapter.

The law on legislation includes, in Chapter I regarding general principles, the reference to sources of atypical law, due to the fact that they are placed above the law and therefore present a quasi-constitutional character. Articles 3 and 6 of the *lifa fa* establish, respectively, that the process of legislation must: a) adhere to the fundamental principles of the Constitution, must be focused on economic development, must adhere to the socialist path, the dictatorship of the people, the *leadership* of the Chinese Communist Party and adhere to Marxism–Leninism, Mao Zedong thinking, the theory of Deng Xiaoping and adhere to the politics of openness towards the rest of the world; and b) start from the current circumstances and establish, in a scientific and reasonable manner, the rights and duties of citizens, legal persons, and other organizations, as well as the powers and responsibilities of public institutions.

It is quite clear that, as already seen in connection with the Preamble to the Constitution, one is faced with references to political theories and ideologies stratified over time and not well harmonized with each other, which however indirectly dictate the conformation of the legal system to the extent that laws must adapt to these theories and ideologies.

On the other hand, the reference to Article 3 of the law on legislation regarding the policy of openness to the rest of the world as a guiding principle of the legislative process further amplifies the possibilities for the CCP to influence the production processes of legislative norms, conditioning its content in various ways.

The desire to avoid that the provisions of the law remain *law in the book*, and instead are *law in action* as required by the objective of the implementation of the *rule of law* in China, seems to be the source of the reference contained in Article 6 of the law on legislation to the current circumstances from which the legislative process has to start in order that such a process can find concrete application, to stem the widespread phenomenon in the PRC (but also characteristic of imperial China) of the so-called manifest laws, declaimed by the legislator but greatly lacking in terms of effectiveness.

Articles 12, 13 and 24 of the *lifa fa*, which establish that the power of legislative initiative to be exercised in the Plenary National Congress and in its Standing Committee (in accordance with their respective competences) falls into the sphere of competence not only of the members of the national people's congress and the members of the relative Standing Committee as foreseen by Article 72 of the Constitution, but also of the State Council as envisaged in Article 89, Number 2, of the Constitution, and moreover (despite the absence of corresponding provisions in the constitutional text) to the Central Military Commission, the Supreme People's Court and the Supreme People's Procuratorate.

A particular significance envelops Article 52 of the law on legislation, which establishes the obligation to publish laws in the Official Journal of the Standing Committee of the NPC, as well as in a newspaper with a national circulation. The official version is, however, that which is published in the Official Journal of the standing national parliamentary body.

The prescription in question is important only if one considers that, previously, the Chinese legal system did not envisage a mandatory form of publication and/or divulgation of laws.[118]

The law on legislation contains important provisions regarding the hierarchy between normative sources of the central state and local legislative sources,[119] with a particular focus on local legislation. Article 63, Paragraph 1, in Section I of Chapter IV of the *lifa fa*, attributes to the provincial plenary congresses, of the autonomous regions and autonomous municipalities, and respective Standing committees, the power to issue local laws, which must conform to the Constitution, state laws (fundamental and ordinary) and administrative regulations approved by the State Council (Central Government). Local legislative competence, as envisaged in Paragraph 2 of Article 63, lies with the *plenums* of the people's congresses, and their Standing Committees, established at the level of the major cities. In this case, local laws, on the one hand, must not conflict with the Constitution, national laws and even provincial laws; on the other hand, they come into force only after approval by the Standing Committee of the Provincial Parliament.

The strengthening of the regulatory power of local self-governments represents thus an objective of the law on legislation, as can be inferred from Article 66 that focuses on the regulatory acts adopted by the self-governing bodies in the national autonomous areas created on an ethnic basis. The aforementioned regulatory provisions may be issued by the People's Congresses of the Autonomous Regions, the autonomous prefectures and the autonomous districts, with the clarification that the provisions of the People's Congresses of the Autonomous Regions are effective, subject to approval by the Standing Committee of the National Parliament, while those adopted at the prefecture and autonomous district level come into force after the control of competence of the Standing Committee of the provincial Parliament.

With regards to the content that the norms approved by the local Parliaments of the areas with an ethnic autonomy may have, Article 66 of the *lifa fa* establishes that they must respect the Constitution, but are susceptible to the introduction of exceptions to the national legislation and administrative regulations of the Central government, unless they are provisions of law or state regulations that have as their specific object the regulating of the

118 The right to publish legal acts and provisions was governed by the regulation on the compilation and publication of collections of laws and regulations, adopted by the Council of State Affairs on 29 March 1990. On this, *see* the comment by R. Bertinelli, *Norme sulla compilazione dei documenti ufficiali e sulla pubblicazione delle raccolte di leggi e regolamenti*, in *Mondo cinese*, n. 78, 1992, 7 ff.

119 On the set up of regulatory sources in China, *see* Hsia Tao-tai, C.A. Johnson, *Law Making in the People's Republic of China: Terms, Procedures, Hierarchy, and Interpretation*, Washington (DC), Library of Congress (Law Library), 1986; P. Keller, *Sources of Order in Chinese Law*, in *American Journal of Comparative Law*, 1994, 711 ff.; D.T.C. Wang, *Les sources du droit de la République populaire de Chine*, preface by Rui Mu & Tsien Tche-hao, Genève, Librairie Droz, 1982.

self-government of ethnic groups in the national autonomous areas established to protect minority rights.[120]

In a similar way to national laws, the legislative acts of local Parliaments must be made known to citizens, via the forms of publication deemed mandatory by Article 70 of the law on legislation.[121]

The hierarchy of the sources of law, and in particular the relationships between national laws, central government regulations, local laws, regulations of autonomous areas and special economic zones, are analytically regulated in Chapter V of the law on legislation. Here, one can find, first and foremost, the reaffirmation, in Article 78, of the principle of the unconditional supremacy of constitutional provisions in the law of the PRC. The following art states that the (fundamental and ordinary) laws of the national parliament and its Standing committee are superordinate both to administrative regulations and to laws adopted by local people's congresses. The regulations issued by the State Council have a superior legal authority and therefore, prevail over the provisions contained in the laws and regulations adopted by the parliaments and local governments respectively. In turn, Article 80 clarifies that local legislation is ranked higher than the regulations issued by equal or lower level governments. Article 81 adds that the rules approved by the organs of the autonomous administration areas and the special economic zones prevail, within the territorial limits of the same areas, over the possibly conflicting rules contained in national laws, administrative regulations and local laws. Article 85 establishes that, in the sphere of each level of normative production, there is a prevalence of a special law on the general law and that of the later law on a prior law. The conflicts that may arise between a special prior law and the later general law are resolved by the Standing Committee of the NPC, which issues an authentic interpretation of the contested provisions. Article 84 affirms in Paragraph 1 that the law provides only for the future, but at the same time provides in Paragraph 2 the possibility to derogate, albeit in exceptional cases, to this essential

120 A notable example was represented by the derogatory provisions, introduced in autonomous areas where ethnic minorities are established, with respect to the implementing provisions of the so-called one-child policy contained in the national law on family planning and birth control in 2001, which incorporated provisions originally approved in 1979. The law of 2001 was, however, amended on the initiative of the III Plenum of the Central Committee of the Party on 12 November 2013 and, therefore, with a resolution adopted on 28 December 2013 by the Standing Committee of the NPC. Further amendments approved by the Standing Committee of the NPC on 27 December 2015, following a similar decision adopted by the Party Central Committee on 29 October 2015, definitively repealed the provisions of the law on population and family planning concerning the "one child" policy, making it possible for Chinese couples, with effect from 1 January 2016, to have (up to) two children (so-called "one couple, two children" new policy). *See* T. Scharping, *Abolishing the One-Child Policy: Stages, Issues and the Political Process*, in *Journal of Contemporary China*, 2019, 327 ff.

121 The characteristics of local legislation in the PRC lead to the view that "as it may be said that the Chinese state is not of a federal nature, it must be recognized that its legal system is not multi-legislative". In this sense, G. Conetti, *Le norme costituzionali che disciplinano le relazioni internazionali*, op cit., 19.

principle in a state based on the *rule of law*, whenever required for the better protection of the rights and interests of citizens, legal persons and organizations.[122]

Finally, at the conclusion of the Third Annual Plenary Session of the XII National People's Congress, the Parliament of the PRC approved on 15 March 2015, with 2,761 votes in favour, 81 against and 33 abstentions, a partial reform of the law on legislation,[123] with amendments that refer in particular to two aspects: a) the introduction of the statutory reserve in the fiscal area and b) the extension of the subjects (entities) that are holders of the local regulatory power, increased from 49 to 288 cities.

1.3.7 The Chinese People's Political Consultative Conference as an Organ of the Parliamentary System

As we has seen before, dealing with the historical profile of the communist China's parliamentary events, the Chinese People's Political Consultative Conference (CPPCC)[124] served as the legislative body of the PRC up until the election of the first National People's Congress in 1954.[125] Starting from that year, and in connection with the approval of the new Chinese Constitution which substituted the 1949 Joint Program, the People's Political Consultative Conference ceased to exercise legislative power, becoming a parliamentary body with high-level consultancy duties compared to the National Parliament. Its historical origin implies that even today one speaks of it as an organization of the united patriotic front of the Chinese people, recalling the role played by both communist and non-communist forces in the struggle against the troops of nationalist China as well as during the phase of anti-Japanese resistance. The CPPCC is still made up of delegates from the CCP and the eight (non-communist) Democratic Parties, as well as representatives of various mass organiza-

122 This latter includes political parties, and therefore also the CCP.

123 *Cf.* G. Mannocci, *Cina - Nuova legge sulla legislazione*, in *Dir. Pubbl. Comp. Eur. Online*, 2015, n. 2 (www.dpce.it); B. Ahl, *Zur Revision des Gesetzgebungsgesetzes der Volksrepublik China*, in *Zeitschrift für chinesisches Recht*, 2015, 241 ff. (& *ivi*, 259-284, the German translation is by M. Martinek, of the Chinese law on legislation); X. Zhang, *Die Änderung des Gesetzgebungsgesetzes der VRCh und die "neue Normalität" der Gesetzgebung in China*, in *Verfassung und Recht und Übersee. Law and Politics in Africa, Asia and Latin America*, 2015, 443 ff.

124 On which *see*, in addition to the works concerning the Chinese parliamentary Assemblies cited *retro* in this same chapter, J. Wang, *Proposing the way forward. CPPCC playing a bigger role in improving the lives of people*, in *Beijing Review*, 2004, n. 38, 16 ff. (CPPCC is the acronym for *Chinese People's Political Consultative Conference*).

125 *Cf.* Para. 1 Chap. I.

tions,[126] non-party figures,[127] members of the Hong Kong and Macao communities, Taiwanese compatriots, and the Chinese overseas.[128]

The fundamental tasks of the People's Political-Consultative Conference are political consultation and democratic supervision, which are carried out via the participation of political parties, mass organizations and public figures in the discussion and administration of State affairs.

Political consultation may regard public policies on economic, social and cultural issues at both national and local levels. Instead, democratic supervision consists of presenting suggestions and criticisms on the actualization of the Constitution, laws and administrative provisions, and more generally on the activities of public bodies, institutions and officials. Participation as a democratic method of deliberation in matters concerning the administration of the State consists in the transmission to the parliamentary bodies (or also to the CCP bodies) of dossiers, inquiry reports, proposals, projects and motions on the main political, economic, social and cultural problems, which require, in the opinion of the CPPCC, the adoption of legal normative acts by the competent authorities. Taking also into account the inspection powers attributed to the National Committee of the CPPCC, it is worth noting that it is, on the whole, a "proactive role, of control and stimulation".[129]

On the organizational and operational level, the Chinese system currently includes a national committee and over three thousand local PPCC committees. The term of office of all the said Committees is five years.

The National Committee of the CPPCC meets in ordinary session once a year. Its institutional vertex includes the figures of the Chairman and Vice-Chairmen, assisted by the Secretary General. During the not short interval between sessions, the advisory functions of the CPPCC National Committee are carried out by its Standing Committee, in a similar way to that which occurs for the National People's Congress and its respective Standing Committee. The local committees of the CPPCC also have standing committees, which exercise the institutional duties of the local committees when they are not in plenary session.

It is the responsibility of the Standing Committee of the National Commission of the outgoing CPPCC to establish the number of members and organizations represented at the next CPPCC at central level. The X CPPCC National Committee now in office includes

126 The main organisations: the League of Young Communists of China, the Pan-Chinese Federation of Trade Unions, the Pan-Chinese Women's Federation, the Pan-Chinese Federation of Young People, the Pan-Chinese Federation of Industry and Trade, the Chinese Association for Science and Technology.

127 Those persons who have distinguished themselves in the fields of culture or art, technology or social sciences, economics, medicine, journalism, publishing, or are representatives of the agricultural sector, religious communities or ethnic minorities.

128 For a total of thirty-four organizations and interest groups currently represented through their delegates in the CPPCC.

129 In this sense, A. Lavagnino, *Le istituzioni "parlamentari" della Repubblica Popolare Cinese*, op cit., 15.

2,238 members.[130] The local committees of the CPPCC are in the current legislature made up of over half a million delegates.

The members of the CPPCC Standing Committees established at the various levels are elected by the plenary session of the National Committee and local committees. Any changes in the composition of the national and local committees of the CPPCC may be effected by the respective Standing Committees during the legislature.

In particular, the Standing Committee of the CPPCC National Committees includes the President, some Vice-Presidents, a Secretary-General and other members. The President of the CPPCC National Committee, who ranks fourth in the hierarchy of public offices in contemporary China,[131] presides over the work of the Standing Committee of the same National Committee. The Standing Committee, in turn, has the functions of management and presidency of the ordinary sessions of the CPPCC National Committee.

1.4 Executive Functions

1.4.1 The President of the People's Republic of China

The constitutional position of the President (*zhuxi*) of in the PRC is the subject of discussion in the public law doctrine of contemporary China.[132]

On the one hand, there are those who believe that the Head of State (*guojia yuanshou*) constitutes a collegial figure, whose powers are exercised by both the President of the Republic as well as the Standing Committee of the National People's Congress. This takes into account both the tradition of state law of socialist countries, which frequently provides (provided) the constitutional design of a collegial presidency in accordance with the model included in the Soviet Constitutions of 1936, the German Democratic Republic of 1968 and the Yugoslavian Federation of 1974, together with also the mainly ceremonial functions and the scant powers attributed to the President of the Republic.

On the other hand, it is sustained with arguments that seem more shareable than those of the afore-mentioned thesis, that the conferral of important and extended powers to the

130 In the previous legislature, the delegates to the CPPCC National Commission totalled 2,093.

131 The President of the X CPPCC National Commission is Jia Qinglin, who succeeded Li Ruihuan who presided over the VIII and IX National Commission. The position of Honorary President of the CPPCC National Commission was attributed, in the course of the evolution of the parliamentary institutions of the People's Republic, to Mao Zedong alone, during the II, III and IV National Commission (these National Commissions were presided over by Zhou Enlai; Mao himself was President of the I National Commission in 1949).

132 *Cf.* Lin Feng, *Constitutional Law in China*, op cit., 122 f. More recently, the work of Xu Chongde, *The Head of State*, Beijing, People's Press, 1982. Finally, *see* Zhang Runhua, *The Constitutional and Legal Development of the Chinese Presidency. The Emperors' New Clothes?*, preface by M.D. Pendleton, Lanham (Maryland), Lexington Books, 2015.

Head of State as a monocratic body represents a simple eventuality in the panorama of comparative constitutional law, which for example, occurs in systems of the United States and France, but not in that of the UK. Moreover, the model of a collegial Head of State was abandoned in the same evolutionary dynamics of the post-socialist law systems, starting from the paradigmatic case of the Russian Federation[133] and more generally in Central-Eastern Europe.[134]

The historical origin of the institutional figure of the President of the Chinese Republic can be traced back to the People's Central Government Committee created in 1949 by the Chinese People's Political-Consultative Conference, since the Chairman of this Committee was at the head of the hierarchy of state bodies, albeit not configurable as an independent body.

The first Chinese People's Constitution of 1954, which replaced the provisional Constitution represented by the Joint Program, contemplated the office of President of the PRC to which some significant powers were attributed, although one cannot speak of a "governing" President.

Internally, the Head of State presided over the State Supreme Conference, which included the highest public authorities, among which the Vice-President of the PRC, the Chairman of the Standing Committee of the National People's Congress and the Prime Minister. Furthermore, the President of the Republic was the head of the armed forces and presided over the historical antecedent of the current Central Military Commission, namely the National Defence Committee.[135] Furthermore, after approval by the NPC or its Standing Committee, the President of the Republic was responsible for the promulgation of laws and decrees, as well as the appointment and revocation of: the Prime Minister, Deputy Prime Ministers, Ministers, the Secretary-General of the State Council, and the Vice-Chairmen and members of the National Security Council. The President of the Republic was responsible for the adoption of formal proclamation acts of martial law and the state of war, as well as the issuing of the mobilization order in the country. Finally, the Head of State was responsible for granting amnesty and pardon, as well as the awarding of medals and state honorary titles.

On an international level, the President of the Republic on the one hand, represented the People's Republic in relations with foreign countries and received diplomats accredited by the PRC. On the other hand, following the deliberation of the Standing Committee of the NPC, the President ratified international treaties and appointed and removed China's plenipotentiary representatives abroad.

---

133 On this point *see* M. Ganino, *Dallo Zar al Presidente. Ricostruzione del modello di governo della Russia fra trasformazioni costituzionali e continuità*, Milano, CUESP, 1999.

134 *Cf.* M. Lesage, *Il modello francese nelle nuove Costituzioni dei Paesi dell'Europa dell'Est*, in S. Gambino (edit.), *Costituzionalismo europeo e transizioni democratiche*, Milano, Giuffrè, 2003, 147 ff.

135 Which we will discussed below, in para. 3 of Chap. IV.

The functions and powers of the President of the Republic were in fact eliminated during the decade of the Cultural Revolution, from 1966 to 1976, leaving the office vacant up until the ultramaoist Constitution of 1975, which also formally suppressed the institutional figure of the Head of State. The infusion of party and state bodies in the management of public affairs was exacerbated by the 1975 Charter,[136] also with regards to the profile now under examination, given that the institutional tasks already attributed to the President of the Republic by the 1954 Constitution, were transferred mainly to the Chairman of the CCP Central Committee, placed under the command of the People's Liberation Army, while for example, the nomination (or, better, confirmation) of the Prime Minister was attributed to the NPC's competence via the (binding) designation of the Central Committee of the Communist Party.

The third Chinese Constitution of 1978, similar to the second Constitution, did not include the office of President of the Republic, but at the same time assigned to the Chairman of the Standing Committee of the National People's Congress some powers that, according to the 1954 Constitution, belonged to the Head of State. Article 26, Paragraph 1, of the 1978 Charter established, in fact, that included among the tasks of the Chairman of the standing body[137] of the National Parliament were the accreditation of foreign diplomats in China, the dispatching and recall of Chinese plenipotentiaries abroad, the ratification of international treaties and the promulgation of laws and decrees adopted by the National People's Congress or its Standing Committee.

The times were ripe for the complete rehabilitation in terms of Chinese political theory of the office of President of the Republic which was subsequently reintroduced into the system of the PRC by the 1982 Constitution.

The distribution of functions among the bodies that make up the structure of the Chinese state therefore includes, according to the regulations contained in Articles 79–84 of the current Constitutional Charter, the institutional figures of the President of the Republic as Head (individual) of the State, as well as the Vice-President of the PRC. Both are elected by the National People's Congress, for a period of five years (similar to that of the national parliament and the local popular congresses). The term of office of President and Vice-President of the PRC could not be renewed more than twice in a row; however, the constitutional amendment approved on 11 March 2018 by the 13th ANP abolished the constraint of the two mandates.[138] A system of *extension* of the aforementioned offices

136 It is no coincidence that it is called "the craziest and shortest of the Constitutions, not only of China"; thus G. Crespi Reghizzi, *Verso il mercato e lo Stato di diritto: recenti riforme costituzionali in Cina*, op cit., 486.

137 That is to say the permanent organ (*changshe jiguan*) of the NPC; *cf.* G. Melis (Ed.), *Costituzione della Repubblica Popolare Cinese*, in *Mondo cinese*, n. 22, 1978, especially 151.

138 2958 votes were in favour, two against and three abstentions. *See* R. McGregor, *Un presidente senza limiti*, in *Internazionale*, March 2018, 40; F. Sisci, *Con Xi a Pechino è tornato l'uomo forte*, in *Limes*, 2018, n. 4, 79 ff.; W. Hurst, *The Abolition of the Two-term Limit: A Sea Change?*, in *Made in China Journal*, 2018, n. 1, 12 ff.; S.L. Shirk, *The Return to Personalistic Rule*, in *Journal of Democracy*, 2018, n. 2, 22 ff. (thematic

is also envisaged. In accordance with Article 83 of the Constitution, the President and Vice-President of the Republic continue to exercise their functions up until the swearing-in of their successors, chosen by the NPC.

The requirements for eligibility for President and Vice-President of the Republic are: holder of Chinese citizenship and political rights, as well as the minimum age of forty-five.

With regard to the functions and powers of the Head of State, they appear to be classifiable within two general categories. On the one hand, from the point of view of internal politics, he promulgates the laws approved by the National Congress or by its Standing Committee. Furthermore, on the basis of the decisions taken by the parliamentary bodies at a national level, he appoints and dismisses the highest offices of the State: Premier, Deputy-Premiers, State Councillors, Ministers, Chairmen of Committees, General Auditor (or Chief Auditor) of accounts and the Secretary General of the Central People's Government. The President of the Republic proclaims a state of emergency[139] and a state of war, issues the mobilization orders, grants pardon,[140] and confers decorations and honorary titles of state.

On the other hand, with regards to international relations, the President of the Republic is responsible for the representation of the PRC in relations with foreign states, as well as the function of receiving diplomats accredited by the Chinese State. In addition, in accordance with the resolutions adopted by the Standing Committee of the NPC, the Head of State: a) appoints and dismisses the plenipotentiaries of the People's Republic of China abroad; and b) ratifies and repeals treaties and major international agreements of which the PRC is a contracting party.

An examination of the functions and powers attributed by the 1982 Constitution to the President of the Republic, compared to those recognized by the 1954 Constitution, highlights the limitations of the role of the Head of State, to the extent that the first Chinese

---

number *China in Xi's "New Era"*); S. Miracola, M. Procopio, N. Missaglia, *Cina: Xi Jinping forever*, Milano, ISPI, 2018 (www.ispionline.it); A. Talia, *"China's Dream Needs Chinese Power": the New Era in Xi's Thought*, in *Reforming China's Constitution, ISPI Dossier*, Milano, 2018 (www.ispionline.it); N. Li, *China's National Legislature Adopts Constitutional Amendment. This is the Constitution's first amendment in 14 years*, in *Beijing Review*, 11 March 2018, www.bjreview.com; E. Menezes de Carvalho, *A New Era for the Chinese Constitution. The amendment to the Chinese Constitution aims to follow the new situation*, in China Today, 15 March 2018, www.chinatoday.com.cn; E.C. Economy, *China's New Revolution. The Reign of Xi Jinping*, in *Foreign Affairs*, May/June 2018, www.foreignaffairs.com; K. Wang, *Apologetics of 2018 Constitutional Revision*, relazione presentata al convegno *Rule of Law and Governance in China at Home and Abroad*, op. cit.

139 The constitutional revision of March 2004 replaced the term "martial law" (*jieyan*) with that of «state of emergency» (*jinji zhuangtai*); on the reasons underlying the lexical modification, *see* G. Crespi Reghizzi, M.E. Delmestro, *La Costituzione della Repubblica popolare cinese si aggiorna*, op cit., 593, text and nt. 77. For the historical notion of martial law in the PRC, *see* D.S. by Silva Cornell, *The Legal Structure of Martial Law in Beijing*, in *China Law Reporter*, 1993, 129 ff.

140 Presidential power to proclaim general amnesties, contemplated by the Chinese Constitution of 1954, was suppressed.

Constitution, in contrast to the fourth, envisaged a substantial and not merely nominal authority for the President of the PRC. In particular, the 1954 Constitutional Charter placed the President of the Republic at the head of the people's armed forces, recognized his power of legislative initiative in the plenary meetings of the National People's Congress and its Standing Committee, as well as the power to convene the State Supreme Conference. These important presidential prerogatives were not reproduced in the 1982 Constitution, which included functions of the Head of State to be exercised almost exclusively on the basis of decisions previously taken by the central parliamentary bodies. It is true, however, that in the Chinese system the real distribution of powers between the superior organs of the State and the Communist Party depends on a multiplicity of factors affecting both constitutional law and political science, with a special focus on the so-called personal unions, that is to say, the frequent occurrence[141] of the accumulation of high state and party functions by one and the same person. The case of the PRC founder Mao Zedong, who was at the same time Secretary General of the CCP, Chairman of the Central Military Commission and President of the Republic,[142] is exemplary in this respect. This, however, still does not explain all. One has only to consider that Deng Xiaoping, undisputed ruler of the Chinese political scene in the eighties and nineties of the last century, instead was Chairman of the Central Military Commission, the highest state office, while he never was Secretary General of the communist party or Head of State. Let us not forget, in fact, that the social, political and juridical institutions of China (ancient, modern and contemporary) are located in the vast and composite area of the "mysterious Orient", surrounded by a halo of exotic charm, positioned on the legal globe, even more than other systems of law such as the Islamic and Hindu systems, in "polarity opposed to that of the West"[143] (and constituting research ground for "a few solitary and romantic explorers of lesser-known legal systems"[144]).

With regards to the constitutional position of the Vice-President of the Republic, he assists the Head of State, and can exercise presidential powers and functions, if delegated to do so by the President. In the case of vacancy (by death or resignation) of the office of

141 In the absence of super-primary norms that establish incompatibilities between the offices of President of the Republic, President of the Central Military Commission and Secretary General of the CCP. The question has been analysed, at least from an evolutionary perspective and in terms of political opportunity, by Chinese constitutional doctrine; *see* Lin Feng, *Constitutional Law in China*, op cit., 127, nt. 40, which reports the views of the jurist Zhu Guobin.

142 The current Head of State, Hu Jintao, elected on 15 March 2003, also covers the three offices mentioned above in the text. For a biographical and political profile of President Hu, *see* B. Mottura, *Il nuovo gruppo dirigente emerso dal XVI Congresso del PCC*, in *Mondo cinese*, n. 113, 2002, 29 ff.

143 *Cf.* L. Moccia, *Prologo breve sulla «originalità» del diritto (tradizionale) cinese e sull'importanza del suo studio in prospettiva storico-comparativa*, op cit., 992 f. *Ivi* the author, on the Orient, he evokes "all that is enigmatic, indistinct and fabulous traverses and envelops it" (*see* 995 ff.).

144 *See* G. Crespi Reghizzi, *Prefazione*, in R. Cavalieri, *La legge e il rito. Lineamenti di storia del diritto cinese*, op cit., especially 9.

the President of the Republic, the role is assumed by the Vice-President. If the office of the Vice-President of the Republic is instead vacant (for the same reasons mentioned above), the national Parliament elects its successor. Finally, if the vacancy of the offices of President and Vice-President of the Republic occur at the same time, their successors are appointed by the National People's Congress. Pending such election, the duties of the Head of State are transiently carried out by the Chairman of the Standing Committee of the NPC.

The constitutional rules on the Vice-President of the Republic clarify that he does not have independent powers, but only those that are subject to delegation by the Head of State. The constitutional text is less clear with regard to the possible functions of an *acting President* of the Vice-President of the Republic, in the hypothesis of temporary impediment of the Head of State. These last functions could be considered or implicit in the superprimary provisions on the powers of the Vice-President as described above, or constituting a constitutional convention.

1.4.2 The State Council (Central or National People's Government) and Local Governments, with a Brief Overview of the Democratic Self-Government System at the Basic Administrative Level

The State Council (of affairs) (Chinese. Guowuyuan) constitutes the superior organ of the state administration, with executive functions of the decisions taken by the superior organ of state power, namely the national parliament and its Standing Committee.[145] The current name of the central government of the People's Republic of China was introduced by the 1954 Constitution, without undergoing changes in the subsequent constitutional texts. Article 13 of the Basic Law on the Central People's Government of the PRC, approved by the first Plenary Assembly of the Political-Consultative Conference of the Chinese people on 27 September 1949 when the Common Program (or Provisional Constitution) was in force, defined the state administrative superior body, the Council of Political Affairs.

The composition of the State Council, amended in March 2018 by the 13th ANP,[146] includes the presence of the Prime Minister, assisted by the Deputy Prime Ministers and

145 On the State Council, *see* Xu Yi-chong, P. Weller, *The Challenges of Governing: The State Council in China*, in *The China Journal*, n. 76, 2016, 1 ff.; Li Shishi, *The State Council and Law-Making*, in J.M. Otto, M.V. Polak, J. Chen, Y. Li (Eds.), *Law-Making in the People's Republic of China*, op cit., 91; B.S.J. Weng (Weng Songran), *The Role of the State Council*, in *Chinese Law and Government*, 1983, n. 2-3, 153 ff. (in the monothematic dossier *Studies on the Constitutional Law of the People's Republic of China*, B.S.J. Weng Ed.).

146 *See* Y. Yuan, *The massive State Council restructuring creates new ministries, cuts or merges others*, in *Beijing Review*, 2018, n. 13, www.bjreview.com; J.G. Mahoney, *Will Big Cabinet Changes Lead to Big Societal Changes? State Council restructuring moves to improve governance, ivi*, 2018, n. 13; *Better-Functioning Government, ibidem*, 2018, n. 14; G.M. Heggelund, I. Stensdal, *Will structural changes in China's bureaucracy save the environment?*, in www.fni.no (20 March 2018). On "unremitting efforts to smoothly promote the

State Councillors, as well as Ministers, Chairmen of the Commissions, the Chief Auditor and the Secretary General. The overall responsibility for government action lies with the figure of the Premier, that of the Ministries and the Committees of the State Council of the respective ministers and the Chairmen. The 1982 Constitution therefore acknowledged in Article 86, Paragraphs 2 and 90, the principle of individual responsibility in the sphere of the national government, in contrast to that which was envisaged in Article 17 of the organic law of the central people's government of 1949 which rigidly implemented a system of collective government and its corresponding collective responsibility.

The Central People's Government is accountable to the National Parliament and, during the intervals between the sessions of the Plenary Assembly, to the Standing Committee of the NPC. The Government is also required to report on its activities to the central parliamentary bodies.

The Central People's Government remains in office for five years, similar to the term of office of the deputies of the National People's Congress. The consecutive mandates of a member of the national government cannot exceed two, for a total duration of ten years.

The work of the State Council, governed by the Organic Law on the State Council of the People's Republic of China approved in 1982, can be held in a permanent session (*changwu huiyi*), attended by the Premier, the Vice-Premiers, the Councillors of State and the Secretary General, as well as in plenary session (*quanti huiyi*).[147] Both sessions are convened and chaired by the Prime Minister. The standing session of the State Council meets weekly, while the plenary sessions are held every two months.

On a functional level, the State Council has the power of legislative initiative in the national parliament and in the Standing Committee of the NPC. The State Council typically issues administrative measures, subordinated to the Constitution and to laws to which they must not be in contrast. Number 1 of Article 89 of the Constitutional Charter establishes that the national government is responsible for the approval of administrative rules and regulations,[148] as well as provisions and measures called decisions (*jueding*) and ordinances (*mingling*). The unitary guidance exercised by the national government over the administrative bodies is not limited to the Ministries and the Committees of the State

institutional reform of the Council of State", *see Chinese Vice Premier Urges Smooth, Unremitting Institutional Reform*, in *Beijing Review*, 2 April 2018, www.bjreview.com.

147 As established by Art. 4 org. law State Council.

148 For the latter, the law on legislation envisages the obligation of publication in the Official Gazette of the State Council. The plurality of the Official Gazettes, edited by the Standing Committee of the NPC and the State Council, to which are added the ministerial and departmental gazettes, certainly does not facilitate the full and timely knowledge of the current law in China, having among other things the PRC assumed international obligations on the subject of simplification of the system of official publication of legal normative acts. *See* R. Cavalieri, *L'adesione della Cina alla WTO. Implicazioni giuridiche*, op cit., 26 ff., which opportunely stresses that the certainty, predictability, transparency and know-how of all legal rules (and not only commercial law) is an essential condition for the progress of the process of modernization of law and the affirmation of legality in post-Maoist China.

Council, but extends both to administrative activities that are national in nature and to the work carried out by the local government bodies at different levels (subordinated to the national government body) of the administrative divisions. A corollary of such a unitary guidance is the power of the central government to modify or annul "improper" acts and measures issued by ministerial bodies, government committees and local state administrative bodies.[149] More generally, the national government has powers to review and approve the employees of public administrations, as well as to appoint, dismiss and train administrative staff, overseeing the progress of administrative activities with the possibility of granting bonuses and imposing sanctions on individual officials.[150]

The State Council is further responsible for performing high administrative management tasks in a large number of areas of the PRC system. For example: a) economic affairs and urban and rural development; b) affairs related to education, science, culture, public health, sport and family planning (*id est*, births); c) civil affairs, public security, administration of justice, and legal controls; d) foreign affairs, with government competence extended to the conclusion of international treaties and agreements; e) national defence; f) the right to the autonomy of minority nationalities; and g) protection of the legitimate rights and interests of both the Chinese abroad and their families, as well as Chinese repatriats.

149 *See* n. 13-14 of Art. 89 of the Constitution.

150 The regulation of legislative sources concerning the public administration is contained in the «Provisional norms on civil servants» which entered into force on 1 October 1993, of which, a reform has been (for some time, in truth) *see* B. Mottura, *La gestione delle risorse umane nella pubblica amministrazione: la formazione*, in *Mondo cinese*, n. 122, 2005, 22 ff.; A. Lavagnino, *La riforma della pubblica amministrazione nella Cina del nuovo millennio*, in L. Lanciotti (Ed.), *Conoscere la Cina*, op cit., 95 ff. The Italian translation, of the original text in Chinese, of the provisional legislation on the public service is available in *Mondo cinese*, n, 102, 1999, 89 ff., and also, at 69 ff. the comment of D. Pilia, *La riforma della funzione pubblica*, added to which, Zhu Guobin, *La réforme de la fonction publique et son évolution en droit chinois*, Aix-en-Provence, Presses Universitaires d'Aix-Marseilles, 1995. On the resistance opposed by the state bureaucracy to change and the process of modernization, *see* S.K. Ma, *Chinese Bureaucracy and Post-Mao Reforms. Negative Adjustment*, in *Asian Survey*, 1990, 1038 ff. Pekingologists equally highlight the possible transition in China from the role of party official to that of state official; *cf.* E. Tran, *Du cadre dirigeant au haut fonctionnaire? Enquête sur l'Ecole du Parti de Shanghai*, in *Perspectives chinoises*, n. 75, 2003, 29 ff. After the amendment of the Art. 27 of the Constitution made by the revision of March 2018, public officials, at the time of taking the service, have the obligation to swear on the Constitution. On the topic *see also*, for the organization of public administration in the PRC prior to the issuance of the 'Provisional Rules' of 1993,J. Burns, *Civil Service in Contemporary China*, in *The Australian Journal of Chinese Affairs*, 1987, 47 ff.; Id., J.-P. Cabestan (Eds.), *Provisional Chinese Civil Service Regulations*, monothematic dossier of *Chinese Law and Government*, 1990-1991, n. 4; Tsien Tche-hao, *Discussion sur la Bureaucratie en Chine*, in A. Giuliani, N. Picardi (Eds.), *L'educazione giuridica*, IV, *Il pubblico funzionario: modelli storici e comparativi*, t. III, *Modelli comparativi. Discussioni sulla burocrazia*, Perugia, Università degli Studi of Perugia, 1981, 273 ff.; J. Cabestan, *L'administration chinoise après Mao: les réformes de l'ère Deng Xiaoping et leur limites*, Paris, Éditions du Centre Nationale de la Recherche Scientifique, 1992. With regard to the bureaucratic apparatus of imperial China, *see* É. Balazs, *La burocrazia celeste. Ricerche sull'economia e la società della Cina del passato*, (1968), Italian translation, Milano, il Saggiatore, 1971; Id., *Chinese Civilization and Bureaucracy. Variations on a Theme*, Preface by J.K. Fairbank, A.F. Wright, introduction by A.F. Wright, New Haven-London, Yale University Press, 1964; P. Corradini, *Ricerche sull'origine e lo sviluppo dei sei dicasteri (liu-pu) dell'impero cinese*, Roma, IsMEO, 1962.

Furthermore, the Central People's Government is responsible for drafting and implementing the national economic and social development plan and the state budget, as well as the organization of the administrative division of provinces, autonomous regions, autonomous municipalities, autonomous prefectures, districts, autonomous districts and cities, being able finally to decide, in conformity with law provisions, the adoption of a state of emergency[151] in a part of the territory of provinces, autonomous regions and autonomous municipalities.

The list contained in Numbers 1–17 of Article 89 of the Constitution on the functions and powers of the State Council, formerly examined, is not to be considered exhaustive, due to the fact that Number 18 of the same article specifies that further institutional competences can be devolved to the national government by the NPC or its relative Standing Committee.

This last constitutional provision proved to be extremely important due to the fact that it was based on the deliberation adopted on 10 April 1985 by the third session of the VI National People's Congress, with which the central parliamentary body delegated the national government to approve provisional measures and regulatory provisions concerning in particular the reforms of the economic system, provided that these provisions issued by the State Council were not inconsistent with the Constitution, national laws and the fundamental principles contained in the decisions taken by the NPC or its Standing Committee. The rules and measures approved by the central government would subsequently then, after an evaluation of the results of the regulatory experiment, be incorporated into the legislative acts of the NPC (or Standing Committee). The described regulatory production mechanism was acknowledged and regulated by Article 56, Paragraph 2, of the law on legislation. The provision in itself, on the contrary, extended the legislative power delegated by the State Council, having established that the national government is entitled to lay down rules in matters reserved for the exclusive competence of central parliamentary bodies, in the absence of norms of primary order in the aforementioned subjects and provided there is a prior authorization decision or delegation adopted by the National People's Congress in plenary meeting or by its Standing Committee. Chinese doctrine, furthermore speaks of a special legislative authority of the State Council, special due to the fact that it is subject to the pre-condition of the existence of the appropriate authorization emanating from the national parliament (or the Standing Committee).[152]

The current Chinese Constitution also regulates, in Article 91, inserted in Section III of Chapter III dedicated to the State Council, the central body for auditing, surveillance and legal-accounting control. The creation of an *auditing body* of the PRC is the responsi-

151 Before the constitutional amendment of 14 March 2004, no. 16 of Art. 89 of the Constitution referred to martial law.

152 *See* Lin Feng, *Constitutional Law in China*, op cit., 139.

bility of the central government. The scope of the audit body is broad, covering revenues and expenditures not only of local Ministries and Governments at the various levels, but also of all state organs and bodies of financial and monetary administration, as well as each institution, enterprise or state organization. In exercising the functions of accounting control, the body envisaged by Article 91 of the Constitution acts in accordance with the Prime Minister's instructions and the law, while enjoying the *status* of an independent institution, not subjected to any interference by administrative bodies, social organizations or physical persons (as established in Para. 2 of the aforementioned provision).

Among the powers of the State Council there is, moreover, that of establishing special government offices, on the basis of provisions that must however be approved by the NPC or, in the intervals between the plenary sessions, by its Standing Committee. In the exercise of such a regulatory power of the national government, special offices for the Affairs of Hong Kong, Macao, Taiwan, the Chinese overseas and special economic zones, were created. The Special Offices assist the Prime Minister in dealing with issues that fall within their respective competence. The adoption of administrative acts and provisions by the special offices of the central government is subject to the approval of the Premier.

Other constituted organs, organisms and institutions directly depend on the State Council. Among them, the main organ is the State Agency for Environmental Protection. The Prime Minister designates the subjects under their guidance. The relative posts rank lower than those of the Ministers, and are not part of the State Council.

If now, panoramically and retrospectively, we analyses the constitutional *status* of the State Council, in the light of the powers attributed to it, one can note that, on the one hand, it carries out an external function in the field of international relations as a representative of the ownership of the State, as well as, on the other hand, a function of internal or "domestic" importance, which in turn takes on a dual nature, being addressed both to the unitary guidance of the administrative apparatus of the State and to the emanation of rules of secondary rank in the hierarchy of sources, and with regards to the implementation of the legislative provisions approved by the central parliamentary bodies (NPC and its Standing Committee) of the People's Republic of China.

With particular regard to the unified guidance of the administrative structures, the difference between the powers exercised by the State Council towards Ministries, Committees of the State Council, bodies and institutions directly dependent on the central government, with respect to those they express towards the local organs of state power, which are also subject, in accordance with the principle of double dependence or subordination, to control and supervision by the local parliaments (and the relative standing Committees) established at the corresponding political-administrative level.

It should be noted that China is witnessing a proliferation of structural articulations by the popular central government, which has led to repeated attempts to reduce, rationalize and "lighten" the organizational structure of the higher organs of state administration.

The path of reforms appears, however, long and complex, if one takes into consideration that the four reform periods carried out in the years 1982–1983, 1988, 1993–1996 and 1998, are still in the transitional phase of progressive application. On the other hand, the objectives pursued are not solely based on the reduction of public administration staff, but also the improvement of the level of professionalism of public sector workers, especially managers and officials, in the fight against rampant corruption in the state bureaucracy,[153] as well as in the modernizing of the entire administrative system of the country, in order that the functions of national and local government represent a complement of the market economy, and not an alternative to it.[154]

From the point of view of normative production, regulatory power lies with the Ministries of the National People's Government, Committees of the State Council, the Chinese Central Bank (or Bank of China), control bodies, as well as other bodies acting under the control or supervision of the State Council. The regulatory provisions thus enacted are however hierarchically inferior to the regulations adopted by the central government. In the case of competing competences, the State Council assumes the initiative to coordinate the related regulatory process, which may lead to the approval of joint administrative regulations. The central government is also responsible for resolving any conflicts that may arise between previous special regulations and following general regulations.

As for the local people's governments, in the light of what has been analysed in the previous paragraph on the functions and powers of the local People's congresses, one can observe that they adopt local regulatory acts to implement the legislative norms issued by the Parliaments of the corresponding political-administrative level. Local legislation is of a higher hierarchical level in the system of sources of Chinese law than that of local regulatory law, approved by the sub-national people's government of the same level, that is to say, by a local subordinate executive, in accordance with the institutional architecture based on the already examined principle of double dependence or subordination.

With regard, thus, to the hierarchy between the administrative norms issued by the local people's governments of the various levels, the provisions adopted by the provincial or autonomous regions are prevalent on the norms adopted by metropolitan governments of cities included in autonomous provincial or regional jurisdictions. On the other hand,

153 *Cf.* F. Sapio, *La corruzione in Cina oggi: alcuni casi recenti*, in *Mondo cinese*, n. 114, 2003, 11.; Id., *Sulla natura "funzionale" della corruzione in Cina*, in M. Scarpari, T. Lippiello (Eds.), *Caro Maestro... Scritti in onore di L. Lanciotti per l'ottantesimo compleanno*, op cit., 1043 ff.; P. Corradini, *Corruzione a Pechino*, in *Mondo cinese*, n. 99, 1998, 11 ff. Re the campaigns of moralization and counter-corruption promoted by the CCP, *see* Yang Fengchun, *Zero Tolerance for Corruption. Punishment and Prevention Form Foundation of the Anti-Corruption Plan*, in *Beijing Review*, 2004, n. 7, 26 ff.; F. Sapio, *La corruzione in Cina: "campagne" e "retizzazione" del fenomeno*, in *Mondo cinese*, n. 124, 2005, 14., where the author examines systemic corruption, implemented by a network of public officials.

154 In this sense, Lin Feng, *Constitutional Law in China*, op cit., 140 ff. (*sub The Establishment of a Modern Administrative System*).

the provision contained in Article 82 of the law on legislation seems to raise some doubts in terms of legal certainty, for which, if there is a conflict between secondary administrative acts, be they central or local regulatory acts, they must be considered as having the same equal legal authority and consequently *ratione materiae* is applied. The conflicts between provisions adopted by different Ministries, or between ministerial source norms and norms issued by local People's Governments, are therefore destined to find a solution on the basis of the precise identification of the respective application area, which may not always be easy given the complexity of the Chinese system design for executive bodies at central and local level.

The obligation laid down by Article 77 of the *lifa fa* to publish the regulations of the central government, ministries and agencies and *authorities* placed under the control of the State Council in the Official Gazette of the State Council, as well as the regulations of the local government in the Official Gazette of the People's Government, is very useful for the purposes of the effective knowledge of administrative regulatory acts.

Lastly, it should be noted that the new *linfa* for the construction of a system of local (socialist) democratic government stemmed from the provisional organic law on the direct election of the Village Committees of November 1987. It is a provisional experimental legislation adopted by the Standing Committee of the IV National People's Congress, which dictates the regulations on the organization and functions of the village Committees. The powers attributed to the management of a village's affairs to the institutional figures of the Head of the Village, the Vice-Head of the Village and the members of the Village Committee seem appropriate to prefigure transparent and effective forms of self-government (or self-management) of rural villages,[155] as well as the progressive emergence of a new local *elite*,[156] especially from the point of view of financial and budgetary issues, of the supply of local public services (e.g. electricity),the provisions for allocating building land and, in general, the regulation of economic activities.

155 On local democratic self-management by village committees in the PRC, *see* Sun Yu, *Il sistema di autogoverno dei villaggi*, in L. Moccia (Ed.), *Profili emergenti del sistema giuridico cinese*, op cit., 101 ff.; M. Zinzi, *La transizione della democrazia rurale nell'esperienza cinese*, in *Percorsi costituzionali*, 2017, 175 ff.; G. Schubert, *La démocratie peut-elle coexister avec le Parti unique? Appréciation nuancée des élections villageoises et cantonales en Chine*, in *Perspectives chinoises*, n. 75, 2003, 16 ff.; J.C. Oi, S. Rozelle, *Elections and Power: The Locus of Decision-Making in Chinese Villages*, in *The China Quarterly*, 2000, 513 ff.; B. He, *Local Democratisation, Governence, and Village Elections in China*, in *Panorama. Insights into Asian and European Affairs* (a series of *occasional papers* published in Singapore by Konrad-Adenauer-Stiftung), 2012, n. 2 (edited in 2013), *Local Politics and Governance*, W. Hofmeister Ed., 61 ff.; K.J. O'Brien, S. Zhao (Eds.), *Grassroots Elections in China*, London/New York, Routledge, 2014.

156 *Cf.* Y. Guo (Ed.), *Local Elites in Post-Mao China*, London/New York, Routledge, 2018.

1.4.3 The Central Military Commission

The unitary power of the Chinese state includes the military component, whose control is attributed to the people who exercise it through the central parliamentary bodies. The 1982 Constitution dedicates Articles 93 and 94 to the upper echelons structure of the armed forces, called the Central Military Commission (CMC). It consists of a Chairman, the Vice-Chairmen and some members elected by the National Parliament, who remain in office for the entire term of the legislature (five years). The Constitution does not establish any limitation to the renewal of the positions of Chairman of the Central Military Commission[157] and its members, unlike that which is established for the highest offices of the State, who cannot hold their office for more than two consecutive terms.[158] The responsibility of the CMC's activity lies with its Chairman, who is accountable to the NPC and its Standing Committee.

In the history of Chinese constitutional law, there has always been a close interweaving of military, state and party institutions.[159] Already in 1925, when the PRC did not yet exist,

157 Most probably for personal reasons, since Deng Xiaoping maintained the CMC presidency uninterrupted for more than two terms.

158 This is the case, as seen earlier in the examination of the respective institutional figures, for the President and Vice-President of the PRC, as well as for the Premier, the Vice-Premiers and the Councillors of State.

159 *Cf.* M. Abbiati, *Come cambia la Cina: la funzione dei militari. Ambivalenza nei rapporti fra esercito e partito*, in *Politica internazionale*, 1979, n. 12, 64 ff. G. Samarani, *La Cina verso il 2000. Potere politico e trasformazioni economico-sociali*, op cit., particularly *sub L'Esercito*, 125 ff. On the People's Liberation Army (PLA) of the PRC, founded on 1 August 1927 with the original name of the Chinese Workers' and Peasants' Red Army, *see* Hu Huang-tai, *The People's Liberation Army*, in *Peking Review* (*Beijing Zhoubao*), 1959, n. 30, 10 ff.; H.W. Nelsen, *The Chinese Military System. An Organizational Study of the Chinesepart People's Liberation Army*, Boulder (Col.), Westview, 1981, 2nd edn; Dong Lisheng (Ed.), *The Cadre Management System of the Chinese People's Liberation Army*, monothematic dossiers of *Chinese Law and Government*, 1995, n. 4 e 5; D. Shambaugh, *Modernizing China's Military. Progress, Problems, and Prospects*, Berkeley-Los Angeles, University of California Press, 2002; Q. Shi, *China's Military Reform: Prospects and Challenges*, Stockholm-Nacka (Sweden), Institute for Security and Development Policy (ISDP), 2014; C. Attanasio Ghezzi, G. Epifanio, *L'esercito popolare di liberazione nel XXI secolo: l'era di Xi Ping e il dibattito sulle riforme*, in *Sulla via del Catai. Riv. sem. sulle relazioni culturali tra Europa e Cina*, VII, n. 10, May 2014 (thematic number *Gli Artigli del Drago. Il pensiero militare cinese tra confucianesimo e realpolitik*, Ed. P. Rosa), 141 ff.; S. Dossi, *Le Forze armate cinesi nel novantesimo anniversario*, in *Mondo cinese*, n. 162, 2017, 13 ff.; Id., *L'Esercito popolare di liberazione fra mutamento della dottrina militare e riforma della struttura di comando: un'ipotesi interpretativa*, in *OrizzonteCina*, 2018, n. 2, 3 ff. For strictly constitutional law studies aspects, *see* J.T. Paltiel, *Civil-Military Relations in China: An Obstacle to Constitutionalism?*, in *Journal of Chinese Law*, 1995, 35 ff. On the distinction between 'core military law' and 'international military law', *see* J. Zhou, *Fundamentals of Military Law. A Chinese Perspective*, Heidelberg, Springer, 2019. Chinese-Maoist ideas on the special relationship between the army and the people have traditionally been 'visualized' through propaganda posters and educational posters (the latter attached to textbooks used in schools); *see* the extensive collection of reproductions of such posters contained in *Chinese Propaganda Posters*. Whit Essays by A. Min, D. Duo and S.R. Landsberger, from the collection of M. Wolf, Köln, Taschen, 2011, *passim*, especially 120 ff. (*ivi* read, *inter alia*, that, according to a phrase attributed to Mao Tse-tung, "An army without culture is a dull army, and a dull army is not able to defeat the enemy"). On the historical aspects (concerning pre-revolutionary China), *see* K. Filipiak, *Civil-Military Relations in Chinese History. From Ancient China to the Communist Takeover*, London-New York, Routledge, 2015.

a Central Military Commission was created within the CCP. The 1949 Joint Program placed the People's Revolutionary Military Commission under the command of the armed forces (Article 20 of the Provisional Constitution). The innovation brought by the first Chinese Constitution of 1954 consisted in the provision, in Article 42, of the National Defence Council, the superior organ of state power in the matter of the armed forces presided over by the Head of State, aided by the Central Military Commission, part of the organizational structure of the CCP. The members of the state vertex of the People's Liberation Army were different from those established in a homologous position within the Party, thus delineating an embryonic form of autonomous military state command in relation to the party military command.

The 1975 Constitutional Charter suppressed the National Defence Council, placing the armed forces under the exclusive leadership of the Communist Party, whose command was attributed by Article 15, c. 2, of the Constitution to the Chairman of the Central Committee of the National Congress of the CCP. A similar approach was acknowledged by Article 19, Paragraph 1, of the third Chinese constitution of 1978.

The current Constitutional Charter has re-established the model acknowledged by the 1954 Constitution. Alongside the Central Military Commission as a state organ, one can find the CMC established within the CCP. However, in accordance with an established practice, the members designated by the NPC to be part of the state CMC are the same members of the CMC of the Party. It is therefore not an institutional union, due to the fact that the state organ is different and (formally) autonomous from the party organ, but rather it is a personal union, with the same subjects who hold both offices.

1.4.4 *The Links Between the Executive Functions of Higher Level, with a View to the Rationalization of the Chinese Form of Government*

The upper echelon structure of the Executive in the PRC seems rather crowded, as one can find, based on the analysis carried out in this paragraph, the President of the Republic, the Prime Minister and the Chairman of the Central Military Commission. The holders of these three offices are all appointed by the National People's Congress, to which they are accountable. In the intervals between the parliamentary sessions, they are accountable to the Standing Committee of the NPC. However, the constitutional text does not outline a regulation of the relations between the three highest organs of the state. Thus, the distribution of functions between them avoids, on the one hand, the concentration of power but, on the other hand, encourages the struggle for power itself.

In consideration of the above-stated, several institutional paths could be envisaged for the rationalization of executive superior functions, via the strengthening of the position of the Head of State, with the conferral of the chairmanship of the Central Military Commission, thus placing the Premier in a subordinate role with respect to the Head of State, in accordance with a model of presidential form of government. Or, on the contrary, strengthening the institutional figure of the Prime Minister, by assigning him the position of Chairman of the CMC, with the consequent reduction of the role of the President of the PRC to that of the nominal Head of the State, lacking substantial powers.

The search for brakes and balances, in this perspective, could then usefully move towards the more precise constitutional regulation of external relations between national legislation and central government, as well as enhancing the top of the Judiciary (*id est*, the Supreme People's Court) as an external balancing limit of possible abuses of the National Executive. In this way, the objectives of rationalizing the form of Chinese government would be pursued in accordance with procedures that appear to be more convincing than the current internal division of executive powers between the offices of President of the PRC, Premier and Chairman of the CMC, formally (and to a full extent) independent from each other.

On the other hand, it is also true that the lack of a constitutional status regulation on the subject of internal relations between the highest offices of the Chinese Executive is overcome, as a matter of fact and by simple agreement, by the prevalence often given to the Chairman of the CMC as occurred during the leadership of Deng Xiaoping, or from the mechanism of the personal union between the positions of Head of State, Chairman of the CMC and the Secretary General of the CCP.

1.5 The Administration of Justice

1.5.1 Judicial Organs in the Chinese Constitutional Law System

Among the six higher organs of unified state power in the PRC, alongside the National Parliament and its Standing Committee, the State Council, the President of the Republic and the Central Military Commission, of which all has already been stated in the previous paragraphs, one can find the structures to which are devolved the judicial functions, represented by the People's Courts and the People's Procuratorates.[160]

160 On the Chinese judicial system, *cf.* B. Liebman, *Authoritarian Justice in China: Is There a "Chinese Model"?*, in W. Chen (Ed.), *The Beijing Consensus?: How China Has Changed Western Ideas of Law and Economic Development*, Cambridge, Cambridge University Press, 2017, 225 ff.; Y. Zhao, *The Courts' Active Role in the Striving for Judicial Independence in China*, in *Frontiers of Law in China*, 2017, 278 ff.; Feng, L.P. Nelson. T.W. Simon, *Judiciary: System, Issues, and Alternatives*, in Id., *China's Changing Legal System*, Basingstoke (UK)/New York, Palgrave Macmillan, 2016, 47 ff.; Y. Li, *The Judicial System and Reform in Post-Mao China Stumbling towards Justice*, Farnham (UK)-Burlington (VT, USA), Ashgate, 2015; L.L.P. Gore, *Limits to Judicial Reform in China*, in *Chinese Journal of Comparative Law*, 2014, 213 ff.; X. He, *Judicial Innovation and Local Politics: Judicialization of Administrative Governance in East China*, in *The China Journal*, n. 69,

Given that the hierarchical administrative appeals are still more numerous in China

---

January 2013, 20 ff.; Y. Li, *Judicial Independenced in China: An Attainable Principle?*, The Hague, Eleven, 2013; C. Mugelli, *Judicial Independence in China: A Comparative Perspective*, in *Acta Juridica Hungarica. Hungarian Journal of Legal Studies*, 2013, 40 ff.; Y. Wang, *Court Funding and Judicial Corruption in China*, in *The China Journal*, n. 69, January 2013, 43 ff.; Id., *The Independence of Judges in China and Germany*, Frankfurt am Main, Lange, 2011; S. Hou, R.C. Keith, *A New Prospect for Transparent Court Judgement in China?*, in *China Information*, 2012, 61 ff.; Y. Qin, *The Current Situation of Chinese Judges: Lost in a Cloud of Conflict and Confusion*, in *Zeitschrift für chinesisches Recht*, 2011, 241 ff.; R.C. Keith, Zhiqiu Lin, *Law and Justice in China's New Marketplace*, Basingstoke (UK)/New York, Palgrave Macmillan, 2001; Zhou Hanhua, *Objectives of Judical System Reform: Establishing an Independent, Open and Dynamic Judiciary*, Oslo, Norwegian Centre for Human Rights (Faculty of Law, University of Oslo), 1999 (*NCHR Working Paper*); R.C. Brown, *Understanding Chinese Courts and Legal Process: Law with Chinese Characteristics*, The Hague, Kluwer Law International, 1997; D.C. Clarke, *Dispute Resolution in China*, in *Journal of Chinese Law*, 1991, 245 ff.; J. Brady, *Justice and Politics in People's China: Legal Order or Continuing Revolution?*, London/New York, Academic Press, 1982; Leng Shao-chuan, *Justice in Communist China: A Survey of the Judicial System of the Chinese People's Republic*, Dobbs Ferry (New York), Oceana Publications, 1967; S. Lubman, *Mao and Mediation: Politics and Dispute Resolution in Communist China*, in *California Law Review*, 1967, 1284 ff.; H. McAleavy, *The People's Courts in Communist China*, in *American Journal of Comparative Law*, 1962, 52 ff.; A. Allen, M.S. Palay, *Economic Courts*, in R.H. Folsom, J.H. Minan (Eds.), *Law in the People's Republic of China. Commentary, Readings and Materials*, op cit., 183 ff.; AA.VV., *La justice en Chine. Des Cent fleurs aux cent codes*, Paris, Maspero, 1979; H. Isaïa, *La justice en Chine*, Paris, Economica, 1978; B. Ahl, *Justizreform in China*, Baden-Baden, Nomos, 2015; K.B. Pißler, *Volksgerichtsorganisationsgesetz der Volksrepublik China*, in *Zeitschrift für chinesisches Recht*, 2012, 52 ff.; Q. Zhang, *Stellung und Rolle des Richters und der Gerichte in China. Eine vergleichende Darstellung aus der Perspektive des deutschen Rechts*, in *Verfassung und Recht in Übersee. Law and Politics in Africa, Asia, Latin America*, 2012, 20 ff.; R. Cavalieri, *L'applicazione della legge straniera da parte dei tribunali della Repubblica Popolare Cinese*, in Id., P. Franzina (Ed.), *Il nuovo diritto internazionale privato della Repubblica Popolare Cinese. La legge del 28 ottobre 2010 sul diritto applicabile ai rapporti civili con elementi di estraneità*, Milano, Giuffrè, 2012, 103 ff.; C. Mugelli, *Indipendenza e professionalità del giudice in Cina*, Firenze, Firenze University Press, 2012; F.R. Antonelli, *Il sistema giudiziario cinese*, in *Mondo cinese*, n. 145, 2011, 84 ff.; M. Mazza, *Le istituzioni giudiziarie cinesi. Dal diritto imperiale all'ordinamento repubblicano e alla Cina popolare*, Milano, Giuffrè, 2010; M. Timoteo, *Il sistema cinese di conciliazione popolare. La giustizia informale in Cina fra tradizione e modernità*, in *Mondo cinese*, n. 71, 1990, 37 ff.; M. Taruffo, *La conciliazione nell'ordinamento cinese*, in G. Crespi Reghizzi, R. Cavalieri (Eds.), *Diritto commerciale e arbitrato in Cina tra continuità e riforma*, Milano, EGEA, 1991, 357 ff.; Id., *L'organizzazione giudiziaria in Cina*, in *Riv. trim. dir. proc. civ.*, 1987, 757 ff.; M. Scarpari, *Recenti discussioni sull'amministrazione della giustizia in Cina*, in *Cina*, n. 13, 1976, 127 ff. Re the evaluation system of judges, *see*, J.J. Kinkel, W.J. Hurst, *The Judicial Cadre Evaluation System in China: From Quantification to Intra-State Legibility*, in *The China Quarterly*, 2015, 933 ff. (in accordance with an *Opinion* of the Supreme People's Court adopted in 2011, thirty performance indicators are used, with the aim of measuring *fairness/gongzheng* 公正, *efficiency/xiaolü* 效率 e *impact/xiaoguo* 效果); J. Zhu, *Making Court systems more efficient and effective: The Chinese Experience*, paper presented at the international conference *The Role of Courts in Evolving Societies*, held in Peking from 25 to 26 May 2018. For a particular analysis profile, *see* J.C. Kinkley, *Chinese Justice, the Fiction. Law and Literature in Modern China*, Stanford, Stanford University Press, 2000. With regard to the conceptions of justice, *see* F. Sapio, S. Trevaskes, S. Biddulph, E. Nesossi (Eds.), *Justice. The Chinese Experience*, Cambridge, Cambridge University Press, 2017. On the history of Chinese judicial institutions, *cf.* P. Paderni, *Recenti studi sull'amministrazione della giustizia e sul diritto nella Cina del XVIII e XIX secolo*, in *Mondo cinese*, n. 97, 1998, 3 ff.; C.C. Huang, *Civil Justice in China. Representation and Practice in the Qing*, Stanford, Stanford University Press, 1996; A. Kormány, "*To Enter a Court is to enter a Tiger's Mouth*". *The role of law in China*, in *Annales Universitatis Scientiarum Budapestinensis de Rolando Eötvös nominatae, Sectio Iuridica, tomus* L, Budapest (*Eötvös Loránd University Faculty of Law*), 349 ff. (the title of the work echoes a Chinese proverbial expression).

than the introductory acts of legal proceedings,[161] it must first be noted that the organs of the judiciary and prosecution judges of the People's Republic are divided into four levels, corresponding to the political and administrative subdivisions of the country. Members of the judiciary are appointed by the same-level People's Congresses, to which they are accountable (as well as to the relevant standing Committees). Article 126 of the 1982 Constitution guarantees the independence of judges from interference by administrative bodies, social organizations and individuals; nevertheless, in Chinese law, the magistracy does not constitute an autonomous power, being a simple functional articulation of the power that belongs entirely to the people and, hence, to the delegates that make up the national Parliament. The National People's Congress and its Standing Committee therefore have the task of issuing binding directives for the application and judicial interpretation of legal norms.

The organization of judicial structures with judicial functions is regulated in detail by the Organic Law on the People's Courts of the People's Republic of China, approved in 1979 and amended in 1983. In implementation of the provisions contained in Article 124, Paragraph 1, of the Constitution, ordinary and special jurisdictional bodies are envisaged; among the latter, the Constitutional Charter expressly mentions the military Courts. The *status* of judicial magistrates is defined in the law on judges of the People's Republic of China, issued by the Standing Committee of the National Parliament and which entered into force on 1 July 1995.[162]

The People's Courts are articulated in levels, as follows: a) Basic popular courts, which include District Courts and County Courts; b) People's intermediate courts; c) High people's

---

161 This was highlighted by, for example, V.R. Palmisano, *The Petitioning system in China*, in *Diritti comparati. Comparare i diritti fondamentali in Europa* (www.diritticomparati.it, doc. dated 22 April 2014). Restrictions on the right to petition have entered into force on 1 May 2014: *see* note entitled 'Kritik an Reform des Petitionsrechts in China – Neue Regelung schürt gewaltsame Proteste', on the website of the *Gesellschaft für bedrohte Völker* (www.gfbv.de, doc. dated 25 April 2014).

162 For the characteristics of the judiciary in China, *see* Tsien Tche-hao, *La formation et le recrutement des juges en République Populaire de Chine*, in N. Picardi, A. Giuliani (Eds.), *L'ordinamento giudiziario*, II, *Documentazione comparativa*, Rimini, Maggioli, 1983, 78 ff.; Tang Teh-hua, *I magistrati e le organizzazioni giudiziarie*, in N. Picardi, A. Giuliani (Eds.), *Ricerche sul processo*, 7, *Il processo civile cinese*, Rimini, Maggioli, 1998, 111 ff. On the need to reform the judicial system of the PRC, especially in order to ensure the independence of judges and combat corruption, *see* Liao Kuangsheng (Liao Guangsheng), *"Independent Administration of Justice" and the PRC Legal System*, in *Chinese Law and Government*, 1983, n. 2-3, 123 ff. (in the monothematic dossier *Studies on the Constitutional Law of the People's Republic of China*, B.S.J. Weng Ed.); H. Koguchi, *Some Observations About "Judicial Indipendence" in Post-Mao China*, in *Boston College Third World Law Journal*, 1987, 195 ff.; Li Yuwen, *Judicial Independence: Applying International Minimum Standards to Chinese Law and Practice*, in *China Information*, 2001, 67 ff.; Jian Fa, *Reforming the Judiciary*, in *Beijing Review*, 2004, n. 42, 18 ff.; Fan Ren, *Calling for an Independent Judiciary, ivi*, 2004, n. 23, 32 ff.; Yu Zonghe, *Judicial Overhaul, ivi*, 2004, n. 18, 28 ff.; Liu Yu, *Reforms for More Rights, ibidem*, 2004, n. 47, 32 ff.; He Weifang, *Judicial Independence Should Come First, ibid.*, 2005, n. 45, 24 ff. (interview by Li Li). Some amendments to the law on judges were adopted by the Sstanding Committee of the National Assembly of the People on 23 April 2019. With regard to the problems of defence (legal assistance) in favour of the less well off, *see* Jian Fa, *Legal Assistance: Government Duty*, in *Beijing Review*, 2004, n. 6, 26 ff.

courts; and d) the People's Supreme Court.[163] The magistrates assigned to such courts are: President, Vice-Presidents, Section Presidents, Section Vice-Presidents and ordinary judges. The sole President of the People's Court is elected directly by the Parliamentary Congress of the corresponding level, while the remaining judges are appointed (and possibly dismissed) by the Standing Committee of the People's Congress.

A peculiar characteristic of the Chinese system of the administration of justice is constituted by the institution, in all the people's courts, of the same number of judicial councils.[164] The members of these bodies are designated (and removed), on the proposal of the President of each people's Court, and by the Standing Committee of the People's Assembly of the same level. As envisaged by Article 11, Paragraph 1, of the Organic Law on Popular Courts of the PRC, the Judicial Councils of all levels carry out their activities in a manner consistent with the principle of democratic centralism. From this it follows that, on the individual issues discussed by the Judicial Council, the President of the People's Court, who is responsible for directing and presiding over the work of the Council itself, has nevertheless the final word. At the meetings of the Judicial Council, the Chief Prosecutor of the People's Procuratorate established at the corresponding level, may also participate, but without the right to vote.

The functions of the Judicial Council consist in the supervision of cases to be decided by the People's Court, with particular regard to the most important or "difficult" civil and criminal cases, as well as the collection and processing of judicial petitions.[165]

The intervention of the Judicial Council in the decision-making phase of individual cases seems to be in contrast with the principle of the so-called internal independence of a judge, due to the fact that it is certainly not a functional interference of organs, organizations or natural persons unrelated to the judicial order (the so-called external independence

---

163 The organization and functioning of the Supreme Court of the PRC are analysed by S. Finder, *The Supreme People's Court of the People's Republic of China*, in *Journal of Chinese Law*, 1993, 145 ff.; T. Zhang, *The Pragmatic Court: Reinterpreting the Supreme People's Court of China*, in *Columbia Journal of Asian Law*, 2012, 1 ff.; R.C. Keith, Z. Lin, S. Hou, *China's Supreme Court*, London-New York, Routledge, 2014; B. Ahl, *Judicialization in authoritarian regimes: The expansion of powers of the Chinese Supreme People's Court*, in *International Journal of Constitutional Law*, 2019, 252 ff. The People's Supreme Court actively participates in the debate on justice reform in China; for example, on 29 October 2013 the Supreme Court published a document (*Judicial Reform Opinion, see* website www.leggicinesi.it) which highlights the need to improve the current regulatory framework in relation to (at least) four aspects, namely: a) protection of the independence of the judiciary (with respect to external interference); b) combatting the phenomenon of corruption; c) review of the current recruitment mechanisms for judges; d) increase in the professionalism of magistrate staff. For the influence of the doctrinal formative on the jurisprudential production of the Supreme Court, *see* J. Jie, *A Study of Effect and Impact of Scholarly Opinions on Judgements in the Spc of P. R. China*, in *Ann. dir. comp.*, 2015, 123 ff. From a comparative viewpoint *see* C.H. van Rhee, Y. Fu (Eds.), *Supreme Courts in Transition in China and the West. Adjudication at the Service of Public Goals*, Berlin, Springer, 2017, and ivi Y. Fu, *The Chinese Supreme People's Court in Transition*, 13 ff.

164 *cf.* X-Y. Li-Kotovtchikhine, *Pragmatisme juridique et contrôle de l'activité judiciarire en Chine post-Mao*, in *Rev. intern. dr. comp.*, 2016, 129 ff.

165 According to the principle of collective management of the work of the People's Courts.

of a judge), but rather constitutes assessments made by a structure belonging to the judiciary. On the other hand, according to Chinese doctrine,[166] the independence of the judiciary must be understood as a principle that refers to the people's courts and not to individual judges. Indeed, Chinese constitutionalists and procedural experts believe that the internal and collegiate evaluation of specific cases by the Judicial Council is useful precisely to prevent any external influences on magistrates. On the other hand, there is a tendency to very hastily examine serial cases by the Judicial Council, whose detailed intervention is limited to causes of greater importance or novelty, especially in view of the controversies on issues related to the development of the (socialist) market economy to which a consolidated jurisprudential production is often lacking and the same judges sometimes find themselves (especially in the lower-level People's Courts) uncertain with regards to the content of the ruling to be adopted. Moreover, the collegial study of jurisprudential precedents by the Judicial Councils in the People's Courts can certainly be of help to individual magistrates, even if the legitimacy and power of the judiciary councils to issue instructions and prepare operational guides for decision-making by the legal entities of the causes assigned to them raises doubts in the eyes of Western justice-public law and procedural law experts.

The sentences are issued by courts in collegial composition.[167] At all the four levels, the People's Courts decide in benches formed by several judges, albeit with the differentiation represented by the fact that the people's Courts of the basic level form benches composed of a togated judge assisted by two people's judges, while the judging benches of a higher level include (not less than) three professional judges.[168] The presence of lay judges in the first-level people's courts is not, however, always requested, due to the fact that Article 10, Paragraph 2, of the Organic Law on the PRC's People's Courts states that in some cases, both civil and criminal, of minor relevance, the decision is taken by a professional single presiding judge. In any case, the appeal decision is pronounced by a collegial judicial body.

From an organizational point of view, the President of each people's Court, or the President of the Section of the very same Court (if such a court operates in several sections) designates the President of the judging bench, with the indication that the bench to which the President of the People's Court or the President of the section belong, are chaired by these latter.[169]

The practice has, moreover, highlighted the clear propensity of councillors, who judge both matters of fact and those of law, to comply with the orientation expressed by the

166 *Cf.* Lin Feng, *Constitutional Law in China*, op cit., 216, text and nt. 36.

167 There are problems in the application of judgments, to the point that, not infrequently, a judge must resort to the authority of the local village leader to obtain the execution of a judicial ruling by the "recalcitrant" defendant, highlighted by G. Cuniberti, *Grandes systèmes de droit contemporains*, Paris, LGDJ, 2011, 2nd edn, 258.

168 This is the principle of the collegiality of judgments.

169 Provisions envisaged by paras. 2-4 of Art. 10 of the Organic Law on Chinese People's Courts.

professional judge member of the college, in a similar well to that of the associate judges in the judging college of people's courts at a higher level who generally accept the approach given in view of the decision of the case by the President of the college itself.

The Chinese courts are normally internally structured in sections specialized in a particular subject. The regulations contained in the Organic Law on the People's Courts of the PRC envisage, in Articles 24, 27 and 31, sections for civil litigation matters, criminal cases and for economic disputes at the courts of all levels, to which are further added specialized sections that can be established within the jurisdiction of the Courts of a higher level in relation to those of the basic level. Going beyond the normative text, the District and County Courts have often created, in a similar way to the Superior Courts (expressly authorized by the law), specialized sections for dealing with administrative litigations. Furthermore, on some occasions, specialized sections for judicial disputes on issues of industrial law and intellectual property, have also been established. This has occurred also at the level of the basic people's courts, for example in the judicial organs of Beijing.

The pyramidal system of the Chinese People's Courts, outlined in the Constitution and clarified by the Organic Law on the People's Courts of the PRC, envisages the attribution of the competence to decide the predominant part of civil and criminal litigation[170] to the jurisdictional bodies with the basic level of jurisdiction, due to the fact that only a few categories of disputes have been subtracted from this jurisdiction and devolved to the intermediate courts of the people or to the people's high courts. In particular, the Intermediate Courts of the People decide, at the first level, the disputes in which foreign elements are involved, that is to say, disputes that are of greater importance for the interests of the territory included in their jurisdiction. In a few remaining cases, the High Courts of the People function as judges of the first instance, with regard to matters of provincial relevance.

The judicial body of last resort in the Chinese system is the Supreme People's Court. It examines appeals against the judgments issued by the High People's Courts and by the Special People's Courts; in some cases it is the first and only level of judgment. Furthermore, in accordance with a reform that came into force on 1 January 2007, the Supreme People's court is responsible for approving death sentence judgments handed down by any court (the so-called review procedure, based on Article 235 of the criminal trial law[171]), even if, in accordance with Article 32 of the Organic Law on the People's Courts of the PRC, this power of approval may be delegated by the Supreme Court to the People's High Courts in the cases of capital punishment for crimes of murder, theft, robbery, rape and damage by explosion, as well as other serious crimes against public safety and social order.[172] On

170 Approximately 90% of cases are decided by people's courts at the basic level.

171 The procedure envisages that the defendant of the convicted person must be listened to; established in Art. 240 in the Code of criminal procedure.

172 From a statistical and quantitative point of view, in China, no less than three thousand death penalty convictions were executed in China, equal to about 74.5% of the total of executions worldwide; *cf.* G.P. Salvini,

average, the Supreme Court annuls 10% of the death sentences handed down in the PRC each year.[173]

The main functions of the Supreme People's Court, however, concern two areas of activity that are different from decision-making in the last instance of the appeal cases. These tasks are outlined in Articles 30 and 33 of the Organic Law on the People's Courts of the PRC, devoted respectively to supervision and legislative interpretation.

The first concerns the monitoring by the governing body of the judicial system on the actions of the ordinary and special courts of justice of the various levels that are subordinated to the Supreme Court.

The second task, of a more complex nature, is regulated, in addition to the aforementioned Article 33 of the organic law on the people's courts (in accordance with the version amended in 1983), in Article 2 of the resolution issued on 10 June 1981 by the Standing Committee of the National People's Congress, containing measures to strengthen the interpretation of the law. This function is based on opinions expressed by the supreme

---

La pena di morte nel mondo, in *Civ. catt.*, 2014, 393 ff.; *Nessuno tocchi Caino, La pena di morte nel mondo. Rapporto 2014* (S. D'Elia Ed., Preface by B. Yayi), Roma, Reality Book, 2014 (in relation to 2013 and the first six-months of 2014), and *ivi see* especially. *sub La pena di morte nei paesi illiberali: Cina, Iran e Iraq i primi paesi boia del 2013*, 5 ff., it states that China is «record holder of executions». With regard to 2015 and the first six months of 2016, the death penalty was executed in China in at least 2,400 cases, which correspond to approximately 59 % of the total worldwide: *cf. Nessuno tocchi Caino, La pena di morte nel mondo. Rapporto 2016* (Ed. E. Zamparutti), Roma, Reality Book, 2016, *sub La pena di morte nei paesi illiberali: Cina, Iran e Pakistan i primi paesi boia del 2015*, 5 ff. The *trend*, however, is in decline, in accordance with the approach *killing fewer criminals promotes social harmony*, on which *see* S. Tresvaskes, *Propagating Justice through Court and Prosecution Work in China*, in *Modern China. An International Journal of History and Social Sciences*, 2017, 156 ff., especially 167 ff.

173 The data emerging in Western studies (*see* the note above) cannot use official information from China, since statistics on death sentences and executions are traditionally secret. In confirmation of this, when, for example, the President of the Supreme People's Court, Zhou Qiang, presented the annual report to the National People's Congress on 10 March 2014, he did not provide any quantitative indication in this regard. On the other hand, it is also noted that the PRC expressed in the UN General Assembly, on 20 December 2012, a vote against the resolution for a moratorium on capital punishment, and that China, in response to requests made on 22 October 2013, during the Universal Periodic Review of the UN Human Rights Council, stated, through its official declaration of 19 March 2014, that it had no intention to abolish the death penalty, or to introduce a moratorium, adding that the Government of the People's Republic of China will continue in the future to keep data secret concerning the identity of those sentenced to death, their total number and the actual executions (immediate execution may sometimes be suspended for the duration of two years, with subsequent commutation of the death penalty in life imprisonment). In any case, it should be borne in mind that an amendment to the criminal code approved by the NPC in 2011 reduced the number of hypotheses of crime that envisage the application of the death penalty to 55, hypotheses that numbered 68 in the original version of the criminal code of 1979, eliminating from the list 13 hypotheses, the latter concerning economic crimes or, in any case, committed without violence (the death penalty is not applicable in China to those who have violated criminal law under the age of eighteen, pregnant women and those over seventy-five years old, unless these older people have committed murder "with exceptional cruelty"). A further amendment of 2015 also eliminated another nine cases of death penalty, which now total 46, (*see*, Amnesty International, *Rapporto 2015-2016 – La situazione dei diritti umani nel mondo*, Roma, AI-Italian Section, 2016, 282).

court judges of the PRC regarding the interpretation of legislative provisions. This exegetical reading of the current legislation can be carried out by the Supreme Court not only if there is a dispute pending before the Court itself, that is, at the request of a High People's Court, but also following the issuance of new legislative provisions and even in the absence of current disputes, that is to say in relation to purely hypothetical assumptions regarding the application of the law. In this third case, the scope of the opinion expressed by the Supreme Court is necessarily general and abstract. It is essential to identify, thus, the exact qualification to be attributed to such interpretative opinions, that is, if they are binding for decisions in future cases, so as to constitute a source of law.[174] The question echoes very similar discussions originating in the former Soviet Union from the directive clarifications approved by the Supreme Court of the Union and addressed to the lower courts, as well as similar documents issued by the Supreme Courts in the (then) socialist countries of Central and Eastern Europe.[175]

---

174 Recently, *see*, H. Yao, *中国民法总则中的法源条款 – 兼论司法解释的法源地位 – Le disposizioni sulle fonti del diritto nella Parte generale del Codice civile cinese. A proposito dell'interpretazione giurisprudenziale quale fonte del diritto*, report of the conference «*Cina e codificazione nel XXI secolo. La parte generale del diritto civile in vigore dal 1° ottobre 2017*», held at the University of Bologna and Rome «La Sapienza» from 3 to 4 October 2017.

175 *See* G. Crespi Reghizzi, *La Corte Suprema dell'URSS: spunti da una recente modifica al suo regolamento*, in *L'Est. Riv. trim. di studi sui Paesi dell'Est*, 1967, n. 4, 198 ff.; Id., *Il cittadino Kirill Krapivin e la legge. Quarantaquattro casi di diritto sovietico*, Milano, Giuffrè, 1983, *sub Introduzione*, XVII ff.; G. Ajani, *Le fonti non scritte nel diritto dei Paesi socialisti*, Milano, Giuffrè, 1985, *sub* VIII, *La Corte Suprema educatrice dei tribunali*, 103 ff.; Id., *Diritto dell'Europa orientale*, Torino, Utet, 1996, 178 ff.; M. Mazza, *Le garanzie del potere giudiziario nell'evoluzione degli ordinamenti* ex *socialisti*, in *Riv. dir. proc.*, 1995, 540 ff. *See also* M. Solina, *Convegno-dibattito sugli aspetti dell'ordinamento giuridico cinese*, in *Il Tommaso Natale (Bollettino dell'Istituto di Diritto Processuale Penale dell'Università di Palermo)*, 1973, 244 f., which analyses the relatively binding value of case precedent in Chinese law. On the use of case precedent in Imperial China, *see* R.R. Edwards, *The Role of Case Precedent in the Qing Judicial Process as Reflected in Appellate Rulings*, in C.S. Hsu (Ed.), *Understanding China's Legal System. Essays in Honor of J.A. Cohen*, op cit., 180 ff. Re the experience of Communist China, *see* Liu Nanping, *"Legal Precedents" with Chinese Characteristics: Published Cases in the Gazette of the Supreme People's Court*, in *Journal of Chinese Law*, 1991, 107 ff. On the directive clarifications of the Supreme Court in the PRC (sometimes approved with the collaboration of other institutional subjects, such as the Supreme People's Public Prosecution Office or the Ministry of Public Security), and the related legal effectiveness, *cf.* G. Crespi Reghizzi, *Il diritto cinese oggi*, paper presented at the conference "*Italia – Cina: il ponte della comparazione giuridica*", op cit., which speaks of supplementary legislation, M. Timoteo, *L'evoluzione storica del diritto cinese: le fonti*, op cit., which refers to the directive clarifications as a (supreme) source of legislative rank; S. Wu, *Le interpretazioni giudiziarie nel sistema penale cinese*, in *Diritto penale XXI secolo*, 2014, 55 ff., according to which the provisions are quasi-legislative; S. Cao, *The legal status of decisions and judicial interpretations of the Supreme Court of China*, in *Frontiers of Law in China*, 2008, 1 ff., which uses the (wide) expression *legislative judicial interpretations and decisions of the Supreme Court*. For a recent adoption of the official interpretation of the Supreme Court, *see* N. Nord, G. Cerqueira, *La codification de la résolution du conflit de lois en China et son interpretation par la Cour suprême: entre progrès et incerttitudes*, in *Journal du droit international*, 2016, 77 ff.; R. Cavalieri, P. Franzina, *A Lei de Direito Internacional Privado de 2010 na Suprema Corte do Povo da China*, in F. Bertini Pasquot Polido, M. Maciel Ramos (coord.), *Direito Chinês Contemporâneo*, São Paulo, Almedina, 2015, 331 ff.

The problem seems to necessitate in the law of the PRC, a solution not dissimilar to that which had been conceived in the Eastern European Communist States, in the sense that the legislative interpretations of the Supreme People's Court do not constitute a real judicial legislation. They are jurisdictional and not regulatory acts, and thus remain unconnected with the sources of law. If this approach seems appropriate to safeguard the primacy of the national parliament in the field of production of legislative provisions, it should however be noted that the opinions of the supreme judges could certainly not be neglected by the lower level courts, due to the fact that in appeals, the controversy would come under the examination of the Supreme Court. To this one must also add that there is a mechanism for a possible request for instructions within the Chinese judicial system, which is based on the fact that the People's Courts have the right to address the Court of Justice at a higher level in the course of the proceedings to obtain a clarifying answer on matters of substantive or procedural law, relevant to the ruling. Also in this case, the opinion expressed by a superior judge will have a decisive influence on the lower judicial body, precisely owing to the possibility of challenging the sentence before the judge who has already expressed his orientation in relation to the dispute.

From this point of view, both the legislative interpretation of the Supreme Court and the responses given by the Superior/Higher Courts to the requests for instructions and interpretations coming from the lower jurisdictional bodies may nullify the function of re-examining the case which is typical of procedural appeals, due to the fact that the judge called to give a ruling on the dispute in reality has already expressed his orientation in the interpretative opinion or in the instructions given in response to the request formulated during the trial by the judge of the subordinate level.

Alongside the people's courts of general jurisdiction, one can find the special courts of the PRC. They are governed by Article 124, Paragraph 1 of the Constitution, which expressly mentions only the military Courts, adding that further special people's Courts may be established. Additionally, the establishment of special courts is envisaged in Article 2 of the 1979 Organic Law on the People's Courts of the PRC, namely, the Railway Courts (or Courts for Rail Transport), the Water Courts (or for River Transport) and the Courts for Forestry affairs. In application of these provisions, the Standing Committee of the National Parliament established with a decree issued on 14 November 1984, the constitution of the Maritime Courts, competent to judge on maritime affairs and in particular on maritime commercial disputes (including those with foreign economic operators).[176] The organs of the maritime jurisdictions, created in the main coastal cities of China, are specialized courts of a single degree/level. An appeal to the intermediate popular courts can

176 *Cf.* L. Zhao, L. Li, *Maritime Law and Practice in China*, London/New York, 2017; Li Wei-Jun, *La justice maritime en Chine*, in *Le Droit Maritime français*, 2008, 362 ff.; G. Naronte, *Med-China. Diritto cinese civile e marittimo. Cina e Mediterraneo: sistemi portuali a confronto*, Milano, Angeli, 2006, 198 ff.

be heard against the judgments issued by the Maritime Courts. In accordance with the principle of double dependence or subordination, the supervision of the Courts of maritime disputes is devolved horizontally to the popular Congresses of the city where the judge of maritime disputes is established and vertically to the intermediate Courts of the territorially competent peoples. Finally, the creation of environmental Courts, constituted in the areas of China where the environmental emergency[177] is greatest, is peculiar. These are specialized courts[178] that exercise, in environmental matters, both civil and criminal administrative jurisdictions.[179]

Two degrees of jurisdiction are provided for by the procedural law of the PRC, in the sense that, as envisaged by Article 12, Paragraph 1, of the Organic law on the People's Courts, the parties can propose a single appeal and the sentence of the second degree becomes final. However, it is possible that new judicial proceedings can be opened on an issue already decided upon in appeal, following a procedural initiative of which both the private parties, based on the recent reforms of civil and criminal procedural law,[180] as well as the State Attorney of the level above that of the Court which issued the decision, are entitled to commence. Moreover, the reopening of the judgment can be requested by the same Court that pronounced the sentence, as well as by the People's Court of a higher level.

177 *See* B. Pozzo, *Tutela ambientale e modelli giuridici: il caso cinese*, in *Riv. giur. ambiente*, 2010, 877 ff.; M. Timoteo, *Diritto cinese e tutela ambientale: un itinerario nella giustizia civile*, in R. Cavalieri, V. Bellomo, S. D'Attoma (Eds.), *Diritto, cittadini e potere in Cina. L'evoluzione del diritto cinese fra tradizione e modelli internazionali, Sulla via del Catai. Riv. sem. sulle relazioni culturali tra Europa e Cina*, VIII, n. 12, March 2015, 163 ff.; S. Novaretti, *Urbanizzazione sostenibile: governance sociale, ambiente e partecipazione pubblica nella Repubblica Popolare Cinese*, in *Rivista quadrimestrale di diritto dell'ambiente*, 2016, n. 1, 3 ff.; M. Zhang, B. Zhang, *Specialized Environmental Courts in China: Status Quo, Challenges and Response*, in *Journal of Energy & Natural Resources Law*, 2012, 361 ff.; S. Wang, *The Status and issues of China's Environmental Courts*, in *Tsinghua Journal of Rule of Law*, 2012, 111 ff.; A. Stark, *Umwelgerichte in China*, Baden-Baden, Nomos, 2017. Re judicial compensation (for damage as a result of environmental pollution), *cf.* N. Coggiola, *Tra il dire ed il fare. Il risarcimento dei danni alla persona da inquinamento in Cina, tra leggi e pratica quotidiana*, in *Pol. dir.*, 2015, 61 ff.; M. Timoteo, *Law and Language: Issues Related to Legal Translation and Interpretation of Chinese Rules on Tortious Liability of Environmental Pollution*, in *China-EU Law Journal*, 2015, 121 ff. On corporate social responsibility (CSR), *see* G. Li, *Tutela ambientale e responsabilità sociale d'impresa nel diritto cinese contemporaneo*, in *Riv. trim. dir. proc. civ.*, 2017, 1335 ff., on CSR in the environmental field (the so-called Environmental Corporate Social Responsibility ECSR). From a comparative viewpoint, *see also* D. Amirante, *Les juges verts: perspectives de droit compare*, in C.-H. Born, F. Jongen (Eds.), *D'urbanisme et d'environnement. Liber Amicorum F. Haumont*, Bruxelles, Bruylant, 2015, 389 ff.

178 Currently about 450.

179 This aspect is higlighted by Y. Zhao, *Innovative measures to improve environmental law enforcement in China*, in *China-EU Law Journal*, 2015, 155 ff.

180 This will be examined immediately, in the next section 1.5.2.

1.5.2 Follows: Judicial Review or Supervision (the Re-Opening of a Trial)

The special procedure for the re-examination of judicial decisions that had become final was originally referred to as judicial supervision, due to the fact that priority was given to the initiative of the People's Procuratorate, and was removed from the will of the private parties of the trial. The current rules of both the civil procedure code adopted on 9 April 1991 and which entered into force on the same date (*cf.* Arts. 177–188),[181] as well as the penal procedure code of 1 July 1979, in force since 1 January 1980 and extensively renewed

181 The Italian translation of the 1991 Chinese civil procedural law, which replaced that of 1982, is available in N. Picardi, A. Giuliani (Eds.), *Ricerche sul processo, 7, Il processo civile cinese*, op cit.; *ivi see*, in particular, the papers of N. Picardi, *Una ricerca sulla giustizia civile in Cina*, VII ff. and Sheng Yu, *Introduzione al processo civile cinese*, XXVII ff. *Cf.* also Zhang Xianchu, *Law of Civil Procedure*, in Wang Chenguang, Zhang Xianchu (Eds.), *Introduction to Chinese Law*, op cit., 409 ff.; Meng Chuncai, *Civil Procedure Law*, in Wang Guiguo, J. Mo (Eds.), *Chinese Law*, op cit., 179 ff.; Wang Shizhou, *Civil Procedure in China*, Alphen aan den Rijn (Netherlands), Kluwer Law International, 2014. On the Chinese civil procedural law of 8 March 1982, which entered into force on 1 October of the same year, *see* F. Münzel, *Die neue Zivilprozeßordnung der Volksrepublik China von 1982*, in *Rabels Zeitschrift für ausländisches und internationales Privatrecht*, 1983, 78 ff., and *ivi* the German translation by the author of the afore-mentioned law (*cf.* 94 ff.). In the perspective of comparative civil procedural law, *see* A. Garapon, D. Schimmel, S. Balme, B. Li, J.-L. Langlois, *Le procès civil en version originale. Cultures juridiciaires comparée. France, Chine, États-Unis*, Paris, Institut des hautes études sur la justice (IHEJ), 2014. Finally, *cf.* W. Gu, *Dispute Resolution in China. Litigation, Arbitration, Mediation and their Cross-interactions*, London/New York, Routledge, 2016.

in 1996 (*cf.* Arts. 203–207),[182] and more recently on 14 March 2012,[183] with amendments to the criminal procedural law[184] approved by the Fifth Session of the Eleventh National

182 On the criminal procedure in the PRC, and the reform which entered into force on 1 January 1997, *see* L. Lupária, Sun Weiping, *Lineamenti essenziali del nuovo processo penale cinese*, in *Riv. it. dir. proc. pen.*, 2002, 1345 ff.; L. Lupária, *Quelques réflexions d'un observateur européen sur le procès pénal chinois*, in L. Cuocolo, L. Lupária (Eds.), *Valori costituzionali e nuove politiche del diritto. Scritti raccolti in occasione del decennale della rivista "Cahiers Européens"*, Matelica, Halley, 2007, 153 ff.; Guang Zhong Chen, *La réforme du droit de la procédure pénale en Chine*, in *Rev. de science criminelle et de droit pénal comparé*, 1988, 1 ff.; Tsien Tche-hao, *Analyse des récents codes pénal et de procédure pénal de la République populaire de Chine*, *ivi*, 1980, 641 ff.; R. Heuser, T. Weigend, *Das Strafprozeßgesetz der Volksrepublik China in vergleichender Perspecktive*, Hamburg, Institut für Asienkunde, 1997; M. Klein, *Kritische Betrachtung der neuen chinesischen Strafprozeßordnung*, in K. Wegmann, E. Franke, M. Klein (hrsg.), *Studien zum chinesischen Recht*, II, op cit., 84 ff.; J. Su, *From "Harsh Justice" to "Balancing Leniency with Severity". The Transformation of Criminal Policy in Contemporary China*, in *Peking University Law Journal*, 2017, 139 ff.; S. Zhang, *Transparency and Legitimacy in Chinese Criminal Procedure. Beyond Adversarial Dogmas*, The Hague, Eleven, 2017; M. Fabri (hrsg.), *Four Criminal Procedure Case Studies in Comparative Perspective. China-Italy-Russia-U.S.A.*, Baden-Baden, Nomos, 2016; X. Fu, *Legal transplant in the Criminal Procedure of China: Experiences and Reflections*, in B. Ackerman, K. Ambos, H. Sikirić (Eds.), *Visions of Justice. Liber Amicorum M. Damaška*, Berlin, Duncker & Humblot, 2016, 437 ff.; Fu Hualing, *Institutionalizing criminal process in China*, in G. Yu Guanghua (Ed.), *The Development of the Chinese Legal System. Change and Challenges*, cit., 26 ff.; Fu Hualing, *Criminal Procedure Law*, in Wang Chenguang, Zhang Xianchu (Eds.), *Introduction to Chinese Law*, op cit., 129 ff.; Gu Minkang, *Criminal Procedure Law*, in Wang Guiguo, J. Mo (Eds.), *Chinese Law*, op cit., 643 ff.; C.W. Lo, *China's Legal Awakening. Legal Theory and Criminal Justice in Deng's Era*, Hong Kong, Hong Kong University Press, 1995; S. Shapiro, *The Law and the Lore of China's Criminal Justice*, Beijing, New World Press, 1990; T.D. Epp, *The New Code of Criminal Procedure in the People's Republic of China: Protection, Problems, and Predictions*, in R.H. Folsom, J.H. Minan (Eds.), *Law in the People's Republic of China. Commentary, Readings and Materials*, op cit., 313 ff.; D.A. Donovan, *The Structure of the Chinese Criminal Justice System: A Comparative Perspective*, in *University of San Francisco Law Review*, 1987, 229 ff.; Leng Shao-chuan, *Criminal Justice in Post-Mao China: Some Preliminary Observations*, in *The Journal of Criminal Law & Criminology*, 1982, 204 ff.; H.J. Berman, S. Cohen, M. Russell, *A Comparison of the Chinese and Soviet Codes of Criminal Law and Procedure*, *ivi*, 1982, 238 ff. Re appeals in criminal proceedings, *cf.* M. Y.K. Woo, *The Right to a Criminal Appeal in the People's Republic of China*, Baltimore, School of Law, University of Maryland (*Occasional Papers/Reprints Series in Contemporary Asian Studies*, n. 1), 1989. Re particular aspects, *see*, H. Chin, *China's Criminal Justice System and the Trial of Pro-Democracy Dissidents*, Baltimore, School of Law, University of Maryland (*Occasional Papers/Reprints Series in Contemporary Asian Studies*, n. 6), 1992. Re the function of a lawyer in a criminal trial, *cf.* C. Shum, *The Role of Chinese Lawyers in Criminal Proceedings*, in *China Law Reporter*, 1989, 213 ff. Re the law on the legal profession in China of May 1996, (the so-called *Lawyers' Law*), *see* Q. Luo, *Autonomy, Qualification, and Professionalism of the PRC Bar*, in *Columbia Journal of Asian Law*, 1998, 1 ff.; J. Hu, *The Development of the Chinese legal profession since 1978*, Department of East Asian Studies, University of Durham (*Durham East Asian Papers*, n. 9), 2000; Lawyers Committee for Human Rights, *Lawyers in China. Obstacles to Independence and the Defense of Rights*, New York, Lawyers Committee for Human Rights Publications Department, March 1998; F.R. Antonelli, *L'esercizio della professione legale in Cina (con particolare riguardo agli studi stranieri)*, paper presented at the conference "*Italia - Cina: il ponte della comparazione giuridica*", op cit.

183 *Cf.* Z. Wang, *The Development and Main Reform of Criminal Procedure Law in China*, in *Chinese Studies*, 2015, n. 4, 20 ff.; J. Chen, *Criminal Law and Criminal Procedure Law in the People's Republic of China*, Leiden, Njihoff, 2013; M. McConville, E. Pils (Eds.), *Comparative Perspectives on Criminal Justice in China*, Cheltenham (UK)/Northampton (MA, USA), 2013; M. Liu, *A Brief Review of the Second Revision of China's Criminal Procedure Law*, in *Social Sciences in China*, v. 33, n. 4, November 2012 (*Special Issue: Focusing on the Revision of China's Criminal Procedure Law in 2012*), 133 ff.; J. Rosenzweig, F. Sapio, J. Jue, T. Biao, E. Pils, *The 2012 Revision of the Chinese Criminal Procedure Law: (Mostly) Old Wine in New Bottles*, Hong Kong, The Chinese University of Hong Kong-CUHK Faculty of Law (Centre for Rights and Justice-CRJ), *Occasional Papers Series*, May 2012; X. Shen, *Giustizia, garantire un processo equo*, in *Cina in Italia*, n. 97,

People's Congress and which became effective from the 1 January 2013,[185] however, allow the parties to take part in this extraordinary appeal, thus it would appear more correct to now speak of the reopening of a trial, due to the procedural impulse of private parties or legitimated institutional entities. It should, however, be stressed that the request to reopen judicial proceedings from private parties does not imply the obligation for the People's Court to accept the request and thus to emit a new sentence, unlike that which occurs in an extraordinary appeal for revision or supervision proposed by the People's Procuratorate, which involves the need for the People's Court to renew the procedure.

2013, 8 ff.; S. Wu, *Il codice di procedura penale della Repubblica Popolare Cinese: gli sforzi verso la giustizia*, in *Diritto penale XXI secolo*, 2013, 3 ff.

184 The current criminal procedural code of the PRC is available, translated in Italian, in *Diritto penale XXI secolo*, 2013, 15 ff. The reform of 2012 (in force since 2013) has been extensive, having affected circa half of the articles of the criminal procedural law. However, it is not easy to find the (however numerous) innovations introduced, since the reform itself has fully renumbered the articles of the criminal procedural code, and therefore the identification of the provisions without correspondence in the old procedural law of criminal law, is not immediately perceived.

185 This last reform of the criminal procedure has a protectionist approach, to the extent that it establishes that illicitly acquired evidence, such as confessions extracted by illegal means (including torture), depositions and the testimonies of the victims they are illegally obtained (especially through violence or threats), must be excluded from the evidence that can be used in a criminal justice trial. The first assessments in the West seem, however, very critical, especially from the point of view of its practical application: *cf.* note of Amnesty International, *Chine. Six mois après son entrée en vigueur, la nouvelle loi ne protège pas les droits fondamentaux*, available at www.amnesty.fr. (doc. published 15 July 2013), where Corinna-Barbara Francis, a jurist specialised in China and East Asia in *Amnesty International*, affirms that «Les améliorations apportées à la loi ne servent à rien si la police et les tribunaux locaux ne les mettent pas en pratique. Malheureusement, il semble qu'il y ait un manque de volonté à ce niveau». Re the Chinese viewpoint *cf.* Z. Guo, *The first step of the long march: implementing the exclusionary rules in China*, in *Asia Pacific Law Review*, 2017, 48 ff. (the author works at *College of Criminal Justice, Center for Criminal Law and Justice, China University of Political Science and Law*-CUPL, Peking). The 2012 reform had a long gestation phase. A first draft revision of the criminal procedural law, published in 2007, was abandoned, above all due to the resistance expressed by the Ministry of Public Security. The next project, presented in August 2011, was submitted to a public consultation, which was attended mainly by lawyers (academics and legal professionals), journalists and members of China's online communities. Throughout the public consultation, many criticisms were expressed regarding the inadequacy of the (proposed) law in relation to protection of human rights, and more generally in terms of the fair balance between efficient and effective crime-fighting, on the one hand, and on the other hand, the requirements of protection of human rights (in particular, it appeared to many that the reform envisaged an expansion of police powers, with the consequent and persistent "weaknesses" of criminal procedure in China.). The new revision project – finally approved, as stated in the text, on 14 March 2011 – was presented to the Standing Committee of the National People's Congress on 24 August 2011. On the public consultation on the revision project published in 2011, *see* J. Rosenzweig, *Disappearing Justice: Public Opinion, Secret Arrest and Criminal Procedure Reform in China*, in *The China Journal*, n. 70, luglio 2013, 73 ff. For a complete empirical study on Chinese criminal justice (and its numerous weaknesses), *cf.* M. McConville, *Criminal Justice in China. An Empirical Enquiry*, Cheltenham (UK)/Northampton (MA, USA), Elgar, 2012. The judgment of G.P. Voena, *Novità e caratteri del codice di procedura penale della Repubblica popolare cinese*, in *Diritto penale XXI secolo*, 2014, 1 ff., is also marked by caution, who states that "only profound political reforms will be able to align the Chinese process system with the parameters of the liberal democratic regimes, even though they appear unlikely in the short term" (*cf.* 15).

The re-opening of a trial can be requested, first of all, by the President of the People's Court who issued the ruling. In this case, the presidential request must be addressed to the judicial Council of the same level. However, bearing in mind that the President expresses his prior consent to the content of the judicial rulings issued by the presiding People's Court, the request to the Judicial Council to open the re-examination procedure appears as a sort of rethinking, almost self-criticism, and therefore does not occur with frequency.

In exercising control over the activities of lower-level people's courts, the Higher level Courts may order the reopening of proceedings that had been concluded before the courts of the underlying level. In any case, the Supreme People's Court has the power of initiative for the reopening of a trial against all people's courts. The new judgment can then take place both before a Higher Court as well as before that which issued the sentence.

In addition to these hypotheses of so-called internal judicial supervision, the law of the PRC acknowledges the important procedural institute of the so-called external judicial supervision under the jurisdiction of the organs of the People's Procuratorate. The prosecutorial intervention aimed at the reopening of proceedings is carried out in almost all cases with regard to criminal rulings. Instead, in civil and commercial litigations, it only occurs in exceptional cases.

An appeal consisting of judicial supervision in civil and economic matters may be lodged within a maximum of two years from the issuance of the ruling. It is proposed before the same People's Court that issued the provision, or before a Court of a higher level. The grounds on which the judicial appeal in question may be based are connected with the infringement of substantive rules, due to the fact that the appellant must show the erroneous and unjust nature of the contested ruling. The non-observance of procedural rules is relevant, for the aforementioned purposes, only if the competent People's Court for the appeal deems that the violation of the procedural law led to the enactment of a judicial sentence with a different content to that which would have been issued with its correct application. Furthermore, only private parties (and not the people's courts and prosecutors) may propose an appeal for judicial supervision based on new evidence. In the latter case, however, the judicial provision against which the appeal is addressed, is not to be considered erroneous or unjust in relation to the evidence known to the judge at the time the ruling was pronounced. On the other hand, an appeal for the reopening of civil court proceedings brought by the parties following the discovery of new evidence has no suspensive effects on the implementation of the contested ruling, thus avoiding even the slightest instrumental and dilatory use of the word appeal or, in short, the misuse or abuse of a trial.[186]

The regulation concerning legitimated subjects and grounds for the reopening of a trial contained in the criminal procedural code is substantially similar to that established

186 Abuse of judicial action, a *sub-species* of the abuse of appeals.

in the civil procedural code. The exception is represented by the failure to provide for an appeal for judicial supervision, initiated by private parties, founded on *err in progress*. The violation of the procedural rule could, even in this case, be included in the broad diction of Article 204 of the Italian Criminal Code, according to which a trial can be reopened upon the appeal of legitimated subjects in the case of an erroneous application of the law made by the contested legal provision. It should also be noted that Articles 30 and 32 of the 1995 Law on Judges of the PRC include the imposition of internal administrative sanctions, of a disciplinary nature, against magistrates who do not comply with procedural rules in the discussion and ruling of cases.

The fundamental problem of the Chinese judicial system remains, however, that of ensuring the effective independence of its judges, which is also proclaimed in Article 126 of the Constitution. As is evident, one cannot speak of a neutral judiciary and impartiality of judges in a legal system which, as in the law of the PRC, envisages a control over judicial activity, also in relation to rulings of individual cases, by the popular Congresses and the administrative/executive bodies of the same level, as well as the CCP's structure constituted at various levels and called the Political and Law Committee, which includes the President of the People's Court and the Chief Prosecutor of the corresponding level, this latter also having tasks of supervision and vigilance of the work of the courts. On the other hand, decisions regarding the assignment of personnel and instrumental resources necessary for the functioning of the People's Courts are the responsibility of the executive bodies of state power at various levels, with possible implications with regards to the independence of the Courts from the organs of local administration. The horizontal dependence of the People's Courts on state and party structures combines with the internal control exercised by the Judicial Committee on the ruling of each case, as discussed above. Vertical dependence implies, as already mentioned, that the lower Courts are bound by the directive clarifications of the Supreme People's Court and, more generally, by the instructions issued by the Higher Courts. Hence, it is also very difficult to identify individual responsibility profiles of judges, given the dense network of subjects who participate in various ways in the conformation of the content of the final judicial provision.

Lastly, as a result of the constitutional revision of March 2018, the supervisory committees system has been created, which have the status of state bodies with the main task of combating corruption. At the top of the system is established the National Supervisory (or Supervision) Commission, whose direction was designated by the ANP on 18 March 2018 Yang Xiaodu (deputy secretary of the Central Disciplinary Commission), which has the same administrative level as the Supreme People's Court and of the Supreme People's Procuratorate. The constitutional reform, anticipated by a local experimentation in the Municipality of Beijing and in the Provinces of Shanxi and Zhejiang started in December 2016, was finally completed through the approval of the supervision law adopted by the PA on 20 March 2018.

1.5.3 *The Organization and Functioning of the People's Procuratorates: The National System of Supervisory Commissions and the Constitutional Reform of 2018*

General supervision in the Chinese system is the task of the People's Congresses, in accordance with the principle of the unity of state power. In light of this organizational rule, already illustrated in the second paragraph of this chapter, there is the need to read the definition that Article 129 of the Constitution and Article 1 of the 1979 Organic Law on the People's Procuratorates give re the role of public prosecutors as state organs that exercise legal supervision. Prosecutorial supervision seems, that is, to be understood correctly as legal supervision in the sense of judicial supervision, albeit with the further clarification that the judicial activity subject to the control by public prosecutors is not only that carried out by the popular courts, but also the set of acts and behaviours concerning public safety and state organs, prisons and all legal places of detention,[187] including re-education camps via forced labour.[188]

The structure of the procuratorates is rigidly hierarchical. There are three levels of public prosecutors, starting with the summit represented by the popular Supreme People's Procuratorate. Below there are the Provincial People's Procuratorate that operate at the level corresponding to the administrative subdivisions of the provinces, autonomous regions and autonomous municipalities. The District People's Procuratorate are set up at the first level of the political-administrative divisions. The people's Congresses Assemblies and the executive/administrative bodies of the same level are distributed along a hierarchical scale of four levels; likewise, the pyramid of the People's Courts is articulated on four levels. The apparent anomaly of the People's Procuratorates that are structured only on three levels is re-dimensioned somewhat considering that Article 2, Paragraph 1, Number 2 of the Organic Law on the People's Procuratorates of the PRC includes the sub People's Procuratorates, or sections of the People's Procuratorates, as branches of the provincial People's Procuratorates set up horizontally at the second level of the parliaments/congresses, governments and people's courts. On the other hand, taking into account that: a) the People's Procuratorates at the provincial and subordinate level can create further local

187 *See* F. Sapio, *Detention and its Reforms in China*, Farnham (UK)/Burlington (VT, USA), Ashgate, 2016; E. Nesossi, S. Biddulph, F. Sapio, S. Trevaskes (Eds.), *Legal Reforms and Deprivation of Liberty in Contemporary China*, Farnham (UK)–Burlington (VT, USA), Ashgate, 2016. For senior Party officials, in the event of responsibility – especially for corruption matters – extra-legal forms of detention are usually (but not always) envisaged; *cf.* F. Sapio, *Sovereign Power and the Law in China. Zones of Exception in the Criminal Justice System*, Leiden, Brill, 2010, which speaks of a "parallel" criminal code. The Chinese criminal code (law) was recently revised, according to the IX Amendment of 29 August 2015, which came into force on November 1 of the same year, precisely in order to tighten the sanctions foreseen for corruption (the so-called anti-corruption norms).

188 *See* C. Wan, J. Gao, *On the Relationship of Legal Supervision and Prosecution, Defense, Adjudication*, in *Frontiers of Law in China*, 2008, 368 ff.

People's Procuratorates, having the particular *status* of agencies or decentralized representatives of the higher People's Procuratorates, if the need arises in industrial, mining, agricultural rehabilitation or forestry areas, provided that there is the approval of the Standing Committees of the National People's Procuratorates at the corresponding level; b) the Military Procuratorates and the Railway Procuratorates are established as Special Procuratorates; and c) other special Procuratorates may be set up on the initiative of the national parliament or its standing committee. It seems apparently obvious to state that the panorama of the local (ordinary and special) People's Procuratorates in the judicial system of the PRC is characterized by a not negligible measure of organizational complexity.

With regards to the appointment and dismissal/removal from office of state public prosecutors, Articles 3 and 20–28 of the Organic Public Prosecutor's Law in the PRC envisage, in implementation of the constitutional text, that every People's Procuratorates is to be managed by a chief prosecutor, designated by the People's assembly of the same level. The head of the Supreme People's Procuratorate assumes the name of Attorney General. The People's Procuratorates are also composed of Deputy Chief Prosecutors, denominated Deputy General Prosecutors if they belong to the People's Supreme Court, and state prosecutors, all appointed and dismissed by the Standing Committee of the Parliament at the corresponding level. The procedure for appointing and dismissing state prosecutors presents the characteristic, not contemplated for the designations of the judges of the popular courts, of the necessity to request the approval of the Standing Committee of the deliberative Congress of the higher level, to which proposals for the designation and dismissal of State Prosecutors must be forwarded by the chief Prosecutor of the People's Procuratorates to which the new appointments or dismissal measures relate. In this way, the judicial supervision body (People's Procuratorate) is subjected in the law of the PRC to the legislative supervision of two people's Congresses, that is to say that of the same level as well as the Standing Committee of the higher-level Parliament.[189]

The problems analysed previously concerning the Judicial Committees established at the People's Courts, with respect to the independence of judges, are even more acute in relation to the Procuratorial Committees created in the context of the People's Procuratorates. The members of the Procuratorate Committees are the Chief Prosecutor (or the Attorney General if it is the Supreme People's Procuratorates), the Deputy Head Prosecutors (or Deputy-General Prosecutors) and the State Procurators. Although the People's Procuratorates perform their functions independently, as established by Article 131 of the Constitution and 9 of the Organic Law on the People's Procuratorates in the PRC, however,

189 In the event of contrast between the nominations/revocations proposed by the People's deliberative Assembly of the level corresponding to that of the People's Procuratorate concerned and the decisions issued in this regard by the Standing Committee of the People's Assembly of higher level, based on the already examined principles of democratic centralism and the double subordination, the choices made by the latter prevail.

in accordance with Paragraph 2 of Article 3 of the same organic law, a Procuratorial Committee is established at each of the People's Procuratorates, which also takes decisions on individual cases, provided that they are important or not easy to resolve, by majority vote. Moreover, if there is a difference of opinion within the Procuratorial Committee between the majority of the voters and the Chief Prosecutor (or the Attorney General in the case of the Supreme People's Court), the final decision lies, in accordance with Article 3, Paragraph 2, last part of the Organic Law on the People's Procuratorates in the PRC, with the Standing Committee of the People's Congress at the corresponding level. Therefore, the close connection that exists in the public-law system of the People's Republic of China between the functions of legislative supervision and those of judicial or prosecutorial supervision appears clearly evident, with the clear predominance of the former over the latter.

On the organizational level, it must still be said that Article 20 of the Organic Law on the People's Procuratorates of China permits the establishment of specialized structures, internal offices and operational representations of public prosecutor's, both at a national and local level. In particular, the Supreme People's Procuratorates acts through, economic, criminal, legal and disciplinary, and prison People's Procuratorates. The regulating of the personnel assigned to the public prosecutor's offices is issued by the Supreme People's Procuratorates, as envisaged by Article 28 of the organic law on the People's Procuratorates. In any case, Article 10 of the same organic law, in reiterating the provisions of Article 133 of the Constitution, states that the Supreme Public Prosecutor is accountable to the NPC and its Standing Committee, while the public prosecutors of the lower levels are accountable to the parliamentary congresses and the standing committees of the same level. Taking also into consideration the hierarchical structure of the procuratorial organs, the Supreme People's Procuratorates exercises a general direction over the local People's Procuratorates and the special People's Procuratorates, while it is the task of the People's Procuratorates of the upper levels to direct those of a lower level (*see* Para. 2 of Art. 10 of the People's Procuratorates organic law).

With regard to the functioning of the People's Procuratorates, the investigative activity for the prevention and repression of crimes takes place under the control of the procuratorial organ, remaining in the general jurisdiction of the security forces, *id est* the police. However, Article 18 of the Criminal Code envisages some crimes for which the investigations are carried out directly by the prosecuting bodies (the so-called direct investigation). Above all, these are crimes committed by public officials, which at the same time harm the collective interest and the rights of citizens. The exact scope of the code requirements on direct procuratorial investigation was first stated in the document adopted jointly by the Supreme People's Court, the Supreme People's Procuratorates and the Ministry of Public Safety on 15 December 1979, supplemented by the additional note of 22 October 1988, as well the partial reform of the criminal procedural code in 1996 by the instructions approved by the Supreme People's Procuratorates on 6 August 1999, in force since 16 September of the same year. Based on these provisions, the People's Procuratorates conduct investigations directly for crimes such as embezzlement, corruption by central and local state administration officials, omission of official deeds, illegal detention, extortion, retaliation and confessions obtained through torture. The subdivisions of these crimes have progressively expanded from twenty-three to fifty-two crimes subject to direct investigations by state prosecutors.

The investigative activities of the public safety authorities are, however, subject to the supervision of the public prosecutors, who decide whether to validate or cancel the measures adopted by the police and implement the legal procedures for the assessment of criminal liability and the punishment of the guilty parties.

Of great importance is the judicial prosecutorial supervision function which is carried out through the appeals system. A public prosecutor can challenge a sentence issued at the first instance by the People's Court of the corresponding level before it becomes final. Once it has become definitive, the ruling of the People's Court is open to appeal for review under surveillance by the People's Procuratorate at a higher level than the Court that pronounced the sentence. The Supreme People's Procuratorate has the power to challenge and submit the rulings issued by the People's Courts of all levels for extraordinary revision.

Procuratorial supervision also extends to the execution phase of criminal rulings, including supervisory tasks on the application of substantive and procedural rules in jails, prisons and forced labour re-education camps.

Among the functions of the Supreme People's Procuratorate there is the inherent interpretation of the new substantive and criminal procedural norms, as occurred with the adoption of the amendments to the Criminal Code in 1997 and to the Code of Criminal Procedure in 1996. The interpretation serves to guide the activities of the public prosecutors at a lower level, and sometimes one can find documents drawn up jointly by the Supreme People's Court and the Supreme People's Procuratorate on the subject of clarifications for the correct application of the normative provisions in the work of a prosecutor. Where there are interpretative interpretations provided separately by the Supreme People's Court and the Supreme People's Procuratorate which are conflicting with each other, the final interpretation is the responsibility of the political-parliamentary body, represented by the Standing Committee of the National People's Congress, as established by Article 2 of the resolution adopted in 1981 by the same Standing Committee on the strengthening and improvement of the mechanisms for interpreting the law.

The independent exercise of the powers of the People's Procuratorates is subject to considerable limitations due to both the institutional setting of the Chinese public law system and to the application practices concerning the administration of justice and, in particular, the repression of crimes. State prosecutors are subject to the supervision of the popular congresses of the corresponding political-administrative level, also in relation to the investigation and handling of specific cases, as well as being subject to the conditioning of the CCP's organs, especially by the Committee on Politics and Law which operates within the framework of party structures at various levels and whose General Secretary is often at the same time the head of the Local Public Safety Bureau. On the other hand, investigations concerning members of the Communist Party can be carried out by the organs of the State Prosecutor only after the matter has been dealt with by the CCP's disciplinary committee of the same level.[190]

As required by Article 135 of the current Constitution, the State Prosecutor's investigations must coordinate with the activities of the public safety organs and with the functions of the People's Courts. From this it follows that state prosecutors are legitimized both to continue the investigations carried out by the public safety offices as well as requesting from them a supplementary investigation. In turn, the police forces have the right to request from the Public Prosecutor of the same or higher level, a new assessment regarding the performance of certain investigations. The People's Courts may decide to defer the examination of a criminal case to the State Prosecutor's Office, if they find evidence of insufficiency, violation of the law or need for further investigation. In any case, the decision of the People's Court is subject to appeal, including review under surveillance or supervision, by the prosecuting authorities.

Lastly, as a result of the constitutional revision of March 2018, the supervisory committees system has been created, which have the status of state bodies with the main task of combating corruption. At the top of the system is established the National Supervisory (or Supervision) Commission, whose direction was designated by the ANP on 18 March 2018 Yang Xiaodu (deputy secretary of the Central Disciplinary Commission),[191] which has the same administrative level as the Supreme People's Court and of the Supreme People's Procuratorate.[192] The constitutional reform, anticipated by a local experimentation

190 *Cf.* X. Guo, *Controlling Corruption in the Party: China's Central Discipline Inspection Commission*, in *The China Quarterly*, 2014, 597 ff., on the *Central Discipline Inspection Commission* (CDIC) and its local branches (*disciplines inspection commissions*, DICs).

191 Yang had previously directed the National Bureau of Corruption Prevention at the State Council.

192 *See* W. Zeng, *Supervision of Power. Supervisory Commissions to Independently Probe Graft Cases*, in *Beijing Review*, 2018, n. 12, www.bjreview.com. According to the sinologist Jerome Cohen, *National Supervision Commission and China's Silenced Legal Elites*, www.jeromecohen.net, «*This is the Inquisition with Chinese characteristics!*»; Id., *Has Xi Jinping Brought China the Inquisition with Chinese Characteristics?*, conference held on 17 April 2018 at the *Sarah Lawrence College* di Bronxville (NY, USA); L. Li, P. Wang, *From Institutional Interaction to Institutional Integration: The National Supervisory Commission and China's New Anti-corruption Model.* in *The China Quarterly*, 2019, published online 27 May 2019. *See also* L. Zhang, *La Chine entre dans une période de contre-réforme au nom de la réforme*, in *Le Monde*, 13 March 2018 (the author is a professor of *Civilisation chinoise* at the *Université de Cergy-Pontoise*-UCP). In the Italian doctrine, *see* R. Cavalieri, *La revisione della Costituzione della Repubblica Popolare inese e l'istituzionalizzazione del "socialismo dalle caratteristiche cinesi per una nuova era"*, op. cit., 277-278; F. Spagnoli, *La riforma della Costituzione cinese: un'analisi della revisione costituzionale del 2018 e dei suoi caratteri principali*, op. cit., 157-161, For the thinking of the President of the PRC Xi Jinping, *see* J. Xi, *A National Supervision System*

in the Municipality of Beijing and in the Provinces of Shanxi and Zhejiang started in December 2016, was finally completed through the approval of the supervision law adopted by the ANP on 20 March 2018.

1.5.4 The Peculiarities of Administrative Justice (the 1989 Law, in Force Since 1990, and the 2014 Law, in Force Since 2015)

Of particular interest is the development, especially recent, of the Chinese disciplining on administrative litigation, also in consideration of the importance of this sector of procedural law as an observation point to evaluate the evolution of general conceptions of law and judicial administration in a socialist country, similarly to that which occurred in the former Soviet Union with the laws of the second half of the eighties of the twentieth century in administrative justice.[193]

Jurisdictional protection against public administrations is covered by the various constitutional documents of the PRC, and precisely by Article 19 of the 1949 (para-constitutional) Joint Program, 97 of the First Constitution of 1954, 27 of the Second Constitution of 1975, 55 of the Third Constitution of 1978, and 41 of the fourth and current Constitution of 1982. However, in the absence of implementation ordinary legislative norms of the constitutional text, the provisions on administrative justice have long remained ignored, due to the fact that they conflict with both the anti-legal orientation of the Cultural Revolution, which looked with the utmost disfavour to the application of legal provisions addressed against public officials and bodies, and furthermore conflicted in general with the typical conception of socialist democracy systems for which employees of public administrations are at the service of the people and cannot perform acts in violation of the rights and interests of citizens and social organizations.

The rigidity of this ideological approach had to, moreover, deal with the abuses of power that occurred with a frequency that is certainly not episodic in Chinese administrative life, reaching the point of a legislative recognition of judicial action against acts, behaviours and omissions of public administrations in Article 3, Paragraph 2, of the Civil Procedure Act (Civil Trial Code) adopted on 8 March 1982. Ordinary judicial bodies (i.e., the People's Courts) called to apply the civil procedural rules in administrative litigations have been progressively equipped, since 1986 and at various levels, with administrative chambers, that is to say specialized sections for the resolution of judicial conflicts between citizens and administrative institutions.

Covering State Organs and Public Servants, in Id., *The Governance of China*, II, Beijing, Foreign Languages Press, 2017, 185.

193 *Cf.* M. Mazza, *Il controllo giurisdizionale della pubblica amministrazione nelle Repubbliche ex sovietiche*, in *Riv. trim. dir. proc. civ.*, 1993, 549 ff.

The widely felt need to reform the system of administrative law (substantive and procedural) of the PRC led, in 1986, to the establishment by the Standing Committee of the National People's Congress of a special research group[194] on administrative legislation, which focused its work on the drafting of administrative law bills.[195] Of these, the most important were the law on administrative sanctions, adopted in March 1996 by the fourth session of the VII NPC,[196] as well as, the Administrative Litigation Law, approved by the second session of the VII NPC on 4 April 1989 and which entered into force (after eighteen months) on 1 October 1990,[197] and subsequently amended, for the first time since its

194 Composed of thirteen members, appointed among university professors in legal matters and other legal experts. The research group was placed under the leadership of Jiang Ping, president of the University of China's political science and law faculty, based in Beijing.

195 On acts, procedures and administrative laws, *see* J.-P. Cabestan, *Administrative Law-Making in the People's Republic of China*, in J.M. Otto, M.V. Polak, J. Chen, Y. Li (Eds.), *Law-Making in the People's Republic of China*, op cit., 175 ff. Re the codification proposal (of Chinese law) of administrative procedure, *see* Z. Li, *La procédure administrative en Chine*, in *Rev. intern. dr. comp.*, 2012, 451 ff.

196 *Cf.* Cai Dingjian, *Introduction to the Administrative Penalty Law of China*, in *Columbia Journal of Asian Law*, 1996, 259 ff.

197 *See* E. Epstein, *Administrative Litigation Law: Citizens can Sue the State but not the Party*, in *China News Analysis*, 1989, 1 ff.; S. Finder, *Like Throwing an Egg Against a Stone? Administrative Litigation in the People's Republic of China*, in *Journal of Chinese Law*, 1989, 1 ff.; B. Potter (Ed.), *The Administrative Litigation Law of the RPC: Changing the Relationship Between the Courts and Administrative Agencies in China*, monothematic dossier of *China Law and Government*, 1991, n. 3; Id., *The Administrative Litigation Law of the RPC: judicial review and bureaucratic reform*, in Id. (Ed.), *Domestic Law Reforms in Post-Mao China*, Armonk (NY), Sharpe, 1994, 270 ff.; S.G. Wood, L. Chong, *China's Administrative Procedure Law: An English Translation with Comments*, in *Administrative Law Review*, 1991, 89 ff.; H.S. Chan, *Judicial Review and Control over Administrative Discretion in the People's Republic of China*, in *Rev. of Central and East European Law*, 1992, 135 ff.; Fa Jyh-pin, Leng Shao-chuan, *Judicial Review of Administration in the People's Republic of China*, Baltimore, School of Law, University of Maryland (*Occasional Papers/Reprints Series in Contemporary Asian Studies*, n. 1), 1992; Lin Feng, *Administrative Law Procedures and Remedies in China*, Hong Kong-London, Sweet and Maxwell, 1996; Id., *Judicial Review in China*, in Wang Guiguo, J. Mo (Eds.), *Chinese Law*, op cit., 63 ff.; Pei Minxin, *Citizens v. Mandarins: Administrative Litigation in China*, in *The China Quarterly*, 1997, 832 ff.; Wang Xixin, *Administrative Procedure Reforms in China's Rule of Law Context*, in *Columbia Journal of Asian Law*, 1998, 251 ff.; A. K.C. Cheung, *China's Administrative Litigation Law*, in *Pub. L.*, 2005, 549 ff.; L. Yu, *Judicial Review on Abuse of Power by Administrative Authority*, in *Frontiers of Law in China*, 2009, 61 ff.; S. Jhaveri, *Transforming "fairness" as a groung of judicial review in Hong Kong*, in *International Journal of Constitutional Law*, 2013, 358 ff.; Y. Li (Ed.), *Administrative Litigation Systems in Greater China and Europe*, Farnham (UK)/Burlington (VT, USA), Ashgate, 2014; Zhong-le Zhan, *The Codification of Chinese Administrative Procedural Law*, in Wen-Yeu Wang (Ed.), *Codification in East Asia*, op cit., 147 ff.; R. Heuser, *Le rôle des tribunaux administratifs dans les litiges entre les citoyens et le gouvernement chinois*, in *Perspectives chinoises*, n. 78, 2003, 18 ff.; Zhang Li, *Le contrôle juridictionnel de la légalité des actes administratifs en Chine. Éléments d'analyse comparée des contentieux administratif chinois et français*, Preface by G. Timsit, Bruxelles, Bruylant, 2009; U. Fragola, *Rudimenti di diritto amministrativo cinese*, op cit., VI, *Cenni sulla tutela giurisdizionale contro gli atti amministrativi nella Repubblica Popolare Cinese*, 107 ff.; M. Mazza, *Il controllo giurisdizionale della pubblica amministrazione nella Repubblica popolare cinese*, in Id., *La giustizia amministrativa in Asia orientale. Linee ricostruttive della circolazione dei modelli di* civil law, common law e socialist law *in area extraeuropea*, Napoli, Edizioni Scientifiche Italiane, 2011, 105 ff.; J.P. de Jorio, *Note minime sull'attuazione dei principi di legalità e buon andamento della P.A. nell'ordinamento della Repubblica Popolare Cinese attraverso il sindacato gerarchico*

adoption, by the law of 1 November 2014 issued by the Standing Committee of the XII NPC and which entered into force on 1 January 2015.[198] Its aim is to achieve two objectives, namely to improve administrative action and to protect citizens' rights effectively.[199]

The regulations contained within the law on administrative trials permits the defence of citizens' rights against public administrations, and represents one of the most interesting aspects in the transition phase of the Chinese system from the *rule of man* to the *rule of law*. The mechanisms of administrative justice contemplated by the Chinese civil procedural law of 1982 were perfected by the law of 4 April 1989, after almost two years of preparatory work and eight main projects,[200] via both popular and politician consultations, academic jurists and practical practitioners of law. The final draft of the law on administrative judicial proceedings opted for a restrictive vision of the judicial review of administrative legitimacy, firstly allowing a review only for administrative acts of a concrete nature with the exclusion, instead, of those abstract. This institutional structure was partially modified by the 2014 reform (in force since 2015), which extended citizen judicial protection against public administrations.

More analytically, it should be noted that from the combined provisions of Articles 1 and 2 of the law on administrative trials that: a) the jurisdiction to decide on the legitimacy of administrative acts belongs to the People's Courts of general jurisdiction; b) Supervision of administrative activity also makes use of the instrument offered by the law on administrative litigation, to the extent that the protection of legitimate rights and interests before administrative authorities permits monitoring the correctness of administrative action against the appellant and, at the same time, for the benefit of the community and the State; and c) a judicial appeal in accordance with the law on administrative trials can be proposed

---

amministrativo (c.d. "supervisione amministrativa") e giurisdizionale, in *Istituzioni, Diritto, Economia. Quaderni di scienze sociali*, 2017, n. 1, *Corruzione e inefficienza nella pubblica amministrazione*, 197 ff.

198 *See* the comment of D. Sprick, *Rechtsstaatsentwicklung durch Gesetzgebung? – Das Verwaltungsprozessgesetz der Volksrepublick China*, in *Zeitschrift für Chinesisches Recht*, 2015, 249 ff., and *ivi*, 284–304, the German translation of administrative procedural law. *Cf.*, in addition, L.X. Yu, *Administrative Procedure Law Revised*, in *Global Legal Monitor* (www.loc.gov), 2 April 2015; T. Chen, *Les «gènes» français du droit des contrats administratifs chinois et de son évolution*, in *Rev. fr. dr. adm.*, 2016, 845 ff.

199 On jurisprudential orientations, *see* the special issue *Chinese Law and Government*, 2017, n. 2, entitled *Administrative Litigation Cases*, with a particular focus on *model, typical, or exemplary cases* (Chinese 典型案例), pronounced by the Supreme People's Court. In 2016, first-level administrative proceedings amounted to 225,000, 13.2% more than in 2015 (*cf.* S. Finder, *An Introduction to Administrative Litigation Cases*, in the special issue cited above op cit., 63 f.). *See also*, B.L. Liebman, M. Roberts, R.E. Stern, A.Z. Wang, *Mass Digitization of Chinese Court Decisions: How to Use Text as Data in the Field of Chinese Law, 21st Century China Center Research Paper No. 2017-01 (Columbia Public Law Research Paper No. 14-551)*, June 2017; *China to Strengthen Work on Administrative Adjudication*, in *Beijing Review*, 3 June 2019 (www.bjreview..com).

200 With an increase in the scope of the text that subsequently became normative, which included forty-nine articles divided into seven chapters according to the project published in November 1988, while the law on administrative procedure includes eleven chapters and seventy-five articles.

by citizens, legal persons[201] and other organizations against decisions by administrative authorities and individual officials; nevertheless, the appeal itself, according to the original draft of the law, could be addressed only against "specific administrative acts", while abstract decisions were removed from the scope of the law on judicial review. However, following the revision of the law on administrative trials which came into force on 1 January 2015, the limit represented by the contestability of only "specific administrative acts" was eliminated, with the consequent expansion of cases in which an appeal before the legal bodies for the protection against the public administration, is possible.

Further provisions of the law on administrative trials circumscribe the operational space. Thus Article 41 establishes five substantive and procedural pre-requisites for the valid establishment of administrative judicial proceedings, represented by sufficient evidence, a specific request for a judicial action, an indication of the legal positions that are assumed to have been violated and their configuration as rights or legitimate interests, the precise mention of the administrative act that is contested and the administrative authority that issued it. Furthermore, Article 25 of the law itself establishes that judicial action must be proposed only against the organ, body or administrative authority, and not instead against the single official who issued the act against which the judicial appeal is addressed. In the hypothesis, thus, of an administrative appeal followed by a judicial appeal, passive legitimation belongs to the higher administrative authority only when the latter has modified the act or administrative provision issued by the lower hierarchical level, otherwise competence remains with the original public authority.

Jurisdictional areas are established by Articles 13–23 of the law on administrative proceedings, which assign the power to decide administrative disputes in the first instance to the People's Courts of the basic level, except for some disputes that are of greater complexity or concern the appeal of acts issued by authorities of a higher rank, in particular the provinces, autonomous regions and autonomous municipalities, which are devolved to the exclusive jurisdiction of the higher courts. This solution adopted by the Chinese legislator favours the access of citizens and organizations to administrative judicial protection, but presents the small inconvenience that the judges called upon to decide on the legitimacy of administrative acts are subject to the supervision of the Executive Committees of the Local People's Congresses, and therefore the acts, measures and behaviours scrutinized by the judges of administrative litigation stem precisely from the holders of the unitary state power and who are in a higher institutional position than those who exercise jurisdictional functions.

---

201 On this concept in the legal system of the PRC, *see* Fu Tingmei, *Legal Person in China: Essence and Limits*, in *American Journal of Comparative Law*, 1993, 261 ff. (the Chinese equivalent of the expression legal person is *faren*).

The (limited) field of intervention of administrative jurisdiction stems from Articles 11and 12 of the law on administrative litigation. Article 11 enumerated eight categories of acts and behaviours (including omissions) subject to the control of judicial authorities, which refer to the personal rights and property of citizens and organizations. Also in this case, the reform of administrative proceedings in force since 1 January 2015 has had an expansive effect of judicial protection, due to the fact that the categories of administrative acts or administrative behaviour that can be challenged before the courts, now amount to twelve. In turn, Article 12 excludes from judicial review four types of administrative acts, among which the provisions concerning civil servants and the acts of the public administrations that cannot be challenged according to the law. As for the nature of the control exercised by the People's Courts on administrative action (or inaction), this is outlined in Articles 5 and 54 of the law on administrative proceedings, an examination of which shows that it is based on a review of legitimacy, subject to the cases of Paragraph 4 of Article 54 that permits an appeal against administrative sanctions based on their allegedly "unjust" character, which implies an assessment in terms not of legality but of reasonableness.

Some interesting aspects of the law on administrative proceedings concern the regulation of conditional jurisdiction (from the prior experience of out-of-court appeal), envisaged by the law only in specific cases without prejudice to the possibility for citizens and organizations to propose a hierarchical appeal before submitting a jurisdictional appeal, as well as the enforcement of judicial decisions issued in administrative litigations, where it is established in particular (in Art. 65, interpreted in light of the explanatory notes adopted by the Supreme People's Court on 29 May 1991, under subsection Number 87) that while the victorious appellant must once again address the judicial authority to obtain compliance with the administrative judicial provision, within three months from the ruling except in cases of a justified delay, the administration instead has the choice to proceed directly with the execution of the judicial provision in its favour, or appeal to the People's Court for its implementation. The practice has, on the contrary, highlighted the tendency towards an "alternative" use of the judicial mechanism by public administrations, in the sense that they use the courts of justice to obtain the compulsory observance of legislative and regulatory provisions that are disliked and unpopular with the citizens directly concerned, such as the one-child policy[202] and the demolition of illegal buildings. It is clear, however, that in these cases one is not in the presence of a judicial sentence to be executed, but of administrative decisions to be implemented out of administrative proceedings.[203] The 2014 reform has, however, reinforced the position of appellants that are victorious in court, to the extent that sanctions are envisaged, including imprisonment (new Art. 69), for

202 *See supra*, in para. 3.6 of Chap. I.

203 As precisely noted by A. K.C. Cheung, *China's Administrative Litigation Law*, op cit., 567.

administrative officials who execute judicial decisions that are unfavourable to public administrations.

In terms of compensation for illegal acts and behaviours by public administrations, Articles 67–69 of the Administrative Litigation Act delineate a rather restrictive regulatory framework. Firstly, it is necessary that the anti-juridical conduct of the organ or public official is deemed to be characterized by malice or guilt, and moreover the amount of compensation must be calculated only on the emerging damage, a direct and current consequence of the administrative illegality, with the exclusion of loss of profit. Secondly, the action *apud judicem* for the restoration of damage is not feasible until after the submission of an out-of-court administrative request, or together with the judicial appeal for the annulment of the administrative act that is deemed to be illegitimate and productive of damage. Thirdly, the judicial petition must be brought against the administrative authority, not the single official responsible for the act or behaviour *contra jus*. Fourthly, the payment of the sum as compensation for damage is by the competent central financial administrative structures, which then submit a request for total or partial reimbursement to the administrative authority against which the victorious judicial appeal has been proposed. The official who carried out the unlawful conduct is subject to the reimbursement action by the administration. However, they: a) may be required to partially reimburse the sum paid for compensation for damage; b) they are not required to reimburse anything, if their behaviour is deemed to have been not intentional nor characterized by gross negligence (remaining immune, therefore, in the case of slight negligence); and c) they are not subject to further liability with respect to the consequences of a patrimonial nature, and hence, in particular, exempt from disciplinary measures or career downgradements. The set of these provisions seems suitable to limit the responsibility of a public administration within the limits of the illegitimate acts carried out by its organs and officials, confirming, on the other hand, the impression that the law on administrative proceedings is aimed at, despite the major openings guaranteed by the 2014–2015 reform, improving the efficiency and effectiveness of administrative action, rather than guaranteeing full protection for the legitimate rights and interests of citizens and organizations.

1.6 Central-Periphery Relations

1.6.1 The Hierarchical System of the Sub-State Territorial Entities in China

The People's Republic of China is still configured from the point of view of regulatory modelling as a unitary state.[204] The superior organs of state power are represented, first,

204 *Cf.* J. Howell, *Reflections on the Chinese State*, in *Development and Change*, 2006, 273 ff.

by the national unicameral Parliament, called the National People's Congress (NPC), and by its Standing Committee, which are both holders of primary regulatory power. National executive power is attributed to the central government, called the State Council and defined as the supreme administrative body of the state. The upper echelons of the ordinary judicial pyramid are the Supreme People's Court and the Supreme People's Procuratorate, respectively for the judging magistracy and the prosecuting magistrature; there are, however, a myriad of special jurisdictions, including military, railway, river, maritime and forestry courts.

Below the superior organs of state power there are the local organs of (political-) administrative decentralization, whose existence on the institutional level appears to be suspended between autonomous aspirations and unitary needs,[205] which now will be examined.

In the course of the historical evolution of the law of the People's Republic of China, via modifications at both the constitutional and legislative levels, there has been the progressive passage from the six levels of local government envisaged between 1949 and 1954, to the five levels covered by the constitutional Charter of 1954, up to the current four levels of decentralized territorial administration. The latter is constituted by the provincial, prefecture, county and district levels.

The first level, the provincial level, includes a plurality of provincial-level administrative units that are placed on the highest rung of the hierarchical scale of Chinese sub-national territorial administrations. There are three types; in fact, in addition to the actual provinces, autonomous regions of a provincial level were established, as well as municipal governments, also of a level equivalent to the provinces and therefore placed directly under the national central government.[206] From a quantitative point of view, the provinces total

---

205 *Cf.* P.B. Potter, *Governance of the Periphery: Balancing Local Autonomy and National Unity*, in *Columbia Journal of Asian Law*, 2005, 293 ff.; Id., *Theoretical and Conceptual Perspectives on the Periphery in Contemporary China*, in D. Lary (Ed.), *The Chinese State at the Borders*, Vancouver/Toronto, University of British Columbia (UBC) Press, 2007, 240 ff.; J.H. Chung, China's Local Administration. *Traditions and Changes in the Sub-national Hierarchy*, London/New York, Routledge, 2009; Id., *China's Local Governance in Perspective: Instruments of Central Government Control*, in *The China Journal*, January 2016, 38 ff.; Id., *Centrifugal Empire. The Anatomy of Central-Local Relations in China*, New York, Columbia University Press, 2016; J. Fewsmith, X. Gao, *Local Governance in China: Incentives & Tensions*, in *Daedalus (Journal of the American Academy of Arts and Sciences)*, 2014, n. 2, 170 ff.; J.C. Teets, W. Hurst (Eds.), *Local Governance Innovation in China. Experimentation, Diffusion, and Defiance*, London/New York, Routledge, 2014; J. Donaldson (Ed.), *Assessing the Balance of Power in Central-Local Relations in China*, London/New York, Routledge, 2017; M. Mazza, *Decentramento e governo locale nella Repubblica popolare cinese*, Milano, Giuffrè, 2009. From a comparative viewpoint, *see* H. Kudo, G. Ladu, L. Pegoraro (Eds.), *Municipi d'Oriente. Il governo locale in Europa orientale, Asia e Australia*, Roma, Donzelli, 2008; A. Harding, M. Sidel (Eds.), *Central-Local Relations in Asian Constitutional Systems*, Oxford, Hart, 2015.

206 It is worth noting that, in contrast to regional law and local Italian authorities, the provinces constitute the decentralized territorial body of greater size and political-administrative importance in the PRC's legal system. *See also* for the diachronic perspective, G. Melis, *Province e distretti cinesi. Attualità e note storiche*, in *Mondo cinese*, n. 23, 1978, 55 ff.; J. Fitzgerald (Ed.), *Rethinking China's Provinces*, London/New York,

twenty-two, the autonomous regions five[207] and the municipal governments of the provincial level four,[208] for a total of thirty-one provincial or equivalent local administrative units.[209]

The second level includes heterogeneous administrative units, represented by prefectures,[210] autonomous prefectures, districts placed under the jurisdiction of the four municipal governments, in turn directly dependent on the central government, as well as the cities whose *status* contemplates their direct dependence on the provincial jurisdiction.

The third level is composed of the counties, flanked by a multitude of territorial entities consisting of autonomous counties, county-level cities, special economic zones (SEZs), industrial, agricultural and forest districts, as well as the districts belonging to the cities directly under the provincial jurisdiction.[211]

The basic level, or fourth level, includes the cities and villages, respectively in urban and rural areas. However, while the first three levels are expressly provided for by Article 30 of the current constitutional charter of 1982, this last rung of the decentralized territorial administration includes non-constitutional entities, which therefore can be freely modified in their institutional configuration, or even more radically, suppressed, by the ordinary legislator.

It is important to note that the Chinese communist system operates a radical rejection of the principle, defined bourgeois and reactionary, of the separation of powers, with the consequence, that each level of decentralized local administration also has the task of appointing and dismissing the President of the People's Court of the corresponding level, as well as the Chief Prosecutor. The judiciary, in fact, does not constitute in China a power

---

Routledge, 2001; D.S.G. Goodman, *China's Provinces in Reform*, London/New York, Routledge, 1997. For an intrasinic comparison *see also*, on the reform of local government in Taiwan analysed from a historical-evolutionary viewpoint, M. Tung-Wen Sun, Ta-Shu Chiang, *The Transformation and Challenges of Local Governance in Taiwan: A Historical Perspective*, in *The Journal of Comparative Asian Development*, 2004, 27 ff.

207 These are the autonomous regional bodies of Inner Mongolia, Tibet, Xinjiang, Guangxi and Ningxia.

208 The *municipal governments* were set up in correspondence with the main cities of China, namely the capital Beijing (Peking), Shanghai, Tianjing and Chongqing.

209 It must be remembered that the authorities of Communist China still regard nationalist China, or Republic of China (Republic of China, ROC), as an integral part of China, as if it were politically united with mainland China. In this light, the PRC's system attributes to the island of Taiwan a legal-administrative status of the provincial level.

210 Recurrent in the legal and political debate of the PRC is the question of redefining the competences of the prefectures, sometimes considered an unnecessary institution, of which some call for their deletion. *See* Voïta, *Rationalizing Administrative Divisions: The Resistance of the Prefecture*, in *China Perspectives*, 2007, n. 3, 140 f.

211 During the 1990s, *performance* indicators for county/municipal or lower level local governments were introduced in the PRC, according to so-called *target-based responsability system* (Chinese: *mubiao zerenzhi*): *cf.* S. Chan, J. Gao (Eds.), *Performance Measurement in Chinese Local Governments*, monothematic issue of *Chinese Law and Government*, 2008, n. 2-3, 1-126, where the importance of *result-focused management and local budgeting* is highlighted.

distinct from the other powers (legislative and executive), since there is only one state/public power with respect to which, it is possible to identify and regulate only functional articulations, including the administration branch of (ordinary and special) justice.

In order to meet the needs of the Chinese multinational state, in which fifty-six nationalities are officially registered, even taking into account that according to data provided by the National Statistics Office of the People's Republic of China, the majority of *Han* ethnicity totals 91.59% of the entire Chinese population,[212] the Chinese People's system has a dimensional modulation of local autonomous governments, in the sense that they possess a triple typology. Integrating now what has already been stated previously, it should be noted that on the first level one can find the autonomous regions of the provincial level, on the second the autonomous prefectures flanked by the autonomous cities of prefecture level and on the third level the autonomous counties to which the autonomous cities of county level are to be added. From the numerical point of view, in addition to the five autonomous regions,[213] there are seventy-seven autonomous prefectures[214] and six hundred and ninety-nine autonomous counties.[215]

It appears evident that the PRC's public law does not accept, in any way, the (Jacobin-) French organizational-constitutional principle of derivation of the free administration of territorial communities, as well as the connected transalpine principle of the ban of protecting one territorial community over the others in adherence to the conception for which the equality of citizens is reproduced on the level of the equality of territorial bodies among themselves, and also when they belong to different levels of political and administrative decentralization.[216] The Chinese system of local autonomies is, instead, rigidly hierarchical, that is, it constitutes a mono-hierarchic system, owing to the fact that decisions are taken by the bodies of territorial authorities of a higher level, that are however binding for those of the lower rungs of decentralization, which are entirely subordinated to the higher level governments. Moreover, if it is true, on the one hand, that the deliberative assemblies of the higher level, namely the provincial, autonomous regional and municipal governments, have legislative power, and that these assemblies as well as the assemblies of lower levels of administrative decentralization may enact regulations, thus having secondary regulatory power, and finally that the approval of secondary-level norms is included in the competence of local (executive) governments, it also corresponds to the truth, on the other hand, that the legislative and regulatory provisions adopted at the level of territorial autonomies may

212 *Cf.* National Bureau of Statistics of China, *China Statistical Yearbook 2002*, Beijing, China Statistics Press, 2002. *See also* above para. 2.8.

213 *See supra*, in this paragraph.

214 Including the autonomous cities of prefecture level.

215 Including the county-level cities that have an autonomy status.

216 In other words, the principle of equal institutional pluralism is affirmed, recognized and guaranteed in the French system of regional and local authorities.

be abrogated, replaced, revoked or cancelled, totally or partially,[217] by either the Standing Committee of the National People's Congress or the State Council, depending on their respective institutional jurisdiction. In this way, the hierarchy between the decentralized bodies is added to the hierarchy between the organs of state power and those of the subnational territorial entities of any level, reaffirming the nature of the People's Republic of China as an example of a unitary state with a weak asymmetric decentralization (at least *on paper* or *de jure*), as well as being characterized by the non-acceptance of the opposing organizational and functional paradigm of a compound state (be it regional or federal).

1.6.2 *The Political-Administrative Decentralization Bodies: Counties, Districts and Cities of Both County and District Level*

In this paragraph one intends to examine in more detail the organizational and functional profiles of the subnational territorial administrations that actually constitute the political-administrative decentralization bodies, due to the fact that they have deliberative congresses directly elected by the local population, while the higher levels make use of indirectly elected deliberative congresses for their institutional functioning, since the respective members are appointed by the deputies of the lower-level congresses, thus acting mainly as organs of the bureaucratic-administrative decentralization (or deconcentration).[218]

As for numerical and demographic dimensions, it is a reality of considerable importance in the People's Republic of China. The county-level counties and cities total over 2,500,[219] with a population of about 900 million. The districts total approximately 25,600 and the cities of the corresponding level, 19,200.

On the historical level, the birth of the People's Republic of China in 1949 did not entail the suppression of the pre-existing counties of the republican era, which were simply renamed people's counties, and equipped with an autonomous people's county government.

---

217 If there is a total or partial contrast with national legislation, whether it is constitutional (super-primary), legislative (primary) or regulatory (secondary), or even "improper" regulations. With special regard to relations between the central government and local governments, Chinese doctrine usually speaks of "administrative interaction"; *cf.* X. Yan, *The People's Republic of China*, in United Nations Economic and Social Commission for Asia and the Pacific, *Local Government in Asia and the Pacific: A Comparative Study*, UNESCAP, Bangkok, a study in collaboration with the *Asia Pacific Section* of the *International Union of Local Authorities* (IULA-ASPAC), available at www.onu.org. (*ivi see* 22).

218 *See, e.g.*, S. Steiner, *Decentralisation and Poverty Reduction: A Conceptual Framework for the Economic Impact*, Hamburg, *Working Paper Global and Area Studies* (edited dal *German Overseas Institute*-GOI/*Deutsches Übersee-Institut*-DÜI), June 2005 (GOI-WP n. 3/05, by the a *Research Unit* «Transformation in the Process of Globalization»), especially 9 f., where a difference, in the author's opinion, exists, between administrative decentralization or deconcentration, political (-democratic) decentralization or devolution, fiscal decentralization and economic or market decentralization, is outlinEd.

219 Of which, approximately, two thousand and ten counties and four hundred county level cities (the so-called county-status cities).

Until 1953, the county's deliberative congresses[220] were elected directly by the population, albeit on the basis of a selective democratic process, as only the peasants, the democratic parties, the mass organizations and the military participated in the elections, with the exclusion, for example of the old landowners, deprived not only of their assets but also their active and passive right to vote. However, in 1953 there was a turning point, subsequently confirmed and, so to speak, rendered official by the 1954 Constitution, by virtue of which, the direct election of the members of the county congresses was cancelled and replaced by the mechanism of indirect election by the members of the elective assembly at the administrative level immediately below. At the same time, a horizontal transfer of powers was made, in the sense of strengthening the competence of the county (executive) governments in accordance with the so-called zero-sum principle, that is to say, with the corresponding decrease of functions and decision-making powers of the (indirectly) elected congress.

In the "animated" period of the Cultural Revolution (or "Great proletarian cultural revolution"), during the decade from 1966 to 1976, inspired by Maoist radicalism and the so-called juridical nihilism, the county governing bodies were not abrogated but simply suspended, "provisionally" replaced by the revolutionary county committees, formed by members that were absolutely faithful to the communist ideology and Maoism, among which representatives of the army, members of the Red Guards, as well as exponents of the working and peasant class. The formal modification followed the revolutionary practice, with Article 22 of the 1975 Constitution abolishing organs and organisms of the People's county government, that were replaced by a single revolutionary committee established in each county. The revolutionary county committees accomplished, at the highest level, the principle of the concentration and indivisibility of the unified state power, since they simultaneously possessed both general and decision-making/individual regulatory authority that were normally shared between the deliberative congress and the executive of the levels of decentralized administration. At the same time, the local revolutionary committees represented the standing body of the local people's congress and the local people's government.[221] This situation of exceptional accumulation of powers and functions by the revolutionary county committees, however, was short-lived, being in fact innovated in 1979 with the restoration of the traditional organs of territorial government of the county, subsequently constitutionalized by the fundamental Charter of 1982 in Chapter III[222] of Section V, sub Articles 95–111, dedicated precisely to the regulating of the people's

---

220 Created under the name of people's representative assemblies, Chinese *renmin daibiao huiyi*.

221 This occurred, of course, at every level of the hierarchy of peripheral administrative subdivisions, starting from the great territorial-fiscal distribution of the provinces. *See* G. Melis, *I nuovi Comitati rivoluzionari provinciali*, in *Mondo cinese*, n. 21, 1978, 85 ff.

222 Entitled "structure of the state"; it follows Chap. I on general principles and Chap. II on the fundamental rights and duties of citizens.

congresses and governments at the local level. The requirements for the creation of a local administrative unit with the *status* of a city have changed over time, being specifically defined in a document approved in 1985 by the State Council (National Government).[223] They envisage the existence of three conditions. Firstly, the city must be the seat of the county government. Secondly, the composition of the population must be such that if the resident inhabitants are less than twenty thousand in total, at least two thousand must carry out their activity in a sector other than that of agriculture. If instead the resident population exceeds the total sum of twenty thousand inhabitants, then the percentage of non-agricultural workers must be more than one-tenth of the entire community of residents. Thirdly, even by way of derogation from the requirements examined above, a city can be established from the point of view of sub-national territorial administrations if the local community represents an important tourist destination, or is an important commercial port, has significant mineral resources or is a main border town. The general trend, at least since the mid-eighties of the last century with the intensification of the industrialization phenomena and consequent urbanization in the People's Republic of China, has been a constant growth of cities, and a consequential decrease in the total number of districts. For example, there has been the passage from 29,502 districts and 17,532 cities in 1995, to the situation described above, and referring to the new millennium.[224]

In a similar way to that which occurred for the counties and cities of the corresponding level, even the existence of the institutional bodies of districts and cities at the district level has been troubled. The district and equivalent administrative structure was contemplated by the nationalist law of Republican China, confirmed in 1949 by the communist law of the People's Republic of China. Thus, in the first evolutionary phase of the law of the People's Republic and according to the 1954 Constitution, the district assemblies (and those of the city) had an executive body called the district or people's city committee. The latter was made up of a variable number of components, not less than three and not more than thirteen, related to the territorial dimensions and the demographic consistency of the population included in the decentralized administrative district. The bureaucratic apparatus placed under the people's or district commission, constituting an embryonic form of the local public function, included on average about ten offices, which took the name of subcommittees. The duration of the institutional mandate given to the members of the people's district or city commission of the same level was two years. In 1958, coinciding with the start of radical reforms that should have constituted a support for the "Great Leap Forward", Maoist extremism wiped out the local district administration

223 The central government provision can be read in Diao Tianding, *Zhongguo difang guojia jigou yanjiu* [Study of Chinese Local Government], Beijing, Masses Press, 1985, especially 215 f.

224 *Cf.* data reported in Y. Zhong, *Local Government and Politics in China. Challenges from Below*, Armonk (NY)/London, Sharpe, 2003, 49.

bodies, replacing them with the model of the people's communes,[225] which, moreover, were entities with functions not only administrative but also (and mainly) economic.[226] Better luck, if compared to that reserved for the district administrations, was to be had instead by the city administrations that had already been established at the district level, since the latter resisted the renewing wind of radicalism, albeit the total number of cities created at the administrative level of the ex-districts suffered a drastic reduction. Time, however, rendered justice to these extreme forms of concentration of political and economic power at the local level, when in 1982, the people's communes were finally dismantled, with the consequent restoration to their full functionality of the district administrations and the cities of corresponding level, which were once again attributed solely tasks of an administrative nature, thus overcoming the adventurous model of the people's communes, To these (less relevant) administrative functions were added – according to a dubious (and double) logic of mixture and simplification, (more consistent) functions of an economic-productive nature.

1.6.3 Village Authorities and "Chinese-Style" Rural Democracy (with a Brief Overview of Local Urban Democracy)

In the history of Chinese law, the situations related to land have always been strongly intertwined with public law. Even before the foundation of the People's Republic of China in 1949, the imperial and then nationalist authorities did not disdain, for the purposes of maintaining public order in the vast rural areas of the country, from the use of informal organs, midway between unofficial law and semi-official law, of local administration at the basic level. After the victory of the Maoist communists over the nationalist forces, the landowners fled to the island of Taiwan, and on mainland China their land was confiscated in favour of the peasants, via the more or less regular application of allocation plans, implemented between 1949 and the early fifties of the last century. However, a process of a progressive publicizing and collectivization of land ownership soon begun. In particular, in 1955 the first agricultural cooperatives were established, which as early as 1958 were transformed into people's communes. These latter replaced, as seen in the previous paragraph, the pre-existing district administrations, and were characterized by the joint development of political, administrative and socio-economic functions. They were organized on two levels, in a military type set-up. Indeed, if the common agricultural community

225 On the Maoist people's comune organizations, *see* the extensive research by M. Zaccagnini, *Modelli di impresa agricola collettiva: le comuni popolari agricole cinesi*, in *Riv. dir. agr.*, 1980, I, 670 ff. (part 1) and 1981, I, 80 ff. (part 2), in addition to M.B.C. Garzia, *La Comune Popolare come strumento egemonico del Mao Tse-tung-pensiero*, in *Mondo cinese*, n. 17, 1977, 33 ff.

226 Historically, the people's communes constituted a new entity that resulted from the fusion of several Agricultural Producers's Cooperatives (APCs).

could be considered a sort of regiment, within it were created production brigades;[227] in other words, the first political, administrative and economic level was represented by the people's communes, while the second level consisted of the production brigades. Also the second level, created in the context of (and subordinately to) the first level consisting of the people's communes, had powers to be exercised on the political, administrative and economic level. In the early eighties of the twentieth century,[228] the agricultural communes were abolished, with the consequent revival of the system of districts. A similar fate was reserved, naturally, for the production brigades, which, moreover, unlike the popular communes, could not count on the pre-existence of an autonomous yet subordinate level of decentralized territorial administration. For this reason, the new post-Maoist Chinese leadership devised the informal solution of replacing production brigades with village committees.[229] The situation was complicated by the fact that two categories of villages were introduced: the first being the so-called integral or geographic villages[230] and the second the so-called administrative villages;[231] the difference consisted in the fact that the geographical villages were single local communities physically separated from any other territorial administrative unit, while the administrative villages constituted in essence unions among villages, often of small dimensions, with a common administrative structure in order to provide essential services to resident citizens. For the purposes of an analysis on village committees, this difference has no particular relevance, due to the fact that the committees in question were set up both in the integral/geographical villages and in the administrative villages.

The question of defining the legal *status* of village committees is certainly not easy to solve, in the absence of any reference to them as a decentralized administrative level in the text of the Constitutional Charter,[232] which indeed contains an indication contrary to their recognition in this sense, to the extent that it considers the districts as decentralized territorial administrations of the basic level (together with the cities of a level equivalent to the district level). However, village committees do exist, and the Chinese Communist Party itself seems to take adequate account of them, having set up special party branches at the village level,[233] in a manner substantially similar to that which has been outlined previously

227 Chinese: *shengchan dadui*.

228 Via provisions adopted in 1983.

229 Chinese: *cunmin weiyuanhui*. In doctrine, *see* J. Unger, *The Decollectivization of the Chinese Countryside: A Survey of Twenty-Eight Villages*, in *Pacific Affairs*, winter 1985-1986, 585 ff.

230 In Chinese, *zirancun*.

231 In Chinese, *xingzhengcun*. For a comprehensive examination of the Chinese political-administrative system of villages, *cf.* Liu Zhenwei, *Nongmin yu nongcun zuzhi jianshe* [*Peasants and the Development of Rural Organizations*], Guiyang, Guizhou People's Press, 1994.

232 Art. 111 of the Constitution speaks of village committees, within the section (V, sub-chap. III) dedicated to local governments, but outside the provisions that directly concern sub-national territorial administrations.

233 Chinese: *dangzhibu*. In dottrina, *see* Z.H. Guo, T.B. Bernstein, *The Impact of Elections on the Village Structure of Power: The Relations between the Village Committees and the Party Branches*, in *Journal of Contemporary*

with regard to levels, rings or steps of local administration expressly covered by the Constitution. However, the creation of a party branch does not appear to be a decisive element, due to the fact that the Statute (or Constitution) of the Chinese Communist Party establishes that a branch of the Party is to be set up, something different and less than the Party Committee, in every work unit or in the places where at least three members of the CCP reside.[234] It is also true, on the other hand, that officials and employees of a village administration are not paid by the state budget and are not considered members of the public bureaucracy, owing to the fact that the village committees are informal organs that give rise to a level of quasi-governmental administration,[235] with the task of implementing policies and decisions approved by both the central authorities and the (other) local authorities of the People's Republic of China.

A closer examination of the village committees highlights, first of all, that they have fewer component units, called village groups.[236] Village committees consist of a number of members ranging from three to six, depending on the size of the resident population. Among them, there is the Chairman of the village committee, who also goes by the traditional name of village chief[237] or Committee manager.[238] In addition, at least one woman must be present in the village committees, dealing with women's affairs, including family planning, as well as a member of the public safety office in the village. The (quasi-institutional) term of office of the members of village committees is three years.

The Constitutional Charter mentions village committees, establishing in the first paragraph of Article 111, that the Chairman, the Vice-Chairman and the other members of the Village Committee are elected directly by the residents of the village itself. However, the implementation of the 1982 constitutional text on the election of village committees

---

China, 2004, 257 ff.; Y. Yao, *Village Elections and Redistribution of Political Power and Collective Property*, in *The China Quarterly*, 2009, 126 ff. For relationships between village elections and the development of intra-party democracy in the People's Republic of China, *see* J. Fewsmith, *Pressures for Expanding Local-Level Democracy*, in *China Leadership Monitor*, n. 12, summer 2004, 1 ff.

234 *See The Constitution of the Communist Party of China*, Beijing, Foreign Languages Press (FLP), 2002 (bilingual text in Chinese-English); Yue Qiwei, *Ru dang xu zhi* [What You Have to Know to Join the Party], Shanghai, Shangahai renmin chubanshe, 2003; Zhang Dejiang, *Several Issues to be Studied and Resolved in Strengthening the Work of Party Building in Non-Public Enterprises*, orig. in *Dangjian yanjiu*, 2000, n. 4, reproduced in *Zhenli de zhuiqiu*, 11 May 2001 and translated in *BBC Monitoring Global Newsline Asia Pacific Political File*, 15 May 2001. It affirmed that "If the Constitution is the charter of socialist legality, the Statute of the CCP is the charter of revolutionary legitimacy, and the reading of the Constitution cannot be in contrast to that of the Statute"; *cf.* C. Donati, F. Marrone, F. Misiani, *Stato e Costituzione in Cina*, Milano, Mazzotta, 1977, 11 (according to the authors, the statutory norms of the PRC's system could be defined as indirect sources of law).

235 This is the conclusion reached, albeit problematically by Y. Zhong, *Local Government and Politics in China. Challenges from Below*, op cit., 159.

236 In Chinese, *cunmin xiaozu*.

237 Chinese: *cunzhang*.

238 Almost invariably, a local official of the Chinese Communist Party is elected manager/head of the village committee.

was decidedly slow and troubled.[239] In 1987, the provisional organic law was approved on village committees, which became a permanent organic law only in 1998,[240] after a pause of more than a decade of reflection due, on the one hand, to fears on the part of the CCP and especially of the Organization Department established in the Central Committee of the Party, who were concerned with the possible expansion of electoral mechanisms directed at the various levels of decentralized territorial administration and, on the other hand, the occurrence of the tragic events of Tian'anmen Square in 1989, with the related further widespread fears among the Chinese leaders of the strengthening of the pluralistic democratic movement that was objectively revolutionary towards the communist principles of organization, both in relation to the superior powers of the State as well as those of the local organs of state power.

On the other hand, the evaluations carried out in the abundant international literature[241] on the election of village committees in the local administration system of the People's

239 *See* B. Alpermann, *Provincial Legislation on Village Elections in China*, in *Zeitschrift für Chinesisches Recht*, 2007, 1 ff.

240 The text, in Chinese, is available for consultation in *Zhonghua renmin gongheguo cunmin weiyuanhui zuzhifa* [*People's Republic of China's Organic Law on Villager's Committees*], Beijing, Zhongguo Falü chubanshe [China Law Press], 1998. For comments in Chinese doctrine, *see* Wang Yongwu, *Shitan cunmin weiyuanhui zuzhifa guanche nan de yuanyin* [*Discussing the Reasons Why it is Difficult to Implement the Organic Law of Villagers' Committee*], in Zhongguo jiceng zhengquan jianshe yanjiuhui (Ed.), *Shijian yu sikao* [*Practice and Reflection*], I, Shenyang, Liaoning daxue chubanshe, 1989, 169 ff.

241 *Cf.*: S. Yu, *Il sistema di autogoverno dei villaggi*, in L. Moccia (Ed.), *Profili emergenti del sistema giuridico cinese*, Roma, Philos, 1999, 101 ff. (translation from Chinese by F.R. Antonelli); K.J. O'Brien, *Implementing Political Reform in China's Villages*, in *The Australian Journal of Chinese Affairs*, n. 32, 1994, 33 ff.; Id., *Villagers, Elections, and Citizenship in Contemporary China*, in *Modern China. An International Journal of History and Social Sciences*, 2001, 407 ff.; J.C. Oi, *Economic Development, Stability and Democratic Village Self-governance*, in M. Brosseau, S. Pepper, S.K. Tsang (Eds.), *China Review 1996*, Hong Kong, Chinese University of Hong Kong Press, 1996, 125 ff.; J. Elklit, *The Chinese Village Committee Electoral System*, in *China Information. A Journal on Contemporary China Studies*, 1997, 1 ff.; S. Chan, *Research Notes on Villager's Committee Elections: Chinese Style Democracy*, in *Journal of Contemporary China*, 1998, 507 ff.; J. Howell, *Prospects for Village Self-Governance in China*, in J.A. Robinson (Ed.), *Villager Committee Elections in China. A Selected Collection of Essays*, Pensacola, *University of West Florida* (*The Carter Center in cooperation with the Florida-China Institute*), 1999, 125 ff.; Id., *Village Elections in China: Recent Prospects, New Challenges*, in *Etudes Rurales*, 2007, 213 ff.; T.J. Shi, *Economic Development and Village Elections in Rural China*, in *Journal of Contemporary China*, 1999, 425 ff.; K.J. O'Brien, L.J. Li, *Accommodating "Democracy" in a One-Party State: Introducing Village Elections in China*, in *The China Quarterly*, 2000, 465 ff.; R.A. Pastor, Q.S. Tan, *The Meaning of China's Village Elections, ivi*, 2000, 490 ff.; B. Alpermann, *The Post-Election Administration of Chinese Villages*, in *The China Journal*, n. 46, 2003, 45 ff.; J.P. Horsley, *A Legal Perspective on the Development of Electoral Democracy in China. The Case of Village Elections*, in C.S. Hsu (Ed.), *Understanding China's Legal System. Essays in Honor of J.A. Cohen*, New York/London, New York University (NYU) Press, 2003, 295 ff.; X. Wang, *Mutual Empowerment of State and Peasantry. Village Self-government in Rural China*, New York, Nova Science, 2003; Q.S. Tan, *Building Institutional Rules and Procedures: Village Elections in China*, in *Policy Sciences*, 2004, 1 ff.; R. Hu, *Economic Development and the Implementation of Village Elections in Rural China*, in *Journal of Contemporary China*, 2005, 427 ff.; M.F. Manion, *Democracy, Community, Trust: The Impact of Elections in Rural China*, in *Comparative Political Studies*, 2006, 301 ff.; Q. Tan, *Village Elections in China. Democratizing the Countryside*, New York, Mellen Press, 2006; G. Schubert, X Chen, *Village Elections in Contemporary China. New Spaces for Generating Regime Legitimacy?*

Republic, with the clarifications previously made regarding the semi-official character of this level of decentralized administration, appear quite discordant, since they range from enthusiastic comments that enhance their value as a fundamental tool of democratic and civil education to considerations much more cautious and almost pessimistic, which underline the almost zero level of competitiveness and genuine democracy of these elections, rigidly "orchestrated" by the Party. A fact, however, appears difficult to contest: that of the villages that have equipped themselves with a village committee. They number, in fact, not more than half of the total number of villages, demonstrating that rural democracy in the Chinese version still has to take important steps towards a complete acceptance in the particular socio-political, constitutional and legislative context of the PRC.

The Village Committees are not the only bodies required by the 1998 Organic Law on Village Self-Government in China. It also includes village congresses and the village representative (or representatives) congresses. Village congresses are,[242] at least on paper, the main decision-making body of the village communities. Participation in such congresses[243] is open to all residents of the village, provided they are eighteen years of age. Therefore, the direct democracy expressed via the village congresses is supported by the indirect or representative democracy of the village committees. As previously stated, the village congress *is* the heart of the local administrative system of the villages. The use of italics, however, seems appropriate and necessary, as although the convening of village congresses is scheduled at least annually, in fact organizational and practical problems related in particular to the difficult mobilization of the entire adult population of the village have meant that in most cases, village congress meetings are actually held when the village

---

Experiences from Lishu County, in *China Perspectives*, 2007, n. 3, 12 ff.; Q. Tan, Q. Xin, *Village Election and Governance: Do Villagers Care?*, in *Journal of Contemporary China*, 2007, 581 ff.; G. Schubert, A.L. Ahlers, *Participation and Empowerment at the Grassroots. Chinese Village Elections in Perspective*, Lanham (Maryland), Lexington Books, 2012. Re the Chinese point of view, *see* Zhang Houan, *Zhongguo nongcun jiceng zhengquan* [*Political Power at China's Rural Basic Level*], Chengdu, Sichuan chubanshe, 1992; Wang Zhenyao, Bai Yihua (Eds.), *Xiangzhen zhengquan ji cunweihui jianshe* [*The Construction of the Township/Town Government and the Villagers' Committe*], Beijing, China Social Press, 1996; Lang Youxing, He Baogang, *Cunmin huiyi he cunmin daibiao huiyi-cunji minzhu wanshan ji chanshi* [*Village Assemblies and Village Representative Assemblies: Efforts to Perfect Village Democracy*], in *Zhengzhixue yanjiu* [*Political Science Studies*], n. 84, 2000, 57 ff.; He Baogang, *Xiangcun xuanju diaocha suibi* [*Investigative Notes on Village Elections*], in *Ershiyi shiji* [*Twenty-first Century*], n. 58, April 2000, 131 f.; T.B. Xiao, *Duowei shijiao zhong de cunmin zhixuan* [*Village Elections in Multi-Perspective*], Beijing, Zhongguo shehui kexue chubanshe [Chinese Academy of Social Sciences Press], 2001; Y. Xu, *Xiangcun zhili yu Zhongguo zhengzhi* [*Rural Governance and Chinese Politics*], Beijing, Zhongguo shehui kexue chubanshe [Chinese Academy of Social Sciences Press], 2003; Y. Xu, J.Q. Xiang, *Cunmin zizhi jincheng de xiangcun guanxi* [*Township-Village Relations in the Process of Village Self-Government*], Wuhan, Huazhong shifan daxue, 2003; Z.H. Tong, *Xuanju shijian yu cunzhuang zhengzhi* [*Election Events and Village Politics*], Beijing, Zhongguo shehui kexue chubanshe [Chinese Academy of Social Sciences Press], 2004.

242 Chinese *cunmin huiyi*, or also *cunmin dahui*.

243 One of the aspects of citizen participation at a local level: *cf.* E. Sancton, Z. Chen (Eds.), *Citizen Participation at the Local Level in China and Canada*, Boca Raton (FL), CRC Press, 2014.

committee is to be elected, so that the members of the congress can assess and approve the work of the committee, this being the main task, entrusted by the organic law on village committees to the equivalent – outgoing congresses,[244] followed shortly thereafter with the vote for the designation of the components of the new village committee.

The difficulties that hindered the creation and, above all, the effective functioning of the village congresses have led to the establishment of additional bodies envisaged in the organic law on *village self-government*,[245] that is to say the representative/village representatives congresses.[246] It is, as is evident from its name, an assembly made up of representatives elected by the residents of the village. The provisions contained in the organic law on the subject of congresses of village representatives are minimal, since they limit themselves to establishing a tendential relationship between voters and elected representatives that conforms to the principle that each group of families numbering between the minimum of five and the maximum of fifteen corresponds to one elected person in the village representative congress. Moving from this quasi-void normative, the village authorities have shown not little imagination in governing the elections of the congress of village representatives, since, by way of example, the (automatic) right to participate in the representative congresses in question is sometimes granted to leaders of local village groups, or members of the popular deliberative congresses of counties, districts or equivalent cities that come from the village, or furthermore the village-level party secretary, in some cases also other village party officials. On average, the proportion established in implementation of the law by local village authorities between the represented and representatives is based on an elected representative for every minimum ten and maximum fifteen families.

Finally, it should be noted that the assessments regarding the functionality of the representative village congresses are discordant, as one has previously seen with regard to the effective democracy of the elections for the designation of the components of the village committees. In any case, the feeling[247] prevails, that in the Chinese perception, the elective

244 They adopt the decisions of their competence according to the rule of the majority. It should be noted that the villages do not have, unlike the four levels of constitutionally guaranteed administrative decentralization (provincial, prefecture, county and district), budgetary autonomy; this fact undoubtedly reinforces the conclusion that the villages themselves do not constitute a formal level of decentralized territorial governance.

245 That is, in the matter of *governing village self-governance*.

246 Chinese: *cunmin daibiao huiyi*, o *cunmin daibiao dahui*. In doctrine, *see* S. Chan, *Villager's Representative Assemblies: Toward Democracy or Centralism*, in *China. An International Journal*, 2003, n. 2, 179 ff.

247 Shared by Y. Zhong, *Local Government and Politics in China. Challenges from Below*, op cit., 169. *Adde* J. Chen, *Popular Support for Village Self-government in China*, in *Asian Survey*, 2005, 865 ff.; Id., *Sociopolitical Attitudes of the Masses and Leaders in the Chinese Village: Attitude Conguence and Constraint*, in *Journal of Contemporary China*, 2005, 445 ff.; Id., Y. Zhong, *Why Do People Vote in Semicompetitive Elections in China?*, in *The Journal of Politics*, 2002, 178 ff.; Id., *To Vote or Not To Vote. An Analysis of Peasants' Participation in Chinese Villages Elections*, in *Comparative Political Studies*, 2002, 686 ff.; Y. Zhong, *Democratic Values Among Chinese Peasantry: An Empirical Study*, in *Journal of Contemporary China*, 2005, 189 ff.; S. Feuchtwang, *Peasants, Democracy and Anthropology*, in *Critique of Anthropology*, 2003, 93 ff.;

mechanism and the decision-making power of the village congresses, power that in essence is similar to that of the village congresses, due to the fact that it is in fact exercised in substitution of the failure of the same congresses, is to be ascribed to the category of official fulfilment or mere formality.[248] Instead, only in some numerically minority territorial realities, where the joint pressure of the organs of the decentralized upper level administration and the party officials operating at the village level is strong, the representative village congress is configured as a *genuine decision-making body*,[249] to ensure that the village's deliberative and governing bodies are efficient, capable of carrying out effective local administrative action and combating corruption.[250]

Nor can one fail to point out that protest movements of the people of the villages against the authorities of local self-government,[251] sometimes take place.

It must be stated, thus, that problems similar to those found for village committees in rural areas appear with regards to the neighbourhood committees in urban areas, as they too – although of lesser comparative relevance than the village committees,[252] are an

---

T.J. Shi, *Voting and Nonvoting in China: Voting Behaviour in Plebiscitary and Limited-Choise Elections*, in *Journal of Politics*, 1999, 1115 ff.

248 A notion that the Chinese render with the word *zouxingshi*.

249 *See* G.Y. Dang, *Cunmin zizhi shi minzhu zhengzhi de qidian ma?* [*Is Village Self-government the Starting Point for Democratic Politics?*], in *Zhanlüe yu guanli*, 1999, n. 1, 88 ff.; L.J. Li, Z.L. Guo, T.B. Xiao (Eds.), *Cunweihui xuanju guancha* [*Observing Village Elections*], Tianjin, Tianjin renmin, 2001; B.G. He, Y.X. Lang, *Xunzhao minzhu yu quanwei de pingheng. Zhejiang sheng cunmin xuanju jingyan yanjiu* [*Searching an Equilibrium between Democracy and Authority. A Study on the Experiences of Village Elections in Zhejiang Province*], Wuhan, Huazhong shifan daxue, 2002; J.J. Kennedy, S. Rozelle, Y.J. Shi, *Elected Leaders and Collective Land: Farmer's Evaluation of Village Leaders' Performance in Rural China*, in *Journal of Chinese Political Science*, 2004, n. 1, 1 ff.; E.M. Niou, *Village Election: Roots of Democratization in China*, in J.F.-S. Hsieh (Ed.), *How Asia Votes*, New York-London, Chatham House, 2002, 18 ff.; G. Schubert, *Village Elections in the PRC. A Trojan Horse of Democracy?*, Institute of East Asian Studies, Gerhard-Mercator-University Duisburg, 2002 (*Project Discussion Paper* n. 19); T.J. Shi, *Village Committee Elections in China: Institutionalist Tactics for Democracy*, in *World Politics*, 1999, 385 ff.; D. Kelliher, *The Chinese Debate Over Village Self-Government*, in *The China Journal*, n. 37, 1997, 63 ff.; A.B. Epstein, *Village Elections in China: Experimenting with Democracy*, in Congress of the United States (Joint Economic Committee) (Ed.), *China's Economic Future: Challenges to U.S. Policy*, Washington (DC), Government Printing Office, 1996, 403 ff. More generally on *participatory decision-making deliberations* in the PRC, *see* J. Unger, A. Chan, H. Chung, *Deliberative Democracy at China's Grassroots: Case Studies of a Hidden Phenomenon*, in *Politics & Society*, 2014, 513 ff.

250 *See, e.g.*, R. Levy, *The Village Self-Government Movement: Elections, Democracy, the Party, and Anticorruption – Developments in Guangdong*, in *China Information. A Journal on Contemporary China Studies*, 2003, 28 ff.; Id., *Village Elections, Transparency, and Anticorruption. Henan and Guangdong Provinces*, in E.J. Perry, M. Goldman (Eds.), *Grassroots Political Reform in Contemporary China*, Cambridge (Mass.), Harvard University Press, 2007, 20 ff.

251 *See* G. Wu, *From the Great Rock to the Eastern Islet. The Politics of Citizen Engagement and Local Governance in China*, in *China Perspectives*, 2008, n. 1, 70 ff. (*Great rock* and *Eastern islet* are the literal meaning of the denomination of two localities of China, namely Taishi and Dongzhou).

252 *Cf.* R. Benewick, I. Tong, J. Howell, *Self-Governance and Community. A Preliminary Comparison between Villagers' Committees and Urban Community Councils*, in *China Information. A Journal on Contemporary China Studies*, 2004, 11 ff.

expression of local democracy with Chinese characteristics (the so-called *urban Shequ-democracy*).[253] In a similar way to the village representative or representatives congresses, in urban areas, congresses of the community representatives (in Chinese, *Shequ*[254]), were established, of which not all the residents in the neighbourhood belong, but their delegates, according to the scheme already seen above regarding (indirect) rural/peasant democracy. The organizational structure of each urban *Shequ* includes, in addition to the Congress of Residents' Representatives, a Committee of urban residents, alongside which operates the local party branch, established at the level of the residents' committee.

The term of office of the members of the Committee of urban residents has a duration of three years, without limitation to the possibility of being re-elected.[255] The Congress of Representatives meets only once a year to discuss and approve the decisions taken by the Residents Committee. The Residents Committee has executive functions; it deals with various aspects of the lives of resident citizens, including issues related to public safety, family planning, culture, education and propaganda, security and social services, health, the environment, policies for the elderly, women and youth, childcare, the disabled, the unemployed and low-income families, and controls and protection for employees of private companies. There is an expansive trend in the tasks assigned to urban residents' committees, which do not correspond to an adequate transfer of financial resources,[256] despite the fact that the functions of these committees are more closely concerned with attributions usually pertaining to the state authorities, rather than territorial self-government. In particular, the residents' committees are in charge of controlling births and payment of pensions, as well as carrying out mediation functions in disputes between resident citizens. In addition, they deal with drug addicts and former inmates, as well as providing psychological assistance to victims of family violence and to those who have attempted suicide.

---

253 On local democracy in the Chinese system, *see* T. Heberer, *Institutional change and legitimacy via urban elections? People's awareness of elections and participation in urban neighbourhoods (*Shequ*)*, in Id., G. Schubert (Eds.), *Regime Legitimacy in Contemporary China. Institutional change and stability*, London/New York, Routledge, 2009, 79 ff.; J. Audin, *Gouverner par la communauté de quartier (*shequ*) en Chine Ethnographie de la bureaucratisation participante des comités de résidents à Pékin*, in *Rev. fr. sc. pol.*, 2015, 85 ff. In the Chinese doctrine, *cf.* M. Deng, *Chuang xin shequ* [*Establish new* Shequ], Beijing, Zhongguo shehui kexue chubanshe [Chinese Academy of Social Sciences Press], 2002; B. Wang, *Juweihui yu shequ zhili. Chengshi shequ jumin weiyuanhui zuzhi yanjiu* [*Residents Committees and Shequ Administration. Studies on the Organisation of Shequ Residents Committees*], Shanghai, Shanghai renmin chubanshe, 2003. For historical precedents prior to the communist revolution, *see* R.R. Thompson, *China's Local Councils in the Age of Constitutional Reform, 1898-1911*, op cit.

254 Plural, *Shequs*.

255 The law on the organization of urban residents' committees dates back to 1989. The first elections for the designation of the members of the residents committee were held only in June 1999, and took place in the urban district of Shenhe, which is located in the city of Shenyang.

256 District and sub-district public offices have more substantial economic resources than those assigned to urban residents' committees; *see* T. Heberer, *Institutional change and legitimacy via urban elections? People's awareness of elections and participation in urban neighbourhoods* (Shequ), op cit., 82, text and nt. 3.

The identifying characteristic that unites the elections for grassroots representatives in rural villages and urban neighbourhoods is typical of authoritarian regimes, that is to say, it appears to be fourfold. Firstly, via the elections, the regime, personified by the Party-State, seeks the legitimization of its power. Secondly, the electoral consultations favour the processes of political socialization of the masses. Thirdly, the elections serve to mobilize the population, both in rural as well as urban areas. Fourthly, the elections aim to contribute to the goal of community integration, especially between Party members and non-CCP citizens, as well as between those who exercise public functions and ordinary members of the local community. If these are the essential aims of controlled participation in local elections in the Chinese people's legal system, it should not be surprising that opinion polls highlight a greater interest of Chinese citizens in economic development than in political democracy.[257]

1.6.4 The Special Regimes of Hong Kong and Macao (After the So-Called Handover)

Since 1982,[258] the autonomous constitutional-legal system of the People's Republic of China also contemplates the possible creation of special administrative regions (SARs). In fact, two special administrative regions were established, namely the Hong Kong SAR (HKSAR),[259] after the return of the former British colony to the Chinese Motherland in

257 *Cf.* T. Heberer, *Institutional change and legitimacy via urban elections? People's awareness of elections and participation in urban neighbourhoods (*Shequ*)*, op cit., 102, text and nt. 46.

258 In accordance with Art. 31 of the Constitution.

259 For the special status (*Basic Law*-BL) of the HKSAR, *see* S.A. Elgebeily, *Hegemony and Post-Colonial Hong Kong Hybridity:* Jūnzǐ, Yi, Li, Xin, *and Concepts of the Rule of Law in a Confucian Context*, in *Chinese Journal of Comparative Law*, 2017, 154 ff.; J. Husa, *'Accurately, Completely, and Solemnly': One Country, Two Systems and an Uneven Constitutional Equilibrium*, *ivi*, 2017, 231 ff.; Lo Pui Yin, *The Judicial Construction of Hong Kong's Basic Law: Courts, Politics, and Society after 1997*, Hong Kong, Hong Kong University Press, 2014; R. Yep (Ed.), *Negotiating Autonomy in Greater China. Hong Kong and its Sovereign Before and After 1997*, Copenhagen, NIAS (Nordic Institute of Asian Studies) Press, 2013; C.H. Chan, *Reconceptualising the Relationship between the Mainland Chinese Legal System and the Hong Kong Legal System*, in *Asian Journal of Comparative Law*, 2011, 1 ff.; Sun Zhichao, *International Legal Personality of the Hong Kong Special Administrative Region*, in *Chinese Journal of International Law*, 2008, 339 ff.; J. Y.S. Cheng (Ed.), *The Hong Kong Special Administrative Region in its First Decade*, Hong Kong, City University of Hong Kong Press, 2007; B. Verri, Common law *con caratteri cinesi. Il diritto nella Regione Amministrativa Speciale di Hong Kong tra flussi linguistici inglesi e cinesi*, PhD thesis discussed 17 March 2015 at the University of Trento; A. Conte, *Le fonti del diritto a Hong Kong dopo il ritorno alla sovranità cinese: un paese, due sistemi giuridici*, in *Riv. trim. dir. proc. civ.*, 2003, 361 ff. For the legislative function, *see* Y. Gu, *Hong Kong's Legislature under China's Sovereignty 1998-2013*, Leiden, Brill, 2015. For the judicial function, *cf.* M. Gu, *Good Governance and Judicial Review in Hong Kong*, in *Chinese Journal of Comparative Law*, 2017, 398 ff.; P.J. Yap, *Twenty Years of the Basic Law: Continuity and Changes in the Geoffrey Ma Court*, in *Hong Kong Law Journal*, 2019, 209 ff.; Lord Neuberger of Abbotsbury, *Judges, Access to Justice, the Rule of Law and the Court of Final Appeal under "One Country Two Systems"*, in *Hong Kong Law Journal*, 2017, 899 ff.; E.C. Ip, *Law and Justice in Hong Kong*, Hong Kong, Sweet & Maxwell, 2016, 2nd edn; R. Tang, *Developing Common Law in Hong*

1997, as well as the Macao SAR (MSAR),[260] set up as a result of the return of its territory to the People's Republic of China by the former Portuguese colonial power in 1999. The special administrative regions have the highest level of self-organization allowed by the Chinese system of sub-state territorial autonomies, as they are governed by the so-called "One country, two systems" (1C2S), a denomination indicating, above all, the characteristic for which the former colonial possessions of Hong Kong and Macao are an integral part of China, albeit with the a not inconsiderable difference that the latter is based on the socialist system while the HKSAR and the MSAR maintain the economic institutions of the capitalist system in force. It is interesting to note, in this regard, that on the one hand, representation on the international level lies solely with the PRC – there is therefore no independent international personality of the special administrative regions – and, on the

Kong, in *Hong Kong Law Journal*, 2016, 761 ff. For the division of responsibilities between the Hong Kong's Court of Final Appeal (CFA) and the Standing Committee of the National People's *Congress* (NPCSC) in Beijing, *see* (from a comparative viewpoint between Art. 267 of the Treaty on the Functioning of the European Union and Art. 158 of the BL of Hong Kong) C. Chan, *Implementing China and Hong Kong's Preliminary Reference System: Transposability of Art. 267 TFUE Principles*, in *Pub. L.*, 2014, 642 ff.; J. Lam, *Rethinking the NPCSC's Power to Interpret the Basic Law*, in *Hong Kong Law Journal*, 2017, 825 ff.; P.Y. Lo, *Enforcing an Unfortunate, Unnecessary and "Unquestionably Binding" NPCSC Interpretation: The Hong Kong Judiciary's Deconstruction of Its Construction of the Basic Law*, in *Hong Kong Law Journal*, 2018, 399 ff.; M. Mazza, *Sguardi dalla Cina (Hong Kong) sul diritto eurounitario: il rinvio pregiudiziale nella prospettiva comparatistica*, in *Dir. pubbl. comp. eur.*, 2016, 465 ff.; previously *see*, v. R. Cavalieri, *La corte di ultima istanza di Hong Kong recepisce l'interpretazione ufficiale degli articoli 22 e 24 c. 2 della Legge fondamentale in materia di immigrazione fornita dal Comitato Permanente dell'Assemblea Nazionale del Popolo della Repubblica Popolare Cinese*, in *Dir. pubbl. comp. eur.*, 2000, 1319 ff. For a comparison with the autonomous regions of Tibet and Xinjiang, *see* B. Chou, *New Bottle, Old Wine: China's Governance of Hong Kong in View of Its Policies in the Restive Borderlands*, in *Journal of Current Chinese Affairs*, 2015, n. 4, 177 ff.

260 *Cf.* S. Shiu-Hing Lo, *Political Change in Macao*, London/New York, Routledge, 2008; P. Cardinal, *The Internationalization of an Historical Autonomy*, in *Boletín Mexicano de Derecho Comparado*, n. 122, 2008, 637 ff. For a comparison with Hong Kong, *cf.* G. Samarani, *La Cina contemporanea. Dalla fine dell'Impero a oggi*, Torino, Einaudi, 2017, *sub* XVII, *Lo status «speciale» di Hong Kong e Macao*, 392 ff.; S. Rodriquez, *Le specialità di Hong Kong e Macao: esempio di bilanciamento tra diversità ed unità*, in G. Rolla (Ed.), *Regimi giuridici speciali di autonomia delle comunità territoriali. Profili di diritto comparato*, Milano, Giuffrè, 2013, 59 ff.; M. Manero de Lemos, *Too late for the Standing Committee of the National People's Congress to Take a Step Back?: The Basic Laws of Hong Kong and Macau as Constitutions of China and the Fall-Off of the "One Country, Two Systems" Principle*, paper presented at the conference, *Constitutional History: Comparative Perspectives*, held at the University of Bologna from 13 to 14 November 2017; E.C. Ip, *Comparative Subnational Foreign Relations Law in the Chinese Special Administrative Regions*, in *Int'l & Comp. L.Q.*, 2016, 953 ff.; M. Sadowski, *Crossroads of the World, Crossroads of the Law: Hong Kong and Macau Legal Systems. Approaching 20 Years Post-Transition*, in *Comparative Law Review*, 1-2016 *online* at www.comparativelawreview.unipg.it; I. Castellucci, *Legal Hybridity in Hong Kong and Macau*, in *McGill Law Journal*, 2012, 665 ff.; M. Morin, *Dualisme, mixité et métissage juridique: Québec, Hong Kong, Macao, Afrique du Sud et Israël, ivi*, 2012, 645 ff. On gambling in Macao, *see* X. Paulès, *Les limites de l'influence du modèle de la Las Vegas dans l'offre de jeux de hasard à Macao: apports d'une mise en perspective historique*, in *Études chinoises*, 2014, n. 2, 129 ff.; the gambling industry has made Macao a sort of "recycling Mecca", as observed by J.P. Cardenal, H. Araújo, *Come la Cina sta conquistando l'Occidente*, (2015), Italian translation, Milano, Feltrinelli, 2016, 64 ff. For a collection of essays, *see* I. Castellucci (Ed.), *The Many Legal Roles for Macau within the People's Republic of China*, Macau, Fundação Macau, 2017.

other hand, the SAR typological scheme is usually prefigured by the authorities of the People's Republic also in the perspective of (future and eventual) reunification with the "rebel sister" Taiwan.[261]

The effective exercise of the autonomy of the special administrative regions, however, is very different, since it took a significant measure in Hong Kong and much smaller in Macao, especially from a jurisprudential point of view. In particular, it must be remembered that the Court of Final Appeal of Hong Kong has repeatedly judged unconstitutional laws, while a similar decision has never been pronounced by the *Tribunal de Última Instância* of Macao.[262]

In any case, the Chinese authorities are currently very careful to prevent any special administrative regions, especially Hong Kong, from gaining independence from the People's Republic of China.[263]

1.7 FUNDAMENTAL RIGHTS, DUTIES AND FREEDOMS

1.7.1 The Historical and Conceptual Framework of Fundamental Rights in the People's Republic of China: The Typically Chinese Characteristics of the Hierarchy Between Constitutional Rights

The rights and duties of constitutional status, provided for by the current Constitution of the People's Republic of China (PRC) approved in 1982, are embedded into a social,

261 On the topic *see*, J.-P. Cabestan, Taiwan, Chine populaire: l'impossible réunification, Paris, Ifri (Institut français des relations internationales), 1995; Id., *Taipei-Pékin: les liaisons dangereuses*, in *Politique internationale*, n. 72, 1996, 43 ff.; Id., *The Cross-Strait Relationship in the Post-Cold War Era: Neither Reunification Nor 'Win-Win' Game*, in Lin Bih-jaw (Ed.), *The Asia-Pacific and Europe in the Post-Cold War Era*, Taipei, Institute of International Relations, 1995, 90 ff.; Id., *Taiwan – Mainland China: Reunification Remains More Impossible Than Ever*, in M.-L. Naeth (Ed.), *The Republic of China on Taiwan in International Politics*, Frankfurt a.M./Berlin/Bern/Bruxelles/New York/Oxford/Wien, Lang, 1998, 51 ff.; Id., *The Relations Across the Taiwan Strait : Twenty Years of Development and Frustration*, in Lau Chung-ming, Shen Jianfa (Eds.), *China Review 2000*, Hong Kong, The Chinese University Press, 2000; 105 ff.; M. Esteban, Democratization of the People's Republic of China and Military Conflict in the Taiwan Strait, in China aktuell. Journal of Current Chinese Affairs, 2007, n. 6, 5 ff.; C. Su, Taiwan's *Relations with Mainland China*, London/New York, Routledge, 2008; *H.-W. Schütte, Entspannung an der Taiwan-Straße: ein Land, zwei Regionen*, in China aktuell. Journal of Current Chinese Affairs, 2008, n. 4, 183 ff. For historical aspects, *see* P. Carioti, *L'incorporazione dell'isola di Taiwan alla Cina, dalla fondazione del "regno" dei Zheng alla formale annessione all'impero Qing, 1661-1683*, in S.M. Carletti, M. Sacchetti, P. Santangelo (Eds.), *Studi in onore di L. Lanciotti*, I, Napoli, Department of Asian Studies of *Universitario Orientale* – Italian Institute for the Middle and Far East, 1996, 185 ff.

262 *See* the comparative analysis of E. Ip, *Hybrid Constitutionalism. The Politics of Constitutional Review in the Chinese Special Administrative Regions*, Cambridge, Cambridge University Press, 2019.

263 *See*, for instance, *Central Government Voices Firm Support for HKSAR's Ban on "Hong Kong National Party"*, in *Beijing Review*, 25 September 2018, www.bjreview.com.

political, philosophical, moral and juridical fabric that privileges the values of order and harmony, with respect to the individual liberties of citizens.[264] And nor can the situation

---

264 On the difficult emergence in China of a new sensibility in terms of individual rights (or fundamental democratic rights), *cf.* J.G. Koeltl, *Civil Rights and Liberties in China*, in *Albany Law Review*, 1982, 740 ff.; R. Dworkin, *Taking Rights Seriously in Beijing*, in *The New York Review of Books*, 26 September 2002, 64 ff.; M. Goldman, *From Comrade to Citizen. The Struggle for Political Rights in China*, Cambridge (MA), Harvard University Press, 2005; D. Kelly, *Approaching Chinese Freedom: A Study in Absolute and Relative Values*, in *Journal of Current Chinese Affairs*, 2013, n. 2, 141 ff.; Z. Zhaou, *Liberal Rights and Political Culture. Envisioning Democracy in China*, London/New York, 2013. In Italian, *see* T. Groppi, *Il perimetro delle libertà e dei diritti nel sistema costituzionale cinese*, in R. Cavalieri, V. Bellomo, S. D'Attoma (Eds.), *Diritto, cittadini e potere in Cina*, op cit., 43 ff.; E. Consiglio, *Sviluppo economico e diritti umani in Cina*, in A. Rinella, I. Piccinini (Eds.), *La costituzione economica cinese*, Bologna, il Mulino, 2010, 57 ff.; T. Groppi, *Tra costituzionalismo globale ed eccezionalismo: diritti e libertà nel sistema costituzionale cinese nel XXI secolo*, in *Federalismi.it. Rivista di diritto pubblico italiano, comparato, europeo*, n. 1/2015, on the *website* www.federalismi.it. With regard to the movement for the protection of rights (Chinese: "*weiquan yundong*"), whose goal is "to affirm the constitutional rights of Chinese citizens" *cf.* F. Sapio, *Gli avvocati per la tutela dei diritti*, in R. Cavalieri, I. Franceschini (Eds.), *Germogli di società civile in Cina*, Milano, Brioschi, 2010, 167 ff.; J. Benney, *Defending Rights in Contemporary China*, London/New York, Routledge, 2013; H. Fu, *Human Rights Lawyering in Chinese Courtrooms*, in *Chinese Journal of Comparative Law*, 2014, 270 ff.; re the growing *public interest litigation* (Chinese: *gongyi susong*) *see* J. Jiang, *Rightful Resistance through Public Interest Litigation in China*, in *Asia in Focus. A Nordic journal on Asia*, 2015, n. 1, 13 ff.:, S. Novaretti, *Social Governance vs. Social Management: Towards a New Regulatory Role for Social Organizations in China?*, in *Opinio Juris in Comparatione. Studies in Comparative and National Law*, n. 1/2017 (www.opiniojurisincomparatione.org), on *evironmental public interest litigation*; Id., Le ragioni del pubblico: le "azioni nel pubblico interesse" in Cina, Napoli, Edizioni Scientifiche Italiane, 2011; Id., La riforma della procedura civile della RPC e le «azioni nel pubblico interesse»: un balzo in avanti? Diritto con «caratteristiche cinesi» e società civile, in Riv. dir. civ., 2013, 343 ff., re the new formulation of Art. 55 of the Civil Procedure Law of the People's Republic, which entered into force on 31 August 2012, which regulates civil actions for the defence of the public interest; Z. Luo, Significato costituzionale delle azioni nel pubblico interesse ambientale in Cina, in Rivista quedrimestrale di diritto dell'ambiente, 2016, n. 1, 33 ff.; C. Wang, *Studio sulla controversia amministrativa di pubblico interesse in materia ambientale, ivi*, 2016, n. 1, 86 ff.; X. Liu, *Valutazione dell'attribuzione dello status di querelante nelle controversie di pubblico interesse in materia ambientale nello scenario del diritto di querela, ibidem*, 2016, n. 1, 190 ff. (for the relative statistical data, *see* Chinese Courts Accept over 800 Public Interest Litigations in 2 Years, in Beijing Review, 15 November 2017, www.bjreview.com). On the principle of legality *chinese-style, see* I. Castellucci, *Rule of Law with Chinese Characteristics*, in *Annual Survey of International and Comparative Law*, 2007, 35 ff.; Id., *Rule of Law and Legal Complexity in the People's Republic of China*, Trento, University of Trento, 2012 (*Quaderni del Dipartimento di Scienze Giuridiche*, n. 103); Id., *L'idea di* rule of law *nella Repubblica Popolare Cinese*, in R. Cavalieri, V. Bellomo, S. D'Attoma (Eds.), *Diritto, cittadini e potere in Cina*, op cit., 59 ff.; G. Ajani, *Fa zhi, Rule of Law, Stato di diritto*, in Id., J. Luther (Ed.), *Modelli giuridici europei nella Cina contemporanea*, op cit., 189 ff.; G. di Plinio, Fazhi (法治). *L'espansione della* Western Legal Tradition *nella Cina del terzo millennio*, in *Iura Orientalia*, vol. VII, 2011, 176 ff.; Id., Rule of law/fazhi (法治): *il diritto in Cina tra WTO e* Asian Values, in *Dir. pubbl. com eur.*, 2011, 326 ff.; V. Accattatis, *Rule of law e democrazia in Cina*, in *Il Ponte*, febbraio 2015, 48 f.; M. Porto, *Cina*, in R. Torino (Ed.), *Sistemi giuridici. Diritto e geopolitica*, Wolters Kluwer-Cedam, Milanofiori-Assago, 2017, 69 ff., *sub Occidente* vs *Cina:* Rule of Law vs Rule by Law, 74 ff., in addition to R. Cavalieri, *Trends and Contradictions of Contemporary Chinese Law*, a seminar held 29 November 2011 at the Faculty of Economics, Libera Università, Bolzano, which favours for the translation of the expression *fa zhi* contained in Art. 5 of the Chinese Constitution of 1982 (amended in 1999) as *rule by law*, rather than *rule of law*; also according to E.W. Orts, *The Rule of Law in China*, in *Vand. J. Transnat'l L.*, 2001, 43 ff., especially 93 ff., the PRC did not follow the *rule of law* (*as a normative and political theory*) but *rule* by *law* (*as an instrument of government*). From a comparative point of view, *see*, K.A. Ziegert, *Is*

regarding respect for fundamental rights be said to have changed substantially as a result of the adoption by the Chinese authorities of two successive national plans on the protection of human rights, the first relating to the two-year period 2009–2010 and the second implemented between 2012 and 2015.[265] On this last point, it is worth pointing out that through the amendments introduced in March 2012 by the National People's Congress (National Parliament) in the code of criminal procedure, explicit mention is made of the protection of human rights in Article 2, in accordance with Article 33 of the current Constitution and in implementation of the same superprimary provision.[266] It remains, however, for now, little more than an auspice for which

the Rule of Law Portable? A Socio-Legal Journey from the Nordic Mediterranean Sea via the Silk Road to China, in P. Bergling, J. Ederlöf, V.L. Taylor (Eds.), *Rule of Law Promotion: Global Perspectives, Local Applications*, Uppsala, Iustus Førlag, 2009 (*Skriften från juridiska institutionen vid Umeå universite*, n. 21), 19 ff.; L.S. Rossi, G. Di Federico (Eds.), *Fundamental rights in Europe and China. Regional identities and universalism*, Napoli, Editroiale Scientifica, 2013. For an intra-Chinese comparison, *cf.* C.V. Chen, Chao-chin Su, Yong-huang Lin, *The Rule of Law in China and Taiwan – Toward "One China, Better Wirtschaftswissenschaften System"*, in *Issues & Studies. An International Quarterly on China, Taiwan, and East Asian Affairs*, 2010, n. 4, 217 ff. Finally, on the relationship between tradition and modernization in Chinese law, *see* L. Moccia, *Le double paradoxe de la modernité en Chine ou de la question du droit, miroir du monde chinois traditionnel et contemporain*, in *Rev. intern. dr. comp.*, 2011, 781 ff.

265 For the point of view of the Chinese authorities on the promotion and protection of human rights in China, *cf.* A. Viviani, *Il rapporto del Governo cinese sullo* Human Rights Action Plan, in *Diritti umani e diritto internazionale*, 2011, 625 ff., commenting on the results of the first national plan on the protection of human rights and respect for internationally accepted obligations (*National Human Rights Action Plan of China, 2009-2010*), presented in Beijing on 13 July 2011 by Wang Chen, Minister of the *State Council Information Office*; re the Chinese academic debate, *see also*, K. Yu (Ed.), *Democracy and the Rule of Law in China*, Leiden, Brill, 2010. For a comparative comparison between the 2009-2010 two-year plan and the second national human rights plan for the period 2012-2015, *see* E. Sorda, *Cina. Pubblicato il secondo piano nazionale per i diritti umani*, in *Dir. pubbl. comp. eur. online*, 2012, n. 3 (www.dpce.it.); R. Toniatti, *La Cina dei diritti umani*, in *AffarInternazionali. Riv. online di politica, strategia ed economia*, at www.affarinternazionali.it (doc. dated 19 July 2012), who observes conclusively that "Il nuovo Piano d'Azione per i diritti dell'uomo – al di là degli impianti concettuale e istituzionale, che rimangono saldamente ancorati a radici culturali e premesse ideologiche del regime – testimonia comunque che il discorso sui diritti dell'uomo si è venuto affermando come un contenuto ineludibile del potere pubblico, presumibilmente anche per motivi di politica interna, oltre che di immagine del paese, che mira ad ottenere maggiore credibilità internazionalethe". Lastly, *see* P. Sun, *Human Rights Protection System in China*, Berlin, Springer, 2013. Finally, worthy of interest is the fact that the Chinese authorities have initiated, also with the collaboration of prestigious foreign academic institutions active in the field of study and protection of human rights, the activation of new university courses dedicated to *human rights*, as evidenced by the recent seminar on *Human Rights Law Teaching at Chinese Universities*, held in Beijing at the *China University of Political Science and Law* from 15 to 23 August 2013, thanks to the support given by the *Norwegian Centre for Human Rights* (created at the Law Faculty of the University of Oslo); the seminar was attended by forty-five Chinese law professors.

266 *Cf.* E. Nesossi, *Giustizia e compromesso: uno sguardo al recente emendamento del Codice di procedura penale cinese*, in *Inchiesta*, n. 177, July-September 2012, 93 ff. (*sub* Dossier *Cina: politica, lavori e diritti*, editied by I. Franceschini and L. Tomba).

> To make their country a new republic, the Chinese people need to transform themselves from subjects of a despotic regime – whether under an emperor or a monopolistic ruling party – into citizens with a republican spirit.[267]

At least two aspects of the Chinese constitutional theory contribute decisively to the compression of the dimension of classical liberties.

On the one hand the constitutional rights of individuals are not considered as pre-existing to the State, but on the contrary they are considered created and recognized by the legal system in relation to the material conditions (structural, according to Marx-Engelsian doctrine) of socio-economic development. The Chinese "colouring" of the Constitution implies that the latter is the source, and not the reflection, of fundamental rights and freedoms.[268]

On the other hand, the communist conception of man and society is clearly oriented, in a similar way to that which occurred before the foundation of the People's Republic of China, on the basis of Confucian moral philosophy, to giving priority to the collective interests of individual rights.[269] In the current Chinese constitutional legal context, therefore, one does not find absolute rights, but only relative rights, which exist and are exercisable respectively, if and in the ways, provided for by law.

In terms of relations between international law and domestic national law, it should be noted that the regulations contained in the Constitution of the PRC prevail, in the case of conflicting rules, on the provisions contained in international treaties ratified by the People's Republic, and only with respect to the laws of the PRC, the rules of conventional international law are endowed with superior legal force in the event of divergence.

Lastly, the Marxist conception of law and the State is based on the values of traditional Asian culture, which places limitations on the fundamental rights of individual citizens in favour of the expansion and full realization of collective or community rights, in order that the convergence of political, philosophical, moral and social elements that characterize extreme-oriental systems in general and in particular the Chinese normative system, determines an overall restrictive and strictly positivistic reading of the juridical positions recognized by the Constitution to private subjects. This is to be viewed, even taking into account that the Government of the People's Republic of China did not adhere to the Bangkok Declaration adopted by the Asian Regional Intergovernmental Conference (Regional *Meeting* for Asia) held from 29 March to 2 April 1993, and attended by the Ministers and representatives of Asian States in preparation for the UN World Conference

---

267 Thus Q. Zhang, *The Constitution of China. A Contextual Analysis*, op cit., 264.

268 As highlighted by A. Rinella, *Il sistema di governo cinese: aspetti nodali*, conference held 30 November at the Department of Law & Politics, Milan State University.

269 For the Chinese perspective re the greater importance of collective rights with respect to individual rights, *cf.* for example Tian Dan, *Rights Perspective*, in *Beijing Review*, 2005, n. 51, 19.

on Human Rights held in Vienna in June 1993, which focused on the issue of so-called Asian values placed in relation to political democracy, fundamental human rights, and collective rights of national and local communities.[270]

---

270 On the legal-constitutional profiles of "(pan) Asian values", *see* F. Tedesco, *I diritti umani alla prova del relativismo. La critica dei "valori asiatici"*, in T. Casadei (Ed.), *Diritti umani e soggetti vulnerabili. Violazioni, trasformazioni, aporie*, Preface by G. Zanetti, Torino, Giappichelli, 2012, 45 ff.; M. Flores, *Storia dei diritti umani*, Bologna, il Mulino, 2008 (rpt. 2012), 299 ff.; T. Groppi, *I diritti umani in Asia*, in C. Amato, G. Ponzanelli (Eds.), *Global Law v. Local Law. Problemi della globalizzazione giuridica* (XVII Biennial Colloquium of the Italian Association of Comparative Law, held in Brescia from 12 to 14 May 2005), Torino, Giappichelli, 2006, 186 ff.; Id., *Costituzioni senza costituzionalismo? La codificazione dei diritti in Asia agli inizi del XXI secolo*, in *Pol. dir.*, 2006, 187 ff.; A.E.-S. Tay, *I "valori asiatici" e il* rule of law, in P. Costa, D. Zolo (Eds.), *Lo Stato di diritto. Storia, teoria, critica*, Milano, Feltrinelli, 2002, 683 ff.; J.D. Ciorciari, *Institutionalizing Human Rights in Southeast Asia*, in *Human Rights Quarterly. A Comparative and International Journal of the Social Sciences, Humanities, and Law*, 2012, 695 ff.; Wu Xiaodan, *The Current Situation and Prospects for Regional System(s) of Human Rights in Asia*, in *Diritti umani e diritto internazionale*, 2012, 45 ff.; D. Kingsbury, L. Avonius, (Eds.), *Human Rights in Asia – A Reassessment of the Asian Values Debate*, Basingstoke (UK)-New York, Palgrave Macmillan, 2008; R. Peerenboom, *Law and Development of Constitutional Democracy: Is China a Problem Case?*, in R. E.D. Schwartz (Ed.), *Law, Society, and Democracy: Comparative Perspectives*, monothematic issue of *The Annals of the American Academy of Political and Social Science*, January 2006, 192 ff.; Id., *Beyond Universalism and Relativism: The Evolving Debates about "Values in Asia"*, in *Indiana International and Comparative Law Review*, 2003, 1 ff.; Id., C.J. Petersen, A. H.Y. Chen (Eds.), *Human Rights in Asia. A Comparative Legal Study of Twelve Asian Jurisdiction, France and USA*, London-New York, Routledge, 2006; B. von Albertini Mason, *The Case for Liberal Democracy in China. Basic Human Rights, Confucianism and the Asian Values Debate*, Zürich, Schulthess, 2005; Chang Yu-tzung, Chu Yun-han, F. Tsai, *Confucianism and Democratic Values in Three Chinese Societies*, in *Issues & Studies. A Social Science Quarterly on China, Taiwan, and East Asian Affairs*, 2005, n. 4, 1 ff.; E.E. Douglas, *The Struggle for Human Rights Versus Stability: The Chinese Communist Party and Western Values Clash*, in *Denver Journal of International Law and Policy*, 2001, 151 ff.; A. Kent, *China, the United Nations, and Human Rights. The Limits of Compliance*, Philadelphia (PA), University of Pennsylvania Press, 1999; R. Weatherley, *Discourse of Human Rights in China. Historical and Ideological Perspectives*, London, Macmillan, 1999; AA.VV, *Menschenrechte in China. Der Staat als Täter*, n. 231 di *Bedrohte Völker – Pogrom* (journal editied by *Gesellschaft für bedrohte Völker*-GfbV, office in Göttingen), 2005; S. Heilmann, *Die Menschenrechtslage und die Perspektiven eines Rechtsstaates in China*, in *China aktuell*, 1999, 587 ff.; G. Paul, C.Y. Robertson-Wensauer (hrsg.), *Traditionelle chinesiche Kultur und Menschenrechtsfrage*, Baden-Baden, Nomos, 1998, 2nd edn. For the philosophical aspects, *see* A. Chiricosta, *Filosofia interculturale e valori asiatici*, Milano, O barra O Edizioni, 2013; E. Fornari, *Globalità, cultura e fine della modernità. Il caso dei "valori asiatici"*, in *Iride. Filosofia e discussione pubblica*, January-February 2004, 163 ff.; Id., *Los valores asiáticos y la nueva escena global*, in *Cuadernos filosóficos*, n. IV/2007, 27 ff. For the position of People's Republic re the Bangkok Declaration, *cf.* M.C. Davis, *Human Rights in Asia: China and the Bangkok Declaration*, in *Buffalo Journal of International Law*, 1995-1996, 2 ff. On the international role of the PRC on the promotion and protection of human rights, *see*, from the Chinese perspective, Chen Xulong, *Reforming Rights Protection. For China, the recently established UN Human Rights Council is a victory of multilateralism*, in *Beijing Review*, 2006, n. 19, 14 f. For the Chinese position with regard to the competence of the UN Security Council on human rights (and, therefore, on the Chinese position concerning international human rights law), *see* F. Couveinhes-Matsumoto, *La critique des principales orientations du Conseil de sécurité par la République Populaire de Chine. Eléments pour une évaluation des effets de la fin de l'hegémonie occidentale sur le droit de la paix et de la sécurité internationales*, in *Rev. générale de droit international public*, 2013, 233 ff., which points out (*cf.* especially 243) the "frontal" adhesion of the People's Republic of China to human rights (since the "Chinese adhesion to human rights is still accompanied by temperaments"). On the East Asian model of human rights, specifically considered in relation to China, *cf.*

From a historical point of view, one should remember that provisions concerning the protection of fundamental human and citizen rights were established from the first constitutional documents of the People's Republic of China. A list of constitutionally guaranteed rights was contained in Articles 4 and 5 of the 1949 Joint Program, which included, among other things, the political rights (active and passive) of Chinese citizens, as well as the classical freedoms of expression, communication and manifestation of thought, assembly, association, press and religion. Chapter III of the 1954 Constitution was entirely dedicated to the fundamental rights and duties of citizens, while important laws were enacted to allow the effective exercise of these rights, as occurred in particular for political rights via the provisions of the 1953 electoral law. However, precisely at the level of effectiveness, there were very serious violations of fundamental rights, with the emergence of anti-rightist campaigns in the second half of the fifties of the last century, which then culminated in the hegemony of the radical left during the period of the Cultural Revolution. The Constitutions of 1975 and 1978 also presented catalogues of fundamental rights and duties of citizens. The 1975 Constitution was approved in a context, decidedly unfavourable for the affirmation of law and legality, represented by the proletarian cultural revolution begun in 1966 and concluded in 1976.[271] The 1978 Constitution, while expanding the number and scope of constitutional provisions on the fundamental rights of citizens governed by Articles 44–59 of Chapter III,[272] was adopted in the difficult moment of the abandonment of the extremist theories of ultra-Maoism. The 1978 Constitutional Charter dictated, among other things, some characteristic norms of the public law system of the People's Republic of China, such as, where it integrated freedom of speech, correspondence, press, meeting, assembly,[273] association,[274] travel, and the freedom to parade, demonstrate and strike,[275] via the recognition of the right to employ "great honesty, great openness, great controversy,

---

C. Ryngaert, *The Long Road to the Entrenchment of Human Rights in China*, in *Studia Diplomatica. The Brussels Journal of International Relations*, 2011, n. 2, 99 ff.

271 *See, si vis*, M. Mazza, *Lineamenti di diritto costituzionale cinese*, op cit., 8 ff.

272 The corresponding norms of the 1975 Constitution were contained in Art. 26-29.

273 Now governed by the law adopted by the National People's Congress on 31 October 1989. *Cf.* J. Polumbaum, *In the Name of Stability: Restrictions on the Right of Assembly in the People's Republic of China*, in *The Australian Journal of Chinese Affairs*, 1991, 43 ff.; K.C. Wong, *Law of Assembly in the People's Republic of China*, in *Asia Pacific Journal on Human Rights and the Law*, 2004, n. 2, 30 ff., to which *adde* : a) in the context of the comparison between the law of the People's Republic of China (PRC) and the law of nationalist China (ROC), K.C. Wong, *Law of assembly in China: People's Republic of China vs. Republic of China*, in *International Journal of the Sociology of Law*, 2005, 215 ff.; b) for the ROC, K.C. Wong, *Law of Assembly in China: The Case of Taiwan*, in *Asia Pacific Journal on Human Rights and the Law*, 2005, n. 1-2, 49 ff.

274 *See* I. Thireau (Ed.), *De proche en proche. Ethnograhie des formes d'associations en Chine contemporaine*, Bern, Lang, 2013 (*Mondes de l'extrême-orient*, n. 20).

275 For an analysis of Art. 28 of the 1975 Constitution, *see* C. Donati, *La libertà di sciopero nella Repubblica popolare cinese*, in *Critica dir.*, 1975, n. 5-6, 190 ff.; with regard to the Constitutions of 1975 and 1978, *cf.* E. Carrabba, *La libertà di sciopero nella legislazione e nella pratica della Rpc*, in *Mondo cinese*, n. 55, 1986, 35 ff.

great wall posters". Or with the clarification that the right to file complaints, accusations and appeals, can not only be prevented or hindered, but is not even to be accompanied by reprisals and revenge. Or moreover, by completing the provision on the right to work of Chinese citizens with the provision for which the State assigns them a job "in accordance with the principle of providing for individuals in a universal framework".

Chapter II of the current Constitution of 1982 perfected the list of fundamental rights and duties, introducing also a significant systematic innovation consisting in the placing of the norms on fundamental rights in Chapter II, immediately after the general principles, and before the discussion dedicated to the structure of the State, contrary to that which occurred in the Constitutions of 1975 and 1978, which dealt with fundamental rights and duties in the final part, followed by a single rule (Article 30 of the 1975 Constitution and Article 60 of the 1978 Constitution) on the national flag, national emblem and capital of the PRC. All of this, limiting this current investigation to the recognition and protection of fundamental rights according to the formal statements of Chinese constitutional documents, that is *on paper* (or in writing), due to the fact that, as is universally known and highlighted by comparative analyses – the affirmation of rights in the Constitution is certainly not equivalent to their actual implementation in the practice of the so-called living law.

It is worth underlining, however, that the dogmatic reconstruction of fundamental rights in the Chinese constitutional system places on a hierarchically superior level the human rights consecrated in the Constitution, which are habitually second-generation, represented by economic and social rights and freedoms, including the rights to food and the fulfilment of the basic needs of life, with respect to the classical rights and liberties of the so-called first generation, such as freedom of expression, the right to meet in assembly and association, religious freedom, freedom and secrecy of correspondence, etc. The same human rights of the so-called third generation, such as the rights of groups, collective-community and development, are considered in the Chinese perspective prevalent over the fundamental human rights of the first generation.

1.7.2 The Catalogue of Citizens' Rights in the 1982 Constitution

The systems for classifying the constitutionally protected rights that have been adopted by the public law of the People's Republic of China are numerous and are characterized by an increasing complexity in the identification of categories and sub-categories. In particular, one can find theoretical positions that distinguish five categories of fundamental rights, in which the rights themselves are grouped according to different methods so as to give life to as many doctrinal approaches, or developments of such theories that have led to an elaboration, in the Chinese People's constitutional dogma, of nine categories of fundamental rights recognized and protected in the 1982 *lex fundamentalis*.[276]

Various opinions, however, agree in sustaining that the constitutional principle of equality of citizens before the law ex Article 33 of the fundamental Charter, is of a higher rank, since it is both a fundamental right and a general principle which shapes the entire Chinese constitutional system. The main moments of emergence in the constitutional text of the general rule proclaimed by Article 33 include the affirmation of the equality between the nationalities of China on the basis of Article 4, between men and women according to Article 48, and between citizens who profess a religion and those who declare themselves atheists according to Article 36. On the other hand, the constitutional principle of equality as a meta-right of the Chinese regulatory system presents a multidimensional nature, acting as a predominantly procedural content right with regard to civil and political rights, while it appears to be of substantial value in relation to socio-economic and cultural rights. From a different point of view, the right of equality in the Chinese Constitution encounters limitations deriving from differentiated treatments justified to the extent of their reasonableness, as is the case with the promotional provisions in favour of working women permitted by Article 48, Paragraph 2, of the fundamental charter.

The importance of the constitutional principle of equality as a fundamental rule governing the entire Chinese regulatory system was also underlined by the fifth *plenum* of the XVI CCP Central Committee, held in Beijing from 8 to 11 October 2005, which examined the guidelines for the approval of the eleventh Five-Year Plan for National Economic and Social Development, for the years 2006-2010.[277] The governing body of the country's political leadership pointed out that the goal of equality of treatment is essential to achieve a harmonious society (Chinese: *hexie shehui,* HS),[278] also via a fair distribution of the tax burden among citizens.[279]

The necessarily interconnected nature of fundamental rights in Chinese law also appears in the regulation of political rights, which include not only electoral rights, but also political

276 *See* He Huahui (Ed.), *Bijiao Xianfa Xue* [*Comparative Constitutional Law*], Wuhan, Wuhan University Press, 1988; Xu Chongde (Ed.), *Zhongguo Xianfa* [*Chinese Constitutional Law*], Beijing, People's University Press, 1996; Xu Chongde (Ed.), *Xian Fa* (*Constitutional Law*], Beijing, People's University Press, 1999; Dong Heping, Han Dayuan, Li Shuzhong, *Xian Fa* [*Constitutional Law*], Beijing, China University of Political Science and Law Publishing House, 2000.

277 *Cf.* Li Jianguo, *Building a Harmonious Society*, in *Beijing Review*, 2005, n. 42, 2; Ni Yanshuo, *More Reforms on Cards to Ensure Equity*, in *Beijing Review*, 2005, n. 42, 8 ff.; M. Miranda, *Il nuovo programma del Pcc per una maggiore equità sociale*, in *Mondo cinese*, n. 125, 2005, 5 ff.

278 *See* L. Choukroune, *Global "Harmonious Society" and the Law: China's Legal Vision in Perspective*, in *German Law Journal*, 2012, 497 ff.; D. Joshi, *Does China's recent 'harmonious society' discourse reflect a shift towards human development?*, in *Journal of Political Ideology*, 2012, 169 ff.

279 For reflections of the principle of equality on Chinese tax levies, *see* Li Jianguo, *The Rule of Law and Human Rights*, in *Beijing Review*, 2005, n. 44, 3; Lan Xinzhen, *Redistributing Wealth Through Income Tax*, in *Beijing Review*, 2005, n. 41, 18 ff.

(or democratic[280]) freedoms concerning the right to freedom of thought and speech, as well as the press, assembly, association, procession and demonstration. On the other hand, individual rights with constitutional significance encounter in the Chinese normative model a double limitation, respectively of an intrinsic and extrinsic nature. The first concerns the procedural modalities prescribed by the Constitution itself or by the implementing laws for the exercise of fundamental rights. The second projects a particular light, with a typical People's Republic connotation, on the actual dimension of rights and freedoms in the constitutional system of the PRC, and is summarized in the provisions of Article 51 of the 1982 Constitution,[281] where it is established that the exercise by Chinese citizens of rights and freedoms provided for by the Basic Law must not in any case be in contrast not only with the legal positions of other citizens but also with the superior interests of the State, society and the community. Individual rights, in other words, are recognized and guaranteed by the Constitutional Charter to the extent that they conform to prevailing collective interests.

Having outlined these general premises, one should remember that the catalogue of individual constitutional rights and freedoms includes the rights of citizenship and electoral, religious freedom, personal freedom,[282] the right to housing, secrecy of correspondence,[283] the right to freedom of thought and the press, the right – to work and the right to rest, the right to retirement benefits and social security. Furthermore, the PRC promotes education and research, protects gender equality, protects marriage and the family, places citizens in charge of defending the homeland, carrying out military service and paying taxes, without neglecting a special consideration for the rights and interests of citizens residing abroad, as well as their family members living in the People's Republic of China.

It is useful, in this context, to carry out some in-depth reflections with regard to matters that present an intense political "colouring" in the legal-constitutional context of the PRC. In the outlined perspective, the following examination is dedicated to freedom of speech and the right of association. It should, however, be stated beforehand that an important particular aspect of the freedom of association in China concerns religious activities and freedom of religious belief. Article 36 of the 1982 Constitution guarantees freedom of religion and related rites, within the limits of their "normality" and provided they are not harmful to public order (*see* Para. 3 of the provision cited above). The detailed regulation

280 In the true sense of classical democracies, *i.e.* inspiration, derivation, liberal and western tradition.

281 In comment of which, *cf.* W. Gellhorn, *China's Quest for Legal Modernity*, in *Journal of Chinese Law*, 1987, particularly 19 f.

282 *See* O. Malmgren, *Art. 37: The right to liberty of person under the Chinese constitution*, in *China-EU Law Journal*, 2013, 35 ff., who highlights the still limited scope of the recognition of constitutional rights in China, since the constitutional provisions become binding on state organs and citizens only after their "transformation" into sub-constitutional legislative sources.

283 With implications on the protection of privacy, *see* Cao Jingchun, *Protecting the Right to Privacy in China*, in *Victoria University of Wellington Law Review*, 2005, 645 ff.

is contained in decree number 426 adopted by the State Council on 7 July 2004 and which entered into force on 1 March 2005.[284] The interpretation of these regulatory rules is the exclusive responsibility of the Department of Religious Affairs of the State Council. There are five officially recognized religious communities in the PRC: Buddhist, Taoist, Islamic, Catholic and Protestant. With regards to Chinese Muslims, there also exists an Islamic Neo-Confucianism. The Orthodox Church has presented an application for recognition, while the Jewish community is not officially recognized. However, there are considerable problems with the effectiveness of protection: the situation is very complicated with regards to religious sects (especially the Islamic, fundamentalist as well as some Christian sects dependent on the Evangelical Churches), the vernacular or folkloric-popular religions and the so called new religions, expressions of oriental mysticism, sometimes in various ways connected to the New Age Movement (NAM) as occurs for the *Falun Gong movement* (Chinese: *Qigong*), the latter also of Buddhist derivation.[285] In particular, the *Falun Gong*

284 *Cf.* Regulations on Religious Affairs (Promulgated by the State Council of the People's Republic of China; effective as of March 1, 2005), in *Chinese Journal of International Law*, 2006, 475 ff.

285 On the various aspects discussed, *see*: X. Zhuo, *Religious Faith of the Chinese*, Berlin, Springer, 2018; *Chinese Christianity*, monothematic dossier *Chinese Law and Government*, 2017, n. 3; C.T. Vala, *The Politics of the Protestant Churches and Party-State in China. God Above Party*, London-New York, Routledge, 2017; X. Yao (Ed.), *Religion in Contemporary China*, London/New York, 2017; M.S. Eire, *China and Islam. The Prophet, the Party, and Law*, Cambridge, Cambridge Unievrsity Press, 2016; Y. Liang (Ed.), *Religious Revival in Ethnic Areas of China*, London-New York, 2016; A. Stewart, *Islamic Revival in Northwest China. Searching for Allah*, London/New York, Routledge, 2016; J.A. Carpenter, K.R. den Dulk (Eds.), *Christianity in Chinese Public Life: Religion, Society, and the Rule of Law*, Basingstoke (UK)-New York, Palgrave Macmillan, 2014; R.P. Weller, *The Politics of Increasing Religious Diversity in China*, in *Daedalus (Journal of the American Academy of Arts and Sciences)*, 2014, n. 2, 135 ff.; X. Li, *Freedom of Religion in China*, in L.S. Rossi, G. Di Federico (Eds.), *Fundamental rights in Europe and China. Regional identities and universalism*, op cit., 133 ff.; A.R. Dicks, *The ownership of Buddhist temples and the civil status of the clergy in China*, in C. Bulfoni (Ed.), *Tradizioni religiose e trasformazioni sociali dell'Asia contemporanea*, Roma, Bulzoni, 2012 (*Accademia Ambrosiana, Asiatica Ambrosiana*, n. 4), 23 ff.; H.H. Lai, *Religious Policies in Post-Totalitarian China: Maintaining Political Monopoly over a Reviving Society*, in *Journal of Chinese Political Science*, 2006, n. 1, 55 ff.; Id., *The Religious Revival in China*, in *The Copenhagen Journal of Asian Studies*, (*see* 18), 2003, 40 ff.; E.R. Carlson, *China's New Regulations on Religion: A Small Step, Not a Great Leap, Forward*, in *Brigham Young University Law Review*, 2005, 747 ff.; A.C. Yu, *State and Religion in China*, Chicago (Ill.), Open Court, 2005; N.N. Chen, *Healing Sects and Anti-Cult Campaigns*, in *The China Quarterly*, 2003, 505 ff.; B. Potter, *Belief in Control: Regulation of Religion in China*, *ivi*, 2003, 317 ff.; M. Dillon, *Religious Minorities and China*, Preface by M. Lattimer, London, Minority Rights Group International (*MRG Report*), 2001; K-F. Daiber, *Konfuzianisches und anderes religiöses Leben in der südwestchinesischen Provinz Yunnan*, Berlin-Münster, LIT Verlag, 2016; A. Melloni, *La Via della Seta e la via del Vangelo*, in *OrizzonteCina*, 2019, n. 1, 14 ff.; A. Andreini, *Il Daoismo tra il XX e il XXI secolo*, *ivi*, 2019, n. 1, 19 ff.; E. Bianchi, *Vitalità, continuità e rinnovamento del Buddhismo nella Cina d'oggi*, *ibidem*, 2019, n. 1, 24 ff.; F. Rosati, *Islam con "caratteristiche cinesi". L'amministrazione della fede e i musulmani nella Repubblica popolare dell'era Xi Jinping*, *ibid.*, 2019, n. 1, 28 ff.; Id., *L'Islam in Cina. Dalle origini alla Repubblica popolare*, Roma, L'Asino d'oro, 2017; A. Giovagnoli, E. Giunipero (Eds.), *L'Accordo tra Santa Sede e Cina. Ii cattolici cinesi tra passato e futuro*, Preface by P. Parolin, Città del Vaticano, Urbaniana University Press, 2019; E. Giunipero, *I nuovi sviluppi nelle relazioni tra Cina e Vaticano*, in M. Miranda (Ed.), *La Cina quarant'anni dopo Mao. Scelte, sviluppi e orientamenti della politica di Xi Jinping*, Roma, Carocci, 2017, 109 ff.; Id., *Chiesa cattolica e Cina comunista dalla rivoluzione del 1949 al Concilio Vaticano II*, Preface by A. Giovagnoli, Brescia, Morcelliana, 2007; Id., *Nuove*

movement, founded by Li Hongzhi and whose public presence in China dates back to 1992, was suppressed by the Chinese government in the summer of 1999.[286]

With reference, therefore, to the right to free expression of thought, verbally and in writing,[287] it constitutes a good point of observation for evaluating the different conception

---

norme per le attività religiose in Cina, in *Mondo cinese*, n. 122, 2005, 33 ff.; J.J. You Guo, *Il cattolicesimo in Cina nel XXI secolo*, in *Civ. catt.*, 2017, 417 ff.; A. Spadaro (Ed.), *Nell'anima della Cina. Saggezza, storia, fede*, with a *Saggio introduttivo* by F, Lombardi, Milano, Àncora/La Civiltà cattolica, 2017; M. Chambon, *I cristiani cinesi tra repressione e aperture*, in J.-M. di Falco, T. Radcliffe, A. Riccardi (Eds.), *Il libro nero della condizione dei cristiani nel mondo*, Milano, Mondadori, 2014, 422 ff.; V. Pagliaro, *L'Islam in Cina e l'onda della Primavera araba*, Preface by F. Géré, Roma, Eurilink, 2013; R. Cavalieri, *Religione e libertà religiosa in Cina: appunti per una ricerca*, in C. Piccinini (Ed.), *Culture e religioni in Asia*, Roma, Bulzoni, 2009 (Accademia Ambrosiana, *Asiatica Ambrosiana*, n. 1), 161 ff.; Id., *La libertà religiosa in Cina*, in V. Possenti (Ed.), *Diritti umani e libertà religiosa*, Soveria Mannelli, Rubbettino, 2010, 221 ff.; G. Fazzini, *Cina: Se il partito teme la fede*, in *Mondo e Missione* (journal edited by Pontificio istituto missioni estere-PIME), February 2006, 13 ff.; S. Testa Bappenheim, *La nuova normativa della Repubblica popolare cinese sulla libertà religiosa*, in *Quaderni di diritto e politica ecclesiastica*, 2006, 391 ff.; Id., *L'attuale situazione della libertà religiosa in Cina*, in *Coscienza e libertà*, 2005, 119 ff.; A. Tamburrini (Ed.), *Rapporto 2005 sulla libertà religiosa nel mondo*, Roma, Aiuto alla Chiesa che Soffre (ACS), 2005, *sub Cina*, 162 ff. In a *media studies* perspective, *see* S. Travagnin (Ed.), *Religion and Media in China. Insights and Case Studies from the Mainland, Taiwan and Hong Kon* London/New York, Routledge, 2016.

286 *See* the detailed discussion by B. Penny, *The Religion of Falun Gong*, Chicago (IL), The University of Chicago Press, 2012, for a complete history of the *Falun Gong* movement. In Italian, *see* L. Sacco, *Diritto costituzionale e libertà religiosa in Cina: il problema Falun Gong*, in *Iura Orientalia*, III, 2007, 175 ff. The activities of the followers, as well as the government repression, seem to continue; *cf.* S. Noakes, C. Ford, *Managing Political Opposition Groups in China: Explaining the Continuing Anti-Falun Gong Campaign*, in *The China Quarterly*, 2015, 658 ff.; Y. Lu, Y. Su, N. Zhou, *Doctrinal Innovation, Resistance, and Falun Gong's Politicization*, in *The China Review*, 2018, n. 4, 41 ff.

287 On the topic *see*: Sun Xupei, E.C. Michel (Eds.), *An Orchestra of Voices. Making the Argument for Greater Speech and Press Freedom in the People's Republic of China*, Westport, Praeger, 2000, which speaks of a socialist press "with Chinese characteristics"; B.L. McCormick, *Recent Trends in Mainland China's Media: Political Implications of Commercialization*, in *Issues & Studies. An International Quarterly on China, Taiwan, and East Asian Affairs*, 2002-2003, 175 ff.; H. de Burgh, *The Chinese Journalist. Mediating Information in the World's Most Populous Country*, London, RoutledgeCurzon, 2003; Id., *Kings without Crowns? The Re-Emergence of Investigative Journalism in China*, in *Media, Culture & Society*, 2003, 801 ff.; Huang Chengju, *Transitional Media vs. Normative Theories: Schramm, Altschull, and China*, in *Journal of Communication*, 2003, 444 ff., on the theoretical models of the (half-way) communication systems in the Marxist state systems; R. Akhavan-Majid, *Mass Media Reform in China: Toward a New Analytical Framework*, in *International Communication Gazette*, 2004, 553 ff.; AA.VV., *Media and Globalization in China*, n. 3, September 2005, by *NIASnytt – Asia Insights* (journal editied by *Nordic Institute of Asian Studies*-NIAS of Copenhagen); B.L. Liebman, *Watchdog or Demagogue? The Media in the Chinese Legal System*, in *Colum. L. Rev.*, 2005, 1 ff.; Id., *Innovation Through Intimidation: An Empirical Account of Defamation Litigation in China*, in *Harv. Int'l L.J.*, 2006, 33 ff.; B.L. Massey, Wei Luo, *Chinese Newspapers and Market Theories of Web Journalism*, in *International Communication Gazette*, 2005, 359 ff.; Pan Zhongdang, *Media change through bounded innovations. Journalism in China's media reforms*, in A. Romano, M. Bromley (Eds.), *Journalism and Democracy in Asia*, London/New York, 2005, 96 ff.; B.H. Winfield, Z. Peng, *Market or Party Controls? Chinese Media in Transition*, in *International Communication Gazette*, 2005, 255 ff.; D. Bandurski, *China's Yellow Journalism*, in *Far Eastern Economic Review*, 2006, n. 5, 49 ff., on the characteristics of "yellow journalism" (*id est*, Chinese); K. Willmann, *Verschärfte Medienkontrolle oder Protektionismus?*, in *China aktuell – Journal of Current Chinese Affairs*, n. 5, 83 ff.; A.C. Lavagnino, *Editoria e stampa in Cina oggi*, in AA.VV., *La letteratura cinese contemporanea: invito alla lettura* (acts of the Rome convention, organised

of democracy in China and in countries of Western legal tradition, even in the presence of constitutional provisions abstractly suitable for allowing the effective implementation of fundamental freedoms in the PRC in accordance with the *standards* common to liberal-democratic legal systems. In this regard, one needs only to consider that the ultra-Maoist Constitution of 1975 established, in Article 13, that the socialist revolution led by the popular masses guarantees the freedom of expression of opinions and the full expression of points of view, also via the great debates and the mural newspapers (Chinese *dazibao*). The current 1982 Constitution envisages, in Article 35, that citizens have freedom of speech, the press, assembly, association, to travel and to manifest in the PRC. However, it is a matter of seeing whether the fundamental human rights of man have entered into the constitutional system of China. The answer, at least in the current state of constitutional evolution of the PRC, is undoubtedly negative. The rights of citizens exist, and are protected at the jurisdictional level, if and within the limits in which they are recognized by the Constitution and by law, reason for which there is no freedom of speech as a natural pre-constitutional law, owing to the fact that, on the contrary, the system can introduce restrictions that are justified by the socialist and collectivistic nature of communist China. From the standpoint of Chinese legal pragmatism, the law constitutes a mere instrument for the implementation of social policies, while it remains true that the best guarantor, interpreter and representative of the interests of citizens is still the State. As a corollary of this, in accordance with Article 53 of the 1982 Constitution, citizens have a duty to observe the Constitution and the laws, manifesting their obedience.

The PRC does not represent, based on the evidence, a state of liberal democracy, but rather a democratic dictatorship of the people, with the consequence that the autonomy of citizens and fundamental individual rights are subordinated to public interests and the collective good. Citizens who do not support the dictatorship of the proletariat become enemies of the people, reactionary, counter-revolutionaries,[288] and can be deprived of the benefit of fundamental rights. Thus, the tension/opposition of collectivist socialism (or community collectivism) *versus* liberal individualism permeates every aspect of the constitutional rights of citizens in the People's Republic. The theory of fundamental rights upheld

by the *Associazione Italia-Cina* and the *Istituto italiano per l'Africa e l'Oriente,* 22 and 23 October 1999), Roma, *Associazione Italia-Cina* (*Quaderni dell'Amicizia*, n. 2), 2000, 24 ff.; Id. (Ed.), *Il drago che parla. La riforma della stampa in Cina* (acts of the Milan convention, 18 January 2005), Milano, *Fondazione Italia Cina*, 2006; from a diachronic perspective, L. De Giorgi, *La rivoluzione d'inchiostro. Lineamenti di storia del giornalismo cinese 1815-1937*, Venezia, Cafoscarina, 2001. Re the Hong Kong *mass-media*, *cf.* J.M. Chan, C. Y.K. So, *The surrogate democracy function of the media. Citizens' and journalists' evaluations of media performance in Hong Kong*, in A. Romano, M. Bromley (Eds.), *Journalism and Democracy in Asia*, op cit., 66 ff.

288 Even if the Constitution, after the revision of 15 March 1999, no longer contemplates counter-revolutionary activity, replaced by the mention of the crimes that harm the security of the State; *cf.* G. Crespi Reghizzi, G. Crespi Reghizzi, *Verso il mercato e lo Stato di diritto: recenti riforme costituzionali in Cina*, in *Dir. pubbl. comp. eur.*, 1999, especially 497.

by the Chinese constitutionalism is therefore based not on the formalistic conception of natural human rights as metaphysical entities with an individualistic and pre-state connotation, but rather on the anti-formalistic, realistic or pragmatic conception of fundamental rights concretely recognized in each legal and social order, based on *standards* of rationality that take into account the graduation of collective values, general objectives to be achieved and (individual and superindividual) interests to be protected that is perceived in every particular social fabric and historical moment. In China, the constitutional rights of citizens are a product of the legal system, and possess an intrinsic political dimension, in contrast with the (vindicated) apolitical nature of individual rights in liberal democracies.

Freedom of speech is limited in the PRC by the necessary adherence to the CCP's political vision. In the absence of a widespread democratic political conscience, the approach to the right to freedom of speech can only be authoritarian,[289] and structural or institutional reforms are not sufficient to create a free market of ideas if the monopoly of political power is maintained by the Communist Party, which also holds – directly or via state bodies – absolute control over the mass media. Free expression of political ideas is not permitted in China; from here stems the use of alternative Chinese tools of political communication represented by anonymous wall newspapers (Chinese *dazibao*), almost a neoliberal form of "mural democracy",[290] or more recently the use of the Internet, governed by numerous laws, regulations and directives,[291] as well as new incriminating types that, having

289 *See*, in fact, T. Wright, *Accepting Authoritarianism. State-Society Relations in China's Reform Era*, Stanford (CA), Stanford University Press, 2010.

290 Hua Sheng, *Big Character Posters in China: A Historical Survey*, in *Journal of Chinese Law*, 1990, 234.

291 *See*: T. Facchin, *Cavalcare l'onda del dissenso: il web cinese, tra mobilitazioni dal basso e nuove strategie di controllo*, in *Inchiesta*, n. 177, July/September 2012, 68 ff.; I. Franceschini, *Cina.net – Post dalla Cina del nuovo millennio*, Preface by M. Del Corona, Milano, O barra O edizioni, 2012; E. Bertolini, *L'"apertura sorveglia": la via cinese alla* governance *e alla censura di internet*, in *Dir. pubbl. com eur.*, 2008, 1063 ff.; S. Bigatti, *Il grande* blog, in *Mondo cinese*, n. 126, 2006, 41.; G. Criveller, *Cina: La rivolta dei cyber-dissidenti*, in *Mondo e Missione*, May 2006, 60 ff.; F. Moneta, *Tecnocin@. Transmedia, videoarte, videogiochi tra Cina, Corea del Nord, Hong Kong*, Milano, Costa & Nolan, 2006 (with regards to the Chinese telecommunications market); F. Rampini, *Chi cambierà chi? Internet in Cina*, in *Aspenia*, n. 33, 2006, 62 ff.; A. Spalletta, *La penetrazione di Internet in Cina*, in *China News – Fuzzy Net. Materiali, analisi, documenti*, n. 3, September 2005, 84 ff.; Li Junqing, *La funzione di Internet nel processo di democratizzazione in Cina*, in *Mondo cinese*, n. 121, 2004, 44 ff.; F. Sapio, *Quarantacinque milioni di piccoli timonieri. Gli internauti cinesi e gli internet café a Pechino, ibidem*, n. 112, 2002, 35 ff.; C. Krönke, M.W. Müller, W. Yu, W.Tian (Eds.), *Paradigms of Internet Regulation in the European Union and China*, Baden-Baden, Nomos, 2018; A. Segal, *When China Rules the Web. Technology in Service of the State*, in *Foreign Affairs*, September/October 2018, online at www.foreignaffairs.com; S. Zhao (Ed.), *Chinese Authoritarianism in the Information Age: Internet, Media, and Public Opinion*, London/New York, Routledge, 2018; Y. Hu, *Three Features of China's Internet Legislation*, in *Chinese Law and Government*, 2016, n. 1, 1 ff.; W. Zhang, *The Internet and New Social Formation in China. Fandom Publics in the Making*, London/New York, Routledge, 2016; P. Sevastik, *Freedom of Expression and Opinion in the People's Republic of China and the Internet*, in *Scandinavian Studies in Law*, 2015, 253 ff.; P. Marolt, D.K. Herold (Eds.), *China Online. Locating Society in Online Spaces*, London/New York, Routledge, 2014; G. Yang, *Internet Activism & the Party-State in China*, in *Daedalus (Journal of the American Academy of Arts and Sciences)*, 2014, n. 2, 110 ff.; H. Zheng, *Regulating the Internet: China's Law and Practice*, in *Beijing Law Review*, 2013, 37 ff.; T. Bax, *Youth and Internet Addiction in China*, London/New

acknowledged the increasingly widespread use of information technology and telematics, are aimed at protecting *privacy*, sanctioning in particular the sale or illicit procurement, as well as the unlawful obtainment of personal information.[292] It is important to bear in mind, however, with regards to the limits of the "revolution" of the Internet in China, that

---

York, Routledge, 2013, on the problem of *internet addiction* (Chinese: *wangyin*), which has led to a sort of "electronic opium" (with the consequent "medicalization" of Internet overuse by "internet-addicted" people, through psychiatric interventions based on hypotheses of "mental disorder"); J. Leibold, *Blogging Alone: China, the Internet, and the Democratic Illusion?*, in *Journal of Asian Studies*, 2011, 1023 ff. (on the "Chinese-speaking blogosphere"); Liu Fengshu, *Urban Youth in China: Modernity, the Internet and the Self*, London/New York, Routledge, 2010; J. Damm, S. Thomas (Eds.), *Chinese Cyberspaces. Technological Changes and Political Effects*, London/New York, Routledge, 2006; Ding Wenlei, *Blogging for Fun and Profit. Should online journals be a money spinner?*, in *Beijing Review*, n. 19, 2006, 26 ff., especially *sub Censorship and Intellectual Blogging*, 27; K. Giese, *Challenging Party Egemony: Identity Work in China's Emerging* Virreal *Places*, Hamburg, German Overseas Institute (Deutsches Übersee-Institut, DÜI), Research Unit: Institute of Asian Affairs, *Working Papers Global and Area Studies*, n. 14, January 2006 (GOI-WP-14/2006) (on the internet "with Chinese characteristics"); Huang Wei, *Internet, the Second Coming*, in *Beijing Review*, 2006, n. 19, 2; T.G. Lum, *Internet Development and Information Control in the People's Republic of China*, Washington (DC), Congressional Research Service (CRS) of the Library of Congress, 2006; Lu Ling, *Online Survivors. Internet cafes must navigate strict government regulations to stay in business*, in *Beijing Review*, 2006, n. 14, 30 f.; Z. Tai, *The Internet in China. Cyberspace and Civil Society*, London/New York, Routledge, 2006; Zhou Yongming, *Historicizing Online Politics. Telegraphy, the Internet, and Political Participation in China*, Stanford, Stanford University Press, 2006; Wu Xu, *Red Net over China: China's New Online Media Order and its Implications*, in *Asian Journal of Communication*, 2005, 215 ff.; W. Guo, *Internet entre État-partie et société civile en Chine*, Paris, L'Harmattan, 2015; S. Arsène, *Internet et politique en Chine*, Paris, Karthala, 2011.

292 *Cf.* S. Wu, *La protezione delle informazioni personali nel diritto penale cinese*, in *Dir. informaz.*, 2013, 307 ff.,a commentary on the VII Novel of the Penal Code, approved by the VII session of the XI Standing Committee of the National People's Congress on 28 February 2009 and which entered into force on the same day. In particular, Art. 7 of VII Novel introduced Art. 253 – criminal code law of the PRC, whose three paragraphs establish that: "The person in charge of the organs of the State or of the financial, health, telecommunications, transport, education or other bodies that, in violation of the state provisions, sells or illegally offers to others the personal information of citizens obtained for reasons of their office or services, shall be punished, if the circumstances are serious, with imprisonment equal to or less than three years and a fine or with arrest and a fine or with a fine. Anyone who subtracts or otherwise unlawfully procures the aforementioned information shall be punished, if the circumstances are serious, in accordance with the preceding paragraph. If an entity commits any of the crimes referred to in the two preceding paragraphs, it shall be punished with a fine, while the direct general manager and the direct manager shall be punished according to the respective paragraphs" (the Italian version of the Chinese text is that contained in S. Wu, op cit., 308). The Chinese criminal code dates back to 1979, but over time has undergone radical and very significant changes especially those of 1997 (as well as those of 2015, on the subject of combating corruption). For example, in this regard, the 1979 text was made up of 192 articles, while now the criminal code includes 452 articles, as well as two attachments. To evaluate the changes, *see* the comparative text of the original criminal code, approved by II Session of the V National People's Congress on 1 July 1979 and which entered into force on 1 January 1980 (Italian translation by S. Wu, *Diritto penale del XXI secolo*, 2011, 133 ff.) and the current text of 30 June 2010, modified by the V session of the VIII National People's Congress on 14 March 1997, subsequently modified by the I–VII Novels, adopted between 1999 and 2009 (Italian translation by S.Wu, revised by the editor of the issue S. Vinciguerra, in *Diritto penale del XXI secolo*, 2010, 85 ff.). On the topic, in particular *see* G. Ajani, *Il diritto penale cinese in trasformazione*, in *Diritto penale del XXI secolo*, 2010, 29 ff., who, *inter alia*, speaks of a «re-codification of 1997» (*see* 32 f.).

> Those who had hoped that it meant the sudden emergence of a civil conscience and of opposition were disappointed. Most Internet users are interested in online game and sales sites or blogs about "lifestyles".[293]

In any case, in the (albeit precarious[294]) spaces of the Chinese media sphere, new opportunities are opening up, for example for investigative journalism, with significant repercussions on freedom of information,[295] pluralism of opinion and (even) expression of criticism and/or dissent.[296] Furthermore, according to data released in 2013 by the *China Internet Network Information Center* (CNNIC, in Chinese, 中国 互联 网络 信息 中心), 64.4% of young people in the PRC regularly surf the Net both to buy, play and also to be informed. Thus they number now over two hundred and thirty two million, or even 45.1% of the global "*netizens*" of the planet.[297] The statistical data of the CNNIC, updated to 2015, show that China is "the country with the largest number of users connected to the Internet".[298] The official statistics of the CNNIC, published in January 2016, also illustrate that in the PRC, 620 million people access the Internet using mobile phones, PDAs, *smartphones* or *tablets* (the so-called mobile web), that is 90% of the total number of Chinese internet users.[299] But control is penetrating. At the beginning of 2014, the President of the PRC (and Secretary General of the CCP) Xi Jinping took over the *Central Internet/Cyber Security and Informatization Leading Group* (*中央 网络 安全 和 信息 化 领导 小组*), to which also the Chinese Premier Li Keqiang as well as Liu Yunshan, former director of the *Party's Department of Publicity* (previously, the *Party's Department of Propaganda*[300]) belong.

---

293 Hence, J.-L. Rocca, *La società cinese*, (2010), Italian translation, Bologna, il Mulino, 2011, 97. Less pessimistic is the evaluation of Y. Zhu, J. Y.S. Cheng, *The Emergence of Cyber Society and the Transformation of the Public Policy Agenda-Building Process in China*, in *The China Review. An Interdisciplinary Journal on Greater China*, 2011, n. 2, 153 ff.

294 As well as being supervised by anonymous online commentators, who are actually agents of the Chinese government; *cf.* R. Han, *Manufacturing Consent in Cyberspace: China's "Fifty-Cent Army"*, in *Journal of Current Chinese Affairs*, 2015, n. 2, 105 ff.

295 Disciplined by the law of 17 January 2007, which entered into force on 1 May 2008. *See* W. Xiao, *La réforme de la liberté d'information en Chine: Analyse des fleux d'information*, in *Rev. intern. sc. adm.*, 2013, 849 ff. The law was approved after five years (2002–2007) of studies and debate (in the essay cited, *difficuté de traiter des demandes d'information sous un régime autoritaire, are critically analyses*). Lastly, on the *right of access to information* (ATI), *cf.* Y. Chen, *Halfway to Freedom of Information. The Legislative and Judicial Protection of the Right of Access to Information in China*, London/New York, Routledge, 2017.

296 *Cf.* L. De Giorgi, *Costruzione del consenso ed espressioni di pluralismo in Cina: il ruolo dei media*, in C. Meneguzzi Rostagni (Ed.), *La Cina luci e ombre. Evoluzione politica e relazioni esterne dopo Mao*, Milano, Angeli, 2010, 40 ff.

297 *See* Z. Nie, *Ai giovani cinesi piace fare surf nel web*, in *Cina in Italia*, n. 101, 2013, 28.

298 *Cf.* G. Negro, *Dalla Grande Muraglia alla "diplomazia di Internet"*, paper presented at the XV Conference of the *Associazione italiana studi cinesi*-AISC, held at the University of Macerata from 24 to 26 settembre 2015.

299 *See* D. Vacatello, *Pechino e la gestione dei nuovi media*, in *Aspenia*, n. 73, 2016, 127 ff., particularly 130-131.

300 *Cf.* J. Goldkorn, *The Chinese Internet: Unshared Destiny*, in G.R. Barmé, L. Jaivin, J. Goldkron (Eds.), *Shared Destiny. China Story Yearbook 2014*, Canberra, ANU (Australian National University) Press, 2015, 106 ff.

Lastly, on 7 November 2016, the NPC approved the new IT security law, which envisages, since its entry into force, in June 2017, stringent conditions and limitations for the use of the internet.[301]

If we assume that the Chinese people's democracy[302] follows the so called *top down* model, in the sense that the political-party elite directs public affairs for the benefit of the people, and therefore the Party, the State, and the (central and local) government realize collective interests as the sum of individual interests, then freedom of speech in the political field poses as a mere possibility of proposing "suggestions" for the better functioning of the government apparatus. The theory of constitutional rights in China, and in particular the institutional configuration of the freedom of speech, are therefore antithetical (a kind of inverted pyramid) compared to the construction of democracy according to the so-called *bottom up* model, for which the self-government of the people requires, as a pre-condition, the widest, most thorough and above all free expression of opinions on the relevant issues to be decided.

Ultimately, in the People's Republic of China, the constitutional freedom of speech is conditioned and limited by the need to comply with the cardinal principles of the Chinese path to socialism, the democratic dictatorship of the proletariat, the lead role of the CCP and the Marx-Leninist thought in the Maoist version. Moreover, in the absence of judicial control of constitutionality, there are essentially no limits for the public authorities in imposing restrictions on freedom of speech, nor does the exercise of fundamental rights appear guaranteed according to Western *standards*.

With regards to freedom of association,[303] it is proclaimed in Article 35 of the 1982 Constitution. The implementation of the constitutional provision took place not via ordinary law, but via administrative regulations. The State Council had approved certain provisional regulations on freedom of association in 1950; these provisions, ineffective

---

301 *See*, for a brief comment on the law, *Cyber-regulation. The noose tightens. Alarm over a new cyber-security law*, in *The Economist*, November 2016, 52.

302 On which *see*, in a vast literature, M. Miranda, *Democrazia con «caratteristiche cinesi»*, in R. Cavalieri, I. Franceschini (Eds.), *Germogli di società civile in Cina*, op cit., 41 ff.; B. Onnis, *Democrazia e autoritarismo nella Cina contemporanea*, in AA.VV., *Autoritarismi e democrazie in Africa e Asia*, Cagliari, Aipsa, 2005, 165 ff. (*Quaderni di studi africani e orientali* of the Historical-Political-International Department, sect. of History and Institutions of Non-European Countries -*Orientalia Kalaritana*); M. Delmas-Marthy, P.-É. Will (Eds.), *La Chine et la démocratie*, Paris, Fayard, 2007 (the work is composed of 894 pg.); Zhou Zhenghuan, *Liberal Rights and Political Culture. Envisioning Democracy in China*, London/New York, Routledge, 2010.

303 On which *see* S. Woodman, *Quelle liberté d'association en Chine? La promotion des organisations à but non lucratif est concomitante d'une restriction de la liberté d'association*, in *Perspectives chinoises*, n. 51, 1999, 17 ff.; Li Yuwen (Ed.), *Freedom of Association in China and Europe. Comparative Perspective in Law and Practice*, Leiden, Nijhoff, 2005. For some observations on the (constitutionally recognized) association law in relation to non-profit organizations (NGOs) in China, *see* Liu Xin, *L'influenza dello sviluppo delle Organizzazioni Non Governative cinesi sul diritto degli organi amministrativo*, in G. Rossi (Ed.), *Stato e società in Cina. Comitati di villaggio, organizzazioni governative, enti pubblici* (acts of the Rome convention, 2 December 2009), Torino, Giappichelli, 2011, 25 ff.

although not formally repealed during the anti-legalistic period (i.e. the "legal nihilism") of the Cultural Revolution, have been replaced since 1980 by over fifty administrative measures adopted mainly by the State Council and the Ministry of Civil Affairs. (MCA). After the attempts, severely repressed by the authorities, to start from the bottom, a genuine (student) democratic movement in China in 1989, culminating in the "incidents" of Tian'anmen Square in Beijing on 4 June of that year,[304] decree number 43 of 25 October 1989, was approved by the State Council, concerning the registration and management of social groups, which was aimed at subjecting to strict state control, all groups and social organizations.

To understand the objectives underlying the government decree concerning freedom of association, social groups and mass or popular organizations, it is sufficient to recall the nature of the strengthening and improvement of the CCP's leadership on the work of the Pan-Chinese Federation of Trade Unions,[305] the League of Young Communists of

---

304 *Cf.*: M. Francisci di Baschi, *Il dramma di piazza Tian'anmen*, in E. Collotti Pischel (Ed.), *Cina oggi. Dalla vittoria di Mao alla tragedia di Tian'anmen*, Roma-Bari, Laterza, 1991, 161 ff.; Wang Hui, *Il nuovo ordine cinese. Società, politica ed economia in transizione*, Preface by E. Masi, (1997), Italian translation, Roma, Manifestolibri, 2006, 19 ff.; M. Oksenberg, M. Lambert, L.R. Sullivan (Eds.), *Beijing Spring, 1989. Confrontation and Conflict. The Basic Documents*, Armonk (NY), Sharpe, 1990, and *ivi* especially. M. Manion, *Reluctant Duelists: The Logic of the 1989 Protests and Massacre*, XIII ff. (*sub Introduction*); R.V. DesForges, Luo Ning, Yen-bo Wu (Eds.), *Chinese Democracy and the Crisis of 1989. Chinese and American Reflections*, Albany (NY), State University of New York Press, 1992; T. Han, J. Li, *Tiananmen Square Spring 1989. A Chronology of the Chinese Democracy Movement*, Berkeley, Institute of East Asian Studies, University of California (UC Berkeley), 1992; C.E. Kobland, Liping Du, Joongrok Kwon, *Influence of Ideology in News Reporting: Case Study of New York Times' Coverage of Student Demonstrations in China and South Korea*, in *Asian Journal of Communication*, 1992, 64 ff.; S. Ogden, K. Hartford, L.R. Sullivan, D. Zweig (Eds.), *China's Search for Democracy. The Student and Mass Movement of 1989*, Armonk (NY), Sharpe, 1992; T. Wright, *The Perils of Protest. State Repression and Student Activism in China and Taiwan*, Honolulu, University of Hawai'i Press, 2001; Zhao Dingxin, *The Power of Tiananmen. State-Society Relations and the 1989 Beijing Student Movement*, Chicago, University of Chicago Press, 2001; J.-P. Béja (Ed.), *The Impact of China's 1989 Tiananmen Massacre*, London/New York, 2011. For a diachronic history of the Chinese democratic movement, *see* J.-P. Béja, *A la recherche d'une ombre chinoise: Le mouvement pour la démocratie en China (1919-2004)*, Paris, Éditions de Seuil, 2004. On the thinking of Chinese intellectuals post-Tian'anmen, *see* E. Pilz, *On the Analysis of Chinese Intellectual Discourses after Tiananmen*, in *Asian and African Studies* (journal editied by *Department of Asian and African Studies*, University of Ljubljana), *Special Issue: Conformity and Dissent in China*, 3 ff.

305 On the rights and organizational system of the Chinese trade union, *see* E. Carrabba, *L'organizzazione sindacale in Cina*, in *Mondo cinese*, n. 52, 1985, 29 ff. (Part I) and n. 53, 1986, 53 ff. (Part II); I. Franceschini, *Tra sindacato ufficiale e organizzazioni della società civile: nuove strategie di tutela dei diritti dei lavoratori nella Cina popolare*, in R. Cavalieri, I. Franceschini (Eds.), *Germogli di società civile in Cina*, op cit., 137 ff.; Id., *Lavoro e diritti in Cina. Politiche sul lavoro e attivismo operaio nella fabbrica del mondo*, Bologna, il Mulino, 2016; M. Zou, *Rapporti di lavoro con "caratteristiche cinesi"? Il diritto del lavoro cinese a un bivio storico*, in *Lav. e dir.*, 2012, 145 ff., especially 155 ff.; Biddulph, S. Cooney, *The Trade Union Law in the People's Republic of China*, in *Melbourne University Law Review*, 1993, 253 ff.; I. Franceschini, *The Broken Belt. The All-China Federation of Trade Unions and the Communist Party in the People's Republic of China*, in *Contemporanea. Riv. di storia dell'800 e del '900*, 2015, 67 ff.; J. Li, *Collective Contracts and Trade Unions in China*, in J. Basedow, S. Chen, M. Fornasier, U. Liukkunen (Eds.), *Employee Participation and Collective Bargaining in Europe and China*, Tübingen, Mohr Siebeck, 2016, 103 ff.; .J. Ye, *Reforming the Regulatory*

China and of the Pan-Chinese Women's Federation, issued on 21 December 1989 by the Central Committee of the Chinese Communist Party, which stated that it is absolutely forbidden for any group, association or organization to express political opinions contrary to those of the CCP.

The sixth plenary meeting of the XIV Central Committee of the CCP, held in October 1996, dealt with the problems related to the improvement of the work of associations and organizations in order to build a socialist spiritual civilization[306] with antagonistic characteristics compared to bourgeois liberalism. The outcome of this ideological debate within the Communist Party was the approval of two important documents: a) the circular of the General Affairs Office of the Central Committee of the CCP and the Office of General Affairs of the State Council concerning the strengthening of the management of social groups and of the people's units external to companies, promulgated as document number 22 of 1996 by the Secretariat of the CCP's Central Committee; and b) the circular of the State Council concerning the instructions of the MCA on the "rectification" of social groups, promulgated by the State Council Secretariat as document number 11 of 1997. Taking a joint position on the manner of governing, in the PRC, freedom of association in the sphere of non-profit organizations with the exclusion of political parties, the Party-State summit organs then established that public authorities must verify a number of aspects relating to the constitution and activity of groups, associations and organizations. They concern: a) the observance by the social groups of the laws, regulations and political directives of the CCP; b) the "political profile" of the subjects who hold institutional and positions of responsibility within groups, associations and organizations; c) the sectors of activity of the associations, with particular attention to the academic exchanges that are carried out in the field of the study of political, economic, juridical and theoretical sciences; d) any sources of funding from outside the Chinese territory that are used by associations and social organizations that carry out research and research activities in the social sciences sector; e) the accession of Chinese associations to independent international organizations; f) participation of foreign persons in groups, associations and organizations established and operating in the PRC; and g) the patrimonial, economic-financial and management status of the social organizations.

Mechanism for the Collective Labour Relationship in China: Diagnosis and Outlook, in U. Liukkunen, Y. Chen (Eds.), *Fundamental Labour Rights in China – Legal Implementation and Cultural Logic*, Berlin, Springer, 2016, 243 ff. For the history of the Chinese labour movement, *cf.* J. Chesneaux, *Les syndicats chinois 1919-1927*, Paris, Mouton, 1965; E.S. Hui, *Hegemonic Transformation. The State, Laws, and Labour Relations in Post-Socialist China, Basingstoke* (UK)/New York, Palgrave Macmillan, 2018; I. Franceschini, E. Nesossi, *State Repression of Chinese Labor NGOs: A Chilling Effect?*, in *The China Journal*, n. 80, 2018, 111 ff. On the role of the trade union representative in labour disputes, *see*, recently E. Signorini, *Le controversie di lavoro nell'Asian arbitration law*, in *Mass. giur. lav.*, 2014, 878 ff. The current *Trade Union Law* was approved in 1992 and amended in 2001.

306 The concept of civilization is recurrent in the examination of Chinese cultural heritage; *see* R. Zhang-Fernandez, *Précis de civilisation chinoise. De ses origines à nos jours*, Paris, L'Harmattan, 2014.

According to the aforementioned documents drawn up by the CCP and the State Council, social organizations are prohibited if they are dangerous for the security of the state and for the common interest of society, something that occurs in particular, in the opinion of the Chinese central party and state authorities, if the said organizations disseminate bourgeois and liberal ideas in the country, or even if they are participants in international or foreign organizations hostile to the People's Republic of China. In any case, social groups, mass organizations and citizens' associations must respect the law and the regulations of sub-legislative rank, nor can they act in such a way as to create "unpleasant" consequences for society.[307]

A cautious loosening of the tension and restrictions that characterize the normative vicissitudes of the freedom of association in the PRC occurred following two events, represented by the XV Congress of the Chinese Communist Party in September 1997 held under the banner of the *slogan* "small Government, large society",[308] which refers to a desired expansionary phase of civil society[309] and, therefore, to the extension of associative life in a climate of greater tolerance, as well as the accession of the People's Republic to the International Covenant on civil and political rights, signed by the PRC on 5 October 1998, in which Article 22 envisages freedom of association.

A new regulation of the matter was adopted by the State Council with two decrees, Numbers 250 and 251, issued on 25 October 1998 and published in the *People's Daily* respectively on 4 and 9 November, 1998. The first of these is dedicated to the registration and management of social groups, the second to the registration and management of people's units outside companies. These measures confirm, first of all, that associations can legitimately operate in the PRC on the condition that they are previously registered in accordance with current legislation. The registration must take place at the Ministry of Civil Affairs, with the caution that if the association or social organization intends to carry out its activity at national level, it is required to register at the MCA headquarters in Beijing. Instead, if the scope envisaged for the action of the constituting association is more circum-

307 Data on regularly registered social groups, organizations and associations are collected by the MAC and published in the Statistical Yearbook of China's Civil Affairs. On the emerging category of the *Party-organized non-governmental organizations* (PONGOs), *cf.* P.M. Thornton, *The Advance of the Party: Transformation or Takeover of Urban Grassroots Society?*, in *The China Quarterly*, 2013, 1 ff.

308 China is, in fact, the country of the slogans (Chinese: *kouhao*): hence G. Crespi Reghizzi, *Il diritto cinese oggi*, paper presented at the conference «*Italia – Cina: il ponte della comparazione giuridica*», op cit. In the literature, *see* the extensive analysis of S. Stafutti, G. Ajani, *Colpirne uno per educarne cento. Slogan e parole d'ordine per capire la Cina*, Torino, Einaudi, 2008. *See also*, recently F. Sapio, *Slogans and Ideological Formulas in China's Political Language*, a conference held 19 November 2015 at «L'Orientale» University of Naples.

309 On the development of civil society, albeit in the context of the Chinese authoritarian regime, *see*, to integrate and update R. Cavalieri, I. Franceschini (Eds.), *Germogli di società civile in Cina*, op cit., J.C. Teets, *Let Many Civil Societies Bloom: The Rise of Consultative Authoritarianism in China*, in *The China Quarterly*, 2013, 19 ff.

scribed to a territorial level, the registration must be done at the corresponding level of administrative division. The purpose, according to the enunciations of the decrees in question, is aimed at guaranteeing the freedom of association of Chinese citizens, protect the rights and legitimate interests of social groups, associations and organizations, and promote the construction of a socialist society in both material and spiritual dimensions.

The control over associations is not limited to their genetic moment, due to the fact that an annual inspection is envisaged by the territorial departments of the Ministry for Civil Affairs. Furthermore, some exemptions from the obligation of prior registration are established. They concern social groups, organizations and associations with respect to which the non-application of the rules on registration formalities is envisaged by means of special measures adopted by the State Council. That is to say, this refers to the popular organizations that are part of the Political-Consultative Conference of the Chinese people, the social groups established and operating within governmental bodies, companies, groups or institutions that have approved their functioning (the so-called second-level or second rank organizations). In particular, the main official mass organizations are exempted from the burden of registration and are represented by: a) the pan-Chinese Federation of trade unions; b) the Pan-Chinese Women's Federation; c) the League of Young Communists of China; d) the Federation of overseas Chinese; e) the Federation of literary and artistic circles; f) the Association of Chinese writers; g) the Chinese scientific association; and h) the Chinese Federation of Industry and Trade.

If we consider, finally, that the administrative regulations of 1998 on the implementation of the constitutional text on freedom of association envisage new and more demanding requirements than in the past to obtain registration, such as: membership of the association or social group of at least fifty individuals or, alternatively, no less than thirty institutional members; the availability for nationwide organizations of a patrimonial fund not less than 100,000 yuan and for local organizations not less than 30,000 yuan; possession by social groups who aspire to registration of the quality of a moral person (Chinese *faren*), and subsequently reflect on the fact that, on the one hand, it was forbidden with a life ban for former political prisoners to set up non-profit organizations and, on the other, the possibility of lodging appeals against the decisions taken by the public authorities on the subject of the creation, modification and extinction of associations, organizations and social groups, was deleted, if we sum up the total of all these factors and elements, it seems reasonable to conclude that the sub-legislative regulating of the constitutionally guaranteed freedom of association is based on strict and restrictive criteria, perhaps even more restrictive than the previous legislation.

1.8 Some Reflections from the Comparative Perspective: Is the *Suis Legibus Uti* Principle Also Valid for China?

If, retrospectively, we look at the historical development of the People's Republic of China's constitutional law, one can find that the victory of the Maoists in 1949 over the nationalists led to the approval of a provisional Constitution, called the "Common Program of the Political-Consultative Conference of the Chinese People". The first Constitution of the People's Republic of China, approved by the National People's Congress in 1954, was in many ways similar to the "Stalinist" Constitution adopted in the Soviet Union in 1936. The second constitution of the People's Republic, issued in 1975, reflected instead the juridical-nihilist climate and the ideological ultra-left approach typical of the period of the Cultural Revolution, i.e. the "renewal" movement called by Mao Zedong "the Great proletarian cultural revolution" and inaugurated by him in 1966, which led to serious violations of human rights, so much so that it could be considered a sort of "holocaust" for the Chinese people. Two years after Mao's death in 1976, the third constitution of the PRC was approved. The Constitution of 1978 marked the abandonment of the ideological ultra-left approach, opening the new era of "Reform and Opening", as well as that of the "socialist modernization". The new ideology, introduced by the will of Deng Xiaoping and labelled as "socialism with Chinese characteristics", was therefore accepted by the fourth People's Republic Constitution of 1982, which is still in force, albeit with the amendments that were subsequently made.

With the Fourth Constitution of 1982 there was a sort of return to the general structure of the first Constitution of 1954. However, the 1982 Constitutional Charter is considered by the Chinese leadership as an improvement of the juridical institutions built on the 1954 Constitution. Deng Xiaoping himself emphasized the role played by the so-called four cardinal principles in the 1982 Constitution. They are aimed, as a whole, at the economic modernization of China, and consist in the pursuit of the "socialist way", as well as the maintenance of the principle of popular democratic dictatorship, in the leadership of the country reserved for the Chinese Communist Party, and finally in Marxist–Leninist–Maoist political thought. The four principles, partially modified in the sense that the fourth principle, i.e. Marxist–Leninist–Maoist thought, was integrated so as to include also the thinking of Deng Xiaoping and the so-called related theory. of the three representations, are still enunciated in the Preamble of the Constitution of People's Republic of China.

The ideological foundations of the Chinese constitutional system are still firmly anchored in socialist thinking. In this regard, a reading is sufficient of the formulation of Article 1 of the 1982 Constitution. This provision states that the People's Republic of China is a socialist state founded on a popular democratic dictatorship led by the working class and based on the alliance of workers and peasants. Ultimately, the old Soviet expression of the "dictatorship of the proletariat" has been "*sinotised*" (i.e. "indigenized", from the

Chinese point of view) by the will of Mao in the new formulation of the "people's democratic dictatorship". But the Marxist–Leninist phraseology remains, with implications on the legal-constitutional level. In fact, the aforementioned wording of Article 1 of the 1982 Constitution contains the implicit attribution of the country's *leadership* to the Chinese Communist Party, which constitutes – according to the Marx-Engelsian theory and Leninist practice, the vanguard of the proletariat, which in turn, is identified in the working class. It follows, according to this (political-) constitutional approach, the position of the CCP that leads the country in representation of the proletariat and for the construction of the socialist society.

The 1982 Constitution has undergone important amendments over time. The amendments were introduced on four occasions, namely in 1988, 1993, 1999 and 2004. As a result of these, the policy of "Reform and Opening" was further elaborated. New concepts have been coined, which appear in logical connection with each other. Thus, the Constitution (or the Preamble) now speaks of the preliminary phase of socialism, socialism with Chinese characteristics, socialist market economy, government of the country through the law (*rule by law*) and the building of the *rule of law* (even if the Chinese expression *fazhiguojia* is probably better translated as a *rule of law*-based state), protection of the private sector of the economy, as well as protection of private property[310] and human rights.

As a result of these important innovations, the People's Republic of China no longer appears, as was originally the case, a totalitarian communist system, which controls every aspect of its citizens' social and economic life, but, with increasing intensity since the late seventies of the last century, following the launch of the defined policy of "Reform and Opening" commissioned by Deng Xiaoping, but rather an authoritarian political system, characterized in one direction by the presence of the single party which is at the same time the Party-State, and on the other hand by the impetuous development of the "socialist market economy", where the private sphere and, above all, the economic activity is now largely freed from the direct control of the Party-State, so that "socialism with Chinese characteristics" could perhaps be called "capitalism with Chinese characteristics". In other words, as has been stated, "The second modernity [understood, this latter, as the period from 1978 to the present] of China, favours economic liberalization, and absolutely not

---

310 *See* finally, L. Xie, *What is constitutional property in China?*, in *China-EU Law Journal*, 2015, 65 ff.; C. Wang, *The Constitutional Protection of Private Property in China. Historical Evolution and Comparative Research*, Cambridge, Cambridge University Press, 2016; S. Qiao, F.K. Upham, *China's Changing Property Law Landscape*, in M. Graziadei, L. Smith (Eds.), *Comparative Property Law. Global Perspectives*, Cheltenham (UK)/Northampton (MA, USA), Elgar, 2017, 311 ff.; A. Putz, *Das Eigentumsrecht in Deutschland und der VR China. Genese, Status quo und Entwicklungsperspektiven aus rechtsvergleichender Sicht*, Baden-Baden, Nomos, 2017; M. Timoteo, *Il trasferimento della proprietà immobiliare nel diritto cinese. Questioni di lingua e diritto*, in *Un giurista di successo. Studi in onore di A. Gambaro*, I, op cit., 863 ff.; X. Xia, *La garanzia costituzionale della proprietà in Cina*, Pisa, Pisa University Press, 2017.

that which is political".[311] This peculiar People's Republic model of neo-liberal transition, without prejudice to the uncertainties of the future,[312] is certainly alternative to the paradigms of the Western legal tradition, since the control mechanisms of the Party and government bureaucracy are always stringent with regards to the great industry, or that is to say, the so-called *big business*.[313]

In the sphere of public law, the constitutional datum must still be read in the double dimension of theory and practice, or, if one wishes, in the dimension of *formalism* ("*law in the books*") and *legal realism* ("*law in practice*"). On the one hand, one reads in the articles of the Constitution that the National People's Congress, that is to say the institution placed at the top of the Chinese system of state organs, is elected by the popular assemblies of the lower administrative levels, which in turn are invested of their respective functions via indirect elections or directly by the people for grassroots administrative rings. However, in the operational reality, all this conceals the non-controversial fact that nominations, at least for the medium-high levels of political representation, are uniquely selected by the Chinese Communist Party.

The implementation of the Constitution took place with the approval of the laws. The judicial system, after the innovations introduced with the policy of "Reform and Opening", has certainly been marked by improvements, above all with regards to the higher level of preparation of its judges, as well as with a substantial extension of litigations. However, in the field of the administration of justice, three fundamental problems remain, represented by: corruption, interference by politicians (party officials) in the issuing of rulings in individual cases, and the difficult enforcement of civil judgments as a result of the phenomena of "local protectionism". An important aspect concerns the function of the courts of justice with respect to constitutional ranked legislation. On the basis of a response issued by the *judicial committee* of the Supreme People's Court in 2001, concerning the dispute *Qi Yuling* v. *Chen Xiaoqi*, at the time pending before the Higher People's Court of the Shandong Province (which had sent a "request for instructions" to the Supreme People's Court),[314] seemed to open up new and unprecedented spaces for the direct application of the Constitution by the Chinese courts, up until perhaps foreshadowing the characteristics of the widespread control of the constitutionality of laws and legal normative acts (including administrative acts). Currently, however, following the new directives approved

---

311 Hence K. Vogelsang, *Cina. Una storia millenaria*, (2012), Italian translation, Torino, Einaudi, 2014, 536.

312 On which *see* R. Irvine, *Forecasting China's Future. Dominance or Collapse?*, London/New York, Routledge, 2016.

313 *See*, in this sense, the broad analysis of C. Li, *China's Centralized Industrial Order. Industrial Reform and the Rise of Centrally Controlled Big Business*, London/New York, Routledge, 2014.

314 *Cf.* R.J Morris, *China's Marbury: Qi Yuling v. Chen Xiaoqi – The Once and Future Trial of Both Education and Constitutionalization*, in *Tsinghua China Law Review*, 2010, 273 ff., in addition to M. Mazza, *Repubblica popolare cinese: Verso l'introduzione del controllo giurisdizionale (diffuso) di costituzionalità degli atti normativi?*, in *Dir. pubbl. comp. eur.*, 2002, 942 ff.

in subiecta materia by the Supreme People's Court in 2008 (which, therefore, replace the instructions given in 2001), there is no doubt that the courts do not have the power to review the constitutionality of laws and administrative provisions, and indeed the courts of the PRC cannot make any reference, in their decisions, to the rules of the Constitution, which are therefore not directly applicable by the courts, with the inevitable repercussions on the inadequate protection of the constitutional rights of citizens,[315] thus constituting, among other things, an obstacle to the judicial protection of human dignity.[316]

If, therefore, the expressions *rule of law* and human rights have now entered the legal lexicon of the People's Republic, the same cannot be said for the term (and the related concept of) "constitutionalism" (i.e. in Chinese, *xianzheng*).[317] Nor is it a merely theoretical question, which is instead revealing of the peculiar Chinese method of "exercising one's own laws" (*suis legibus uti*). This is demonstrated, *inter alia*, by the fact that the writer, human rights activist and intellectual Liu Xiaobo,[318] a supporter of the need to introduce the principles of liberal constitutional democracy in China and, therefore, committed to collecting signatures for the manifesto known as "Charta 08" (Chinese: "零八 宪章")[319] (its name evoking the document "Charter 77" prepared by Czechoslovak dissidents in the seventies of the last century), was subjected to a criminal trial on charges of sedition ("Anti-state subversion",[320] and following the judicial proceedings, Liu himself – winner of Nobel

315 On this topic *see*, G. Zhu, *Weak Courts, Weak Rights: Assessing the Realisation of Constitutional Rights in PRC Courts*, in *Hong Kong Law Journal*, 2013, 713 ff.; D. Han, F. Mélin-Soucramanien (Eds.), *Le contrôle de constitutionallité en France et en Chine*, Paris, Dalloz, 2014; W. Wang, *La mise en œuvre d'un contrôle efficace de constitutionalité en China*, in *Rev. fr. dr. const.*, 2014, 413 ff.; Id., *Le contrôle de constitutionnalité en Chine au regard de l'expérience française*, prefazione di A. Roux and B. Jin, Aix-en-Provence, Presses Universitaires d'Aix-Marseille, 2014; Y. Wang, *Verfassungskontrolle in China. Eine historische und politische Darstellung*, Berlin/Münster, LIT Verlag, 2016. On future prospectives *see also*, M. Mazza, *Un modello confuciano di giustizia costituzionale per la Cina del XXI secolo?*, in *Dir. pubbl. comp. eur.*, 2014, 1002 ff.; J. Fan, *Constitutional Transplant in PRC: The Communism Russian Legacy and Globalized Era Challenge*, a paper presented at the international conference of the *BRICS group in the spotlight. An interdisciplinary approach*, in *Federalismi.it. Rivista di diritto pubblico italiano, comparato, europeo*, n. 20/2014, on the website www.federalismi.it.

316 This was revealed recently, Z. Li, *Vers l'avènement de la dignité humaine en Chine: d'un droit civil à un principe constitutionnel*, in B. Feuillet-Liger, K. Orfali (Eds.), *La dignité de la personne: quelle réalités? Panorama international*, Preface by M. Delmas-Marty, Bruxelles, Bruylant, 2016, 389 ff.

317 In China, after the 18th CCP Congress in November 2012, a lively debate is ongoing re the compatibility between constitutionalism and socialism with Chinese characteristics: *see* H. Piquet, *Le «rêve chinois» en question: le débat sur le constitutionnalisme in Chine*, in *Rev. fr. dr. const.*, 2014, 389 ff.; D. Cai, *Transformation sociale et développement du constitutionnalisme en Chine*, in *Rev. fr. adm. pub.*, n. 150, 2014, 327 ff.

318 On whom, as an intellectual personage, *see* Varriano, *Xiu Liaobo: l'eresia della coerenza*, paper presented at the conference *Studiosi eretici. Anticonformismo, autonomia di giudizio e oppressione ideologica in tempi remoti e studi recenti*, held from 19 to 20 May 2015 at the Department of Asia, Africa and Meditterraneo of "L'Orientale", University of Naples.

319 *See "China's Charter 08" [unofficial translation by Perry Link]*, in *The New York Review of Books*, 15 January 2009.

320 For details of the accusation, *see* P. Barbieri, *Gli intellettuali e il carcere*, in *Quilibri. La rivista di chi legge*, May/June 2016, 21 f., especially 22.

Peace Prize in 2010[321] – was sentenced in December 2009 to eleven years in prison (a sentence confirmed in appeal in February of the following year).[322]

Even in the light of the afore-mentioned judicial case, one can conclude that, in view of a comparative analysis of the forms of contemporary constitutionalism, the experience of the People's Republic is still part of social-communist constitutionalism, namely Marx-Leninist constitutionalism, due to the fact that the principle of the separation of powers and *checks and balances* mechanisms are both absent in the system of the People's Republic. If, then, one adds that civil rights and fundamental human rights are guaranteed subject to their recognition by the State, and that there is also no judicial control over the constitutionality of legislative acts and the measures adopted by the Government, one reaches the current nature of authoritarian status of the People's Republic of China, which cannot even be considered as a hybrid constitutional regime, in which elements of liberal constitutionalism coexist with aspects of the so-called hybrid constitutionalism, given the absolute preponderance of the Party-State in the functioning of public structures,[323] resulting in the Constitution of the PRC assuming a merely semantic or nominal value,[324] rather than a real normative value.[325]

---

321 *Cf.* T. Benedikter, *Conferimento del Nobel per la pace al dissidente cinese Liu Xiaobo*, on the website www.gfbv.it. (doc. dated 9 December 2010). Liu is the first Chinese personage (residing in China) to have been named Nobel Peace Prize.

322 On the criminal proceedings against Liu Xiaobo, *see* J.-P. Béja, H. Fu, E. Pils (Eds.), *Liu Xiaobo, Charter 08 and the Challenges of Political Reform in China*, Hong Kong, Hong Kong University Press, 2012. On 26 June 2017, Liu Xiaobo was released by the Chinese authorities for health reasons; the following 13 July, Liu died in the hospital (*see Liu Xiaobo. A dying dissident*, in *The Economist*, July 2017, 41; G. Chen, *Liu Xiaobo e la dittatura del partito unico*, in *Internazionale*, July 2017, 18). For an analysis of the distinction between declared dissidents, who are usually harassed and persecuted by the Chinese authorities, and critical intellectuals, who are more or less tolerated (depending on the periods) E. Frenkiel, *Parler politique en Chine. Les intellectuels chinois pour ou contre la démocratie*, Paris, PUF, 2014.

323 The so called *Party-run China.*

324 Using the categories developed by K. Loewenstein, *Political Power and the Governmental Process*, Chicago (IL), University of Chicago Press, 1957, 147 ff.

325 Naturally, nothing prevents, and this is indeed the wish in the West, that the "nominal" Constitution evolves into a "normative" Constitution, as (well) highlight. Groppi, *Tra costituzionalismo globale ed eccezionalismo: diritti e libertà nel sistema costituzionale cinese nel XXI secolo*, op cit., 16 f., test and nt. 62; M. Delmas-Marty, *Constitutions, Constitutionnalisation*, in M. Delmas-Marty, R. Guillaumond (Eds.), *La constitutionnalisation du droit en Chine et en France. Rétrospective, perspectives, prospective*, Paris, Pedone, 2017, 9 ff., and *ivi* see *sub Des Constitutions virtuelles aux Constitutions réelles*, 11 ff. However, the premises – even those recent – do not seem encouraging. The directive adopted by the CCP in April 2013 (unpublished), supplemented by the (recent) subsequent party directive n. 9 of August 2013 (the latter published in September of the same year), both addressed to the Chinese universities in relation to teaching in political and juridical subjects, contain the enunciation of seven issues that are forbidden by university teaching (the so-called seven taboos of higher education, or seven subjects off limits for teaching). However, in the first place on this list, aimed at opposing (by prohibition) "ideological dangers", appears "western constitutional democracy", (*see* H. Piquet, *Le «rêve chinois» en question: le débat sur le constitutionnalisme in Chine*, op cit., 402 ff.).

Undoubtedly, important steps forward in the direction of the construction of the *rule of law* (*Fazhi*) in China have been made, among which emerges the inclusion in Article 33 of the Constitution, modified in 1999, of the assertion that the State respects and protects human rights, as well as the approval of the law on legislation of 2000, relevant in terms of the hierarchy of the sources of law. However, the absence of a normative dimension of the Constitution, which still has an essentially political-programmatic nature, prevents the realization of the guarantee of the Constitution (in the Kelsenian sense), i.e. the introduction of a control (not "political", but jurisdictional and effective) of the constitutionality of the laws.

In conclusion, the fact is that, according to me, the constitutional legitimacy of the Chinese institutional system subsists and has characteristics of peculiarity, indeed of uniqueness. This, in the sense that power is divided, with the attribution of political power to the Party and juridical-administrative power to the State, according to the model of the Party-State. The "constitution" of the Party establishes the perimeter of the Constitution of the State, giving rise to a dual constitution,[326] with the first (i.e. the party constitution) which establishes the evolutionary dynamics of the second (i.e. the state Constitution).[327] Within these institutional and organizational parameters,[328] Chinese "constitutionalism" itself can be considered legitimate.[329]

---

326 On which *see* S. Wang, *Emergence of a Dual Constitution in Transitional China*, in *Hong Kong Law Journal*, 2015, 819 ff., which considers Chinese constitutionalism to be influenced by Maoism and Sovietism, but not by Western legal thought. Contemporary Confucianism (*cf. supra*, in numerous places) obviously must not be neglected; *see* J. Chan, *Confucian Perfectionism. A Political Philosophy for Modern Times*, Princeton (NJ), Princeton University Press, 2015. *Cf.* also B. Mottura, *Il costituzionalismo è un valore occidentale? Riflessioni su un dibattito dell'era di Xi Jinping*, paper presented at the *X Dies Academicus* held in Milan from 19 to 21 October 2017 at the Class of Studies on the Far East of the Accademia Ambrosiana, on the topic of *Interpretazioni reciproche della diversità in ambito etico e giuridico*.

327 *Cf.* J.C. Mittelstaedt, *Understanding China's Two Constitutions: Re-Assessing the Role of the Chinese Communist Party*, in *Social Science Research Network* (http://ssrn.com), doc. dated 14 September 2015.

328 Which, moreover, presents a division with respect to the determining elements of the systems ascribable to the socialist family; *see* L. Pegoraro, *Approccio classificatorio "fuzzy" ed elementi determinanti nel diritto costituzionale comparato*, in P. Borsellino, S. Salardi, M. Saporiti (Eds.), *L'eredità di Umberto Scarpelli*, Torino, Giappichelli, 2014, 85 ff., especially 112. *See also* that which was states *ante, sub Introduction*.

329 *See* L.C. Backer, *The Party as Polity, The Communist Party, and the Chinese Constitutional State: A Theory of State-Party Constitutionalism, Penn State Legal Studies Research Paper No. 05-2009*; Id., *Party, People, Government, and State: On Constitutional Values and the Legitimacy of the Chinese State-Party Rule of Law System*, in *Boston University International Law Journal*, 2012, 331 ff. (where is stated at 331, that «The people speak through the Party but act through the State»); X. Ding, *Law According to the Chinese Communist Party: Constitutionalism and Socialist Rule of Law*, in *Modern China. An International Journal of History and Social Sciences*, 2017, 322 ff.; J.-P. Cabestan, *The Party runs the show: how the CCP controls the state and towers over the government, legislature and judiciary*, in W.Wo-Lap Lam (Ed.), *The Routledge Handbook of the Chinese Communist Party*, London/New York, Routledge, 2018, 75 ff., and *ivi* also E. Pils, *The Party and the law*, 248 ff.

1.9 Appendix: The Institutional Design of the "Other" China – A Brief Account on the Constitutional and Legal System of the Republic of China/Taiwan

1.9.1 General and Historical Background

Taiwan is quite a useful misnomer: useful because it is both a toponym (indicating the roughly 36,000 km^2 sub-tropical island previously known as Formosa, in the North-Western Pacific Ocean, next to Mainland China, home to over 23 million people, and where the official language is Mandarin Chinese) and an ethnonym ("Taiwanese" actually, reminding of the identity conundrum experienced by the islanders, itself intertwined with the wider issue of recognition and relationship with – the rest of? – China); and a misnomer because it simply is not the proper name for the subject of this section.

As a matter of fact, the subject of this section has more than one denomination, depending on the institutional nature of the interlocutor and on what political environment it finds itself in: in sport events and in APEC meetings the country is called "Chinese Taipei"; vis à vis the WTO it is called "Separate Customs Territory of Taiwan, Penghu, Kinmen and Matsu"; newspapers and passers-by call it simply "Taiwan"; the few countries that recognize it, and its own government – albeit reluctantly – officially have to call it the "Republic of China" (*Zhonghua Minguo*), or simply the ROC.

The reasons that explain this abundance of names for the same political entity boil down to limited international recognition and the troubled relationship with the People's Republic of China (*Zhonghua Renmin Gongheguo*, PRC), which in turn owe to the peculiar historical developments of this land that, to be understood, deserve a brief account.

Ethnic Chinese or Han (*Hanzuren*) began migrating to Taiwan, already long-inhabited by Austronesian indigenous people (or Taiwanese aborigines, currently around 530,000, or 2.3% of the total population) as early as A.D. 500. The island became a base for trade for Dutch then Spanish traders since 1624, then it was briefly and partially ruled by the Koxinga-established Kingdom of Tungning/*Dongning* (allegiant to the already-overthrown Ming dynasty (1368–1644)), from 1661 to 1683, when it was eventually annexed by China's Manchu dynasty, the Qing (1644–1912), that kept it until 1895. China was then forced to cede Taiwan in perpetuity to the Empire of Japan after a military defeat and the Treaty of Shimonoseki: the island remained a Japanese colony for 50 years, until the end of the Second World War and Japan's unconditional surrender on 2 September 1945, when Taiwan was handed back to China and the Treaty of Shimonoseki was nullified. Meanwhile, in Mainland China, the Qing dynasty had been substituted by the Republic of China at the beginning of 1912, an event followed by a long period of turbulence and internal political instability. In 1949, civil war in the Mainland resulted in the Communist victory over the Nationalist forces. Generalissimo Chiang Kai-Shek (Jiang Jieshi, 1887–1975), the leader of the Nationalist party (Kuomintang/*Guomindang*, KMT),[330] and 2 million of his followers and troops fled to Taiwan ("Mainlanders" nowadays make up roughly 13% of the population) and re-established the KMT-led ROC central government there, proclaiming Taipei the provisional capital of Nationalist China, declaring Martial Law and readying for a take-over of China that never came to be. In the following decades the island has prospered economically, and has been democratized since the late 1980s. Since then, Taiwan and mainland China have had distinct legal and political systems.[331] The "Statute for Agriculture, Mining, Industry and Commerce During the Extraordinary Period" (1938) and the "Temporary Provisions Effective During the Period of General National Mobilization for the Suppression of Communist Rebellion" (1942) gave KMT-led authorities the power to control resources, as well as establish political dominance over freedom of news, speech, press, communication, assembly and association during wartime, installing a de facto dictatorship in Taiwan.[332]

The PRC officially replaced the ROC in the United Nations Organization in 1971 (Resolution 2758), and the UN expelled the representatives of the Nationalist government from its organs and organizations: more and more countries followed suit by switching recognition and, as to April 2019, the ROC is officially recognized by only sixteen UN member states (out of 193, plus 2 observers) and by the Holy See, its only diplomatically in Europe.

Martial Law was terminated in 1987 and the Period of National Mobilization officially ended on 1 May 1991: with democratization taking place and with various constraints of the constitution lifted, reforms proceeded swiftly, along with the integration of western legal concepts into ROC Law.[333] A thaw between the two sides of the Taiwan Strait ensued and the first official talks regarding reunification were held, where both sides committed to uninterrupted dialog, symbolized by the so-called "1992 Consensus", often rendered as

---

330 The other major party in the ROC, the Democratic Progressive Party (DPP) seeks detachment from China and advocates, with varying degrees of vehemence and resolve, independence of Taiwan from the ROC. The DPP currently ruling, holds the majority of seats in the legislature since 2016, its former chairwoman Tsai Ying-wen (Cai Yingwen) is the President of the ROC since the same year, and the current premier belongs to the party as well.

331 The relevant literature, from both the political and legal points of view, is extremely vast. For an assessment, by this author, of the intertwining between Party and State in the PRC, *see* M.E. Delmestro, *The Communist Party & the Law: an outline of formal and less formal linkages between the CPC and the other legal institutions in the People's Republic of China*, in *Suffolk University Law Review*, 2010, Vol. XLIII, n. 3, 681-700.

332 For a general overview, *see* Wang Tay-sheng, *The Legal Development of Taiwan in the 20th Century: Toward a Liberal and Democratic Country*, in *Pacific Rim Law & Policy Journal Association*, 2002, N. 3.

333 The first free elections took place in 1996, and in 2000 Chen Shui-bian, a DPP politician, was elected president, the first in Taiwan not belonging to KMT.

"'One China', with each side maintaining its own interpretation of its meaning".[334] The question of eventual reunification between Taiwan and Mainland China has morphed into the question about independence, and is still the dominant political issue, as political and diplomatic pressure from the PRC limits the ROC's ability to engage in the international arena.

Having provided this necessary historical overview, a closer look the main constitutional and legal features of the ROC in Taiwan can be taken. From the point of view of comparative law, the legal system of the ROC is mainly a branch of the European Continental Law system (Civil Law): in Qing China, the German Civil Code was introduced in the later years of the dynasty, emulating Japan, and it later formed the basis of the law of the ROC, which remains in force today in Taiwan. In addition, Korea and Taiwan, former Japanese colonies, have been directly influenced by the Japanese legal system[335] itself. This Civil Law backbone is only laced with traces of traditional Chinese customary law.[336] In line with the Civil Law tradition, the law in the ROC is centred around six main legal collections, known as the "Six Codes" (*Liu Fa*):

1. the Constitution (*Xianfa*);
2. the Civil Code (*Minfa*);
3. the Code of Civil Procedure (*Minshi susong fa*) and associated laws;
4. the Criminal Code (*Xingfa*);
5. the Code of Criminal Procedure (*Xingshi susong fa*) and associated laws;
6. the Administrative laws (*Xingzheng fa*).

The current Constitution of the ROC is the 5th since the founding of the Republic,[337] was enacted on 25 December 1946, promulgated on 1 January 1947 and officially adopted on 25 December 1947. For a fundamental statue duly aspiring to have substantial force, the ROC Constitution did not enjoy an easy life: it was repealed on 1 October 1949 in Mainland China with the founding of the PRC; and its provisions guaranteeing civil and political rights were "frozen" and made inert in Taiwan due to the "Temporary Provisions" and the Martial Law mentioned earlier. After the lifting of the Martial Law in 1987 and the repealing of the Temporary Provisions in 1991 the Constitution exited abeyance, only to

334 The "1992 Consensus" has been questioned by the then DPP Chairwoman Tsai Ying-wen soon after her election as President of the ROC in 2016, prompting a sudden cooling and hardening of China's attitude towards Taiwan.

335 At the beginning of the Meiji Era in the second half of the XIX century, Japan made European legal systems, especially the civil law of Imperial Germany and France, the primary models for its own legal and judicial system.

336 *See* Chiu Hungdah, Fa Jyh-Pin, *Taiwan's Legal System and Legal Profession*, Baltimore (MD), University of Maryland School of Law, 1994.

337 An English translation of the ROC Constitution can be found in the Laws and Regulations Database of the ROC, at: https://law.moj.gov.tw.

almost immediately be amended to reflect the territorial loss of Mainland China (dating back to 1949) and to ease cross-Straits relations.[338]

The Constitution, a 175-article, 14-chapter-long document (plus a preamble) already envisioning the ROC as a unitary semi-presidential constitutional republic (mixing presidential, parliamentary and cabinet systems), finally also came to form the basis for a multi-party democracy. The Constitution incorporates (and positively mentions) the "Three Principles of the People" (*San Min Zhuyi*), Sun Zhongshan's (Sun Yat-sen, the Founding Father of the ROC, 1866-1925) core ideological legacy, also hellenized as the doctrine of "Tridemism": the three principles are roughly translatable in English as Nationalism (*Minzu Zhuyi*), Democracy (*Minquan Zhuyi*), and People's Welfare or Well-being (*Minsheng Zhuyi*). The Three Principle have constituted the ideological base of the KMT since its origins and, despite being stressed and revered until the 1990s, they nowadays are met by the general populace either with indifference or with the preference to reinterpret them in a local Taiwanese context rather than in a pan-Chinese one.

The Constitution embodies the ideal of sovereignty of the people, guarantees human rights and freedoms, designs a political system with five branches and a local self-government system, ensures a balanced division of powers between the central and local authorities, and stipulates fundamental national policies. Starting in the 1990s, seven waves of constitutional amendments (1991, 1992, 1994, 1997, 1999, 2000, 2004) radically altered various aspects of the state institutions of ROC: these revisions and amendments, collectively known as the "Additional Articles of the Constitution of the ROC",[339] were one of the main instruments of democratization and constitute a still semi-detached legal corpus laying down the reformed institutional framework presently in force in the ROC.[340]

338 The Additional Articles of the Constitution of the ROC use the term "Free Area (of the ROC)" to refer to the territories under the jurisdiction of the government of the ROC, namely the island groups of Taiwan, Penghu, Kinmen, Matsu and minor islands and islets. The remaining part of the territory of the ROC, under communist control, is called "Mainland Area". These terms have been retained to the present day in the ROC legislation. The Additional Articles delegate numerous rights to exercise the sovereignty, including that of electing the President and the Legislature, to citizens residing in the "Free Area". These terms were first used with the promulgation of the first set of amendments to the Constitution in 1991 and have been retained in the most recent revision, ratified in 2005. Pursuant to Art. 10 of the Additional Articles (promulgated on 1 May 1991), the ROC enacted the "Act Governing Relations between the People of the Taiwan Area and the Mainland Area" to serve as the main legal tool for the interaction between inhabitants of both sides of the Strait. These provisions configure the ROC as a country that claims in principle sovereignty over the entirety of its ancestral territory, but that constitutionally and legally self-restrains its jurisdiction and authority to a fraction of it.

339 An English translation of the articles, apart from the database mentioned above, can also be found here: https://english.president.gov.tw/Page/95.

340 A partial account of the scholarly debate at the time of the last wave of amendments can be found at: www.wilsoncenter.org/sites/default/files/No125.pdf.

1.9.2 Political System, Government, Judicial System and Administrative Divisions

As hinted above, the principle of the separation of powers was (and is still to a remarkable extent) taken so seriously in the ROC Constitution that state power there is penta-partite, rather than tri-partite as in virtually all the countries that employ that principle. Instead of simply displaying the usual division between Legislative, Executive and Judiciary power, there are two additions: Examination power and Control/Audit power. This constitutional "oddity", probably the most striking and unique feature of the ROC political system, can be tracked back to the ancient Chinese tradition of Imperial Examinations (*Keju*) to gain access to the Civil Service, and to the system of supervision and public censors employed by various dynasties, two peculiar and revered institutions that republican China saw fit to be somehow retained in the new legal framework. Until the 2005 entry into force of the last wave of constitutional amendments, this five-power/five-branch constitutional structure was mirrored by a seven-institution makeup: the Presidency and the National Assembly, both representing the unity of the country and the totality of state power, and the five branches, embodied by the five Yuan/*Yuan*. Following the constitutional revisions started in the 1990s, the National Assembly has been abolished but the five-branch/five-Yuan system has been retained, even though the authority and functions allocated have been recalibrated so that the architecture now resembles a bit the more familiar threefold system.

Table 1 Organizational chart of the main state institutions of the ROC prior to the reforms.

President and Vice-President			**National Assembly**	
Office of the President, National Security Council			**334 delegates representing "all of China"**	
Elected by the National Assembly, 6-year term, 2-term limit			**Approves constitutional amendments introduced by the Legislative Yuan**	
Executive Yuan	**Legislative Yuan**	Judicial Yuan	Examination Yuan	**Control Yuan**
Premier	Unicameral, 3-year terms	15 justices	21 app. members, 6-year terms	223 elected members
Ministries	225 seats		2 Ministries	1 Ministry

In **bold**: elected central state organs with parliamentary powers. App.: appointed.

Table 2 Organizational chart of the main state institutions of the ROC after the reforms.

		President and Vice-President		
		Office of the President, National Security Council		
		Direct election, 4-year term, 2-term limit		
Executive Yuan	**Legislative Yuan**	Judicial Yuan	Examination Yuan	Control Yuan
Premier	Unicameral, 4-year terms	15 justices	21 app. members, 6-year terms	29 appointed members
Ministers	113 seats		2 Ministries	1 Ministry

In **bold**: elected central state organ with parliamentary powers. App.: appointed.

- National Assembly (*Guomin Dahui*). Its main functions were to elect and recall the president and vice-president, and to amend the Constitution. After passing the last amendments to the Constitution and thus exhausting its purpose of existence (not without debate and clashes with the Legislative Yuan), the National Assembly (then made up of 334 delegates) voted to abolish itself in 2005 and to transfer its functions to the Legislative Yuan (*see below*).
- President (*Zongtong*). The president is head of state and commander-in-chief of the armed forces, represents the nation in foreign relations, and is empowered to appoint the members of four out of the five Yuan, including the president of the Executive Yuan, or premier. The president and vice-president are directly elected since 1996, serve terms of four years and may be re-elected once only. Most past presidents have been the leaders of the ruling party, thus enhancing the president's powers well beyond what was constitutionally conceived, and making the political system presidential in practice, despite the fact that the Constitution set forth a mixed presidential, cabinet and parliamentary system. Through both constitutional revision and practice, the system now is often described as semi-presidential, with the presidency seen as the locus of political authority, leading to conflicts with the premier and the Legislative Yuan in case of different political orientation of those organs.[341]

  Interestingly, the president or vice-president can be dismissed from office (*jiezhi*) in two ways: removal (*bamian*) in case of mischarge of political responsibilities, and impeachment (*tanhe*), in case of mischarge of legal responsibilities. Removal is achieved through a popular ballot after an ad hoc decision is passed by the Legislative Yuan, but cannot be invoked in the first year of the presidency; when unsuccessful, it cannot be initiated again during the remainder of the term. Impeachments as well is initiated by

341 Until 2016, the Legislative Yuan has always been controlled by a KMT-led, "pan-blue" majority. President Lee Teng-hui (Li Denghui, president: 1988-2000), despite belonging to the KMT had frequent disputes with his party. President Chen Shui-bian (Chen Shuibian, president: 2000-2008) belonged to the DPP.

the Legislative Yuan but decided by the justices of the Judicial Yuan, sitting as Constitutional Tribunal (*Xianfa Fating*).

- Executive Yuan (*Xingzheng Yuan*). It comprises eight ministries and several commissions and agencies, whose heads are appointed by its president (the premier, the second most important political figure in the ROC,[342] and second in the presidential line of succession, after the vice-president) and form the Executive Yuan Council, commonly referred to as the Cabinet. The premier bears overall responsibility for formulating and implementing programs and must report regularly to the Legislative Yuan. Neither the president's appointment of the premier nor the premier's appointment of ministers are subject to confirmation by the Legislative Yuan.
- Legislative Yuan (*Lifa Yuan*). The unicameral ROC legislature is made up of 113 legislators elected for 4-year terms,[343] who cannot concurrently hold posts in any other branch of the system. Besides reviewing and enacting legislation, the legislature conducts hearings on policy matters, examines budgetary bills and monitors government agencies. Presidential appointments of the fifteen grand justices of the Judicial Yuan and of the members of the Examination Yuan and Control Yuan must be confirmed by the Legislative Yuan.

  Constitutional amendments, previously within the purview of the now-abolished National Assembly, must now be proposed by at least one-fourth of lawmakers, adopted by three-fourth of the members present, and approved by the voters through a nationwide referendum (ballots must be cast by an absolute majority of voters, with at least a one-half approval rate).
- Judicial Yuan (*Sifa Yuan*). It operates the nation's system of courts and is similar in organization and functions to judicial organs in most Western political systems. It is composed of a Council of Grand Justices (15 judges), that acts as a Constitutional Court, and a Committee on the Discipline of Public Functionaries.[344] The justices provide rulings on the following categories of cases: a) interpretation of the Constitution;

342 Between 1975 and 1978, when Chiang Ching-kuo (Jiang Jingguo, Chiang Kai-shek's son and political heir) was concurrently premier and head of the ruling KMT, most observers regarded him as the nation's central political figure, rather than president Yen Chia-kan (Yan Jiakan), and the formal political system as more a cabinet or parliamentary one. Under president Lee, president and premier (Hau Pei-tsun/Hao Baicun) were locked in a dispute that evolved in a minor constitutional crisis since the president could at that time only appoint but nor remove the premier from office. The legal relationship between president and premier was altered following the 1997 amendments, which strengthened the president, pushing the system slightly towards the presidential end of the typological spectrum.

343 Seventy-three legislators are elected under the first-past-the-post system in single-member constituencies. Thirty-four are elected under the supplementary member system on a second ballot, based on nationwide votes (any party which receives 5% or more of the party vote can enter the Legislative Yuan). For each party, at least half of the legislators elected under this system must be female. Six seats are elected by aboriginal voters through single non-transferable vote in two three-member constituencies.

344 That serves as a check on decisions made by the Control Yuan involving impeachment and dismissal cases of public officials.

b) uniform interpretation of statutes and regulations; c) impeachment of president and vice-president; and d) declaring the dissolution of political parties that act in violation of the Constitution. The main functions are interpreting the Constitution (decisions require a three-fourth majority of the members present) and unifying the interpretation of laws and ordinances (simple majority suffices). The fifteen Grand Justices serve for either four or eight years.

A very controversial and crucial decision[345] was made by the Council in June 1990, an interpretation of the Constitution that caused senior parliamentarians (delegates of the National Assembly and members of the Legislative Yuan not elected by the electorate in Taiwan, but rather politicians fossilized in office from the time before the ROC's government exile on the island) to have their tenure ended by the end of 1991. The decision was not well-received among those affected, but it was eventually executed and it had a momentous impact on the political reform and democratization process.

The Judicial Yuan represent the apex of the Justice System pyramid, the second tier of which is two-fold, as a distinction is made between the general Supreme Court (in charge of civil and criminal cases) and the Administrative Supreme Court[346] (in charge of administrative cases). The middle tier is composed of the Taiwan High Court (with four detached territorial branches) and the Fuchien High Court, while the lower tier is made up of twenty-one district courts, nineteen in Taiwan and two in Fuchien (*Fujian*). There are also two specialized courts, the Taiwan Kaohsiung Juvenile Court and the Intellectual Property Court.

According to the Law Governing the Organization of the Court, prosecutors' offices form part of the court at the same level of trial, with a Prosecutor-General office attached to the Supreme Court, Chief-Prosecutor offices attached to High Courts and District Courts, etc.

- Examination Yuan (*Kaoshi Yuan*). Is responsible for managing the ministry of examination and the ministry of civil service, and the civil service system in general. It has responsibility for compiling and administering civil service examinations used to recruit officials and various personnel (governmental, but not only); the employment and management of civil service personnel; and the setting of criteria for evaluating, promoting and compensating government employees. It had been made a separate branch, independent from the other branches of state power, in order for it to remain politically unpartisan and neutral, and to maintain the same high status that the civil service had

345 *See* Decision 261 (21/06/1990) of the Constitutional Court www.judicial.gov.tw/constitutionalcourt/p03_01_printpage.asp?expno=261.

346 Administrative litigation employs a "Two Level Two Instance System" procedure: the High Administrative Court is the court of first instance (trial of facts), while the Supreme Administrative Court is the appellate court.

enjoyed in China since ancient times. Its members are appointed by the president, with the consent of the Legislative Yuan, for six years.

- Control Yuan (*Jiancha Yuan*). Formerly one of the three elected institutional bodies (223 members originally) in the ROC, it is patterned after the ancient censorate. Originally, a sixth Yuan, the Auditing Yuan (*Shenji Yuan*) was established in 1928, but in 1931 it was downgraded to the current Ministry of Audit and incorporated into the Control Yuan. Prior to the reforms, the Control Yuan used to have to approve the presidential nominations for president and vice-president of the Judicial Yuan and Examination Yuan: it is nowadays empowered to impeach and censure officials and audit government agencies and has currently twenty-nine members appointed by the president with the approval of the Legislative Yuan. The Control Yuan is periodically the subject of debates about its abolition and/or streamlining.[347]

The territory under the jurisdiction of the ROC includes two archipelagoes (Matsu/*Mazu* and Kinmen/*Jinmen*), formally belonging to the province (*sheng*) of Fujian,[348] and the province of Taiwan (the island itself – by far the bulk of the total area and population of the republic – plus archipelagoes and minor islets). The ROC, a unitary state, is administratively divided into five levels. The first level includes the two provinces (whose provincial governments have been streamlined in 1956 (Fujian) and 1998 (Taiwan) respectively) and six special municipalities directly under the central government (*zhixiashi*).[349] The second level includes three cities (*shi*) under the provincial government of Taiwan (alternatively called "county-level municipalities") and thirteen counties (*xian*) under the two provinces, eleven under Taiwan and two under Fujian, respectively. The third level includes mountain indigenous districts, districts, county-administered cities, urban townships, rural townships, and mountain indigenous townships. The fifth level is that of neighbourhoods. If the two ghostly provincial governments – existing nowadays almost only in name and for statistical purposes – are disregarded, there are twenty-two primary administrative units under the central government. The peculiar one-plus-five institutional structure that we find at the central level is not replicated at the local level, where a much simpler Mayor/City Council or Magistrate/County Council dynamic is instead apparent.

347 The most recent of such moves is reported, among other sources, here: *Control Yuan nominees for its abolition*, in *Taipei Times*, 13 January 2018, accessible at http://news.ltn.com.tw/news/focus/breakingnews/2310647.

348 The bulk of Fujian province stays under the jurisdiction of the government of the PRC.

349 Taipei/*Taibei* City and New Taipei City, the two main urban areas in the country, are both special municipalities. The remaining four special municipalities are Kaohsiung/*Gaoxiong*, Taichung/*Taizhong*, Tainan, and Taoyuan.

1.9.3 *Rights and Duties of the Citizens*

As a modern well-meaning constitution, the Constitution of the ROC, modelled on Western counterparts, provides the guarantees that are expected of it. The Constitution states that the ROC, founded on the Three Principles of the People, shall be a democratic republic of the people, to be governed by the people and for the people and the sovereignty of the Republic of China shall reside in the whole body of citizens (Arts. 1 and 2). The Constitution also states, in Chapter II ("Rights and Duties of the People", Arts. 7–24) that all citizens of the Republic of China, irrespective of sex, religion, race, class, or party affiliation, shall be equal before the law (Art. 7). The Constitution states also that the people shall have freedom of residence and of change of residence, freedom of speech, teaching, writing and publication, freedom of privacy of correspondence, freedom of religious belief, and freedom of assembly and association (Arts. 10–14). The Constitution further states that the people shall have the right of existence, the right to work and the right of property, the right of presenting petitions, lodging complaints, or instituting legal proceedings, the right of election, recall, initiative and referendum, and the right of taking public examinations and of holding public offices (Arts. 15–18). The people shall have the duty of paying taxes in accordance with law, the duty of performing military service in accordance with law, and have the right and the duty of receiving citizens' education (Arts. 19–21). As mentioned above, these constitutional guarantees were legally inert until the beginning of the 1990s, when the country ditched dictatorship.

Despite its alignment with mainstream political systems, the situation in the ROC/Taiwan presents a few peculiarities, and displays – not differently from any other jurisdictions in the world – lights and shadows. The voting age in the ROC is 20 (18 for referenda) while most countries in the world (PRC included) set it at 18, but young men are still subject to military conscription (unlike the PRC). These somehow conservative attitudes are mirrored by the attitude towards soft drugs, like cannabis, the status of which is still illegal and strictly enforced, and by capital punishment (the ROC is one of the fifty-six retentionist countries in the world). Another feature not in line with modern liberal constitutionalism is the criminalization of adultery: Taiwan is one of the few non-Islamic jurisdictions in the world, along with twenty-one USA states and the Philippines, where marital infidelity is punishable with jail (in Taiwan up to one year). On the bright side of the spectrum is the attitude towards sexual minorities: same-sex sexual intercourse is legal, discrimination due to sexual orientation is prohibited by law since 2007, and on 24 May 2017 the Constitutional Court ruled that the current marriage laws are unconstitutional and that same-sex couples should have the right to marry.[350] A feature that puzzles observers

350 The court has given the Legislative Yuan a maximum of two years to amend the Civil Code or enact ad hoc laws so that same-sex marriage is legally recognized. According to the court ruling, in case of failure to do so by 24 May 2019, same-sex marriage will automatically become legal, potentially making the ROC the

of the ROC-guaranteed and now cherished liberties, is the emergence of a free-for-all, free-wheeling press, praised for its freedom but also criticized for its not-so-occasional lack of standards and for its idiocy.[351]

first country in Asia to allow it. *See* Decision 748 (24/05/2017) of the Constitutional Court. www.judicial.gov.tw/constitutionalcourt/EN/p03_01.asp?expno=748.

351 An account on Taiwanese media can be found in: M.E. Delmestro *L'incontro tra Xi Jinping e Ma Ying-jeou visto da Taiwan*, in M. Miranda (Ed.), *Politica, società e cultura di una Cina in ascesa: L'amministrazione Xi Jinping al suo primo mandato*, Roma, Carocci, 2016, 87 ff.

2 Japan[*]

2.1 A Brief Constitutional History of Japan

In the history of Japanese law, three documents have the name "Constitution" (*kenpo*). The first is the so-called "Seventeen-Art. Constitution" (*Jushichijo Kenpo*) of 604: more than an actual constitutional text, it is a collection of moral precepts and maxims (of Buddhist and Neo-Confucian inspiration) addressed to the rulers.[1] It contains some principles relevant to the law, including the pre-eminence of imperial power (also via the recommendation that only the Emperor is entitled to impose taxes), as well as suggestions for use by officials in charge of administering power. Although some conservative scholars attribute to this document the value of "Constitution" in the proper sense of the term, a greater majority of scholars identify nineteenth century, and more precisely the year 1889, as the moment when Japan began to have a real constitutional charter.

This is not to say, however, that a state system was missing: dating from the seventh century, there is evidence of "codifications" in administrative matters. However, there is the need to make a series of clarifications. First, with reference to the regulatory production of the Asuka (538-710) and Nara (710-794) eras: although historians often use the term "code", it is obvious that these legislative collections cannot be considered on a par with the European codifications of the eighteen and nineteenth centuries, and therefore the term must be understood in an improper sense. Furthermore, any analysis of the legislation of the time must be carried out bearing in mind that most of the original sources have been lost, and therefore historians have relied on subsequent editions and reconstructions. In fact, there are reports of four *ritsuryo* (*ritsu*: criminal law, *ryo*: administrative rules). However, of the first of these, known as *Omiryo* (Code Omi), compiled between 662 and 668 AD and dedicated only to administrative rules, its existence is contested; of the second, the *Asuka kiyomihararyo* (Asuka kiyomihara Code, also dedicated only to administrative law), there is concrete evidence in historical documents, but the original text is missing. The first complete text of which there is a direct testimony is the *Taiho ritsuryo* (Taiho Code) of 701 AD. For this reason, it is appropriate to refer not only to the "history" of the codifications, but also to their "mythology".[2]

---

* This Chapter has been translated from Italian. The translation was not made by the Authors. *Status Iuris*: December 2017.

1 C. Steenstrup, *A History of Law in Japan until 1868*, Leiden, Brill, 1996, 16-17.

2 G.F. Colombo, *Tra norma e principio: storia, mitologia, ed eredità dei codici di epoca Nara*, in A. Maurizi (Ed.) *La cultura del periodo Nara*, Milano, FrancoAngeli, 2012, 9-17; M.C. Migliore, *I documenti ufficiali del periodo di Nara*, Rome, La Sapienza Orientale, 2011.

Having clarified the above, one can thus enter into an analysis of the rules, which, as mentioned, denote an adhesion to the Chinese model, but with some significant differences.[3] If one analyses comparative law scholarship on the subject, one can note how the originality of the Japanese system has been simplistically flattened, and how the analyses of jurists do not adequately enhance the peculiarities of Japan. It is quite evident how this approach, obviously motivated by the need to be concise, omits highlighting some of the discrepancies between the Chinese and Japanese models.

First of all, the most macroscopic difference concerns the figure of the sovereign: in China, starting from the complete theorization carried out by Mengzi,[4] the legitimation of the ruler derived from the so-called "Mandate of Heaven". The emperor of China, therefore, was not a deity, but he enjoyed the favour of Heaven, a favour that could be "revoked" in the case of conduct that did not conform to his role as sovereign. In Japan, this concept was never accepted: the emperor was the direct descendant of the Sun Goddess Amaterasu Omikami, and as such did not need any further investiture other than his divine status deriving from his ancestry, nor would the question of his behaviour, more or less virtuous, ever arise. Thus, at no time in the history of Japan (at least until 1946), was the sovereignty of the emperor to be contested, even if, as is known, for long periods the substantial exercise of power was to be exercised by other subjects. First, the court aristocracy and then the military would deprive the emperor of effective power. Over the course of many centuries of Japanese history, there would be a peculiar dissociation between the formal ownership and the actual exercise of sovereignty. Hence, it appears legitimate with reference to these periods to define the emperor as a sovereign (in the technical sense of *superiorem non recognoscens*) and not monarch (in the sense of a subject that encompasses executive, legislative and judicial powers). At the *nadir* of his power, the emperor would be granted only the possibility of awarding honours and changing the calendar. This originality of the Japanese model is of paramount importance, since the role of the emperor will be a distinctive and constant feature of the entire legal system. From a philosophical point of view (but also with regards to the general theory of the state), Japan's ruler is not, as in China, at the top of the human hierarchy, but is above it, and external to it.

---

3 Western manuals tend to underestimate these differences. *See, e.g.*, K. Zweigert, H. Kötz, *Einführung in die Rechtsvergleichung auf dem Gebeit des Privatechts*, Tübingen, Mohr Siebeck, 1971, Italian translated by B. Pozzo (Ed.) *Introduzione al diritto comparato*, Giuffré, Milano, 1998, 367: "Japan, as well as Korea and Indochina, soon fell into the sphere of influence of the most refined Chinese culture. Towards the V century AD, Chinese calligraphy arrived in Japan, while Buddhism spread in the following century. The Japanese rulers of the VII and VIII centuries were great admirers of Chinese intellectual life, were acquainted with Chinese literature and art, converted to Buddhism and reorganized their state according to the Chinese model, creating a hierarchy of salaried officials and, as the Chinese emperors had already done, transformed their position into that of absolute and omnipotent rulers. Even the most ancient Japanese laws, known to us, a great resemblance to those of the Chinese T'ang dynasty."

4 372-289 BC known in Europe as Mencius, he was the most famous Confucian thinker after Confucius himself.

From the conservation of the sacred role of the sovereign, which remained integral following the adoption of the Confucian system, also derive some structural characteristics of the hierarchy of the state: in particular one can observe a prevalence of the Ministry of Cult over the State Council. Historians attribute this prevalence precisely to the dual sacred and civil significance of the emperor.[5]

Another fundamental difference between the Chinese and Japanese model concerns the recruitment of administrative officials. As is well known, the *ritsuryo* system, as indeed the affiliated Tang system, envisaged a hierarchy of officials. In Imperial China, however, the public administration positions were accessed through a system of selection competitions, theoretically open to anyone who wanted to participate.

Japan, in a much more aristocratic way than China, never opted for this system of recruitment. Thus, it selected officials based on their birth status and not merit, officially placing this last requirement even after personal characteristics. It was in fact the court nobility first and then the military that were to constitute the backbone of Japanese public administration.[6]

In this respect, in addition to considerations on the elitist management of public affairs, one can also draw conclusions on the social pyramid: the absence of the institute of competitions precluded, in Japan, even this limited form of social mobility. With the entry into force of the *Yoro ritsuryo* (Yoro Code, enacted in 752 - but the text had already been ready since 720), Japan's first major legislative phase was completed. The codifications of the period were soon to fall into desuetude in favour of the laws of feudal lords and local customs. They were however never formally repealed, thus remaining in force, though only

---

5 G. Sansom, *A History of Japan to 1334*, Tokyo, Tuttle Publishing, 1969, 68-69. The bipartition of the state structure basically saw four ministries subject to the Minister of the Left (the Ministry of the Centre, *i.e.* the connection between the sovereign and the general administration, the Ministry of Ceremonies, the Ministry of Civil Affairs, the Ministry of Affairs of the subjects) and four to the Minister of the Right (the Ministry of Military Affairs, the Ministry of Justice, the Ministry of the Treasury, the Ministry of the Imperial House). Furthermore: the protohistory of Japanese law, prior to the adoption of Chinese calligraphy, has been reconstructed by archaeologists and anthropologists. On the basis of these reconstructions, it is thought that archaic law was a religious right, based therefore on the identity between moral-religious precept and juridical norm. *See* H. Oda, *Japanese Law*, Oxford, Oxford University Press, 2nd edn, 1992, 12-13 (the third edition [2009], omits the part concerning ancient history).

6 The Japanese social hierarchies are considered far more rigid than the Chinese. This greater impermeability of the system becomes particularly clear in the Tokugawa era. "La separazione fra le classi era dettagliatamente regolata, attraverso codici di comportamento che definivano doveri, prerogative, ruoli, atteggiamenti esteriori propri di ogni classe e sotto-classe, così da produrre una cristallizzazione sociale ancora più stringente di quella derivante dal codice etico-sociale della Cina confuciana. D'altra parte, nel contesto giapponese non funzionava neppure quell'elemento di elasticità del sistema che in Cina era rappresentato dalla possibilità di ascendere, tramite il superamento degli esami di stato, alla classe più elevata dei letterati. Nel Giappone del neoconfucianesimo Tokugawa, infatti, l'accesso alla classe di vertice, quella dei samurai, era bloccato dal principio del bungen, ossia il principio dello status definitivo, immutabile per ogni individuo" (M. Timoteo, *Il contratto in Cina e in Giappone nello specchio dei diritti occidentali*, Padova, Cedam, 2004, 89). This situation made Tokugawa Japan a "rule by status" system: *cf.* J. W. Hall, *Rule by Status in Tokugawa Japan*, in 1 *Journal of Japanese Studies* 39-49 (1974).

on the books, until the legislative reforms of the Meiji era (1868-1912). The eclipse of imperial power in favour of the military aristocracy (culminating in the establishment of the shogunate) was in fact to lead to the disregard of the *ritsuryo*.

This is not the right place to summarize the long legislative history of medieval and pre-modern Japan, but it is useful to make two notations of a systemic nature. The first: contrary to what is often reported in the manuals of comparative law of a general nature, in Japan and especially in the Edo period (coinciding with the Tokugawa shogunate,[7] 1603-1868), but also well before then,[8] the country was equipped with a series of laws, obviously different in terms of content, scope and style compared to the Western experience, but still present. Moreover, especially in the period dating from the eighteenth century, Japan was to witness the establishment of a structured judicial system (albeit managed by administrative officials without a specific legal preparation).

The second: the Tokugawa shoguns did not consider it necessary to consecrate their power in a document, not even in a constitutional sense. On the one hand, this is consistent with the historical period (in Europe and the United States too, constitutional charters begin to appear at the end of the eighteenth century), on the other, this is also understandable in the light of the ambiguous ownership of power between the shogun and the emperor.

It is therefore precisely with the Meiji era that Japan acquires its first true constitutional charter.

In order to accurately describe the birth of the Constitution of 1889 (also known as the "Meiji Constitution" or "Constitution of the Japanese Empire") there is the need to outline, at least briefly, the history of the period in which this document was born.[9]

In 1853, the apparition, in the bay of Tokyo, of the American naval fleet led by Commodore Matthew Perry triggered a series of events that led to the opening of the country,

7 A large collection of legal documents from the Tokugawa period is collected in the dated but still fundamental work of J.H. Wigmore, *Law and Justice in Tokugawa Japan. Materials for the History of Japanese Law and Justice under the Tokugawa Shougunate 1603–1867*, Tokyo, University of Tokyo Press, 1890.

8 F.K. Upham, *Mythmaking in the Rule of Law Orthodoxy*, in *30 Carnegie Endowments for International Peace Working Papers 1*-33, 22-23 (2002): "In the Middle Ages, when the English were still throwing litigants into rivers to see if they would float, Japan had developed a legal system to adjudicate competing land claims that valued procedural regularity, the right to confront hostile witnesses, and objective third-party adjudication based on evidence instead of magic or divine ritual. Even during the Tokugawa period, seen largely as the heyday of neo-Confucian authoritarianism and the flat prohibition of the legal profession, formal legal institutions were overloaded with lawsuits, legal advice was a significant industry, and legal justice was not impossible for even the most downtrodden. By number of cases, commercial matters and debt collection cases dominated, but the courts were used for disputes concerning property rights and personal status as well. For the period preceding the Tokugawa, Upham refers to J. Mass, *The Development of Kamakura Rule, 1180-1250*, Stanford, Stanford University Press, 1979."

9 *Amplius*, G.M. Beckmann, *The Making of the Meiji Constitution, the Oligarchs and the Constitutional Development of Japan, 1868-1891*, Lawrence, University Press of Kansas, 1957; J. Banno, *The Establishment of the Japanese Constitutional System*, London, Routledge, 1992; K. Takii, *The Meiji Constitution. The Japanese Experience of the West and the Shaping of the Modern State*, D. Noble (Tr.), Tokyo, International House of Japan, 2007.

to the stipulation of unequal Treaties with the Western powers and, in 1868, the collapse of the Tokugawa shogunate and the restoration of imperial power.

Emperor Meiji, realizing the backwardness of the local law compared to the much more evolved Western legal systems, believed it essential to provide Japan with modern and structured laws, such as to be thus considered on a par with the European and American powers.

Japan was however not devoid of a local normative substratum. The Tokugawa shogunate had indeed established a system of courts to administer criminal justice, as well as civil justice (an aspect frequently underestimated in texts on Japanese law).[10] Nonetheless, the law of pre-modern Japan was considered unsuitable for transformation or transfusion into an evolved legal system, due to the fact that it was based on poor and fragmented normative material (the reference text was still the *Kujikata Osadamegaki* of 1742, a two-volume collection of norms and precedents used by administrative officials who administered justice[11]). Thus, there was the need to turn to foreign models. In choosing the system from which to draw inspiration, the Japanese preferred to turn to the systems of European-continental civil law rather than *common law*, for two reasons: the first, because the rules of *common law* are based on a long tradition of precedence, and therefore the model was ill-suited for the development of a new system; and secondly due to the fact that the *civil*

10 Y. Hiramatsu, *Tokugawa Law*, in 14 *Law in Japan* 1-48 (1981).

11 The *Kujikata Osadamegaki* has been described by various scholars: "Written Decisions for Lawsuits; the nearest thing to a code achieved by the Tokugawa regime; completed under Yoshimune, eight Shogun (1742)", D.F. Henderson, *Conciliation and Japanese Law. Tokugawa and Modern*, Tokyo and Seattle, University of Tokyo Press, 1965, 288; "It was only in 1742 that a systematic code was enacted. This code was a compilation of acts and precedents and comprised two volumes: the first being a compilation of various acts, and the second mainly covering civil and criminal law. It is interesting to note that the second part of the osadamegaki was a secret code, accessible only to three commissioners and other senior officials of the Shogunate: it was considered unnecessary to let ordinary people know the contents of the code" (Oda, *Japanese Law*, 18-19); "[...] They created a new *ritsu ryo* type of legislation, the *Kujikata Osadamegaki*, in 1742. These laws had *ritsu* type administrative provisions and *ryo* type penal provisions. After 1472, the motor of economic and social change introduced threads of movement into the tightly knit system, occasioning social legislation directed largely at the increasingly unsettled merchant and farmer classes. This legislation also restricted the recourse to the legal system" (M.K. Young, C. Hamilton, *Historical Introduction to the Japanese Legal System*, in M. Matsushita, *Japan Business Law Guide*, Sydney, CHH International, 1988, chap. I; "The main legislative text of the time, Osadamegaki, summarized, in extremely essential terms (81 articles the first book, 103 articles on the second), a series of rules elaborated by Shogunal courts in the early Tokugawa period in the wake of the autochthonous jurisprudential tradition." M. Timoteo, *Il contratto*, 93); "In 1742, that which is considered the third great document of the authoritative law of the Japanese tradition, the Kujikata Osadamegaki (Rules written for the judicial procedures) was promulgated, after the Ritsuryo and the Goseibai Shikimoku. It is a codification composed of two parts, on the basis of the structure of the ancient Ritsuryo, of which the former contains administrative rules, the second mainly rules of a criminal nature. The work, which was conceived as a manual of instructions for use by the bakufu (bugyo sho) courts for their proceedings, and was not accessible to the common public, represented the ultimate crystallization of the trial system that had been defined since the Kamakura era. Among other things, there was a detailed regulating of access to Shogunal courts [...]", G. Ajani, A. Serafino, M. Timoteo (with the collaboration of H. Chen, A. Ortolani, P. Rossi), *Diritto dell'Asia orientale*, Torino, Utet, 2007, 86-87.

law model, based on organic and coherent texts, better lent itself to imitation in a short time. However, the vast historical and institutional affinity with European-continental countries should also not be underestimated.

Within the various models of *civil law*, initially the French model was considered better, also in the light of the success of the Napoleonic codification, and therefore the first legal texts (in particular the Penal Code and Code of Criminal Procedure) were drafted with the collaboration of a French jurist (Prof. Gustave Boissonade) and were based on the French model. However, also thanks to the experience of study directly carried out in Europe by Japanese scholars, it soon became clear that there was no "ideal" model, and hence, the legislator decided to draw on other experiences, particularly those of the Germanic area. Hence, the Code of Civil Procedure (1890) and the Commercial Code (which had to wait until 1899 to enter into full force) came into being, thanks also to the assistance of a German consultant (Prof. Hermann Roesler).[12]

With regards to constitutional law, the idea of giving the country a Constitution was acknowledged already in the early years of the Meiji era (some historians, however, have a different view on the subject). In truth, in the urgency of the Restoration, an attempt was made to restore the ancient *daijiokan* system, according to which the Emperor, the supreme and absolute monarch, governed with the help of ministers and advisors. However, it soon became clear that such an archaic system was ill-fitting with the demands of the radical modernization of the country.

Other attempts, respectively based on the translation of the Dutch Constitution of 1815 commissioned by a *daimyo* (feudal lord) of the South of Japan, and a first draft of the Prussian model in 1872, were unsuccessful.

The decisive step towards the adoption of the Constitution was made with an imperial rescript of 1881, with which the Emperor undertook to "donate" a constitutional charter to his subjects and convene the first Parliament by 1890.[13]

In order to identify an adequate model, studies were also undertaken in the context of the first diplomatic missions sent by the Emperor to the Western powers. Nobles, politicians, and scholars were sent to the various nations deemed to be "evolved" (the United States, the British Empire, the Germanic Empire, Prussia, France, etc.) also with the aim of studying their legal-constitutional systems.

---

12 The Civil Code was to have a separate legislative history. Amplius, S. Ono, *Comparative Law and the Civil Code of Japan (I)*, in XXIV *Hitotsubashi Law Review* 27-45 (1996); *Id.*, *Comparative Law and the Civil Code of Japan (II)*, in XXV *Hitotsubashi Law Review* 29-52 (1997); A. Ortolani, G. F. Colombo, *La cultura giuridica italiana in Giappone*, in M. K. Gesuato (Ed.) *Ricerca, scoperta, innovazione: l'Italia dei saperi*, Tokyo, Istituto Italiano di Cultura, 2014, 22-42; B. Jaluzot, *Les origines du Code civil japonais*, in 20 *Zeitschrift für Japanisches Recht/Journal of Japanese Law* 121-146 (2015).

13 C.G. Tamás, *The Birth of the Parliamentary Democracy in Japan: An Historical Approach*, in 17 *Zeitschrift für Japanisches Recht/Journal of Japanese Law*, n. 33, 146-167 (2012).

The main architect of this operation was Hirobumi Ito (1841-1909), a dominant figure of the reform season (he was the first Prime Minister of Japan, and was to hold the office for a further three times in the Meiji period). He spent periods of study in the German-speaking area, particularly in Austria and in Prussia, and ultimately it was probably him who made the final decision as to which constitutional model to follow.[14]

The chosen model of inspiration was the Prussian model, since in Prussia Japan found some similarities with itself regarding the paternalistic-authoritarian idea of the state, with the sovereign at the head of the nation. Moreover, Prussia had recently emerged from a transition from a predominantly agricultural country to an industrial power, and even in this Japan found affinities. There remained, however, a profound difference between the figure of the Emperor and that of the Kaiser: no Western ruler in fact held the same divine role, nor were they invested with the same sacral and mystical value as the Tenno of the Japanese Empire.

The Prussian model, however, still seemed the most appropriate, and was thus effectively followed for the drafting of the Constitution of the Japanese Empire of 1889 (literally the "Constitution of Great Japan", also known as the Meiji Constitution). From a formal point of view, it was composed of a Preamble and seven titles or chapters:

i. The Emperor
ii. The Rights and Duties of Subjects
iii. The Imperial Diet
iv. The Ministers of State and the Privy Council
v. The Judicature
vi. Finance
vii. Supplementary Rules

The Meiji Constitution is a typical example of *Charte octroyée* ("A Constitution granted from above") of the nineteenth century: the Constitution of 1889 was considered a sort of benevolent gift of the sovereign to his subjects. Particularly notable is the Preamble of the Constitution, which celebrates the imperial dynasty, reigning over Japan as a direct descendent of divinity. Even the very day of its promulgation, 11 February, is a tribute to tradition: it is in fact the conventional date of the ascent to the throne of the first Emperor.

From a technical point of view, as it can be expected, the entire constitutional charter rotated around the fundamental figure of the Emperor, an absolute sovereign who committed himself to respecting the Constitution, but who ultimately held the three powers (Art. 4), legislative (albeit with the consent of the Imperial Diet), executive, and to some extent also judicial power (albeit obviously a judiciary existed for the purpose, but it was

14 G.M. Beckmann, *The Making of the Meiji Constitution, the Oligarchs and the Constitutional Development of Japan, 1868-1891*, op. cit.

in the name of the Emperor and not according to the law that the judges pronounced their sentences (Art. 57). And thus, the Emperor who obtained his sovereign power from his divine ancestry (Art. 1), who is sacred and inviolable (Art. 3), could count on the "assistance" of the Diet (Art. 5) and the Government, as his advisory body. The Emperor was also the supreme head of the armed forces (Art. 11).

Another important and aristocratic institution was the privy council, a non-elective body composed mainly of members of the nobility.

Chapter II, dedicated to the rights and duties of subjects (note, not citizens), is strongly unbalanced towards the obligations towards the State. Explicitly declared is the obligation to pay taxes (Art. 19) and to serve the State in arms, if conscripted to national service (Art. 20), but in reality most of the rights are conditioned by the interests of the community. Some commentators wanted to read in this a product of the neo-Confucian vision of society, in which the idea of subjective law is absent and interpersonal relationships and institutions are governed by a dense network of obligations.

From the point of view of fundamental freedoms, the juridical mechanism to make Shinto the state religion without making it explicit is particularly ingenious: the result is that a Japanese subject was thus theoretically granted religious freedom (note, as an individual choice, but not as a freedom to publicly profess a religious belief), but practically forced to participate in the rituals of Shinto.

The authors of the 1889 Charter in fact intended to outline a clear demarcation between the freedom to choose one's faith and publicly practising one's religion: Article 28 of the fundamental charter safeguarded the individual choice of a faith, but not its public externalization. Shinto was an exception, but not as a religion: participation in its ritual practices was, in fact, considered (since the first years of the Constitution) not a public expression of the creed, but a real civic duty. The consequence was that not only subjects could openly profess Shinto, but were even required to do so. It should however be pointed out that the political-religious mixture was strengthened and exploited during the Meiji (1868-1912) and Taisho (1912-1926) eras, and in the first phase of the Showa era (1926-1945) up until the end of the Second World War, with the creation of a "State Shinto" only partially coinciding with the traditional religious phenomenon. The result of this operation, in the wake of the constitutional text, on the one hand favoured Shinto in comparison to any other religion, but on the other, it equated it to a civil, traditional phenomenon, linked to the organization of the State, favouring its social aspects and even penalizing those more truly religious.

Additionally, in Chapter II, and always with regard to the emphasis on duties over rights, Article 32 relating to the military duties of Japanese subjects stands out. From the literal formulation, it seems that the duties as a member to the armed forces prevail over constitutional rights.[15]

That being said, the Meiji Constitution still marks an important turning point in the modernization of the country also from the perspective of the fundamental individual rights. In fact, with the 1889 Charter, some key principles of modern systems were introduced in Japan, such as the right to a fair trial (Art. 23) before a pre-established state judge (Art. 24). Clearly, for the most part, the rights are tempered by an exercise or benefit of such rights in accordance with the laws of the State. Hence, freedom of movement (Art. 22), inviolability of the home (Art. 25), secrecy of correspondence (Art. 26) and freedom of speech, assembly and association (Art. 29) are guaranteed on condition that they do not clash with the law.

As already mentioned, the Emperor necessitated the consent of the Diet to legislate. Chapter III of the Meiji Constitution is dedicated to this institution.

The Diet consists of an imperfect bicameral composition,[16] the House of Peers and that of the Representatives (Art. 33). As a tribute to the idea of an aristocratic nation underlying the whole constitutional design, the democracy of the parliament is decidedly contained. The first of the two branches of the Diet is in fact composed of members of the imperial family and other nobles, while the second is elected. The Constitution, however, does not specify the electoral mechanisms, delegating the purpose to a specific legislation (Art. 35). The first laws in this area were structured in such a way as to grant electoral rights only to males who declared a certain annual income. The result was that in the first elections of the Diet, those entitled to vote amounted to circa 2% of the total population of Japan. Subsequently, in 1925, the right to vote was extended to all adult males.

One can therefore see how the Meiji Constitution was suitable to the idea of the state in the hands of a small elite.

In general, the Meiji Charter is a "prudent" constitution, which traces the essential lines of a state that is still young and not fully formed, and does not intend to precisely define rights, duties and an institutional system. This is in line with the dominant model of "granted" Constitutions and in particular with the Prussian model, the primary inspiration of the Meiji Constitution.

Alongside the Constitution, the Imperial Household Law (also of constitutional rank) regulated the family matters of the ruling house, and in particular the succession rules to the Chrysanthemum Throne.

---

15 Art. 32 in fact states "Each and every one of the provisions contained in the preceding Articles of the present Chapter, that are not in conflict with the laws or the rules and discipline of the Army and Navy, shall apply to the officers and men of the Army and of the Navy" (emphasis added).

16 S. Wrbka, *The Research Commission on the Constitution and the Upper House Issue*, in 11 *Zeitschrift für Japanisches Recht/Journal of Japanese Law* 105-130 (2006) (110).

With the definitive approval of the Commercial Code (1899), the system of sources of Japanese law assumed its current structure. At the top of the sources of law is the Constitution, and under it the ordinary laws (the most significant of which are, of course, the five codes).

The following period, marked by the revision of the so-called Unequal treaties to which Japan had been subjected in the second half of the nineteenth century, and since its debut as an international power, especially following the victories in the Sino-Japanese War (1894-1895) and the Russo-Japanese War (1904-1905), did not see significant changes from a constitutional point of view. With the advent of the nationalist period, however, there was a loss of power of the democratic institutions (even if not complete) to the benefit of the military, culminating in the attack on Prime Minister Inugai in 1932 and in a coup attempt in 1936. However, despite the turbulent political events that led Japan to nationalism (historians are divided over the legitimacy of the term *fashizumu*, "fascism" to indicate the militarist phase)[17] and the substantial exclusion of civil authorities from the country's government, the constitutional charter was never amended. The scant detailed structure of the norms of the 1889 Constitution also permitted the possibility to act without excessively forcing the institutional context. Moreover, in the absence of a real control of the constitutionality of the laws on the part of the judicial system, possible contrasts between primary and superprimary norms were less evident.

The role that the Emperor had during the nationalist phase is very controversial and the legal consequences of the behaviour of the sovereign have also been the subject of a wide and heated debate, as will be mentioned below.

The defeat in the Second World War of Japan and the consequent allied (*rectius*: American) occupation of the country led to a series of fundamental reforms from the point of view of law, and in particular of constitutional law.

Among the first measures taken by the SCAP (*Supreme Commander for the Allied Powers* – the official rank taken by the commander in chief of the occupation forces, the US General Douglas Mac Arthur) there were the dissolution of the army and navy, the dissolution of large industrialist groups known as *zaibatsu* (and identified by the American occupiers as traditional allies of the nationalists) and the redistribution of land properties.

Moreover, the SCAP also imposed on the Emperor to pronounce a famous speech (known as the *Tenno no ningen sengen*, New Year's Eve 1946) in which the Japanese ruler formally renounced his divine nature and declared himself, to all intents and purposes, a mere human being.

As mentioned above, the Meiji Constitution is very clear in establishing that the Emperor is the supreme head of the army and navy, and therefore, theoretically, should be respon-

17 The positions of historians are amply illustrated in F. Gatti, *Il fascismo giapponese*, Venezia, Cafoscarina, 1997.

sible for the command and action of the armed forces. However, when the occupants started the Tokyo Trial (the *International Military Tribunal for the Far East* or IMTFE, the equivalent of the Nuremberg Trial for East Asia), they took the decision to exclude not only the Emperor, but all the members of the Imperial House from the trial.[18] This decision, which still generates not a few perplexities from a strictly juridical point of view, was equally dense with political significance: to rebuild Japan, the occupiers thought it better to maintain an institutional continuity through the maintenance of the imperial figure, albeit, as will be seen, in a role and with extremely different powers compared to the previous phase.

The fundamental idea of the SCAP was to democratize Japan, in every respect, and understandably the pivot around which to rotate the whole operation was identified in the superprimary source of law, the Constitution.

It should be noted in this regard that the Potsdam Declaration (or Proclamation of the terms for the Japanese surrender) of 26 July 1945, issued by the American, British, and Soviet heads of state, envisaged some specific characteristics in the unconditional surrender of Japan. In particular, the tenth point of the Declaration required the country to

> remove all obstacles to the revival and strengthening of the democratic tendencies of the Japanese people. Freedom of speech, religion and thought, as well as respect for fundamental human rights, will be established

In order to put these principles into practice, it was necessary to replace the aristocratic Meiji Constitution with a document that could lead the Japanese legal system towards democratization.

The background of the current Constitutional Charter is fascinating, and shows how institutions can be modelled also as a result of mere accidents of history.

The SCAP had urged the Japanese government to provide for the complete revision of the Constitution without delay, in order to make it a suitable text to forge, and at the same time, reflect the new democratic course of the country. The government therefore created a commission of experts for the reform of the Constitution, which, however, misunderstanding (probably not in complete bad faith) the American instructions, focused on preserving, as much as possible, the Meiji constitutional system. Therefore, they worked on a draft that maintained the central role of the Emperor as effective ruler of the country,

---

18 The Tokyo Trial is still a fundamental precedent in international law, since for the first time international laws have been applied to a state (for example, those concerning the treatment of prisoners of war) not because the country in question had joined these treaties, but because they covered fundamental subjects, and as such binding, irrespective of adhesion. Another innovative element of the Tokyo Trial is the conviction of civil servants for military crimes. *Amplius*, Y. Totani, *The Tokyo War Crimes Trial: The Pursuit of Justice in the Wake of World War II*, Cambridge (MA), Harvard University Press, 2009.

strengthening however the powers of the Diet and the ministers, and widening the scope of fundamental rights and freedoms.

On 1 February 1946, a national newspaper published the entire draft of the new Constitution as elaborated by the government commission: the disappointment of the SCAP in the face of such a document was immense. The occupying authorities decided to take the matter directly into their own hands and formulate their own draft. The basis for this work was essentially a note by General MacArthur, containing three pivotal points: popular sovereignty (keeping the figure of the Emperor, albeit deprived of real powers), the abolition of the nobility and, a unique case in the world constitutional landscape, renunciation of the country to possess an army and the right of belligerency.

A parallel committee of experts of the SCAP worked incessantly for eight days and eight nights, between 4 and 12 February 1946, on a draft that was compatible with the resolutions of the occupants. And thus, the fundamental legal document, the *Grundnorm* of a country, was written in a few hours, by people recruited in a hurry and without a preliminary study on the appropriateness or feasibility of a "legal transplant".[19] As will be seen below, this norms, evidently conceived by Americans but applied in the Japanese context, were to cause many application problems,

The Japanese commission was specularly surprised and critical of the American draft, but the SCAP was adamant and the Japanese government had to adapt. The Constitution was approved by the Diet in 1946 and subsequently entered into force on 3 May 1947. Formally a simple revision of the Meiji Constitution, in reality the new constitution has almost no resemblance to the previous document.

From the moment of its approval in 1946, a strong ideological-intellectual opposition (especially from exponents of the nationalist right) began to take root against the Constitution, seen as a real imposition of the occupiers, a foreign charter designed by foreigners, far-flung from Japanese ideology. Some criticisms also related to the methods of approval of the Constitution: the fact of conceiving the new text as a mere revision of the Meiji Constitution was considered incompatible with the intrinsic mechanisms of revision of the Constitution (envisaged by Art. 73 of the 1889 Charter) However, some considerations in support of the acceptance of the Constitution are opportune: first, during the period of examination of the draft in the Japanese Diet, there was a period of 50 days in which the elected representatives of the people had the possibility to examine and revise the text. Moreover, the Constitution is in fact completely in line with the principles of the Potsdam

19 As stated, the current Constitution of Japan was in fact written by the supreme command of the allied occupation forces: so it is not surprising that such a constitution charter has very little that is "Japanese". *Amplius*, G.D. Hook, G. McCormack, *Japan Contested Constitution. Documents and Analysis*, London and New York, Routledge, 2001.

Declaration that Japan formally accepted in their surrender. Finally, the Constitution has been in force since 1947 in its original form, without any changes.[20]

There remain some peculiarities and criticalities, which will be examined in the following chapters, but to consider the Constitution an "imposition" is substantially inaccurate.[21]

2.2 The Current Constitution: Important Characteristics

The 1947 Constitution consists of a preamble and eleven chapters (or parts), and in particular:

The Preamble

- Chapter 1: The Emperor
- Chapter 2: Renunciation of War
- Chapter 3: Rights and Duties of the People
- Chapter 4: The Diet (or Parliament)
- Chapter 5: The Cabinet
- Chapter 6: TJudiciary
- Chapter 7: Finance
- Chapter 8: Local Self-Government
- Chapter 9: Amendments
- Chapter 10: Supreme Law
- Chapter 11: Supplementary Provisions

Although the Constitution is, as previously mentioned, formally a mere amendment of the Meiji Charter, and partly also follows the structure of the previous document, the content is radically different.

It is sufficient to make a quick comparison between the respective preambles of the two Constitutions[22] to see how the difference is substantial.

First, let us analyse the Preamble of the 1889 Charter:

---

20 On the prospects for constitutional reform, *see* G.F. Colombo, S. Donati, *La proposta di riforma della Costituzione giapponese. Tentazioni nazionalistiche o ricerca dell'identità?*, in *Dir, pubbl. comp. eur. online*, 2017, 831-843; E. Bertolini, *La nobiltà della sconfitta: considerazioni sulla revisione costituzionale nipponica*, in *Dir. pubbl. comp. eur.*, 2014, 1813-1837.; S. Matsui, *Fundamental Human Rights and 'Traditional Japanese Values': Constitutional Amendment and Vision of the Japanese Society*, in 13 *Asian Journal of Comparative Law* 59-86 (2018).

21 K. Inoue, *MacArthur's Japanese Constitution: A Linguistic and Cultural Study of Its Making*, Chicago, University of Chicago Press, 1991; H. Tanaka, *A History of the Constitution of Japan of 1946*, in H. Tanaka (Ed.), *The Japanese Legal System: Introductory Cases and Materials*, Tokyo, University of Tokyo Press, 1976; T. Kataoka, *The Price of a Constitution: The Origin of Japan's Postwar Politics*, New York, Crane Russack, 1991.

22 *Amplius*, L. Beer, J.M. Maki, *From Imperial Myth to Democracy: Japan's Two Constitutions*, Boulder, University Press of Colorado, 2002.

> Having, by virtue of the glories of Our Ancestors, ascended the throne of a lineal succession unbroken for ages eternal; desiring to promote the welfare of, and to give development to the moral and intellectual faculties of Our beloved subjects, the very same that have been favored with the benevolent care and affectionate vigilance of Our Ancestors; and hoping to maintain the prosperity of the State, in concert with Our people and with their support, We hereby promulgate, in pursuance of Our Imperial Rescript of the 12th day of the 10th month of the 14th year of Meiji, a fundamental law of the State, to exhibit the principles, by which We are guided in Our conduct, and to point out to what Our descendants and Our subjects and their descendants are forever to conform. The right of sovereignty of the State, We have inherited from Our Ancestors, and We shall bequeath them to Our descendants. Neither We nor they shall in the future fail to wield them, in accordance with the provisions of the Constitution hereby granted.

And now, for a comparison, let us analyse the Preamble of the current Constitution:

> We, the Japanese people, acting through our duly elected representatives in the National Diet, determined that we shall secure for ourselves and our posterity the fruits of peaceful cooperation with all nations and the blessings of liberty throughout this land, and resolved that never again shall we be visited with the horrors of war through the action of government, do proclaim that sovereign power resides with the people and do firmly establish this Constitution. Government is a sacred trust of the people, the authority for which is derived from the people, the powers of which are exercised by the representative of the people, and the benefits of which are enjoyed by the people. This is a universal principle of mankind upon which this Constitution is founded. We reject and revoke all constitutions, laws, ordinances and rescripts in conflict herewith. We, the Japanese people, desire peace for all time and are deeply conscious of the high ideals controlling human relationship, and we have determined to preserve our security, and existence, trusting in the justice and faith of the peace-loving peoples of the world. We desire to occupy an honoured place in an international society striving for the preservation of peace, and the banishment of tyranny and slavery, oppression and intolerance for all time from the earth. We recognize that all peoples of the world have the right to live in peace, free from fear and want. We believe that no nation is responsible to itself alone, but that laws of political morality are universal; and that obedience to such laws is incumbent upon all nations who would sustain their own sovereignty and justify their sovereign relationship with other nations. We, the

> Japanese people, pledge our national honour to accomplish these high ideals and purposes with all our resources.

From a formal point of view, the Constitution manifests its main "peculiarities" (which will be examined in detail) in Chapter I (the Emperor) and II (renunciation of war). The rest of the Constitutional Charter reveals no particular reasons of surprise or originality to public law experts.

The cardinal points of the new Constitution are essentially three, in accordance with that which was established by the SCAP: a) popular sovereignty; b) respect for fundamental rights and the equality of all citizens; c) pacifism and the renunciation of war.

The concept of popular sovereignty does not present any particular criticality for an interpreter: it is nevertheless necessary to acknowledge the presence of the figure of the Emperor in the Constitution, and this, as will be discussed later, has caused a series of misunderstandings with regards to the ownership of sovereignty in Japan. The wording of the preamble, however, leaves no doubt that sovereign power resides in the citizens. In a similar way to that of the other parliamentary democracies, the exercise of popular sovereignty takes place through elections, and therefore through a parliamentary system based on political parties.

With regards to fundamental rights, the Japanese Constitution envisages a wide range of rights, and in this, once again, it is considerably different to the previous text of the Meiji Constitution that was focused more on the system of duties. The current Constitution expressly envisages the respect of human rights as such, and a wide range of individual rights: in this sense, the provision of some very broad formulations stand out, for example the "right to happiness" contained in Article 13, which has been used over the years as the basis of a wide range of legal claims: for example, child visitation rights, not expressly provided for by the Civil Code, was invoked via the direct application of Article 13 (but up until now without success).

Another of the peculiarities of the Japanese Constitution is its longevity: it has been in force, in its original form, for over 70 years, despite its controversial origin and despite repeated debates related to the advisability of amendments, the text has never been changed. This also depends on the intrinsic rigidity of the Constitution, which envisages a very complex procedure for possible changes: Chapter 9, solely composed of Article 96, outlines that in order to amend the text, there is the need for a vote with a majority of two-thirds of the members in each house of the Diet, following which, a confirmatory referendum is envisaged which must result in a favourable vote of the absolute majority of the voters. Only at the end of this referendum can the Emperor promulgate (promptly and without the possibility of refusing) the constitutional amendment. This system has, over the decades, made it very difficult to change the text of the Constitution: the technical reasons are obvious, as a parliamentary majority of two-thirds in both branches of the Diet has in fact rarely occurred. Furthermore, a special harmony between the governing parties and the population is necessary, due to the fact that a favourable parliamentary vote does not lead to any result without the support of a popular referendum.

2.3 The Figure of the Emperor in the Constitution

In the contemporary international scene, currently only one person legitimately carries the title of "Emperor", and it is precisely the Emperor of Japan. As previously mentioned, however, the figure of the Emperor and his legal framework have changed greatly throughout history.

In ancient times (fifth to eleventh century), and before the coming into force of a real Constitution, the Emperor (first of the Empire of Yamato, in central Japan, and then of the whole country) was *de facto* and *de jure* the Head of State, holder of supreme power, head of the sacred rites, as well as the deities. With the Meiji Restoration of 1868, the Emperor had begun to become a constitutional monarch, up until, with the Meiji Constitution of 1889, his figure was formally regulated and framed as an organ of the state, although he preserved his divine nature and a series of sacral functions. The 1947 Constitution changed this picture forever.

In the current system, the Emperor is present and regulated by Chapter I of the constitutional charter. The presence of this figure has generated, for many years, an intense debate on the form of state of Japan: is it a constitutional monarchy or a parliamentary democracy? The existence of the Emperor, to whom moreover, a series of powers and prerogatives not dissimilar from other constitutional sovereigns (such as the monarch of the United Kingdom) are entrusted, could make one think of the first hypothesis; however, a reading of Article 1 of the constitutional text (together with the Preamble) disperses any doubt regarding the ownership of sovereignty. Here is the text of the article in question:

> The Emperor shall be the symbol of the State and of the unity of the People, deriving his position from the will of the people with whom resides sovereign power.

Hence, it is quite clear that the formal ownership of sovereignty is in the hands of the people, who exercise it through their regularly elected representatives in the Diet. As stated, however, the Emperor retains a series of significant functions and prerogatives, which include: the appointment of the Prime Minister and the Chief Justice of the Supreme Court (Art. 6); the promulgation of any constitutional amendments, laws, government decrees and treaties; the convocation of the Diet; the dissolution of the House of Representatives; the call for general elections; the appointment and revocation of the Ministers of the State and ambassadors; the granting of amnesties and pardons; the conferment of honours; welcoming and receiving ambassadors and foreign ministers; and the performance of ceremonial functions.

Therefore, beyond some purely formal tasks (for example the conferral of honours or the welcoming of ambassadors), at a first glance, it would seem that the Emperor has (still) significant power. In reality, the totality of the prerogatives that the Constitution assigns to the Emperor are merely formal: for example, the appointment of the Prime Minister simply acknowledges the result of the elections and is resolved in the designation of the *leader* of the victorious party or coalition. Likewise, the promulgation of legislative measures takes the form of a formal ratification of the procedure, without the Emperor having any real power to modify the measure in question. Nonetheless, the presence of the Emperor in the constitutional text, is significantin itself.

The survival of the imperial figure is also accompanied by the mention of the Imperial Household Law (probably of ordinary rank, even if the question is debated in doctrine), adopted in 1947 in execution of Article 2 of the Constitution.

The new legislation, which replaced the homonymous Law of 1889, was also elaborated with a view to drastically reducing the weight of the imperial aristocracy. The effects of this reform have also led to the dramatic narrowing of the possibility of ascending to the throne. Articles 1 and 2 of the Law of 1947 deal precisely with the rules of succession:

> Article 1. "The Imperial Throne of Japan is succeeded to by male descendants in the male line of Imperial Lineage."
> Article 2. "
> 1. The eldest son of the Emperor
> 2. The eldest son of the Emperor's eldest son
> 3. Other descendants of the eldest son of the Emperor
> 4. The second son of the Emperor and his descendants
> 5. Other descendants of the Emperor
> 6. Brothers of the Emperor and their descendants
> 7. Uncles of the Emperor and their descendants."

In the event that there are no members of the Imperial House among those mentioned in the previous paragraph, the member of the Imperial House with the closest degree of kinship will ascend to the throne. In the hypothesis, precedence will be given to the older family line, and in the case of the same degree, to the oldest member.

As can be seen, according to the current rules of succession only a male heir can ascend to the throne. The elimination of collateral lines from the Imperial House meant that the number of members of the family shrunk in a sensitive way, currently consisting of 18 members, including 5 males and 13 females. The Imperial House of Japan is thus faced with a shortage of male heirs, as well as, the fear of a prospect of shrinking to a few units within two generations.

The risk is therefore that, in a few years, the Throne of Chrysanthemum will not have a legitimate heir apparent under the law. Regardless of the issue closely related to the succession to the throne, there is still the problem of a rapidly shrinking family: the possibility that the Imperial House will be drastically reduced in a few decades is very real. This is likely to happen very early, due to the fact that in accordance with Article 12 of the Law, in the event that a female member of the family marries someone outside the family itself (and the fact is unlikely to happen otherwise!), they lose their status of member of the Imperial House.

There is a further point to consider: in order to open a family branch (or lineage) within the family, an authorization from the Imperial House Council is required, a body foreseen by Chapter V of the Law (Arts. 28-37). This authorization can however be granted only to males. Therefore, considering that six of the family members are over 70 years old and that, of the nine members of the Imperial House under the age of 35, there are eight Princesses, it is clearly evident that, due to age and marriage, the family is bound to shrink.

The question of succession has been addressed several times, and in the years prior to 2006 (the year of the birth of Prince Hisahito), the proposal to allow female descendants to ascend to the Chrysanthemum Throne was repeatedly addressed. Curiously, during the debate on the subject, the argument of the conflict with Article 14 of the Constitution was often kept in the background, and the real engine of any change was to ensure the continuation of the imperial line, uninterrupted for 125 generations from 660 BC (at least according to tradition). In November 2005, an advisory committee of the then Prime Minister Koizumi had suggested the urgent need for a legislative reform aimed at allowing the women of the Imperial House both to succeed to the throne and to establish their own branches of the family. The birth of His Highness Hisahito on 6 September 2006 made the matter less urgent, and the Government decided not to present the proposed reform to the Diet.

The problem of how to ensure a worthy numerical consistency to the Yamato Dynasty, however, remains (as was pointed out to the then Prime Minister Noda by the *Kunaicho Chokan* or Grand Majordomo of the Imperial House Agency on 5 November 2011), and the Japanese legislator is currently studying two concurrent legal proposals, one more liberal and one more conservative. According to the first proposal, the women of the Imperial House would be allowed to maintain their status even after marriage and open their own branches: the ordinary consorts would become members of the family, and the children of such couples would be members of the imperial family. To achieve this, a rather incisive reform of the Law of 1947 is needed, focusing in particular on the modification of Articles 12 and 15 (the latter specifies that ordinary male citizens cannot become members of the Imperial House). The less extensive proposal, on the other hand, advocates the simple possibility for the female members of the family to preserve membership in the Imperial House even after marriage.

The need to expand the numerical consistency of the imperial family is not only given by concern over succession (and none of the two proposals under discussion deals with this problem), but by the fact that the Emperor and his relatives are required to perform a series of functions, sometimes only of a protocol or courtesy nature, but sometimes imposed by the law. Under the Constitution, it is the Emperor who promulgates the laws, appoints the Prime Minister and the Chief Justice of the Supreme Court, meets foreign ambassadors, etc. In case of temporary disability, the task passes to another family member (and happened recently, during Emperor Emeritus Akihito's illness).

It should be noted that the 1947 reform might seem "traditional", but in effect under the 1889 Act, Princesses retained their status even after marriage. The contemporary law is therefore more restrictive and "masculine" than the original Meiji legislation. Moreover, the idea of an Empress is well documented in Japanese (also juridical) culture: the last case was that of Empress Go-Sakuramachi, on the throne from 1762 to 1770. After all, does not the Yamato Dynasty descend from a Goddess (the Sun Goddess Amaterasu Omikami)?

2.4 Constitutional Pacifism

Article 9 is one of the most known (and controversial) provisions of the Japanese constitution, and is unique in the international scene. In this regard, it is useful to report the article in its entirety:

1. Aspiring sincerely to an international peace based on justice and order, the Japanese people forever renounce war as a sovereign right of the nation and the threat or use of force as means of settling international disputes.
2. In order to accomplish the aim of the preceding paragraph, land, sea, and air forces, as well as other war potential, will never be maintained. The right of belligerency of the state will not be recognized.

It can be clearly seen that this provision goes well beyond the rejection of war contained, for example, in the Italian Constitution: not only does Japan commit itself to rejecting war as a tool for resolving international disputes or, to use the words of Von Clausewitz, as "a continuation of politics by other means":[23] the country is constitutionally prohibited from possessing a war potential. This is an element of uniqueness, which according to some commentators poses some serious problems of contrast between internal constitutional

23 Von Clausewitz, *Della guerra*, Milano, Mondadori, 1997.

law and public international law, which recognizes the right to self-defence to any sovereign state.

As mentioned, the Japanese Constitution is the oldest in the world in its original form, having not undergone any changes in the 70 years of its history: Article 9 is therefore still in force in its original form, as desired by the allied occupiers and accepted by the Japanese authorities during the occupation. However, a diachronic analysis of the interpretations given to this article, and in particular of recent developments in this regard, easily illustrates how the disposition has been progressively eroded through a heterogeneous series of measures, and how the current interpretation of the constitutional text is totally in contrast to the precise content of the norm. This contrast places the country, and in particular the Government, in the position of having to choose between addressing the question of the modification of the text or accepting cohabitation with a constant constitutional violation. The first choice, however, is rendered impracticable for a series of technical and international political reasons. With regards to the technical reasons, the Japanese Constitution is, as previously stated, one of the most rigid in the world, and should ever the necessary parliamentary majority to make a change be ever reached, Article 9 is still popular with the population. Consequently, at least for the moment, even a partial abrogation of constitutional pacifism would probably fail the test of the confirmatory referendum of Article 96. In addition to the aforementioned issues related to the constitutional review process, there are important non-technical considerations of international politics: a change of Article 9 would be considered a challenge by other countries in the area, in particular Korea, the People's Republic of China and Taiwan. In fact, significant issues are still open with these countries, related to the Japanese occupation before and during the Second World War, a brutal occupation that left deep open wounds, which were not remedied either by the Tokyo Trial or other special tribunals for war crimes.

A brief historical overview highlights how Article 9 has been progressively emptied of meaning, both through the creation of a remarkable war potential, and through interpretations increasingly distant from the spirit and the letter of the constitutional provision.

In the years immediately following the entry into force of the Constitution, Japan was subject to the Allied occupation, and the presence of the US military essentially rendered the problem of having an army irrelevant, at least as far as national defence was concerned. The situation began to change with the Korean War in 1950: the commitment of the American army on the one hand, and the need for the United States to have loyal allies in East Asia meant that, as early as 1950, the Japanese government (upon suggestion from and encouraged by the American occupiers) decided to create a military contingent known as the National Police Reserve. This military force was expressly qualified as "police" in order not to contravene Article 9, which, naturally does not prohibit the maintenance of internal public order. In 1952, simultaneously with the Peace Treaty of San Francisco, Japan and the United States stipulated the Treaty of Mutual Cooperation and Security, according to which American forces were formally authorized to be stationed on Japanese territory pledging to defend the country in case of external aggressions.[24] At the same time, the National Reserve was upgraded and renamed "National Security Forces", and a naval force was added.

A fundamental moment in the evolution of the system was 1954, when Japan reorganized the National Reserve with a law establishing the "Self-Defence Forces" (land, naval and air). The denomination is not accidental, and also denotes a change in approach with regards to Article 9, via the application of a hermeneutic syllogism whose validity is, in the most benevolent hypothesis, doubtful. The interpretation is as follows: each sovereign State is granted the right to self-defence in the event of an attack; Japan is a sovereign state; Japan is granted the right to self-defence. This interpretation obviously robs Paragraph II of the Constitution of its meaning, which does not simply envisage the rejection of war, but a real renunciation of possessing armed forces. The advocates of this thesis, however, believe that due to the fact that self-defence is an intrinsic prerogative to the nature of sovereign state, it can be considered one of the fundamental principles of international public law, and therefore cannot be limited by national provisions, all be they of constitutional rank.[25]

More sophisticated interpretations have obviously been attempted to argue that the "absolute pacifism" imposed by the literal spirit of Article 9 is actually to be interpreted in the context of a broader framework, and therefore, despite the peremptory text, the presence of armed forces is constitutionally tolerable. One of the interpretations is based precisely on a balance between two principles contained in the Constitution, namely Article 9 and the Article 98(2), which envisages a scrupulous compliance with international treaties. This balance should be read, for example, in the light of Japan joining the United Nations, in two ways. On the one hand, Japan (under the application of Art. 98) could be called to participate in UN peacekeeping missions,[26] but on the other hand, to do so, it would obviously necessitate having military forces at its disposal: a rigorous application

24 H. Honma and others, *United States Forces in Japan: A Bilateral Experience*, in D. Fleck, S. Addy (Eds.), *The Handbook of the Law of Visiting Forces*, Oxford, Oxford University Press, 2011.

25 H. Nasu, *Art. 9 of the Japanese Constitution Revisited in the Light of International Law*, in 9 *Journal of Japanese Law/Zeitschrift fuer Japanisches Recht*, n. 18, 50-66 (2004). Japan, in reality, has armed forces that number circa 250,000 people, and is among the top ten countries in the world for the size of military spending (currently, in seventh position with circa $46.3 billion in annual spending, 3.2% of global military investments. Source: *Stockholm International Peace Research Institute*, www.sipri.org). In 2007, the Ministry of Defence was formally constituted. On the Ministry's website (www.mod.go.jp) the explanation provided is precisely the following: "Since Japan is an independent state, it is recognized beyond doubt that the provision in the Art. 9 does not deny the inherent right of self-defense that Japan is entitled to maintain as a sovereign nation".

26 K. Arai, *The Pacifist Constitution of Japan and Participation to UN operations*, conference held on 23 October 2018 at the University of Siena (with introduction by T. Groppi and conclusions by M. Perini).

of Article 9, according to this reading, would therefore be in contrast with Japan's international obligations.

The Charter of the United Nations has been used by a part of Japanese legal scholarship also to justify the balancing between the rejection of war and the right to self-defence. It has been pointed out that this balancing is present in the founding document of the international organization, which, in Article 2(4) establishes a clear rejection of war (but also of the threat of the war) and Article 51 that states that every nation has the right to self-defence. This interpretation, however, tends to underestimate or even ignore the power of Paragraph 2 of Article 9.

Another reading aimed at balancing constitutional values is that which links pacifism with the Preamble of the Constitution itself, which establishes the right of peoples to live in peace, free from fear. The impossibility to defend oneself, if not by means of partisan forces composed of the civilian population or the police, would make the right of the Japanese to live in peace and free from fear non-existent.

This is not the place to deepen the long evolution (and the progressive strengthening, until becoming the ninth army for military potential in the world) of the Self-Defence Forces, and therefore it seems appropriate to focus on recent times.

In the 1990s, Japan participated for the first time in the post-war period, in compliance with a UN resolution, in a logistical support operation to international military troops during the Iraq War. This circumstance has already raised criticisms and doubts of interpretation: although the Japanese contingent had limited itself to non-combat functions, the presence of Japanese soldiers abroad had been considered by many to be incompatible with Article 9. The legal framework in which this occurred is the UN Peacekeeping Participation Act, under which active participation of Japanese contingents in international operations was permitted, but only in compliance with a number of specific conditions, that is to say: the existence of a "ceasefire" between the parties in conflict; their consent to the transaction; the neutrality of Japanese forces; the immediate withdrawal of troops in the event that the previous conditions are lost; the minimum use of force to safeguard the lives of those involved. As has been pointed out, in essence the law provides for the possibility for Japan to send troops only in conditions of safety, i.e. in cases where the usefulness of the presence of a military contingent is doubtful.

Once again, in November 2001, Japan sent troops supporting the US-led coalition troops in Afghanistan. This time, the contrast was even wider due to the fact that the allied operation had not been legitimated by a UN resolution: therefore, the constitutional argument of Article 98 of the Japanese Constitution became even less convincing in the light of the United Nations Statute, but still retained some possible validity under the Treaty of Mutual Cooperation and Security between Japan and the United States. Despite the criticisms and despite the obvious doubts arising from the contrast with Article 9, the intervention was legitimized by a specific legislation, a special law on counter-terrorism measures, with which the right to "collective self-defence" of Japan and its allies, was further expanded and codified.

Finally, in 2014, the Government led by Shinzo Abe promoted and adopted a sort of "authentic interpretation" of Article 9, according to which Japan has the legitimacy to participate in what was qualified as "collective self-defence": therefore, according to this reading, the country is allowed to send military contingents in international peacekeeping operations. Even before this decision, Japan had taken part in operations under the aegis of the United Nations, but with logistical support functions: from 2015 onwards, instead, it was permitted to send fighters. It is evident that this interpretation leads to a reading of Article 9 that is immensely distant from its text, but due to the technical and political issues mentioned above, a revision of the Constitution is neither probable nor expected, at least in the short term. Nevertheless, this interpretative provision has given rise to a compact reaction from the academic environment, which with very few exceptions has acknowledged that the Government's work is not compatible with the constitutional text. In particular, it has been noted that, according to the constant-permissive interpretation of the presence of armed forces for self-defence purposes, the only circumstance in which the use of the war potential is foreseen is in the event that there is a direct attack on Japan. The terminology used in the interpretation of the Government instead speaks more generically of "circumstances that endanger the existence of Japan" (*sonritsukikijitai*). This definition, which is vague and with variable contours, raises a series of questions that are not easy to resolve: is the danger of international terrorism a circumstance of this kind? Likewise, is the experimentation of long-range weapons of destruction in North Korea another circumstance of this kind? Moreover: the new interpretation allows Japan to take part in international coalitions, and thus also, for example, in joint exercises with other nations. The formal inclusion of the country in a multilateral contingent could give rise to doubt, regardless of the real functions of the Japanese troops, of a belligerent state, as such prohibited by the Constitution. The opinion of Japanese doctrine therefore leaves no room for doubt: the interpretation of the Government is unconstitutional, and to allow Japan the initiatives envisaged, would necessitate, inevitably, a modification of the text of the Constitution itself.

The population has also reacted with hostility to this initiative, and for the first time in many years in the country, there have been mass popular demonstrations against the government.

Over the decades, and especially after the end of the Allied occupation, the contradiction between the presence of armed forces in the country and the provision of Article 9 has been repeatedly raised, not only in public debates and in parliament but also before the courts of the State.

The first and most significant case in this regard is known as the "Sunakawa case", of 1959.[27] In 1957, some pacifist protesters had violated the perimeter of an American military base on Japanese territory (precisely, in the Sunakawa locality, on the outskirts of Tokyo): a series of criminal charges were brought against the protestors, one of them based on a special law designed to protect the US bases in the archipelago. The accused in question brought a legal action against the State, based on the following motivation: the presence of a military contingent, even non-Japanese, on the national territory violates the provision of Article 9, due to the fact that in this way Japan is nevertheless "maintaining" a military potentiality. As a result, both the United States-Japan treaty and the special law on which the charges were formulated would have been unconstitutional.

The Court of First Instance upheld the above-mentioned thesis, and pronounced in favour of the plaintiffs. However, the State proposed a direct appeal to the Supreme Court, which affirmed the constitutionality of the contested norms and treaty, and, within nine months, the State obtained its desired ruling.

The argumentation of the Japanese supreme judges was based on two lines of reasoning: the first aimed at a critical reading of the constitutional text; the second (and most important) in terms of jurisdiction of the judicial system.

Based on the first argument, according to the Supreme Court, Article 9 imposes a restriction on the maintaining of *Japanese* armed forces. Therefore, the presence of military contingents from other nations, albeit with the backing and economic support of Japan, would not therefore violate the constitutional provisions. The second argument, on the other hand, became known as the "political act theory": according to this interpretation, the decision to stipulate an international treaty is a substantially "political" decision, and therefore falls within the sphere of executive and legislative power. According to the judges, it would therefore have been inappropriate for the judiciary to enter into the merits of the Treaty: the only condition on which this could have happened would have been in the case of a "manifested unconstitutionality" of the international agreement, which, in the circumstance under scrutiny, was not the case. Ultimately, the only true "judge" of this type of decision could only be the people, who, through the election of their representatives, could have given indications regarding the country's international policies. The "political act theory" has been challenged by generations of constitutionalists in the country, who have little doubt in declaring that it was a convenient decision to avoid international tensions with Japan's most important partner. The ruling is also significant owing to the fact that it is the first, and only, time in which the Supreme Court declared that Article 9 does not prohibit self-defence.

---

27 H. Wada, *Decisions Under Art. 9 of the Constitution-The Sunakawa, Eniwa and Naganuma Decisions*, in 9 *Law in Japan* 117-128 (1976).

2.5 Legislative Power: The Parliament

Legislative power is exercised by the Parliament (*Kokkai).* The term is composed of two characters: the first, "*kuni/koku*", is the character of "Country, nation", the second, "*au/kai*" is the character of "meeting, association". A more or less literal translation of "*Kokkai*" could therefore be "National Assembly".

The Japanese legislative assembly is often called "Diet", probably under the influence of the choice made in the first English publications dating back to the Meiji period, which translate the Japanese "*Kokkai*" of the time with "Diet".

The reasons for this choice are to be found in the doctrine that arose around the Meiji Constitution. As seen previously, the Constitution promulgated in 1889 was drafted on the Prussian model. In the Japanese text we can find the expression "*Teikoku Kokkai*" ("Imperial Parliament", Art. 33 and ff., Meiji Constitution). Commentaries in English used the term "Diet" as a translation of "*Kokkai*": for instance, this linguistic choice was followed by one of the first works on the Meiji Constitution written by a Japanese author in a Western language: Hirobumi Ito's "*Commentaries on the Constitution of Japan*".[28] The author, referring to the legislative assembly of Japan, uses repeatedly the expression "(Imperial) Diet", in addition to "Houses". The use of "Diet" must be analysed in the light of the historical and political context of Japan in those years, when Japan was a young state and the political class of that time wanted, through these terminological choices, to affirm their ideological affinity with the Prussian state model. The use of the English term *Diet* perfectly suited this goal: it signalled which model government elites looked at when they created the foundations of the state, and which model to follow in the future. In the wake of the English example, the use of the nearest linguistic equivalent spread in other languages. For instance, in Romance languages such as French, Italian and Spanish, the Japanese legislative body is commonly called Diète (French) or Dieta (Italian and Spanish). With the defeat in world war II and the more or less forced democratization of the country, the character of the State and the structure of the Parliament designed by the new Constitution changed radically with respect to the past. While the choice to use "Diet", a term with well-defined connotations, before 1947 responded to specific ideological-political purposes, nowadays it sounds obsolete and it is difficult to find convincing reasons for perpetuating this terminology. The only reasons for the use of "Diet" may be respect for the existing literature, and the fact that the *Kokkai* refers to itself as "Diet" in English documents. Provided that the use of "Diet" can be considered correct when it refers to the two Houses of the Legislative Assembly of the Meiji Constitution, it seems appropriate to stress the substantial change occurred in 1947 by making an analogous change in the terminology.

---

28 H. Ito, *Commentaries on the constitution of the Empire of Japan*, M. Ito (Tr.), Westport, Greenwood Press, 1889.

The most appropriate choice in our opinion can only fall on the neutral term used in jurisprudence and social sciences to indicate modern legislative assemblies: "Parliament".

In this chapter, therefore, the Japanese *Kokkai* is called Parliament. The Constitution dedicates to the Parliament the norms referred to in Title IV (Arts. 41-64).

2.5.1 The Two Houses: Structure

The Japanese Legislative Assembly is a bicameral Parliament, composed of a lower house, or House of Representatives (*Shūgi'in*), and a higher house, or House of Councillors (*Sangi'in*) (Art. 42).

According to the Constitution, the Parliament is the highest body of state power and the only legislative body of the state (Art. 41). Both houses are elected, and their members represent the nation (Art. 43). Like in all modern democracies, the members of the Parliament do not represent exclusively their constituency but the entire nation, without imperative mandate.

The House of Representatives is the heart of the Japanese Parliament and of the political life of the nation. It casts the votes of confidence for the candidate for Prime Minister. The laws are approved by a majority of both houses, but in the event of a dissenting vote by the House of Councillors, the House of Representatives can force bills into laws by approving them in a second reading by a majority of two-thirds of the members present at the vote (Art. 59).

The House of Councillors can be considered the higher house of the Japanese Parliament, although its functions do not differ radically from those of the House of Representatives. When the same party or coalition controls both houses, the House of Councillors does not play a significant role. On the contrary, when the political forces dominating the House of Representatives do not have a two-thirds majority in the House of Councillors, it can be a challenge for the government, and sometimes it can slow down the legislative process in a decisive manner.

2.5.2 The Electoral Law and Rulings on Electoral Districts Colleges

The Constitution does not regulate in detail the number of members of the houses, leaving the details to ordinary law: "The number of the members of each House shall be fixed by law (art. 43, par. 2)". This legislative source is the Public Offices Election Act (*Koshoku senkyo ho*, L. 100 of 1950, hereinafter "Election act"). The House of Representatives currently consists of 465 members, the House of Councillors of 242 (Art. 4, Election act).

The members are elected via mixed systems, slightly different from each other, decided via ordinary law (Art 47[29]). No one can be a member of both houses at the same time (Art. 48). Members of the Parliament enjoy immunity from arrest for the period in which the Parliament is sitting and are not responsible for the opinions or votes expressed in the Parliament (Art. 50 and 51).

Two hundred eighty-nine members of the House of Representatives are elected in single-member constituencies; the remaining 176 are elected from proportional lists organized on the basis of eleven large regions.[30] The mandate of the representatives lasts four years, unless the Prime Minister prematurely dissolves the House of Representatives. This power, rarely used in the past, has been used with great political skill in recent times. Japanese citizens over the age of 25 are eligible for election to the House of Representatives.

As for the House of Councillors, 146 members are elected in plurinominal districts mirroring the administrative divisions, while the remaining 96 are elected from a national proportional list. The term of office of the councillors lasts six years, but the composition of the House of Councillors changes partially every three years, owing to the fact that every three years elections are held to elect half of its members (Art. 46 of the Constitution). The House of Councillors is therefore in some respects the House in which the political preferences of the country are more closely reflected, since elections are held (if there is no early dissolution of the House of Representatives) at shorter intervals than those of the House of Representatives. On the other hand, since the mandate of the councillors lasts six years, it possesses a certain political inertia that can mitigate sudden changes in the country's political preferences. An example of this mechanism is represented by the elections of December 2012, won overwhelmingly by the Liberal Democratic Party of Abe, who gained a solid majority in the House of Representatives. Despite this victory, the LDP did not have an equally overwhelming majority in the upper house, due to the opposition councillors elected in 2010 and whose mandate has lasted until 2016. The age at which one can stand for election to the House of Councillors is 30.

The right to vote for both houses was set in 1945 at 20; in 2015 it was extended to those over 18 years of age. Thus, in the elections for the House of Councillors in the summer of 2016, for the first time in Japan more than two million voters of 18 and 19 years of age had the right to vote. Adults who have been registered as residents for at least three months in a municipality are registered in the local electoral lists and may exercise their right to vote.

A little known institution survives in Japan: the electoral deposit system. It was introduced in 1925, and despite the post-war reforms, it has never been abolished.

29 "Electoral districts, method of voting and other matters pertaining to the method of election of members of both Houses shall be fixed by law."

30 Art. 13, Election act.

According to the Election act (Art. 92 and ff.), every candidate for the elections, or their political party, must deposit a sum of money to the State at the time of the announcement of their candidacy. The sum is not just symbolic: 3 million yen in the case of candidates in single-member constituencies of the House of Representatives or in the plurinominal constituency of the House of Councillors, or 6 million yen in the case of candidates in proportional lists. Both sums must be deposited if a candidate runs in the single-member constituencies and in the proportional list.[31] After the elections, only the winning candidate obtains a full refund of the sum they deposited; unelected candidates can obtain a refund of all or part of the sum, if they reach a certain number of votes;[32] in case the votes received below a certain threshold, the candidates lose their money.

A very delicate issue, with important political implications, and the subject of several pronouncements of unconstitutionality by lower courts and the Supreme Court, is that of the malapportionment of the various electoral districts of the Archipelago resulting in vote disparity. Due to internal migration from rural areas to the more economically and socially attractive urban centres, the Japanese countryside has undergone a gradual and constant depopulation. The disparity between the population size of rural and urban districts colleges has therefore widened over the years, thus leading to the recent situation in which large but sparsely populated rural districts elect the same number of candidates of urban districts with a population up to four times bigger.[33] This is a clear violation of the principle of voter equality: residents in the districts with few voters exercise a much "heavier" vote than voters in the most populated districts. This situation of inequality was already clear from the 1960s, and the electoral law, which set the boundaries of the districts, began to be challenged before the Supreme Court, with plaintiffs claiming its unconstitutionality. In 1976, the Supreme Court issued its third ruling of unconstitutionality precisely on this issue,[34] but did not go as far as to declare the elections null and void.[35] After this ruling,

---

31 The amounts correspond, respectively, to 24,000 and 48,000 euro. The deposit of sums of money is also required in local elections for governor and mayor, with the sole exception of members of local assemblies (Art. 92 Election act).

32 In the case of uninominal districts for the House of Representatives, the threshold is 10% of valid votes. In the case of plurinominal districts for the House of Councillors and proportional lists, the rules are more complex and depend, besides the absolute number of valid votes, on the number of candidates. *See* Art. 93, Election act.

33 In 1947, the maximum disparity between districts colleges of the House of Representatives was about 1 to 5. Y. Hasebe, *The Supreme Court of Japan: Its Adjudication on Electoral Systems and Economic Freedoms*, in 5 *International Journal of Constitutional Law* 296-307 (2007), 301.

34 Ruling of 14 April 1976, n. tsu 75. It shows that the inhabitants of the Chiba 1 district are 4.99 times more numerous than the district of Hyogo 5.

35 The Court adopted the doctrine of the so-called "Ruling in (special) circumstances" (*jijo hanketsu*), according to which it declares the unconstitutionality of the provision in question, but not the nullity of the consequences deriving from it. Some judgments of the lower courts have recently declared the nullity of the elections, but they have not been confirmed by the Supreme Court, which so far adopted decisions that can be summarized as "unconstitutional, but valid". S. Matsui, *Why is the Japanese Supreme Court So Conservative*, in 88 *Washington University Law Review* 1375 (2010).

many governments have promised reforms aimed at limiting such disparities within an "acceptable" 2:1 disparity ratio, but these projects are made difficult by demographic fluctuations and by the reluctance of the ruling Liberal Democratic Party to dismantle a system that so far has secured it a block of easy and loyal votes from the rural areas.

2.5.3 *Legislation*

The Japanese Constitution adopts and adheres strictly to the principle of the separation of powers of the state. The Constitution declares that Parliament is the only body with legislative power. In fact, the picture is partly different, as in many liberal democracies: the Parliament is indeed the body that exercises the legislative power, but many laws it approves are of governmental origin. The position of supremacy enjoyed by ministerial officials with respect to members of the Parliament is a theme frequently mentioned in the works that analyse the relations between popular sovereignty and bureaucratic elites in Japan. The following paragraphs will present the basics of legislative procedure in Japan.

Bills are presented by members of Parliament, and must be supported by at least 20 representatives or 10 councillors.[36] A custom established to thwart attempts of minority factions within the parties from presenting their bills, and confirmed by a precedent of a lower court, requires the support of the entire parliamentary group to which the proponent of the law belongs.[37] Article 72 of the Constitution and Article 5 of the Cabinet Act[38] envisage the possibility that the government presents bills to Parliament: in this case the Prime Minister, not the individual ministers, submits them to the Parliament.[39] This is in fact very frequent. The bills presented by the government become law with a frequency around three times higher than the bills of parliamentary origin.[40]

After the bill is formally submitted to one of the houses, the competent committee examines it.[41] If the committee approves the text, it is presented to the House in plenary for discussion and voting.

The quorum for the validity of the sessions of each House is one third of the members (Art. 56). The discussions are public, unless two-thirds of those present request that the discussion and voting be conducted in secret (Art. 57). The text approved by a House is

---

36 These thresholds are respectively raised to 50 representatives or 20 councillors in case the law envisages budget expenditures. *See* the Diet (Parliament) Act, Art. 56.

37 S. Matsui, *The Constitution of Japan. A Contextual Analysis*, Oxford and Portland, Hart, 2011, 78.

38 Naikaku ho, Act 5 of 1947. Art. 5 states that "The President of the Cabinet presents draft bills, the budget and other bills to Parliament as a representative of the Cabinet (...)."

39 Bills are drafted by the important Cabinet Legislation Bureau (*Naikaku hoseikyoku*), on which *see infra*.

40 S. Matsui, *The Constitution of Japan. A Contextual Analysis*, op. cit.

41 In the House of Representatives and in the House of Councillors, there are commissions, established on areas of competence mirroring that of ministries; at the time of writing there are 17 commissions in each house.

sent to the other House, where it is examined with the same procedures. If there are changes in the text approved, the bill must be re-examined and approved in its new version by the other House. Bills approved in their identical form by both Houses become laws. The the House of Representatives however can force a bill into law even with the opposition of the House of Councillors, if it approves for a second time, with a majority of two-thirds, a bill not approved by the House of Councillors.[42]

2.6 EXECUTIVE POWER: THE GOVERNMENT

2.6.1 *The Provisions of the Constitution: Composition, Designation and Votes of Confidence*

Chapter 5 of the Constitution, titled "The Cabinet (*Naikaku*)" is dedicated to executive power. The Cabinet is composed of the Prime Minister and the other ministers, in accordance with the provisions of the law (Art. 66) and has executive power as outlined by the Constitution (Art. 65). In order to prevent the possibility of heading down the same path that led to the military dictatorship in the 1930s, the current Constitution explicitly provides that the Prime Minister and the other ministers must be civilians ("*bunmin*").[43] The Cabinet is collectively responsible to the Parliament (Art. 66 para. 3).

The Prime Minister is appointed by the Parliament from among its members, via the resolutions of each of the two houses. In the event of a disagreement on the appointment, the nomination of the House of Representatives is deemed the nomination of the Parliament (Art. 67). The Constitution thus establishes a very close bond between Parliament, and in particular the House of Representatives, and the government. Moreover, the Constitution eliminates all kinds of actual control by the Emperor over the executive: the Emperor is in charge only of the formal appointment of the Prime Minister (Art. 6). In the practice established under the current Constitution, the leader of the party who holds the parliamentary majority becomes Prime Minister. The internal struggles between party factions and the elections for the presidency of the Liberal-Democratic Party ("*Jiyū Minshu To*",

---

42 A negative vote or the lack of an affirmative vote within 60 days from the decision of the House of Councillors are considered as a rejection.

43 An attentive reader will not fail to notice the apparent inconsistency between the provision of Art. 9 that prohibits the maintenance of military forces of land, sea and air (widely commented above, para. 4), and this article which reiterates that ministers cannot be members of the armed forces. This latter provision, apparently superfluous, must however be interpreted in the sense in which, at the time of the entry into force of the Constitution, it precluded the appointment as Minister of State of former members of the armed forces. Subsequently, it is the foundation of the prohibition to appoint officers of the so-called Self-defence forces as ministers of state. *Cf.* S. Matsui, *The Constitution of Japan. A Contextual Analysis*, above notes 36, 93. *See below.*

often abbreviated as "*Jiminto*") have a deep impact on the constitutional architecture of the country. With the exception of few short periods, the Liberal-Democratic Party has remained in power since 1955.[44] However, until the years 2000 and with few exceptions,[45] the Japanese Prime Minister never was strong and charismatic figure, due to the fact that he (so far there has never been a female Prime Minister in Japan) had also to act as a connecting point between the party factions, usually without a clear popular legitimation.

The Prime Minister appoints the ministers, and can remove them from office at his own discretion (Art. 68). This faculty has been exercised with a certain frequency. The decisions of the Cabinet are adopted in a collegial manner: each minister must therefore affix their own seal on all the decisions of the Cabinet. In the event of disagreement with the refusal of a minister to give his consent to a proposal, the Cabinet cannot adopt a decision by majority: the only way to have a decision approved in the event of a stubborn opposition of one minister is the substitution of the dissenting minister.[46] The Prime Minister has the power to decide whether to allow a minister to be subject to criminal proceedings during the period in which the minister is in office (Art. 75 of the Constitution).

The Cabinet Act provides that the maximum number of ministers is 15, which can be increased in exceptional circumstances to 19.[47] The Constitution provides that the majority of the ministers shall be chosen from among the members of the Houses, stressing the strong link between the government and the Parliament.

The Constitution does not have detailed provisions on the vote of confidence, but does have some provisions on the vote of no confidence. Strictly speaking, a newly formed government is under no obligation to present itself to the Parliament to obtain a vote of confidence, but is obliged to resign if the House of Representatives passes a vote of no confidence or rejects a vote of confidence (Art. 69). The only exception is when the House

---

44 M.M. Mochizuki, *Managing and Influencing the Japanese Legislative Process: The Role of Parties and the National Diet*, 1982, PhD dissertation, Harvard University, 1982; Matsui, *The Constitution of Japan. A Contextual Analysis*, 103.

45 Since the 2000s, Jun'ichiro Koizumi and Shinzo Abe are examples of Japanese Prime Ministers with a great charisma and considerable political capital.

46 This eventuality may sound like an extreme example, but it occurred in 2005, under the Koizumi cabinet. The way in which the crisis was managed raised doubts of constitutionality. *See* Matsui, 94; *id.*, 102 n. 14.

47 These limits were lower in the past, but were raised in recent times following the 2011 Tohoku earthquake and tsunami, when a ministry for reconstruction was added, and in 2013 after the choice of Tokyo as the host city for the 2020 Summer Olympics, when a minister for the Olympics was added. At the time of writing, in addition to the Prime Minister, there are 19 ministers, entirely chosen from among the members of Parliament. They are: the Minister of Finance, Minister of Internal Affairs and Communications, Minister of Legal Affairs, Minister of Foreign Affairs, Minister of Education, Culture, Sport, Science and Technology, Minister of Health, Labour and Welfare, Minister of Agriculture, forests and fisheries, Minister for the Economy, Trade and Industry, Minister for the Territory, Infrastructure, Transport and Tourism, Minister for the Environment, Minister for Defence, Cabinet Secretary, Minister for Reconstruction [for the areas hit by the earthquake 2011], Minister for Administration Reform, Minister for Okinawa and the Northern Territories, Minister for Economic Recovery, Minister for Equal Opportunities, Minister for Population Growth, Minister for the Tokyo Olympics.

of Representatives is dissolved within 10 days from the passing of the vote of no confidence, in which case the government remains in office until a new Prime Minister is chosen by the newly elected House of Representatives.

2.6.2 *The Powers of the Prime Minister and Ministers*

The powers of the Prime Minister and the Cabinet are listed summarily in Articles 72 and 73. The first states that the Prime Minister, acting as a representative of the Cabinet, presents bills, reports to Parliament on internal and foreign affairs, and manages and controls public administration. Article 73 provides that, in addition to general administrative functions, the Cabinet has the following functions: to faithfully execute laws and administer state affairs; manage foreign affairs, conclude international treaties, with the prior or subsequent authorization of the Parliament; manage public administration on the basis of the principles established by law; prepare the state budget and present it to Parliament; issue Cabinet orders ("*seirei*"), which however cannot include criminal provisions; and decide on amnesty and other extraordinary measures of clemency.[48]

In practice, the Prime Minister and the Cabinet have executive functions, in a manner substantially similar to most liberal democracies based on the parliamentary system.

Dissolving the House of Representatives is among the most important powers of the Prime Minister. The dissolution is formally proclaimed by the Emperor (Art. 7.3), but substantially the decision rests with the Prime Minister. Elections must be held within 40 days from the date of dissolution, and the first session of the House must take place within 30 days from the date of the election (Art. 54). As previously seen, on the occasion of the election of a new House of Representatives, the government is obliged to resign, and after the elections the new Parliament must proceed to appoint the Prime Minister, according to the ordinary rules. The power to dissolve the House of Representatives before its ordinary 4 years term is a critical power, which can lead to significant political victories.[49] It should be noted that there are no explicit provisions in the constitutional text to justify the total discretion of the decision regarding the early dissolution of the House, but despite doubts voiced by some scholars, it is permitted and has been used under the current Constitution. The thesis supporting the admissibility and the discretionary nature of the power to dissolve the House of Representatives is backed by a precedent of the Supreme Court of 1960. In this case, Gizo Tomabechi, a former member of the House, claimed the unconstitutionality

48 According to Art. 7.6, the provisions of clemency must be performed by the Emperor, on behalf of the people, with the advice and approval of the Cabinet.

49 The most recent example of a clever and in some ways bold use of this power is the dissolution by Prime Minister Shinzo Abe in the autumn of 2014. There are no provisions that prevent the Parliament from reappointing as prime minister the same person who dissolved the House. This is what happened in 2014, when Abe was appointed again by the newly elected House, in which Abe had maintained a solid majority.

of the dissolution occurred in 1952, due to the fact that it was decided without a vote of no confidence or of a decision by the Cabinet, and demanded the payment of the salary as a Representative that he did not receive as a result of the early dissolution. The judges of the Supreme Court technically did not decide on the merits, stating that the decision on the early dissolution of the House of Representatives was a high-level political decision, which, in accordance with the principle of separation of powers, cannot be assessed by the judiciary, but in fact the dissolution was not declared unconstitutional and Mr. Tomabechi lost the case.[50]

2.6.2 The Cabinet Legislation Bureau

The Cabinet Legislation Bureau (*Naikaku hosei kyoku*, hereinafter CLB) is an internal body within the Prime Minister's office and it is not part of the Cabinet. It is one of the most important, most prestigious and most influential institutions in the Japanese administration.[51]

A first "Legislative Bureau" (*Hosei kyoku*) in Japan was created in 1875, but the real antecedent of the current body was established in 1885. It adopted the French Council of State as a model, and incorporated functions of assistance to the government and to the supreme administrative court. Under the Meiji Constitution, the Legislative Bureau was responsible for approving the acts of ministers, both normative acts and acts related to internal matters, and for supervising the activity of the Privy Council.[52]

With the introduction of the new Constitution, the bureau was abolished and its top officials purged. With the end of the US occupation in 1952, it was promptly re-established. It is now composed of personnel transferred by the ministries for at least five years: more than one post is reserved for the most important ministries (Finance and Legal Affairs), while some other ministries are not represented. The prestige associated with holding a position in the CLB implies that after the end of their mandate the staff of the Bureau does not return to the Ministry to which they came from; their career usually continues via various forms of *amakudari*[53] or in senior positions in the administration, in some cases even as judges of the Supreme Court.

---

50 Peter J. Herzog, *Japan's pseudo-democracy*, Folkestone, Japan Library, 1993, 30 and ff.; S. Matsui, *The Constitution of Japan. A Contextual Analysis*, op. cit., 103.

51 Another sign of its importance is that the Director General of the CLB is the highest paid bureaucrat in the administration. On the CLB, see R.J. Samuels, *Politics, Security Policy, and Japan's Cabinet Legislation Bureau*, in *JPRI Working Paper No. 99* (2004).

52 See R.J. Samuels, *Politics, Security Policy, and Japan's Cabinet Legislation Bureau*, in *JPRI Working Paper No. 99* (2004).

53 The term "*amakudari*" literally means "descending from the sky", and indicates the practice of appointing public officers and high-ranking bureaucrats to well-paid and highly visible positions, but with little prac-

The Bureau performs two main functions: first, in its advisory capacity, it offers opinions to the Cabinet as a collective body, as well as to individual ministers. Furthermore, it painstakingly examines bills, international treaties and other documents of the government in order to make a prior check on their compliance with the Constitution and the legislation in force, and to control the style, the language, the structure and in general the quality of the drafting. This control of course is not mandatory, but it has become a deeply-rooted practice and in fact it is an obligatory step. For bills originating from ministries, after a preliminary double examination, the competent Minister presents the bill to the Cabinet for approval and submission to the Houses, where it follows the normal legislative procedure. In this case, the Director of the CLB may appear before the Parliament together with the ministers to provide answers on the bills of ministerial origin.

Due to its tasks, structure and the technical expertise of its staff, the Bureau enjoys a high reputation even in the courts of the country. The opinion-giving activity includes opinions on the interpretation of laws and opinions also given to the Parliament on issues that may be of constitutional relevance. Thus, the control of constitutionality, in theory entrusted to each judge and ultimately to the Supreme Court, is in fact partially performed by this Bureau: in the rare cases in which the Japanese courts declared a provision to be unconstitutional, the provision was often of parliamentary origin or dating back to the period prior to the entry into force of the current Constitution.[54]

2.7 Judicial Power

Chapter 6 of the Constitution (Arts. 76-82) outlines the basic norms concerning the judicial system and trials. Article 76 states that "The whole judicial power is vested in a Supreme Court and in such inferior courts as are established by law". The law governing the judiciary, the powers of the lower courts, and many detailed aspects of the Supreme Court is the Courts Act (Law 59 of 1947).

Article 76 par. 2 prohibits the establishment of special courts and the attribution of jurisdictional powers to the government or its organs or agencies. If the meaning of the second part of the provision is clear, the first part must be interpreted as the provision that precludes the reintroduction of administrative tribunals, similar to those that existed up until the Second World War. Paragraph 3 states that all judges exercise their power independently and according to their conscience, and are bound only by the Constitution and the laws. The right of access to the courts cannot be violated (Art. 32). In particular, the

tical everyday tasks, in companies or private or public institutions. On the phenomenon *cf.* C. Jones, *Amakudari and Japanese Law*, in 22 *Michigan State International Law Review* 879 (2013).

54 Y. Hasebe, *The Supreme Court of Japan: Its Adjudication on Electoral Systems and Economic Freedoms*, op. cit.

Constitution includes the fundamental right of citizens to claim compensation from the State or from other public bodies, in the forms established by law, as compensation for losses incurred as a result of an unlawful act carried out by a public official. The law that governs the matter in detail is the State Redress Act (*Kokka baisho ho,* Law 125 of 1947).

2.7.1 *The Supreme Court*

The structure of the Supreme Court is outlined briefly by Article 79, which describes its fundamental features, leaving to ordinary law the task of regulating the details. The appointment of the Chief Justice of the Supreme Court, however, is found not in the chapter dedicated to the judiciary but in the chapter dedicated to the Emperor, in Article 6: it is in fact the Emperor, upon designation of the Cabinet, who appoints the Chief Justice of the Supreme Court. In practice, the Emperor has no say in choosing a candidate, nor a veto power: his role does not go beyond a simple ratification of the government's decision. Article 79 of the Constitution outlines that the justices of the Supreme Court, unlike what occurs for the Chief Justice, are appointed by the government, without the intervention of the Emperor, but it does not specify their number. The Courts Act mandates a total number of 14. (Art. 5 par. 3, Courts Act). Since the 1970s, six judges have been chosen among the judges of lower courts, two among the prosecutors, two among the members of the public administration, while the remaining five seats have been filled by university professors and lawyers. This allocation of seats guarantees that the "bureaucratic" component always has a majority, both in the Grand Bench, as well as in the Petty Benches.[55]

The appointment of each judge is confirmed by popular vote on the occasion of the first general elections for the House of Representatives following the appointment (Art. 79 par. 2). A judge is removed if the majority of voters express a vote for the dismissal. Up to now, this has never occurred. The term of office of judges of the Supreme Court expires when they reach the age of 70 (Art. 50, Courts Act).

The Supreme Court normally gives decisions through its petty benches (*shohotei*), i.e. panels composed of five judges (Art. 9 and ff. Courts Act). When matters of particular importance are to be decided, or when there are conflicting precedents for which an authoritative decision is necessary to resolve the issue, all 15 Supreme Court judges decide together the case, forming what is called the Grand Bench (*daihotei*). An unique feature among all the judges of all the courts of the Archipelago is that the judges of the Supreme Court have the duty to express their own opinion in the decisions of the cases in which

55 As noted by Repeta, the composition of the Supreme Court in its first two decades of operation gave more space to the "liberal" components, *i.e.* lawyers and professors, but this structure was altered at the turn of 1970, giving rise to the current, more conservative composition. L. Repeta, *Reserved Seats on Japan's Supreme Court*, in 88 *Washington University Law Review* 1713 (2010).

they participate (Art. 11 of the tribunal). A significant proportion of the judgments and decisions published on the website of the Japanese Supreme Court contain concurring or dissenting opinions.[56] This provision is linked to the aforementioned provision of Article 79 of the Constitution, which states that on the occasion of the first elections for the House of Representatives following their appointment, the judges of the Supreme Court should be subject to the popular judgment to be confirmed in their office. If there were no information on the positions adopted in the cases in which they participated, it would not be possible for the voters to evaluate the work of the judges. In practice however, public opinion and the mass media and in some ways also practitioners and academics are not especially interested in the positions of individual judges. There are basically two reasons for this popular disinterest: on the one hand, the Supreme Court is rarely called to decide on cases of great popular interest, and in the few cases where it had the possibility, it hid behind the theory of the "political decision" (*see below*) to toss the question back to the political authorities. Furthermore, Supreme judges are forbidden from conducting any electoral campaign activity for the purpose of their confirmation. The results of the popular consultations held in accordance with Article 79 of the Constitution, in most cases resulted in between 6% and 9% of the votes cast requesting the removal of a judge, with a minimum difference between the results relating to the various judges. The removal from office seems therefore to be a hypothesis almost completely theoretical and there have been proposals for the abolition of this provision.[57] However, since the judges' evaluation is mandated by a constitutional rule, it seems unlikely that this institute will soon be reformed, given the rigidity of the procedures for the amendment of the Japanese Constitution.[58]

2.7.2 The Lower Courts

The High Courts, eight in all the country, plus six branches, sit in panels of three judges and rule on appeals against judgments in criminal and civil matters of the District Courts or of Family Courts, or in criminal matters of the Summary Courts. High Courts also have exclusive jurisdiction over disputes concerning administrative matters and in particular over electoral matters, crimes of insurrection or other crimes against the State, and over

56 Between 2001 and 2007, between 9% and 17% of the rulings and decisions published on the website of the Japanese Supreme Court contained minority opinions, *i.e.* concurring or dissenting opinions; between 2008 and 2010 the percentage rose up to over 30%. *See* A. Ortolani, *Junin toiro*, in R.R. Cavalieri and G.F. Colombo, *Il massimario. Proverbi annotati di diritto comparato. Liber amicorum in onore di Gabriele Crespi Reghizzi*, Milan, Giuffrè, 2013.

57 T. Izumi, *Concerning the Japanese Public's Evaluation of Supreme Court Justices*, in 88 *Washington University Law Review* 1769 (2010).

58 *Ibid.*

appeals against decisions by independent administrative authorities such as the Patent Office, in which cases the panel consists of five judges.

For all other civil and criminal cases, the court of first instance is the District Court. There are 50 District courts in the country, with 203 branches. The jurisdiction of each court corresponds to their respective administrative district (*to-fu-ken*), with the exception of the island of Hokkaido, which is divided into four judicial districts. Furthermore, these courts have jurisdiction over appeals against decisions in civil matters of the summary courts. As a rule, the judge is a single judge, with the exception of appellate judgments and cases concerning the most serious crimes, when a panel of three judges decides the case. Since 2009, a form of citizen participation in criminal trials has been introduced. Hence, for serious offenses (about 3% of criminal cases) the panel includes a majority of lay judges.[59]

Hierarchically subordinated to the District Courts, there are 438 summary Courts, which judge civil cases of limited value[60] and minor offenses.

Family Courts are located with each District Court or its branch, with Summary Courts and in 77 more locations. Family Courts judge in matters of family, succession, personal status and juvenile delinquency.

A section of the Tokyo High Court specializes in questions relating to intellectual property.

2.7.3 *Judges*

Until 2005, access to the legal professions, including that of judge, took place via a very selective national examination.[61] For most of the post-war period, the percentage of suitable candidates stood at around 2% of the candidates, with an average number of successful candidates in the period 1960/1990 of approximately 500 each year, progressively moving up to 1,183 in 2002. After the examination, the successful candidates undertook a two-year internship at the Institute for Legal Practice, managed by the Supreme Court, which included periods of study and periods of law practice. Finally, after a final examination aimed primarily at creating an internal ranking for the purpose of assigning posts, the so-called "Practitioners" embarked on a career as a judge, prosecutor or lawyer.[62]

---

59 *See above*, para. 6.

60 As of February 2011, the limit value of the dispute is 1,400,000 jpy.

61 On the legal professions, *see* G. F. Colombo, *Giappone*, in A. Negri (Ed.), *Sistemi giuridici nel mondo*, Torino, Giappichelli, 2010, 252 and ff.

62 On the formation of jurists, *cf.* K. Rokumoto, *Legal Education*, in D.H. Foote, *Law in Japan: A Turning Point*, Seattle, University of Washington Press, 2011, 190; A. Riles and T. Uchida, *Reforming knowledge? A Socio-Legal Critique of the Legal Education Reforms in Japan*, in 1 *A Socio-Legal Critique of the Legal Education Reforms in Japan (March 23, 2009). Drexel Law Review* 3 (2009), 3; C.P. Jones, *Japan's New Law Schools: The Story So Far*, in 14 *Zeitschrift für Japanisches Recht* 248-256 (2009), 248.

Since April 2004, about 70 schools for legal professions, established with the major universities of the Archipelago, offer a three-year limited-access study program.[63] Attendance at these so-called "Law Schools" is today the main channel for access to the legal professions.

Judges of the lower courts are appointed by the government from a list of names prepared by the Supreme Court (Art. 80, *see below*). The term of office is 10 years, after which it can be renewed at intervals of ten years, until reaching the age limit, set at 65 years of age.

2.7.4 *The General Affairs Bureau of the Supreme Court*

In addition to its judicial activity, the Supreme Court plays a crucial role in the administration of justice in Japan via its administrative structure. First of all, it influences the provisions regulating trials contained in the codes of procedure by issuing supplementary rules on the functioning of the courts and internal regulations. A very delicate function is the appointment, confirmation and transfer of judges, managed by the General Secretariat (*Saiko Saibansho Jimu Sokyoku*). The appointment of new judges (as associate judges) for the first ten-year term and their confirmation in service for successive terms is formally the task of the government, upon proposal of the Supreme Court (Constitution 80). In fact, the government usually ratifies the list prepared by the General Secretariat, which thus has almost complete control over the judicial body. The criteria used to select candidates on the list are not known, and the Supreme Court has long considered this power to be entirely discretionary; since 2003, a commission composed of magistrates, lawyers and academics supports the Supreme Court in the extension of the list of judges to be confirmed, but the criteria used to evaluate the judges are not entirely clear.[64]

The General Secretariat is responsible for another very important task, namely the three-year transfers of judges. Assignments in major urban centres, in higher courts, or as the President of the Court are associated with greater prestige and career opportunities than positions in in rural areas of lower courts or family courts. Moreover, living in bigger cities brings with it various material advantages, rather than being confined in rural areas. The Secretariat thus controls the career of judges, and via these transfers sends clear signals on which judges deserve career advancement, and which do not. The evaluation criteria on the basis of which the General Affairs Bureau compiles the rankings among judges and

63 Law Graduates can skip the first year and start attending from the second year of the course. The first graduates of the so-called "Law School" took the entrance examination for the legal professions in 2006.

64 S. Matsui, *The Constitution of Japan. A Contextual Analysis*, op. cit., 125. On the Commission for the appointment of lower courts judges *see* D.H. Foote, *The Supreme Court and the Push for Transparency in Lower Court Appointments in Japan*, in 88 *Washington University Law Review* 1745-1763 (2011).

decides transfers and promotions, is a topic of central importance in the discussion on the independence and integrity of Japanese courts.

Judges staff the General Secretariat, in order to guarantee the independence of the judiciary from the interference of political power. Transfers to the Bureau itself, where judges do not perform judicial but purely administrative functions, are among the most prestigious and are a sign of the bureaucratic nature of the Japanese judiciary. All the General Secretaries of the Bureau were later appointed judges of the Supreme Court. There is also the case of a Supreme Court Chief Justice who spent only 8 years, on a career of 36, in courtrooms, and the remaining 28 in administrative positions.[65]

At the end of the ten-year term, judges are usually confirmed in service until retirement at 65 (Art. 50 of the Courts Act). Only two cases of non-confirmation are known, and in both cases this was not due to a government decision but to the fact that the General Affairs Bureau did not include the names in the list presented to the government. One case involved a judge who, for family reasons, refused a transfer.[66] The best-known case concerns Judge Miyamoto, a member of the leftist organization *Seinen Hôritsuka Kyôkai* (Association of Young Lawyers), who did not appear on the list presented to the government in 1971, and in April 1972 ceased to be a judge. However, it is to be mentioned that these numbers might not tell the truth because in some cases, anticipating their non-reconfirmation, the judges resign. The cases of substantial non-reconfirmation may, in this sense, be more.[67]

A highly debated question, connected to the dynamics that regulate the reconfirmation and transfer of judges, concerns the question of the autonomy of judges from political power. On this delicate problem, several scholars of the Japanese system have recently expressed their opinions, supporting opposing views. According to the analysis of Ramseyer and Rasmusen, the judges who judge against the government on various matters are regularly punished by the General Affairs Bureau of the Supreme Court via appointments to less prestigious offices and less brilliant careers.[68] Haley, while recognizing the conservative character of the Japanese judiciary, denies that there are direct political influences on the judges and declares the Japanese judges among "the most honest, politically independent, and professionally competent in the world today".[69]

---

65 C. Jones, *In the Best Interests of the Court: What American Lawyers Need to Know About Child Custody and Visitation in Japan*, in 8 *Asian Pacific Law and Policy Journal* 166 (2006), 173 n. 20.

66 The law guarantees judges the right to refuse transfers during their 10 years term. Of course, the refusal of a transfer, as in the case mentioned, may cause a reaction on the part of the General Affairs Bureau.

67 One of these recent cases is that of the former judge Kaoru Inoue, now a lawyer and prolific author of vitriolic essays on the Japanese legal and judiciary system. *See* C. P.A. Jones, *Japan's Crazy Judges*, in *Journal of Japanese Law/Zeitschrift fuer Japanisches Recht*, 2008.

68 J.M. Ramseyer, E.B. Rasmusen, *Measuring Judicial Independence: The Political Economy of Judging in Japan*, Chicago, University of Chicago Press, 2003.

69 J. O. Haley, *The Japanese Judiciary: Maintaining Integrity, Autonomy, and the Public Trust* in D.H. Foote, *Law in Japan: A Turning Point*, Seattle, University of Washington Press, 2011, 99.

2.7.5 *The Control of Constitutionality: General Characteristics*

The influence of the common law model on the Japanese Supreme Court is also evident from the way in which it has interpreted and developed its powers regarding the control of constitutionality. In the first years of its establishment, it repeatedly stated that according to the Constitution, it has no power to assess the constitutionality of a provision in an abstract manner, but only to declare its unconstitutionality where such a provision is referred to in a judgment. The ruling of the plenary bench of 7 July 1948 first stated this principle citing the American Constitution and the famous *Marbury v. Madison* case; these principles were to be confirmed later and would become established case-law.[70] The influence is however only partial: it has been noted that in the United States it is possible to file an appeal to the judicial authority to obtain the declaration of unconstitutionality of certain rules and measures aimed at avoiding its concrete application, while in Japan this is not permitted.[71]

On the practical side, constitutional issues can be raised during a trial in which the rule deemed unconstitutional must be applied, or, in the event that the constitutionality of an administrative provision is claimed, an individual must act with an administrative request[72] or with a claim for compensation against the State.[73]

2.7.6 *A Conservative and Useless Court?*

It cannot be said that the Supreme Court and its control on the constitutionality of laws play a significant role in the living law of the country. Up to now, the Supreme Court has exercised its control of constitutional legitimacy with extreme caution, and up to May 2016, there have been only 10 cases in which it has declared a provision of law to be unconstitutional.[74]

---

70 S. Matsui, *Why is the Japanese Supreme Court So Conservative*, op. cit., 1378.

71 S. Matsui, *The Constitution of Japan. A Contextual Analysis*, op. cit., 141.

72 That is a petition submitted on the basis of the Law on proceedings in administrative cases (*Gyosei jiken sosho ho*, Law 139 of 1962).

73 Regulated by the Law on State Compensation (*Kokka Baisho Ho*, Law 125 of 1947).

74 Besides these 8 cases, the following two must be mentioned: the judgment of 4 September 2013 which declared unconstitutional the provision of Art. 900 of the civil code on succession, which stated that legitimate children were entitled to a double portion of inheritance compared to illegitimate children, and the judgment of 16th December 2015, which declared unconstitutional the provision of Art. 733 of the civil code regarding marriage, in the part in which it prohibited divorced woman from remarrying before 180 days had elapsed from the date of the divorce. In the latter case, the Supreme Court declared that a 100-day time limit would be reasonable to resolve possible disputes over the presumption of paternity, limiting as far as possible the difference in treatment between men and women regarding the period, that had been exclusively applied to woman, who were not allowed to remarry. On the day of the judgment, the Ministry of Legal Affairs issued a circular incorporating the contents of the sentence.

Perhaps the most well-known area in which the Supreme Court has been called to decide is that linked to Article 9 and to the so-called Japanese "constitutional pacifism". The Supreme Court, despite some rulings on the point made by lower courts,[75] has so far avoided taking a clear position on the constitutionality of the Self-Defence Forces and of the security treaty between Japan and the United States. It was a case on the constitutional legitimacy of the 1951 security treaty between Japan and the United States that offered the Supreme Court the chance to enunciate the doctrine of the "political question", which has already been discussed (para. 4). Since then, the cases concerning Article 9 are decided, or rather they are not decided, referring directly or indirectly, to this precedent.

It should be noted, however, that the pronouncement of unconstitutionality applies exclusively to the case before the court, and the action of the legislator is necessary, via ordinary procedures, to remove or amend the unconstitutional provision. It is clear that such a mechanism deprives the Court of the power to act effectively pronouncing judgments that declare immediately null and void the provisions declared unconstitutional. For instance, the rule that punished more severely the murder of the direct ascendant than a simple murder, declared unconstitutional in 1973, was changed only in 1994 with the linguistic reform of the penal code (*see below*, para. 8).

Likewise, the rulings with which the Court declared, as noted above, with an ambiguous expression, the state of unconstitutionality of the boundaries of the electoral districts due to the imbalance between the population represented in them, did not invalidate the elections, nor did they push the legislator or the government to rectify the situation within a reasonable time limit. These rulings are a clear sign on the one hand, of the will of the Supreme Court to keep as far away as possible from issues that may have politically sensitive side effects, while on the other hand, reveal the lack of effectiveness of its rulings. From a certain point of view, judicial review in Japan does not play an important role, so much so as to be defined a failure.[76] The reasons for this may be numerous: cultural, historical, or based on political influence, and the arguments brought to support these reasons lend themselves to different interpretations and criticisms.[77] A complementary perspective emphasizes the institutional elements that influence the decision-making process and the outcomes of the judicial review of the Supreme Court. Firstly, it highlights that all regulatory measures are carefully examined, before their entry into force, by the Cabinet Legislation Bureau, which can thus highlight any profiles of unconstitutionality so that they may be eliminated. This sort of preventive control is made more effective by the frequent exchange of personnel between the Ministry of Justice, the Cabinet Legislation Bureau, and the

---

75 *Cf.* the rulings in *The Japanese Legal System. Cases, Codes, and Commentary*, C.J. Milhaupt and others (Eds.), New York, Foundation Press, 2006, 205 ff.

76 D.S. Law, *Why Has Judicial Review Failed in Japan?*, in 88 *Washington university law review* 1425 (2011)

77 S. Matsui, *Why is the Japanese Supreme Court So Conservative*, op. cit.; D.S. Law, *Why Has Judicial Review Failed in Japan?*, op. cit.

judges actually working in the courts. Finally, the bureaucratic and hierarchical structure of the judiciary constitutes another important institutional reason for the extremely cautious and conservative approach towards the control of constitutionality.[78]

2.8 Fundamental Rights and Freedoms

From a merely "quantitative" point of view, within the Japanese Constitution, the chapter on the rights (and duties) of citizens is that which is composed of the largest number of articles: this consistency was interpreted as being a deliberate assertion of the importance of rights in the new constitutional structure of the country. And moreover, respect for fundamental rights was, as previously seen, one of the pivotal points on the basis of which the SCAP gave impetus to the drafting of the Charter.

The list of rights deserving of constitutional protection is long and detailed, and does not reserve particular surprises to the comparatist: it ranges from the right to life and freedom (and the pursuit of happiness), to the principle of formal and substantial equality before the law, freedom of religion, freedom of assembly, etc.

This broad formulation, of obvious American inspiration, outlines a series of perceptive principles that require interpretation in order to be put into practice. The following are some known cases in which the protection of fundamental rights[79] has been brought to the attention of the courts. The selection of the cases treated is arbitrary and linked to the skills of writing, but nevertheless takes into account the most famous decisions on the subject, of interest from a comparative point of view, and is aimed at providing a *bouquet* of cases of constitutional relevance: there is therefore no claim of completeness.

2.8.1 The Right to Equality: Gender Discrimination in the Workplace[80]

The provision of Article 14, which establishes formal and substantial equality before the law, has been invoked to protect numerous situations of actual or perceived inequality in the most disparate areas of law, from family to work.

---

78 The characterization of the Supreme Court as a conservative, bureaucratic and illiberal organ is not shared by Fujita, who was a justice of the Supreme Court from 2002 to 2010. T. Fujita, *The Supreme Court of Japan: Commentary on the Recent Work of Scholars in the United States*, in 88 *Washington University Law Review* 1507-1769 (2011).

79 In Italian on the subject, *see* E. Bertolini, *La tutela dei diritti fondamentali in Giappone. Studio storico-giuridico tra tentazioni occidentali e radicamento asiatico*, Napoli, Jovene, 2011.

80 This paragraph is based on the paper by G.F. Colombo, *Suzuki Setsuko e le altre: la lotta per le pari opportunità nel diritto del lavoro in Giappone*, in M.C. Juillon and others (Eds.), *Al di là del cliché: rappresentazioni multiculturali e transgeografiche del femminile*, Milano, FrancoAngeli, 2012.

The representation of the feminine in Japan, is often flawed, in the perspective of the average "Western" observer (that is to say, not endowed with a specific cultural preparation on the subject), by a series of clichés that prevent a correct understanding of the complex Japanese reality. When it comes to women and law, the stereotype is twofold: in addition to the already mentioned simplistic perception of the female condition in Japan, there is a further distortion given by a reductive, contradictory schematization, of which the Japanese legal system has suffered until very recent years.[81] This is not the place to investigate a more than 50-year debate on the subject: for the purposes of this discussion, it is sufficient to only mention another cliché regarding the relationship between law and society in Japan, which is:the Japanese are reluctant to act judicially for the protection of their own rights,[82] in particular in areas such as labor or family law.

To the stereotype of the woman who supinely accepts male primacy in the workplace, is added to that of a person unable to assert their rights with the proper instruments of the judiciary.

In truth, modern Japanese legislation had in fact some "machismo" traits that made it at least more difficult for women to obtain the protection of their subjective situations by means of the formal resolution of litigations. This occurred mainly in family law and succession, where the legislation adopted in the Meiji period, and in particular the Civil Code,[83] had – at least rethorically - intended to partially preserve the Tokugawa model based on the cohesion of the house (*ie*) around the figure of the male householder.

The traditional structure of the *ie* was therefore partly acknowledged by the codicistic norms. From the point of view of the concrete rules, one could note the power of the head of the family to expel members who were in disagreement with his decisions, also in terms of marriage, the total pre-eminence of the firstborn male, as well as a general unfavourable treatment of the female components of the family.[84]

---

81 The attitude of "generalist" scholars towards Japanese law has been brilliantly defined as "schizophrenic" by A. Ortolani, *Il giri e la mentalità giuridica giapponese*, in *Rivista di diritto civile*, n. 3, 371-388 (2009).

82 This is probably the most controversial issue in comparative law with reference to the Japanese system. For a summary of the very long debate on the subject I recommend referring to G.F. Colombo, *Oltre il paradigma della società senza liti. La risoluzione extra-giudiziale delle controversie in Giappone*, Padova, Cedam, 2011.

83 The Civil Code, which came into force in 1898 after a long and heated debate, was essentially based on the structure of the German Code (BGB, which was to come into force in Germany in 1900 but whose text was already ready by the date of the Japanese legislation), including the division into chapters and a general part. As for the contents, although the Germanic imprint is predominant, some French influences can be found (in particular in the ways of transfer of ownership) and the *common law* model. Amplius, *A History of Law in Japan since 1868*, W. Röhl (Ed.), Leiden, Brill, 2005.

84 For example on the subject of primogeniture, which, as mentioned, belonged to the male heir. The importance of having a male descendant in the family is also found in the large and detailed legal provision on the possibility of adopting the husband of the daughter, a situation that frequently occurred if the family did not have biological male descendants. Another example is the different legal regime of marital infidelity, which was considered much more seriously if done by women. In the reconstruction of the legal system of the Meiji era, some scholars have contested that these provisions could have a real and effective discriminatory scope, owing to the fact that, for example, the sanctions applied by the head of the family were mostly

Legislative discrimination against women was formally swept away by the Constitution of 1947, which has among its pivotal principles equality before the law, and expressly prohibits discrimination on the basis of (also) gender (Art. 14).[85]

Since the Constitution is the superprimary source of the legal system, it became necessary to modify the primary legislation in contrast with the new constitutional provisions. As a consequence, Books IV and V of the Civil Code (family and succession) were completely reformulated, and the elements of primacy of the male in the family nucleus, were eliminated.[86]

Furthermore, from the viewpoint of the modernization of local law, in 1947, the Labor Standards Law was also approved, which was however formulated (perhaps deliberately) in a rather unhappy manner as regards equality between male workers and female workers. In Article 4 in fact, this law establishes the prohibition of discriminatory treatment based on gender, but only with regard to salaries.

It is quite clear that a protection limited to the mere economic treatment was not sufficient: a comprehensive reading of the legal system, however, permitted the possibility of an extensive interpretation of the principle of equality. This interpretation, however, in a working culture not very favourable to women, was not adopted and indeed, there were numerous examples of semi-institutionalized discriminatory behaviour.

Dating from the second half of the 1950s of the twentieth century, in fact, the practice of drawing up, in companies (and especially large companies), a series of internal rules of conduct, which were usually signed by the worker at the time of employment, was established. These regulations often envisaged a set of discriminatory rules against female workers.

In this sense, among the most common provisions, one could find those that required the recruitment of only licentiatewomen (graduates were considered unsuitable), the default contractual status at the lowest level in the company hierarchy and the invariable assignment to simple tasks, without decision-making responsibilities (e.g., typist, receptionist, etc.).

However, the most evident discriminatory disposition in these documents (*nota bene*, not secret *memoranda*, but official company documents that workers were formally obliged

---

symbolic (in particular *see* J.M. Ramseyer, Odd Markets in *Japanese History: Law and Economic Growth*, Cambridge, 1996, 80-108). The brilliant and very careful analysis of these scholars, however, omits to take into account the fact that to eradicate a widespread behaviour in society, there is the need to adopt a law of contrast (this principle is the basis of the so-called *affirmative action*), while instead a law mildly condescending with tradition would probably achieve the aim of maintaining the *status quo*.

85 On the overall relationship between gender and law in Japanese legislation, fundamental reading is the essay by M. Kamiya, «Women in Japan», in 20 *University of British Columbia Law Review* 447-469 (1986).

86 Observing the current Civil Code of Japan, the comparative law scholar will not find particular provisions in this matter. There remains a small residue of tradition in Art. 897, which envisages that for succession in possession of the objects of cult of ancestors, code rules do not apply, but rather traditional rules.

to subscribe to) was the mandatory resignation for female employees in the event of marriage or filiation.

These regulations, as mentioned coming into force in the second half of the 1950s, were mostly accepted as a binding rule for almost a decade.

In 1960, Sumitomo Cement (a company which produced building materials and connected to the huge Sumitomo corporate group) hired a young woman, Setsuko Suzuki.[87] Consistent with the practices of large corporate groups, Sumitomo Cement also had internal regulations, in line with the above; these regulation envisaged, among other things, the obligation for female workers to resign in the event of marriage.[88] In 1963, Ms. Suzuki married, but refused to resign and therefore, on 17 March 1964, she was dismissed for not having complied with the regulation.

Setsuko Suzuki, however, did not accept this decision and contrary to expectations decided to act judicially for the protection of her rights by initiating legal action before the Tokyo District Court.

Ms. Suzuki's case was based essentially on the combined reading of Articles 14 (equality and prohibition of discrimination) and 24 (the constitutionally guaranteed right to marry) of the Constitution, and 1.2 and 90 of the Civil Code.

If Articles 1 and 90 of the Code contain provisions that are widely diffused in most the legal systems, namely the general principle of good faith and the prohibition of abuse of the law (Art. 1) and the sanction of nullity for legal transactions contrary to public order (Art. 90), Article 2, on the other hand, is more surprising, and contains a rule specifically inserted during the post-constitutional review of the code with intentions of affirmative action. This article, in fact, affirms, *inter alia*, that the rules of the Code must be interpreted also in the light of "the fundamental equality between the sexes".

Ms. Suzuki therefore argued that the obligation to resign entailed an unfair economic sacrifice for female workers, and that therefore the regulation involved discrimination and therefore was void on the basis of the aforementioned constitutional and legislative provisions.

The company defended itself in court with a wide and articulated series of arguments: first of all, the legislative text forbids only wage discrimination, and therefore Sumitomo's conduct could not be deemed anything but virtuous, due to the fact that it not only permit-

---

87 In the reconstruction of the *Sumitomo Cement* case, I consulted the excellent report by F.K. Upham, *Law and Social Change in Postwar Japan*, Cambridge (MA), Harvard University Press, 1987, 129-140. *See also* C.W. Brown, *Japanese Approaches To Equal Rights for Women: The Legal Framework*, in 12 *Law in Japan* 29-56 (1979).

88 The Sumitomo Regulations of 1958 stated: a) only female workers with a high school diploma will be hired; b) female workers will be hired with the lowest possible level of classification; c) only tasks that do not involve decision-making responsibilities will be entrusted to them; d) female workers will not be granted job changes or transfers; e) female workers will be asked to sign an irrevocable letter of resignation in case of marriage or attainment of the thirtieth year of age.

ted female workers to receive an economic treatment equivalent to that of male colleagues, but did so despite their much lower contribution in terms of commitment and responsibility. In doing so, the company, as a benevolent gesture, permitted its female workers to set aside a sort of "company dowry" in view of a future marriage.

In addition, Sumitomo argued that it is common knowledge that after marriage (or filiation) the productivity of workers falls dramatically, and therefore it was legitimate for the company to protect itself against these problems.

Finally, Sumitomo's lawyers claimed that, based on the system of sources of Japanese law, if the law does not expressly regulate a specific case, it is necessary to refer to custom. And in this case, its internal regulations were in line with the most common practices, customs and even "national traditions" and hence, perceived, by male workers and female workers alike, as fair and reasonable, and even natural.

Therefore, if the internal rules of Sumitomo are discriminatory, affirmed the defence, they are towards male workers, who are forced to see their female colleague paid more for less burdensome jobs. The only way to rebalance this treatment was therefore that of compulsory resignation.

The Tokyo Court decided in favour of the plaintiff.

According to the reasoning of the judges of the capital, the reference made by Sumitomo to custom as an integrative source was improper. Instead, there was the need to refer to the general spirit of the system as a whole, a spirit that can also be deduced from Article 14 of the Constitution and Articles 1, 2 and 90 of the Code, which in fact constitute perceptive and hermeneutical norms of general scope.

Therefore, although the Court admits that the 1947 Law expressly prohibits only economic discrimination, it considers that non-discrimination is a general and cardinal principle of the legal system, declared, respectively, in the relationship between the State and citizens, in Articles 14 of the Constitution, and in the already cited code-related norms in the relationships between private individuals. Any individual or general agreement that introduces discrimination is therefore invalid according to Article 90 of the Civil Code, and therefore without any legal effect.

Parenthetically, the judges also stated that the assertion that female workers are less productive after marriage or filiation was completely apodictic unless supported by specific and circumstantial evidence. Moreover, they added, that such a drop in productivity could also occur in relation to male workers.

The Tribunal admitted that there was a category of female workers to whom the obligation of virginity was an absolute must: that of the virgins of the Shinto shrines!

The Sumitomo Cement case is considered by many to be the *leading case* in the field of workplace discrimination. The principles expressed in this judgment were applied in at least 20 other similar disputes, and, although there were decisions to the contrary, they contributed to an important and irreversible change in Japanese working practices. Consequently, such provisions in internal regulations (very widespread and peacefully accepted in the 1960s) disappeared completely by 1980. However, despite the symbolic importance of the Sumitomo case, and the jurisprudence generated by it, forms of discrimination remained, both at an informal level (and therefore difficult to measure), as well as at the formal level. Even in judicial proceedings, some objectively discriminatory behaviours were considered lawful: for example, it was considered lawful, in case of collective redundancies, to prefer female workers with children to male colleagues. Moreover, the decisions were given modest limelight in the Japanese press, and for this reason too, they had a limited impact on the social perception of the phenomenon.

Obviously, overtime, legislation was amended and improved several times.

Some significant milestones in the Japanese legislative process are Japan's accession to the *Convention on the Elimination of All Forms of Discrimination Against Women* (CEDAW) in 1980 and the (partially consequent) approval in 1985 of the Equal Employment Opportunity Law. This law, known by the English acronym of EEOL, has been amended several times and, especially in its 2006 version, explicitly takes into consideration various forms of indirect discrimination. The 1947 Working Conditions Act has also been amended several times, and the 2003 version devotes a part to protecting female workers in the event of pregnancy.

This therefore is the normative (and jurisprudential) situation.

Undoubtedly, the contribution of the battle of Susuki Setsuko and that of other women workers who decided and have decided to assert their rights judicially has been significant in improving the institutional situation on this point. However, the Japanese situation still presents considerable critical issues, which make the country very backward in comparative terms with other industrialized nations, necessitating much more decisive actions aimed at ensuring substantial equality.[89]

2.8.2 *Use of the Surname*

Another area in which the Supreme Court of Japan has recently rendered a judgment regarding gender discrimination and the freedom to marry ratified by Article 24 of the Constitution, is that of the use of the surname. According to Article 750 of the Civil Code, at the time of registration at the municipal office of the necessary documents for marriage, the future spouses must choose a common surname, which will automatically become that of the children born during the marriage. Although Article 750 do not specify that the wife should take the surname of her husband, in practice this happens in the vast majority of

89 D. Tidten, *Equality-Oriented Policies in Japan*, in 17 *Zeitschrift für Japanisches Recht/Journal of Japanese Law* 51-76 (2012).

cases,[90] thus realizing, according to some, a *de facto* discrimination. The issue has been widely debated, and since 2010 a bill is pending with the Diet to permit each spouse to maintain their own surname. Recently, in December 2015, the Supreme Court, sitting in Grand Bench, ratified the constitutionality of the provision in question.

The action was proposed by two different groups of women, the first of whom had changed their surname at the time of marriage but continued to use the maiden name in everyday life (though not in official documents); the second group, instead, was made up of future brides who had been refused the registration of their marriage documents at the competent municipal offices due to the fact that they had refused to make a choice regarding their surname. The reasons for the protest were based on three constitutional provisions, namely: Article 13 on the fundamental rights of individuals (including, according to the prevailing interpretation, the right to a name); Article 14 on equality; and the Article 24 on the freedom to marry, which must be based exclusively on the consent of the spouses.

The applicants argued that having to obligatorily choose a surname resulted in the deprivation of one's name, and therefore that Article 750 was in contrast with Article 13 of the Constitution. The fact that in the vast majority of cases, it is the wife who adopts the surname of the husband contrasts instead with Article 14; finally, the provision that the marriage is not valid and effective if the choice of a common surname is not undertaken is in conflict with Article 24, according to which only the consent of the spouses is what matters.

The Supreme Court rejected, by majority, the appeal.

The motivations of the supreme judicial body dealt with each single cause of encumbrance. In particular, with reference to the alleged contrast with Article 13, the Court affirmed that the right to a name as an individual right does not entail the right to keep one's own surname after marriage, and that the requirement to choose a common family name is legitimate, due to the fact also there it is a necessity for identifying a family unit.[91] In the ruling, the judges explicitly acknowledged a different identity (and bureaucratic-administrative) value to first names and surnames.

With regard to the second grounds of appeal, the Supreme Court confined itself to pointing out rather dryly that Article 750 was gender-neutral, and explicitly permitted the husband to adopt the wife's surname. That this, in practice, does not happen, cannot be considered, according to the supreme judges, a matter of unconstitutionality, simply because *de facto* is not *de jure*, and it is not the judicial power's task to try to remedy a practical situation.

---

90 S. Matsui, *The Constitution of Japan. A Contextual Analysis*, Oxford and Portland (OR), Hart, 2011, 180.

91 On the importance of identifying the family nucleus *see* C. Danwerth, *Basic Principles of Japanese Family Law*, in 16 *Zeitschrift für Japanisches Recht/Journal of Japanese Law* 273-248 (2011).

Finally, as regards the "obstacle" to marriage constituted by the obligation to choose a common surname, the Supreme Court asserted that it is a formal fulfilment that does not prevent the celebration of marriage itself for those who desire to marry. Nevertheless, even in the majority opinion, one can note that the judges hope for a reform that takes into consideration the possibility for spouses to keep their own surname, in line with the proposed law.

The ruling was however accompanied by the dissent of five judges out of fifteen. Three of them, in particular, sustained, that in the current state of affairs, the legislative provision, although apparently neutral from the gender point of view, legitimized and supported a systematic violation of women's rights, being women, frequently the economically and socially weaker part of the marriage union. According to them, it was not sufficient for the Supreme Court to maintain a neutral attitude, but it must be activated to restore equality: until the Diet decides to provide legislative provisions, there was the need to plug a situation which, in effect, entails a violation of equality and places an unacceptable restriction on the right to marry sanctioned by Article 24 of the Constitution.

2.8.3 *Restrictions on the Possibility of Remarrying*

Another famous case in which a code-related provision on the subject of marriage was accused of being unconstitutional for violation of Articles 14 and 24 of the Constitution concerns Article 733 of the Civil Code, regarding the prohibition for women to remarry for a period of 180 days following the dissolution of the previous marriage (both due to divorce and death of the spouse), a prohibition that does not exist for men. The *rationale* of the norm is evident: to avoid that any pregnancies started in the previous marriage, end during the new. According to the Japanese system, in fact, within 300 days after the dissolution of a marriage, paternity of any children is presumed to be pertaining to the previous husband (Art. 772). The same provision, however, envisages that a child born within 200 days of a new marriage is to be presumed of the new husband, and therefore there is a range of potential conflict.

The law has been repeatedly attacked in court, due to the fact that, for obvious biological reasons, it does not concern the male components of a couple: it therefore includes a violation of Article 14 on equality (in this case of gender) and Article 24, as an undue restriction on the possibility of marriage.

The issue was recently dealt with by the Supreme Court, with its ruling of 16 December 2015.[92] The situation concerned a woman who, as a result of a divorce, wanted to remarry quickly, but had not been able to do so because of the provision of the code. The plaintiff stated that the disputed provision had as its *rationale* not the certainty of paternity, but

92 *Minshu*, Vol. 69, n.8 (Supreme Court, Grand Bench, 15 December 2016), case n. 1079 (O) of 2013.

the imposition on woman of a period of mourning in the event that she remained a widow. Moreover, modern technologies permit verifying paternity beyond any doubt, and the provision of the code would not come into potential contradiction even with a period of prohibition limited to 100 days: the six-month restriction was therefore exorbitant and unreasonable even in the case in which the aim was the prevention of doubtful attributions of paternity.

Initially, the Supreme Court dealt with the problem by denying that the contested provision had any "moralizing" value, but simply permitted an undisputable attribution of paternity. It was true, the judges conceded, that modern technologies (and in particular the DNA test) make it possible to dispel any doubt, but the procedure for using these means was not always simple and straightforward. In the event of disputes regarding paternity, in fact, legal proceedings can be opened, which therefore require a judicial intervention and a complex procedure, during which the situation remains in a state of doubt, harming, above all, the child. The Court acknowledged that the period of 100 days proposed by the plaintiff would permit a compliance with the code, but also acknowledged that a "not unreasonable" limitation of the possibility of a new marriage fell within the discretion of the legislator, and therefore the question was not a matter to be resolved by the magistracy, but rather by the Parliament. The judges acknowledged that the provision of a period of time in which a new marriage is forbidden is progressively disappearing from the legal systems of the world (and this leads to interesting comparative considerations on the German system, on which, the original Japanese Civil Code, was modelled), but, beyond this observation, it confined itself to refer the question back to the field of politics, for the legislator to evaluate the possibility of any changes.

The recent decision was therefore in line with the consistent jurisprudence of the Supreme Court.

Incidentally, the proposal to reduce the period of prohibition of remarrying to 100 days from the current six months, together with the proposed reform on the use of a common surname examined above, had been lying dormant in the Diet for some years now. After the Court issued its decision, however, the law was eventually amended to reflect the judgment by the Supreme Court.

2.8.4 *Succession*

As repeatedly stated, the constitutional structure introduced by the Charter of 1947 has had a particularly disruptive effect on the norms relating to family law and succession.[93]

93 C. Danwerth, *Principles of Japanese Law of Succession*, in 17 *Zeitschrift für Japanisches Recht/Journal of Japanese Law* 99-118 (2012); S. Matsui, *The Constitution and the Family Law of Japan*, in H.N. Scheiber (Ed.), *Japanese Family Law in Comparative Perspective*, Berkeley, The Robbins Collection, 2009.

However, some residues of the previous regulations still remained. One of the most notable examples was constituted by Article 900 of the Civil Code, which envisaged that, in the event of a succession of legitimate children and children born out of wedlock,[94] the latter receive half of the quota due to the former. This provision, although not unique in the comparative landscape, was considered a legacy of the Japanese in favour of the legitimate family.[95] Obviously, the law in question has been attacked for its violation of the principle of equality of Article 14, but until very recently the Supreme Court had always confirmed its validity, based on two lines of reasoning. According to the first type of reasoning, the Constitution establishes the need to treat homogeneous situations equally, but does not impose the same obligation for objectively or subjectively different situations. The jurisprudence of the Supreme Court had consistently declared[96] the non-unconstitutionality of the differential treatment on the basis of the fact that a child born in wedlock and a child born out of wedlock are in subjectively different positions, and therefore the law does not discriminate but rather limits itself to recognizing this diversity. Furthermore, Article 900 is not intolerably discriminatory due to the fact that, in any case, it recognizes the legal protection of a child borne out of wedlock, thus not leaving it completely unprotected; the problem is moreover tempered by the fact that the rule regulates legitimate succession, but a will can easily rectify the situation in most cases. All this was justified also in light of the prevalence given to marriage as a fundamental institution in the Civil Code (and in the constitutional system).

A consequence of this provision was that couples who did not intend to marry but who lived together in a *more uxorio* regime, in the presence of children executed a procedure made possible by the ease with which in Japan, it is possible to enter into and dissolve a marriage. On the occasion of the birth of a child, the couple then registered their marriage, and, obtained through this the legitimizing effect, divorcing a few days later, thus returning to a relationship of cohabitation but having thus given their offspring, the status of a legitimate child.

In 2013, the Supreme Court decided, in United Sections,[97] to change its orientation, with a pronouncement that markedly breaks with previous jurisprudence and which definitively ratifies the unconstitutionality of Article 900, which was definitively modified shortly thereafter.

94 Considering the expression in Japanese (*chakushutsudenaiko*), probably "illegitimate" would be a more correct translation.

95 M. Ahlefeldt, *Less than Family: Surrogate Birth and Legal Parent-Child Relationships in Japan*, in 16 *Zeitschrift für Japanisches Recht/Journal of Japanese Law* 65-96, 79-79 (2011).

96 For example, with the *Minshu* ruling, Vol. 49, No. 7 (Supreme Court, Grand Bench, 5 July 1995), case no. 143 (Ku) of 1991.

97 *Minshu* Vol. 67, No. 6 (Supreme Court, Grand Bench, 4 September 2013), case no. 984 (*Ku*) of 2012.

The action had obviously been proposed by a subject, a child borne out of wedlock of the deceased, who had received a halved share of the inheritance compared to that received by the legitimate children.

The ruling of the Supreme Court initially analysed the circumstances in which Article 900 (formerly Art. 1004 of the Pre-reform Code) had been drafted, and continued with a description of the historic Japanese family and society, stating that, at the time the action was proposed, the cultural context of the country had radically changed and that new forms of the family (including nuclei composed of a single person but also couples who do not wish to marry) now constituted a fundamental component of the social fabric: it was therefore necessary to take this into account with appropriate forms of legal protection.

Moreover, the ruling added that Japan was bound by a series of international treaties, some of which in force in the Japanese system for only a few years,[98] not to discriminate on the basis of the birth of an individual: the Court therefore considered that the previous jurisprudence was somehow justifiable in the light of the socio-juridical context of the time, but that the time had come for a revision of the norm. Moreover, this change had already been registered in other sectors, such as that of the family register: in 1994 and subsequently in 2004, two administrative regulations had led to the elimination of the specific indication of the fact as to whether a child was legitimate or not, from the registration at the competent municipal offices. In the light of these circumstances, therefore, the Supreme Court considered it appropriate to change its consolidated orientation after several decades, and in this case the legislation was amended accordingly very quickly.

2.8.5 *Criminal Law*

Criminal law is one of the areas in which the contrast with constitutional norms regarding equality before the law has taken place with the most peculiar, paradigmatic modalities of the hesitations of the Japanese system in the face of constitutional reforms that stem from judicial activism. The most famous case concerns the provision of (the now repealed) Article 200 of the Criminal Code, relating to patricide as a specific offense that is more serious than murder. This provision had survived the reforms of the Second World War and constituted a residue of the legislation of the previous period, which envisaged, as mentioned, the figure of the male householder as the backbone of the family structure, and as such worthy of respect and recognition by the law.

98 In particular, the International Convention on the Rights of the Child of 20 November 1989, which Japan ratified in 1994.

The case[99] that led to the revision of Article 200 is extremely famous, and has often been commented on by international observers:[100] it concerned the terrible story of a daughter who had murdered her father after years of abuse and violence suffered at his hands. The Court of First Instance accepted the thesis proposed by the defence according to which the provision of a more severe punishment for patricide compared to murder (with the obvious consequences related to the statutory minimum punishment of the sentence and the possibility of obtaining a conditional suspension of the punishment), constituted a violation of Article 14 of the Constitution. The decision is quite interesting, also owing to the fact that it constitutes a historical-comparative reconstruction of the contested provision, starting from none other than ancient Chinese law, arriving at the *Ritsuryo* and Tokugawa law: the deep connection is with the *ie* system, which however had been repealed with the advent of the new constitutional framework. The judges also acknowledged that this provision is not unique to the law of East Asia, but found a correspondent in Roman law, where the *pater familias* was particularly respected. The ruling, however, also acknowledged that this approach had almost completely disappeared in the contemporary context, and even Japan should align itself with this trend. The judges therefore acknowledged the rationale behind the norm, and had no hesitation in admitting that the murder of a forefather is a particularly repugnant crime: however, they considered the legislative treatment disproportionate, which envisaged severe penalties (the death penalty or life imprisonment), so severe that this did not permit an effective toning down of the sentence even in cases of exceptional circumstances. For this reason, the Court declared Article 200 to be unconstitutional on the grounds that it violated Article 14 of the Constitution, and ordered its non-application in the case in question.[101]

As seen, however, the "American style" widespread control of the constitutionality of Japanese law did not entail the elimination of the norm from the law, but only the transmission of the documents to the competent institutions (in particular to the Diet), in order to activate the legislative procedure of the revision of the norm. The first consequence of the ruling in question was that the Ministry of Justice initiated, a few days after the constitutional ruling, an amnesty campaign for subjects who had been convicted under Article 200, which is worth remembering, was still fully in force. The legislative procedure was extremely long, in the opinion of some commentators due to the resistance of the Diet, then dominated by the conservative Liberal Democratic Party. The reform of the criminal

99 27 *Keishu* 265 (Supreme Court, Grand Bench, 4 April 1973), case no. 1310 of 1970.

100 Among the many, C.F. Goodman, *The Rule of Law in Japan: A Comparative Analysis*, Alphen aan den Rijn, Kluwer Law International, 2008, 178.

101 The practical result, in the circumstance, was that the defendant was convicted of simple homicide (with all the extenuating circumstances), receiving a sentence tenuous enough to allow the conditional suspension of the sentence.

law in the sense advocated by the Supreme Court occurred only in 1995, 22 years after the ruling in question.[102]

2.8.6 *Minority Rights*

Although Japan is known, in an excessively simplistic manner,[103] as an extremely homogeneous country in terms of population, there are a number of ethnic, social and religious minorities in Japan.[104]

However, by way of example, in the archipelago, the indigenous populations of northern Honshu and Hokkaido, known as the *Ainu*,[105] are of an ethnic lineage that is different from the majority of the Japanese, and have a different culture and tradition. Since the unification of the country, these communities have been considered as being "barbaric" by the central power, and were bitterly contrasted, to the point of being confined to a limited geographical area, the island of Hokkaido. During the Meiji Restoration, when the country was trying to give itself a strong national identity, these populations were subjected to various persecutions, sometimes intentional, sometimes incidental. Examples of the first type are offered by various regulatory measures, such as the introduction, in 1876, of criminal sanctions to prohibit the use of tattoos, earrings and other ornaments, typical of the Ainu, as well as, in 1880, the prohibition to perform the ritual funeral typical of this population, namely the burning of the house of the deceased. For an example of the second type, it is sufficient to recall the various rural property reforms that characterized Japan in the late nineteenth century. In particular, two measures specifically intended for the redistribution of land in Hokkaido (the Hokkaido Land Regulation and the Hokkaido

---

102 Another provision of the Penal Code which has been contested before the Supreme Court is that of Art. 177, relating to sexual violence, which states that victims of violence may be only women: in the case of men, the provision concerning obscene acts is applied. However, the Court confirmed the legitimacy of the rule, on the basis of two motivations: the first, is that the body of women is different from that of men; the second, that in the statistically more frequent hypothesis the victim is a woman (Supreme Court, Grand Bench, 24 June 1953, *Keishu* 1366). In the criminal procedure, there is another series of elements of dubious constitutionality, especially in light of the pervasive powers entrusted to the *kensatsukan*, a figure equivalent to our Public Prosecutor. Moreover, the police detention period (before, therefore, a formal charge) can last up to 23 days, an exorbitant length of time compared to the equivalent institution in other democratic countries. For a general discussion on the peculiarities of police law and the Japanese criminal procedure *see* D.T. Johnson, *The Japanese Way of Justice. Prosecuting Crime in Japan*, Oxford, Oxford University Press, 2002.

103 R. Caroli, *Il mito dell'omogeneità giapponese: storia di Okinawa*, Milano, FrancoAngeli, 1999; M. Weiner, *Japan's Minorities: The Illusion of Homogeneity*, London and New York, Routledge, 1997.

104 Some scholars recognize the existence of (discriminated) minorities on a health basis, for example HIV patients. This is the position of E. Feldman, *The Ritual of Rights in Japan. Law, Society, and Health Policy*, Cambridge, Cambridge University Press, 2000.

105 R. Siddle, *Ainu: Japan's Indigenous People*, in *Japan's Minorities: The Illusion of Homogeneity*, London and New York, Routledge, 1997.

Land Purchase and Sale Regulation, both of 1872) had a disruptive effect on the rights of this ethnic minority. Indeed, the Ainu, not being accustomed to a system of individual ownership of land, but rather a collective ownership, not having internalized the family registration system (a necessary requirement for presenting an application for land allocation) and being mostly illiterate in the complex Japanese ideographic language (and thus unable to submit the appropriate registration applications), found themselves essentially deprived of their lands. It was only in 1899, with the Hokkaido Aboriginal Protection Act, that the central institutions dealt with the problems of poverty and discrimination afflicting the Ainu. The law in question, which also tamponed some emergencies (for example, by granting land for cultivation and providing specific medical assistance) was however completely insufficient to solve the problems of the native population, and the process of cultural assimilation proceeded (even through the educational system, which gave priority to the Japanese language) until very recent times. In 1977, to preserve the little that remained of the culture of the natives, a population now reduced to a few thousand units, a Law for the promotion of Ainu culture was enacted.[106]

The Supreme Court did not deal with the matter. Instead, the matter was dealt with by the Sapporo District Court, in a famous case,[107] concerning the expropriation of the land of an Ainu community for the construction of a dam. According to the plaintiffs, territorial deprivation was a threat to the preservation of the cultural heritage of the community in question. The judges did not acknowledge the reasoning and validity, underlying the arguments presented (although they did invalidate the expropriation only for some land plots): the ruling, however, is laudable in its attempt to reconstruct diachronic interactions with the *wa-jin*[108] of the various legislative and regulatory provisions that related to the Ainu dating from the late Kamakura period (beginning of the forteenth century). The ruling also duly mentioned the International Covenant on Civil and Political Rights,[109] which, on the protection of minorities dedicates, *inter alia*, Article 27.

The question of the "rights of the Ainu", which has fascinated generations of juridical anthropologists is, at present, far from being a primary research topic for scholars of Japanese law. Nevertheless, due to its peculiarity, it was considered appropriate to cite it here.

Another "Japanese" minority (in the sense of being made up of Japanese citizens) that has historically been discriminated against is the so-called *burakumin*. In pre-modern

106 Advisory Council for Future Ainu Policy, *Final Report*, 2009.

107 1598 *Hanrei jiho* 33, District Court of Sapporo, 27 March 1997. The sentence is translated, by Mark Levin, in the volume *The Japanese Legal System. Cases, Codes, and Commentary*, C.J. Milhaupt and others (Eds.), New York, Routledge, 2006, 267-279.

108 Term used to counter the Japanese belonging to the most widespread ethnic group with the Ainu (also, obviously, Japanese from a nationality point of view).

109 It became law in Japan in 1979 (Treaty 7 of 1979). *See* on its ratification L. Repeta, *The International Covenant on Civil and Political Rights and Human Rights Law in Japan*, in 20 *Law in Japan* 1-28 (1987).

Japan, there existed a social class, obviously *mutatis mutandis*, vaguely comparable to the outcaste of India. They were called *eta*, and were considered "impure" for religious reasons: although some were employed in activities such as agriculture, most of the members of this social group exercised professions associated with death (gravediggers, tanners, butchers, etc.). Both according to the Shinto faith and Buddhism, contact with dead bodies is deeply contaminating: the *eta* were therefore separated from the rest of the population, and were forced to live in separate places and were subjected to a long series of restrictions.[110]

With the advent of the Meiji Restoration and with the legislative provisions aimed at eliminating class distinctions, even the *eta* were integrated into the common population, and yet, since they were easily identifiable (also due to their peculiar registration within the family registers), they continued to suffer discrimination and were referred to as *burakumin*, literally "villagers", but in this case with a vaguely derogatory meaning of "ghetto residents".[111]

At the end of the 1960s of the twentieth century, specific legislation was promulgated to alleviate the disadvantageous conditions in which the *burakumin* still found themselves, particularly in terms of housing and access to essential services.[112] The law, initially intended as a provision of a provisional nature of ten years, was renewed several times until 2002: on that date, considering that the purpose set by the provision had been achieved, the law ceased its effectiveness. If the question has really been resolved is nevertheless the subject of debate among scholars, activists and non-governmental organizations. Although there has been an undeniable improvement in the conditions of *burakumin* and in many parts of Japan there are no reports of discrimination, in the Kansai region, there are still discriminatory attitudes and behaviours towards members of this social group.

During the post-war period, the associations for the protection of the *burakumin* were characterized by a lively activism, which in some famous cases also assumed violent overtones:[113] this is the reason why the best-known rulings on the subject of discrimination of this category are of a penal nature. In particular, the most commented ruling, concerns the case of some activists who had kidnapped some school teachers, guilty, according to

110 *Amplius*, F.K. Upham, *Ten Years of Affirmative Action for Japanese Burakumin: A Preliminary Report on the Law on Special Measures for Dowa Projects*, in 13 *Law in Japan* 39-73 (1980), 39-40.

111 As Upham also reports, the term became known to the international public thanks to the essay, in English, R. Yoshino, S. Murakoshi, *The Invisible Visible Minority: Japan's Burakumin*, Osaka, Osaka Liberation Institute, 1977. *See also* I. Neary, *Burakumin in Contemporary Japan*, in M. Weiner (Ed.), *Japan's Minorities: The Illusion of Homogeneity*, London and New York, Routledge, 1997.

112 Law on special measures for assimilation (Law 60/1969). F.K. Upham, *Ten Years of Affirmative Action for Japanese Burakumin: A Preliminary Report on the Law on Special Measures for Dowa Projects*, op. cit., 39 prefers to keep, as is clear from the title, the words *Dowa*, which emphasizes the aspects of affirmative action.

113 F.K. Upham, *Instrumental Violence and Social Change: The Buraku Liberation League and the Tactic of Denunciation Struggle*, in 17 *Law in Japan* 185-205 (1984).

the activists, of having disseminated material of discriminatory nature on the occasion of the election of union representatives.[114] Although the defendants were subsequently convicted in the second instance (the first instance ruling had ended with acquittal), the element that is important to underline is that the tribunals entrusted with dealing with the issue, acknowledged the relevance of the discrimination suffered by the *burakumin* and considered it a mitigating circumstance, if not even (as occurred before the District Court) a justification.[115]

2.8.7 *Foreigners' Rights*

When addressing the issue of the rights of "foreigners" in Japan, one must first reflect on the definition of "foreigner": in fact, in the country, a series of individuals live, who were born and raised in Japan by parents who, in turn, were born and raised in the archipelago, who are, however, not technically Japanese citizens.

Over the years, another minority subject to discrimination, is constituted precisely by citizens of Korean and Taiwanese origin residing in Japan. In this case, however, it is difficult to establish whether this category can be deemed a Japanese or foreign minority, for reasons that will be subsequently explained.[116]

During the period of imperialistic expansionism, the Japanese Empire had incorporated the territories of Korea and Taiwan, and many of the inhabitants of these areas had moved to the archipelago, of their own free will but also in the context of forced migration policies aimed at ensuring sufficient (semi-slave) industrial manpower during the war effort. Japan had also set up separate registers for subjects residing in the Korean and Taiwanese regions: all were subjects of the Empire and were therefore considered, to all intents and purposes, Japanese, but were differentiated on the basis of their registration in the various territorial registers.

At the end of the conflict, many Japanese had to leave the conquered territories and returned to the motherland. Conversely, a conspicuous number of Koreans and Taiwanese returned to their countries of origin, but many remained in the archipelago. Furthermore, the provision of differentiated family registers meant that, due to mixed marriages, quite a few Japanese had been registered as Koreans or Taiwanese. With the defeat in the war

---

114 782 *Hanrei jiho* 22, District Court of Osaka, 3 June 1975 and 996 *Hanrei jiho* 34, High Court of Osaka, 10 March 1981. Both cases are translated and commented on by Upham in F.K. Upham, *Ten Years of Affirmative Action for Japanese Burakumin: A Preliminary Report on the Law on Special Measures for Dowa Projects*,op. cit., 54-68.

115 In a manner not dissimilar to that in which the so-called cultural defence is used in criminal matters. *Amplius*, A. Dundes Renteln, *The Cultural Defense*, Oxford, Oxford University Press, 2005.

116 S. Matsui, *The Constitution of Japan. A Contextual Analysis*, op. cit., 177-178, favours for the second hypothesis.

and the consequent renunciation of the territories of Korea and Taiwan, the original citizens of these territories were considered as "foreigners", and hence they were not granted Japanese citizenship. The problem was further exacerbated by the fact that, according to the Law on nationality, Japan does not recognize the institute of *jus solis* (birthright citizenship), and consequently also the children of these subjects (born in Japan and often in the so-called "motherland", having never set foot outside Japan, and furthermore not speaking any other language, other than the Japanese language) are considered foreigners, with all that this entails in terms of visa, entry procedures in the country, etc. (although they are granted permanent residence, or more precisely "special permanent residence" due to their peculiar situation).

The legal treatment of these subjects has been a source of discriminatory problems for decades.

Dating from the first years after the end of the war, individuals originally denominated Japanese citizens but who had been first deprived of their citizenship following a mixed marriage, and the subsequent loss of the occupied territories, had acted in court to re-obtain their *status* as citizens of Japan. The Supreme Court, in a famous case[117] that successively became the *leading case* in the matter, however, denied the possibility for these subjects to reacquire their citizenship, arguing that the loss of the such a citizenship was a simple consequence of the Treaty of San Francisco and therefore did not constitute a constitutional violation.

Other famous cases related to this problem regarded the requirement of nationality to participate in public tenders. For example, a Supreme Court ruling concerned the issue of a person born in Japan in 1950 but of Korean citizenship stemming from the aforementioned circumstances. To take part in a promotion procedure within a Tokyo Metropolitan Government structure, required Japanese citizenship: the applicant, therefore, had been automatically excluded from the public competition. In 2005, the Supreme Court[118] recognized that this had not occurred in violation of Article 14 of the Constitution, and that no discrimination had happened in this regard.

Hence, it is not difficult to imagine that the lack of inclusion of individuals of Korean or Taiwanese origin, created a question of "minority" in relation to such individuals.

Recently, Koreans living in Japan have been the subject of two important rulings on incitement to racial hatred. For years, in the country, the so-called *hate speech* had been widely tolerated due to the protection afforded by the right to freedom of expression, envisaged by the Constitution (Art. 21). The case, decided first by the District Court of Kyoto and subsequently appealed and definitively closed before the Court of Appeals (or

---

117 15 *Minshu* 657, Supreme Court (Grand Bench), 5 April 1961, 1955 (O) 890.

118 1380 *Saibansho jiho* 59, Supreme Court (Grand Bench), 26 January 2005, 1998 (*Gyo-Tsu*) 93. The sentence is partially published, in the translation of Ari Nishitani, in *The Japanese Legal System. Cases, Codes, and Commentary*, op. cit., 279-286.

High Court)[119] of Osaka, concerned the activities of a group of right-wing anti-Korean extremists, who had organized a series of protest demonstrations in the vicinity of a Korean school in the city of Kyoto related to the use of a park near the institute for sport. Due to the fact that the protests had become verbally very heated, with explicit instigations of violence and very heavy racial insults, the company that ran the school had decided to take legal action. The petitions presented before the court were of two types: first of all, the school requested compensation arising out of tort, where the tort consisted of protests and some videos broadcast on the Internet. In addition to this, a provision was requested that ordered the defendants to cease all disturbance activities.[120]

The Kyoto Court upheld the plaintiff's petition mainly on the basis of the application, via Article 98(2) of the Constitution, of the International Convention on the Elimination of All Forms of Racial Discrimination of 1965, of which Japan has been a member since 1995. Among the various obligations deriving from the Convention, there is, sanctioned in Art. 6, that of guaranteeing the possibility of legal action in state courts for the cessation of any discriminatory behaviour: it derives, according to the reasoning adopted by the court, that this obligation does not only exist in the state, but directly also applies to judicial organs.

As previously stated, the ruling was appealed, but the High Court of osaka upheld the first instance ruling. From the point of view of a constitutional analysis, the judges had explicitly taken into consideration Articles 13 and 14 of the Constitution, and the necessary nature that they envisage when compared to Article 21 on the right to freedom of expression.

The sentence is very important due to the fact that it is the first significant case in which the problem of *hate speech* was addressed so directly and decisively by the judicial system.[121]

---

119 The use of the terminology "High Court" to translate the original Japanese *koto saibansho* is not fully convincing. Undoubtedly the word *koto* ("superior") is not dissimilar to "High", however it is clear that the translation into English is simply a cast of the term *High Court* used by English language doctrine in reference to the Japanese judicial system. The creation of the system of courts in Japan, however, took place based on first the French model and subsequently on the German model, therefore the words "Court of Appeal" appear to be correct – if not even better. *See*, on the topic, *A History of Law in Japan Since 1868*, op. cit., 655-681; G.F. Colombo, *Nomophilacy and Beyond: Comparative Reflections on Judicial Precedents by Supreme Jurisdictions in Italy and Japan*, in 2 *European Journal of Comparative Law and Governance* 281-315, 288 (2015). On the general problem of translations relating to judicial systems and means of encumbrance, *see* S. M.F. Geeroms, *Comparative Law and Legal Translation: Why the Terms Cassation, Revision and Appeal Should Not Be Translated...*, in 50 *The American Journal of Comparative Law* 201-228 (2002).

120 In the sentence there are a series of very interesting procedural problems related to the passive legitimization of the extreme right group and to the configurability of the protests as an unlawful act in accordance with Art. 709 of the Civil Code, but are not of particular interest from the point of view of the constitutional protection of fundamental rights. *Amplius*, T. Wakabayashi, *Hate Speech and Legal Restrictions in Japan*, in 19 *Zeitschrift für Japanisches Recht/Journal of Japanese Law* 249-263 (2014).

121 S. Matsui, *The Constitution of Japan. A Contextual Analysis*, op, cit., 196 doubted the configurability of a condemnation of incitement to hatred, unless, of course, this did not materialize in a genuine incitement to commit crimes.

Connected to this problem, there is the question of the acquisition of Japanese citizenship, proverbially difficult to obtain. As previously mentioned, Japanese citizenship is obtained only via *ius sanguinis*, but sometimes this principle is also subject to restrictions. In particular, in 2008 there was a famous ruling by the Supreme Court[122] that led, a few months later, to a revision of the law on nationality.[123]

The facts of the case are as follows: a Philippine woman had given birth to a child from a Japanese man. The couple was not married, but the father had recognized the child after birth. However, this did not entail the acquisition of citizenship for the child, since, in the case of post-birth recognition, the Law on Nationality required that the parents be united in marriage in order to grant citizenship.[124] The mother and son were subsequently issued with an expulsion order and were forced to leave the country.

Both the decision to refuse citizenship and the deportation order were challenged. It is more interesting to observe the first reason for complaint, which was put forward based on a violation of Article 14 of the Constitution on the question of equality. The Supreme Court indeed accepted this thesis.

According to the judges, it was certainly true that it fell within the discretion of the legislator to establish the requirements for obtaining Japanese citizenship (as also expressly stated in Art. 10 of the Constitution), and this discretion could not be arbitrary, but had to operate in accordance with criteria of reasonableness. The Court noted that the *reasoning* of the law identified in the family an element of stability and therefore of closer connection to the country and its culture, but nevertheless this motivation was not sufficient to legitimize the norm. In this case, in fact, the different treatment offered to the child of a Japanese citizen on the basis of the fact that their parents were not married constituted an excessive and exorbitant discrimination with respect to the respective situations, also due to the fact that the possible nuptial bond of the parents was not something on which an offspring can have control. The Supreme Court also acknowledged that citizenship, in addition to being important in itself, is the key to access a range of other rights, particularly in terms of assistance from the state (*see below*). The text of the ruling also referred to the aforementioned International Covenant on Civil and Political Rights and to that on the Rights of the Child as a further stimulus to more egalitarian legislation.[125]

---

122 2002 *Hanrei Jiho* 3, Supre Court, 4 June 2008. The case is commented by H. Nasu, *Constitutionality of the Japanese Nationality Act: A Commentary on the Supreme Court's Decision on 4 June 2008*, in 13 *Journal of Japanese Law* 101-116 (2008). In Italian *see* E. Bertolini, *La legge sulla cittadinanza: profili problematici e recenti dubbi della Corte Suprema*, in G.F. Colombo (Ed.), *Giappone: un diritto originale alla prova della globalizzazione*, Venezia, Cafoscarina, 2011.

123 *Kokuseki-ho*, Law n. 147/1950.

124 The question would have been different if the child had been recognized *before* birth, because at that point it would have automatically been a Japanese citizen *iure sanguinis*.

125 In the dissenting opinion of the judges Yokoo, Tsuno and Furuda, however, this reference is criticized because it does not pertain to the intrinsic reasonableness of the national legislation. H. Nasu, *Constitution-*

The aforementioned ruling led, as stated, to the revision of the Law. With a simple change, the legislator eliminated the requirement of marriage between the parents, and therefore the Supreme Court's approach became a law of the state.[126]

This ruling leads to a final, important issue: that of the rights of foreigners in Japan. In fact, recently, the issue has been the subject of an important ruling,[127] widely criticized due to the fact that it effectively excludes foreigners residing in the country from social assistance.

The question concerns an interpretation of the Law on social assistance of 1950. The beneficiaries of welfare measures, according to the text of the legislation, are "citizens" (*kokumin*), but the constant interpretation of the Ministry of Health had envisaged, since 1954, that even foreigners residing in the country could benefit from the same treatment, and had instructed the local authorities responsible for providing such services to comply with their interpretation (in order to also address the problem of the Chinese and Korean minorities mentioned above). In 1990, the interpretative provision (that is to say, the circular of the Ministry of Health) was the subject of a revision aimed at limiting the categories of "foreign" beneficiaries, substantially acknowledging the possibility of receiving state assistance to persons in possession of a permanent residence status or similar situations.[128]

In 2009, a woman of Chinese origin (and therefore not a Japanese citizen, but simply in possession of the special permanent residence) had applied to receive the benefits of the law, but her request had been rejected: it is worth outlining, however, that the reason for refusal was not related to her *status* as a resident alien, but to the fact that she had savings that did not justify the granting of care. The woman filed an appeal with the competent Court of the territory, which rejected the application not on the merits, but for lack of procedural standing. According to the court, in fact, the 1950 law stated that only citizens have the right to social assistance and care. The plaintiff, in the first instance had therefore appealed, and the Fukoka High Court had accepted her reasons: not only did the appeal judges recognize the legally binding value of the 1954 circular, but they also referred to Japan's accession to the 1951 Geneva Convention on Refugees, with which the country, according to the Court, had committed itself to guaranteeing to certain categories of foreigners, a certain level of welfare benefits. Therefore, the appellant was entitled to that which she had requested.

---

ality of the Japanese Nationality: A Commentary on the Supreme Court's Decision on 4 June 2008, op. cit., 106.

126 Y. Okuda, H. Nasu, *Amendment of the Japanese Nationality Act*, in 14 *Zeitschrift für Japanisches Recht/Journal of Japanese Law* 285 (2009).

127 J.C. Fisher, *'We the Kokumin': The Constitution, International Law and the Rights of Foreigners in Japan*, in 20 *Zeitschrift für Japanisches Recht/Journal of Japanese Law* 109-135 (2015).

128 Permanent residence (including spouses), special permanent residence, long-term residence and foreign citizens married to Japanese citizens.

The case reached the Supreme Court, which adopted the reasoning of the Court of First Instance and thus stated that "foreigners" did not have a real right to welfare benefits provided by the Law of 1950. The interpretation of the Supreme Court did not imply that the competent territorial authorities could not however grant such benefits, but deprived foreign residents of the possibility of taking legal action in the event that their requests were denied. According to the supreme Japanese judiciary, an administrative act such as the Ministry's circular could not contradict the wording of the normative text. Many commentators have viewed this ruling as being highly discriminatory versus foreigners, even if, in practical terms, the interpretation was to have a very limited impact on the rights of non-Japanese residents in the archipelago.[129]

2.8.8 Religious Freedom and the Separation Between State and Religion[130]

The separation between the State and the Church and the general affirmation of the secular nature of the State are principles contained, explicitly or implicitly, in numerous contemporary constitutional charters. These provisions, however, usually combine in a dogmatic model of religion, in which civil organs and religious institutions are clearly distinct and differentiated. The question becomes further complex in the case in which there is a profound interaction between secular authorities and worship administration. And even more delicate connotations and problems are found where religion and tradition cohabit, intertwine or are not well distinguished.

These two latter situations, which inevitably complicate the relationship between State and Church, both occur in contemporary Japan. The legal collocation of Shinto also appears difficult to understand for the Western observer who does not have a profound knowledge of the uniqueness of the Japanese religion.

First of all, the Japanese are known for the ease with which they practice more religions syncretically: in particular, in the daily life of a Japanese citizen, the combined influence of at least Shinto and Buddhism can be found.[131] Moreover, the fact that the Emperor of Japan is also the supreme head of the Shinto clergy cannot be underestimated, and, until a few decades ago, his divine nature was not only not denied or opposed by civil laws, but it was even hinted at in the Constitution of 1889. This latter document placed Shinto in a

---

129 J.C. Fisher, *'We the Kokumin': The Constitution, International Law and the Rights of Foreigners in Japan, supra* n. 125, 115.

130 This paragraph is based on the paper by G.F. Colombo, *Laicità dello Stato e Shintoismo nella giurisprudenza costituzionale giapponese*, in *Ambrosian Asia*, Roma, 2011.

131 A contemporary Japanese proverb states that "we are born shinto, we marry Christians and die Buddhists". The high rate of marriages celebrated with Christian rites (almost 35% in the metropolitan area of Tokyo and almost 25% in that of Osaka) is given by the fact that a Christian ceremony, especially the Catholic ceremony, is considered to be scenically more gratifying.

position of absolute privilege, even if it did not explicitly qualify it as a state religion.[132] The authors of the 1889 Charter in fact intended to outline a clear demarcation between the freedom to choose one's own religion and the practice in public of such a religion: Article 28 of the fundamental charter defends the right to the individual choice of a faith, but not its public externalization.[133] Shinto was an exception, but not due to the fact that it was a religion: participation in its ritual practices was, in fact, considered (since the early years of the Constitution) not a public expression of faith, but a real civic duty. The consequence is that not only could subjects openly profess Shinto, but moreover they were even required to do so.[134] To this, one must add that the functional and personal mixture of the head of state with the religious vertex of Shinto had generated, in Japan before the Second World War, a complex situation of cohabitation between a modern legal system and a traditional notion of sovereign.[135]

The political-religious mixture was strengthened and exploited during the Meiji and Taisho (1912-1926) eras and in the first phase of the Showa era (1926-1945) until the end of the Second World War, with the creation of a "State Shinto" only partially coinciding with the traditional religious phenomenon.[136] The result of this operation, part of the

132 The constitutional was however, only the culmination of a series of measures aimed at favouring the native religion: in 1871 the Government had already enunciated, through the Proclamation of the Great Doctrine, that "the way of the gods" guided State action. Furthermore in 1871, with two decrees of the Great Council of State, a hierarchical system was introduced for Shinto shrines and their priests were awarded the status of public officials. In 1872, the Ministry of Religion had involved Shinto priests in civil activities, through the Authority for Spiritual Guidance.

133 *See* the position of H. Roesler, legal advisor of the Meiji government, editor of the Code of Civil Procedure of 1890 and the Trade Code of 1899, as well as principal assistant of the Japanese authors of the Constitution. Roesler, in the drafting of the Constitution, expressed himself on the problem of religious freedom: "The freedom of religious belief does not include the right of public exercise of any faith [...]. By the Japanese Constitution the public exercise of religion is not freely permitted, but remains entirely under the existing laws and ordinances [...]. A State religion may be established on the basis of national faith, and privileges may be accorded to such religion or to others related therewith" (J. Siemes, *Hermann Roesler's Commentaries on the Meiji Constitution*, in 19 *Mounmenta Nipponica* 37-65, 55-57 (1964).

134 This situation inevitably implied a compression of the freedom of worship, even individual, of the faithful of different religions, who were obliged to celebrate Shintoist rituals. As noted in H. Hardacre, *Shinto and the State 1868-1988*, Princeton, 1989, 120, "Thus, if a person refused a talisman from the Ise Shrine or doubted the truth of Shinto myth [...], such actions could be taken as a dereliction of civic duty, even though no national law required anyone to do any of these things."

135 A consequence of this conflict can be found in Art. 28 of the Meiji Constitution, according to which the Japanese were granted religious freedom "on condition that [...] does not conflict with his duties as a subject".

136 "Shinto and State Shinto are not identical. The Japanese imperial government created and implemented the religion, or system, of State Shinto in a time period that corresponds roughly with the resumption of the imperial government until Japan's defeat in World War II, from the mid-nineteenth century to the mid-twentieth century," K. Yamagishi, *Freedom of Religion, Religious Political Participation, and Separation of Religion and State: Legal Considerations from Japan*, in *Brigham Young University Law Review* 919-941, 922 (2008). The creation of an official de facto religion closely linked to Shintoism was initially conceived as an instrument for the reaffirmation of imperial power and to foster cohesion and patriotism after the fall of the Tokugawa Shogunate (which had instead elevated Buddhism to the rank of religion of the state).

constitutional text, on the one hand favoured Shinto over any other religion, but on the other, it assimilated it to a civil, traditional phenomenon, linked to the organization of the State,[137] favouring its social aspects and even penalizing those more strictly religious.[138]

At the end of the war, Japan found itself under the government of the allied occupation forces (SCAP), mostly from the United States. Owing to the fact that the State Shinto was recognized as a contributory factor in the nationalistic drift and legitimation of Japanese military expansionism, the occupiers decided that this epiphenomenon should be eliminated from the country, and they adopted a series of measures aimed at secularising Japan, first of all via the severing of the links between political and religious power. In particular, on 15 December 1945, General Douglas MacArthur, commander in chief of the occupation forces, issued a document known as the "Shinto Directive" ("Directive on the Abolition of Governmental Sponsorship, Support, Perpetuation, Control, and Dissemination of State Shinto and Shrine Shinto "), which ordered the closure of state institutions dedicated to religious formation, prohibited any nationalistic or militaristic propaganda related to the Shinto and purified the scholastic system from any religious reference.[139]

However, the most important provision on this subject is undoubtedly Article 20 of the 1947 Constitution, which established the strict principle of a secular state (as well as guaranteeing religious freedom).

Hence, the peculiar difficulty in applying the constitutional precept to Japan is also the result of the aforementioned historical fact: the Constitution of 1947 was in fact drawn up, in the first instance, by US experts, based on principles eminently Anglo-Saxon, with a very limited focus on the specific characteristics of the country. The consequence of this other-directed "legal transplant"[140] is an imperfect (according to the canons of the western observer, one intends) application of constitutional norms.

To accurately comprehend the nature of the problem, one must start from the textual data. Hence, there is the need to analyse Article 20 of the Constitution, which states:

Amplius, S. Murakami, *Japanese Religion in the Modern Century*, in E. H. Byron (Tr.), Tokyo, University of Tokyo Press, 1980, 20

137 Shinto was in fact placed under the jurisdiction of the Ministry of the Interior, while issues related to all other religions were assigned to the supervision of the Ministry of Education.

138 Already in 1882 the priestly prerogatives of the cult had been severely limited with two notes from the Ministry of Internal Affairs. "Furthermore, the State prohibited Shintoist from recruiting new members or practicing Shinto funeral rites and limited the subsidies to shrines to ten percent of legitimate expenses. Thus, although it is commonly believed that the national government protected Shinto, the reality for Shinto believers was very different. The fact is, the established State Shinto was more concerned with civic duty than religious ritual, and even legitimate Shinto religious rituals were regulated by the State." H. Kobayashi, *Religion in the Public Sphere: Challenges and Opportunities in Japan*, in *Brigham Young University Law Review* 683-710, 688-689 (2005).

139 *Amplius*, L.S. Wittner, *MacArthur and the Missionaries: God and Man in Occupied Japan*, in XL *The Pacific Historical Review* 77-98 (1971); H. Hardacre, *Shinto and the State 1868-1988*, op. cit. 136-137.

140 On the notion in general of *legal transplant* (here used in the imperfect sense) *see* A. Watson, *Legal Transplants: An Approach to Comparative Law*, Atlanta (GA), University of Georgia Press, 1993.

1. Freedom of religion is guaranteed to all. No religious organization will receive privileges from the State nor exercise any political authority.
2. No person shall be compelled to take part in any religious acts, celebration, rite or practice.
3. The State and its organs shall refrain from religious education or any other religious activity.

In addition to Article 20, Article 89 assumes a particular importance in relation to the question:

No public money or other property shall be expended or appropriated for the use, benefit or maintenance of any religious institution or association, or for any charitable, educational or benevolent enterprises not under the control of public authority.

The *black letter rule* seems to leave no doubt. By adopting a strict hermeneutic canon, the constitutional text did not allow overlapping State and religious organs, institutions or manifestations. However, as Nipponists know very well, much more than comparatists, the Japanese *Grundnorm* has often subjected to at least questionable or even forced interpretations, and this happened also in the case of the constitutional text on religion. Above and beyond political or intellectual exegesis,[141] the constitutional text has been repeatedly analysed in court. As is well-known, in Japan, the control of constitutionality is not entrusted to a specific judicial body, but is distributed, according to the US model of widespread constitutional control, throughout the system of the courts, so that even a judge of the first degree can expose the unconstitutionality of a law or behaviour. However, questions of constitutionality, due to their particular importance, usually retrace the appeal mechanism up to the third degree of judgment, namely that before the Supreme Court. Here, a series of four decisions, between 1977 and 2002, where the Supreme Court of Japan assumed an explicit position on the question of the relationship between state and religion, will be analysed.

The first ruling worthy of note concerns the blessing of a construction site and is from 1977.[142]

In 1965, the mayor of the city of Tsu, in the province[143] of Mie had instructed some Shinto priests to celebrate a ritual (known as *jichinsai*) to bless the construction of a new

141 The debate on the Constitution (and its possible revision) is not a monopoly of the political class, but often finds space in newspapers, magazines, etc. who report the main initiatives.

142 *Kakunaga v. Sekiguchi* (known to Western scholars as *The Shinto Groundbreaking Ceremony Case*), *Minshu*, Vol. 31, n. 4, 533. The ruling is fully translated by Frank Upham in L. Beer, H. Itoh, *The Constitutional Case Law of Japan, 1971-1990*, Seattle (WA), University of Washington Press, 1996, 478-483. It is also found in extracts in *The Japanese Legal System. Cases, Codes, and Commentary*, op. cit., 226-230.

143 Although the translation of the term *ken* commonly used to describe the areas in which Japan's main administrative structure is articulated, is "prefecture", the most attentive historiography is inclined to translate into "province". R. Caroli, F. Gatti, *Storia del Giappone*, 12th edn, Roma-Bari, Laterza, 2016.

school building, spending 7,663 yen of the municipal budget. A town councillor had subsequently filed a lawsuit against the mayor of the city, claiming a violation of Article 20, Paragraph III, of the Constitution and asking for the reimbursement of the amount paid (the 4,000 yen paid to the officiants and the donation of 3,663 yen) and compensation of 50,000 yen for the suffering caused by having to participate in the ceremony. The District Court of Tsu had rejected the claims, claiming that the ritual in question had a purely traditional value, and not intrinsically religious. Moreover, the court added that the plaintiff had not been forced to attend the ceremony and thus could not claim a violation of his personal religious freedom, nor a sufferance.

The Nagoya High Court, nominated to address the matter following the appeal (*koso*) by the plaintiff, modified the sentence of the first instance, affirming the full religious nature of the *jichinsai* and therefore the unconstitutionality of the use of public money. In stating their reasons for the ruling, the judges highlighted how the ceremony had been faithfully celebrated in accordance with the dictates of State Shinto.

The Supreme Court, where an appeal had been lodged (*jokoku*) by the mayor of Tsu, definitively decreed (sitting in Grand Bench, with a very narrow majority) the non-violation of the Constitution. According to the judges, the text of Article 20 cannot and must not be read in a literal sense, owing to the fact that an authentic, clear, and complete separation between state and religion would not only be impossible, but would even lead to distortions and discriminations.[144] Therefore, according to the Supreme Court, a "physiological contamination" exists between civil and religious institutions: the tolerable intensity of this osmotic relationship is however difficult to ascertain and entrusted to vague and ambiguous parameters, such as the concept of "reasonableness", to be determined according to the concrete and specific circumstances of each individual case.[145] The Court must decide

144 "The Provisions on Religion-State Separation are essentially an institutional guarantee; that is to say, they do not directly guarantee freedom of religion per se, but attempt to guarantee it indirectly by securing a system in which religion and the State are separate. However, religion involves more than private, personal belief; it is accompanied by a broad array of external social aspects and thus comes into contact with many sectors of social life, including education, social welfare, culture, and folk customs. As a natural result of this contact, the State cannot avoid association with religion as it regulates social life or implements policies to subsidize and support education, social welfare, or culture. Thus, complete separation between religion and State is virtually impossible in an actual system of government. Furthermore, to attempt complete separation would inevitably lead to anomalies in every area of social life. For example, it would cast doubt on the propriety of extending to religiously affiliated private schools the same subsidies that are given to nonreligious private schools, and it would call into question the propriety of State assistance to religious groups for the maintenance and preservation of cultural assets such as shrine and temple buildings, Buddhist statues, and the like. To deny such support would amount to imposing a disadvantage on these entities because of their religious affiliation; in other words, it would amount to discrimination on religious grounds. Similarly, to prohibit all prison chaplaincy activities of a religious nature would severely restrict inmates' freedom of worship. As these examples demonstrate, there are certain inherent and inevitable limits to the religion-State separation guaranteed by the Provisions."

145 "When the principle of religion-State separation is embodied in an actual system of government, given that the State must accept some degree of involvement with religion according to the particular societal and

following the criterion of the *purpose-effect test*, according to which the purpose and the effect of each conduct must be evaluated, taking into account common perceptions. And in this case, the supreme judges (as mentioned, only by majority) affirmed that the ritual performed on behalf of the mayor of Tsu consisted of an exclusively traditional celebration: although the fact that that originally the *jichinsai* was a religious ceremony was not disputed, the Supreme Court deemed that the sacral value was to be now be considered surpassed. At most, one could attribute to the event an apotropaic function.[146]

The ruling in question was accompanied by two robust and articulated dissenting opinions.

The first, signed by five judges, cautioned against the dangers of a broadly discretionary interpretation in such a delicate question. The dissenting judges, retracing the events that led to the adoption of the *Shinto Directive* and Article 20 of the Constitution, affirmed that the principle of religious freedom was substantially without effect unless accompanied by

cultural characteristics of the nation, the question then becomes [a balancing of interests]: under what circumstances and to what degree can such a relationship be accepted while remaining consistent with the guarantee of religious freedom which is the fundamental objective of the system. From this perspective, the principle of religion-State separation, which forms the basis of the Provisions and serves to guide their interpretation, demands that the State be religiously neutral but does not prohibit all connection of the State with religion. Rather, it should be interpreted as prohibiting conduct that brings about State connection with religion only if that connection exceeds a reasonable standard determined by consideration of the conduct's purpose and effects in the totality of the circumstances [...]. Art. 20, Paragraph 3 of the Constitution stipulates that 'The State and its organs shall refrain from religious education or any other religious activity.' Using the above discussion of the principle of religion-State separation to interpret this language, "religious activity" should not be taken to mean all activities of the State and its organs which bring them into contact with religion, but only those which bring about contact exceeding the aforesaid reasonable limits and which have a religiously significant purpose, or the effect of which is to promote, subsidize, or, conversely, interfere with or oppose religion."

146 "Nevertheless, although the groundbreaking ceremonies (known as *jichinsai*, among other names) that are traditionally performed at the start of construction work to pray for a stable foundation and workers' safety had religious origins in their intent to pacify the gods of the land, there can be no doubt that this religious significance has gradually waned over time. In general, although the ceremony includes prayer for safety and a firm foundation at the start of construction, the proceedings have become a formality perceived as almost completely devoid of religious meaning. Even if the ceremony is performed in the style of an existing religion, as long as it remains within the bounds of well-established and widely practiced usage, most people would perceive it as a secularized ritual without religious meaning, a social formality that has become customary at the start of construction work. Although the Groundbreaking Ceremony was conducted as a Shrine Shinto rite, for most citizens, and for the Mayor of Tsu City and others involved in sponsoring the event, it was a secular occasion with no particular religious meaning, because such a ceremony is well within the bounds of general usage widely observed over many years.Furthermore, in actual practice, the construction workers themselves who are particularly concerned with safety consider it indispensable, as a general custom, to mark the start of work with a ceremony sponsored or attended by the owner of the building and including a ritual like the one in this case. In light of this practice, together with the public attitudes discussed above, it is clear that the building owner had a very secular motive for holding the customary Groundbreaking ceremony: meeting the demand of construction workers to observe a social formality that has become customary at the start of work, thereby ensuring its smooth progress."

the rigid separation between the state and religion.[147] They also criticized the approach taken by the majority, affirming that, even if a total separation was impossible, there was the need to try to obtain, with careful specific evaluations, an osmosis that was as limited as possible. This choice should be made by distinguishing, in a tangible way, activities with a simple religious origin, completely blurred over the years, from those with a current and effective relevance of worship via the application of an "ethnological criterion" (as suggested in the appeal). In the case of the city of Tsu, the dissenting judges, analysing the nature of the ceremony and its concrete development, had no hesitation in acknowledging the undoubtedly religious value of the ceremony performed.[148]

The second dissenting opinion, signed by Judge Fujibayashi (on that occasion as President), supported even more drastic positions against the majority decision. He affirmed that it was essential to stick to the rigid constitutional text, preventing the State and its organs from participating in activities that were only abstractly attributable to religion:[149] this clear abstention was the necessary prerequisite for the protection of minority rights.[150] The judge did not contemplate how it could be possible to deny religious significance to a ceremony that was not celebrated "as such", that is, as a traditional manifestation for its own sake, but in order to bless, with a supernatural intervention, the safety of the work.[151] He therefore regretted the decision taken by the majority of the judging bench.

---

147 "The Constitution of Japan incorporated the ideas of the Shinto Directive in contemplation of the bitter experience of the harmful effects of close association between the State and Shinto under the Meiji Constitution's guarantee of religious freedom. That guarantee, as shown above, was incomplete despite the importance of freedom of belief as a basic human right. The separation of religion and State is essential to secure that right. Thus, in addition to the unconditional guarantee of religious freedom in the first section of Paragraph 1, Art. 20, the Constitution of Japan adopted the provisions cited above to secure a complete guarantee. Reviewing the above history, the principle of religion-State separation embodied in the second section of Paragraph 1 and Paragraph 3 of Art. 20 and in Art. 89 would require absolute separation. In other words, the State should be secular: religion and the State are mutually independent with no connecting ties, and the State neither allows religious influence in its affairs nor interferes in religious matters."

148 "In our opinion, the Groundbreaking Ceremony clearly constitutes religious activity under art. 20, par. 3. Moreover, there are absolutely no grounds as described above for allowing such activity in this case. The Groundbreaking Ceremony therefore violates Art. 20, Paragraph 3 of the Constitution and should not be permitted."

149 Moreover, according to Fujibayashi, the difference between rituals, even if only very abstractly religious and traditional customs, is very clear: "Of course, we must recognize that there are various observances which were originally religious but which no longer have any religious meaning in society. The Japanese still place New Year's pine decorations outside their gates to bring good luck, although the custom seems to be declining year by year. We can also readily accept that customs like the Dolls' Festival and Christmas trees are meaningful as family treats that parents provide for children, or as observances to foster goodwill within a group. These customs have probably lost all religious significance."

150 "When the power, prestige, and financial support of the State or of a local public body is present behind a particular religion, this gives rise to indirect pressure on members of minority religions to submit to the religion that has received public recognition."

151 "But can we regard the performance of the Groundbreaking Ceremony under the circumstances described by the Court of Appeals merely as a way of bringing good luck or a form of entertainment? As the majority notes, those who are involved in the building work and who are thus particularly concerned with safety

The decision concerning the city of Tsu is relevant due to the fact that, under the current Constitution, the Supreme Court ruled on Paragraph III of Article 20, thus weakening its scope and concluding, as previously highlighted, by affirming a "physiological" mixture between state and religion.

The ruling also established what would become the criterion used to evaluate similar situations that were submitted to the attention of the judiciary, i.e. the aforementioned *purpose-effect test*. The judges affirmed here, for the first time, that the parameters to be considered for judging whether a conduct violated the constitutional precept were: the place where the event takes place, the reaction of the average individual before the fact, the subjectively religious purpose of the person who undertakes the activity, existence and scope of a (objectively) religious content, and the effect or influence that the event may have on the average individual.[152]

The second ruling, regarded the process of "deification" of aman belonging to the Self-Defence Forces, and is dated 1988.[153]

---

consider it indispensable to hold a groundbreaking ceremony incorporating rites as in this case, and the sponsors comply with this demand, regardless of their own wishes, to ensure the smooth progress of the work. It is inconceivable that the ceremony in the present case was held merely for the sake of the banquet that traditionally follows it. Something is here that cannot be understood in terms of mere customary practice. In other words, if consideration for workers' safety was the only concern, then given proper supervision and today's advanced building techniques, scientifically, nothing further would be necessary. However, a desire to ensure safety beyond human powers makes it necessary to rely on something other than human agency. If this is not religious, what is? Even if the Mayor of Tsu City, who sponsored the Groundbreaking Ceremony, is not a believer in any religion, the ceremony does not lose its religious character, inasmuch as it was an essential requirement to satisfy the construction personnel's wish for a level of safety not attainable by human powers."

152 The method in question has similarities with the so-called "Lemon Test", elaborated by the United States Supreme Court in the *Lemon v. Kurtzman* case, 403 U.S. 602, 612-613 (1971). This very famous case, concerning the financing by the State of Pennsylvania in favor of some religious schools, fixed the parameters on the basis of which the legislation (and more generally, the action of public institutions) had to be evaluated in religious matters, *i.e.*:

- the action/provision must have a secular institutional purpose;
- the action/provision must not have as its main effect the advancement or the inhibition of religion;
- the action/provision must not result in the "excessive involvement" of public institutions with religion.

In truth, these parameters are more similar to those, although analogous, adopted, even if with a different result, by the Supreme Court of Japan in the case of *Japan v. Nakaya*, which will be discussed below. On *Lemon v. Kurtzman*, R.S. Alley, *The Constitution and Religion: Leading Supreme Court Cases on Church and State*, Amherst, Prometheus Books, 1999; On the evolution of the jurisprudence of the US Supreme Court towards the abandonment of the *Lemon Test, see* H.M. Kritzer, M.J. Richards, *Jurisprudential Regimes and Supreme Court Decisionmaking: the Lemon Regime and Establishment Clause Cases*, in 37 *Law & Society Review* 827-840 (2003).

153 *Japan v. Nakaya*. The ruling is completely translated by F. H. Miller e H. Itoh L. Beer, H. Itoh, *The Constitutional Case Law of Japan, 1971-1990*, op. cit., 495-500 and in the database of the Supreme Court of Japan, www.courts.go.jp/english/judgments/index.html. It is also partially found in *The Japanese Legal System: Cases, Codes, and Commentary*, op, cit., 234-240. First of all, the English term Serviceman, commonly translated as "military" or "combatant", cannot be rendered with the usual transpositions in Italian, since the members of the Self-Defence Forces of Japan strictly could not be called "soldiers" (*see above*). Moreover, the ritual of "deification", through which the subject of the emperor died to defend the country is consecrated

In 1968, Takafumi Nakaya,[154] a member of the Japanese Self-Defence Forces, died in a car accident while on duty. In March 1972, the Yamaguchi's office of the Friends of the Self-Defence Forces Association forwarded a request to the local Shinto temple to hold a collective "deification" ceremony of 27 members of the Self-Defence Forces, including the deceased Takafumi. On 5 April 1972, Nakaya's wife, Yasuko Nakaya, formally expressed her opposition to the inclusion of her late husband in the ceremony. Indeed, being of Christian faith, she felt her religious soul offended by the ritual. Despite Mrs. Nakaya's opposition, the Shinto ritual took place, and on 5 June 1972, the widow was notified that her husband's spirit had been deified.

Yasuko Nakaya, thus, decided to take legal action to obtain the revocation of the initial request for a collective ritual, and demanded monetary compensation from the Association and the Government. The presence of the Government among the defendants was due to the fact that the administrative-bureaucratic preparation of the ceremony was carried out with the significant contribution of the regional government office.

The District Court partially pronounced in favour of the plaintiff, sentencing the Association and the Government to pay compensation, but rejected the petition for the revocation of the request. The unsuccessful defendants appealed against the sentence to the Hiroshima Court of Appeal. The judges of the second degree partially confirmed the initial sentence, albeit, excluding the position of the Association that, owing to the fact that it was a private organization, it had no constitutional duties of abstention from religious activities. The Government subsequently filed an appeal before the Supreme Court.

Once again the Supreme Judge of Japan established that there had been no violation of Article 20 of the Constitution.

The majority of the judges, in the wake of the 1977 decision, affirmed that the constitutional ban did not affect all the activities connected with religion, but only those aimed at promoting, privileging or, on the contrary, oppressing a specific creed. Once again, the reference aimed at highlighting not only the action per se, but its consequent perception in the "public".[155] Indeed, the Supreme Court acknowledged that the main purpose of the intervention of the local administration was that of "improving the moral and social recognition of the members of the Self-Defence Forces", and therefore that the purely religious function was "marginal or even absent".[156]

---

kami protector of the nation, would require a broad explanation of this practice, an explanation that goes beyond the scope of this work.

154 Nakaya himself did not actively profess any religion and was married in a civil ceremony.

155 "When we examine whether a certain action constitutes religious activity, we should decide objectively following common sense and considering various factors such as place of the action, the public's evaluation, intent, purpose and religious feelings of those who act, its effect and influence to the general public, etc."

156 "The actual actions of the Regional Office staff cooperating with the Veterans Association up until the application, which were as stated above, had indirect relation with the religion and their purpose and intention were assumed to be to raise the social status and morale of SDF members, as aforementioned;

However, the decision had to deal with other and much more important arguments raised during the trial, and in particular the question of whether Mrs Nakaya's juridical sphere had been damaged by the celebration of the ritual to which she had been opposed. The conclusion of the judges was negative, due to the fact that, recognizing as a "right" to the widow "that others should refrain from commemorative events in memory of her husband, would have constituted a violation of religious freedom. Consequently, albeit acknowledging the plaintiff's "discomfort", the Court categorically rejected the claim that this feeling could have any legal importance.[157] Due to the fact that no-one had forced Nakaya's widow to attend the Shinto ceremony, and furthermore no-one had prevented her from commemorating her husband according to the dictates of Christianity, constitutionally protected freedom had been respected. The conclusion of the judges was therefore in the sense of establishing, in essence, that the content of Article 20 of the Constitution complements a prohibition aimed, or rather a limitation imposed on the State rather than a right granted to citizens. Furthermore, this prohibition was watered down by the already adopted approach on the basis of which, not all abstractly religious activities were banned.[158]

Although the ruling referred to the precedent of *Kakunaga v. Sekiguchi*, it manifested a different analysis of the parameters adopted to accomplish the *purpose-effect test*. In fact, the principle elements, taken in consideration by the Court in the Nakaya case, were the

---

hence it should be said that they had little religious feelings and that it was not the activity which would be considered by the general public as having effect of drawing attention to a specific religion or of sponsoring, promoting, encouraging a specific religion or suppressing or interfering with other religions. Therefore the actions of the Regional Office staff cannot be regarded as constituting religious activities though they did relate to religion."

157 "However, when one's religious peacefulness is disturbed by religious activity of others, though it is natural for him to feel uncomfortable for that and to wish not to be disturbed any more, if we admit such a person to seek legal relief such as compensation or injunction on the ground of infringement of religious feelings, then, instead, it will obviously come to harm the religious freedom of others. The guarantee of freedom of religion requires tolerance for religious activities of others that are inconsistent with the religion that one believes in as long as such activity does not disturb his or her freedom of religion through compulsion or by giving rise to disadvantages. The same is true for cases of reminiscence or memorial of one's deceased spouse. Because the freedom of religious activity such as to choose someone for an object of faith or to worship someone with one's religion and to pray for the peace of his spirit is guaranteed to every person. The interest to live a religious life under a quiet religious atmosphere, which interest the original judgment recognized as the religious personal right, is of the nature that could not be recognized immediately as a legal interest."

158 "The provision of separation of the State and religion in paragraph 3, Art. 20 of the Constitution, which is known as a provision of the institutional guarantee, *does not guarantee the religious freedom itself directly to individual persons, but rather it is an attempt to indirectly guarantee the freedom of religion by setting forth the parameters of actions which the State and its organs may not conduct* (the Grand Bench judgment of the Supreme Court, *supra*). Therefore, the religious activity of the State or its organs which violates this provision should not necessarily be deemed unlawful in relation to individual persons unless the activity directly infringes upon their religious freedom as guaranteed by the Constitution, e.g., by imposing restriction on their exercise of religious freedom in violation of the first sentence of paragraph 1 of the said Art. or by compelling individuals to attend religious activities in violation of paragraph 2 of the said Art." (emphasis added).

limits of the action of public officials (that is to say, to what extent involvement of institutional subjects in religious activities is granted) and the effect of the conduct implemented in terms of promotion, support or, conversely, oppression of a religious belief.

The main decision was accompanied by four separate opinions: one supplementary,[159] two shared and one dissenting.

The concurrent opinions, albeit sharing the majority decision, diverge, in part, on the motivation. Of particular interest is the second opinion, signed by Judge Sakaue, who rejected the notion of the nonexistence of a legal basis to the claim of a surviving spouse to see their religion respected in the commemoration of a deceased relative: however, in the case in question, the widow's wishes had to be counterbalanced by those of the other family members, who were in favour of the Shinto veneration.

The dissenting opinion of Judge Ito arose in the wake of the already *dissenting opinion* of Judge Fujibayashi in the case of the city of Tsu, which was expressly mentioned. The judge did not criticize the reasoning of the majority according to which the religious character of a rite depended on the purpose, the effect and the result of the rite. However, he challenged the concrete application of this method. In particular, Judge Ito did not perceive how a purely religious significance could be denied to the controversial commemoration, whose realization had been made possible thanks to the assistance of a peripheral administration of the State;[160] therefore, the petition of Nakaya's widow was worthy of approval.

This decision was widely reported by Western specialists. In particular, numerous pages were spent on the true or presumed iniquity of the ruling. However, the comments were mostly of a socio-political rather than a technical-legal nature.[161]

---

159 Signed by magistrates Takashima, Yotsuya and Okuno, it confines itself to noting that the public administration involved should have maintained a more appropriate behaviour, without recognizing profiles of unlawful conduct.

160 The dissenting opinion notes in fact that there were secular alternatives to the contested ceremony: for example, the eventual erection of a memorial of Takafumi. A civil celebration would have nevertheless obtained the declared purpose (improving the morale and social recognition of the members of the Self-Defence Forces) without violating the constitutional precept. The "deification" of the spirits of the fallen instead, is without a doubt a religious ritual.

161 Some of the most decisive reprimands are found in N. Field, *In the Realm of a Dying Emperor*, New York, Pantheon, 1991, 107-154. To tell the truth, rather than focusing on the technical defects of the sentence, Field disputes the political significance of the decision taken, viewing it, as a manifestation of clear support for the Japanese militarism. "The significance of the suit brought by Mrs. Nakaya Yasuko lies beyond the merely legal: the case reflects the incommensurateness of judicial capability and judicial will with the challenges she issued to Japanese militarism, to the Japanese treatment of religious minorities, and to the situation of women in Japanese society [...]." (108) An analysis more meditated and attentive to the purely legal aspect is found in E.N. Weeks, *A Widow's Might: Nakaya v. Japan and Japan's Current State of Religious Freedom*, in *Brigham Young University Law Review* 691-730 (1995) In this paper, the author highlights similarities and differences between the criteria adopted in the *Nakaya* case and those followed by the Supreme Court of the United States of America in similar cases, above all, in the *Lemon v. Kurtzman* case,

A change in direction by the Supreme Court occurred in a ruling of 1997, and regarded some donations made in favour of the Yasukuni Shrine.[162]

In the period between 1981 and 1986, some subjects holding public offices for the Province of Ehime had made donations to the YasukuniShrine[163] and other Shintoinstitutions using public money. Moreover, the disputed emoluments had not been generically transferred to the sanctuaries, but had received an expressed ritual qualification.[164]

---

and comes to the conclusion that the main defect in the decision of the Japanese magistrates is not so much in the sentence, but in having artfully contracted the reasoning on the most delicate points.

162 Anzai *et al.*v. Shiraishi *et al.* (known to Western scholars as nota *The Yasukuni Donation Case* or the *Ehime Tamagushiryo Case*), *Minshu*, Vol. 51, No. 4, 1673. The ruling can partially be found also in *The Japanese Legal System: Cases, Codes, and Commentary*, op. cit., at 235-245. The ruling is cited in almost all recent contributions on the subject, and is incidently discussed in more general papers, such as Y. Abe, *Secularization: Karel Dobbelaere and Japanese Sociology of Religion*, in R. Laermans and others (Eds.), *Secularization and Social Integration Papers in Honor of Karel Dobbelaere*, Leuven, Leuven University Press, 1998, and has been the subject of some specific comments (such as S. Morimura, *Freedom of Religion and the Separation of State and Religion: A Japanese Case Study*, in 31 *Hitotsubashi Journal of Law and Politics* 23-30 (2003). The ruling is also commented, from a blatantly US perspective, by F.S. Ravitch, *Japanese Prime Minister's Visits to the Yasukuni Shrine Analyzed under Articles 20 and 89 of the Japanese Constitution*, in 22 *Michigan State International Law Review* 713 (2013).

163 The Yasukuni Shrine (靖国神社, Yasukuni Jinja) (literally "National Peace Sanctuary") is a Tokyo shrine dedicated to the souls of soldiers and other people who died fighting in the service of the country. The sanctuary is a source of considerable controversy since there are 1068 war criminalsamong the fallen commemorated (whose names are noted in the Shrine's Book of Souls). Among these there are 14 "class A war criminals" *i.e.*, people convicted of crimes against peace during the Tokyo Trial (on which, we recommend consulting the excellent essay by Y. Totani, *The Tokyo War Crimes Trial: The Pursuit of Justice in the Wake of World War II*, op. cit.,). The visits to the sanctuary by members of the Government have been the cause of protests both inside Japan and abroad, and China and South Korea have repeatedly protested against these visits since the first post-war visit, by the then Prime Minister Yasuhiro Nakasone in 1985. Despite the controversy, the former Prime Minister Jun'ichiro Koizumi made annual visits during his tenure from 2001 to 2006, with consequences also challenged in court, precisely in the perspective of an undue mix between politics and religion, *see* E. Bertolini, *Giappone: l'Alta Corte di Osaka giudica incostituzionale la visita del premier Koizumi al santuario shintoista di Yasukuni*, in *Diritto pubbl. comp. eur.* 1733-1734 (2005). Each episode is followed by numerous legal actions taken against the Government. However, even before the legal action against Nakasone's visit, there had been a previous appeal against a provision by the Iwate Province that required the heads of government to visit Yasukuni. The District Court of Morioka had declared the provision in accordance with the Constitution, considering that even the Prime Minister was granted individual freedom of conscience. The Sendai High Court instead deemed the provision unconstitutional. The lawsuits filed against Nakasone's visits were rejected in the first instance or on appeal. For the most part, this was due to the fact that they were proposed as compensatory actions, and therefore, not recognizing a compensable damage, the claims were rejected. In the appeal, the Fukuoka Court noted, *obiter*, that the visits were unconstitutional, while the Court of Osaka limited itself to questioning it in dubious terms. Koizumi's visits again provoked a range of legal actions. Suits were filed at the courts of Tokyo, Osaka, Chiba, Takamatsu, Fukuoka and Naha. All the actions were rejected, again because the judges did not find compensable damage. However, during the appeal, the Fukuoka and Osaka Courts expressly considered the visits to be unconstitutional. *Amplius, ibid*; C.-P. Su, *The Constitutional Debates on the YasukuniShrine and the Separation of Religion andState in Japan*, in 2 *National Taiwan University Law Review* 1-20 (2007).

164 The donations have been qualified as *tamagushi-ryo, kumotsu-ryo* and *kento-ryo*. The first two ritual offerings are offered to the Shinto gods made on the occasion of the spring and autumn festivities, while

The competent court of first instance decreed the unconstitutionality of these donations, asserting the undisputed religious nature of the gesture and the consequent support to the Shintoist sanctuaries. The High Court, however, decided in relation to the conduct in question's compliance with the Constitution. The appeal judges deemed that, despite the religious qualification of the donations, they could be considered, in the general perception, as simple gestures of "social courtesy", simply aimed at "consoling the families of the dead" commemorated in the sanctuaries. The emoluments, however, did not violate the constitutional ban due to the fact that they did not favour or discriminate against any particular religion.

The Supreme Court, for the first time, ruled instead in favour of the unconstitutionality of the act, in violation of Article 20 and, above all, violation of Article 89.

The specific ritual qualification of donations, according to the judges of the last resort, could not be underestimated: the fact that offerings of a sacred nature were made on the occasion of religious ceremonies[165] implied the direct participation of public officials in activities prohibited by the Constitution.[166] Basing itself on its own precedents, the Supreme Court did not reject its criterion of "reasonableness" and reference to "general perception". Indeed, in this case, the judges took the opportunity to further elaborate in detail the principles on the basis of which the so-called *purpose-effect test* should be performed, namely: the place where the event takes place, the perception of the average individual in relation to its religious nature, the existence of a possible intention, purpose or religious awareness of the plaintiff and finally the influence that the fact may have on the average individual.

Therefore, on the basis of the usual parameters, the Court affirmed that the matter submitted to its judgment was very different from the case of the city of Tsu of 1977, due to the fact that the blessing of a building site was primarily a secular event, whose original religious significance had gradually thinned down over the centuries.[167] In this case, instead,

---

the third is accompanied by the lighting of votive lamps with the name of the offerer during a ceremony to commemorate the dead.

165 "Now, it is a judicially noted fact that holding ceremonies are the main religious activities for Shinto, that the main points of the Spring and Autumn Ceremony or Memorial Ceremony are religious rites according to the Shinto tradition, that they are among the most important traditional ceremonies held by each shrine, and that the memorial ceremony has almost the same religious rite and takes place on the largest scale among ceremonies held by Yasukuni Shrines. Moreover, it is clear that each shrine has regarded *tamagushiryo, kumotsuryo*, and *kentoryo* as having religious meanings, because *tamagushiryo* and *kumotsuryo* are offered to the Shinto god when religious rites are held at the thime of the Spring and Autumn Ceremony or memorial ceremony, and because, when *kentoryo* is offered, lights with the contributors' names are displayed within the precincts of the shrines at the time of the Mitamasai ceremony."

166 "According to these facts, it is clear that the prefecture was involved in important religious ceremonies held by specific religious groups."

167 In reality these differences do not appear evident to all commentators. Regarding the doubts of some interpreters *see* C.-P. Su, *The Constitutional Debates on the Yasukuni Shrine and the Separation of Religion and State in Japan*, op. cit., 15.

the sacral nature of the donations was indisputable, and hence, from this stemmed the violation of Article 20, Paragraph III,[168] and Aricle 89[169] of the Constitution.

As expected, the decision was accompanied by several additional,[170] concurring and dissenting opinions.

The three concurring opinions added significant elements of investigation.

The first opinion, signed by Judge Sonobe, cautioned against the poor objectivity and effectiveness of the *purpose-effect test*, based on criteria that were too debatable to provide a valid evaluation parameter. Moreover, he considered the decision of the majority on the conflict with Article 20, Paragraph 3, of the Constitution, to be superfluous: according to him, it would have been much more appropriate to have ruled solely on the basis of the violation of Article 89.[171]

The second opinion, signed by Judge Takahashi, outlined some passages of the majority opinion and the decision of 1977, asserting that the reasons given to justify a "physiological contamination" between State and religion had actually been presented in an instrumental way. By way of example, he used the hypothesis of a religious school to which funds normally granted to other scholastic institutions,[172] are denied: the fact that such support can (should) be granted did not imply a denial of the separation between state and religion, but only a respect for the obligation of non-discrimination on the grounds of worship.[173] However, continued Takahashi, the point of view of "physiological contamination" contained a genetic defect of approach: according to the judge, the correct

168 "Based on the above consideration, it is reasonable to assume that these offerings by a local government to Yasukuni Shrine or Gokoku Shrine, as mentioned above, constitute prohibited religious activities under Art. 20(3) of the Constitution, because the purpose of the offerings had religious significance and the effect of the offerings led to support or promotion of a specific religion, and the relationship between the local government and Yasukuni Shrine or other shrines caused by these offerings exceeded the reasonable limit under the social and cultural conditions of Japan. Thus, these disbursement were illegal because they were made to religious activities prohibited by the art."

169 "It is clear that Yasukuni Shrine and Gokoku Shrine are religious organizations as stipulated by Art. 89 of the Constitution, and, as mentioned above, it is assumed that these offerings of tamagushiryo to Yasukuni Shrine and Gokoku Shrine resulted in a special relationship between the local government and those shrines that exceed reasonable limits under the social and cultural conditions of Japan. So the expenditure was in the category of payment of public funds prohibited by this art. and thus illegal."

170 Signed by the judges Ono and Fukuda. The first aims above all to underline how, in evaluating the conduct of public officials, the subjective element must be completely ignored, and therefore the defence alleged by one of the defendants of having made donations with a non-religious purpose was of completely irrelevant. The second, instead, emphasizes how Shinto should not benefit from preferential treatment compared to other religions.

171 "[…] Since the expenditure in this case apparently violated Art. 89, I do not have to judge whether the expenditure violated Art. 20(3) or not. I think is desirable to avoid official judgements concerning religious problems as much as possible. 'All the power of a statesman should not and cannot relieve the soul' (John Locke, '*The establishment of the modern tolerance and religious freedom*')."

172 Example used by the judges of the *Kakunaga v. Sekiguchi* case.

173 "Thus, I do not think that these examples are anomalous situations resulting from total separation, and I do not hesitate to interpret the separation of state and religion as total separation in spite of these examples."

perspective was the opposite, i.e. to consider any overlap, even apparent, between public institutions and cult as pathological in as such, admitting a proof to the contrary.[174] The judge then proceeded to caution against the risks of a judgment based on a supposed "common" perception: the law, he stated, should not follow social parameters, but stick to the literal content. The risk was that of permitting unlawful conduct for the simple reason that they are (or had become) socially acceptable. The opinion concluded with a notation related to the *purpose-effect test* stating it was a vague and unreliable method[175] that had led to different results in objectively similar situations.

The third shared opinion was that of Judge Ozaki. He believed that all religious conducts, even if carried out with legal purposes[176] by public subjects, should be considered unconstitutional if alternative secular behaviours to achieve the same purpose exist. He also affirmed that contamination must be avoided, and that the guideline to be observed was that of considering all actions abstractly connected with religion to be illicit, permitting an exceptional permissive regime.

The dissenting opinions were signed by Judge Miyoshi (President of the United Sections) and Judge Kabe.[177]

The first opinion, permeated by a certain rhetorical view, intended to show how the gestures of respect for the fallen for the country could not be qualified as religious even though they are expressed through sacral behaviours. Judge Miyoshi highlighted how, although the sanctuary of Yasukuni was certainly a Shintoreligious institution, most of the people who visit it do not go to pay homage to the divinities of the Japanese native religion, but go there to commemorate their deceased relatives. He stated that most citizens regard the sanctuary as a symbolic place in memory of the fallen, and not as a religious institution. Applying some parameters of the purpose-effect test, Miyoshi highlighted how the intent of the contested donations was purely secular[178] and perceived as such by the average individual.[179] The opinion is relevant from at least three other points of view: firstly, the amount of the donations should also be assessed to establish their possible lawfulness.

---

174 "Thus, I do not think that these examples are anomalous situations resulting from total separation, and I do not hesitate to interpret the separation of state and religion as total separation in spite of these examples."

175 "Like a scale without graduation."

176 For example, support for the families of the fallen, official motivation for donations to the Yasukuni shrine.

177 The dissenting opinion of Judge Kabe is aimed at a different application of the *purpose-effect test*, according to which the correct decision should have been in the sense of the constitutionality of the emoluments. He underlines that the method used by the Court is in any case improper, because it is based on abstract and not objectively verifiable factors.

178 "We should understand that the intent or purpose of the expenses was to console the war bereaved, as well as to remember and mourn the war dead. Most people understand so."

179 In truth, the dissenting opinion in question goes further, making a logical leap, and evaluating the effect on the average citizen in terms of positivity: "Thinking of the expenses' effect or influence on ordinary people, we can see the positive effect and influence to mourn the war dead, to console the war bereaved, and to pray for world peace. On the other hand, we never see the effect or influence of aiding encouraging, or promoting any specific religion, nor the effect or influence of oppressing or intervening in any one."

In this case, a few thousand yen had to be considered an insignificant sum. The second relates to the relationship between religion and pacifism: Judge Miyoshi believed that the emoluments at the Yasukuni shrine had been assessed with particular rigor due to the fact that also the fallen in the Second World War, including 14 "class A war criminals"[180] are also venerated in the shrine. Finally, even the dissenting judge, while supporting the constitutionality of the donations, stated that he would have felt more "at ease" if they had been donated on a personal basis.[181]

In 2002, the Supreme Court finally expressed itself on the constitutional legitimacy of the procedure of the Emperor's coronation, a ritual known as *Daijosai* (2002).[182]

In 1991, some citizens of the Kagoshima Province took legal action to obtain the declaration of unconstitutionality of the provincial governor's participation in a ceremony to celebrate the emperor's coronation.[183]

The Supreme Court, confirming the lower degree rulings, declared the constitutionality of the behaviour. Consistently with its own precedents, the supreme judge of Japan affirmed that Article 20 of the Constitution did not prevent all contacts between the State and religion, but only those that exceeded a reasonable limit, taking into account the purpose and the effect of the actions, in accordance with the parameters already set out in the decisions commented above.[184]

---

180 *See supra.*

181 The problem of personal action arises regularly whenever the Prime Minister of Japan visits the Yasukuni Shrine. Often, the visit of the Head of Government is accompanied by the simultaneous declaration that the visit is carried out individually and not in an official capacity.

182 1999 (Gyo-Tsu), No. 93. *Minshu*, Vol. 56, No. 6, at 1204. *See also* the comment of S. Matsui, *The Supreme Court and the Separation of Church and State*, in II *International Journal of Constitutional Law* 534-545 (2004)

183 The participation of the civil bodies at this celebration was also the subject of debate in Parliament. In particular, a parliamentarian (Yasuko Takemura, from Hokkaido Province), posed a series of questions to representatives of the Government on the opportunity to use public money for ceremonies related to the coronation.

184 "The doctrine should be understood to prohibit the involvement of the state with the religion which exceeds the reasonable limit in relation to the basic goal of the institution, i.e. the guarantee of the freedom of religion, in the light of the social and cultural conditions of Japan by taking into consideration the purpose and effect of the act which represents the involvement with the religion. In the light of the doctrine of the separation of the state and religion understood in this way, 'religious activities' in the context of Art. 20, para.3 of the Constitution does not mean every activity of the state and its agencies which is related to religion, but only those whose level of involvement exceeds the reasonable limit as mentioned above, and more specifically, acts whose purpose is religious, and its effect is to assist, enhance, promote, or suppress, interfere with religion. Whether a given act qualifies as a religious activity as mentioned above should be determined objectively and in accordance with the socially acceptable sense, not being solely influenced by the appearance of the act, but by taking into consideration the place the given act has taken place, the religious assessment of the general public of the act, the intention, purpose and the existence and the level of the religious consciousness of the person in performing the given act, the effect and influence the given act would have on the general public and other circumstances."

The Court did not deny any religious significance and function to the *Daijosai* ceremony, nor did it deny that the provincial Governor took part in a sacred ritual;[185] however it considered the socio-cultural and traditional aspect of the celebration to be prevalent, and affirmed that the participation of public figures in the celebrations was a gesture of social courtesy. Furthermore, the sentence tracked a possible further legitimization of participation, obtainable from Article 1 of the Constitution. Due to the fact, as stated in this article, the Emperor is "a symbol of the State and of the unity of the people", the governor had paid homage not to the Emperor-god, a descendant via an unbroken succession line of the Sun Goddess, Amaterasu Omikami, but rather to the (constitutional) symbol of the unity of the nation.[186]

Unlike previous decisions, the *Daijosai* ruling was unanimously adopted by the judging bench (moreover in simple session, not in joint session).

Finally, in two recent cases, the Supreme Court dealt with the subject, with a different outcome. Both cases regarded the granting of use of public land to some associations of citizens, soil that was also used for religious purposes (that is to say, the presence of Shinto shrines). In the first case,[187] the territorial body had granted ownership of the land to a residents association; in the second case,[188] instead, it had granted free use of the land.[189] In the second case, the lack of a payment in money has led to the violation of Article 89.

The afore-mentioned and commented rulings permit the drawing up of some recapitulatory considerations.

First of all, they seem to reveal a certain reticence of the Supreme Court in assuming a clear and definitive position on the subject. The limited number of existing rulings is

---

185 "According to the facts lawfully established by the original instance court, Daijo-sai is a ceremony in which the emperor gives thanks to the ancestors and the gods in heaven and the land for peace and the harvest of various crops and, for the state and the populace, prays for peace and the harvest, and was conducted in a Daijo-palace with Shintoist installations in accordance with the Shintoist ritual. Therefore, the participation and the vowing of the jokoku appellee who is the governor of the Kagoshima Prefecture have an involvement with religion."

186 "However, according to the facts lawfully established by the original instance court, (1) Daijo-Sai is an important traditional ceremony of the imperial household normally performed at the time of the succession of the throne since the 7th century although there were occasional interruptions, (2) the jokoku appellee, invited by the Imperial Household Agency, merely participated in a Yukiden Kusen-no-gi ceremony together with the heads of the three powers, ministers and the heads of the local public organisations and vowed, (3) <u>the participation of the jokoku appellee in the Daijo-sai ceremony was intended to celebrate the enthronement of the emperor who is the symbol of integration of the nation and the Japanese people</u> on the occasion of the traditional ceremony of the imperial household at the time of the succession to the throne by the emperor as a social courtesy of a person who holds a public office as a governor of the local public organisation." (underlining added)

187 64(1) *Minshu* 128, Supreme Court, 20 January 2010, 19 (gyo-tsu) 334.

188 64(1) *Minshu* 1, Supreme Court, 20 January 2010, 19 (gyo-tsu) 260.

189 Both decisions are commented (somewhat laconically) by A.B. Van Winkle, *Separation of Religion and State in Japan: A Pragmatic Interpretation of Art. 20 and 89 of the Japanese Constitution*, in 21 *Pacific Rim Law & Policy Journal* 363 (2012).

indicative, *inter alia*, of the prudential approach of Japanese jurisprudence: often cases end in the first or second degree courts without a constitutional ruling by the Supreme Court,[190] sometimes applying the so-called "political act theory", according to which the judiciary cannot and must not rule on the political work of the organs of the state.[191] And even when this filter is exceeded, and controversies are presented before the Supreme Court, they are resolved with the application of the *purpose-effect test*, which (as repeatedly noted) is a poorly defined criterion, equipped with a variable geometry, to the point of leaving the judges of the last resort, a wide decision-making discretion.

Secondly, one can note how the constitutional text has undergone, since the first rulings, an interpretation clearly discordant with the intent of the authors of the Constitution. As stated at the beginning, the wording of the rule leaves no room for doubt, and the examination of the documents prodromic to the drafting of Article 20 confirms the original desire to prevent any mix of state and religion. The question of whether this interpretation can be consonant with the Japanese "common feeling" is an extra-technical evaluation that is the task of a sociologist and not of a jurist.

Finally, the conservative approach of the Supreme Court is evident, perhaps aimed more at preserving tradition than at applying the norms.[192]

It is not clear whether the Supreme Court is willing to change its approach with respect to its precedents, despite the (shared) observation of the imperfection of the *purpose-effect test*. Even doctrine has repeatedly stressed that the issue of relations between state and religion requires greater clarity and, probably, an approach that adheres more to the literal wording of the norm. To this end, a proposal was even proposed to adopt a primary legislation that outlines in case studies the specific implementation of the clear but abstract principle contained in the Constitution;[193] nevertheless the hypothesis seems hardly prac-

190 *See supra* concerning the rulings on the visits by Prime Ministers to Yasukuni.

191 This theory has been repeatedly used by the Japanese courts to avoid having to pronounce on the subject of Art. 9, and is effectively summarized in a famous maxim of the Court of Appeal of Sapporo "[...] the problem of whether or not the existence, and so on, of the Self Defence Forces conforms to Art. 9 of the Constitution is a decision concerning state governance, and as a political act of the Diet and Cabinet would ultimately be entrusted to the political judgment of the entire people. It should not be construed to be a matter that courts are to determine." Court of Appeal of Sapporo, 27 *Gyosai reishu* 1175, in L. Beer and H. Itoh, *The Constitutional Case Law of Japan, 1971-1990*, op. cit., 122.

192 This conduct of the Japanese Supreme Court has been the subject of numerous investigations. Refer to D. Law, *The Anatomy of a Conservative Court: Judicial Review in Japan*, in 87 *Texas Law Review* 1545 (2009) ("One might characterize it as 'conservative' in the sense of being so passive or cautious that it almost never challenges the government. Alternatively, or in addition, one might characterize it as 'conservative' in the sense that it happens to share the ideological views and preferences of Japan's long-ruling conservative party, the Liberal Democratic Party (LPD). What is clear, however, is that label fits") and to the ample bibliography mentioned therein.

193 K. Yamagishi, *Freedom of Religion, Religious Political Participation, and Separation of Religion and State: Legal Considerations from Japan*, op. cit., 937, "Japan's Diet should enact a code embodying specific implementation of the religious freedom and separation of religion and state guarantees of the Constitution of Japan. Japan's tradition and history is such that state and religion are connected comparatively easily.

ticable, also due to the fact that, beyond an objective technical complexity in the enumeration of a closed list of behaviours, it does not seem that the theme has priority in the political agenda of the Parliament. It remains to be seen (with a dubious attitude) if the result of the recent elections will have some influence on issues such as this, often on the border between law and ideology.[194] One last consideration remains: the Japanese Constitution still leads us to ponder upon a concept of religion rather distant from the dogmatic concept typical of monotheistic religions, where tradition, sacredness, ritual and national feeling merge. The effective application of "western" norms in such a culturally distant context undoubtedly arouse the interest of the interpreter.[195] Also in the perspective of *de iure condendo*, the Japanese experience can help to reflect on an essential point in the light of the evolutionary currents of world law: the problem of legal transplants is indeed intensified in all those sectors in which the norm is to be grafted into a substratum traditional tenacity, and the results can sometimes be surprising, and very distant from those for which the norm was conceived. The adoption of hetero-directed solutions is useless if not executed with extreme attention to the culture of the recipient country.

Earnest watch is required. A. Proposal for a New Code Because religion ably functions to unify masses of people and imbue them with collective feelings, political power cannot help having interest in this ability. Once, State Shinto was a support of the Japanese integration and nationality; it unified the Japanese in a way that perhaps has not been possible since. Its ends, however, were disastrous. Japan must continue to prevent present and future religious affiliation that state actors could utilize to cause serious wrong. As has been demonstrated, the judicial body whose function would be to play this role has not developed precedent that will protect the Japanese via the Constitution. In most cases, the principle of separation of religion and state helps freedom of religion because it prevents the state from promoting one religion to the threat of other religions. However, under the Japanese Constitution's allowance of religious political participation, which is included in the guarantee of freedom of this new code would formulate regulations concerning that which the state and its organs shall not do and that which is a violation of the religion and state provision. One of the most important provisions required by this suggested code is a section that proscribes the misuse of religion for political ends. In such a section, the code will specifically prescribe in detail what constitutes a violation of the separation of religion and state guarantee of the Constitution. This section will ensure that separation of religion and state will not be eroded. It will preserve the constitutional guarantees that prohibit the use of religion by the state and the use of political authority by religious organizations. Without a code to protect our constitutional guarantees, the Supreme Court's precedents represent ineffective protection, and further erosion remains likely."

194 D. Law, *The Anatomy of a Conservative Court: Judicial Review in Japan*, op. cit., "If the Court is conservative, that is ultimately because the government is conservative, and so too are a majority of the nation's voters. It is implausible that any judiciary could defy an ideologically aligned government and electorate for any meaningful period of time."

195 Imagine that a Japanese citizen, married in Japan with a traditional shintoist ritual (as is customary), then divorces. If this subject then wanted, after their conversion to Christianity, to marry again, would the original Shintoista celebration be considered a "religious marriage" and therefore incompatible with a another Christian wedding? NB. in Japan the problem of the annulment of a "canonical" marriage (in the sense, this time, improper, in the most absolute way!) does this not arise in any way, and therefore in fact there is no suitable instrument for an extra-civil dissolution of the bond.

2.9 Language and Law in Japan

2.9.1 National Symbols: Language, Anthem and Flag

The language of Japan is Japanese. In public schools the first language taught is Japanese. The language used in the courts and in the Parliament, the language of laws and rulings, is Japanese. In law faculties and in schools for the legal professions, legal education is generally given in Japanese. The state administration speaks and operates as a rule in Japanese.

If on the one hand, these observations may seem obvious, on the other hand, in legislation, and firstly in the constitutional text, there are no references to Japanese as the official language of Japan. In some statutes one can find the term "*kokugo*" [national language] which is universally interpreted as a synonym of the Japanese language.[196] In other texts, the legislator chose the more unambiguous "*nihongo*", literally "Japanese language".

Thus Article 21, Paragraph 5, of the Law on School Education (law 26 of 1947) lists among the objectives of school education, the "approach to reading, and the development of the basic skills necessary to understand and correctly use the national language (*kokugo*), indispensable for the needs of everyday life". Other legal texts refer explicitly to the Japanese language [*nihongo*]. Thus, Article 74 of the Court Act (No. 59 of 1947) states that "In the court, the Japanese language shall be used".

In the codes of procedure, due to the different period in which they were drafted, to a different sociolinguistic sensibility and legislative style, the provisions concerning the language follow different lexical choices. The language provisions are found in the articles concerning the cases involving the intervention of the court interpreter: the code of criminal procedure, which came into force in 1948, uses the most antiquated "*kokugo*":

> When the court has a person who is not proficient in the national language [*kokugo*] make a statement, it shall have an interpreter interpret it. (Art. 175 of the Code of criminal procedure, Act 131 of 1948)

On the contrary, the most recent code of civil procedure, promulgated in 1996 (Act 109 of 1996), states in Article 154: "If a person participating in oral arguments is unable to communicate in Japanese [*nihongo*] [...] arrangements are made for an interpreter to be present at oral arguments".

These provisions are relevant where a party involved in a trial does not speak Japanese. If the problem is of relatively minor importance in the case of civil proceedings, but it is

196 Thus, in Japanese public schools, Japanese as a subject is called *kokugo*.

very important in the case of criminal proceedings. The Constitution, in Article 37 par. 1 and 2, provides that:

> In all criminal cases the accused shall enjoy the right to a speedy and public trial by an impartial tribunal. He shall be permitted full opportunity to examine all witnesses, and he shall have the right of compulsory process for obtaining witnesses on his behalf at public expense.

Furthermore, as a signatory of the International Covenant on Civil and Political Rights (ICCPR), Japan is required to ensure that the accused is "informed promptly and in detail in a language which he understands of the nature and cause of the charge against him" (Art. 14(3) point (a) ICCPR), and to guarantee "the free assistance of an interpreter if he cannot understand or speak the language used in court" (Art. 14(3) point (f), ICCPR).[197]

The constitutional text contains no rules regarding two other more important national symbols of national identity: the anthem and the national flag. In the immediate post-war period, it was generally forbidden to show the Japanese flag without prior authorization. This prohibition was partially abolished by MacArthur on 2 May 1947, the day before the entry into force of the Constitution,[198] and totally abolished in 1949. Despite this, due to the association of these symbols with the military dictatorship of the 1930s, this matter remained a legislative taboo for over 50 years, governed de facto via the guidelines of the Ministry of Education.[199] In 1999, the legislator finally filled this gap with the Law on the national flag and the national anthem (Law 127 of 1999), which officially acknowledged the flag commonly known as *Hinomaru* (a red disc in a white field; the official name of the flag, also used in the law is *Nisshoki*) as the national flag, and the hymn *Kimigayo* as the national anthem. The flag of the rising sun (*Kyokujitsuki*), in which 16 red rays stem from the central red disc on white background, was used as a symbol of Japan and by the Japanese imperial army. It is still used, in some variants, by the Self-Defense forces.

2.9.2 *The Language of the Constitution*

The style of legislation, rulings and doctrine, and of all legal texts has undergone a radical evolution over the past 150 years. Its watershed can be represented by the drafting of the current Constitution.

---

197 I. Nakane, *Language Rights of Non-Japanese Defendants in Japanese Criminal Courts*, in N. Gottlieb, *Language and Citizenship in Japan*, New York and London, Routledge, 2012, 155.

198 Supreme commander for the Allied powers Government section, *Political Reorientation of Japan: September 1945 to September 1948*, 1976.

199 R. Goodman, I. Neary (Eds.), *Case Studies on Human Rights in Japan*, Tokyo, Japan Library, 1996, 81.

The texts of law before the Second World War were written in an extremely formal style, and in some respects, they were already obsolete at the time of their promulgation. Their style, called *katakana-bungotai*, makes use of syntactic structures of the classical language or exclusively of the written language, and presents all the "connective tissue" of the Japanese language, i.e. verbal endings, prepositions and other particles, written in the *katakana* syllabary. In addition, *kanji* may appear in forms barely recognizable to the inexperienced reader. These grammatical, syntactical and graphic features make these texts complex and difficult to understand.

The current Constitution, promulgated in 1946, was the first text written in the less formal style called *kogotai*, literally "colloquial style". In the texts, the Sino-Japanese characters are mixed with the *hiragana* characters, there is the use of expressions closer to the spoken language, and there are punctuation marks. In fact, both the first draft of the new Constitution prepared in January 1946 by the Shidehara Government Commission chaired by Joji Matsumoto, but rejected by MacArthur in the early days of February 1946, and the first Japanese translation of the draft prepared by the Americans were written in the old, formal style.[200] Only after the pressure exerted by some members of the Cabinet Legislation Bureau, by the occupation forces and by the public opinion,[201] it was decided to use the colloquial style for the document. The choice was not easy: according to Matsumoto, the use of colloquial Japanese would have diminished the dignity of the document; other officers, however, did not disapprove of the idea of the adoption of a more modern style. The choice on the modern colloquial style was given the final push by the consideration that it would not have been possible to draft, or better to translate the American draft in time to produce a document in classical Japanese with a stylistic refinement worthy of the role played by the fundamental charter of the country. The Constitution was therefore written in modern Japanese, thus exalting its democratizing function. The draft, which thanks to its innovative style, surprised many Japanese, was published on 17 April 1946. In line with the tradition of Japanese collective responsibility, the final choice was not attributed to any individual in particular.[202]

The fact that the Constitution, a charter hierarchically overriding all the other laws of the State, was written in the colloquial style, marked the change in the style of legislation as a whole: almost in a similar way to a relationship between people in flesh and blood, an ordinary law adopting a more formal language would be perceived as being "higher in status" than the supreme charter and would commit, in a certain sense, an act of imperti-

200 K. Inoue, *MacArthur's Japanese Constitution: A Linguistic and Cultural Study of Its Making*, Chicago, 1991, 14-29.

201 For example, the Union of movements for the national language of citizens (*Kokumin no kokugo undo renmei*) presented a series of recommendations for the constitutional charter to be written in colloquial style. *See ibid.*

202 S. Koseki, *The Birth of Japan's Postwar Constitution*, Boulder, Westview Press, 1997, 137.

nence. All the laws following the publication of the draft of 1946 were therefore written in the colloquial style. This change, however, caused a fracture within the legal system: since the laws prior to the Second World War were not automatically repealed nor "translated" into modern Japanese, but continued to be in force in their original form, two very different linguistic styles started coexisting. The most famous and important example of this situation was the Japanese Civil Code. It was originally promulgated in 1898, and written according to the conventions of the era, in *katakana-bungotai*. The reforms of the US occupation government, aimed at the emancipation of women and the abolition of the patriarchate, profoundly reformed Chapters 4 and 5 of the code dedicated to the family and successions, which were therefore entirely rewritten in the style of the Constitution. Hence, up until 2005, the Japanese civil code appeared written in two very different ways: Books 1, 2 and 3, respectively on general rules, things and obligations, were written in the antiquated *katakana-bungotai* style and the amended Books 4 and 5, on persons and successions in *hiragana-kogotai*. In this case, the legislator rectified the stylistic misalignment via the linguistic reform of 2004, which rewrote the first three chapters in the modern, colloquial form.

3 Korea

3.1 The Institutional and Juridical Traditions of Korea

3.1.1 From Its Origins to the Political Unification of Korea

The anthropic presence throughout the Korean peninsula has archaeologically been proven since the Paleolithic age, no less than forty or thirty thousand years ago. In the Neolithic age, circa 10,000 to approximately 4,000 years ago, the peninsula was scattered with small human communities, initially organized on the basis of small clusters and clan groups, often living in caves or in small groups of dwellings dug into the ground, on near arable land. These small communities developed a society and a culture based on community principles and on animistic and shamanistic cults and rites. This reality of very ancient autochthonism combined with that of peoples of Mongol or Siberian origin, who migrated to the peninsula during the third and second millennium BC, thus giving rise to the current Korean ethnic group.[1]

The clans were often grouped into greater tribal units towards the end of the Neolithic period (circa 2000-1000 BC), an age that eventually faded into the local Bronze Age (eighth to fourth century BC), characterized by a partially new culture introduced by successive migrations of Mongol and Siberian peoples, and by a more complex and stratified social organization, with proto-urban agglomerations and a number of fortified cities.

---

1 There are not many legal texts on Korean law in Italian: A. Serafino, chapter *Corea Tradizionale e Repubblica di Corea*, and chapter *Repubblica Popolare Democratica di Corea (Corea del Nord)*, in G. Ajani, A. Serafino, M. Timoteo, *Diritto dell'Asia orientale*, Torino, Utet, 2007; I. Castellucci, *Corea*, in R. Cavalieri (Ed.), *Diritto dell'Asia orientale*, 2nd ed., Venezia, Cafoscarina, 2019, 131 ff. Korean history books in the English language are also relatively few; many Korean classical sources are collected, in two volumes, in P.H. Lee, Wm. T. de Bary (Eds.), *Sources of Korean Tradition*, Vol. I (from the beginning of the sixteenth century), New York, Columbia University Press, 1997; and in Y. Ch'oe, P.H. Lee, Wm. T. de Bary (Eds.), *Sources of Korean Tradition*, Vol. II (from the eighteenth to the twentieth century), New York, Columbia University Press, 2000. A history of Korea is in C.J. Eckert, K. Lee, Y.I. Lew, M. Robinson, E.W. Wagner, *Korea Old and New: A History*, Seoul, Ilchokak Publishing for the Korea Institute, Harvard University, 1990; this booklet contains, condensed and updated, the text of a previous book on Korean history, of some success, published for the first time in 1961 and translated into English in 1984: K. Lee, *A New History of Korea* (translated into English) by E.W. Wagner and E.J. Schultz), Seoul, Ilchokak and Harvard University Press, 1984. M. Riotto, *Storia della Corea. Dalle origini ai giorni nostri*, Milan, Bompiani, 2005 is very beautiful and complete in Italian. For a brief summary *see also* M. Riotto, *Atlante storico-geopolitico della Corea*, in *I quaderni speciali di Limes – rivista italiana di geopolitica*, 2011 n. 1, *Corea, la guerra sospesa*, 37 ff. re-published in an updated version in *Limes*, 2016 n. 12, *La Corea è una bomba*, 113-130. The quotes of this work below refer to the 2011 version.

Small kingdoms sprung up from the small cities, via conquests or federation, with political structures dominated by priest-kings of divine ancestry. Among them, a semi-mythological and ancient Chosŏn kingdom in Manchuria and in the entire peninsula,[2] and followed by the historical Chosŏn kingdom, with the capital near the current Pyongyang.[3] The latter, known to both Korean and Chinese sources, resulting from the federation of several fortified cities, reached a significant extension around the fourth century BC; it came in contact and also military confrontation with the neighbouring Chinese state of Yen and was strongly influenced by Chinese culture, as revealed by the use of the title of *tan'gun wanggŏm*, containing the Chinese word *wang* (king), to indicate its head – a semi-divine sovereign associated with a cult of the Sun.[4]

The increased interaction with China from the fourth century BC marks the passage of Korean societies into the Iron Age, and a change in the social organization of the Chosŏn kingdom – militarily weakened, hybridized by Chinese elements, in marked decline in the third to second century and finally destined to succumb to the power of the Chinese Empire in 108 BC. This was followed by the fragmentation of the ancient Chosŏn into several tributary kingdoms of the Chinese Empire, an empire which was to continue until the modern age to have a role of hegemonic power and not entirely external in the events of the Korean peninsula.

After a series of complex political and military events, both among the various communities of the Korean peninsula and with the Chinese, Mongolian and Mongols, contemporaneously to the Chosŏn decline, at least six or seven significant kingdoms, between the Korean peninsula and Manchuria (first to third century AD), began to emerge and consolidate, originating from confederations of smaller communities. They were aristocratic states, governed by councils of nobles (probably the heads of the towns and confederate communities) residing in the fortified cities. There were processes of centralization of government functions, with the inheritance of the title of king and the emergence of centralized administrative structures based on the Chinese model, while maintaining the aristocratic structure of society; and with the specialization of the functions of connection with the deities, no longer the prerogative of the king but now the prerogative of the shamanic caste. Sources speak of few embryonic strict laws, and simple governments run

2 M. Riotto, *Atlante*, op cit., 37.

3 The Korean terms are reshaped according to the McCune-Reischauer method; the common names known in the West with simple Romanizations are rendered according to the most common use (*e.g.*, Pyongyang rather than P'yŏngyang; Kim Jong Il rather than Kim Chŏng-il). The names of the authors cited in the note are reported according to the use made by the author himself; and therefore according to the Western use of indicating the first name of the surname, as is frequent for South Korean authors (*e.g.*, "K. Lee, YI Lew"), or according to the traditional Asian use to indicate the surname before the first name (*e.g.*, "Ahn Choong-yong").

4 C.J. Eckert, K. Lee, Y.I. Lew, M. Robinson, E.W. Wagner, *Korea Old and New: A History*, op cit., 11.

by the leaders.[5] Around the first century AD, the role of two of these kingdoms, the Puyŏ and the Koguryŏ, became important. They were aristocratic and centralized states, in conflict amongst themselves and with the neighbouring Chinese state of Chin – with the Chinese often in excellent relations with the former and opponents of the latter.[6]

Further aggregation processes finally produced, between the third and fourth centuries, the expansion of the Koguryŏ in Manchuria and in the north of the Korean peninsula, at the expense of the Chinese and Puyŏ, and the division of the central-southern part of the peninsula between the two great kingdoms of Paekche and Silla, initially with the presence of a third and smaller kingdom Kaya (or Gaya, or Karak), a federation of clans with marked Buddhist traditions, born in first century AD,[7] politically very influenced and finally incorporated by Silla in the fifth century. They were hereditary, aristocratic, militarily strong kingdoms, well organized from the administrative point of view, greatly influenced by the bulky Chinese neighbour and by Buddhist thinking – originally with the Mahāyāna doctrines, to which were then added local doctrines, the result of contamination with Taoist doctrines and with ancestral and shamanic local elements.[8]

Thus began the period commonly referred to as the period of the "Three Kingdoms" – referring to Koguryŏ, Paekche and Silla, which was to last until the nineth to tenth century.

Koguryŏ, the major entity and the most northerly, after absorbing other political realities was now a vast kingdom between Korea and Manchuria, bordering the Chinese Empire, often with tense relationships and sometimes in open conflict with it dating from the first century AD (as well as with the Korean but pro-Chinese kingdom Puyŏ, later incorporated by Koguryŏ), but with a king who now assumed the Chinese title of *wang*.

---

5 From M. Riotto, *Storia della Corea*, op. cit., Chap. II. In the *Cronache dei Tre Regni*, classic Chinese of the third century AD, is reported (Vol. 30, paras. 840-853) a description of the uses and customs of the main Korean communities, all represented as simple communities of courageous men, strong, lovers of drinking, music and dance, and of attractive women. The Puyŏ kingdom is represented as the only Korean community with prisons and ritual procedures for the imposition of public sanctions on the occasion of religious ceremonies; all the others had repressive systems based on private revenge. Sources reported in English translation in *Cf.* P.H. Lee, Wm. T. de Bary (Eds.), *Sources of Korean Tradition*, Vol. I (from its origins to sixteenth century), New York, Columbia University Press, 1997, 7-13.

6 C.J. Eckert, K. Lee, Y.I. Lew, M. Robinson, E.W. Wagner, *Korea Old and New: A History*, op cit., 15-17; in the nelle *Cronache dei Tre Regni*, Vol. 30, Puyo is represented as the only community whose members showed deference to the Chinese authorities, as well as that with a more sophisticated administrative organization.

7 Sources narrate of a king who founded the kingdom by marrying a princess of Ayutthaya (Thailand), and a kingdom organization based on a *soft* government, certainly based on the authority of the king but not on the use of force, according to the precepts of the *yin-yang*: *Samguk yusa* (Memories of the Three Kingdoms, a classic of the eighteenth century written by a literary Buddhist monk, Ilyon or Iryeon), second book; English translation, T.H. He, *Samguk Yusa – Legends and History of the Three Kingdoms of Ancient Korea*, Yonsei University Press, 1972; the fragments to which the text refers are also reported in P.H. Lee, Wm. T. de Bary (Eds.), *Sources of Korean Tradition*, op cit., 13-17.

8 *Cf.* The excerpts from the third book of the *Samguk Yusa* in P.H. Lee, Wm. T. de Bary (Eds.), *Sources of Korean Tradition*, op. cit., 48-53.

In the years 372-372, Koguryŏ introduced a series of reforms, becoming officially Buddhist and at the same time founding a real Confucian academy and with the adoption of a code of administrative laws. At the beginning of the fifth century, the capital of the kingdom was established near today's P'yŏngyang.[9]

Paekche too, in the central region of the peninsula, was organized according to Chinese models, with the royal government subdivided into six departments and a sophisticated hierarchy for royal officials;[10] it would become an officially Buddhist kingdom by royal decree, from the end of the fourth century.

Silla, in the south-eastern region, stabilized its institutions at the beginning of the sixth century, based on the Chinese model too, with the title of *wang* for the sovereign and an administrative code, adopting at the same time the Buddhist religion; Silla created its own Confucian academy during the seventh century, and a rudimentary system of examinations for the access of young aristocrats to public careers in 788.[11]

Alongside the government institutions inspired by the Chinese model remained an aristocratic political and strongly hierarchized structure – as in the case of Silla, the most Buddhist of the three kingdoms,[12] in which society was formally stratified into two levels of the so-called nobility "Of bones" (the royal lineage), three other levels of aristocracy, further subdivided into degrees, and finally three levels of organization of non-noble subjects.[13] All three kingdoms were however characterized by the continuing presence of the noble councils – *Hwabaek*, in Silla – in historical continuity with the ancient councils of the tribal-based federations, called to deliberate with the sovereign on all the most important issues.[14]

These were centuries of complex power games between the Korean "Three Kingdoms" and China – the northern Chinese kingdoms during the fragmentation of the empire known as the "Chinese Middle Ages", in the third to sixth centuries, and then the Reconstituted empire. The political and cultural influence of China was overwhelming in the Korean kingdoms, in which hierarchies of officials-letterati, alongside the military hierarchies, sprung up and became powerful; a situation which remained as such until 1910. The oldest cultural substratum of the peoples of the Korean peninsula, and a significant presence of Buddhism in the aristocracy and in the political, institutional and juridical thinking of the three kingdoms, in addition to the peculiar political dynamics within the Korean

---

9 M. Riotto, *Storia della Corea*, op. cit., Chap. III. .J. Eckert, K. Lee, Y.I. Lew, M. Robinson, E.W. Wagner, *Korea Old and New: A History*, op. cit., 26.

10 *Ibid.*, 24

11 M. Riotto, *Storia della Corea*, op. cit., Chap. IV, para. 1.

12 *Cf.* P. H. Lee, in P.H. Lee, Wm. T. de Bary (Eds.), *Sources of Korean Tradition*, op. cit., 34-35.

13 J. Eckert, K. Lee, Y.I. Lew, M. Robinson, E.W. Wagner, *Korea Old and New: A History*, op. cit., 32-33.

14 A reference to the Hwabaek of Silla is in the first book of *Samyuk Yusa*; P.H. Lee, Wm. T. de Bary (Eds.), *Sources of Korean Tradition*, op cit., 23; J. Eckert, K. Lee, Y.I. Lew, M. Robinson, E.W. Wagner, *Korea Old and New: A History*, op. cit., 34.

peninsula societies, became the main differentiating factors between the institutions and law of Korea and China.

The outlines of the dynastic vicissitudes of Korea as a unitary kingdom would be influenced by political and military events concerning China, the peoples of the north, then also Japan and by the end of the nineteenth century by also Russia and the Western powers. Moreover, it bestowed a dynamic that was entirely internal to the Korean *elite*, which witnessed the opposition of different ideologies of government at various times: initially, with the contrast between more characterized ideologies in the Buddhist sense and others more in the Confucian sense; then characterized by the greater or less adhesion to the precepts of "pure" Confucianism. Above all, Korean history is characterized by various moments of weakness of the ruling families with respect to the aristocracy, a marked internal political pluralism, and from a certain point, with a widespread tendency to use the Confucian ideology as a banner and instrument for access to political power and for the preservation of such power.

In the era of the "Three Kingdoms", although not yet a unified national conscience, an awareness of a marked cultural unity in the Korean peninsula began to form, characterized by historical, linguistic, religious and artistic elements. It was the Silla kingdom that succeeded in unifying under its own control almost the entire peninsula in 668, remaining thus the dominant kingdom in Korea for circa two centuries. Meanwhile, the exiles of Koguryŏ retreated to a vast area between the north of the Korean peninsula and Manchuria, subjugating local populations and giving birth in 713 to a kingdom called Parhae, multiethnic and stratified, with the Korean aristocracy in a dominant position over local ethnic groups. Parhae governed a vast area of Manchuria for over 200 years, also expanding into the Chinese Empire, with which it was to have variable relationships: initially conflicting, then of closeness and interchange, drawing inspiration for the development of its model of government – largely, a replica of the T'ang.[15]

In Korea, almost entirely unified by Silla, the victorious dynasty maintained and extended its model of aristocratic and Buddhist government to the entire peninsula, giving rise to a kingdom characterized by exceptional social and technological economic development, a sort of golden age, as well as by the development of Korean culture and Korean Buddhism, with monks travelling in China, India and elsewhere, giving life to several local schools of thought, with different levels of sophistication and destined for the different levels of Korean society.[16]

Chinese influences persisted, too, for example with the importation of the code of the laws of the imperial T'ang dynasty of 624, and in general with the strengthening of the

15 C.J. Eckert, K. Lee, Y.I. Lew, M. Robinson, E.W. Wagner, *Korea Old and New*, op. cit., 55. M. Riotto, *Storia della Corea*, op. cit., Chap. V.

16 M. Riotto, *Storia della Corea*, op. cit., Chap. IV para. 3; *Id.*, *Atlante*, op. cit., 41.

royal, Confucian and rationalist element against the aristocracy,[17] thus generating a Syncretic Korean culture: Confucian, Buddhist, Taoist – syncretism that also characterized the governing ideology of the coeval Chinese imperial dynasty T'ang[18] – innervated by ancestral animist and shamanic elements of the local culture.[19]

The interaction and tensions between the different visions of the world linked to that complex of cultural elements characterized Korean history for the following centuries, and was always to be at the centre of political contradictions and critical events of the hermit kingdom until 1910.

Towards the middle of the nineth century, the Silla dynasty began to decline, manifesting its inability to govern a country characterized by increasing instability: the Buddhist ideal, based on the acceptance of reality awaiting eternal salvation, and the tendency towards the conservation of lineage-based power structures entered into conflict with the Confucian ideal, that was more rational and innovative from the point of view of the government of public affairs, morals and *governance* rules to be applied to earthly life.

Added to this, there was also the tension between the aristocrats of the highest nobility, the so-called "bone" nobility, with their private armies and their elite units formed by young aristocratic warriors, even monks or in any case of Buddhist formation (the so-called *hwarang*), on the one hand, and that of the literary officials, still aristocratic but of less rank, probably not carriers or bearers of their own political interests, closer to the king and to the service of a more centralizing vision, on the other. The excessive economic weight of military expenditures and in general of this double *governance* apparatus, burdened by taxation on the exhausted populations, exacerbated these tensions.[20]

Towards the end of the nineth century, the Silla kingdom disintegrated and new kingdoms were born: "New Paekche" and "new Koguryŏ" or Koryŏ – the name assumed in

17 *Ibid.*, 46-52.

18 Zhang Sheng, in a report to the Chinese Academy of Social Sciences, presented a research on the Taoist and Buddhist element in the T'ang codification in which he analysed the structure of codification and the contents of numerous norms, noting in it the clear presence of the Taoist element, absent in subsequent dynasties. This scholar of the Academy of Sciences noted that all the legal codes of the T'ang adinsatism were characterized by the presence of exactly 500 articles, a number of high symbolic value in the Taoist and *yin-yang* doctrines of the time, a characteristic no longer found in any of successive dynastic codifications. Zhang Sheng, 形 神 俱 妙 的 唐律: 立法 技术 与 治平 理念 的 统一 (*The Tang Code: Unity of Legislative Techniques and Ideas of State Governance*), presented at the CASS *Annual Forum on the Rule of Law* on 4-5 November 2016 ; unpublished collection of *papers.*

19 *See* the excerpts from the third book of *Samguk Yusa* in P.H. Lee, Wm. T. de Bary (Eds.), *Sources of Korean Tradition*, op cit., 48-53; *see also* C.J. Eckert, K. Lee, Y.I. Lew, M. Robinson, E.W. Wagner, *Korea Old and New*, op. cit., 36-40; C. Choi, *East Asian Jurisprudence*, Seoul, National University Press, 2009, op. cit., 66-69.

20 *Id.*, Chap. 4 and especially 51-52. M. Riotto, *Storia della Corea*, Chap. III; *Id.*, *Atlante*, op. cit., 41.

honour and in declared continuity with the Koguryŏ kingdom, of which the name Koryŏ is an abbreviated form.[21]

It was this latter, led by King Wang Kŏn, to conquer first Silla and then the "new Paekche", reuniting the peninsula in 935. The elite of Korean lineage of Parahe – another succeeding kingdom of the first Koguryŏ, returned to the south in 926, integrating into the élite of the emerging new pan-Korean state, after having lost the territories of Manchuria and its domination over the relative indigenous peoples due to an attack by the peoples of the north, the Mongols of the Khitan, successfully held at bay, up until that point. Wang Kŏn became the *T'aejo*, the Great Ancestor, a title acknowledging him as the founder of the new Koryŏ dynasty (918-1392), and the first reunited king of Korea, with the capital Kaesong.[22] Indeed, the current name of the country derives from the name of the dynasty.[23]

Koryŏ was a new state, compared to Silla, characterized by the initial political prevalence of the elite of Confucian-educated literati on the most conservative aristocratic-military apparatus. It differed in its organization, undoubtedly certainly more markedly inspired by that of the Chinese Empire and the neo-Confucian ideas born in the age of the imperial Song dynasty,[24] with a sophisticated administrative apparatus, including at the level of the central government, the six departments of the Chinese tradition (personnel, war, taxes, punishments, rites, public works) and a peripheral territorial organization, articulated in regions, provinces or military zones, in turn subdivided into several levels of minor territorial units.[25]

However, the central role of Confucianism as a government ideology was not absolute. Buddhism continued to be the state religion and maintained its important political role

21 *Koryo Dinasty*, in P. Stearns (Ed.) *Encyclopedia of World History*, 6th edn, New York, Houghton Mifflin Harcout, 2001, 156-157.

22 M. Riotto, *Atlante*, op. cit., 41.

23 That Marco Polo called Cauli or Cauly: M. Polo, Il Milione, Chap. 79 in the edition edited by V. Bertolucci Pizzorusso, Milan, Einaudi, 1975; Chap. LXVII in the 2006 Fabbri edition with an introduction by M. Ciccuto.

24 C. Choi, *East Asian Jurisprudence*, Seoul, National University Press, 2009, op cit., 48-65.

25 C.J. Eckert, K. Lee, Y.I. Lew, M. Robinson, E.W. Wagner, *Korea Old and New*, op cit., 70 ff.; M. Riotto, *Storia della Corea*, op cit., Chap. VI; *Id.*, *Atlante*, op cit., 43-46. It is worth mentioning – not only as a curiosity – the emergence of an academic dispute in relation to the origins and historical history of the Kogury dynasty and kingdoms, and therefore also in relation to the legitimacy of the Kory dynasty: Chinese scholars have proposed for some years – also with the active *sponsorship* of the Beijing government in financing research by the Academy of Social Sciences on the subject – a re-reading of the Kogury's story as a story within the Celestial Empire, based on the geographical location of the kingdom and its historical relations with the Empire, also characterized by periods of cooperation, enslavement or tax; and the reception of Chinese *governance* models that can be read as evidence of integration into the empire. One can imagine the Korean. What is at stake is not only the Korean national identity but also political and economic interests linked to the Chinese provinces of Manchuria and to the Korean ethnic populations living there; *see* Chŏn Pyŏnggon, *Political Implications of China's North East Project, National Unity, Social Stability*, in *Chingguk munje yŏn'guso*, Seoul, 2011; reported by A. De Benedittis, *Koguryŏ, ovvero la storia scritta dai grandi*, in *I quaderni speciali di Limes – rivista italiana di geopolitica*, 2011 n. 1, *Corea, la guerra sospesa*, 161-164.

in the aristocracy continued.[26] A general culture and a class of government, influenced by both doctrines, developed. In this period, a system of public exams for access to administrative offices was introduced, with a growing number of young aristocrats who studied to prepare for their government career, creating an intellectually homogeneous ruling class, sufficiently organized to become, over time, a driving force for its own political interests. At the same time, the importance of the Buddhist and aristocratic clergy grew, and territorial networks of organizations able to express their own political and even military capacity developed around the monasteries.[27]

The dynasty maintained good relations with the Chinese Song Empire, and often difficult relationships with other neighbouring nations, in particular with the people of Manchu and Mongolia.

Towards the end of the twelfth century, after a period of military revolts and shogun governments, order was re-established and a new class of government was born, which ended up reincorporating into the ruling *elite*, in addition to the military, the civilian officials of Confucian extraction, but with an inverted balance of power in favour of the latter, giving rise to the *yangba*n class ("two branches" officials). A political alliance was also rebuilt with the Buddhist clergy.

The twelfth and thirteenth centuries were also centuries of external tensions and conflicts, with the people of Manchuria and Mongolia, present beyond the northern border. During the thirteenth century, when the Chinese Empire was invaded and then permanently ruled by the Mongol Yuan dynasty, based on a mixed Confucian and Buddhist model, Korea was invaded by Mongolia. Heavy conditioning in domestic politics was imposed on the kings of the Koryŏ dynasty, also via a Yuan policy based on the marriages of Korean kings with the daughters of the Mongol emperors, to institutionalize and emphasize the authority of the latter over the former.[28]

The enrichment of the most important families linked to the imperial power and the *elite* of the Korean government was accompanied by a general impoverishment of the country, due both to the economic policy of the vertexes and to a worsening of the security conditions, due to the widespread operation of raiders on the territory and Japanese pirates along the sea routes.

The parable of the Koryŏ was marked by these external pressures and internal tensions, and by growing conflicts between the civil administrators, in a position of pre-eminence, and the military cadres, conflicts that led to increasing political instability, the birth of private militias, and periods of military rule. The cyclical instability of Korean politics, due to the multiplicity of the souls of its elite, re-exploded towards the end of the thirteenth

26 C. Choi, *Law and Justice in Korea – South and North*, Seoul, National University Press, 2005, 82.

27 C.J. Eckert, K. Lee, Y.I. Lew, M. Robinson, E.W. Wagner, *Korea Old and New*, Chap. 6.

28 M. Deuchler, *The Confucian Transformation of Korea – A Study on Society and Ideology*, Cambridge, Ma., Harvard University Press, 1992.

century, this time characterized by a conflict between the noble elite linked to Buddhist traditions and the Mongolian emperors, also Buddhists, and a new emergent middle-class of officials-scholars, intellectuals linked to nationalist and neo-Confucian ideals.[29]

In the second half of the fourteenth century, the collapse of the Yuan emperors and the emergence of the Ming dynasty was the occasion for a radical change in Korea. King Kongmin of Koryŏ, in alliance with the Ming, drove the Mongols out of the peninsula. On the internal level, he reformed the kingdom, eliminating many ancient privileges of the highest lineage aristocrats and creating a new, more Confucian government apparatus with cadet rank literati-officials, less attached to the great aristocratic families who had supported the Yuan.

However, this was not sufficient: the internal tensions between the two factions, pro-Ming and pro-Yuan, remained and the relationship between the Koryŏ and the Ming emperors remained difficult and ambiguous.[30] In 1392, General Yi, a hero of the campaigns against Japanese pirates, sent to the border by the last Koryŏ king to resist a Chinese attack, instead turned against the king and founded a new ruling dynasty, taking the name Chosŏn – corresponding, as we recall, both to a mythological kingdom as well as the name of the most important of the ancient protohistoric kingdoms of Korea.[31]

The capital was transferred to Hanyang (Seoul). Furthermore, a very important land reform was implemented, with the lands taken away from the great noble families and reassigned to the State and its new ruling class, now possessing political, military and economic power. Legal and administrative reforms were initiated and innovations in culture and science promoted.[32] The Chosŏn dynasty, the longest in all of Asia, reigned in Korea until 1910.

3.1.2 *The Chosŏn Dynasty and the Stabilization of Korean Institutional and Juridical Thinking*

Over the course of more than 500 years, the modern Korean declination of state Confucianism was defined, as well as its relationship with the administration and the law as a tool of government. The exposure to Chinese culture and political and social models was, by now, strong and continuous, with total acknowledgment of the Confucian government

29 M. Riotto, *Storia della Corea*, op cit., Chap. VI; *Id.*, *Atlante*, op cit., 45.

30 C. Choi, *East Asian Jurisprudence*, Seoul, National University Press, 2009, op. cit., 70-71.

31 Koryŏ and Chosŏn are two strongly evocative names in the Korean mind, associated with the idea of the unity of the nation: Chosŏn is still today the name of Korea in North Korea (in the south the name in use is Hanguk); Air Koryo is the name of Northern Korea's national airline.

32 C.J. Eckert, K. Lee, Y.I. Lew, M. Robinson, E.W. Wagner, *Korea Old and New*, Chap. 8. M. Riotto, *Storia della Corea*, op cit., Chap. VII.

models and the Ming laws.[33] Indeed, the Korean sovereigns maintained a tributary and good-neighbour relationship with the Ming Emperors, based on Confucian canons (according to which the Chinese emperor was the elder brother of the other sovereigns of Asia). Furthermore, economic and cultural exchanges continued for most of the period. The relationship between Buddhist thinking and Confucian thinking, which had characterized the political events and the dynastic alternations of the Silla and Koryŏ kingdoms, took a certain turn in favour of Confucianism with the end of the Kory dynasty: the new Chosŏn Kings opposed Buddhism, that has always been associated with the aristocratic forces that had so often challenged royal authority in Korean history.[34]

With the Chosŏn dynasty, neo-Confucian rationalist thinking became dominant at the public level, with central importance attributed to knowledge and study. The new reigning house initiated a grand program of affirmation of national identity based on works commissioned by the government in scientific, artistic and legal-administrative matters.

However, the process of assimilation to the neo-Confucian model was not a process of total homologation: the Ming law code certainly became a general application also in Korea, already towards the end of the Koryŏ period and certainly with the Yi/Chosŏn dynasty. The T'aejo, at the very moment of his assumption of the royal function, proclaimed in an edict that the country would be governed through the enactment of its own legal codes, not via radical reforms but via the configuration of the laws previously in force, "Respecting the established enactment of the royal ancestors"[35] (*Jojong Seongheon*). This principle permitted an evolution of the relatively slow legislative system: the "laws of the ancestors" preserved traditional, shamanic, Buddhist, Taoist elements in the system, resisting the innovativeness of neo-Confucian thinking, characterized instead by a rationalist component that encouraged the revision of the laws, to adapt them to the changing needs of changing times.[36]

Two famous works stem from this period, the *Chosŏn kyŏngguk-chŏn* (administrative code of Korea) and the *Kyŏngje yukchŏn* (the six government codes, 1397), in a Confucian imprint but with great emphasis on the traditions and ancient Korean laws, approved and subsequently revised and expanded between the end of the fourteenth century and the beginning of the fifteenth century.[37] These works gathered together the fruits of the experience of the last Koryŏ period, and were consolidated and integrated into the *Kyŏngguk*

33 D.H. Chung, *The Establishment of the Early Chosŏn Political System*, in J.B. Duncan, J.C. Lee, J. Lee, M. Ahn, J.A. Dawey (Eds.), *The Institutional Basis of Civil Governance in the Chosŏn Dynasty*, Seoul, The Academy of Korean Studies, 2009, 113-136.

34 M. Riotto, *Storia della Corea*, Chap. VII, para. 11.

35 C. Choi, *Law and Justice in Korea – South and North*, Seoul, National University Press, 2005, 67-72.

36 *Ibid.* More generally, *see* the entire Chap. 2, *Traditional Law in Korea*, of the cited volume.

37 M. Riotto, *Storia della Corea*, op cit., Chap. VII; C.J. Eckert, K. Lee, Y.I. Lew, M. Robinson, E.W. Wagner, *Korea Old and New*, 107. Doo Hee Chung, op. cit.

Taechŏn (Great National Code) of 1485,[38] in which the principle of the applicability of the Ming Code as a common law was legislated.[39]

Even the dominant governing doctrines of the Chosŏn era, albeit in a neo-Confucian frame of thought, continually contained a certain irrationalist component, signalling the need to combine law, Confucian rationality, tradition and sentiment within the legal discourse and government.[40] The legal-administrative model remained more or less unchanged until almost the end of the Chosŏn experience. The main laws, of Confucian style but with clear influences linked to the local tradition and the royal standard, underwent a few occasional reforms, always in the name of continuity,[41] up to the last with a certain outlook, the *Taejŏn Hoet'ong* (updated great code) of 1865-1866, which innovated a previous Taejŏn T'ongp'yŏn (Comprehensive great code) of 1785.[42]

The introduction (1446) of a Korean national alphabet, still used today, desired by King Sejong the Great, also dates from the early Chosŏn period. It is based on twenty-eight phonetic symbols, and its introduction permitted abandoning the use of the much more complex Chinese script, based on ideograms, aiding thus the diffusion of national culture. This should be taken *cum grano salis*: fifteenth century Korea remained a relatively small country, with a predominantly agricultural economy and a restricted ruling class; only the examination system, both for civil functions and access to army cadres, permitted a limited "social elevation" up to within the upper echelons of society. Political power at the beginning of the Chosŏn dynasty was still fragmentary, with the power of the sovereign initially balanced by the presence of various councils of nobles, officials, military, who were established, strengthened, replaced and finally abolished in 1414, to make room for a simpler royal government, whose structure reproduced, for the most part, that of the previous dynasty based on the "six ministries" of the Chinese tradition.[43]

The ruling class of the *yangban*, the "two branches" literati-officials, civil and military, organized and governed the country on the basis of the Chinese model, Confucian doctrines and written laws, becoming the new aristocracy. The *yangban* become a cohesive class, possessing political as well as economic power, via the allocation of royal lands. They were isolated from the rest of the country socially and also physically, with the creation of special neighbourhoods or villages for their residences, and private schools for the young, who subsequently sat the state exams. They implemented a corporate policy and restricted access to their ranks, even with hereditary foreclosures, for example for three generations

38 D.H. Chung, *The Establishment of the Early Chosŏn Political System*, op cit., 115-116.
39 C. Choi, *Law and Justice in Korea*, op cit., 127.
40 *Ibid.*, 88-109.
41 M. Zimbardo, *Corea*, in R. Cavalieri (Ed.), *Diritto dell'Asia orientale*, Venezia, Cafoscarina, 2008, 125 ff., 128.
42 M. Deuchler, *The Confucian Transformation of Korea – A Study on Society and Ideology*, Cambridge (MA), Harvard University Press, 1992, 341 nt. 100.
43 D.H. Chung, *The Establishment of the Early Chosŏn Political System*, op cit., 117-136.

of descendants for officials sanctioned due to certain conduct; and promoted the formation of a minor caste of lower-ranking officials.[44]

The country lived a long period of relative tranquillity, thanks to its good relations with the Chinese Empire, and a certain internal stability, linked to the improvement of the administration and a significant reduction of the tax burden on the people, stratified in officials, the free, servants and in the Korean version of the *outcasts* or untouchables, formally free people but destined to inherit the less respectable trades.[45]

Buddhist doctrines lost much of their ancient public importance, with the ban on founding new temples and the confiscation of all lands and slaves of their monasteries in 1406. There were some returns of Buddhism in public life in later centuries, and some attempts to give life to syncretic doctrines that would reconcile the Buddhist faith with Taoism, local doctrines and Confucianism.[46] However, Buddhism remained present, albeit undercover, in Korean society and culture and, along with ancestral elements of the animist and shamanic type, in the religion of the Korean people.

The periodically re-emerging internal instability of the country recurred in coincidence with the weakening of the Ming emperors and the aggressive attitude of the Japanese, which resulted in an invasion of Korea in 1592; on the internal front, the conflict was within the *yangban* class, throughout the sixteenth century; in particular, among the most authoritative families established in the capital and rural officials without prestigious families behind them, the *sarim*, proponents of a neo-Confucian doctrine that we could define as being extremist or fundamentalist – an only apparent oxymoron – in relation to the correct government of public affairs,[47] which at the end of the sixteenth century completely controlled the government and administration of the country.[48]

The conflict for political power was marked by intrigues, conspiracies, purges of officials (in particular the *sarim*), with the royal house actively involved in power games. A singular element that emerged in Korea in this period was the birth in the rural areas of numerous private Confucian academies (*sŏwŏn*), a fact completely unknown in Chinese history. They were evidently possible institutions in a political context of decentralized power, functional to the rural caste of the *sarim*, in a political conflict between factions that all affirmed themselves to be bearers of the authentic Confucian ideal. The Royal Confucian Academy

44 S.M. Lee, *The Government Service Examinations of the Chosŏn Dynasty*, in J.B. Duncan, J.C. Lee, J. Lee, M. Ahn, J.A. Dawey (Eds.), *The Institutional Basis of Civil Governance in the Chosŏn Dynasty*, op cit., 63 ff., 68-69; M. Riotto, *Storia della Corea*, op cit., Chap. VII

45 M. Riotto, *Atlante*, op cit., 46-48; C.J. Eckert, K. Lee, Y.I. Lew, M. Robinson, E.W. Wagner, *Korea Old and New*, Chap.9.

46 M. Riotto, *Storia della Corea*, Chap. VII, para. 11.

47 M.J. Chung, *The Political and Social Roles of the Sŏwŏn in the Chosŏn Dynasty*, in J.B. Duncan, J.C. Lee, J. Lee, M. Ahn, J.A. Dawey (Eds.), *The Institutional Basis of Civil Governance...*, op cit., 21-59.

48 C. S. Song, *The Power Structure of* Sarim *(士林) Politics in the Chosŏn Dynasty*, in J.B. Duncan, J.C. Lee, J. Lee, M. Ahn, J.A. Dawey (Eds.), *The Institutional Basis of Civil Governance...*, op cit., 137 ff., 152.

lost a large part of its ancient role of teaching, while maintaining instead a role for the preparation for the examination of access to the civil service.[49]

In the seventeenth century, the instability of the region reached maximum heights with the collapse of the Chinese Ming dynasty, which ceded the imperial throne to the lords of the Qing dynasty in 1644. The Korean vicissitudes followed the same fate, with political enslavement to the new rulers of the Celestial Empire, while maintaining the formal independence of the kingdom, and the political domination of the caste of the *sarim*, structured in the seventeenth to eighteenth centuries around small rural agnatic communities residing in villages endowed with their own *sŏwŏn* for the education of the children and youths of the clan.[50]

A long period of isolation began in Korea, which lasted for over two hundred years. In this period there were very few contacts between Korea and the non-Chinese world, due, in most cases, to the activity of Western missionaries. The kingdom witnessed a slow decline, marked by social disintegration, serious economic impoverishment, and the emergence of elements of instability linked to Christianity and other local or syncretic cults, often subject to ruthless repression.[51]

With the decline of central power, centrifugal forces of all kinds resurfaced: even the *sŏwŏn*, the Confucian private academies, had become, in the eighteenth, a widespread counterpower to the royal house, as well as shelters for conscripts, and illegally collected taxes. During the eighteenth century, the royal government forbade the foundation of new *sŏwŏn*, and abolished many of those in existence.[52] However, it was only in the second half of the nineteenth century that the central government succeeded in destroying about 3,000, recovering large estates, and thus discovering circa 100,000 draft dodgers.[53]

In the second half of the nineteenth century, the undisputed hegemony of China over Korea was questioned by Japan, interested in Korea for the purposes of its geopolitical agenda and by some segments of the Korean *elite* also interested in opening up[54] and approaching the Land of the Rising Sun. The Korean establishment, led by *Taewŏn'gun* – the powerful father of King Kojong, and as regent during the minor age of the future sovereign in the decade 1864-1873, and the rural elite of the *yangban*, linked to an isolationist policy, contrary to Christians, the Japanese, Westerners, and the neo-Confucian orthodoxy, resisted the winds of change that had already rocked China and Japan.[55]

---

49 M.J. Chung, *The Political and Social Roles of the Sŏwŏn in the Chosŏn Dynasty*, op. cit.

50 *Ibid.*, 57.

51 M. Riotto, *Storia della Corea*, Chap. VII, para. 5.

52 M.J. Chung, op. *cit.*, 21 and 59.

53 M. Riotto, *Storia della Corea*, Chap. VII, para. 5.

54 C.J. Eckert, K. Lee, Y.I. Lew, M. Robinson, E.W. Wagner, *Korea Old and New*, op cit., Chap. 13 entitled *Growth of the Forces of Enlightenment.*

55 Op.cit., 192-198.

A naval accident deliberately provoked by the Japanese government in 1875 justified a Japanese military landing on Korean soil and the imposition of the *unequal treaty* of Kanghwa of 1876, with Korea obliged to accept harsh conditions to maintain an independence of pure facade compared to the Japanese empire. The stipulations of treaties of diplomatic and commercial openings with the main Western powers thus quickly followed.[56] The traditional structures now began to show signs of wear and tear.

The contrasts between the *Taewŏn'gun* and the rural *elite* of the *yangban,* on the one hand, and the national government of King Kojong and the political-social forces that supported the idea of a process of opening, on the other, became very intense, resulting in internal clashes and attempts at coups d'état in the years 1881-1884, followed also by the sending and permanence of both Chinese and Japanese troops in the capital Seoul.[57] The *Taewŏn'gun* was forced into exile in China after a failed coup in 1882, and returned to Korea only three years later.

The Chinese Empire was, by now, in an irreversible crisis. Japan emerged as a political and military power in the region, with a victorious war over China (1894-1895) due precisely to the dispute over the control of the Korean peninsula. The conflict originated as a result of a Japanese armed intervention in the peninsula following a peasant revolt characterized by religious and xenophobic elements, and by the aversion of the rebels to both the decadent national government and the Japanese presence on Korean soil.[58]

The influence of Meiji Japan and a certain opening also to the West brought new legal ideas in the years between the nineteenth and twentieth centuries, the period of the so-called *Kabo* Reform (the name of the year 1894, in which it was launched, in the traditional Korean calendar),[59] with the implementation of new institutional and normative models of Japanese origin – and therefore also, in a minor and more indirect way, of Western origin, especially of German derivation in the legal field, including the transformation of the state into a constitutional monarchy with a government structure inspired by that of the Japanese government, and a codification of criminal law based on the Japanese code of 1882.[60]

New political conflicts arose stemming from the growing Russian influence at the Korean Court, and with open conflicts between the various factions within the Korean *elite* – including between the king and the *Taewŏn'gun,* with the latter finally placed under arrest by the king, his son, leading – to the assassination of Queen Min in 1895. Popular

56 *Ibid.*, pp. 200-204.

57 C.J. Eckert, K. Lee, Y.I. Lew, M. Robinson, E.W. Wagner, *Korea Old and New*, op. cit., 204-207 and 210.

58 Op. cit., 216-222.

59 M. Zimbardo, *Corea*, op. cit., 129. C.J. Eckert, K. Lee, Y.I. Lew, M. Robinson, E.W. Wagner, *Korea Old and New*, op. cit., 224.

60 A. Serafino, *Corea Tradizionale e Repubblica di Corea*, in G. Ajani, A. Serafino, M. Timoteo, *Diritto dell'Asia orientale*, Turin, Utet, 2007, P.C. Hamh, *Korean Jurisprudence, Politics and Culture*, Seoul, Yonsei University Press, 1986, pp. 126 and ff.; M. Zimbardo, *Corea*, op. cit., 129.

anti-Japanese riots and uprisings followed; in February 1896 King Kojong was exfiltrated from the royal palace guarded by pro-Japanese forces, and took refuge in the Russian embassy and the process of the *Kabo* reforms came to a halt.[61]

The royal house increasingly proved itself to be inadequate to the economic and political challenges of the new times, both those internal ones as well as those related to the new geopolitical context and the power plays in the North Asian chessboard by the world powers.[62] For example, King Kojong reacted to these challenges, in 1897, by proclaiming an unrealistic *Daehan Jeguk*, Great Empire of Korea, above all to assert its total independence both from the Japanese Empire and the Ming Empire, of which Korean kings were tributaries, and proclaiming himself obviously Emperor.[63] Kojong attempted to start a season of Western-inspired economic and administrative reforms.[64]

With the military defeat of 1895 and the unstoppable decline of the Chinese Empire, the only serious obstacle for the Japanese government to control of Korea, was Russia, which Japan defeated militarily in 1905.[65] Korea remained, at that point, defenceless, and Japan established a protectorate, passing with the consent of England and the United States, to the full annexation of the peninsula and the establishment of a colonial regime on August 22, 1910, which was immediately followed by the abdication of Emperor Sunjong, son of Kojong and last sovereign of the Yi/Chosŏn dynasty, on 29 August of the same year.[66]

3.1.3 1910 to 1953

The Japanese invasion put an end to the Chosŏn kingdom in 1910 and a period of a hard colonization of Korea began, which ended with the defeat of Japan at the end of the Second World War.

On the same day of the abdication of Emperor Sunjong, the Japanese Imperial Diet enacted the law on the laws and regulations for Korea;[67] a colonial governorate was established (*Chōsen Sōtokufu*, "General Government of Korea" in Japanese) that responded directly to the Diet. The colonial model, also given the geographical proximity, was aimed at a rapid and close assimilation of Korea into the Japanese economic-social fabric.[68] In Korea, Japanese law was applied, now codified according to German models, together with

61 C.J. Eckert, K. Lee, Y.I. Lew, M. Robinson, E.W. Wagner, *Korea Old and New*, op. cit., 228-230.
62 C.J. Eckert, K. Lee, Y.I. Lew, M. Robinson, E.W. Wagner, *Korea Old and New*, op. cit., 204-214.
63 M. J. Seth, *A History of Korea: From Antiquity to Present*, Lanham (MD), Rowman & Littlefield, 2010, 225; M. Riotto, *Storia della Corea*, op. cit., Chap. VIII, para. 7.
64 J.G. Cho, *The Industrial Promotion Policy and Commercial Structure of the Taehan Empire*, Seoul, Jimoondang Publishing Co., 2006, *passim*.
65 S.H. Lee, *La guerra di Corea*, Bologna, Il Mulino, 2001, 19.
66 M. Riotto, *op.loc.ult.cit.*; *Id.*, *Atlante*, op. cit., 49.
67 M. Zimbardo, *Corea*, op cit., 129.
68 C.J. Eckert, K. Lee, Y.I. Lew, M. Robinson, E.W. Wagner, *Korea Old and New*, op cit., 254-260.

the ordinances of the Governor General, directly appointed by the Emperor, which also had legislative value. The General Government was divided into seven departments including one for Justice; a judicial pyramid was established on three levels.[69]

A model of an administrative state was implemented with a complex, invasive and centralized government, with a very large Japanese bureaucracy. The Governor appointed the local administrators of the 13 provinces, 218 counties, 18 cities, 2,262 villages, and 2 islands.[70]

An intensive cultural assimilation program was launched, with the teaching of Japanese language and culture in all schools; a land reform, with registration and assignment on the basis of legal titles of all lands for tax purposes (with the consolidation of aristocratic assets to the detriment of all those classes of non-nobles who had always used land under the traditional law). Economic, infrastructural, industrial and financial reforms were implemented, continuing those already undertaken under the Japanese influence at the end of the previous century. These reforms guaranteed the control of the General Government over strategic resources and finance, obviously in favour of imperial interests and Japanese economic groups, while still permitting the development of Korean businesses and economic groups. Two Japanese banks dominated the country's finance.[71]

The abrupt and heterodirected modernization of the country was accompanied by a harsh repression of dissent and the control of newspapers, intellectuals, religious leaders, and the loyalty of a part of the old *yangban* elite, generating a variety of positions, pro- and anti-integrationists, a *divide et impera* functional to Japanese interests. The model worked quite well for the whole of the 1910s.[72] Dating from 1919, the episodes of nationalist rebellion began to be stronger and more frequent; in 1919 a Korean government in exile was established in Shanghai, whose first president was the pro-American Syngman Rhee. In the 1920s, Korean nationalist movements proliferated, both at home and abroad, not only of traditional character but also of communist, socialist and pro-Western Wilsonist inspiration.[73] Instead nationalist movements of traditionalist inspiration prevailed in Korea, and subsequently also of communist inspiration: with the support of the Soviet and Chinese communist parties, these movements played an important role in the anti-Japanese guerrilla war until the end of the Second World War.[74]

The war started in Manchuria by Japan in 1931, changed the perspective of the clash between Korean nationalists and the imperial government, inserting it into a broader scheme: the Korean government in exile, now led by Kim Ku (close to nationalist China),

69 M. Zimbardo, *Corea*, op cit.,130.
70 C.J. Eckert, K. Lee, Y.I. Lew, M. Robinson, E.W. Wagner, *Korea Old and New*, op cit., 258.
71 *Ibid.*, 260-273.
72 *Ibid.*, 260 ff.
73 S.H. Lee, *La guerra di Corea*, op cit., 20-22; C.J. Eckert, K. Lee, Y.I. Lew, M. Robinson, E.W. Wagner, *Korea Old and New*, op cit., 276 ff.
74 S.H. Lee, *La guerra di Corea*, op cit., 22-26.

and his political opponent Syngman Rhee, pro-American, could now bring the Korean question to international forums and agendas.[75]

World War II led to the end of Japanese colonialism in East Asia, and also in Korea. The Soviet Union and the United States of America, who invaded the peninsula at the time of the collapse of Japan in August 1945, stationed themselves, above and below the 38th parallel, administrating in trust the two parts of the country. For some years now, the Korean question had come to the attention of the powers at war, and at the 1943 Cairo conference, the United States, Britain and Nationalist China agreed that at the end of the conflict there would be an independent Korean state, without clarifying if immediately, however, and indeed inserting vague terms in this regard in the resolution.[76] The resolution was also accepted by the Soviet Union, and after August 1945, the prevailing idea in the chancelleries of the four powers was that there should be a joint mandate of the administration in trust of the peninsula.

The Korean people obviously hoped for an immediate birth of a sovereign state. In 1946, a People's Republic of Korea was born, from a politically heterogeneous popular movement initially called "the Committee for the preparation of Korean independence"; the People's Republic was initially inspired by a non-communist left-wing reformism, but its political base was also extended to sectors of the right linked to the great land and industrial interests, with the moderate Syngman Rhee being appointed president. It was, however, a Republic, destined to be short-lived. In the years 1946-1947, there was a deadlock in the negotiations for the establishment of the trusteeship, and with the start of the cold war, the division of the country became permanent along the line of the 38th parallel. In in the south, the American military government refused to recognize (1946) the People's Republic that had arisen just one month before. The Republic of Korea (often referred to by the Anglo-Saxon acronym ROK) was born in 1948, with the support of the United Nations, with Syngman Rhee as president. At the same time, north of the 38th, the Democratic People's Republic of Korea in the North (DPRK), was founded, under a partial Soviet control and recognized by the fledgling People's Republic of China. The Northern Republic was led by the young Kim Il Sung, *leader* of the anti-Japanese guerrilla war, formed both with the Maoist forces and subsequently with the Soviet army, who became the Secretary of the Korean Workers' Party. Kim's political goal was that of an independent, reunited and communist Korea.[77]

---

75 M. Riotto, *Atlante*, op cit., 50; S.H. Lee, *La guerra di Corea*, op cit., 20-22.

76 S.H. Lee, *La guerra di Corea*, op cit., 33-47; C.J. Eckert, K. Lee, Y.I. Lew, M. Robinson, E.W. Wagner, *Korea Old and New*, op cit., Chap. 18, 327 ff.

77 S.H. Lee, *La guerra di Corea*, op cit., 33-47; C.J. Eckert, K. Lee, Y.I. Lew, M. Robinson, E.W. Wagner, *Korea Old and New*, op cit., Chap. 18, 327 ff. On the figure of Kim Il-Sung, amongst the many, *see* D.S. Suh, *Kim Il Sung: North Korean Leader*, New York, Columbia University Press, 1995; A. Lankov, *From Stalin to Kim Il Sung: The Formation of North Korea 1945-1960*, New Brunswick, NJ, Rutgers University Press, 2002.

The local, regional and global situation was incandescent, with the boundary between the two Koreas marking one of the points of maximum friction between the geopolitical blocks of the Cold War; the northern country was well organized and with a certain degree of harmony and interpenetration between the political, governmental, police and the people; while in the south, the state and the government reproduced a model of democratic state imposed by the United States and moreover allied to the Japanese, somewhat distant from the historical and social reality and the feelings of many Koreans.[78]

In June 1950, North Korean troops, with the support of the Allied People's Republic of China, invaded the southern country, facing the armies of the UN, almost only US and South Korean forces, starting a bloody war that ended in 1953 with an armistice, and the creation of a demilitarized zone (DMZ) along the 38th parallel.[79]

The two Koreas formally still do not recognize each other today. Both states are endowed with constitutional norms that place reunification among the objectives of the Country, and are equipped with specifically dedicated ministerial apparatuses. The gathering impetus manifested by both parties at the end of the 1950-1953 conflict seems to have given way, over time, to a more pragmatic and wait-and-see attitude, certainly with much more modest results: in the more than sixty years following the armistice there have only been, amongst the ups and downs of politics in and between the two countries, some initiatives and negotiations aimed at reopening channels of communication, some more or less ephemeral economic cooperation initiatives, and some of a cultural or social type, for example allowing some family reunifications. The political events of 2018 indicate the possibility of an upcoming peace treaty, which also formally sanctions the end of the Korean war, and of a progressive rapprochement between the two countries of the peninsula.

3.1.4 A Synthesis and Possible Interpretation of Yesterday's and Today's Korea

Some elements of Korean history strike the observer of Asian affairs, allowing them to characterize it for descriptive purposes – *this is the methodological key proposed here to illuminate the specificity of the legal and government culture of Korea* – in terms of variation compared to the best known imperial Chinese model; and subsequently with respect to those of the Soviet Union and the People's Republic of China for North Korea, and to those of Japan and the West for South Korea. The various attempts to implement those

78 S.H. Lee, *La guerra di Corea*, op cit., 46-47.

79 The literature on the Korean war is vast. Among the works already mentioned, S.H. Lee, *La guerra di Corea*, op cit., *passim*; C.J. Eckert, K. Lee, Y.I. Lew, M. Robinson, E.W. Wagner, *Korea Old and New*, op cit., 327-346.

models of government were nevertheless characterized by specifically Korean elements, of which a strong trace in the society and institutions of the two Koreas today, remain.

The first, almost banal, observation consists in taking note of the frequent condition of the Korean peninsula and its political communities, of a weak entity close to (the interests of) one or more great powers: China and the Mongolian kingdoms, then China and Japan, then Russia, then the Soviet Union and the United States of America in the twentieth century. There has historically been a source of strong external interference in Korean affairs, from tributaries to Chinese emperors to occupations by the Japanese and American, to Russian and Chinese influences in the North; and therefore of nationalist or even xenophobic sentiments.

A second aspect, connected to the first, is linked to the historical isolation of the "hermit kingdom", which generated an ethnic and cultural homogeneity that has no equal in other places in the world, and which only recently manifests a divergence, linked to political events here and beyond the 38th parallel. This element also contributes to the maintenance of deep nationalist sentiments, and to nourishing the idea of reunification among many.

A third aspect is related to a certain historical precariousness of the internal political equilibrium, even in the long periods of stability, with important ideological fractures within the ruling *elites* from time to time. It seems rational to significantly relate these factures to the different cultural traditions, in many ways bearers of opposite visions of the world and social organization, simultaneously present in the Korean peninsula; and to the same localism, political and ideological pluralism inherent in a society that is a small but very polycentric and rural society, as demonstrated by the presence, unknown in China, of numerous private Confucian academies scattered throughout the country.

Fourth: the Korean national consciousness was born in the time of the Three Kingdoms, and reached a first peak with the almost unification of the peninsula by Silla, an officially Buddhist kingdom characterized by high cultural and political-administrative sophistication, even if in the north of the peninsula and in Manchuria, meanwhile, existed a Parhae kingdom, more multi-ethnic and closer to the Confucian model, which introduced an element of complexity in the events of Korean unity, more widely achieved with the Kŏryo dynasty, and completely, with Korea which expanded to its borders maintained until 1945, only in the fifteenth century, in the Chosŏn age.

The prevalence of Confucian thinking and the exclusion of Buddhism from public life was officially established only in 1392, the beginning date of the modern Chosŏn kingdom. Yet, one has also seen how the process of assimilation to the neo-Confucian model, beyond the will officially expressed in this regard by the *T'aejo*, was not a process of total homologation: the Ming law code became of general application even in Korea, and yet the *T'aejo* himself at the time of his assumption of the directing function announced that the country would be governed with its *own* legal codes, "respecting the established enactment of the royal ancestors" (*Jojong Seongheon*) convinced that traditional laws were fair and just, and that new legislation even when it seems to solve a problem, always produces unpredictable negative effects.[80]

This principle produced a system of government and legislation at least partly against change: the "laws of the ancestors" preserved within the system, the traditional cultural, shamanic, and Buddhist elements, and on balance, a certain basic political and socio-economic immobility, opposing some resistance to the neo-Confucian thinking only just declared dominant by the *T'aejo*, inspired instead by the need to adapt the tools of government to situations and times, to produce an optimal government action.[81]

Compared with China, Buddhism officially exits public *governance* circa four centuries later – in China with the exiting of the stage of the T'ang dynasty, at the beginning of the tenth century (even if it reappeared for circa a century with the Mongolian Yuan dynasty), in Korea in 1392. Considering however the preservation of traditional cultural elements within the Yi/Chŏson legislation, one is given back the overall image of an ethnically and culturally homogeneous country, governed by a culturally homogeneous *elite*, even if politically pluralist, and that of a very slow evolving society.

It was a society that, thanks to its long self-imposed isolation made possible by geopolitical conditions, largely maintained its characteristics of ancient aristocratic and rural, localist and nationalist, isolationist society, founded on a syncretic shamanic-Buddhist-Taoist-Confucian culture until almost the end of the nineteenh century. It was a society also characterized by persistent and widespread irrationalist elements, demonstrated by the proliferation in that century not only of Christianity but also of many other syncretic cults, often with a significant political impact, sometimes accompanied by the relative repressive activities of the government.

In cultural and governmental terms, Koreans are often characterized as being more Chinese than the Chinese, so to speak, more neo-Confucians than the neo-Confucians;[82] and perhaps it is true, considering the deep rootedness, and compared to China, comparatively greater, given the small size of the country, of Confucian culture and the idea of personal and social improvement through study.[83] This is even more true considering also the sophistication of Confucian thinking in its Korean ramification, the social order in the Chŏson period, which C. Choi characterizes as "a model Confucian society",[84] and the political weight acquired over the centuries by the caste of the *yangban* literati: "they attained control over warriorclass, functionary officials, royal family, and palace eunuchs. These feats were not even completed in China, where the civil bureaucracy first developed.

80 C. Choi, *Law and Justice in Korea*, op cit., 70-71.

81 *Ibid.*, 67-72.

82 A. Serafino in G. Ajani, A. Serafino, M. Timoteo, *Diritto dell'Asia orientale*, op cit., Chap. X para 2., *Il diritto e la cultura confuciana*, 251 ff., and the literature ivi cited in the footnotes.

83 Today, South Korea is still the most literate and on average the most educated country in the world – and this is also true, as far as we know, of North Korea.

84 C. Choi, *East Asian Jurisprudence*, op cit., 95 ff.

It is likely to be more than the literate class of China, powerful enough to collectively check royal authority".[85]

At the same time, the Koreans are still more Buddhist and more irrationalist (one uses this term due to the fact that one does not have a better one; in Western terms one could say: idealistic or romantic) than the Chinese, with a certain historical aptitude to seek harmony in traditional and ancestral elements, and to incorporate or generate cults of various kinds.

Part of the Chinese and much of the Western narrative, by way of simplifying, often describe the history of Chinese thinking on the art of government via an opposition, that between the lawmaking and Confucian approaches. The historical literature on Korea tends to simplify the description of political dynamics with the ideological opposition between Confucianism and Buddhism.

Both simplifications have an element of truth and a certain pedagogical utility, but they are certainly destined to be overcome if the study becomes deepened; such a deepening is not possible here, but what seems possible to affirm, albeit one is aware of introducing a further simplification, is that in comparison, Korean legal and governmental thinking is historically more inclined than Chinese thinking of making or detecting a synthesis of the polarities involved, seeking and conceptualizing the balance in ideologies and the instruments of government considered from time to time rather than the opposition/tension between them. One of the main debates in the legal literature of the Chŏson age, resuming and developing a few centuries later, themes of the Neo-Confucian Chinese literature of the Song period,[86] was that on the relationships between *them* and *those*: between thought and energy, reason and sensation, morality and desire, ritual (in the Confucian sense) and nature (a more central concept in Buddhist thinking), between fact considered in the abstract and in the context of all its circumstances, between rule and exception, between having to be and being, so to speak; and the solutions reached are always narrated in terms of synthesis; the search for the *Dao*, the overcoming of apparent contradictions through practical, effective solutions, inspired by the realization of cosmic harmony.[87]

Korean history is full of duality in equilibrium (perhaps precarious): starting obviously from the two dominant philosophies of Confucianism and Buddhism; from the political power of the Buddhist priest aristocracy which generated a counter-power to that of civil power; from the caste of the *yangban* (aristocratic officials, originally "of the two branches",

---

85 S.M. Lee, *The Government Service Examinations of the Chosŏn Dynasty*, in J.B. Duncan, J.C. Lee, J. Lee, M. Ahn, J.A. Dawey (Eds.), *The Institutional Basis of Civil Governance in the Chosŏn Dynasty*, op cit., 97.

86 Mainly by Zhu Xi (or Chu Hsi, 1130-1200), perhaps the greatest of the Chinese neo-Confucian philosophers; W.T. Chan, *Chu Hsi: Life and Thought*, Hong Kong and New York, The Chinese University Press and St. Martin's Press, 1987; *Id.*, *A Source Book in Chinese Philosophy*, Princeton (NJ), Princeton University Press, 1964, 588.

87 C. Choi, *East Asian Jurisprudence*, op cit., Chaps. 2, *Medieval Jurisprudence*, 43 ff., and 3, *Modern Jurisprudence*, 78 ff., particularly 53-62 and 93-103.

civil and military, caste that contains the relative Confucian and Buddhist cultural *background*). The *taijitu*, an ancient symbol of Taoism and the *yin-yang* philosophy, stands out even today in the flag of the Republic of Korea.

Even the role of the law and its relationship with virtue and custom is in the Korean mentality, a less dialectical and disruptive role, compared to that of the Chinese legislation, and aimed more instead at clarifying the traditional rules, "respecting the established enactment of the royal ancestors",[88] innovating only the strictly necessary and in accordance with the needs of popular feeling and effective government.[89] All in a harmonious whole, conforming to the Buddhist principle of *wu wei*, of inaction: there is wisdom and success in government when there is no need to act, when the law is respected without the need to apply it. A certain idea conforming to the Confucian doctrine, in which a virtuous government is theorized, conducted chiefly by example,[90] but also shared, from a point of view that appears opposite, from the purest and oldest legist ideology.[91]

Beyond the pedagogical simplifications, and the obvious differences in the means to be used to achieve the ideal of effective government, the two Confucian ideologies also have many points of contact and juxtaposition, and find a possible synthesis in a frame of Taoist, *yin-yang*, Buddhist thought,[92] of which Korean history offers an example.

> Koreans demanded from life the feeling of being alive in the exchange network of deep affection and emotion with other human beings and in the situation of riding with the rythm of nature in relative harmony and peace… law signifies

88 C. Choi, *Law and Justice in Korea – South and North*, Seoul, National University Press, 2005, 67-72. The phrase reproduced in the text is reported by the author quoted in English and in quotation marks, referring to sources of Korean legal literature cited in the note.

89 *See, e.g.*, the thinking of the Korean philosopher Yi I (or Yulgok, 1536-1584); *see* C. Choi, *Law and Justice in Korea*, op cit., 97-101; *Id.*, *East Asian Jurisprudence*, op cit., 100-103; Y. Ch'oe, P.H. Lee, Wm. T. de Bary (Eds.), *Sources of Korean Tradition*, Vol. II (from seventeenth to twentieth century), New York, Columbia University Press, 2000, 145-157.

90 "To govern is to be just. If the guide is just, who will dare to act unjustly?" (Confucius, *Dialogues*, 12.17); "To govern, what need is there to kill? If you want good, the people will be good. The virtue of the gentleman/lord is that of the wind, the virtue of the people is that of the grass. The grass bends to the wind" (*Dialogues*, 12.19).

91 *See, e.g.*, *Shang Jun Shu* (The book of the lord of Shang) the most famous work of the law school, dating back to the fourth century BC, in which the art of government is exposed with numerous discourses on the nature and function of the law: "If punishments are heavy and rigorously applied, then people will not dare to try (how far they can go), with the result that, in the state, there will be no people punished" (Chap. 18, *Rewards and Punishment*); "light offences should be punished heavily; if light offences do not appear, heavy punishments will not come. This is said to be abolishing penalties by means of penalties, and if penalties are abolished, affairs will succeed" (Chap. 14, *Making Orders Strict*); available at the website *Chinese Text Project*, online library of pre-modern Chinese texts compiled in crowd-sourcing, administered by D. Sturgeon of the Harvard University at https://ctext.org.

92 *See also* C. Choi, op cit., *East Asian Jurisprudence*, 34-42.

> the failure of princely virtue, and the administration of justice is premised upon the breakdown of harmony and peace.[93]

This idyllic approach to life and society according to some, however, would have rendered Korea, after centuries of stable isolation, unable to face the aggressiveness of the radically different Western/Japanese perspective, introduced by force, in the late nineteenth century.[94]

It is possible that the secular isolation of Korea, associated with the high level of intellectual sophistication of its higher classes and the essentially rural and polycentric socio-economic reality of the country in the Chŏson period, produced intellectual, political, civil and military litigious elites, with a vision of themselves and their historical role, perhaps excessive, with respect to the actual geopolitical dimension of the country and their individual roles within it; and even their serious difficulty in realizing this situation.[95]

The story of King Kojong seems an extraordinary synthesis of this situation. Surrounded by three of the world's greatest empires, and with the new American empire still far away but already well present in the north-Asian chessboard, in a climate of great geopolitical instability, he decided in 1897 to proclaim an empire of his own, probably accelerating the end of the long Chŏson parable as the ruling dynasty and the end of the nominal independence of Korea.

The debate on these issues is still very much alive in South Korea, and has much to do with the different ideological positions on national tradition and foreign influence, especially that of Japan, from the second half of the nineteenth century. What is certain is that the Koreans, traditionalists deep-down, innovators when the need arises, compared to China, have demonstrated to know how to equip themselves much more quickly, in this, following a dynamic similar to that of Meiji Japan, in the face of major socio-economic and political changes, all be they hetero-imposed, of the late nineteenth century, perhaps due to a lower inertia, compared to China, due to the smaller size and the greater ethnic and cultural homogeneity of the country, or perhaps also due to the historical aptitude of Korea, conscious of its fragility, to adapt quickly to a (new) domination.[96]

---

93 This description, a clear and effective synthesis of Buddhist, Taoist and Confucian principles, is reported by C. Choi op cit., *Op.ult.cit.*, 240, juxtaposing two passages taken from P.C. Hahm, *Korean Jurisprudence, Politics and Culture*, Seoul, Yonsei University Press, 1986, p. 289 and p. 177; P.C. Hahm, as well as being a politician and diplomat, of traditionalist orientation, was one of the most important philosophers of the South Korean law of the twentieth century.

94 C. Choi, op cit., 240, once again reporting the thinking of P.C. Hahm.

95 M. Riotto, *La Corea non è un paese*, in *Limes*, 2016 n. 12, *La Corea è una bomba*, 31-44, *passim*, points out the structural inadequacy and lack of contact with the reality of the Korean elites of the dynastic period, and a certain inclination towards taking, at critical moments, the wrong decisions; and a tendency of the phenomenon to reproduce itself today – with the presence at the socio-psychological level of a problem of self-esteem and national identity crisis, perceived in the southern country since 1948 and (increasingly more acute) even today.

96 M. Riotto, op.cit., 39.

The recent history of Korea now provides, again, oppositions and violent contrasts, after the country was invaded and divided into two parts by foreign hands. The two Koreas represent some of the contradictions experienced over the centuries by the country at a granular level, today as fugitives from the law of *Dao* to manifest themselves, in a historical moment of acute crisis, as two separate aggregates, one cannot now know whether forever, or for how long (but, in any case, probably, still for quite some time).

Some contradictions today certainly arouse amazement, such as that between the country most isolated in the world and that of the country most "connected"; between the always dark city in satellite images (Pyongyang) and that with the most "eco-hi-tech" (Seoul); between a very poor country, supported by a dilapidated industrial apparatus, and one with a very advanced economy. Between two countries, where one "boasts" a GDP fifteen times lower than the other and a bad record on human rights, yet gathers oceanic crowds that hail its leaders (in part genuinely, beyond the well-known repressive capacity of their government); while the other, rich and advanced, suffers a serious crisis of identity, with millions of citizens on the streets of Seoul in 2016, an extraordinary event, demanding the resignation of their president and daughter of president, for having ruled the country under the influence or the guidance of a shaman-friend, with shadows of economic corruption,[97] a story followed by the impeachment of the president and the criminal conviction for the vice president and designated heir of Samsung.

Only the sum of all the historical, ideological and cultural factors, and the internal and external political and military events can provide the right keys for an interpretation: looking back, there are recurrent dynamics, between ethnocentrism, conservation and isolationism on the one hand, and innovative and oriented to openness forces, on the other. The two Koreas today express these two orientations, which are very reminiscent of the political events of the late nineteenth century, which in turn reproduced even older dynamics, with the *Taewŏn'gun* leading the nationalist and isolationist forces and King Kojong oriented towards the opening versus Japan and the western powers.

Western literature on the laws of Korea usually narrates the legal history of Korea until 1945, followed by that of the Republic of Korea, dedicating only a short chapter or paragraph to North Korea.[98] This approach can/should be overcome, even if it understandable given the known difficulties in accessing information on the Democratic People's Republic of Korea, and perhaps also due to the prevalent interests of the Western comparators, which generates a perhaps incomplete perception of the historical process, and the relationship

---

97 *Ibid.*

98 A. Serafino, chapter *Corea Tradizionale e Repubblica di Corea*, e chapter *Repubblica Popolare Democratica di Corea (Corea del Nord)*, in G. Ajani, A. Serafino, M. Timoteo, *Diritto dell'Asia orientale*, Torino, Utet, 2007; M. Zimbardo, capitolo *Corea*, in R. Cavalieri (Ed.), *Diritto dell'Asia orientale*, Venezia, Cafoscarina, 2008, 125 ff.

between continuity and discontinuity between Korean history up to 1945 and the separate histories of the two Koreas of today.

In fact, it seems that it is precisely the Northern Country, with its political and government institutions and its ongoing inaccessibility, to have preserved "unencoded", for example in the use of a more "pure" Korean language, the most significant part of Korean historical heritage and the profound archetypes of political and social organization. This, obviously does not rule out that this cultural heritage is also present in the Southern Country, ready to re-emerge where and to the extent that political conditions permit.

3.2 The Institutions and Law of North Korean

3.2.1 *Methodological Premise*

Describing North Korea is notoriously difficult, in general. Even more so, is the attempt to describe the legal system, due to the political circumstances of this country which, on the one hand, make its operating mechanisms opaque, while on the other, render it a country characterized by a system of *governance,* (we prefer this broader term albeit, in this context, an inadequate concept of a legal system), based essentially on the *law of politics* and on specific Korean elements of *rule of tradition.*[99]

It is not yet possible and in any case, it would not be sufficient to carry out a scientific analysis of the law of North Korea using only the usual approach of a jurist and the official or academic legal sources. Access to sources is very difficult, and even more so, is access to information on how the country is actually governed; the available sources are not always neutral or sometimes completely reliable. There is the need to collect all kinds of data, and carefully analyse and systemise this data: from every piece of news, from a journalist source or a travel report, a government source or an NGO, various North American or South Korean research centres, or the small business community that interacts with the country, a wiki source or a blog on the net, the news provided by defectors or the *intelligence* diffused by other governments, and from private conversations: all this information produces a jigsaw, whose overall design is not yet fully known.[100]

99 The reference is obviously to the tri-partition of the classification systems proposed in U. Mattei, *Verso una tripartizione non eurocentrica dei sistemi giuridici*, in *Studi in memoria di Gino Gorla*, Milan, Giuffré, 1994, 775 ff.; in English, U. Mattei, *Three Patterns of Law: Taxonomy and Change in the World Legal Systems*, 45 (2007) *American Journal of Comparative Law*, 5 ff.

100 We have chosen here to cite the normative and doctrinal sources, and some of the main literary sources of various kinds stemming from particularly qualified authors. Some statements that may appear unsupported by specific sources will normally be the result of the concordant indication of multiple sources not particularly qualified (*e.g.*, blogs of organizations with various political agendas, which in turn refer to unspecified sources); this type of source was avoided, as far as possible, unless the diversity of concordant sources and

Possible keys to the understanding of the political-institutional reality of North Korea – bearing in mind that here the discussion is at least partly Popperian, composed of plausible hypotheses, pending criticisms, verifications, falsification of facts, all expected and welcomed – can be given by a comparison, in particular, with the kingdom Chŏson, the USSR and People's Republic of China. Useful indications can also stem from a comparison with the events of the southern country, especially in the years immediately following the end of the Second World War, when the distance between the two models of government, economy and legal systems, was less than today, and from the opportunities for interaction between the two countries. In relation to the economic, administrative and juridical reforms registered in the Northern Country, a comparison with the current experience of China, from which many of the incorporated institutional and legal models originate, is certainly useful.

3.2.2 *Political and Constitutional Framework*

The DPRK was founded in 1948 as an authoritarian state based on the doctrine of orthodox communism and on nationalistic ideas, with an initial system modelled on the Soviet system; above all, it was born around the charismatic figure of the nation's father Kim Il Sung, who died in 1994 but still has under the North Korean Constitution of 1998 the title of "Eternal President", which obviously can no longer be attributed to others.

The Workers' Party of Korea (Chosŏn Rodongdang), also known outside Korea with the Anglo-Saxon acronym WPK, guides and oversees everything. This includes also two minor parties that in 1946 had formed together with the WPK, the Democratic Front for the Reunification of the Fatherland,[101] and that today do not have any independent political role, in accordance with a model also seen in the People's Republic of China, where eight minor parties operate under the supervision of the Communist Party. In this typically socialist vision and structure, characterized by the absence of *checks and balances* and no theory on the separation of powers, the administrative apparatus does not represent in itself a "power", but instead performs functions instrumental to the implementation of

---

their overall agreement with the picture reconstructed by means of the most traditionally considered reliable sources, renders the data reported well known among "authorized personnel". We are aware of the exercise of patience and trust that we ask of our readers. The alternatives would have been to flood the work with notes with evanescent references to websites, or not to write this piece.

101 This is the Social Democratic Party of Korea and the Chondoista Chongu Party, originally of a religious and nationalist character; they have, respectively, less than 10% and less than 55% of the seats in the SPA, compared to almost 90% of the seats occupied by WPK members; *see*, as part of the publication of the Interparliamentary Union, the *Constitutional and Parliamentary Information* of the Association of General Secretaries of Parliaments, 3rd series, n. 163, first semester 1992, 3 ff., in which is reported an extract in English of the minutes of the SPA with the description of the parliamentary system of the DPRK made by the Deputy Secretary of the Presidium at the time of his assuming office.

the political will of the people, the sole possessor of the sole possible power, which transforms political power into decisions via its politically conscious avant-garde: the Communist Party in the USSR and in China, and the Workers' Party in North Korea.[102]

The state, however, is also founded, and especially over time, on the *Juche* (or *Chuche*) ideology,[103] elaborated and advocated by Kim Il Sung, and then expanded in content and range of action by his son Kim Jong Il: *Juche* literally means pride, self-confidence, self-esteem, self-awareness (in the national sense). A theoretical ideology that is also sometimes applied in a maximalist way, without any subjection, at least on a formal level, with respect to the neighbouring USSR and China, with which relations are not always be easy.

The foundation and organization of the state have been expressed with changing principles in the various constitutional texts that have characterized the system in the last decades, but never diverting from the influence of a profound nationalist ideology.

The first constitutional text of the Democratic People's Republic of Korea was promulgated in September 1948 by the newly constituted Supreme People's Assembly, after a brief planning phase carried out with the help of Soviet jurists. The Supreme People's Assembly, the legislative body of the state, was established on the model of the Supreme Soviet of the Soviet Union and determined the dissolution of the representative organs formed after the end of the Japanese occupation.[104]

As in the Soviet (and Chinese) model, it was the Presidium of the Supreme People's Assembly that determined the fundamental decisions concerning the political and economic direction, as a representative body of the state in both domestic and foreign politics.

The constitutional history of North Korea recalls from a historical point of view what had been the evolution of the Soviet system, starting from the New Economic Policy, up to the Stalinist Constitution of 1936. Even in the North Korean constitution of 1948, there was the need to reach a series of compromises, admitting the coexistence of principles of socialist law with the recognition of private property and freedom of trade,[105] pending the transformation of society to be accomplished through the necessary and interlocutory phase of socialism until the advent of communism.

The subsequent Constitution of 1972 formalized the profound changes that marked society in the following years: in the preamble, the abrogation of the right of private property was definitively established and the achieved goal of the transition to a pure

102 As confirmed by the Constitutions and statutes of the relevant parties, and by their respective national constitutions.

103 Sometimes the term is rendered, in Korean, with the word *Jaju*.

104 Including the People's Provisional Committee, established in February 1946 and dissolved one year later, succeeded by the People's Assembly of North Korea.

105 Costitution of 1948, Arts. 5, 8, 19.

socialist system through the removal of the antagonistic elements still contained in the 1948 text, was emphased.[106]

The 1972 Constitution, called the "Socialist Constitution of the Democratic People's Republic of Korea"[107] sanctioned the consolidation of the absolute power of Kim Il Sung, establishing *ad hoc* the presidential office of Head of State, with a four-year term without limits of re-election;[108] it outlined in Article 1 that North Korea was "an independent socialist state", in the historical phase probably of the greatest political and economic success of the Northern Country, after having reached a fair level of industrialization and economic and social progress[109] that permitted Kim also to proudly distance North Korea from both the communist superpowers. The *Juche* philosophy was formally incorporated into the text[110] (in conjunction with the reference to the Marxist-Leninist ideology) and significant changes were made in the field of citizens' rights, now completely surrounded by the collectivist principle,[111] which also constituted the basis of the entire educational system. Citizen was substituted on a terminological level by the "mass",[112] as the owner of active and passive legal positions, in contrast to that which had been established by the constitutional text of 1948, in which the fundamental rights of individual citizens were enumerated, if only formally. The organization and activities of the state organs were subjected to the principle of "democratic centralism,"[113] which determined the hierarchical submission of all authority to that superior, without the provision of checks or balances between the various organs of the state.

The 1972 constitutional text also established the constitution of the People's Central Committee of the People,[114] whose president coincided with the figure of the head of state, thus strengthening the predominant position of Kim Il Sung.

The international collapse of the socialist system at the end of the 1980s and the consequent failure of the system of mutual assistance between socialist countries led to a serious economic, social and political identity crisis within the Korean nation. The need for survival

---

106 *See* Art. 6 ("*The class antagonisms and all forms of exploitation and oppression of man by man are eliminated forever*") and, as regards the achieved goal of a modern and efficient centralized and planned economic system, Art. 24 ("*The historical task of industrialization has been successfully achieved*").

107 It should be noted that the 1948 Constitution does not mention the socialist state in any part.

108 1972 Socialist Constitution, Arts.88, 89.

109 The data is known and undisputed in literature; up to the beginning of the 1970s of the twentieth century, it was commonly held that the general economy and the welfare of the citizens were for much of North Korean society better than it was in the southern country, not to mention the comparison with the still very backward Chinese economy; *See, e.g.*, J.J. Suh, *Origins of North Korea's Juche*, Plymouth, Lexington, 2013, 18-20.

110 1972 Socialist Constitution, Art. 4.

111 1972 Socialist Constitution, Art.68, for which citizens must show a high degree of collective spirit, take care of their collective organization and support the revolutionary aspect of the interests of the motherland.

112 1972 Socialist Constitution, Arts. 12 and 13.

113 1972 Socialist Constitution, Art.9.

114 1972 Socialist Constitution, Arts. 100-106.

in a completely altered international situation led North Korea to change its foreign policy and to adopt, above all towards South Korea, a dialogue approach. The constitutional precept concerning the goal of reaching a reunification of the Korean peninsula via revolutionary means gave way to the idea of a peaceful reunification; in the 1992 amendments to the 1972 Socialist Constitution, the *Juche* ideology was formally raised to an autonomous constitutional principle.[115] The 1992 text introduced a series of further important changes at the ideological level, among which stands out the expounding of Marxism-Leninism among the constitutive doctrines of the state. The term "dictatorship of the proletariat" was replaced by that of the "dictatorship of the people's democracy", overturning the principle that, in the socialist revolutionary process, the dictatorship of the proletariat is placed at a more advanced and evolved level than the latter.[116] Additionally, in these amendments, technological progress, research, and the independence of the national economy were emphasized and a new phase of opening the economy towards the outside was also ratified at constitutional level.[117]

In this new context, in order to consolidate power in the hands of his successor and son, Kim Jong Il, a National Defence Commission was set up, separate from the People's Central Committee, giving Kim Jong Il the positions of Commander-in-Chief of the forces armies and that of the President of the National Defence Commission.

On coming to power after his father's death, Kim Jong Il unveiled a new tendency towards institutional equilibrium. In order to secure an undisputed legitimacy, in the subsequent Constitution of 1998, he reaffirmed the proclamation of his father, Kim Il Sung, as founder of the Republic, Father of Socialist Korea and, as already mentioned, Eternal President of the Republic.[118]

The effort to capitalize on the "sacred" reputation of his father (certainly endowed with a greater charisma than his son) allowed Kim Jong Il to gain access to power, after the period of mourning, in a country where his father Kim Il Sung continues to "reign" together with him in an idealistic manner. The persuasive force of the new provisions contained in the 1998 Constitution was strengthened with the attribution of the content of the constitutional text to the already deceased Kim Il Sung. The new document envisaged a drastic

---

115 Amendments to the 1992 Socialist Constitution, Art. 3 ("*The Democratic People's Republic of Korea is guided in its activities by the Juche idea, a world-centred perspective on the people, a revolutionary ideology aimed at achieving the independence of the masses*").

116 *Cf.* D.K. Yoon, *The Constitution of North Korea: Its Changes and Implications*, in 27 *Fordham International Law Journal*, 2003, n. 4, Art. 2; The author believes that these contradictions are the consequence of a slowdown in the revolutionary impulse due to the new situation of vulnerability of the nation.

117 Amendments to the 1992 Socialist Constitution, Art. 37 ("The State will encourage the institutions, companies and associations of the Democratic People's Republic of Korea which will establish and manage joint ventures with legal or physical persons from foreign countries"). It should be noted that since 1984 a basic regulation on the establishment of joint ventures was envisaged, but in fact it was inhibited by not enjoying constitutional recognition at the time.

118 Socialist Constitution of 1998, Preamble.

limitation of the institutional bodies and determined the centralization of power in the hands of a few government figures, among which Kim Jong Il stands out, whose authority became total and undisputed, thanks to the numerous political and institutional roles held simultaneously.[119] The political leadership of the Workers' Party on all the state apparatus and on the Korean people was confirmed.[120] *Juche* doctrine remained the only relevant ideology, in a state based on a model that one can define praetorian, nationalist and (in theory) autarchic.[121]

In the Constitution of 1998, there was also some openness to the recognition of property and private economic activity: in addition to that of the state and the cooperatives, for the means of production, now extended to "social organizations", the citizen owned property was acknowledged solely aimed at satisfying "simple and individual" needs, and the exercise of commercial activities by citizens, although indicated as secondary or collateral in the economic model ("side-line activities"), via the reference to the products of vegetable gardens for domestic use[122] of farmers in cooperatives and to "other legitimate economic activities",[123] and even with the recognition of intellectual property rights (Art. 74).[124] In addition, a corporate accounting system was introduced for public companies with the constitutionalization of the economic concepts of costs, prices and profits.[125]

The Constitution of 1998 was subsequently followed by the Constitution of 2009, the so-called "Sŏn'gun Constitution", with the constitutionalization of the homonymous principle, "first of all, the military element", already launched and implemented during the previous decade, which integrated and modernized the *Juche* idea, promoting not only the centrality of the military apparatus in the North Korean society, with a predominance also on the political centrality of the WPK,[126] but also a "militant" style for all citizens (Arts. 60 and 61 of the Constitution of 1998). *Juche* and *Sŏn'gun* remained the only constitutionally relevant ideologies.[127]

---

119 Including that of General Secretary of the Workers' Party of Korea, the President of the National Defence Commission and the Commander in Chief of the People's Army.

120 1998 Constitution, preamble.

121 Arts. 58-61 of the 1998 Constitution place defence at the centre of the political community, with the National Defence Commission at the centre of the military and institutional system.

122 It is very significant that the first official recognition of the private sector of the Chinese economy was that concerning the private activities of the farmers concerning the products of the vegetable gardens assigned to private use.

123 1998 Constitution, Art. 24, para. 3 (English translation in appendix to C. Choi, *Law and Justice in Korea*, op cit.).

124 D.K. Yoon, *The Constitution of North Korea: Its Changes and Implications*, in 27 *Fordham International Law Journal*, 2003, n. 4, Art. 2, 1289 ff., 1303.

125 Art. 33 Costitution of 1998.

126 *See* V. Cha, B. Hwang, *The Structure of Government*, in R.L. Worden (Ed.), *North Korea: A Country Study*, Federal Research Division, Library of Congress, 5th edn. 2008, Chapt. 6, 187-193.

127 Art. 3 Constitution of 2009 (English translation on a government website): "The DPRK considers the chuch'e idea and the military-first idea, which are person-centred worldviews and revolutionary ideas for achieving the independence of the popular masses, as the guiding principles of its activities"; *See also* Arts. 58-61 for

In the same Charter of 2009, the principle for which the Chairman of the National Defence Commission was the highest office of the State,[128] was constitutional. The position of "Eternal Chairman" of the National Defence Commission and that of Eternal General Secretary of the Workers' Party were thus attributed to Kim Jong Il by the Congress of the Workers' Party in the spring of 2012,[129] after his death a little unexpected in December 2011; his young son and successor Kim Jong Un was then named "First *Chairman*" of the National Defence Commission and the party.[130]

In the Constitution of 2009 any reference to the communism still present in Articles 29 and 40 (economics and culture, respectively), was also eliminated, confirming the socialist nature of the state and the persistence of a system of dictatorship of popular democracy led by the WPK, and the obligation for every citizen to safeguard the political and ideological unity and solidarity of the people. Moreover, the necessary observance by every citizen of a socialist "style" and the abandonment of "outdated" lifestyles, was reaffirmed.[131]

The reference to the construction of a communist society was also removed from the WPK statute, in 2010: the country's ideological foundations remained the national Juche ideology and the Sŏn'gun policy, with the party leader automatically acquiring the position of president of the Central Military Commission (a powerful party organ, different from the CMD of the state apparatus); the ideological indication was updated with reference to the guiding ideas of "Kimilsungism-Kingjongilism."[132]

There were further constitutional amendments, in quick succession, in 2012, 2013 and 2016, following the death of Kim Jong Il, which perhaps caught the country partially unprepared with regards to his succession.

The 2012 constitutional text was attributed to the joint paternity of Kim Il Sung and Kim Jong Il, with the express acknowledgment of the latter as the founder of the North Korean state and political leadership; and the position of First Chairman of the NCD, assigned to Kim Jong Un, was introduced. The constitutional text also placed emphasis on declaring North Korea as a state with nuclear weapons. The 2013 amendment established

a more detailed description of the *sŏn'gun* vision. But already Arts. 58-61 of the 1998 Constitution place the defence at the centre of the political community, with the National Defence Commission at the centre of the military and institutional system. For an analysis of the relationship between *Juche* and *Sŏn'gun*, from the North American think-tank *The Korean Economic Institute of America, see* H.S. Park, *Military-First Politics (Songun): Understanding Kim Jong-il's North Korea*, in KEI *Academic Paper series* 2, n. 7 (2007).

128 Chap. VI of the 2009 Constitution, commonly known as the "*Songun* Constitution".

129 KCNA (the news agency of the North Korean state): *WPK Conference Decides to Hold Kim Jong Il in High Esteem as Eternal General Secretary of WPK*, 11 April 2012.

130 *DPRK's Kim Jong Un elected first chairman of National Defense Commission*, on the website of the Chinese newspaper *People's Daily*, http://en.people.cn/90777/7786837.html, 14 April 2012 (accessed 28 December 2016).

131 Art. 42, Constitution of 2009.

132 Amendment of the statute voted in the 2012 WPK Conference.

that the *Ku'msusan* Sun Palace, Mausoleum of Kim Il Sung and Kim Jong Il, was an eternally sacred site for all Koreans.[133] The 2016 amendment instead led to the replacement of the former National Defence Commission at the vertex of the institutions with the new State Affairs Commission.[134] A party congress, again in 2016 (the first after thirty-six years), confirmed the *leadership* of Kim Jong Un with the new title of Chairman of the party,[135] completing the transition started with the death of Kim Jong Il.

3.2.3 *Juche, Sŏn'gun, Kimilsungism-Kimjongilism*

An analysis of political and normative data in North Korea cannot ignore the verification of the content of *Juche* doctrine, as an interpretive canon of the juridical, political and economic choices of the country. The verification of the system of sources of law can indeed constitute a useful element for the verification of the influence of the *Juche* idea (and of Marxism-Leninism) in the field of interpretation of the law and in the organization of the North Korean legal system as a whole.

The incorporation in Asian societies of the principles of Marxism-Leninism has, in fact, often been met with resistance (or been subjected to deviations from the original ideology) due to a deep and rooted traditional substratum that stands as an element of continuity in the various historical epochs. The principles of European socialism have been characterized by differentiated evolutionary lines in the countries of Asia, thus even with reference to Chinese socialism, if placed in relation to the Korean situation and even in the presence of significant moments of convergence,[136] it is prudent to refrain from thinking in homogenization terms.

---

133 Amendment of the 2009 Preamble of the Constitution.

134 Constitution of 2016, Art. 100 ff. This constitutional change seems to indicate Kim Jong Un's intention to give the party renewed centrality with respect to the armed forces. The new leader, much younger than most members of the country's military and administrative political vertexes, seems to have been able to overcome the initial perplexities of many – earning loyalty especially from the military apparatuses, continuing the *Sŏn'gun* policy and the nuclear program – affirming at the end of a complex transition what seems now an absolute power. *See* A. Fiori, *Piccoli leader crescono*, in *Limes* 12/2016, *La Corea è una bomba*, 45 ff. The start of Kim Jong Un's leadership was characterized by the "double development" policy, both nuclear and economic, also through legislative and administrative reforms to stimulate and attract investments; Central Committee of the WPK of 31 March 2013, reported in *White Paper on Human Rights in North Korea* of 2014, Korea Institute for National Unification. Recent indications such as Kim Jong Un's speech at the beginning of 2017 seem to confirm a policy characterized by less attention to the *sŏn'gun* principle in favour of economic development policies.

135 A. Fifield, *At Four-Day Congress, North Korean Leader Proves His Strength*, in *The Washington Post*, 9 May 2016 (accessed 29 December 2016).

136 However, historical similarities between the two countries can be found. In particular, the parallel between the *Chollima* Movement in North Korea and the "Great leap forward" in China; between the *Juche* ideology and the Maoist doctrine of *self-reliance*; in terms of collectivization of farms, the *Chongsanri* models in North Korea and the Maoist model of *Dazhai*. In this regard, always see the work of S.C. Yang, *The North*

The ideological parable of North Korea has been intimately connected to the "philosophical" Juche concept and its meaning, not cultured but in common use.

Generally translatable with the idea of self-esteem and self-reliance, the term does not coincide with the birth of an ideology. Used by Kim Il Sung since the 1920s, when he was, together with other Korean Resistors, engaged in the struggle for the liberation of Korea from the Japanese occupation, the term *Juche* referred mainly to the anti-Japanese sentiment, already widespread since the *Kanghwa* treaty (1876), and was often placed in relation to Koreans who had not been able to preserve the territorial and cultural integrity of the nation during the foreign occupation. At that time, it was not easy to distinguish the embryo of an ideology from the mere use of contingent declamatory formulas, but in all probability, the evolution of the instrumental interpretation of the term began, that characterized the guidelines of the domestic and foreign policy of North Korea in the aftermath of the division of the peninsula.[137]

Historical events thus probably constituted the first justification for the *Juche* idea. The entire history of the Korean peninsula is a history of occupations and exploitation (by the Chinese, Russians, Mongolians, Japanese, and the Americans): the Koreans believe that these experiences have made their people the most qualified for the development of an ideology that exalts (the desire of) the self-determination of the nation.[138]

Other factors subsequently influenced the evolution of the concept, including the continuing American military presence in South Korea after the 1953 armistice and the need to consolidate a balance, at the time precarious, between Pyongyang, China and the USSR (formalized by the North Korean government following the declaration of a pact of equidistance), factors that also permitted Kim Il Sung to consolidate his personal power.[139]

The *Juche* philosophy subsequently evolved to establish the centrality of the figure of the supreme leader, the *Suryŏng*, around which the political system developed, *suryŏngje*;[140] and become radical in an ethnocentric sense of national superiority, whose natural presup-

---

and South Korean Political Systems: A Comparative Analysis, Elizabeth (NJ), Hollym International, 2nd edn, 1999, 219-265.

137 J.J. Suh, *Origins of North Korea's Juche*, Plymouth, Lexington, 2013, *passim*, and especially Chaps. 1, 2, 3.

138 On the question of the perception of the Koreans as the most legitimized people to propose nationalistic petitions, *cf.* D.S. Suh, *Kim Il Sung: North Korean Leader*, New York, Columbia University Press, 1995.

139 The historical conjuncture offered the opportunity for Kim Il Sung to try to definitively legitimize his position and to demonstrate the ideological superiority of North Korea compared to the South. A scan of the events traces a common pattern, in which the seizure of power follows expansion of legitimacy through ideology and political education. The Juche ideology, at the beginning a propaganda tool of a feeling of aversion to external factors, tends to transform itself into official political ideology through the exasperation of nationalistic sentiment. In this regard, *cf.* H.S. Park, *Human needs and Political Development: A Dissent to Utopian Solutions*, Cambridge (MA), Schenkman, 1984.

140 Y.C. Chung, *The Suryŏng System as the Center of* Juche *Institution*, in J.J. Suh, *Origins of North Korea's Juche*, op cit., 89 ff.

position also lies in the fact that Korea appears as the nation with the highest degree of ethnic homogeneity in the world.[141]

With regard to the complex evolutionary process of the *Juche* ideology, there are those who have proposed a temporal scan in five main phases, underlining how the philosophy reveals itself without a constant conceptual structure (unlike for example Marxism).[142] Starting from the phase in which the ideological emphasis was placed in the anti-repentance sentiment, the *Juche* idea would later establish its theoretical base on the anti-hegemonist element (this refers in particular to the adverse reaction to the US expansionist policy), to then turn out to be an expression of a strong nationalistic feeling, propagandized within a socialist system endowed with a notable paternalistic connotation.

At the same time, numerous ramifications of the *Juche* ideology have been elaborated to concretely guide the social and economic development of the country through orientations, operative instructions and so on, for various sectors; for example, developing *Juche* organizational and technical doctrines and guidelines for industrial agriculture, a certain success in the years preceding the economic crisis of the 1990s of the twentieth century.[143]

The most recent perspective seems to configure a broader ideology and *Weltanshauung*, centred on the essential components of human behaviour, such as conscience (*Uisiksong*), creativity (*Changuisong*) and self-determination (*Jajusong*).[144]

Other important elements can also be highlighted as representing the Juche ideology, such as a declaimed reaction to the previous Korean social structure, rooted in the foundations of Confucianism; but in truth a clear discontinuity between the new interpretation of *Juche* philosophy and the previous moral and social order proposed by Confucianism is not so easy to trace.

The same premise of the *Juche* philosophy, in fact, which recalls the centrality of man in the universe, capable of transforming society and nature, reveals strong affinities with the Confucian ideal of independent social being (*Jaiusong*), both theories aimed at affirming not so much the self-determination solely of an individual, but of the entire

141 The data is quite well known, and can be found for example in the statistics reported since the late 1970s in G. Kurian, *The Book of World Rankings*, New York, Facts on File, 1979.

142 H.S. Park, *North Korea, The Politics of Unconventional Wisdom*, Boulder (CO), Lynne Rienner Pub, 2002. The author points out that the changing nature of the Juche idea is considered a positive element by the Koreans, who emphatically believe that a living ideology must change in the same way that every living being changes.

143 C.A. Yu, *The Rise and Demise of* Juche *Agriculture in North Korea*, in J.J. Suh, *Origins of North Korea's Juche*, op cit., 119 ff.

144 As the "engine" of human behavior, *Uisiksong* needs the creativity of human actions (*Changuisong*) for the realization of its principles. Creativity directs man to achieve the goals that make it possible to achieve the ideal principles in different historical contexts. The idea of *Jaiusong* is reflected instead more in social organization. Self-determination manifests itself on an individual, group and national level and is closely connected with the principles that regulate the organization of work. *Cf.* H.S. Park, *Juche as a Foreign Policy Costraint in North Korea*, in *Asian Perspective*, n. 1, 1987, 11.

nation, structured according to principles of hierarchy, paternalism, and loyalty. Another concrete parallelism can be found in the idea of a leader of the nation legitimated by a divine mandate. The same preamble to the 1998 "Kim Il Sung" Constitution describes the role of the father of the homeland also in very neo-Confucian terms, with references to the Great Leader, believer in the people "as in heaven" (according to other translations in English, "the people is my God"), who dedicated his life to the people "taking care of them and guiding them with a noble politics of benevolence."[145] The Preamble of the 2016 Constitution reports a similar sentence with extended reference to Kim Jong Il. The traditional brush of the literate, is in fact in the symbol of the WPK, in addition to the hammer and sickle of socialist and communist tradition.

It has already been mentioned how Kim Jong Il launched the *Sŏn'gun* policy dating from the 1990s of the twentieth century, later constitutionalized in 2009 and aimed at doctrinally integrating the *Juche* idea by making *Juche* and *Sŏn'gun* the only national ideologies.[146] After Kim Jong Il's death, the statute of the WPK, the Constitution and other fundamental political documents were updated with wider references to the guiding ideas of "Kimilsungism-Kingjongilism."[147]

Today, Kim Jong Un seems to pursue objectives of improving the economy of the country, but without renouncing the extremist approach based on the political tradition of *Juche* and *Sŏn'gun*, affirming rather the *status* of a nuclear power country: the militarization of the state was proposed as the only way to guarantee independence to Korea (historically characterized in foreign policy as "a shrimp between two whales") in the face of interference from nearby and distant powers.

Kimilsongism-Kimjongilism, in its two ideological and historical components of *Juche* and *Sŏn'gun*, precisely intercepts the two oldest and most profound historical aspirations of the Korean nation: independence/self-determination and an effective military defence.

This ideological package reinforces the political legitimacy of the leader, already endowed with his own dynastic legitimacy, who, despite a thousand difficulties, succeeds in obtaining the respect of foreign powers and maintaining the honour of the nation high, underlining the difference with that which occurs in South Korea, represented in the north as a servant country of the invaders. One cannot underestimate the importance of this element of national pride in the Korean mentality, when analysing the resilience and the degree of popular consensus, surprising for many Westerners, which the North Korean *leadership* has enjoyed for nearly seventy years.

---

145 This is signalled by C. Choi, *Law and Justice in Korea*, op cit., 339-340. The essence of the *suryŏngje* in a symbiosis of socialism and Confucianism is also highlighted by Y.C. Chung, *The Suryŏng System as the Center of* Juche *Institution*, op cit., 91.

146 Art. 3 Constitution of 2009; H.S. Park, *Military-First Politics (Songun)*, op cit.

147 Amendment of the statute voted in the 2012 WPK Conference.

3.2.4 *A Sui Generis Model*

The characterization of North Korean society as a socialist and Confucian society, plastically represented in the symbol of WPK, reveals only a part of the truth. To the north of the 38th parallel, it can be stated that an atavistic diffidence towards foreigners, and a strong nationalism, condensed in the *Juche* ideology and in the *Sŏn'gun* politics, has been maintained to a significant extent, together with and a social and political organization that also manifests Korean anthropic-socio-psychological archetypes with deep roots in the country's shamanic and Buddhist culture.

The nationalistic element linked to an ancient specificity and cultural homogeneity is revealed by the recurring presence through the centuries of certain facts, places and legitimizing names often very ancient, of a supernatural or mythological nature, starting from the very names of Korea, Chŏson and Koryŏ, recurrent in the mythical and then historical realms, and still today used to indicate, respectively, the Korea in/of the North and the generically national element.[148]

The authoritarian and absolute government of the *Suryŏng* finds wide legitimacy in the cult, certainly superior to that found in China at the apex of Maoism, of the personality of the *leaders*, in their dynastic and partly supernatural legitimization, in their places and birth dates that become elements of the national identity and national holidays: all of this, assimilates the worship of North Korean leaders to a secular religion, of the state, which has occupied the wide spaces that Korean culture has always reserved for the irrational, the supernatural, the religious, a deliberate choice by Kim Il Sung, born in a very religious Christian family, who repressed Christians and Buddhists with the aim of becoming the only supreme authority for the Koreans, replacing the other deities. According to Korean propaganda, Kim Il Sung was superior to Christ in love, to Buddha in benevolence, to Confucius in virtue, to Muhammad in justice. He fought 100,000 battles, created and keeps alive all material and spiritual things in Korea,[149] owing to the fact that the Korean race is "too pure and virtuous to survive in this evil world without a great and fatherly leader."[150]

Worthy of note and of importance, is the figure of Kim Il Sung, officially characterized as a semi-divine figure, "Human Deity", "the Sun of the nation", as well as, in Confucian style, "Father of all Koreans".[151] His deeds and teachings are part of the education of every

---

148 As in the case of the North Korean airlines, Air Koryo, the Koryo Link cellular network, etc.

149 *See* V. Cha, *The Impossible State: North Korea, Past and Future*, London, The Bodley Head, 72-74.

150 B.R. Myers, *North Korea's Race Problem: What I Learned in Eight Years Reading Propaganda from Inside the Hermit Kingdom*, in *Foreign Policy Magazine*, March–April 2010, 49-52. Note the assonance and substantial coincidence, on this point of North Korean propaganda thought, with that already mentioned (*supra*, note 94 and relative text) of a well-known South Korean intellectual, and one of the major historians of twentieth century law, of the traditionalist area, of that country: P.C. Hahm, cited by C. Choi, *East Asian Jurisprudence*, op cit., 240.

151 S. Ryang, *Reading North Korea: An Ethnological Inquiry*, Cambridge (MA), Harvard East Asian Monographs, 2012, 17-20.

North Korean from an early age. The official calendar of the *Juche* era starts from 15 April 1912, the date of his birth and obviously a national holiday. The year 2016 corresponds to the Juche year 105. A manual of Ten Principles based on total devotion to the Great Leader, and since 2013 also to his son Kim Jong Il, regulates the daily life of all North Koreans.[152]

Kim Jong Il was born in 1941, during the anti-Japanese guerrilla war, according to the official narrative, on Mount Paektu, one of the sacred places of Korean tradition and identity (where *Tan'gun*, founder and first king of the first mythical Chŏson kingdom in 2333 BC, was presumed to have been born), still a destination for visits, rather than, as in reality, in Habarovsk, in Soviet Siberia. In the official narrative, his birth was accompanied by prodigies such as the passage of a comet, lightning and thunder, an iceberg in Lake Paektu that split, the flight of a swallow in the middle of winter, and the winter sky that lit up with a double rainbow.[153]

Kim Jong Il is therefore the "son of God", and superhuman himself: the "bright star of Mount Paektu", son of the "Sun of the nation". Being the superhuman son of a quasi-God, his birth announced by a comet, the fact that his mother Kim Jong Suk is also the object of civil veneration, especially by North Korean women (while this is not the case for the second wife of Kim Il Sung), the Ten Principles, highlight the legitimizing presence of various symbolic elements of the Christian tradition. The sacredness of the two *leaders* and the images or objects that represent them is also prescribed in the Ten Principles, and very seriously sanctioned at the political and police level, recalling the Buddhist traditions of Thailand in mind, and the heavy penalties that result from an insult, even accidental, to the image of the sovereign (there is a risk of very severe prison sentences, for example, by tearing a page of newspaper or trampling a banknote that bears his images).[154]

---

152 Here are some of the principles of 1974: "3. We must make absolute the authority of the Great Leader comrade Kim Il Sung. 4. We must make the Great Leader comrade Kim Il Sung's revolutionary ideology our faith and make his instructions our creed. [...] 8. We must value the political life we were given by the Great Leader comrade Kim Il Sung, and loyally repay his great political trust and thoughtfulness with heightened political awareness and skill". And here are some of 2013: "2. Venerate the Great respected comrades Kim Il Sung and Kim Jong Il as the Great Leaders of the Party and of the People, as the Eternal Suns of Juche. 3. Make the authority of the respected comrades Kim Il Sung and Kim Jong Il and of the Party the absolute one. Be ready to defend them. 4. Arm yourself with revolutionary ideas of the Great respected comrades Kim Il Sung and Kim Jong Il and with the fulfilment of their ideas: the line and the policy of the Party. 5. Defend the principle following unconditionally the commandments of the Great respected comrades Kim Il Sung and Kim Jong Il as well as Party line and its policy".

153 J. Becker, *Rogue Regime: Kim Jong Il and the Looming Threat of North Korea*, Oxford, Oxford University Press, 2005, 91.

154 Anecdotes in this regard are reported in many journalistic and scientific sources. In the commentary apparatus on the Third Principle (2013 version: "3. Make the authority of the respected comrades Kim Il Sung and Kim Jong Il and of the Party the absolute one. Be ready to defend them") the following rules are reported: "Portraits, plaster figures, bronze statues and emblems of the respected and beloved Great Leader, publications that include the Great Leader's portrait, works of art symbolizing the Great Leader, signboards with the Great Leader's instructions, and the party's basic slogans shall all be treated with respect and protected at all costs" (Art. 3.6); "Meaningful books and relics of the history of the revolution, which are imbued

The superhuman legitimacy of the *Suryŏng* follows a high degree of acceptance of the facts of earthly life on the part of the people, with a consensus and even an enthusiasm and a sincere devotion to their *leaders* in spite of all adversities, beyond the repressive element present in that society, that do not cease to amaze many Western observers.[155]

Times undoubtedly change even in North Korea, and it would have been difficult to have the excessive repetition of certain iconographic elements also legitimizing the young Kim Jong Un; but, undoubtedly the construction of his myth is underway. Extolling his military and governing virtues (after his grandfather and his father, respectively "Great Leader" and "Dear Leader", he is often referred to as the "Great Successor" or "Respected Marshal"). The fact remains that even the transition in his favour, which must not have been easy, as far as we know,[156] was accompanied by the appointment of his late father as Eternal *Chairman* of the National Defence Commission and the WPK's Eternal Secretary General, and the joint writing by his father and his grandfather of the 2012 Constitution that legitimizes his power, reproducing elements already seen in the previous dynastic transition.[157]

Overall, that of North Korean, is an authoritarian, hierarchical and militarized political system, undoubtedly also due to the fact that it is connected to a state of tension or permanent conflict, with a dynasty of leaders who are certainly superhuman if not rather semi-divine, endowed with a supernatural legitimacy, as well as a legitimizing force that goes beyond their earthly life. "Sun of the Nation" sovereigns that are reminiscent of the Japanese emperors, the *elites* of kings and Buddhist warrior monks of Korean history and going

---

with the Great Leader comrade Kim Il Sung's great revolutionary history and achievements, shall be handled and maintained with respect and protected at all costs". (Art. 3.7).

155 As reported by all observers and writers who have dealt with North Korea; *see, e.g.*, H.L. Hunter, *Kim Il Song's North Korea*, Westport CT, Greenwood-Praeger, 1999, 262. *See* V. Cha, *The Impossible State*, op cit., 9-10, points out that even the defectors continue to demonstrate in nine cases out of ten feelings of a North Korean national identity, rather than a Korean identity; and in 75% of cases also sincere affection towards the figures of Kim Il Sung and Kim Jong Il.

156 The four constitutional reforms testify in five years, the numerous purges and death sentences, including that of his uncle Jang Sun Taek (and according to the South Korean and Western press also of many of his family), indicated by analysts as the main advisor of Kim Jong Il in his later years, and "regent" alongside the young Kim Jong Un after the death of the former; and the celebration of the first Congress of the party after 36 years to consecrate his role at the highest political level; the murder in February 2017, in still mysterious circumstances, of Kim Jong Nam, Kim Jong Un's older brother: initially considered the predestined to succeed his father, and then fell into disgrace and forced into exile between Macao and Beijing, had good relations with Beijing and was thought could still constitute a political threat to the younger brother. The new leader, much younger than most members of the country's military and administrative political summits, seems to have been adept at overcoming the initial perplexities of many – earning loyalty especially in the military, continuing the Sŏn'gun policy and the nuclear program – affirming what seems to be an absolute power.

157 In the 2016 Constitution Preamble Kim Il Sung and Kim Jong Il are described together as the "sun of the nation" and the "star of reunification".

further back in time, the king-soldier-priests of the ancient Korean solar cults in the Bronze Age.

The North Korean socialist society has long been, and still is, stratified in a caste system (*Songbun*), in accordance with a system desired by Kim Il Sung and adopted by the WPK in 1957. It classifies citizens according to their demonstrated or perceived loyalty, or that of their families during the years of anti-Japanese resistance, to the cause of national independence and the party: "friends", "uncertain", and "enemies".[158] Based on one's classification, in principle immutable in the course of one's life, stem duties, expectations, and limits to existential possibilities: access to education and to the various occupations and careers is regulated by one's classification; citizens belonging to the third group cannot reside in Pyongyang, in other major cities, in areas near the borders, nor become members of the WPK.[159]

Within the three groups, there is obviously a further stratification, normally linked to the bureaucratic status and work position of the individual. The severity of the system partly eased after the end of world communism, and especially with the economic crisis of the 1990s; a greater number of economic-social opportunities and upgrading have become available as economic opening progresses.[160]

The cast structure of society has a quite direct historical antecedent with that of the Chŏson dynasty, where the people, below the families of the so-called "bone" nobility, were divided into the three macro-castes of officials, municipalities, and servants and the outcast.[161]

Even more clear is the historical connection with the Chŏson age, of the North Korean legislation of the early 1970s of the twentieth century, regarding collective criminal liability, which for certain serious crimes involves penalties not only for the offender but also for the two generations subsequent to them.[162] And likewise that on political responsibility, which in North Korea also falls in many cases on the children, as seems certain from the information of various kinds regarding imprisonment in the labour camps, generating a real caste of outcasts in North Korean society. All seems to be in clear continuity with some Chŏson penal/administrative rules, which for example precluded participation in examinations for descendants of particular categories of persons (immoral women, *yangban*

158 Resolution of the WPK of 30 May 1957.

159 H.L. Hunter, op cit., 3-11; A. Lankov, *North of the DMZ: Essays on Daily Life in North Korea*. Jefferson (NC), McFarland & Co. 2007, 66-67.

160 A. Lankov, *North Korea's New Class System*, in *Asia Times Online*, www.atimes.com, 3 December 2012. Accessed 30 December 2016.

161 C.J. Eckert, K. Lee, Y.I. Lew, M. Robinson, E.W. Wagner, *Korea Old and New*, Chap. 9.

162 M.J. Chung, *The Political and Social Roles of the Sŏwŏn in the Chosŏn Dynasty*, in J.B. Duncan, J.C. Lee, J. Lee, M. Ahn, J.A. Dawey (Eds.), *The Institutional Basis of Civil Governance...*, op cit., 64-67.

concubines) or for the children of those responsible for certain crimes (such as embezzlement by officials).[163]

It seems to be possible to say that North Korea has strongly maintained the Chŏson traditions regarding the centrality of the family element, not only in the sociological sense but also in the political sense and with respect to important criminal and administrative legal aspects. Membership in a family has effects that, for better or for worse, transcend the life of the individual and are transferred to their relatives and descendants, whether it be the *Suryŏng*, whose close relatives occupy prominent positions in the public apparatus,[164] or the last citizen/subject.

Family relationships in Korea are important, as the Yuan Mongolian emperors comprehended well in implementing their Korean policy through marriages with the Kŏryo kings. Sometimes they are complex and dangerous relationships, as evidenced by the turbulent events of the regents during the anomalies of the dynastic process: that of the *Taewŏn'gun* in the late nineteenth century, the recent episode of Jang Sun Taek, uncle of the young Kim Jong Un, during the transition in the aftermath of the death of Kim Jong Il, the existential parable and the assassination in 2017 of Kim Jong Nam, brother of the Respected Marshal: all, signal a tendency to intra-family conflict within the *elites* that does not seem so equally marked in the histories of China and Japan.

The familism, personalism and other elements previously discussed that characterize the society, politics and North Korean institutions render the system monolithic and impenetrable from the outside, susceptible to complex internal dynamics that can emerge especially in the dynastic passages, and to a lesser extent, changes in the political cycle related to the renewal of the SPA and the major offices in the Party. These dynamics involve instrumental and, if necessary, rapid changes in the constitutional, institutional and legislative framework based on the contingent political needs of the *leaders* (see the various constitutional changes, and the various denominations of the top institutional and political offices, previously discussed). This trend does not exempt the territorial *governance* structures, with reported incidents of special territorial organizations and systems that follow changing political guidelines and in some cases the political trajectories of individual characters.

The institutions and the few laws, generally quite modelled on the Chinese example, are therefore characterized by this instrumental nature, realizing a model that can be characterized as substantially that of the *rule of men/rule of politics*, with some limited but slowly increasing applicability of the *rule by law* model in the sectors of international economic activity.

---

163 *Ibid.*

164 Many close-knit leaders have traditionally played leading roles in the North Korean institutional and political system; *see* V. Cha, B. Hwang, *Government and Politics*, in R.L. Worden (Ed.), *North Korea: A Country Study*, Federal Research Division, Library of Congress, 5th edn, 2008, 183-187.

The "private law" activities of North Korean citizens have become ever increasingly important. In fact, they became necessary after years of economic crisis that had slowed down and then interrupted towards the end of the twentieth century, the public system of distribution to the citizens of goods/assets, which provided for all their needs, and that today continues to do so but only in a small way. A "grey" market economy, initially officially non-existent but, between highs and lows, tolerated and finally legalized since 1998 but still today officially marginal (with the vegetable gardens for the farmers and the "sideline activities" referred to in Art. 24 para. 3 of the Constitution) and unofficially even encouraged, has becomes more and more important with the birth of unofficial markets of all kinds in which the North Korean market economy is developing – with dynamics at least partly already seen in China, South Korea, Vietnam, Taiwan.[165]

The phase of simple sales or exchanges of agricultural products by farmers has been overcome for years (Art. 24 para. 3 of the Constitution), with the ever-increasing presence of an emerging urban class, perhaps the first nucleus of a future middle class modelled on the Chinese socio-economic example, which lives and thrives through entrepreneurial activities outside the official system of state policy and economy, with lifestyles, purchases of expensive goods (e.g. cars) and levels of unimaginable expenses for the country's workers and peasants. All of this, maintaining, necessarily, good relations with all the political, administrative and control systems.[166] Overall, this has helped to determine, together with the agricultural reforms of some success in recent years, a noticeable general economic progress in the country.[167]

Future developments include a certain degree of legalization of all these activities, which will correspond to a certain degree of abandonment of the unofficial ways of public *governance* of the phenomenon, and private management of individual activities and disputes.

---

165 All the writings of the last years, of an academic or journalistic nature, refer to the emergence of a grey market economy after the collapse of the public distribution system, with operators able today to significantly improve their economic position through, and in general, with a society that is visibly changing in a market sense, A. Lankov, *North Korea's New Class System*, op cit.; F. Abt (Swiss businessman who conducted various entrepreneurial activities in North Korea), *a Capitalist in North Korea*, Hong Kong, Tuttle, 2014, *passim*; J. Everard (formerly British Ambassador to North Korea), *Only Beautiful, Please*, Stanford (CA), The W. H. Shorenstein Asia Pacific Research Center, 2012, *passim*; *Id.*, *The Markets of Pyongyang*, in Korea Economic Institute, 6 *Academic Paper Series*, January 2011, Art. 1.

166 Reported from all sources. The tolerance or acquiescence of government and police apparatuses is the result of both a political indication from above and of reported corruption phenomena. North Korea is constantly, in the last or second last place, together with Somalia, in the world ranking of the countries with the highest corruption index (or with the lowest index of absence of corruption) produced annually by the NGO Transparency International; www.transparency.org.

167 A. Lankov, *Kim Jong-un's Recipe for Success: Private Enterprise and Public Executions*, in *The Guardian*, 7 October 2015, www.theguardian.com/world/2015/oct/07/north-korea-recipe-for-success-economic-liberalisation-public-executions. It denies the economic success stated above by the South Korean academic Lee Chongkoo, *Autoinsufficienza, la via del nord all'autarchia*, in *Limes* 2016 n. 12, *La Corea è una bomba*, 73 ff.

3.2.5 Fundamental Rights

The various rewritings of the fundamental charter of the DPRK have never changed the collectivist principle that regulates the enjoyment of rights by individual citizens.

North Korea has adhered to many of the main international human rights conventions: the country is endowed with laws of internal legal infrastructures formally intended to implement the dictates of the Universal Declaration of Human Rights and the International Covenant on Civil and Political Rights, or has revised them during the last decade. Therefore, in addition to the Constitutional Charter, there are also laws such as the judicial system, procedural codes, the penal code and the laws for the execution of criminal law, public security laws, laws on administrative sanctions, administrative litigation, a general law on civil law and family law, succession, civil liability, a law on the profession of a lawyer, and so on. Many internal laws incorporate international law in the field of cultural and social rights, including a relatively large employment and social security legislation, the protection and education of minors, health, the environment and others.[168]

The idea of "fundamental rights", introduced in the Constitution of 2009 with the new Article 8[169] is however expressly subject to the collectivist principle, and to the idea of development of the rights of each individual via the priority collective development of the society produced by socialism.[170] Simultaneously, the application of laws is also subordinate and instrumental to political directives, all in accordance with a model already seen in action in the People's Republic of China, with today's level of development of the legal dimension, in real terms and not merely declamatory, perhaps comparable with that of the People's Republic in the early 1980s of the twentieth century.

In practice, the existence of a totalitarian repressive regime prevents each citizen, in practice, from benefiting from the usual list of fundamental rights contained in the Constitution and individual protection, especially through legal means. The subordination of rights to the collectivist principle is almost complete and implemented through policies, to an extent and with methods outside and beyond any international *standard*.[171]

---

168 A list of North Korean laws implementing international law on fundamental rights can be found in *White Paper on Human Rights in North Korea* del 2014, Korea Institute for National Unification, 80-90.

169 "The State shall safeguard the interests, respect and protect the human rights of the working people".

170 The articles 62 ff. Constitutions of 2009 and 2016 constitute the chapter dedicated to the fundamental rights of citizens; Art. 63 states "In the Democratic People's Republic of Korea the rights and duties of citizens are based on the collectivist principle: 'One for all and all for one'." Para. 2 of Art. 64 in addition states "In the Democratic People's Republic of Korea the rights and freedoms of citizens shall be amplified with the consolidation and development of the socialist system."

171 This is the result of a UN Commission of Inquiry published in 2014; report text and other details on the website of the *UN Office of the High Commissioner for Human Rights*, www.ohchr.org; *see also* the *White Paper on Human Rights in North Korea* annually produced (in South Korea) by the Korea Institute for National Unification, rich in data and news; the latest available is 2015.

It seems that a significant percentage, variable depending on the sources, but at least 1%, of the population of the country is interned in labour camps for common or political reasons, including conduct such as access to illegal information (radio, television, South Korean, Chinese, Western media). This often happens in the absence of any legal framework and substantial or procedural guarantees, and for very long terms or for life. Illegal arrest and detention often involve entire households, including children, and not just the perpetrators of real or alleged crimes, implementing a principle of responsibility extended to the group (*yeon-jwa-je*, "guilt by association").[172]

In these detention centres, which officially do not exist, it is reported that people are kept alive in sub-human living conditions and in total violation of every standard, subject to torture and abuse of all kinds, doing forced labour and dedicating themselves to procuring food and all other fundamental needs.[173] Various sources, investigative journalism, accounts of defectors and fugitives,[174] also show how in these camps, families are born and children are born, destined to grow up working from an early age (the camps are actually quite large territorial areas, microcosms with a complex socio-economic organization, also equipped with rudimentary schools).[175]

The problem of human rights violation in North Korea is a very serious problem which, together with the nuclear issue, generates for the country, which officially denies any such problem,[176] condemnation, isolation and sanctions.[177]

Naturally, one of the objectives pursued (this does not necessarily mean achieved) with the adherence to international conventions and with the adoption of legal instruments on fundamental rights can certainly be to lighten the climate of general condemnation for the country at an international level. Another of the effects, perhaps of longer duration, entirely desired or not, of the construction of an internal legal infrastructure could however be the actual improvement of the situation in this regard, where and when the internal political conditions permit. However, all will probably be very tied to economic dynamics, and to the need for the country's *elite*, in part in conflict with that of encouraging economic development, to maintain a cast-iron grip over the country. There is not sufficient data to make predictions either on the results or on the times.

---

172 2014 UN Commission of Inquiry, 227-228.

173 2014 UN Commission of Inquiry.

174 Among the best known, Kang Chol-Hwan, P. Rigoulot, *The Aquariums of Pyongyang*, London, Atlantic Books, 2001; B. Harden, *Escape From Camp 14*, London, Pan Books, 2013. News of this kind must obviously be examined carefully and with every reservation, but the quantity of converging accounts is an objective fact to be taken into account. *See also* V. Cha, *The Impossible State*, op cit., 162 ff.

175 Commission of Inquiry of the N.U. 2014, especially 243; B. Harden, *Escape From Camp 14*, op cit., *passim*.

176 "There is no 'human rights issue' in this country, as everyone leads the most dignified and happy life"; KCNA (the official North Korean news agency), 6 March 2009.

177 With frequent discussions on the violations of human rights in North Korea also in the UN Security Council, accompanied by resolutions of condemnation, requests for activation of international criminal proceedings for crimes against humanity, and more.

3.2.6 *Governments and Institutions*

The North Korean institutional and juridical system can be described as the combination of the Soviet model of Stalinist origin, the Chinese model, roughly implemented, in the periods just before and shortly after the "Maoist cultural revolution" (1966-1976), and that of traditional and political elements, exclusively Korean.[178]

North Korea is, constitutionally, a people's republic that expressly defines itself as "socialist" and based on the "democratic dictatorship of the people". The national political community is characterized by the three pillars of the Party, in a position of pre-eminence, the armed forces and the state apparatus.

The armed forces, which in the USSR were certainly part of the state apparatus and included in the hierarchical structure of the government, are in a more grey position in China. They were founded well before the creation of PRC, as an armed wing of the Party. Today they are undoubtedly part of the Chinese state and subject to the political leadership of the Communist Party, but are constitutionally and institutionally external to the government apparatus, under the guidance of the Central Military Commission, a constitutional body external to the State Council (the Chinese government). The North Korean model imitated, up to the constitutional reform of 2016, the Chinese model, with the National Defence Commission which had an external and politically superior position to that of the government, as had already appeared in the previous constitutions and was clearly formalized in the 1998 Charter and still more in the *Sŏn'gun* Constitution of 2009. The constitutional reform of 2016 replaced the NDC with a State Affairs Commission, a wider body, envisaging a National Defence Committee only in time of war.[179]

The *Presidium* or Standing Committee of the Supreme People's Congress, the legislative body, is, according to the classic communist model of the People's Republic of China, the organ that expresses political and institutional leadership in all the governmental apparatus within the State. After the assignment to Kim Il Sung of the country's eternal presidency (1998), the *Chairman of the Presidium*[180] served as Head of State[181] until the constitutional reform of 2016, which created the State Affairs Council, assigning to its President, the position of Head of State.[182]

---

178 P. Goedde, *Law "Of Our Own Style": The Evolution and Challenges of the North Korean Legal System*, in 27 *Fordham International Law Journal*, 2003, n. 4, Art. 1, *passim*; R.L. Worden, *North Korea: A Country Study*, Federal Research Division, Library of Congress, 5th edn, 2008.

179 Constitution of 2016, Art. 103.

180 Role held at the time by Kim Yong Nam, while Kim Jong Il held the position of *Chairman* of the Party and of the National Defence Commission.

181 V. Cha, B. Hwang, *The Structure of Government*, in R.L. Worden, *North Korea: A Country Study*, Federal Research Division, Library of Congress, 5th edn, 2008, Chap. 6, 196-203.

182 Constitution of 2016, Art. 100 ff.

The structure of the apparatus of government mirrors to an extent that of China, albeit in a slightly simplified form, being based on three "main" levels of government: central, provincial (9 provinces and three/four cities, with continuously changing data, with a status equivalent to that of a province), district or county; and finally a fourth local level (for individual city districts or single villages in counties) which perform only administrative functions of the simplest type.[183] The model of government is similar to the Chinese model characterized by the absence of "checks and balances", and by the distribution of administrative power and functions of the State according to horizontal flows within each level: the elective assembly body represents the community of reference, and its elective mandate represents a political cycle within it. The elective body, in principle, carries out regulatory, political, nomination and supervision functions on the work of executive, judicial and public prosecutor's bodies at the same level, functions, in practice, often carried out by standing committees and by central and local government bodies.[184]

The Supreme People's Assembly, elected with a five-year mandate and in ordinary session twice a year, therefore appoints the *Chairman* of the State Affairs Council, the Prime Minister and the ministers; its *Presidium* executes legislative activities, the authentic interpretation of all laws, even those issued by the Supreme People's Assembly in plenary;[185] the model reproduces, quite faithfully, as stated, the Soviet and Chinese models.

Financial flows for the functioning of the institutional apparatus are also horizontal, with the central and local assembly bodies that approve the budget of all the institutional bodies at the corresponding level, proposed by the local government. The governing bodies at the various levels also recruit and administer civil servants at their corresponding level, including judges and public prosecutors.[186]

The "horizontal" distribution of the governance functions at the various levels is supplemented by a "vertical" administrative supervision, carried out by each administrative body of the upper level on the corresponding organs of the lower levels.

Juxtaposed to this complex grid of institutional power flows exists another constituted by the party apparatus and also characterized by the same levels, and by territorial and functional partitions. The party provides the principal cadres to the state administrations and exercises political supervision over their work.[187]

The judiciary consists of the two pyramids of the judiciary and public prosecution, structured on three levels: central, provincial and basic, corresponding to the three highest levels of the general institutional scheme, while it is not present at the lower level of the

183 V. Cha, B. Hwang, *The Structure of Government*, op cit., 196-203; *Understanding North Korea 2014*, publication of the South Korean Ministry for Unification, Part II, *Political System and Governing Principles*.

184 *Understanding North Korea 2014*, publication of the South Korean Ministry for Unification, 73 ff.; M. Zimbardo, *Corea*, op cit., 162-163.

185 *Ibid.*

186 *Ibid.*

187 V. Cha, B. Hwang, op cit., 187-193; 208 ff.; *Understanding North Korea 2014*, op cit., 67 ff.

administrative offices of villages or neighbourhoods.[188] Benches, in the first instance, are composed of a judge and two people's councillors.[189] In addition, there are also special military judges, judges for the administration of the railways, and an arbitration committee for maritime disputes.[190]

In addition to the "ordinary" territorial structure of the North Korean institutional apparatus, various "special" areas exist, in which socio-economic experiments open to the market economy and attraction of foreign investments, operate, along the lines of the Special Economic Zones (SEZs) of the People's Republic of China, promoted by Deng Xiaoping, which, since the late 1970s, have witnessed a growth of the Chinese "socialist market economy". In these areas there are special laws and local regulations which tend to be aimed at encouraging foreign investments and the development of industrial and commercial activities.

The number and denominations of these areas has changed considerably in the last twenty years or so. Essentially, only a few SEZs operated, in areas subject to specific South Korean investments: the industrial park of Kaesong (2002), developed and managed essentially by Hyundai, following cooperation agreements between the two Koreas, in which the manpower is from the North of the country and the corporate executives from the South, governed by special regulatory instruments issued by both countries, and no longer operational, since January 2016, due to political tensions; the Rason area, the first Economic and Trade Zone (1991), in the north-east near the border with China and Russia; and the tourist area of Mount Kumsan (2002).[191]

In the first decade of the twentieth century, a SAR was founded in the city of Sinuiju, in the north-west of the country bordering China, reproducing or trying to reproduce a model of immense autonomy, with its own legislative, executive and judicial bodies, its own policy on the movement of people, goods, services and capital, and in general a socio-political and economic model different from that of the *Mainland*, to which only the authority on foreign affairs, defence and business of national importance remained. Sinuiju's SAR was also based on a Basic Law (a quasi-constitutional specification, *Kibonpŏp* in Korean), in a similar way to the two Chinese SARs of Hong Kong and Macao, and with an official coat of arms similar to that of the two Chinese regions.[192] The SAR, established

188 M. Zimbardo, *Corea*, op cit., 163; V. Cha, B. Hwang, capitolo *The Structure of Government*, op cit., 196-203.

189 M. Zimbardo, *Corea*, op cit., 163.

190 *Ibid.*

191 V. A. Abrahamian, C. Melvin, *North Korean Special Economic Zones: Plans vs. Progress*, online on the North Korea news and analysis site (run by a North American-South Korean research program) 38North.org, 23 November 2015, http://38north.org/wp-content/uploads/2015/11/38-North-SEZ-Plans-v-Progress-112315.pdf; *see also* the site of information and analysis *North Korean Economic Watch*, which reports in detail and well indexed news also official on each of the areas in question. www.nkeconwatch.com/category/economic-reform/special-economic-zones-2/.

192 On the SAR in Hong Kong and Macao, *see* I. Castellucci, *Legal Hybridity in Hong Kong and Macau*, in 57 *McGill Law Journal*, 2012, n. 4, 1, 665-720.

in 2002, has never really started, having suffered a fatal arrest due to the personal events of its key player: a Sino-Dutch businessman who had obtained the institution, and his appointment as a first governor, thanks to his personal relationship with Kim Jong Il, who fell into political and judicial disgrace in China shortly after the establishment of the Korean SAR.[193] The area was renamed the International Trade Zone in 2013.

Dating from 2013, the model seems to have transformed into the creation of a greater number of less autonomous Special Areas, even smaller than the few established in the first wave. To date, there are a total of about fifteen areas of various names, including those of the International Trade Zone, the International Tourist Zone, the High Tech Development Zone, and the currently most widespread of the Economic Development Zones (EDZs).[194]

The economic results do not seem exciting to date, when comparing the North Korean experience with that of the Chinese areas in the 1980s of the twentieth century: the Korean special areas are created, extinguished, scrape along, and often change denomination, often also in relation to the personal events of prominent figures.[195] Foreign investment is lower than expected, probably due to an insufficient government strategy for the development of these areas, and a low level of certainty regarding the applicable rules and their stability.[196]

The objectively detectable *trend*, however, is that of a slow growth, as well as an increase in the number of these special areas, and certainly of a slow cultural and economic *spillover* effect, even within the "common" North Korean society.

3.2.7 *The Normative Sources and the Legal System*

A manual, "The Ten Principles for the Establishment of the One-Ideology System," published by Kim Jong Il in 1974, in which Kim Il Sung is placed at the centre of the political system, with a full interpenetration between the nation and the *Suryŏng*, and suggestive

193 F. Tertitsky, *The Ill-fated Sinuiju Special Region*, on the website of data research and news on North Korea NKNews.org, 27 January 2015, www.nknews.org/2015/01/the-ill-fated-sinuiju-special-region/.

194 *See* A. Abrahamian, C. Melvin, *North Korean Special Economic Zones: Plans vs. Progress*, op. cit., *passim*; *see also North Korean Economic Watch*: www.nkeconwatch.com/category/economic-reform/special-economic-zones-2/. It should be noted that in literature the terms SEZ and EDZ are also used in a generic and fungible way to indicate any other type of area.

195 In addition to the already cited case of Sinuiju, *see also* the un-developing story of the SEZ of Hwanggumpyeong and Wihwa, initially, part of a project to create special areas along the border with China promoted by Jang Song Taek (the uncle of the leader, regent after the death of Kim Jong Il, purged in 2015): A. Cathcart, *In the Shadow of Jang Song-taek: Pyongyang's evolving SEZs Strategy with the Hwanggumpyeong and Wihwa Islands*, Academic Papers Series 2014, on the website of the Korea Economic Institute of America, 19 June 2014, www.keia.org/publication/shadow-jang-song-taek-pyongyang's-evolving-sez-strategy-hwanggumpyeong-and-wihwa-islands.

196 A. Abrahamian, C. Melvin, *North Korean Special Economic Zones*, op cit., *passim*.

tones, between politics and mysticism, is the basis of the daily life of all North Koreans, and is the ultimate source of any political or legal rule.[197]

The ten principles are accompanied by a commentary and more detailed rules. They are studied in schools, the workplace and political indoctrination centres. They were revised and "re-launched" in 2013, incorporating the figure of Kim Jong Il and his ideology, on an equal footing with that of Kim Il Sung, and strengthening the political role of the WPK, whose directives are stated immediately after those of the leader in the list of political sources.[198]

In addition to these sources, the picture is completed by the so-called "Instructions" by Kim Il Sung, related to various sectors of the economy and social life, often issued by the Great Leader during inspections in localities and production sites (the so-called "on-the-spot guidance") and still today in force. Their political binding nature, superior to that of any party law or directive, is consecrated in the Ten Principles, and was extended in 2013 to the instructions of Kim Jong Il.[199]

After Kim Il Sung's death, the problem of the potentially unlimited effectiveness of these instructions over time, arose. The problem of their modification or revocation was resolved through a posthumous interpretation of the leader's thinking, referring to the constitutional precepts of 1998 on the eternal Presidency assigned to Kim Il Sung, in order to allow its evolutionary interpretation and adaptation to new circumstances, obviously inspired by the Eternal president – the then living leader Kim Jong Il. The same mechanism is reproduced today, with the figure, the thinking and instructions of Kim Jong Il consecrated in the Ten Principles, and his son Kim Jong Un, dynastically invested in the role of *leader*.

The importance of this type of directive, beyond the formal value of a source of law, which in a political system such as that of North Korean may not be a very important subject, has remained central to this day: this can be seen from the official photographs of the visits and inspections in the field of Kim Jong Un, circulating also abroad with relative abundance, in which invariably one can see elders and decorated generals, senior officials and managers always intent to take notes in small notebooks.[200]

---

197 *White paper on Human Rights in North Korea* 2014, op cit., 84-85.

198 All available analyses agree on the purpose of the review, to stabilize the political legitimacy of Kim Jong Un as a new leader and to reinforce the party's role (with respect to the pre-eminent role of the armed forces of the *Sŏn'gun* period); K.S. Oh, *Main Contents of Revised Version of Ten Principles and Their Political Significance*, the Political Development and Policy, Seoul, Sejong Institute, 2013, 13; *White paper on Human Rights in North Korea* 2014, op cit., 90-91, F. Tertiskiy, *The Party's Ten Principles Then and Now*, in NKNews.org, 11 December 2014, www.nknews.org/2014/12/the-partys-10-principles-then-and-now/; Kang Mi Jin, *NK Adds Kim Jong Il to 'Ten Principles'*, in *DailyNK*, 9 August 2013, www.dailynk.com/english/read.php?num=10828&cataId=nk01500.

199 Principles Nos. 4 and 5, both in the original draft of 1974 and in the 2013 revision.

200 The *White Paper on Human Rights in North Korea* del 2014, op cit., 84-85, reports statistics resulting from interviews with North Korean defectors on the perceived importance of regulatory sources in North Korea,

It goes without saying, that legislation is an apparatus of norms of a political rank lower than the cited sources, and that it has an instrumental nature and a vocation to politically oriented and supervised application, in the political tradition of communist and socialist countries, and as very clearly expressed by the *Dear Leader* himself: "Our laws are important weapons for the realization of our national policies".[201]

The laws are issued by the Supreme People's Assembly or by the *Presidium*, regardless of the point of view of the subject and without any difference in hierarchical value. In fact, it is the *Presidium* that produces most of the laws, while the Supreme People's Assembly, in session once a year, only approves the budget laws and those of greater ideological importance, imitating the Chinese model.[202]

Since 1994, two parallel legal systems exist regarding the authorized economic activities on the state territory: the national laws and the so-called exceptional laws.

National laws have a general application and tend to preserve aspects of limitation and subjection to the collectivist principle of individual economic rights. The exceptional laws recognize certain rights in relation to the economic activities regulated therein, or in relation to activities that may be performed in some "special" geographical areas (the various SEZ, SAR, EDZ, ITZ, etc.). Both the former ("common exceptional laws") and the latter ("special exceptional laws") are configured as exceptional regimes, permitting economic activities and interaction with non-national citizens and entities that are otherwise not permitted.[203]

Presumably, as in China too, more and more problems of coordination between the two types of rules, and increasing infiltrations of the "exceptional" economic model in the "national" civil society, will emerge.

On the one hand, with regards to national law, the general subordination of the law to the ideological and political element is known, ascertained and based on an intense process of socialization and indoctrination of society.

On the other hand, the bringing together of the principles of international commercial law within "exceptional laws", applicable in limited special areas, permits an exception to the national system without, at least on paper, any violation of the precepts imposed by ideological orthodoxy, following the Chinese example from the era of Deng Xiaoping onwards.

Thus the laws intended for the regulation of foreign trade and foreign investments seemed to have been characterized, starting from the early 1990s, by a sort of "technical permissiveness" that permitted the adoption of solutions that were progressively more

---

which roughly confirm the following hierarchical structure (descending order of importance): Ten Principles – Instructions – Party Guidelines – Constitution, Penal Code and other laws.

201 Kim Jong Il, *On Strenghtening Socialist Lawful Life*, Pyongyang, KWP Publishers, 1989, 11.

202 V. Cha, B. Hwang, *Government and Politics*, in R.L. Worden, *North Korea: A Country Study*, Federal Research Division, Library of Congress, 5th edn. 2008, 196-199.

203 D.C. Zook, *Reforming North Korea: Law, Politics and the Market Economy*, in 48 *Stanford Journal of International Law* 131 (2012), 131 ff., 156-182.

conciliatory with the rules of international trade regulation. The technical neutrality of these precepts permitted a doubling of the functions of the law, which on the one hand, presents itself with a sufficient technical (and persuasive) character to the external interlocutor, while in practice, it is subordinated in its application to the procedures of the ministerial bodies for the political and administrative supervision of economic activities and external relations, the general residual of the "national" norms, with a consequential applicability of the socialist mechanisms of supervision and control, and, finally, to the normal applicability of litigious or national arbitration procedures in the absence of negotiated resolutions in disputes between foreign investors and North Korean public entities.[204]

The "national" laws include a relatively wide range of normative acts that affect the areas of administrative, penal, civil and economic law (for example, banks and insurance), the civil procedure, penal procedure and that for administrative appeals;[205] the notary and the legal profession are regulated by law, with lawyers who, in a similar way to China until 1996, are still public officials, assigned to individual cases by their professional supervision body.[206] The number of lawyers with technical skills is increasing;[207] laws increase in quantity and quality, and are published, even in collections; since 1999, at the Kim Il Sung University of Pyongyang law courses have been run, in which students also study Soviet and Chinese law;[208] there is also a Pyongyang Business School in which the Master program teaches an "Introduction to International Commercial Law and Practices" using materials in English.[209]

The technical language and the conceptual structure of civil, procedural and penal law, beyond the level of sophistication undoubtedly very different, is always that, typical of all North-East Asia, of German-Japanese matrix, which in the course of the twentieth century was also exported to Mainland China, Korea (and then to the two Koreas), and Taiwan, with colorations of legal socialism, where applicable. There is a law on civil law, dated 1990, based on the model of the "General Principles of Civil Law" of 1986. It is not a complete civil code, in the sense intended on the European continent, but principles that, in turn, refer to the pandectist model, consisting in a sort of simplified and politicized version of the general part of the BGB and the basic principles of the main areas of civil

---

204 D.C. Zook, *Reforming North Korea*, op cit., 160.

205 C. Choi, *Law and Justice in Korea*, op cit., 344-349.

206 P. Goedde, *Law "Of Our Own Style": The Evolution and Challenges of the North Korean Legal System*, in 27 *Fordham International Law Journal*, 2003, n. 4, Art. 1, 1277, indicated between 500 and 1000.

207 P. Goedde, in *Law "Of Our Own Style"*, 2003, indicated between 500 and 1000.

208 M.P. Spina Jr., *Brushes with the Law: North Korea and the Rule of Law*, in Korea Economic Institute, 2 *Academic Paper Series*, June 2007, n. 6, *passim*; Yonhap Press Agency, Seoul, *North Korean Handbook*, Armonk NY, Sharpe, 2003, 152-153.

209 A photo of the materials distributed in the course is published on p. 205 of F. Abt, *A Capitalist in North Korea*, op cit.

law, with contents also inspired by the Soviet Civil Code of 1964, for example in dealing with property (which may be of the State, of cooperative entities, and citizens for consumer goods and personal use only). The Civil Law Act consists of 271 articles and four parts: the first with general principles, rules on subjects and negotiation deeds; the second, on property; the third, on mandatory relationships; and the fourth on civil liability. There are separate laws on family law (1990) and on successions (2002), reflecting Korean rules and traditions. The code of civil procedure is dated 1976, and was revised in 1994, with provisions typically inspired by the "rule of politics", which indicate in the political guidance of the country, the source of the principles applicable in court, or which permit the public prosecution organ to intervene in any civil trial to protect public interest, or to annul a trial and restart it with an "extraordinary appeal" in the event of a "erroneous"[210] decision. The year 1995 saw the enactment of a law on private international law for matters of property, family and succession, established, it seems, to regulate the successor relationships of the citizens of the Korean diaspora, in particular in Japan.[211]

Even with the rapid changes of recent years, the system of "national" laws is still a fairly primordial socialist legality system, in terms of quantity and quality of laws, and due to their perceived importance and objective social role. The majority of public and private activities in North Korea are regulated through political, administrative and traditional channels; the collective interests of intellectuals, soldiers, peasants and workers are protected through these channels by a series of political-administrative hierarchical apparatuses controlled at the vertex by the Supreme Procuratorship.[212] The role of the courts, in addition to the exercise of criminal jurisdiction is still, typically, almost only that of dealing with divorce cases.[213]

For the remainder, the volume of "national" legal activities in the civil sector is still small or minimal, as also seen in the evolution of the Chinese model of the 1970s and 1980s of the twentieth century. It can be considered plausible that even in North Korea, a juridical system modelled on the Chinese model, and operating on principles similar to those of the socialist model of legality, one could say, of political legality, or *Juche* legality, develops along trajectories associated with progress in the socio-economic context.[214] Indeed, by solidly maintaining the dimensions of control and repression for as long as

210 J.H. Roh, *On North Korean Laws*, Chap. 6, available on the website of the *Columbia Law School*, www2.law.columbia.edu/course_00S_L9436_001/2005/class.doc (accessed 11 January 2017). Those described in the text are all mechanisms, moreover, also envisaged in the Civil Code of China. C. Choi, *Law and Justice in Korea*, op cit., 345-346.

211 C. Kim, *The 1995 Private International Law of North Korea*, in 29 California Western International Law Journal, 1998, n. 1, Art. 6, 205 ff.

212 V. Cha, B. Hwang, *Government and Politics*, in R.L. Worden, *North Korea: A Country Study*, Federal Research Division, Library of Congress, 5th edn, 2008, 201. Yonhap, Seoul, *North Korean Handbook*, op cit., 151.

213 *Ibid.*

214 M. Marumoto, *North Korea and the China Model: The Switch from Hostility to Acquiescence*, in Korea Economic Institute, 2 *Academic Paper Series* (May 2007), n. 5.

possible, to counter the possible political instability linked to economic openness, in a game even more complex than that conducted in China by the Communist Party since 1978, and still in progress.[215]

3.2.8 The "National" and "Exceptional" Economic Laws

After the Second World War, under the auspices of the Soviet military authorities, North Korea began its economic revolution, which was subject not only to the principles of socialism but also to the ideological implications of *Juche* philosophy. Land tenure reform[216] freed North Korean peasants from all ties with the old landowners and became a symbol of the revolution. The formation of a new class of farmers coincided with the founding of the socialist movement, which supported Kim Il Sung in the establishment of a Soviet-style regime. The growth of the economy, however, was frozen by the Korean conflict, at the end of which the North Korean government chose the path of collectivizing economic activities via a schedule marked by three progressive moments.[217]

More recently, global economic dynamics have pushed North Korea to search for alternative solutions, including a special mechanism of economic development based on a new management method, theoretically less politicized and more managerial, of public companies, called the "rational low-wage system", which was later paralyzed by the managerial inefficiency of companies, the lack of incentives in the agricultural sector and by an excessive protection of the internal market.[218]

The new paradigm of Chinese law was also accepted in North Korea as a model that combines the maintenance of a socialist plan economy and an external economic market

215 *Ibid.*

216 Formally inaugurated with the promulgation of the *Land Reform Act* of 5 March 1946 following the determination of the economic policy guidelines indicated by the North Korean Provisional People's Committee on 8 February 1946. Art. 5 of the document provided for the confiscation of all the lands previously owned by the Japanese landowners and the consequent distribution of land to peasants who were deprived of it or had only a small part of it.

217 A three-year plan (1954-1956), a five-year plan (1957-1961) and a seven-year plan (1961-1967), respectively aimed at the unification of all production units in cooperatives, also aimed at balancing the agricultural sector with the industrial, until the provision of the socio-economic conditions necessary for the industrial development envisaged for the early 1960s. *See* on the topic H.T. Son, *Socialist Transformation of Agricolture in Our Country*, Pyongyang, Academy of Science Publishing House, 1960; C.S. Lee, *The Socialist Revolution in the North Korean Countryside*, in *Asian Survey*, October, 1962, 9-22; P. Rudolph, *North Korea's Political and Economic Structure*, New York, Institute of Pacific Relations, 1959; T. Shabad, *North Korea's Post-war Recovery*, in 25 *Far Eastern Survey*, June 1956, n. 6, 81-91.

218 S. Kim (Ed.), *The Economy of the Korean Democratic People's Republic*, Kiel, German Korea-Studies Group, 1979, and in particular on the mechanism of the *rational low-wage system cf.* J.D. Park, *Economic Special Area in North Korea*, Seoul, Korean Development Institute, 1996. The thoughts of Kim Il Sung on the subject are contained within the work written by Kim Il Sung himself, *On the Management of Socialist Economy*, Pyongyang, 1992, 271.

cooperation, endowed with the necessary framework of legality, and also the possible internal development of a socialist market economy,[219] already operative, even if in a "grey" area of the legal system, and clearly visible in the main cities of the country.[220]

This influenced North Korea, which promulgated the aforementioned constitutional amendments in 1998, which confirmed the cautious tendency towards a policy of openness to international markets, together with the apparently irresistible tendency to a programed control of activities and the sectoralization of the areas concerned.

With regards to administrative and economic laws, both "national" and for the special economic zones, the reference model is mainly the Chinese model, re-proposing the classic model of socialist legality in its simplest and most pragmatic epiphany, and roughly the development trajectories and content of the Chinese legislative apparatus since 1978. The first North Korean law in the field of non-socialist economy was the law on *Joint Ventures* of 1984, along the lines of the 1978 law in China, with the same subject matter.[221]

The subsequent laws on unplanned economics also follow the Chinese path: a first series dates back to 1992-1993, and was initiated by a law on socialist trade, which permitted some limited commercial activities to citizens, and the first general law on foreign investments (1992) and subsequent implementations (and a revision in 1999); the law on foreign commercial enterprises; numerous legislative documents on the taxation of foreign companies; the law on foreign currency exchange; the law on foreign capital banks, and the land rental law (all of 1993).

The North Korean economic laws often include the Chinese model also in their content, in similar but often simpler legal texts than the originals,[222] often containing the indication of a few general principles, rather than many detailed rules, the identification of the competent authorities and/or supervision of regulated activity, and wide application spaces left to political or administrative discretion.

The intersection of different theoretical elements at the level of the guiding concepts, of Soviet-style socialism but conditioned by traditional Korean elements on the one hand and the *Juche* philosophy on the other, theoretically sharpens the interpretative problems also with respect to the Chinese model, where a Korean judge or official could and still today apply the norm that conforms to the canons of "classic" socialism, incline towards a "mixed" version of concepts or privilege *Juche* philosophy orientations stemming directly

219 M. Marumoto, *North Korea and the China Model*, op cit., *passim*.

220 A. Lankov, *North Korea's New Class System*, op cit.; F. Abt, *a Capitalist in North Korea*, Hong Kong, op cit., *passim*; J. Everard, *Only Beautiful, Please*, op cit.; *Id.*, *The Markets of Pyongyang*, op cit.; A. Lankov, *Kim Jong-un's Recipe for Success: Private Enterprise and Public Executions*, op cit.

221 E. Y.J. Lee, *Development of North Korea's regime Governing Foreign Business Cooperation: A Revisit Under the New Socialist Constitution of 1998*, in 21 *Northwestern Journal of International Law*, Fall 2000, n. 1, 199-242, 203.

222 *See, e.g.*, the two laws on banking and insurance activities, respectively of 2006 and 1995, simplified versions of the corresponding Chinese laws of 1995.

from the national or central government authorities' *leadership* instructions. In fact, there is the need to go to the source, that is, to the competent official, going beyond the simple normative text, the *law in the books*, to know the specific response of the legal system to any practical problem.

Many of the laws on economic matters, however, have been revised frequently in recent years, reflecting a rapidly changing context.[223]

In the following years, the country endowed itself with a certain number of laws to regulate important aspects of economic activities, reaching the year 2000 with around sixty laws and regulations,[224] now well over a hundred, and continuing in the following years in the construction and the reform of the legal system, the promotion of economic activities and the launch of study programs for officials and students in this regard.[225]

The recent period 2008-2011 witnessed another "legislative wave", with the issuing or reform of laws on banking, insurance, intellectual property, *joint ventures* (*equity* or *contractual*), companies (and banks) in which foreigners totally or partially participated, and on bankruptcy. Laws were enacted on customs and tax matters, this latter being really "exceptional", given that the country claims the merit of being the only country to have achieved the socialist goal of having completely abolished taxes. And, with such a "national" characteristic (certainly destined to disappear with the development of the internal market economy), it goes without saying, that no "national treatment" was guaranteed to foreign investors.[226]

The country has recently equipped itself with legislative instruments to combat money laundering (2016). Even this legislation, such as those on human rights and the adoption of other similar initiatives, could have a "diplomatic" function, as well as a substantial function, to permit the country access to membership and the facilities of foreign and international financial institutions, such as for example the Regional Development Banks. It seems that the request for adherence as observer to the Asia Pacific Group, regional organization of the FATF, and the anti-laundering law of 2016, were founded precisely by the need to start on a path that led to access to investment financing instruments made available by the Asian Infrastructure Investment Bank promoted by the Beijing government, to which North Korea has not yet been admitted for its known problems of financial opacity.[227]

---

223 To remain in the example described in the previous note, the 1995 Insurance Law was revised in 2002, 2005 and 2008; and many more of the laws mentioned in this paragraph.

224 Ahn Choong-yong (Ed.), *North Korea Development Report* 2002/2003, (Seoul, Korea Institute for International Economic Policy (KIEP), 2003, 469-470; E.Y.J. Lee, *Development*, op cit.

225 M. Marumoto, *North Korea and the China Model,* op cit.

226 M.P. Spina Jr., *Brushes with the Law: North Korea and the Rule of Law*, in Korea Economic Institute, 2 *Academic Paers Series*, June 2007, n. 6, 4.

227 B.O. Babson, *Could the New Asian Infrastructure Investment Bank Change the Dynamics of Economic Engagement with North Korea?*, in 38north.org, website on North Korea of a North American-South Korean

A 1999 law, revised in 2008, regulated arbitration in the field of international economic cooperation: the applicability of the *lex causae* chosen by the parties or that with the closest connection to the case was envisaged, taking into account the uses.[228] For the remainder, the law include common provisions on the international scene; it stated that foreign arbitration awards must be recognized and executed according to "the relevant law of the DPRK",[229] and indicated the causes of refusal of the execution of a foreign award in a list that is sufficiently compliant with that in Article V of the 1958 New York Convention,[230] of which however North Korea is not a party. The North Korean law did not permit, as also occurs in Chinese law, *ad hoc* arbitration, providing only for administered arbitration.[231]

3.3 The Institutions and Law of South Korea

3.3.1 *Political and Constitutional Framework*

After the Second World War, the country was governed by a US military government (USAMGIK) until 1948, when the Republic of Korea (ROK) was born. The government and the institutional system are inspired by Western models, especially the presidential model of the United States of America,[232] and a political system based on the principles of Western democracies, crystallized in the first Constitution of the country of 1948.

The first president of the ROK was Syngman Rhee, historically close to the United States of America. In spite of his liberal past, he immediately launched an authoritarian policy, characterized by a monarchical management of the country, almost a new King Chŏson, and the use of any means to suppress political opposition, including a law on national security (1948) which made it possible to suppress any voice of dissent, well beyond the declared political objective of defending the country from the communist threat.[233] This included constitutional reforms in 1952 and 1954, aimed at prolonging the presidential term and subsequently seeing it renewed, strengthening his powers.[234]

The entire political and constitutional history of the country until the end of the 1980s of the twentieth century was characterized by tensions between the conservative forces of

research program), 26 May 2015, http://38north.org/2015/05/bbabson052515/; H.Y. Choi, *North Korea Adopts Anti-Money Laundring Law*, on the website of research and news on North Korea NKNews.org 18 May 2016, www.nknews.org/2016/05/north-korea-adopts-anti-money-laundering-law/.

228 North Korean law on international economic arbitration, Art. 45.

229 North Korean law on international economic arbitration, Art. 64.

230 North Korean law on international economic arbitration, Art. 65.

231 North Korean law on international economic arbitration, Art. 18.

232 M. Zimbardo, *Corea*, op cit., 132.

233 C.J. Eckert, K. Lee, Y.I. Lew, M. Robinson, E.W. Wagner, *Korea Old and New*, op cit., 347-349.

234 A. Serafino, chapter *Corea tradizionale e Repubblica di Corea*, in G. Ajani, A. Serafino, M. Timoteo, *Diritto dell'Asia orientale*, Torino, Utet, 2007, 253.

the authoritarian and military governments, and the opposition forces that pursued an opening of the political system towards the model of Western democracies. The most conservative forces, aided by the "cold war", of which the Korean War of 1950-53 was a "hot" epiphany, and in general the volatility of the security situation on the Korean peninsula, permitted maintaining control of the country, or recovering it quickly on occasions when the political system seemed to open up in the direction desired by the opposition.

A first opportunity occurred in 1960, with the end of the Rhee government and a new constitutional reform, aimed at strengthening the counter-powers compared to those of the president. The electoral defeat of Rhee was unexpectedly due to Rhee's advanced age and the poor grip of his heir apparent Yi Ki-bung (whose son, Rhee had adopted, as a public demonstration of a manifest political continuity, in the wake of Korean tradition, through the family and dynastic element). The electoral result of Yi was lower than expected, and also obtained via fraud and abuse; student revolts followed, which then became a popular uprising in April 1960, characterized by clashes between police and students, with numerous deaths and injuries. The United States of America, which until then had tolerated Rhee, publicly condemned him; 300 university professors stood before the National Assembly as a manifestation of solidarity to the students. The head of the armed forces refused to execute the presidential order to shoot the demonstrators. Rhee resigned, which was followed by the collective suicide of the entire Yi Ki-bung family and then the departure of Rhee to Hawaii.[235]

A brief period of euphoria began, with a constitutional reform that introduced a parliamentary model with a bicameral parliament. The reformist season was however short, and on balance, not very convincing.[236] In 1961, a coup led to the long military government of Park Chung Hee, general of the Korean army, culturally and militarily formed under the Japanese colonial regime, and influenced by the model of the colonial power. The National Assembly was dissolved, followed by constitutional reforms (1962 and 1969) aimed at restoring the initial presidential model,[237] with the creation of an invasive police and intelligence apparatus, capable of guaranteeing the control of the country.[238]

Park governed as president from 1962, continuing his policy of repression of all political opposition. With the growing voices of dissent in the country, and after a very painful electoral victory (1971), Park declared the state of emergency, and in 1972, martial law once again, with the suspension of the Constitution and new dissolution of the National Assembly. He subsequently launched a state reform program called "Yusin", "restoration" (the same word as the Japanese "Meiji"). At the end of 1972, a new Constitution was pro-

235 C.J. Eckert, K. Lee, Y.I. Lew, M. Robinson, E.W. Wagner, *Korea Old and New*, op cit., 352-355.
236 *Ibid.*, 356-359.
237 M. Zimbardo, *Corea*, op cit., 133.
238 C.J. Eckert, K. Lee, Y.I. Lew, M. Robinson, E.W. Wagner, *Korea Old and New*, op cit., 361-362.

claimed with markedly authoritarian characteristics and very extensive powers assigned to the President, whose office could be renewed without limits.[239]

Overall, the Park regime lasted for almost two decades thanks to the combination of a number of factors: the political-economic support of the United States, which since 1978, had direct command of a major part of the South Korean armed forces;[240] an internal policy that generated urbanization; a strong economic progress based on a model that one can define as corporate; a significant middle class that guaranteed a certain popular support; and the threatening presence, but useful to national cohesion, of the Northern country, with its vision of national reunification.[241]

Repression of political dissent increased, even abroad, making extensive use of security services, but however, generating some problems in relations with the United States. In 1979, the presence and activities of underground student protest movements became stable, strong and widespread political elements in Korean society. There was also a growing dissent within the government forces, on how to manage the protests. Park was killed in October 1979 by the head of his intelligence. The Prime Minister declared the immediate application of martial law. Within ten months, after serious political-military events, including serious and bloody clashes between the army, the police and political opponents, General Chun Doo Hwan assumed the presidency of the country and established a new military government. A new constitution was produced, approved by a plebiscite, according to which Chun Doo Hwan was thus re-elected President (1981).[242]

General Chun attempted to reactivate the *Yusin* model, characterized by strong presidential powers and economic leadership. His public figure, however, unlike that of Park, was not much appreciated. He was generally considered to be unwise, arrogant, and some of his family members were involved in financial scandals. Park was instead generally respected and considered a capable President, also known for his austere lifestyle and his family model of Confucian virtue. In addition, his wife, much loved by the Koreans, had been killed by North Korean agents in an attempt to assassinate Park in 1974. His daughter

239 M. Zimbardo, *Corea*, op cit., 133-134; C.J. Eckert, K. Lee, Y.I. Lew, M. Robinson, E.W. Wagner, *Korea Old and New*, op cit., 365.

240 The South Korean Armed Forces have been subjected, since 1950, to the formal command of the United Nations; and in fact to the North American command. A joint US-ROK command for the Korean armed forces was created in 1978, headed by a North American official. In the years 2006-2007 the two countries decided to pass over to the ROK, the command of military operations, even in wartime, from April 2012; *South Korea Military Doctrine*, on the website GlobalSecurity.org, 2 March 2009 (accessed 18 January 2017). The presence of the American ally is still important in terms of presence and intensity of cooperation, and in accordance with vital South Korean interests in relation to the DPRK nuclear program and in general for the stability of the whole region: *see Global Korea: The National Security Strategy of the Republic of Korea*, official document of the Presidency of the country of 2009, especially 15 ff.; J.H. Bae, A. Denmark (Eds.), *The U.S.-R. O.K. Alliance in the 21st Century*, Seoul, Korea Institute for National Reunification, 2009, *passim*.

241 C.J. Eckert, K. Lee, Y.I. Lew, M. Robinson, E.W. Wagner, *Korea Old and New*, op cit., 365-367.

242 *Ibid.*, 368-375.

Park Geun-hye assumed many tasks of the First Lady after the assassination of her mother, with great devotion to the figures of her parents, gaining the profound respect of the Koreans,[243] becoming President, herself, in 2012.

The repetition of the *Yusin* authoritarian model seemed, in short, no longer suited to the times and to the South Korean society. Chun's police control became unsustainable, and within a few years the protests of the civil society become very strong. A new political opposition was born in the country within the student movements, of neo-Marxist orientation and strongly opposed to the neo-colonial relationship of the country with the North American power. Chun, who in 1987 nominated his successor *in pectore*, General Roh Tae Woo, as the candidate for the 1988 presidential elections, faced with the growing severity of the protests and clashes, and probably in the face of American threats to remove political support from him, was forced to accept, in June 1987, a surprising proposal made publicly by Roh, to immediately start the reforms required by the opposition, to release the activists detained for political reasons (including the future president Kim Dae Jong), restoring civil and political freedoms.[244]

The Constitution was once again modified, this time to guarantee political and electoral rights, with a reform shared between the political forces, after which the country went to the polls. Roh Tae Woo was elected President, with the opposition, divided into two parties that obtained 27-28% of the votes, compared to the 37% obtained by Roh.

The successive presidents of the country have all been non-military and regularly elected, with a normal political alternation between the two main parties. The country has undertaken a new direction, very different from that held until then.

3.3.2 The Constitution and Fundamental Rights

After the 1987 reforms, the country seemed to have started a new season characterized by rapid civil and political progress, as well as economic progress. The reforms followed decades of repressive governments, the absence of the *rule of law*, constitutional changes brought about by political-military emergencies and dubious legitimacy,[245] and serious violations of fundamental rights, paradoxically justified with positivist doctrines of criminal law and national security laws, directly modelled on those of Japan during its bellicose period and those of Nazi Germany.[246]

243 *Ibid.*, 377.

244 C.J. Eckert, K. Lee, Y.I. Lew, M. Robinson, E.W. Wagner, *Korea Old and New*, op cit., 379-384.

245 Hahm Chai-hark, *Rule of Law in South Korea: Rhetoric and Implementation*, in R. Peerenboom (Ed.), *Asian Discourses of Rule of Law*, London and New York, Routledge, 2004, 385-416, 403 ff.; A. Serafino, *Corea tradizionale e Repubblica di Corea*, op cit., 254; D.K. Yoon, *New Developments in Korean Constitutionalism: Changes and Prispects*, in 4 *Pacific Rim Law & Policy Journal*, 1995, 395 ff., 400.

246 C. Choi, *Law and Justice in Korea*, op cit., 380.

The new course permitted the country to reach high or very high positions in all the most important statistical surveys and international indices related to economic development, innovation, protection of social and human rights, administrative transparency, and *rule of law*.[247]

The 1987 constitution is a rigid charter, based on the principles of popular sovereignty, the protection of fundamental and social rights, political pluralism and the separation of powers and *checks and balances*, according to a semi-presidential model, the pursuit of the reunification of the Korean peninsula by peaceful means, the free market albeit with an important role of *governance* for the State, the protection of trade union rights, and in general the central role of the law in the government of the country.[248]

The Constitutional Court was activated in 1988.[249] The models adopted by the previous constitutions were that of an *ad hoc* constitutional committee, formed by judges of the supreme court and members of the parliament (the Constitutions of 1948, 1972 and 1980). These committees, in reality, decided very few cases or were non-existent or inoperative. Judgments of constitutionality were entrusted to the Supreme Court (1962 Constitution). The Court foreseen in the 1960 Charter was never activated due to the coup of that same year.[250]

The Court established by the 1987 Constitution, consisting of nine judges (three appointed by the President, three by the parliament, and three by the president of the Supreme Court) in office with renewable six-year terms,[251] had jurisdiction over the constitutionality of the laws (after referral by a judge from the Supreme Court),[252] on the

247 Among the main global indexes and statistics, all available on the web, the UNDP *Human Development Index* (hdr.undp.org), the *Bloomberg Innovation Index* (www.bloomberg.com), the World Bank's *Ease of Doing Business Index* (https://data.worldbank.org/indicator/ic.bus.ease.xq), the UNESCO *Education for All Development Index* (www.unesco.org), the PISA index and the OECD reports on *Education at a Glance 2016*, on the website www.oecd.org/education/; the *Rule of Law Index* of the *World Justice Project* (www.worldjusticeproject.org), in which the country was in 19th place in 2016, and the *Rule of Law index* in the *World Governance Indicators* of the World Bank (info.worldbank.org), in the 75-90% range in 2015. Some important indices, although high in absolute terms on a global scale, but lower than the other indices recorded in the country, reflect some characteristics of the Korean society and economy: in the *Control of Corruption* index in the World Bank's *World Governance Indicators* (info.worldbank.org) of 2015, the country reports a position in the mid-range of 50-75%. The country is also 37th in the *Corruption Perception Index 2015* (www.transparency.org). The country, on the other hand, has medium or even low positions in many indices on the quality and protection of the environment: 43rd in 2014 and 80th in 2015 in the *Environmental Performance Index* (joint project of the EU Commission, the *World Economic Forum* and Yale University (https://epi.yale.edu).

248 M. Zimbardo, *Corea*, op cit., 135-136.

249 *Ibid.*, 136-137.

250 *See* the website of the Constitutional Court of the Republic of Korea and in particular the historical page, full of information: http://english.ccourt.go.kr/cckhome/eng/index.do.

251 Constitution of 1987, Art. 112.

252 The judgment on the constitutionality of regulations and administrative acts falls instead within the jurisdiction of the Supreme Court; Hahm Chai-hark, *Rule of Law in South Korea: Rhetoric and Implementation*, in R. Peerenboom (Ed.), *Asian Discourses of Rule of Law*, London and New York, Routledge, 2004, 389.

conflicts of attributions between powers of the State or between State and local authorities, the dissolution of political parties, or cases of *impeachment.*[253]

The Constitution also envisaged a direct constitutional appeal, homologous to the German *Verfassungsbeschwerde*, in which a citizen could directly appeal to the Constitutional Court to protect a constitutional right violated by a law or an administrative act, and in the adversarial discussion with the entities involved, obtain, in a very short time, a declaration of unconstitutionality of the law or the disputed administrative action. The decision binds all the legislative power and the administrations of the country, rendering the law obsolete or unlawful act and if necessary forcing a revision of the administrative action declared illegitimate.[254]

3.3.3 Government and Institutions

The 1987 Constitution, of 130 articles, in addition to the final provisions, outlined a semi-presidential political-institutional system. The document was structured in eleven Chapters: general provisions, rights and duties of citizens, the National Assembly, Executive power (President, government, advisory bodies, ministers, and audit commission), judicial apparatus, constitutional court, elections, local autonomies, the economy, provisions on constitutional changes, transitional and final provisions.[255]

The office of President was elected by universal suffrage, with a non-renewable five-year term. Emergency powers were exercised by the President with presidential acts subject to parliamentary approval, or ratification in the case of urgent acts adopted in the impossibility of convening the parliament.[256] The National Assembly, unicameral, was elected by universal suffrage with a mandate of four years. The government ("State Council") was composed of ministers and led by a Prime Minister, nominated by the president and subject to parliamentary approval, that could not be a serviceman.[257] The Prime Minister and the State Council responded to the President, who was also responsible for a number of independent agencies, including those for intelligence, financial supervision, the fight against corruption, and others.[258]

Among the constitutional bodies, the 1987 Constitution envisaged three bodies that reflected the history, political situation and the Confucian culture of the Country: a National

253 1987 Constitution, Art. 111; *see also* the website of the Court.

254 Art. 68 Constitution of 1987; *see* the page concerning direct judgment on the website of the South-Korean Constitutional Court: http://english.ccourt.go.kr/cckhome/eng/jurisdiction/jurisdiction/constComplaint.do#none.

255 M. Zimbardo, *Corea*, op cit., 134-137.

256 1987 Constitution, Arts. 76 and 77.

257 Constituion 1987, Art. 86.

258 *See* the official website of the South Korean government Korea.net (www.korea.net).

Security Council, a Consultative Council on "democratic and peaceful" Reunification, and an "Advisory Council of Elder Statesmen", presided over by the President immediately prior to the one in office, if present, who "could" be assigned the task of "advising the incumbent president on important affairs of state."[259]

The Constitution envisaged only two articles on local self-government, limiting itself to its competence on local administrative affairs, the regulatory power "within the limits of laws and regulations" and the need for an elected assembly body. It assigned to ordinary law the determinations on elections, organization, powers, and the activities of local governments.[260]

The territorial articulations of the public apparatus envisaged a first level constituted by eight provinces, seven metropolitan cities with the status of provincial level, the city of Seoul which had an autonomous and special status, and by a province with special autonomy constituted by the island of Jaju. The lower level of territorial governance was that of the 227 counties or cities or districts (in turn equipped with sub-municipal subdivisions), corresponding to elected councils and local governments with heads elected for four-year terms, that could be renewed.[261]

The organization of the Judiciary is based on a judicial pyramid articulated on three levels, from the Supreme Court to the basic level, with the juxtaposed required organs, from the Supreme Public Prosecutor's office to the basic level. There are six ordinary Upper Courts (one in reality, on the island of Jeju, is a section of that in Gwangju), with jurisdiction of appeal and which normally judge with benches of three togated judges. The ordinary courts are eighteen in number, and judge in most cases in monocratic composition. Subsequently, there are a hundred "municipal courts" that deal with civil and criminal cases (civil disputes worth up to 20 million *Won*, crimes involving arrest of up to thirty days, and administrative proceedings with penalties of up to 200,000 *Won*). There are judges specialized in matters of administration, family, intellectual property, and a system of military tribunals, whose sentences are appealed before the Supreme Court.[262]

The *Chief Justice* of the Supreme Court is nominated by the president, subject to parliamentary approval, with a non-renewable six-year mandate. He recommends the appointment of the other judges of the Supreme Court, also nominated by the President of the ROK with parliamentary approval and with mandates of six years, but renewable. Ordinary judges are appointed by the Chief Justice with the approval of the conference of judges of the Supreme Court. Their term of office lasts ten years, and is renewable. They

259 Arts. 90-92.
260 Arts. 117 and 118.
261 *See* the official website of the South Korean government Korea.net (www.korea.net). Local government page.
262 M. Zimbardo, *Corea*, op cit., 150-151.

must judge "independently, according to conscience and in accordance with the Constitution and the laws."[263]

The absence of a *life-tenure* for judges, hired without a public competition and nominated with ten-year mandates, deviates from the statist tradition typical of both the civil law model and most of the Asian and Confucian cultures. Literature indicates the absence of *life-tenure*, together with the organizational and disciplinary power of the heads of the Chief Justice who permits "punitive" transfers, as an element of control perceived as limiting the independence of judges.[264]

3.3.4 *Legal System*

The system is structured according to the Germanic-Japanese model of the so-called *roppō*, the "six codes" (the Constitution, the civil, commercial and penal codes, and the two ritual codes), a model also reproduced in nationalist China and then transferred to Taiwan.

The South Korean Constitution of 1948 was followed by the civil code (1960) and commercial code (1962), in the wake of a German *civil law* tradition introduced in East Asia via the Japan of the Meiji age at the end of the nineteenth century, well established during the twentieth century, and still characterizing the system in the twenty-first century.[265] At the same time, in Korea as in all Asian systems, the influences of a juridical thought more linked to the values and the richness and varied cultural and juridical traditions of Asia,[266] are present and growing.

The theory of sources follows that of the Germanic model, with the usual hierarchy established between the Constitution, laws and regulations, and with international treaty law and those generally acknowledged that enter directly into the system at the level of ordinary law.[267] In the administrative sphere, the perceived quasi-omnipotence of the administration is noted, in accordance with the Japanese conception.[268]

---

263 Arts. 103-105 Constitution.

264 M.J. Trebilock, R.J. Daniels, *Rule of Law reform and Development: Charting the Fragile Way to Progress*, Cheltenham/Northampton (MA), Elgar, 2008, 101; C.S. Yang, *The Judiciary in Contemporary Society: South Korea*, in 25 *Case Western Reserve Journal of International Law*, 1993, 303 ff., 312 (which, however, shows data from 1980, in a completely different context).

265 C. Choi, *On the Reception of Western Law in Korea*, in 9 *Korea Journal of Comparative Law*, 1981, 141-167; *Id.*, *East Asian Jurisprudence*, op cit., 317 ff.; M. Rehbinder, J. Sonn (Eds.), *Zur Rezeption des deutschen Rechts in Korea*, Baden-Baden, Nomos, 1990.

266 C. Choi, *East Asian Jurisprudence*, op cit., Part II, *Theory of East Asian Jurisprudence*, 295 ff.

267 1987 Constitution, Art. 6.1.

268 C. Choi, *Law and Justice in Korea*, op cit., 325.

There is no principle of the binding nature of judicial precedents, but the persuasive authority of jurisprudence is acknowledged, in particular that of the rulings of the supreme court, of legitimacy and regularly published, is particularly high.[269]

The civil code or civil law, *Minbŏp*, of 1958, in force since 1960, consists of about 1100 articles, divided into five books in accordance with the German-Japanese model (the same Japanese code was also in force in Korea in the colonial period): a general part, property, bonds, family, and successions. However, the 1958 legislator considered the Japanese code to be too individualistic for the Korean traditions: this code leaves more space, compared to the colonial code, to the autochthonous traditions especially in the fourth and fifth books, in matters of family and succession. These questions were subsequently subjected to various reforms to make the code more suited to the needs of the times. Among these reforms stands out that concerning the head of the family, a male subject originally endowed with managerial powers over the other family members, with consequences also inherited by status and patrimony in favour of the first-born male. These norms were toned down in 1989 and subsequently eliminated by the Constitutional Court in 2005.[270] This also occurred with regards to matters of marriage, traditionally and legally forbidden among blood relations (Art. 809 of the civil code), with the application of the principle that prohibits unions between subjects with the same surname and belonging to the same *clan*. The consequent social problem was very serious, due to the presence in Korea of very few surnames (proof of the homogeneity of ethnicity, historical isolation and the ancient feudal structure of the country).[271]

The ban was suspended with various special laws dating from 1978, and finally overturned by the Constitutional Court in 1997.[272] Even divorce, traditionally non-existent in a society such as that of Korea, appeared in the 1970s of the twentieth century, and then exploded with the urbanization of society and the adoption of social models and a contemporary popular culture inspired by Western culture and the overcoming of old schemes and taboos. A 1989 reform made divorce less discriminatory and punitive towards women.[273]

269 H.C. Kim, I. Cho, *South Korean Law Research on the Internet*, on the website *GlobaLex* of the Hauser Law School Program of the New York University, www.nyulawglobal.org/globalex/South_Korea1.html.

270 H. Yang, *A Journey of Family Law Reform in Korea: Tradition, Equality, and Social Change*, in 8 *Journal of Korean Law*, December 2008, 77-94.

271 The three most common surnames in South Korea (Kim, Lee and Park) pertain together to almost half of the citizens of the country; the ten most widespread, circa 65%. The surnames in total used in the year 2000, out of a population of about 48 million, were 286; surnames to be combined with membership in about 200 clans. Kim is the most common surname, held by circa ten million South Korean citizens; J. Zwetsloot, *Everything you ever wanted to know about Korean surnames*, on the website korea.net, 12 August 2009, http://www.korea.net/NewsFocus/Culture/view?art.Id=75090 (accessed 24 Janauary 2017).

272 M. Zimbardo, *Corea*, op cit., 138-139.

273 K. C. Lee, *Confucian Ethics, Judges and Women: Divorce under the Revised Korean Family Law*, in 4 *Pacific Rim Law and Policy Journal* (1995), 479-504.

The criminal law system is based on a substantial code (1953) which follows the German model. The Korean characteristics are evident in the provision of cases (many today repealed) linked to traditional culture and morality (from adultery to wearing long hair or dressing in an indecent manner) and, above all, in particularly severe penalties in relation to numerous cases of political, opinion and national security crimes. These characteristics appear both in the codes and in the law of 1948 on national security, a law still partly in force even in the presence of a lively debate on its maintenance.[274]

The death penalty, formally still in force, has in fact no longer been applied since 1997. Death sentences continue to be issued that are not executed, while numerous bills of law are pending in parliament for the abolition of the death penalty.[275] For some years now, trial with a jury for some crimes has been introduced experimentally.[276]

There are many, and growing, North American influences in the country's legal system, in addition to the institutional architecture, with a semi-presidential system with separate elections for the presidency and for the renewal of the parliament: the joint-interest of the North American military apparatus with the national apparatus and the presence of institutions that in their organization and even in some cases in the name, recall the American models (the best known and discussed case, of course, is that of KCIA, the country's central intelligence agency).

The North American influences are evident in many areas of commercial law, although codified according to the continental model in 1962: for example, the reforms of company law (a reform in 1984, and others subsequently), and insurance and maritime trade (1991).[277] Employment law has also been influenced by American models, which remained largely unenforceable at the time of the "dictatorship of development". Only recently has the system moved towards a better implementation of the protections envisaged for workers.[278]

The reforms which followed the 1997 financial crisis also introduced elements of global North American-inspired law, especially with reference to company law, accounting, the transparency of economic and financial activities, and the regulation of the economy. However, there is a fairly widespread perception of the lack of effectiveness of the reforms introduced after 1997, as previously stated, owing to the persistence of deeply rooted institutional and cultural mechanisms that at least partly produce resistance to the introduction of global-western inspired operational and legal models.[279]

274 M. Zimbardo, *Corea*, op cit., 145-149; C. Choi, *Law and Justice in Korea*, op cit., 326.

275 *Amnesty International Report 2013*, 152.

276 R.Y. Park, *The Globalization of Jury Trial: Lessons and Insights from Korea*, in 58 *American Journal of Comparative Law*, Summer 2010, 525-582; S. Kim, J Park, K. Park, J.S. Eom, *Judge-Jury Agreement in Crominal Cases : The First Three Years of the Korean Jury System*, in 10 *Journal of Empirical Legal Studies*, Marzo 2013, 1, 35-53.

277 M. Zimbardo, *Corea*, op cit., 144-145.

278 C. Choi, *Law and Justice in Korea*, op cit., 326.

279 *See supra*, para. 4, Economy and society.

The country is however, increasingly actively involved in global economic circuits, and certainly the economic and legal reforms of the last twenty years have introduced changes, both cultural and operational, despite the heavy inertia of the system. The debate on the national economic model and its possible overcoming or improvement, is lively.

The South Korean economy, markedly *export-oriented* and globally "connected", could not but produce the country's accession to the main conventions of international commercial and economic law, among which the 1958 New York Convention on the recognition and execution of the arbitration awards, the ICSID Convention of 1966 on the settlement of disputes related to foreign investments, and the 1980 Vienna Convention on the International Sale of Goods.[280] The country has signed but as yet not ratified, the New York Convention (2005), on the use of electronic communications in international contracts.

The law on foreign investments in 1998 abolished the licensing mechanisms for the activities of foreign investors, permitting them, as the Koreans, to start activities on the basis of a simple communication.[281]

The 1999 Arbitration Act, which regulates both domestic and internal arbitration, both institutional and *ad hoc*, is in line with globally prevalent continental-inspired models,[282] with reasonably advanced content[283] and with the 1958 New York Convention referred to as a *standard* for the recognition of foreign Arbitral Awards.[284]

3.3.5 *Access to the Legal Professions*

The recent tendency of the system to incorporate legal models of North American origin is particularly evident in the case of training and the rules for access to the legal professions.

Access to all legal professions, lawyers, prosecutors and judges, did not formally require a degree in law. Up until 2007, the only requirement was the passing of a very selective state examination (with 3-5% of the candidates promoted) followed by the completion of a two-year internship with a final examination at a national institute for judicial research and training managed by the Supreme Court, the *Judicial Research and Training Institute*. A number of those who passed the internship were selected to perform the functions of

280 Which the ROK joined, respectively, in 1973, in 1967 and in 2004.

281 M. Zimbardo, *Corea*, op cit., 145.

282 The arbitrator may, for example, appoint his own technical advisors (*Arbitration Act* of 1999, Art. 27); while no *discovery* mechanisms are foreseen.

283 For example, on the law applicable to merit, which will be chosen by the parties taking into account the uses, or in defect, the one most closely related to the case (*Arbitration Act* of 1999, Art. 29); or the possibility for the referee to issue interim measures (Art. 18) on request of a party, together with the equal right of the party to request them from the competent court in support of the arbitration proceedings (Art. 10); or the reasonable flexibility granted in relation to the seat of the procedure and the place of the hearings (Articles 21 and 25) or the language used (Art. 23).

284 Arbitration Act 1999, Art. 39.

judges or prosecutors, while others could access the profession of lawyer. This determined ranks composed of young judges, relatively lacking in social experience.[285] Relatively low wages and burdensome roles make it common to see young judges becoming mature lawyers.[286] To resolve some shortages of staff, the Supreme Court sometimes appointed expert lawyers for the positions of judge.[287]

The difficulty of passing the entrance examination produced a very small forensic class, compared to the population, as is also the case in Japan.[288]

Various proposals to reform the mechanisms of access to forensic professions have been put forward since the 1990s, creating a state of tension in the system between the need for innovation and that of keeping the number of qualified subjects limited.[289]

In 2007, the system of access to the legal profession changed radically, with the transformation in the following years of the law faculties into *graduate law schools* based on the North American model, with a limited number of schools (25, where numerous courses are active, in substance and methods, in the tradition of *common law*), with a limited total number of candidates admitted each year (2000). After *Law School*, there is the requirement to pass a "Lawyer Admission Test" (different from the national exam for the forensic professions of the old system) with percentages of passes around 75%. After the reform of access to the profession, in 2013, there were 16,500 lawyers working in Korea out of a population of 50 million citizens, one in about three thousand, still few, compared to Western jurisdictions, but many more than in the past. Circa 2,500 of these are judges and 1,700 are prosecutors. Judges and prosecutors are also appointed with the new system, respectively, by the *Chief Justice* and the *Chief Prosecutor*, who select candidates from among the best students. The old system of access to the profession work in parallel with the new system up until 2017.[290]

The legal profession, traditionally adhering to the model of small law firms or single lawyers, has been transformed in the last decades also acquiring a global dimension, with large associated firms, also international, especially in major cities, and with greater spe-

285 C.S. Yang, *The Judiciary in Contemporary Society*, op cit.; C.R. Kim, *The National Bar Examination in Korea*, in 24 *Wisconsin International Law Journal* (2006), 1, 243 ff., note on 246, how the modalities of the national exam, are not the best to select suitable personnel for the challenges of our time.

286 C.S. Yang, *The Judiciary*, op cit.

287 O.S. Jin, *South Korea*, report in *Asian-American Law Students' Association* 10 April 2004, *in Cornell Law Library, Scolarship@Cornell Law: A Digital Repository – Overview of Legal System in the Asia-Pacific Region* (2004).

288 C.R. Kim, *The National Bar Examination in Korea*, op cit., 246, indicates a total of circa 10,000 people who passed the exam, on August 2005, on a South Korean population of circa 48 million people: one for every 4,500 people.

289 C.R. Kim, *The National Bar Examination in Korea*, op cit., *passim*.

290 B. Stevenson, *How to Practise in South Korea*, on the website of the English *Law Society*, http://communities.lawsociety.org.uk/international/regions/north-asia-and-the-pacific/south-korea/how-to-practise-in-south-korea/5044557.fullarticle.

cialization of professionals,[291] and a 2009 law (FLCA – "Foreign Legal Consultant Act") which regulates the activities of foreign legal advisors, enabling their advice in Korea on the law of the jurisdiction of origin and on international law, and advocacy in international arbitrations in which these rights are applicable.[292]

The small number of legal professionals (judges and lawyers) still corresponds, however, to the best Confucian tradition of resolving conflicts through channels other than the judicial channel. Traditionally, disputes are resolved via socially recognized authorities, such as the village elders or other authoritative persons for the parties involved in the quarrel, or via the intervention of the police or public officials, according to the classic paternalistic approach of the Confucian administration model. This can be seem also via the work of the judges, who are always very active in mediating between the parties (who can appear in court even without the assistance of a lawyer) for the purpose of a conciliatory solution.

Even with the new system of access to legal professions, the numbers remain comparatively low, compared to Western contexts. This confirms the fact that the use of the formal law is, in an Asian context, only one of society's governance systems, preferentially aimed at regulating interests and positions of public order in which the intervention of the judge is necessary: administrative and criminal law, status issues, divorce, private interests in areas characterized by significant technical complexity (e.g. intellectual property), and international economic activities. However, even in these contexts it endures the more or less marked influence of other social regulators.[293]

Despite the now evident "legalization" of Korean society[294] and the pronounced Westernization/Americanization of the legal system, most Korean people remain deeply rooted in mentality, attitudes and tradition, with the result of a hybrid, segmented and stratified legal environment.[295] While the official and professional law is large and growing, both within the system and in the Korean society, a law and public institutions of Germanic-Japanese inspiration, strong recent normative, institutional and cultural elements of Anglo-American origins, and profound Confucian, Buddhist, shamanic, authentically Korean elements, still coexist and negotiate their respective areas of effectiveness, a legal complexity

291 B. Stevenson, *How to Practise in South Korea*, op cit.; M. Zimbardo, op cit., 154-155.

292 Art. 24, *Foreign Legal Consultant Act* 2009.

293 A wide and complete overview, historical and geographical, on the cultural elements that traditionally influence the law in northeastern Asia is in C. Choi, *East Asian Jurisprudence*, op cit., *passim*.

294 Hahm Chai-hark, *Rule of Law in South Korea: Thetoric and Implementation*, op cit., 396 ff., 392-395, 407-409.

295 C. Lee, *Talking about Korean Legal Culture*, 38 *Korea Journal*, n. 3, 45-76; C. Choi, *Traditional Legal Culture and Contemporary Legal Consciousness in Korea*, in Japan Committee of Research Committee for Sociology of Law (Eds.), *Legal Culture: Encounters and Transformations*, Tokyo, Japanese Association of Sociology of Law, 1995, 123-130.

that seems appropriate to describe with reference to the models of legal pluralism and, in particular, according to the scheme of semi-autonomous socio-juridical fields.[296]

3.3.6 Economy and Society

A first timid modernization of the Korean economy began towards the end of the Chŏson period, coinciding with the opening of the country to external influences, especially Japanese and then Western. The process underwent intense acceleration during the Japanese colonization, which transformed the Korean society by urbanizing its *elites*, and in part infiltrating its language, culture and models of socio-economic and juridical organization. Even after the Second World War the evolution of the South Korean economy followed the Japanese model quite slavishly, with whom the cultural and economic ties remain strong, despite the political tension linked to the colonial past and the conflicting feelings generated by it in the Korean society. Syngman Rhee himself had a personal attitude of strong hostility towards Japan: only after the end of his presidency did the two countries sign a treaty (1965) ending hostilities, thus restarting an intense economic cooperation.[297]

The new world order following the Second World War also saw the Southern Country included, in a similar way to Japan, in the geopolitical orbit of the United States of America and the overlapping of the political-economic model of Japanese origin, present in both countries, of ideas, institutions, and laws originated in North America (e.g. the striking case of the Japanese constitution of 1947, or that of the land reforms implemented by the US military government in Korea over the years 1945-1948): "as a consequence of the events outlined... the organization of South Korean society consisted of a 'backbone' coming out of the German legal system and the 'flesh' of American social perspectives. These influences combined to produce an inhibiting effect on the active development of an indigenous Korean legal culture."[298]

US interests in the region and their political and military presence in Korea, even stronger since the 1950-1953 war, have helped bring together American ideas and capital, and the development of significant economic cooperation between the two countries, ultimately generating a modern market economy and significant economic development. The Vietnam war was also an opportunity for a strong increase in economic cooperation, as well as political and military cooperation, between the United States and South Korea.[299]

296 S.F. Moore, *Law and Social Change: The Semi-Autonomous Social Fields as an Appropriate Subject of Study*, in 7 *Law & Society Review*, n. 4 (Summer, 1973), 719 ff.

297 C.J. Eckert, K. Lee, Y.I. Lew, M. Robinson, E.W. Wagner, *Korea Old and New*, op cit., Capitolo 20, *Economic Development in Historic Perspective, 1945-1990*, 388 ff.

298 C. Choi, *Law and Justice in Korea*, op cit., 326-327.

299 C.J. Eckert, K. Lee, Y.I. Lew, M. Robinson, E.W. Wagner, *Korea Old and New*, op cit., 395-399.

Most of the Japanese period industrial infrastructure was located north of the 38th parallel, and certainly until the 1960s of the twentieth century, the Northern country had a more significant industrial infrastructure, while the south lived on agriculture, light industry and external aid. The old land elite, forced to reinvent itself after the reforms of the USAMGIK and Rhee, and the merchant class born in the Japanese colonial period, initiated the industrial and economic miracle that took place in the early 1960s, during the presidency of General Park.[300] This miracle was made possible by the ability of these elites to combine modernity and tradition in economic activities, the favourable geopolitical condition and a wide availability of low-cost but skilled and committed labour, with which to create one of the most dynamic economies in the world.

The role of the cultural context in this "miracle" cannot be underestimated: the role of Confucianism in the social and economic development of some Asian "tigers" is widely dealt with in literature.[301] But there is no analysis of the role in South Korea, for the same ends, of Buddhism, shamanism and Christianity. I think it is probable that the complexity of Korean culture, on the one hand that generates tensions, on the other hand generates greater flexibility and reactivity to the new,[302] even a certain social "liquidity" of the elites, which has always permitted the country to adapt quickly to the form of its "container", so to speak.

The South Korean economy of the Park era is often characterized in literature as a model of "guided capitalism,"[303] characterized by a marked leadership, with five-year plans starting in 1962 and strong government interference in the activities of economic operators as well as a strong protectionism in international relations, tolerated especially by the United States, despite the tariff concessions granted to South Korean products for political reasons, albeit in a decreasing way, until the end of the 1980s.[304]

The Korean model of economic development has at its core a very close cooperative/corporate relationship between state, economic groups and trade union representatives. It is a model characterized by a very active state, which plans and directs production and other economic activities including the private sector, and finance and taxation, in pursuit of economic development according to public planning. It does so by also implementing extra-legal channels of public governance, of a political and administrative type, which

300 *Ibid.*, 400-401.

301 For the Korean experience – with its dominant neo-Confucian culture and the associated social centrality of memberships in social groups of every kind, family, territory, school, company, *affective networks*, – *See, e.g.*, Lew Seok-Choon, Chang Mi-Hye, Kim Tae-Eun, *Affective Networks and Modernitu: The Case of Korea*, in D.A. Bell, Hahm Chaibong (Eds.), *Confucianism for the Modern World*, Cambridge, Cambridge University Press, 2003, 201 ff.

302 C.J. Eckert, K. Lee, Y.I. Lew, M. Robinson, E.W. Wagner, *Korea Old and New*, op cit., 409.

303 *Cf. e.g.*, M. Doral, M. Patrono, *Chaebol and Korea's Industrial Finance*, in 5 *Journal of Global Initiatives: Policy, Pedagogy, Perspective* (2010), n. 2, Art. 7.

304 *Ibid.*, 397-406.

include, as also occurs in Japan, informal networks, personal, clan or purely economic and the administrative phenomena typical of the *haengjeong jido* ("administrative guide", equivalent to the Japanese *gyosei shido*) and *jeongbu jisi* ("government order").[305]

The model presents a marked osmosis between public function and private industry, with frequent passages by politicians and senior administrative officials and army officers holding important and usually well-paid positions in private or quasi-public companies with which they previously had regulatory or supervision relations; that is to say, former officials acting as unofficial interactions between regulators and regulated persons, a phenomenon also known in Korea with the Japanese term *amakudari* ("descent from the sky") or with the phrase *nakhasan insa* ("parachute appointment").[306]

Also typical of the Korean model, are the presence of large national economic conglomerates controlled by large families, the *chaebol*, the Korean word equivalent to the Japanese *zaibatsu*: in both languages, more or less, "economic clan".

In the years between the two world conflicts the *zaibatsu* (especially the four major "clans": Mitsubishi, Sumitomo, Mitsui and Yasuda) had proved to be centres of economic and political power that heavily influenced the policies of the imperial government. These were economic and financial conglomerates controlled by individual families, via vertical corporate control structures; each of the great *zaibatsu* controlled at least one large bank, a significant part of the war industry, and the heavy and light industry of the country, as well as service activities of all kinds, and had tens or hundreds of thousands of employees. It is evident how the internal logics of these economic groups and their operations in the country were little influenced by Western ideas on the *rule of law*, and much by those traditional of Japanese culture.[307]

The American military government in Japan proceeded after the Second World War to the administrative closure of the Japanese *zaibatsu*. However, the Japanese economic fabric soon reorganized the conglomerations in a new form known as *keiretsu* ("network or business system"), structures with a non-juridically top-down and vertical organization, but fluid and reticular, constituted in major cases around a bank, and governed through cross-shareholdings, the sharing of top management personnel, strategies, financial,

305 C. Choi, *Law and Justice in Korea*, op cit., 325.

306 S. Lee – S.Y. Rhyu, *The Political Dynamics of Informal Networks in South Korea: The Case of Parachute Appointments*, in 21 *The Pacifc Review* (2008), n. 1, 45-66; J. Cho, *Korean Amakudari: Bureaucratic corruption in Korea*, in 4 *East Asian Review* (2000), 83-96. The perception of the Korean media is that of an increasing phenomenon, compared to the decrease that is recorded in Japan: Yoon Ja-young, *AIIB fiasco stems from 'parachute appointments'*, in *The Korea Times* (www.koreatimes.co.kr), 11 July 2016; Yoon Chang-hee, *Let's end 'parachute appointments'*, in *Korea JoongAng Daily* (www.koreajoongangdaily.joins.com), 6 June 2013 (accessed 23 January 2017).

307 G.D. Allinson, *Japan's Post-war History*, Ithaca (NY), Cornell University Press, 1997, *passim*.

industrial and commercial transactions, and the presence of unifying identity elements for all their employees.[308]

Formally, in short, the new *keiretsu* respected the law of the victors, but they essentially reconstructed the banned political-economic-social structures, and the traditional rules on their political and economic management.

The current Korean phenomenon was born with the end of the Japanese colonial occupation and developed during the presidency of Rhee, with some Korean families that succeeded via political-economic processes not always very clear, to acquire the properties that had already belonged to the colonial authorities and the Japanese *zaibatsu* operating in Korea, thus obtaining a very significant, rapid and relatively inexpensive initial capitalization.[309]

The Chaebol reproduced to a large extent the model of the *keiretsu*, with some important differences: on the one hand, the permanence of vertices of the economic groups directly managed by the big families of Korean capitalism, with less relevance than the Japanese *keiretsu* of professional managers and therefore with a more centralized, personalist and familist governance; while, on the other hand, the possession of banks and financial activity remained excluded from the scope of possible activities for the *chaebol*, and firmly controlled by the State via the nationalization of banks in the early 1960s. This strengthened the governance of the generals in relations with the *establishment* of the large families and industrial-economic conglomerates (contrary to that which had occurred in Japan before the Second World War), with which they maintained close, and in various ways, personal relationships.[310]

The government had total control over the economy through economic planning, finances, tax flexibility, and licensing processes that made it possible to select the activities entering the system.[311] The *Chaebols*, on the other hand, cooperated loyally with the government and followed its formal and informal directives in pursuing common system goals.[312] The state policy of economic development, from the era of General Park onwards,

308 R.V. Gerald, *Comparing Japan (Keiretsu) and Korea (Chaebol) Economic Efficiency on their Financial Structures*, in 1 *European Journal of Contemporary Economics and Management*, December 2014, n. 2, 102 ff., especially 104; G. Ming, H. Lai, *Knowing Who You Are Doing Business with in Japan: A Managerial View of Keiretsu and Keiretsu Business Groups*, in *Journal of World Business*, 1999, 423 ff.; D. Flath, *Shareholding in the Keiretsu, Japan's Financial Groups*, in *The Review of Economics and Statistics*, 1993, 249 ff.

309 C.J. Eckert, K. Lee, Y.I. Lew, M. Robinson, E.W. Wagner, *Korea Old and New*, op cit., Capitolo 20, *Economic Development in Historic Perspective, 1945-1990*, 388 ff.

310 The position of strength in that period of the Korean government compared to the chaebol – even more marked than that of the Japanese government compared to keiretsu – is reported in the literature.

311 C.J. Eckert, K. Lee, Y.I. Lew, M. Robinson, E.W. Wagner, *Korea Old and New*, op cit., Capitolo 20, *Economic Development in Historic Perspective, 1945-1990*, 405 ff.

312 *E.g.*, the direct involvement of Hyundai in the implementation of the "Sunshine policy" towards North Korea is known, with very high investments for the construction of the industrial park in the special area of Kaesong.

provided these conglomerates with low-cost finance, political and trade union support, and access to world markets.[313] The economic groups, in turn, generously supported the political class, and determined the outcome of elections.[314]

Within the economic groups, there was a strong sense of belonging/identification, Confucian and quasi-family, of all the workers towards the company, with a work environment and a corporate culture characterized, on the one hand, by benevolent paternalism, with benefits, recreation activities and holidays organized by the company and on the other, by strong group ties between the employees and their total dedication to the corporate cause.[315]

Today, the largest Korean *chaebol* produces about 80% of the Korean GDP, and provides the Korean society with most of the goods and services of all kinds (hospitals, schools, mortuary rooms, residential buildings, automobiles, home appliances, insurance, media, culture, leisure). The five main Korean Chaebols (Samsung, Hyundai, LG, SK Group, GS Group) today produce well over half of the country's GDP. An important part of the large domestic economic transactions in South Korea still takes place according to intragroup logic, and principles different from those of free competition.[316]

The South Korean economic model permitted the country's economic *boom*. However, it has generated increasing tensions both internationally and internally, especially since the 1980s of the twentieth century, with the overwhelming inclusion of South Korean economic groups in global economic dynamics. At an international level, global protests grew over the success of Korean exports, due in large measure to state financial aid and the difficulties of foreign companies in accessing the Korean domestic market due to the already mentioned distortion phenomena and anticompetitive practices. The State began to withdraw from the direct management of the economy, leaving some more room for the principles of the free market with the first laws of economic and financial reform, and

---

313 Lee Sang eun, *Si scrive Corea si legge Chaebŏl*, in *Limes*, 2016 n. 12, *La Corea è una bomba*, 145 ff.; C.J. Eckert, K. Lee, Y.I. Lew, M. Robinson, E.W. Wagner, *Korea Old and New*, op cit., 388 ff.; R.V. Gerald, *Comparing Japan (Keiretsu) and Korea (Chaebol) Economic Efficiency on their Financial Structures*, op cit.

314 "Collusion" and "corruption" are very recurrent terms in literature to define the relationship between conglomerates and government; *see, e.g.*, P.S. Lee, *Economic Crisis and Chaebol Reform in Korea*, in APEC Study Center, Columbia Business School, *Discussion Paper Series* n. 14, October 2000, 3-4; R.V. Gerald, *Comparing Japan (Keiretsu) and Korea (Chaebol) Economic Efficiency on their Financial Structures*, op cit., 107.

315 Lee Sang eun, *Si scrive Corea si legge Chaebŏl*, in *Limes*, 2016 n. 12, *La Corea è una bomba*, 145 ff.

316 Lee Sang eun, *Si scrive Corea si legge Chaebŏl*, op cit., 147. The data is variable according to the sources, but it is reported with these orders of magnitude in all the statistics and financial analysis on the main specialized information organs, also available on the web; *see, e.g.*, Kwon Eun-jung, *Top Ten Chaebol Now Almost 80% of Korean Economy*, in *The Hankyoreh*, 28 August 2012, www.hani.co.kr; K. Kato, *Top Four Chaebol Generate 90% of South Korean Conglomerate Profits*, in *Nikkei Asian Review*, 10 April 2014 (www.nikkei.com); Chiang Min-hua, *Chaebol's role in South Korea's Economic Development, EAI Brief* n. 1153 14 July 2016, Singapore, East Asian Institute (www.eai.nus.edu.sg).

the opening up towards foreign countries.[317] From the internal point of view, tensions and petitions for greater economic and social justice stemmed from small and medium-sized enterprises, strangled by an impossible competition with large groups and condemned to live at minimum subsistence levels, or embed themselves, in a legal or economic sense, in the activities of one of the great conglomerates.[318]

The 1987 Constitution, while indicating a model of free market economy, – "The economic order of the Republic of Korea shall be based on a respect for the freedom and creative initiative of enterprises and individuals in economic affairs", maintained, however, all the traditional, Korean and Confucian elements of the control and the harmony of the economic system: "The State may regulate and coordinate economic affairs in order to maintain the balanced growth and stability of the national economy, to ensure proper distribution of income, to prevent the domination of the market and the abuse of economic power, and to democratize the economy through harmony among the economic agents."[319]

It was to be the Asian financial crisis of 1997 that revealed the structural inefficiencies and weaknesses of the Korean system, severely affected by the excessive expansion of production and the excessive weight and poor quality of the indebtedness of the conglomerates, with many bankruptcies (including Daewoo), in spite of the mantra of many on the "too big to fail".[320]

The presence and development of the *chaebol* led to the transformation of the Korean economy during the twentieth century, from a predominantly agricultural economy to one of the most advanced industrial economies, and this is probably the most representative feature of the country's economic model. There are Chinese, Western, Japanese and Korean elements: an imperfect, consociate market economy with opaque mechanisms; *clans* with vast economies led by families/"quasi-sovereign" dynasties, quite independent but usually cooperative with the authority of the State, with which a relationship of trust and exchange was generated that is not easily qualified in socio-economic and juridical-institutional terms via Western schemes, an economic and social environment characterized by circles and dynamics at various levels, with very strong loyalities of the personal/informal, political, and administrative type, in this order, that prevail over the normative element.

If the internal conditions and geopolitical needs, in particular the need for the United States of America, to cultivate another strong and rich Western outpost, similar to Japan, in the region had justified the efforts of the 1960s to make the South Korean economy

317 S.W. Chang, K.S. Shin, *Contribution on the ROK*, in K. Pistor, P.A. Wellons (Eds.), *The Role of Law and Legal Institutions in Asian Economic Development 1960-1995*, Oxford/New York, Asian Development Bank & Oxford University Press, 1998, 73 ff. and especially. 75-76.

318 P.S. Lee, *Economic Crisis and Chaebol Reform in Korea*, op cit., 18.

319 Paras. 1 and 2 of Art. 119 of the 1987 Constitution.

320 P.S. Lee, *Economic Crisis and Chaebol Reform in Korea*, op cit., *passim*; R.V. Gerald, *Comparing Japan (Keiretsu) and Korea (Chaebol) Economic Efficiency on their Financial Structures*, op cit., *passim*; M. Doral, M. Patrono, *Chaebol and Korea's Industrial Finance*, op cit.

grow, towards the end of the twentieth century, with the globalization of the markets, the access of Korea to the WTO (1995, but the country had been a member of the GATT since 1967), and with the strong socio-economic changes taking place in the country, calls came from numerous parties for the model of the "guided capitalism" of the big conglomerates to leave (more) space for a more open, free and transparent economy.

Even the International Monetary Fund, intervening in the rescue of the country after the 1997 crisis, conditioned the aid for the start of structural reforms of the system, and mainly the reform of the *chaebol*.[321] Despite the introduction, since then, of various rules aimed at prohibiting or limiting intra-group anticompetitive activities, cross-trade exchanges, non-transparent accounting practices, and other conduct typically close to the heart of *chaebol* operations, something has changed but not much: the South Korean economic situation has seen an overall increase in the level of economic concentration and the share of domestic product originated in the *chaebol*, without yet producing major improvements for small and medium-sized enterprises.[322]

South Korea's recent problems are typical of an advanced post-industrial society: slowing-downs in economic growth, financial crises (the crisis in 1997 and that which started in 2007-2008), an aging population, environmental deterioration, social inequality and even some more widespread doubts about the validity of the legendary national educational system.[323] The country found itself at the end of the twentieth century, in the midst of the full blown out globalization, with serious problems with regards to its political-economic system, very similar to those found in Japan before the Second World War. After having been "more Chinese than the Chinese for centuries", the Koreans are today to be "more Japanese than the Japanese", in the implementation of a political-economic model that seems increasingly inadequate to the challenges of the times.[324]

---

321 P.S. Lee, *Economic Crisis and Chaebol Reform in Korea*, op cit., 10-15.

322 Lee Sang eun, *Si scrive Corea si legge Chaebŏl*, op cit., *passim*; R.V. Gerald, *Comparing Japan (Keiretsu) and Korea (Chaebol) Economic Efficiency on Their Financial Structures*, op cit., *passim*; M. Doral, M. Patrono, *Chaebol and Korea's Industrial Finance*, op cit.; P.S. Lee, *Economic Crisis and Chaebol Reform in Korea*, op cit., *passim*.

323 Considered by many to be excessively competitive and stressful for young people (with a high suicide rate directly linked to competition), as well as generating an excessive number of unemployed graduates, and finally for a possible bureaucratization/mediocration/corruption of the system itself. M. Riotto, *La Corea non è un paese*, op cit., in *Limes*, 2016 n. 12, *La Corea è una bomba*, 31-44, 33; *see also* the numerous press sources mentioned in this regard in the "Education" section of "South Korea" of *Wikipedia*.

324 "The conglomerates, in fact, had grown so large that they reached the point where they could exploit the national economy for their own benefit. They had grown strong enough even to place the financial industry under their control. The Chaebol enjoyed unrestrained market power and expansion, which caused enormous damage to the Korean economy. These harmful effects included: excessive and illegal debt financing; boundless expansion of capacity; charging excessively high prices; driving rival firms and small industries out of business through predatory tactics; suppressing technological improvements; persuading government to restrict new entry or open market policies; speculation in real estate and the stock market; and illegal inheritance or transfer of property"; *see* P.S. Lee, *Economic Crisis and Chaebol Reform in Korea*, op cit., 2.

Inadequacies can be found, on the one hand, in the most recent events of the economy, as demonstrated by the Hanjin case, another "too big to fail" conglomerate, which collapsed in August 2016, and in the general doubts on the functionality and sustainability of the economic model in the country. On the other hand, these inadequacies can be found in political events such as that which hit President Park Gaun-hye (daughter of General Park), elected in 2012 with great enthusiasm popular and suspended from office with a parliamentary vote at the end of 2016 to undergo a trial of impeachment – for having (apparently) oriented her decisions of government on the basis of the influences and indications of one of her friends (and in the past, already a friend of her father) endowed with shamanic skills: a counsellor of the occult state, in the best case; a hidden president or a presidency under protection, according to others. Park Gaun-hye had organized significant money movements in favour of her friend via informal pressures on large national economic groups.[325]

The parliamentary decision on the suspension and impeachment followed, without prejudice, the parliamentary hearing broadcast live on television, and relaunched by the media around the world, of the leaders of the nine main *chaebols* of the country, who obviously denied the hypothesized payments of billions of *won* in favour of the foundations of the president's "councillor".[326]

Beyond the outlines and details of a scandalistic type, the story is the negative epitome of the Korean economic and social model that generated the extraordinary economic progress of the country during the twentieth century: a model linked to an irrationalist, familist society, linked to charismatic hierarchical figures and to the very opaque operation of large family-based economic conglomerates, animated by a large number of *affective networks* of all kinds, between private persons, the state and private persons, between companies and the state, and between companies and companies, operating in every political, social and economic area, with equal or superior importance in certain cases to that of the public institutions.[327]

In the spring of 2017 following the impeachment, President Park was deposed by the Constitutional Court, with unanimous vote (8-0); the political elections saw the predictable defeat of the conservative party and the victory of the progressive Moon Jae-in, son of exiles of the North and a supporter of a new policy of opening towards the northern country. In the summer of 2017, Samsung's vice president and designated heir was sentenced by a five-year prison sentence in Seoul for corruption, in connection with the story of the president and her shamanic friend – a decision that has historical political and cultural significance which goes far beyond any ordinary judicial decision.

---

325 M. Riotto, *La Corea non è un paese*, in *Limes*, 2016 n. 12, *La Corea è una bomba*, 31 ff., 43-44.

326 *Grilled in Seoul: South Korea's Chaebol Bosses Face Parliament*, editorial, *The Economist*, 10 December 2016, http://www.economist.com/news/business/21711502-lee-jae-yong-samsung-was-most-intensively-interrogated-south-koreas-chaebol-bosses-face (accessed 24 January 2017).

327 *See* Lew Seok-Choon, Chang Mi-Hye, Kim Tae-Eun, *Affective Networks and Modernity*, op cit.

The story reignited the debate on the functionality of the political-economic model, demonstrating that the reforms adopted since the 1980s, despite having started a phase of undoubted transition to a freer economy,[328] had not affected the structure and the deep roots, also confirming the centuries-old political resilience of the most important Korean clans in maintaining their positions, resisting pressure and sometimes subtracting themselves from the sovereign's political control when he tried to make himself more invasive against them. There also seems to emerge in the society of South Korea, a certain crisis of identity and national pride, a meandering and sociologically significant lack of self-esteem,[329] due to the inadequacy of the State in the face of internal powers, which can also be read in the continuity to historical events, with the country's always strong political-economic dependence on external powers.[330]

3.3.7 Competition

In a political-economic system such as that of Korea, legislation on monopolies and competition cannot but be one of the central points of accumulation of systemic tensions of different markets and economic "worlds", but with a wide contact area in which frictions and petitions of economic and social justice are generated, with a direct impact not only on the economy but also on the real free use for all citizens of their constitutional rights as well as economic initiative. After the financial crises of 1997 and 2008, the demands of economic reforms have been particularly pressing, also producing some results.

The regulation in this area began with the "Monopoly Regulations and Fair Trade Act" (MRFTA) of 1980, repeatedly reformed or amended over the years. The MRFTA established the *Korean Fair Trade Commission* (KFTC), an independent government agency dedicated to the enforcement of sector legislation, whose acts are appealable to the Seoul Superior Court. The legislation is aimed at preventing and combating monopolies, cartels, excessive concentrations of economic power, abuses of dominant positions, anticompetitive activities and activities that harm the consumer. The instructive and sanctioning powers assigned to the KFTC include those of imposing sanctions, issuing prescriptions, making public the violations of the law, starting the prosecution, applying leniency rules in case of cooperation from the perpetrators of the violations detected, and much more.[331]

328 S.W. Chang- K.S. Shin, contribution on the ROK in K. Pistor, P.A. Wellons (Eds.), *The Role of Law and Legal Institutions in Asian Economic Development 1960-1995*, op cit., 78-79.

329 M. Riotto, *La Corea non è un paese*, op cit., *passim*.

330 C.J. Eckert, K. Lee, Y.I. Lew, M. Robinson, E.W. Wagner, *Korea Old and New*, op cit., Capitolo 20, *Economic Development in Historic Perspective, 1945-1990*, 412-418 ff.

331 H. Lee, *Development of Competition Laws in Korea*, in *ERIA Discussion Paper Series*, Economic Research Institute for ASEAN and East Asia, November 2015, *online*: http://www.eria.org/ERIA-DP-2015-78.pdf, 5 ff. (accessed of 24 gennaio 2017).

The most recent reforms of the MRFTA and other more specific regulatory acts try to combine the needs, on the one hand, to preserve the functionality of the large *chaebols* and their operational modalities, protecting them from a predictable flood of "bottom-up" legal actions, and, on the other, to protect Korean SMEs in meetings and clashes with large economic groups, pursuing "economic democratization" and the "shared growth" of the country.[332]

The normative and regulatory system in this matter and the implementation approach of the KFTC is therefore developed on two well-differentiated levels: a level, one could define as "horizontal", of competition, concentrations and monopolies, on which the regulation of the relations between companies of the same type and size order, in competition with each other, is set out; and another level that is "vertical" in which the dynamics of economic groups and companies of different sizes, operate. In short, it is the plan in which the interaction between the level of conglomerates and that of SMEs, is regulated; for example via the regulation and the exercise of various types of supervision and moral suasion by the KFTC in subcontracting relationships.[333] This binary model – or, better, orthogonal model, achieves a compromise, the only possible solution in the socio-economic and political reality of the country: a compromise that, in the face of both internal and internal requests, tries to govern different types of economic conflict separately, in defence of the economic status quo and national assets.[334]

The "horizontal" control operates at the highest levels of the economy as a formal regulatory petition, that is added to those already present in the system at both the formal and informal levels, at the social, economic and/or political level. This means that in fact,

332 The existence of the structural problems of the Korean economy and the search for solutions inspired by prudence and gradualness in government action are obtained, for example, from the rigid and very programmatic formulations of Arts. 1 and 3 of the MRFTA (text in English available on the KFTC website, www.kftc.go.kr): Art. 1 "The purpose of this act is to promote fair and free competition, to encourage thereby creative enterprising activities, to protect consumers and to strive for balanced development of the national economy, by preventing any abuse of market-dominating position by enterprisers and any excessive concentration of economic power, and by regulating undue collaborative acts and unfair trade practices." Art. 3: "(1) The Fair Trede Commission shall establish and implement action plans to promote competition in markets in which monopoly or oligopoly situations have continued for a long time in relation to supply or demand of goods or services. (2) The FTC may give opinions to the heads of the relevant administrative agencies as to the introduction of competition or other measures necessary to improve market structures, where it appears necessary for the Commission to carry out action plans under paragraph (1)."

333 S.H. Jeon, *Using Competition Policy to Promote "Shared Growth" in Korea*, in V.Y. Zhang (Ed.), *Competition Policy in Asia: Essays on Recent Developments*, op cit., 241-243.

334 H. Lee, *Overview of Current Antitrust Enforcement in Korea*, in V.Y. Zhang (Ed.), *Competition Policy in Asia: Essays on Recent Developments*, independent publishing platform CreateSpace, 2015; available also at http://ssrn.com/abstract=2626159, 63 ff. "Economic democratization" and "shared growth" were also central themes in the 2012 election campaign, and in the political platforms of both candidates for the presidency. *See* Y. Jung, G.J.H. Choi, *Recent Developments in Korean Competition Law Enforcement*, Available *online* at the website of *Competition Policy International Journal*, 16 September 2015, www.competitionpolicyinternational.com/recent-developments-in-korean-competition-law-enforcement/ (accessed 24 January 2017); H. Lee, *Development of Competition Laws in Korea*, 18-19.

beyond the growing number of cases of enforcement of the MRFTA and the now global standing of the KFTC, it is currently neither probable nor frequent that large national groups will resort to it to resolve any conflicts between them, nor that recourse to the KFTC is the most suitable instrument to settle these conflicts. Nor does it seem likely that Korean SMEs will frequently do so to resolve "horizontal" conflicts amongst each other.[335]

Many of the best known cases decided by the KFTC, some of great worldwide resonance, concern in effect, the activities of large foreign-controlled multinational groups, and their disputes with national companies or they are procedures to protect SMEs and consumers.[336]

The *Korean Fair Trade Commission* in its "vertical" regulation activities, moreover, operates, one could say *cum grano salis*, almost like a sort of SME ombudsman, or perhaps as a Confucian official of the Choson age, trying to solve the problems of SMEs with higher-level economic groups, via "Confucian" mechanisms of encouraging the parties to find a conciliatory solution, These "vertical" activities also include the monitoring of the subcontracting market by the KFTC and awards, incentives and tax benefits for large groups reporting good year-to-year fair trade assessments in subcontracting to SMEs, rather than with the use of the extreme ratio of the strict application of rules, regulations and sanctions.[337]

335 K. Shin, *The Treatment of Market Power in Korea*, in 21 *Review of Industrial organization*, 2002, 113-128, http://dx.doi.org/10.1023/A:1019617325739 (accessed 24 January 2017), *passim*. The existence of a double regulation plan is also present in China, for different reasons – but are they really quite different, in a political and socio-economic sense? – with the state companies legally removed from the enforcement of the 2007 Antimonopoly Act (AML) to which Chinese and foreign private companies are subject. The regulation of the economic activity of Chinese public enterprises remains a predominantly political affair; as well as any "vertical" economic conflict between SMEs and public companies. The need for regulation and enforcement of the Chinese AML among private companies, which is instead normatively possible, is not in fact very often feasible at the level of SMEs, for reasons of cost, culture, economic interest, other than for the uncertainties and dysfunctionality of the system. This follows a very gradual enforcement of legal principles, and still today limited mainly to the activities of large foreign economic groups; I. Castellucci, *Rule of Law and Legal Complexity in the People's Republic of China*, Trento, 2012, Chap. 3, para 4, *Competition*, 129-133, and literature ivi cit Ed. Well known cases have involved Microsoft, Apple, Sony, Warner, Coca-Cola and other multinational groups in recent years, as opposed to national groups. The cases are published, also in English, on the KFTC website.

336 Well known cases have involved Microsoft, Apple, Sony, Warner, Coca-Cola and other multinational groups in recent years, as opposed to national groups. The cases are published, also in English, on the KFTC website.

337 H. Lee, *Development of Competition Laws in Korea*, op cit., 12; S.H. Jeon, *Using Competition Policy to Promote "Shared Growth" in Korea*, in V.Y. Zhang (Ed.), *Competition Policy in Asia: Essays on Recent Developments*, op cit., 241-243.

3.4 The Political Reunification of the Korean Peninsula

3.4.1 *National Reunification and the Economic Rapprochement Between the Two Koreas*

National reunification is a formal issue on the agenda in the two countries, both with constitutional provisions[338] in this regard and specific Ministries, as well as being part of in the strategic objectives of the WPK and the internal political debate in the southern country.

An initial agreement between the two countries, not binding and not bearing the official names of the two States (to avoid questions regarding the absence of mutual recognition), was signed in 1971 by representatives of the two governments, with the aim of easing tensions, creating mutual trust and promoting a *peaceful* process of reunification.[339]

The document envisaged the cessation of mutual threats and defamation, and military incidents, the establishment of a direct line of communication and a coordination committee between the two governments. In short, the recognition of the *status quo* on both sides was formalized, already at that time and today with the countries still formally at war, since 1950, committing them to coexistence. The agreement, even if never binding, has certainly been overtaken by events; what remains, excluding the not (yet?) occurred reunification, is the first official contact between the two States and a mutual recognition of the state of affairs.[340]

The now very consolidated state of affairs is as follows: the pragmatism of the elite of the DPRK has resulted in the abandonment for decades of the implausible idea of a reunification *manu militari*, with an extension to the reunified country of the North Korean model, replicating the dynamics of the reunification of Vietnam. It seems unlikely, at least in this historical moment, that the southern country and the entire region will witness a sudden political collapse or change of regime in the northern country, as many analysts

338 In particular, Art. 4 of the Constitution of the Republic of Korea (ROK, South Korea) of 1987 provides that the same "will seek the unification, formulating and undertaking a policy of peaceful reunification on the basis of the principles of freedom and democracy". No provision concerning the economic relations between the two Koreas is contained in the text, thus demonstrating in the constitutional document the absence of programmatic declarations on the probably most sensitive point towards the path of progressive economic integration. This will be partially remedied with the signing of the 1991 agreement. *See* H. Kim, *Unification Policies of South and North Korea 1945-1991: A Comparative Study*, Seoul, National University Press, 1992. The Constitution of North Korea indicates in its preamble national reunification as the supreme goal of all Koreans, and the great Companions Kim Il Sung and Kim Jong Il as "the sun of the nation and the polar star of national reunification".

339 The formally entitled "Joint Statement of North and South" of 4 July 1971.

340 B.C. Koh, *The inter-Korean agreements of 1972 and 1992*, in 16 *Korea and World affairs*, 1992, 3, 473 ff.

thought until not many years ago.[341] On the other hand, even in the southern country, an absorption of the northern country, on the model of German reunification, has been considered by the majority for over a decade as being too expensive, even with risks of political instability, possible movements of refugees, and national and regional humanitarian crises.[342]

The political and economic rapprochement between the two Koreas, a question perhaps more plausible than the latter and today somewhat, of the reunification, raises important problems of harmonization of the norms dedicated to the economic system. In this regard, the two Koreas signed a historic bilateral agreement in 1991 for "reconciliation, non-aggression and exchanges and cooperation,"[343] which came into force in 1992 but has remained without a broad implementation, initially shared by the two parties.[344]

The analysis and evaluation of this agreement cannot ignore the tenor of the economic principles envisaged by the constitutional evolution in the Democratic People's Republic of Korea from 1992 onwards; among these, the reiterated principle of a national economy consisting of a socialist and independent planned economy, based on the *Juche* state doctrine. Among the numerous provisions that began to delineate the outline of the national economic system,[345] a "progressive transformation of Marxist-Orthodox Leninist juridical theory"[346] was envisaged. If previously the principle regulating the country's international relations was based on the theory of peaceful socialism[347] expressed by Lenin and incorpo-

341 *See also*, J.H. Kim, *Preparing for the Possible: Korea Integration Proposals in the Event of a Sudden Collapse of North Korea or Sudden Reunification*, paper presented at the conference *The Korea project at the University of Southern California*, Korean Studies Institute, Los Angeles, 2010.

342 M. Kang, H. Wagner (Eds.), *Germany and Korea: Lessons in Unification*, Seoul, Seoul National University Press, 1995, *passim*, and especially, D.K. Choi, *Legal Aspects of Present South-North Korea Relations and Beyond*, *ivi*, 208-234. All the available analyses agree on the impracticality and excessive costs of a "German" absorption, which the Seoul government officially states not to pursue.

343 *Cf.* M.K. Kim, *The Treaties on Basic Agreement Between the South and the North*, Seoul, 1992.

344 C. Choi, *Law and Justice in Korea*, op cit., 331, speaks of "very little improvement… both sides have not shown any sincere efforts to carry out this agreement".

345 The concept of an independent national economy was expressed for the first time by Art. 19 of the North Korean Constitution of 1992, while t Art. 26 of the same document defined the independent national economy as the solid foundation for the happiness of the people and for the independent development of the country.

346 As highlighted by E. Y.J. Lee, *Legal Issues of Inter-Korean Economic Cooperation under the Armistice System*, The Hague/London/New York, Kluwer, 2002, 98. Art. 37 envisages that the State encourages the institutions, companies, organizations of the country towards the establishment of joint ventures and the provision of cooperation of companies with commercial companies and foreign persons.

347 A theory that presents numerous points of encounter with the Juche thought, especially where the right of peoples to decide their own destiny is sanctioned, in the most rhetorical and anthropocentric vision of man and the nation as two aspects of a unity that is free to pursue self-determination. Comment on Art. 29 of the Constitution of the Soviet Socialist Republics of 1977; I. Kavass, I. Christian, *The 1977 Soviet Constitution: A Historical Comparison*, in *Vanderbilt Journal of Transnational Law*, 1979, 539. Regarding the application of the principle of socialist pacifism in foreign policy *cf.* M. Liebman, *Leninism under Lenin*, London, Johnatan Cape, 1975.

rated into the Soviet constitutional texts of 1918 and 1977 (Art. 28), after the institutional and economic changes that have taken place in the main socialist countries since 1980,[348] the assumption has lost its antagonistic value compared to the progressive and significant new economic relations with foreign countries.

Article 15 of the Basic Agreement on inter-Korean co-operation set the goal of an integrated and balanced development of the national economy and the well-being of the entire population.[349] A norm of high programmatic and symbolic value, it should have led to a legal redevelopment of the contracts that had until then intervened between the two Koreas, with the provision of a domestic market in a context of "provisional" national separation. The principle seemed to open a breach in the persistent tendency towards North Korean isolation, probably relying on the Korean ethnic homogeneity and, consequently, not contradicting the principles of the *Juche* ideal, to whose conformity, the whole Korean nation as a whole, can legitimately aspire.[350]

This principle norm was followed, with the Protocol of Chapter III of the Basic Agreement, a detailed regulation for a wide range of areas of cooperation.

Following the signing of the agreement, the Republic of Korea redefined the structure of the law on foreign commercial law,[351] devoting itself actively to the drafting of subsequent political documents in support of the dialogue process,[352] interrupted periodically, and again recently, by political tensions, as well as redefining internal legislative acts to regulate the various aspects of relations with the North Country and its citizens, including laws to regulate protection and support for refugees from the North Country, family and succession issues, and the promotion of family reunifications.[353]

The recent "North Korea Human Rights Act" stands out, with which the ROK regulates the institutional activities aimed at monitoring the situation of fundamental rights in North Korea and promoting their protection through planning, coordination and implementation

348 Consider Art. 18 of the Constitution of the People's Republic of China, where it is expected that foreign companies can invest in China and organize themselves under different forms of commercial cooperation with Chinese companies. For a comment *cf.* W. Kraus, *Private Business in China: Revival between Ideology and Pragmatism*, London, Hurst, 1991; S. Steward, *Joint Ventures in the People's Republic of China*, in 4 *Advances in Chinese Industrial Studies*, Greenwhich (CT), JAI Press, 1994.

349 Including the joint exploitation of resources, the trade in goods and products regulated as if it were a domestic trade and the initial establishment of joint ventures between companies of the two countries.

350 M.K. Kim, *The Treaties on Basic Agreement between the South and the North*, op cit, *passim*.

351 On amendments to this legislation *cf.* E.S. Lee, *The Development of Laws to Regulate Foreign Trade in the Republic of Korea*, in *The Transnational Lawyer*, 1997, 269. On the subject, *cf.* also S.H. Song (Ed.), *Korean law in the Global Economy*, Seoul, Bak Young Sa, 1996.

352 Consider the "Measures for Revitalization of Inter-Korean Economic Cooperation" of 8 November 1994, which also included the "pilot" employment of North Korean workers in projects for the construction or exploitation of resources in third countries, the visit of technicians from the Republic of Korea in North Korea for technology transfer operations and the opening of "joint" commercial offices in North Korea.

353 The laws in this regard are readily available in English on the website of the South Korean government's National Law Information Centre, which has a key word search system – *e.g.*, "north korea" – www.law.go.kr (accessed 24 January 2017).

and political, diplomatic and humanitarian activities, study and research, as well as implementing efficient forms of exchange and cooperation with international organizations and NGOs.[354]

The highest point in the relations between the two Koreas was certainly the period of the so-called Sushine policy (1998-2008), promoted by the president of the southern country, Kim Dae Jung, who, as a result, received the Nobel Peace Prize in 2000. There were two summit meetings between the presidents in 2000 and 2007, other political meetings at ministerial level, and a better level of socio-cultural and economic dialogue and interaction. The Olympic delegations of the two countries also paraded together in the opening and closing ceremonies of the 2000, 2004 and 2008 Olympics, under a single white flag with the image of the entire Korean peninsula, bourne by athletes from the two countries. It was also a period of the most interesting political and legislative activities for the cooperation between the two countries, and the launch of some joint economic initiatives, such as the Kaesong industrial park.

After the Sunshine policy period, relations between the two countries worsened considerably, returning to a cold war mode, with some serious military incidents; and with the acceleration of the North Korean nuclear program, followed by international sanctions and the increased isolation of the Pyongyang government, a government that sometimes manages to annoy with its own initiatives, military tests and warlike declarations also the Chinese government, today its main ally (as well as one of the main economic partners of the southern country) on the regional and global chessboard, and the negotiating table created to tackle the nuclear issue (the "Six-Party Talks"), involving Russia, China, the United States, Japan and the two Koreas – whose work has been suspended since 2012.

The election in 2017 of President Moon Jae-in, the son of North Korean exiles and a supporter of a renewed policy of opening up to the North – promptly renamed Moonshine policy by the media around the world – has led to a possible improvement of North-South relations. After a spike in tension in the second half of 2017, with direct reciprocal threats of nuclear attacks between DPRK and the United States of America, 2018 opened with a moment of great relaxation, initiated by the leaders of the two Koreas on the occasion of PyeongChang Olympic Games in South Korea. This was followed by summit meetings between the two leaders, and a historic summit in Singapore between Kim Jong Un and North American president D. Trump. The dialogue started included the declared suspension of the DPRK nuclear program and the US-ROK joint military exercises, and with the planning of economic, social and family reunification initiatives between the two Koreas.

The key words "reunification" and "denuclearization" of the Korean peninsula are on the table and are spent in official statements, probably with a certain declamatory

354 *See* the *North Korean Human Rights Act*, website of the National Law Information Center (accessed 24 January 2017).

emphasis: it seems conceivable that the parties' objective in a reasonable time and political horizon is to start a gradual process to improve the stability of the region and its reciprocal relations – with the total denuclearization of the peninsula and the reunification of the Koreas as more ideal objectives than, at least in the state, concretely achievable.

3.4.2 *Possible Models of Reunification*

Beyond the contingent situation and concerns for the stability of the region, the two countries are constitutionally obliged to have reunification on their agenda, and to officially imagine the possible model, that sooner or later, more or less sincere or by mistake, they could find themselves having to apply.

Since the 1980s of the twentieth century, the dominant idea in the political-economic circles of the South has been that of a peaceful rapprochement and an open supranational union between the two States: an entity that maintains two governments and two political-economic systems; cultural political and social economic cooperation as a way to create a single market and a commonwealth with some coordination bodies; reunification with one sole constitution, political system and government, being a more distant objective.[355]

The North Korean vision, on the other hand, was that of a confederal state with a central federal government, with areas that differ from the economic, social and juridical point of view.[356] It seems, however, that the model proposed by the southern country had become acceptable to Kim Jong Il during the period of sunshine politics, as revealed by the president of South Korea Kim Dae Jung after the meeting with Kim Jong Il of 2000, with his referred willingness to consider a model similar to a "confederation of one people with two systems and two governments."[357]

The examples of Chinese reunification immediately come to mind, with the peaceful return of Hong Kong and Macao (and sooner or later of Taiwan, in the Chinese perspective) to the motherland according to the all-Chinese model of *One Country, Two Systems*, already considered and almost implemented in DPRK with the Sinuiju SAR affair. This is a peaceful model, suitable to protect the motivations of the two ruling elites, originating in

355 *See* the website of the South Korean Ministry of Unification, which presents the "Unification Policy" and the "Korean National Community Unification Formula" of Seoul (http://eng.unikorea.go.kr); S.H. Jwa, C-I. Moon, J.H. Roh, *Constitutional Handbook on Korean Reunification*, Seoul, Korea Economic Research Institute, 2002, passim; T.H. Kwak (Ed.) *Korean Reunification: New Perspectives and Approaches*, Seoul, Kyungnam University Press, 1984, passim; C. Choi, *Law and Justice in Korea*, op cit., 330-331; this author refers on p. 325 how during the presidency of Kim Dae Jung, a draft of constitution for the reunified country, still kept secret, had also been prepared.

356 J.K. Park, *North Korea's Democratic Confederal Republic of Koryo: A Critique*, in T.H. Kwak (Ed.) *Korean Reunification: New Perspectives and Approaches*, op cit., 69-83.

357 Also Kim Dae Jung, *Peace on the Korean Peninsula and East Asia*; Singapore Lecture Series, 20 (2000), Singapore, Institute of South East Asian Studies, 7.

a friend of the northern country but a friend and great economic partner also of the southern country, as well as historical political partner of the Korean kingdoms.

The social and economic gap created in over seventy years of separation has certainly eased the ethnic ties considerably and diminished the cultural homogeneity between the two Korean peoples;[358] those in the south certainly do not seem generally inclined to bear the costs of a reunification all on their shoulders. However, one cannot rule out the re-emergence of an underground tendency towards reunification, strong on both sides, of an ancient nation that has been divided as a result of the military activities of foreign powers. A lightening of the security framework guaranteed by the great powers, a certain economic opening to the north, and the start of a serious cooperation between the two countries could produce an economic, cultural and social rapprochement, and then also, in a distant future, at least some implementation of the principle of *one people, two governments, two systems.*

The South Koreans, in a crisis of pride and self-esteem,[359] could borrow a little from their northern cousins, in exchange for some of their economic well-being.

Unless something unexpected happens, naturally.

358 All the sources on the subject report the discomfort and difficulties of the insertion of the North Korean defectors in the society of the south, and the sense of hostility or indifference of a significant part towards the former.

359 M. Riotto, *La Corea non è un paese*, in *Limes*, 2016 n. 12, *La Corea è una bomba*, 31-44, *passim*.

4 South-East Asia

4.1 Introduction: Composite Juridical-Institutional Character of the Area and Common Aspects

South East Asia, which includes the Indo-Chinese promontory and the Malay archipelago (once called Insulindia), is an extremely varied area.

It is varied from an economic point of view, given the different degree of development of its national economies. According to the indicators provided by the World Bank, Cambodia, Laos, Vietnam, Burma, East Timor and the Philippines are among the countries with a medium-low income, Thailand, Malaysia, Indonesia and the Philippines are among those with a medium-high income and Singapore with a high income, among the richest countries in the world.

It is varied from a cultural point of view, due to the fact that the area has been subject to a complex stratification, owing to the overlapping of influences of different cultures, Chinese, Hindu, Islamic and, most recently, Western culture, during the colonial era.

Finally, it is varied from a legal and institutional point of view: in terms of the sources of law, only two countries have followed the Anglo-Saxon *common law* model (Singapore and Malaysia), the others having followed the *civil law* model. These models, derived from the colonial era, were subsequently combined in various ways with the juridical tradition of the region (be it based on customs, or of a Confucian or Islamic origin). With regards to the institutional systems, there are two constitutional monarchies (Cambodia and Malaysia), two socialist republics (Laos and Vietnam), two presidential republics (Indonesia and the Philippines), a semi-presidential republic (East Timor), two parliamentary republics (Singapore and Burma) and a military regime (Thailand, following the May 2014 coup d'ètat).[1]

In such a composite and heterogeneous context, it is however possible to identify some common aspects: beyond the obvious geographical proximity, the colonial domination borne over the centuries (with the exception of Thailand) and the economic growth recorded in the last decades (with the 1997 grave setback, known as the "Asian tiger crisis"), there is the need to take into consideration membership of ASEAN (*Association of Southeast*

1 For a general legal framework on the countries in the area, *see* the following texts: M.B. Hooker, *A Concise Legal History of South East Asia*, Oxford, Clarendon Press, 1978; E.A Black, G.F. Bell, *Law and Legal Institutions of Asia: Traditions, Adaptations and Innovations*, Cambridge, Cambridge University Press, 2011; A. Harding, *Global Doctrine and Local Knowledge: Law in South East Asia*, in *International and Comparative Law Quarterly*, vol. 51, n. 1, 2002, 35-53; L. Sempi, *Diritto del Sud-est asiatico*, in R. Cavalieri (Ed.), *Diritto dell'Asia orientale*, Venezia, Cafoscarina, 2008; G. Ajani, A. Serafino, M. Timoteo, *Diritto dell'Asia orientale*, in R. Sacco (Ed.), *Trattato di diritto comparato*, Torino, Utet, 2006.

Asian Nations), founded in 1967 by Indonesia, Malaysia, the Philippines, Singapore and Thailand. ASEAN, which now includes the Brunei sultanate (which became a member in 1984), Vietnam (1995), Laos and Burma (1997), Cambodia (1999) and East Timor (2017), has an amalgamating value, having, for over 40 years, favoured cooperation and intergovernmental assistance, with the stated aim of accelerating the economic progress of its member states and increasing the stability of the region.[2]

It is also worth mentioning the debate surrounding the so-called Asian values, that emerged precisely in this area: the expression was in fact coined in 1980 by Lee Kuan Yew, the then Prime Minister of Singapore, and later adopted by other figures on the Asian political scene, including the Malaysian Prime Minister Mahathir, and legitimized in the Bangkok Declaration, a document drawn up in 1993 by the *leaders* of the Asian countries participating in the World Conference on Human Rights. The universality of fundamental rights was thus questioned in the name of the cultural peculiarities of the area (superiority of the common good with respect to individual interests, the search for mediation and good-naturedness in resolving disputes, etc.). This debate, nevertheless, lends itself to a series of criticisms, *in primis* that of a sort of alibi for evading the demands for full and effective protection of human rights.[3]

4.2 The Philippines

4.2.1 *Brief Constitutional History*

The Philippines experienced a very long period of colonization, which inevitably left its mark on the country from a cultural and juridical point of view.

Before the arrival of the colonizers, the traditional law of the natives was founded mainly on unwritten customs, applied by the *Datu*, the head of the local communities, called *Barangay*. The presence of some written codifications has been reported, even in the pre-colonial era, the *Maragtas* Code, applied on the Island of *Panay*, and the *Kalantiao* Code: their actual existence, however, is still debated today.

---

2 For some interesting reflections also of a geopolitical nature on ASEAN and on the strategic importance of the area: F. Mazzei, V. Volpi, *Asia al centro*, Milano, Egea – Università Bocconi Editore, 2014.

3 On the comparison between Asian values and human rights, *see* the following contributions: J. Habermas, W. Rehg, *Remarks on Legitimation through Human Rights*, in *Philosophy and Social Criticism*, vol. 24, n. 2-3, 1998, 157-171; R. Peerenboom, *Beyond Universalism and Relativism: The Evolving Debates on "Values in Asia"*, in *Indiana International & Comparative Law Review*, vol. 14, 2003, 1ff; T. Groppi, Tania, *Costituzioni senza costituzionalismo? La codificazione dei diritti in Asia agli inizi del XXI secolo*, in *Pol. dir.*, 2006, 187-221; A. Sen, *La democrazia degli altri. Perché la libertà non è un'invenzione dell'Occidente*. Milano, Mondadori, 2004, 67 ff.

The long chapter of the history of the Philippines concerning the colonial period began in the sixteenth century, with Magellan, who discovered this archipelago in 1521, and the subsequent expeditions ordered by Philip II of Spain (to whom the Philippines owes its name): from that moment on until 1898, the Philippine archipelago was subject to Spanish domination, then passed under US power (from 1898, with a very brief continuity solution, represented by the fleeting experience of a Republic led by General Emilio Aguinaldo), and finally the Japanese occupation (in the period between 1941 and 1944). The colonial experience ended only after the Second World War, in 1946, with the proclamation of independence and the establishment of the Republic.

This historical circumstance was accompanied by a phase of political instability, followed by a period of "constitutional authoritarianism" under Ferdinand E. Marcos. On 21 September 1972, Marcos proclaimed martial law, beginning a period (1972-1986) of intense discontent, during which, Benigno Aquino, the leader of the opposition, was assassinated.

The year 1986 can be considered a turning point in the history of the country: political elections were called, which ended with accusations of significant vote-rigging by the outgoing president and led to a popular non-violent uprising (the so-called *People Power Revolution*), until the ousting of Marcos, who was forced into exile, in the same year.

The Constitution, promulgated the following year, marked the return to legality and democracy.

The Philippine legal system presents hybrid characteristics, adding together elements of the Spanish model, still prevalent, with others referable to the American model, more present in the area of commercial law, with others still of Islamic law.

Therefore, legislative sources are the source of the law; furthermore, according to the American example, even a legal precedent is endowed with a binding force (the judgments of the Supreme Court, in fact, bind the courts of lower rank). Moreover, judicial power produces norms via some specific regulatory interventions, such as the *Rules of Court*, issued by the Supreme Court, which regulate the matters of civil and penal procedure, replacing in fact the relative codes.

As in other countries of the area, with the exception of Malaysia and Indonesia, in the Philippines too, a non-predominantly Muslim country, but moreover Christian (Catholics representing more than 80% of the population), Islamic law on a personal basis is applied: for those who profess the Muslim religion (a rather small minority, concentrated in some areas south of the country, especially on the island of Mindanao), the *Code of Muslim Personal Laws* of 1977, is applied before the Sharia courts, previously mentioned.[4]

4 V. M.O. Mastura, *Legal Pluralism in the Philippines*, in *Law & Society Review*, vol. 28, no. 3, 1994; *Law and Society in Southeast Asia*, 1994, 461-476.

Lastly, it is important to underline the role that the two former colonial powers, Spain and the United States, still play in the Philippine legal landscape: Spanish legislation and American law (both of a legislative or judicial nature), in fact, continue to exert a persuasive power, where it is not otherwise possible to find a rule applicable to the case in question.

The Spanish legal tradition is still present in today's Philippine law: in particular, in the area of civil law, where a 1950 Spanish-inspired code is in force. The Spanish imprint becomes more remarkable in terms of successions, property and obligations, while contractual matters are more affected by the influence of the US *common law*.

4.2.2 The State Powers and the Local Administration[5]

The 1987 Constitution – still in force today – is the fundamental law of the Philippines, the third constitution since the proclamation of independence, after that of 1973 and that with a "provisional" nature of 1986.

In light of the Constitution, the Philippines is today, a presidential Republic, based on the American model, differentiating only in the fact that it did not implement the federal form of state.

The Head of State is the President of the Republic, elected directly by the electorate for a non-renewable term of six years and invested with executive power (Art. VII of the Constitution). Alongside the President, the Government exercises the executive function, whose members are appointed by the President himself, together with some independent agencies, such as the Central Bank and the *Securities and Exchange Commission*, as is also the case in the United States.

Legislative power is entrusted to Parliament, consisting of two Chambers, the Senate (with only 24 senators, elected for 6 years, of which half the number are renewed every 3 years) and the House of Representatives (297 deputies, of which 238 elected with a mandate of 3 years with a uninominal system, to which is added the 20% of elected members representing minorities elected with a proportional system). Since 2003, with the *Overseas Absentee Voting Act*, the right to vote was extended to the many Philippine citizens residing or temporarily abroad, estimated at over ten million.

Judicial power is also modelled according to the American paradigm: at the vertex, the Supreme Court operates, composed of a President and fourteen judges, who are entrusted with overseeing the constitutionality of laws and other normative acts and the appeal judgment on rulings issued by the lower courts (courts of appeal and regional courts).

---

5 R.C. Pangalan, *The Philippine "People Power" Constitution, Rule of Law, and the Limits of Liberal Constitutionalism*, in R. Peerenboom (Ed.), *Asian Discourse of Rule of Law*, London/New York, Routledge, 2004, 371-384.

A famous ruling on constitutional legitimacy (*Tanada v. Angara*, 272 SCRA 18, 2 May 1997) concerned the accession of the Philippines, in 1995, to the *World Trade Organization*. On this occasion, the Supreme Court, examining some principles, in particular, those of national treatment and the most favoured nation clause, placed at the core of the whole WTO system, in relation to Articles II, Section 19, and XII, Sections 10 and 12 of the Philippine Constitution, declared that these provisions had a mere programmatic value, and hence were not immediately binding for judges, but acted as guidelines for the legislator. Furthermore, it refuted the notion that the Philippine Constitution, read as a whole, embodied an isolationist policy: with this, it excluded, that stemming from the constitution, the Philippine state was prohibited from taking part in the processes of globalization and internationalization of exchanges, such as those favoured by the WTO.[6]

The Supreme Court also has the power to regulate in matters of judicial organization and the power to appoint and control all the judicial personnel (Art. VIII of the Constitution).

In the Philippine judicial system, some special courts are also contemplated, such as military courts, Sharia courts, which apply Muslim law, a tribunal in charge of tax matters and the *Sandinganbayan*, which judges crimes committed by Public Administration.

Justice traditionally represents one of the weak links in the Philippine legal system: trial times are quite long and the category of judges, poorly paid, are held in a scant professional and moral consideration. It must also be said that some flaws are more evident than in other countries, due to the greater freedom of the press.

In accordance with Article X of the Constitution, the territory is divided into provinces, cities, municipalities and *barangayas* (villages). Each level has regulatory and financial autonomy. Mindanao, an island south of the Philippine archipelago, where the population is predominantly Muslim, is an Autonomous Region: it thus exerts legislative power in the matters identified in Article X, Section 20 of the Constitution, including administrative organization, taxation, cultural heritage, family relationships, and urban and rural development. Even the Cordilleras, a mountainous region located in the north of the country, features in the same art. as an autonomous region, but this status has never been officially acquired as a result of the negative outcome of the referendums involving the population in 1990 and 1998.

4.2.3 *Fundamental Rights and Freedoms*

In the list of rights and freedoms, the Philippine Constitution is characterized, in relation to the constitutions of the area in question, by its length and completeness, also contem-

6 For the full text of the sentence: http://elibrary.judiciary.gov.ph/thebookshelf/showdocs/1/34805 (last accessed on May 13, 2019).

plating the so-called third generation rights (the rights of the disabled, consumers, and those related to the environment, etc.). In the catalogue of rights too, the American influence emerges, previously noted in the design of the Philippine institutional structure: it is sufficient to recall the guarantees foreseen in trials (the right to a defence, etc.) to note such an influence.

The Philippine Constitution expressly affirms the principle of human dignity (Art. II, Sect 11, which states that the State "values the dignity of the human person and guarantees full respect of human rights"): this provision is strengthened by the presence of a special commission, the *Human Rights Commission*, which has the functions of investigating human rights violations, envisaging, in a precautionary manner, measures for the protection of rights and providing for the legal assistance of those whose rights are violated, the inspection of prisons and other facilities used for detention, the monitoring of the Government's activity in fulfilling its international obligations, recommending measures for the promotion of human rights and compensation to victims of violations (Art. XIII, Sects. 17 and 18).

Precisely from the point of view of this last constitutional provision, the Law (*Human Rights Victims Reparation and Recognition Act*) launched in 2013, also has a symbolic, and not only, importance, which provides for forms of reparation for violations of human rights perpetrated under the regime of the 1972 Martial Law (ordered by the then president Marcos and which remained in force up until 1986).

4.3 INDONESIA

4.3.1 *Brief Constitutional History*

From many points of view, the huge Indonesian archipelago is of great importance, which is not limited to the area, that of South-East Asia, to which it belongs: Indonesia is today the largest Islamic majority in the world. It is the first economy in Southeast Asia and is the third most populous country in Asia.

Indonesia too, in a similar way to the other countries in the area in question, has a history marked by colonial experience: from the seventeenth century until the Second World War it was, in fact, under Dutch domination and for some years it endured the Japanese occupation. Independence was gained on 17 August 1945, under the guidance of Sukarno, who became the first president of the Indonesian republic. In the same year, the Indonesian Constitution, still in force, although revised, was promulgated. This text is strongly influenced by the ideology promoted by Sukarno, which one finds expressed in the five principles of *Pancasila* (an expression of Sanskrit origin meaning "five principles"), identified as: faith in the one God, a just and civilized humanity, national unity, representative democracy and social justice.

After the events of the decade straddling the end of the twentieth and the beginning of the twenty-first century, that is to say, the financial crisis of 1997, the fall in 1998 of Suharto (the successor of Sukarno) after 32 years in power, the secession of East Timor, the rise of the separatist movement in the province of Aceh (a conflict concluded with a peace agreement in 2005), the natural disasters of the *tsunami* (2004) and the earthquake on the island of Java (2006),[7] subsequently, Indonesia embarked on a new phase of political growth and socio-economic development.

The process of democratization in Indonesia occurred via repeated reforms of the Constitution: thus, the 1945 text was subjected to far-reaching revisions, in particular, on several occasions, between 1999 and 2002. Despite the substantial progress made on the road to democracy, some scholars have pointed out that the democratic transition would have been more rapid, if only it had pursued with greater determination, the crimes and various kinds of abuses committed during the regime established by Suharto.[8]

Indonesian law offers numerous point of interest due to the fact that it is the result of completely different substrates: the most dated being that of pre-colonial times, and of a prevalently customary nature (*adat*).[9] The customs formed and handed down orally in the various local communities still survive today, for example in the field of agricultural law, especially in some regions, outside the island of Java.

To this substrate, that of the colonial era was superimposed, which was influenced by the Dutch influence (the Dutch Civil Code and Commercial Code are still partially in force), and finally the superimposition of the substratum that can be qualified as "national", dating back to the period after independence.

To this, there is also the addition of Islamic law, which is applied with reference to personal status (family law and succession, in particular) for Indonesian citizens of the Muslim faith, who represent the large majority of the population (about 87%, according to the data provided by the 2010 census).[10]

With reference to the institution of marriage, therefore, for the majority of the population, the Sharia (Islamic law based mainly on the Koran and the Sunnah, i.e. the stories regarding the life of the Prophet Muhammad) is applied, together with the legislation

---

7 On the impact of natural disasters on the protection of fundamental rights in Indonesia, *see* N.Y. Puspita, *Legal Analysis of Human Rights Protection in Times of Natural Disaster and Its Implementation in Indonesia*, in *ASLI Working Paper Series* n. 13, 2010.

8 M. Draper, *Justice as a Building Block of Democracy in Transitional Societies: The Case of Indonesia*, in *Columbia Journal of Transnational Law*, vol. 40, 2002, 391-418.

9 On this topic, the reference text is represented by the work of Hooker: M.B. Hooker, *Adat Law in Modern Indonesia*, Kuala Lumpur, Oxford University Press, 1978.

10 On the role of the *Sharia* in today's Indonesian law, *see* H. Federspiel, *Islamic Values, Law and Expectation in Contemporary Indonesia*, in *Islamic Law and Society*, vol. 5, 1998, 90-117.

adopted by the Indonesian authorities in 1974 (*National Marriage Act),* with the declared purpose, and only partially achieved, to reduce "child" marriages, raising the minimum age for marriage, and to limit arbitrary divorces and the phenomenon of polygamy. Regarding inter-religious marriages, which the *National Marriage Act* does not prohibit nor expressly permit, the Indonesian Supreme Court has acknowledged the existence of a regulatory vacuum, which makes it difficult to obtain registration of interfaith marriages before the administrative authorities, inducing spouses to alternative solutions, such as the celebration of marriage abroad or the conversion of one partner to the faith of the other.

4.3.2 The State Powers and the Local Administration

Under the constitutional profile, Indonesia is a presidential Republic: the President is, contemporaneously, the head of state and the head of the government, as well as commander in chief of the armed forces. He is elected, together with his deputy, directly by the people for a five-year term, renewable only once (Art. 7 of the Constitution). The President also has extensive powers of appointment and dismissal of the Council of Ministers, which together with the president, exercises executive functions.

The Parliament – originally denominated the People's Consultative Assembly – is bicameral (*Majelis Permusyawaratan Rakyat*, MPR), and is composed of the People's Representative Council (*Dewan Perwakilan Rakyat*, DPR), composed of 550 elected members with a five-year term, and by the Representative Council Regional (*Dewan Perwakilan Daerah*, DPD), also elected by universal suffrage for five years. Parliament, which meets in joint session at least once every five years (Art. 2 of the Constitution), has the power to amend the Constitution and to impeach the President in accordance with one of the hypotheses specified by Article 7A of the constitution, (high treason, corruption or another serious crime, unethical behaviour or loss of the qualifications necessary to hold the office). The People's Representative Council approves laws together with the President, while the Regional Representative Council promotes legislative proposals on regional autonomy and the relationship between central government and local government and exercises advisory functions on issues concerning taxes, religion and education, but it is not invested with legislative power.

At the top of the "official" hierarchy of the sources of law, ratified by the People's Consultative Assembly in 2000, is the Constitution, composed of only 73 articles and rigid in nature, due to the fact that any modifications to the constitution require the presence of two-thirds of the members of Parliament and approval by an absolute majority (Art. 37 of the Constitution): the Constitutional Court (*Mahkamah Konstitusi*), established after the constitutional amendment of 2001 (Art. 24C of the Constitution) ensures observance of the Constitution. However, the process of checking constitutional legitimacy is not regulated by the Constitution itself, but by implementing legislation. Moreover, this control can only concern the laws subsequent to 19 October 1999, the date of the first constitutional review after the fall of Suharto and the beginning of the process of democratic transition.

Beneath the Constitution are the political directives adopted jointly by the two Houses, followed by the law (called *Undang-Undang*, UU), government regulations, presidential decrees and finally regional regulations. In continuity with the tradition of *civil law* borrowed at the time of Dutch domination, judicial precedent is devoid of binding force and is therefore not counted among the sources of law.

The Indonesian judicial system is structured according to three degrees of jurisdiction: the *State Courts* (*Pengadilan Negeri*) are courts of the first instance, the upper courts (*Pengadilan Tinggi*) act as appeal tribunals and the Supreme Court (*Mahkamah Agung*) acts as the judge of legitimacy in the last instance and controls and supervises the lower courts. The judges who make up the Supreme Court are appointed by the President on designation by the Judicial Commission of the DPR (Art. 24A of the Constitution).

Parallel to the ordinary courts, some special jurisdictions have been set up in administrative, military and commercial matters (since 1998). The latter judge, in particular, bankruptcy cases, intellectual property and competition.

As in other countries of Muslim faith, Islamic courts also operate in Indonesia that apply the *Sharia* to the people of Muslim faith, in disputes concerning family law and succession. It should be noted that in the region of Aceh, which as a result of the separatist claims and an agreement with the central authorities and which benefits from a special autonomy, the *Sharia* is also applied in criminal law.

Indonesian justice is permeated by some chronic defects, linked to the slowness of trials and flaws in the professional preparation, reliability and morality of its judges.

In line with the approach observed in the rest of the area, there is also a greater propensity for an amicable solution to disputes in Indonesia: conciliation and mediation with regard to judicial and arbitration resolutions, are preferred.

Since 2003, as anticipated, the Constitutional Court came into operation, an institution introduced into the Indonesian Constitution with the amendments of 2001 and invested with the power to control the constitutional legitimacy of laws, as well as the power to settle disputes arising between state bodies (Art. 24C of the Constitution). The nine judges of the Constitutional Court are appointed for one-third by the Supreme Court, one third by the Representative Council of the People and for another third by the President.

Article 18 of the Constitution solemnly proclaims Indonesia as a unitary state. Its territory is divided into provinces, districts (*kabupaten*) and municipalities (*kota*). Following the reform introduced in 2001, local authorities enjoy wide regulatory autonomy, with the exclusion of matters reserved for the central government.

4.3.3 *Fundamental Rights and Freedoms*

Fundamental rights and freedoms are included in the Constitution, but with a series of limitations that vary their scope in various ways: firstly, they are enunciated only after the nine initial chapters, dedicated to the system of the state. The list of political, economic and social rights, although very broad, is not supported by the guarantee of non-modifiability: in fact, the material limits envisaged for constitutional revision do not concern fundamental rights, but exclusively the unitary form of the State (Art. 37 of the Constitution).

Indeed, there is a limitation clause on legislative power, owing to the fact that the law may limit the exercise of rights and freedoms, but "for the sole purpose of guaranteeing respect and recognition of the rights of others and to respond to the needs that, in a democratic society, arise on the basis of morals, religious values, safety and public order" (Art. 28J of the Constitution).

Some rights (the right to life, freedom from torture and slavery, freedom of thought and conscience, religion, recognition of the quality of a person before the law and the right not to be tried on the basis of a subsequent retroactive law) cannot however be limited under any circumstances (Art. 28 of the Constitution).

After the 1999 reform, particular emphasis was given to the principle of human dignity, to which repeated reference is made (see Art. 34 of the Constitution, in which it is taken as a reference parameter for social *welfare* interventions by the State).

Given the variety of cultural identities present on the territory, the provisions that the Indonesian Constitution dedicate to the theme of their protection are interesting: on the one hand, it states that "cultural identities and the rights of traditional communities are respected in accordance with the development of the times and civilizations" (Art. 28I, para. 3 of the Constitution); on the other, the right of ethnic minorities to speak their own language is recognized, imposing upon the State the duty of respecting and preserving local languages (Art. 32, para. 2 of the Constitution).

Precisely this profile presents problematic aspects, considering the difficulties encountered by the Indonesian authorities in dealing peacefully with, above all in the past, the remonstrants and protests of the rebel separatist movements. In particular, the Aceh region (north of the island of Sumatra), was the scene of violence and violations of fundamental rights, as stigmatized by many parties.[11]

---

11 *See* Bar Association of New York, *Law under Siege: The Struggle to Prosecute Human Rights Abuses in Aceh, Indonesia*, in *The Record*, vol. 57, 2002, 307 ff.

4.4 East Timor

4.4.1 *Brief Constitutional History*

The territory of East Timor consists mainly of the eastern half of the island of Timor, hence its name: the remaining portion of the island is part of the Indonesian territory. The Portuguese settled there during the sixteenth century, due to its location along the trade routes, making it its own colony. The long period spent under Portuguese domination left as a legacy, a widespread Catholic religiosity that makes East Timor the only country, along with the Philippines, with a Catholic majority (circa 98% of the population, according to 2015 data) in an area predominantly of Muslim faith.

After the proclamation of independence from Portugal in 1975, East Timor was occupied by Indonesian troops, who claimed sovereignty over the region and declared it officially the twenty-seventh province of Indonesia. Despite the condemnation of the United Nations, the civilian population and the Fretilin (*Frente revolucionária do Timor Leste independente*, the political organization that had led the country to independence) were subjected to harsh repression by the Indonesian government, which also adopted a massive immigration program aimed at forming an indigenous pro-Indonesian Muslim *elite* and, at the same time, to "dilute" the local community, predominantly of the Christian faith.

The independence of East Timor from Indonesia was recognized internationally in 2002, after a transition phase, during which local administration was provisionally assigned to the UN, as part of the "INTERFET" mission (*International Force for East Timor*).[12] After overcoming a coup attempt in 2008, the country is now experiencing a phase of greater stability and consolidation of its young democracy.

Lastly, East Timor became a member of the World Intellectual Property Organization (WIPO, with effect from the end of 2017) and started the procedures for joining ASEAN and the WTO, a sign of its willingness to fully become a part of the international community.

4.4.2 *The State Powers and the Local Administration*

The Constitution, which dates back to 2002, the year of official independence from Indonesia, is characterized by the solemn affirmation with which it opens (immediately after the Preamble): "The Democratic Republic of East Timor is a democratic, sovereign,

12 On the phase of the assertion of East Timor independence with respect to Indonesia, *see* R.S. Clark, *East Timor, Indonesia and the International Community*, in *Temple International and Comparative Law Journal*, vol. 14, 2000, 75 ff.; M. Mazza, *Aspetti e problemi della storia istituzionale di Timor Est. Profili costituzionalistici, sistema partitico e linee di sviluppo politico-amministrativo*, in *Dir. pubbl. comp. eur.*, 1999, 1382 ff.

independent and unitary state, based on the *rule of law*, on the will of the people and respect for the dignity of the human person" (Art. 1 of the Constitution).

The recent past of East Timor, as expected, is echoed within the constitution: hence, declamations abound in favour of the principles of self-determination of peoples and of solidarity with other peoples fighting for independence (Arts. 8 and 10 of the Constitution).

The constitutional charter is very long (consisting of 170 articles) and rigid: revision requires, in fact, the approval of a very large majority (4/5 of the parliamentary assembly) or the passing of six years since the last revision.

From the institutional framework outlined emerges a republic in the form of a semi-presidential government, according to the Portuguese model. The President, elected directly by the people, is the guarantor of the independence and unity of the country, but also of the good functioning of the institutions. The Parliament is unicameral and consists of 65 members elected directly by the electoral body for a five-year term. Among its duties, first of all, is the approval of the laws of the State. The following matters fall within the exclusive legislative power of the State: citizenship, national territorial borders, associations and political parties, the electoral law (Art. 95 of the Constitution). In addition, the Parliament is responsible for the approval of the budget, the ratification of international treaties, and the proposal for a referendum on matters of national interest.

At the vertex of the judiciary is the Supreme Court of East Timor.

Administrative decentralization is the basic principle of the country's territorial organization (Art. 5 of the Constitution). The norm, however, refers back to the law, the determination of the administrative responsibilities of the local levels (districts, sub-districts and villages, *suku*) in which the territory is divided. Among the 13 districts, Oecussi Ambeno (an enclave in the north-western part of the island of Timor, in Indonesian territory) and the island of Ataúro (north of the capital Dili) enjoy a special status.

4.4.3 Fundamental Rights and Freedoms

From the point of view of the catalogue of fundamental rights and freedoms, the Constitution adopts solutions that qualify as being "modern", owing to the fact that it also includes the so-called rights of the third generation, such as the right to the protection of personal data, in accordance with Art. 38 of the Constitution, and provides greater guarantees, since it excludes the subject of citizens' rights, freedoms and guarantees from the possibility of constitutional revision (Art. 156 of the Constitution).

A limitation of rights, guarantees and fundamental freedoms acknowledged by the Constitution is permitted, envisaged via an expressed constitutional provision (Art. 24 of the Constitution), exclusively by law and in order to safeguard constitutional rights and interests.

Finally, worthy of interest is the norm that invokes the Universal Declaration of Human Rights for the purpose of interpreting the fundamental rights recognized by the Constitution itself (Art. 23 of the Constitution).

4.5 MALAYSIA

4.5.1 *Brief Constitutional History*

After a long period of colonial domination (first Portuguese and Dutch, and subsequently, for over a century and a half, British domination), Malaysia achieved independence in 1957 and is now a federal state, composed of thirteen Member States, of which eleven are located in the Malay Peninsula (West Malaysia) and two (*Sabah* and *Sarawak*) on the island of Borneo (Eastern Malaysia), as well as three "federal territories" (*Kuala Lumpur, Labuan, Putrajaya*).

However, since 1965, Singapore has not been part of the Malaysian federation, having declared secession on that date and having become an independent republic.

Malaysia is a federal-based constitutional monarchy, with very original characteristics in the framework of contemporary forms of state: at the head of the country, there is a monarch (denominated *Yang di-Pertuan Agong*, supreme head), chosen, according to criteria of rotation and opportunity, from among the hereditary sultans of the monarchical states (nine out of thirteen) that make up the Malaysian federation. The sultans themselves choose who among them will be the federal monarch for a five-year term. In the remaining four non-monarchical states, the role of Head of State is played by a Governor (*Yang di-Pertua Negeri*), designated by the federal monarch for a four-year term.

4.5.2 *The State Powers and the Local Administration*

The Malaysian institutional framework outlined by the Constitution of 1957 (subsequently reformed on several occasions) is inspired by the principle of the separation of powers, in accordance with the particular declination that this assumes in the English model.[13] The Federal Parliament, according to the English tradition, consists of three organs: the Sovereign and the two Chambers, represented by the Senate (*Dewan Negara*) and House of Representatives (*Dewan Rakyat*).

---

13 H.P. Lee, *Constitutional Conflicts in Contemporary Malaysia*, Kuala Lumpur, Oxford University Press, 1995; K. Y.L. Tan, Li-Ann Thio, *Constitutional Law in Malaysia and Singapore*, Singapore, Butterworths Asia, 1997; A. Harding, *The Keris, the Crescent and the Blind Goddess: The State, Islam and the Constitution in Malaysia*, in *Singapore Journal of International and Comparative Law*, vol. 6, 2002, 154 ff.; Id., *The Constitution of Malaysia: A Contextual Analysis*, Oxford/Portland (OR), Hart, 2012.

The Sovereign has the power to promulgate laws, granting his consent.

The Senate, largely composed of persons nominated by the Sovereign among prominent personages of the economic and cultural world, has a limited power to postpone laws.

The House of Representatives, the only federal legislative body directly elected by the people, has the power to enact laws, even without the consent of the Sovereign and the Senate.

The principle of the separation of powers operates not only at the federal but also at the state level. Within each individual federated state, the parliaments are unicameral, and directly elected.

The Federal Parliament passes a vote of confidence in the Government, which exercises executive power: it is the Sovereign who confers the mandate to the Prime Minister (*Perdana Menteri*), who, in turn, appoints his ministers, choosing from among the deputies and senators (Art. 43 of the Constitution).

The Constitution divides by subject the legislative competence of the Federation and the Member States. The Federation is responsible for foreign affairs, defence, internal security, criminal law, procedural law, the judiciary (except for the Islamic courts), citizenship, a large part of civil, commercial and financial law, transport and communications, education, health, labour, publishing and other minor subjects.

On the other hand, the land tenure regime, Islamic law, agriculture, forests and local administration are included in the exhaustive list of matters under the jurisdiction of the individual States. The two states of Borneo have a broader legislative autonomy than the other federated States.

Furthermore, a set of matters is assigned to the shared competence of the Federation and the Member States: social *welfare*, scholarships, the protection of flora and fauna, urban planning, etc. In the event of a conflict between federal and state legislation in one of these matters, the Federation predominates.

Each member state of the federation has its own Constitution, which is flanked by the Federal Constitution, referred to as the "supreme law" (Art. 4 of the Constitution). The control of the constitutionality of the laws is entrusted to the Federal Court.

The Constitution is only partially rigid: constitutional revision requires a two-thirds majority in each of the two Chambers. However, some matters (although important, as they are closely linked to the federal nature of the State, such as the admission of a State in the federation, the alteration of the borders of the States, the change of the federal capital, the composition of the second Chamber) are subject to a "flexibilization" clause and can be changed with a simple ordinary law (Art. 159 of the Constitution).

In a subordinate position with respect to federal and state laws, there is the so-called *delegated* or *subsidiary legislation*, that is to say, the legislation issued by the Government or by other bodies delegated by Parliament.

Based on the English *common law* model, judicial precedent also has a binding effect. Hence, English law is among the sources of Malaysian law (of judicial or legislative matrix, in force on the date of 1949, 1951 or 1956), which, according to the *Civil Law Act* of 1956 (Art. 3), finds application in civil disputes in a subsidiary manner or in the presence of a legislative gap. The same applies to criminal law (Art. 5, Code of criminal procedure).

Malay law attributes a certain space to customary law, referring to local, Chinese, Islamic and Hindu customs.

Islam is proclaimed the official state religion, although religious freedom is guaranteed by the Constitution (Art. 3 of the Constitution). Islamic law is applied only to Muslim citizens, who represent more than half of the country's population (61.3%, according to a 2010 census). This law is applied by a system of Islamic courts, parallel to the "ordinary" judiciary system.

The Malay judicial system is organized on a federal basis: the first instance courts are the two *High Courts* (one for West Malaysia and one for East Malaysia), which adjudicate the most serious criminal cases and the most economically significant civil cases, and the *Magistrates' Courts*, responsible for minor civil and criminal cases. The *Magistrates' Courts* are flanked by the *Subordinate Courts, Sessions Courts, Penghulu's Courts* and *Native Courts*. In the second instance, the *Court of Appeal* and the *High Courts,* pass judgments on the rulings issued by the *High Courts* and *Magistrates' Courts*.

Finally, at the vertex of the judiciary, is the Federal Court, which judges in appeal against the rulings issued by the *Court of Appeal,* in addition to exercising control over the constitutionality of laws and settling conflicts arising between States or between the States and the Federation.

In the past, there was the possibility to appeal to the English *Privy Council,* as a legacy of the colonial period: this possibility, however, was not permitted, in succession, in 1978 (for issues in criminal and constitutional matters) and in 1985 (for those in civil matters).

The judges of the Federal Court and *High Courts* are appointed by the Sovereign, on the recommendation of the Prime Minister and after consultation with the *Conference of Rulers* (composed of the sovereigns of the nine monarchies of the Federation). The President of the Federal Court, as the head of the judiciary, directly oversees all Malaysian courts.

4.5.3 *Fundamental Rights and Freedoms*

In terms of the constitutional protection of rights and freedoms, the Malaysian Constitution offers a catalogue of rights that cannot be classified as "long", with regards to the number of protected legal positions and the details of the rules pertaining to such positions (only 7 articles, out of a total of 181, are dedicated to rights).

Moreover, the Malaysian Constitution places some significant limitations on the exercise of rights: first of all, in the presence of some enumerated reasons, the freedoms recognized in Articles 9 and 10 (movement, expression, association and assembly) may be limited by the Parliament with an ordinary law.

Secondly, broad powers are acknowledged to public authorities in the event in which the Sovereign proclaims a state of emergency: such an event justifies the compression of the fundamental liberties of expression, association, assembly and permits preventive detention for a period of three months (Arts. 149-151 of the Constitution). In this regard, the *Internal Security Act* (known as ISA) adopted in 1960 to deal with the communist uprisings of that period was strongly criticized: the ISA was used to quell the dissent and ensure control over the country and remained in force until 2012, the year in which the *Security Offences (Special Measures) Act* was adopted. The new legislation did not fail to arouse protests due to its use against civil rights activists. Since 1969, a "provisional" law (Emergency Ordinance) has been in force permitting preventive detention, in order to guarantee crime prevention and public order: international organizations for the protection of human rights have denounced the extensive use of the afore-mentioned instruments by the Malaysian authorities.

Finally, the principle of equality (Art. 8 of the Constitution) is substantially limited in the privileges and special guarantees acknowledged by Article 153 of the Constitution to the *Bumiputera* (Malaysian nationals): these privileges, which include guaranteed quotas in public employment, the issuance of government licenses for commercial activities and so on, raise serious problems in a varied and multi-ethnic society such as that of Malaysia.

4.6 Singapore

4.6.1 Brief Constitutional History

Today, a multi-ethnic and lively city-state, Singapore (whose name derives from Sanskrit: *Singa*, lion, *pure*, city, city of the lion, the national symbol) was a colony of the British crown from 1826 to 1959, with a brief interlude represented by the Japanese domination during the second world war. It joined the Malaysian federation for a short period (starting in 1963), but declared secession only two years later, proclaiming itself independent on 9 August 1965.

On that occasion, Singapore adopted as a provisional constitution a series of acts: the Constitution of the Singapore State of 1963, the *Independence Act* of 1965 and some parts of the Malaysian Constitution. Subsequently, the Singapore authorities did not adopt a completely new constitution, but merely amended the text of 1963. Hence, the Singapore Constitution still remains a "composite" constitution, recently amended in 2016.

The political history of Singapore is marked by the long permanence in power of Lee Kuan Yew and his People's Action Party (PAP), whose government had a clear Confucian stamp, as well as being paternalistic. The particular electoral system (which includes, among other things, co-optation and presidential nomination), the absence of an effective opposition, until 1981 formally absent in Parliament too, and the intransigence of the Government towards political opponents have, up to now, prevented the establishment of real democratic debate in the country. Hence, Singapore is considered by most to be an authoritarian state. In fact, the PAP is still firmly at the helm of the country without there ever having been an alternation in government: it has 82 out of 91 deputies (considering only those elected) in Parliament and Lee Hsien Loong, son of Lee Kuan Yew has been continuously the Prime Minister since 2004. Lee Kuan Yew, himself, was Prime Minister from 1959 to 1990, a *senior minister* from 1990 to 2004 and, finally, "*minister mentor*" from 2004 until 2011.

Singapore law can be placed among the *common law* legal systems, i.e. those characterized, among other things, by the binding nature of judicial precedent. As is often the case with countries that have experienced and been subjected to colonization, Singapore followed the model of the power that had colonized it. Consequently, the English matrix is clear in the system of the sources, the legal language and in the regulating of the various institutes.[14]

In the legal landscape of the country, however, the British model is combined with Confucian thinking, of Chinese origin. From this stems a certain preference for personal and political relationships with respect to legal rules. Thus, here, as in China and other countries with which Singapore shares common philosophical traditions, the *rule of law* struggles to take root.

4.6.2 *The State Powers and the Local Administration*

Singapore is a republic with a parliamentary government: the Parliament, depositary of legislative power, is unicameral with 101 deputies. Of these, only some are elected by direct and universal suffrage, the others being co-opted by the Parliament itself (six in all), nominated (up to a maximum of nine) by the President or elected by the *group representation constitutions*, representative bodies of minority ethnic groups in the country. A speaker presides over the parliamentary assembly, as occurs in the English system.

The Government is placed at the head of executive power and responds to Parliament along with its Prime Minister who must be chosen from among the deputies.

14 K. Y.L. Tan, Li-Ann Thio, *Constitutional Law in Malaysia and Singapore*, Singapore, Butterworths Asia, 1997; K. Y.L. Tan, *The Singapore Legal System*, Singapore, Singapore University Press, 1999; K. Y.L. Tan, *The Evolution of Singapore's Modern Constitution: Developments from 1945 to the Present Day*, in *Singapore Academy of Law Journal*, vol. 1, 1989, 1-28.

The President of the Republic, elected directly by the electorate for a term of six years, has mainly representative powers. They must have Singapore citizenship, be 45 years of age, and be a person of "integrity, good character and reputation", but above all they should not be a member of a political party (Art. 19 of the Constitution). The Constitution favours a certain rotation in the representation of the main ethnic groups that make up the varied population of the city-state (Chinese, Malay, Indian or other minorities): Article 19 expressly envisages that eligibility for election is reserved for members of the communities that have not been elected to the presidential office for any of the five most recent terms. Following a constitutional review in 1991, aimed at increasing its institutional weight, the President was given a veto power over some governmental acts.[15] Since 2017, the President of Singapore, is Halimah Yacob, the first woman president in the history of the country.

As stated in Article 93 of the Constitution, judicial power is in the hands of the Supreme Court and the lower courts. The former is constituted by the *High Court* and the *Court of Appeal*, while the latter is made up of the *District Courts* and *Magistrates' Courts*.

Judges are appointed by the President on the recommendation of the Prime Minister, except for the President of the Supreme Court who is chosen discretionally by the Head of State alone. Judges at the lower-level courts possess minor guarantees, due to the fact that they can be revoked or removed from office by the decision of the executive. Unlike in other countries, the judges of Singapore are not career judges, since in most cases they perform judicial functions for periods of less than 15 years. However, a reform of the judicial system has been underway for a several years, aimed at guaranteeing greater specialization also for the lower courts.

A Sharia court is active in Singapore, with jurisdiction over family matters (marriage, engagement, divorce, dowry payment, etc.). It is possible to appeal against the decisions of this court to an *Appeal Board*, composed of three people of Muslim faith, selected by the Chancellor of the Supreme Court from a presidential nomination list. The rulings of the *Appeal Board* are final.

The Singapore justice system is judged to be efficient overall, especially when compared to the others in the South East Asia area. The judgments before the courts are relatively short and the introduction of technology (the hearing of texts via videoconference, the electronic storage of minutes, etc.) in proceedings has helped to reduce times.

The possibility of addressing the *Privy Council* in London was abolished several years ago (1994).

The arbitration resolution system of disputes, especially in the commercial sphere, is also quite developed in Singapore. Other forms of dispute resolution, alternatives to the judicial resolution (the so-called ADRs, *Alternative Dispute Resolutions*) are very

15 *Cf.* on this point, J. Tsen-Ta Lee, *Singapore's Elected President: An Office that Is Still Evolving*, in *Singapore Management University School of Law Opinion Series Paper*, n. JL2, 1-4, 2016.

widespread, in line with the Confucian tradition that favours the amicable solution of the disputes.

4.6.3 *Fundamental Rights and Freedoms*

Only eight articles of the Constitution (out of a total of 163) are dedicated to the enumeration of fundamental rights and freedoms: Part IV of the Constitutional Charter includes freedom of expression, assembly and association, circulation, the principle of equality and non-discrimination and freedom of religion. In this regard, a regime of separation between religious faiths is envisaged, according to which every citizen is required to declare their faith (before the age of eighteen this choice is made by the parents) and, in light of the option, receive the related religious education and practice their faith; no citizen is obliged to participate in worship activities of religious faiths other than their own (Art. 16 of the Constitution).

To a small list of rights is added the provision of penetrating limits that can reach the point of actually emptying these rights of their substance: for example, freedom of expression can be compressed by law by the Parliament in the interest of the nation's security, friendly relations with other countries, public order, morality or to protect the Parliament and the Courts from offences (Art. 14 of the Constitution).[16]

Furthermore, Article 150 gives the President, the right to proclaim a state of emergency: this circumstance legitimizes any derogation from the constitutional provisions, except those relating to religion, citizenship and language.

In a similar way to Malaysia, the *Internal Security Act* of 1960 was applied and is still applied in Singapore today. This act permits detention without trial (up to two years, with the possibility of a prolongation of the detention) where the President on the advice of the Cabinet deems a person to represent a danger to the security of the country. In the past, this legislation was used to counter terrorism, but many doubts arise in doctrine on the question of maintaining this legislation, with respect to the possibility of resorting, instead, to the instruments offered by the Penal Code and *Terrorism (Suppression of Bombings) Act.*[17]

---

16 On the balance between individual rights and collective interests as outlined by the Singapore Constitution, *see* J. Tsen-Ta Lee, *Rediscovering the Constitution*, in *Singapore Law Review*, vol. 16, 1995, 157 ff. On the judicial protection of fundamental rights in Singapore: J. Tsen-Ta Lee, *Protecting Human Rights: The Approach of the Singapore Courts*, in *Singapore Management University School of Law*, Research Paper No. 49/2015.

17 J. Tsen-Ta Lee, *The Past, Present and Future of the Internal Security Act*, in *Singapore Management University School of Law*, Opinion Series n. JL3/2012.

Finally, the "reinforced" procedure envisaged for constitutional revision (a two-thirds majority is required both in Parliament and for the referendum) concerns not the rules on rights, but those on the organization of the State (Art. 5 of the Constitution).

The picture does not improve when passing to the practical application plan: for example, freedom of expression and assembly are strongly limited by prohibitions and restrictions of various kinds (necessary authorizations for public gatherings with more than five people, a ban on the organization of open air assemblies by political parties and so on).

4.7 Thailand

4.7.1 *Brief Constitutional History*

Thailand has a long history marked by independence, being the only country in Southeast Asia not to have experienced colonial rule. Since the fourteenth century, it reached a unitary structure under the name of the Kingdom of Siam and was able to weave a dense network of trade relations with neighbouring countries and Western powers. It was only in the nineteenth century, that it had to partially renounce full sovereignty over its territory, following bilateral agreements with which the British authorities imposed the granting of some privileges, including the liberalization of trade and extraterritoriality for British subjects, subtracted from the jurisdiction and subject to the law and jurisdiction of the British consular authorities. As previously mentioned, however, Thailand was able to escape the imperialism of Western colonial powers, due to a number of concurrent factors: its geographical location, a strategic buffer between the area under French control and that of British domination, the skilled diplomacy of its monarchs and its policy of modernization.

Today, Thailand is still a monarchy. The current monarch (King Maha Vajiralongkorn, officially named *Rama* X, who succeeded King Bhumibol Adulyadej in 2016) is the descendant of the long-standing *Chakri* dynasty, which rose to power in 1782, with the first *Rama*, Thong Duang. The transition from an absolute monarchy to a constitutional monarchy occurred in 1932, following a non-bloody revolution that led to the promulgation of the first Thai Constitution. From that moment onwards, Thailand has seen the succession of nineteen different constitutions, a circumstance that highlights the strong instability that distinguishes the Thai political system,[18] confirmed by recent events: the coup d'etat

18 The most complete work on Thai constitutional history is A. Harding, P. Leyland, Peter, *The Constitutional System of Thailand: A Contextual Analysis*, Oxford/Portland (OR), Hart, 2011.

in September 2006, when the army deposed the government of Thaksin Shinawatra,[19] the subsequent dismissal of the prime minister, Somchai Wongsawat, in 2008, the removal from office of Prime Minister Yingluck Shinawatra (Thaksin's sister) by the Constitutional Court in 2014 and the military coup in the same year.

In spite of the accentuated discontinuity in the constitutional history of the country, the Thai constitutions have, however, maintained a fixed framework, represented by the form of monarchial-constitutional government, on which various mechanisms of *check and balances* between the fundamental powers of the state have been grafted from time to time. Constitutionalists have grouped the nineteen constitutional charters into three categories: a) "elected legislature" constitutions, in which the Parliament is elected directly by the electoral body; b) "mixed legislature" constitutions, where the Parliament is partly appointed by the executive (or in any case in such a way as to guarantee the Government's control over the parliamentary assembly) and "absolute executive" constitutions, where Parliament is completely absent or is appointed entirely by government.

The Constitution plays the role of superprimary source together with the constitutional laws (for example, that relating to the Royal Protocol). Beneath there are the ordinary laws, followed gradually by the royal and ministerial decrees, as secondary sources of law, and, finally, the regulations issued by the other local administrations. Tradition and analogy assume relevance as subsidiary sources, coming into consideration only in the event of a legislative gap.

Primarily based on written legislation, Thai law can therefore be equated to the legal systems belonging to the Roman-Germanic family: judicial rulings are not binding, although the decisions of the Supreme Court are endowed with considerable prestige and, consequently, also of persuasive effectiveness.

4.7.2 *The State Powers and the Local Administration*

The Constitution currently in force, the nineteenth in the history of Thailand, is the product of the military coup that took place in 2014 and brought to power a military junta that drafted a new constitutional text, subsequently approved with a popular referendum in 2016 and finally promulgated, with some successive amendments, by the king the following year.

The new constitutional text can be traced back to the "mixed legislature" constitutions: of the two Chambers that make up the Parliament, the *House of Representatives* is composed

19 For a reading on these institutional changes and the consequences on a constitutional level, *see* F. Munger, *Constitutional Reform, Legal Consciousness, and Citizen Participation in Thailand*, in *Cornell International Law Journal*, vol. 40, 2007, 455-475 and T. Ginsburg, *Constitutional Afterlife: The Continuing Impact of Thailand's Postpolitical Constitution*, in the *International Journal of Constitutional Law*, vol. 7, 2009, 83-105.

of 500 deputies directly elected by the people, 350 with the majority system, 150 with the proportional system (Arts. 83-92 Constitution), while the Senate is made up of 200 senators, appointed by and from among personages with experience and professionalism in various sectors of society (articles 107-113 of the Constitution). The term of office for the two branches of the Thai parliament does not coincide: a four-year term for the deputies, and a five-year term for the senators. What the text of the Constitution does not say explicitly is that the shadow of the influence of the military forces currently in power in the country markedly falls upon the nomination of the senators.[20]

The King is the head of state, a position endowed with a symbolic value (as a representative of the identity and unity of the nation), rather than of effective powers on the political level.[21] Succession takes place in the hereditary line. He is assisted in his duties by a privy council whose members are nominated by him. The president of this privy council acts as regent pending the proclamation of the successor to the throne at the moment of the death of the sovereign or in other cases of a vacant throne without other *pro tempore* rulers.

The executive is represented by the Council of Ministers, which must obtain the confidence of the Parliament. Leading the ministerial team is the Prime Minister, who cannot remain in office for a period of more than eight years, regardless of whether they are consecutive or not. The Council of Ministers is jointly accountable for its work; each minister is also *individually* liable to the *House of Representatives*, who after approval of a motion of no confidence may remove him from his office. The removal of a minister from his office also falls within the King's prerogatives, on the proposal of the Prime Minister.

The Thai justice system is organized on three levels: the courts of first instance, the Courts of Appeal and the Supreme Court. Administrative jurisdiction is entrusted to the Administrative Courts of the first instance and a Supreme Administrative Court.

The Constitutional Court supervises the constitutional legitimacy of laws and regulations. It is composed of 9 judges, appointed by a special selection committee: this appointment must receive approval from the Senate by an absolute majority of its members and be countersigned by the King. Nominations can be promoted by ordinary judges on the request of one of the parties. The rulings of the Constitutional Court are effective *erga omnes*. An individual citizen whose constitutionally guaranteed rights have been violated by the law may bring an action before the Court, as established by Article 213 of the Constitution.

---

20 In doctrine there are those who openly speak of illiberal constitutionalism: *see* E. Mèrieau, *The Legal-Military Alliance for Illiberal Constitutionalism in Thailand*, M. Bünte, B. Dressel (Eds.), *Politics and Constitutions in Southeast Asia*, London/New York, Routledge, 2016, 140-160.

21 Regarding the evolution of the role of the sovereign in the Thai constitutional system, *see* P. Panikabutara Coorey, *King's Influence on the Rule of Law in Thailand, UNSW Law Research Paper* No. 2010-30, 1-13.

In light of the constitution, thus, the judiciary and judges are guaranteed independence: the appointment, removal from office, disciplinary sanctions and promotions of individual judges are referred to a judicial commission, presided over by the President of the Supreme Court and composed of togated and non-togated members (Art. 196 of the Constitution).

The resolution of disputes in Thailand, as in other countries of Confucian tradition, frequently takes place in a friendly and conciliatory way: conciliation is therefore the preferential and most widespread instrument for settling disputes in civil and commercial matters.

With reference to administrative decentralization, the Thai territory is divided into 76 provinces (*changwat*), with financial and organizational autonomy, districts, sub-districts and villages. Two districts, the capital Bangkok and the tourist centre Pattaya, enjoy a special autonomy.

4.7.3 *Fundamental Rights and Freedoms*

The catalogue of rights in the Constitution of 2017 is long and articulated, as in those that preceded it, in 1997[22] and 2007. As often happens in more recent constitutions, this catalogue includes a series of new generation rights (the right to privacy, right of access to information, protection of consumers etc.), taken from previous texts of 1997 and 2007.

Furthermore, with Article 25, the Constitution recognizes and protects not only the fundamental rights expressly established by the Constitution itself, but also those recognized implicitly, provided that their exercise is not prohibited or subject to restrictions by the Constitution or the law or represents a danger to security, public order or morality or, ultimately, violates the rights and freedoms of others.

The principles of human dignity and equality are specifically outlined: to this end, Article 27 contemplates the possibility of positive actions to overcome inequalities and achieve substantial equality.

The constitutional text expressly contemplates the right of individuals and the community to use and preserve in a sustainable way natural resources, the environment and biodiversity (Art. 43 of the Constitution).

In order to guarantee a broader protection of rights and promote their knowledge and respect, in continuity with the 2007 Constitution, the *National Human Rights Commission* was envisaged, whose members are appointed by the King based on the proposals of the Senate. This Commission can send recommendations and remarks to the Parliament and the Council of Ministers, as well as an annual report; however, these duties encounter a

22 On the Thai Constitution of 1997, *see* B.B. Uwanno, D. Wayne, *The Thai Constitution of 1997: Sources and Process*, in *University of British Columbia Law Review*, 1998, 227 ff.; A. Harding, *May there be Virtue: 'New Asian Constitutionalism' in Thailand*, in the *Australian Journal of Asian Law*, vol. 3, 2001, 24 ff.

limit in the interests of the country and of the community, which the Commission must take into account in the performance of its functions (Arts. 246-247 of the Constitution).

In accordance with Article 96 of the constitution, persons suffering from mental disorders, those persons to whom the right to vote has been revoked, prisoners and Buddhist monks and novices, are excluded from the electorate. Furthermore, drug addicts (Art. 98, No. 1 of the Constitution) and those holding shares in the properties of newspapers or other mass media are also excluded from the active electorate. The provision is a clear reference to the conflict of interests for which Thaksin Shinawatra, Thai Prime Minister from 2001 to 2006 and businessman, owner of a financial holding company and a television network, found himself at the centre of a bitter controversy.

To date, the most critical aspects in the protection of fundamental rights appear to be the unrecognized protection for asylum seekers from the neighbouring countries, Laos and Burma (due to the fact that not having ratified the 1951 Geneva Convention on the Protection of Refugees, Thailand considers them to be illegal immigrants), the strong restrictions on the exercise of the rights of assembly and expression imposed to silence the dissent manifested towards the military junta in power, as well as the violence linked to the protests of the separatist groups operating in the south of the country, resulting in numerous fatalities above all among the Malaysian nationals.

4.8 VIETNAM

4.8.1 *Brief Constitutional History*

The history of Vietnam is marked by the influence of different cultural models, even more so by legal models, that have overlapped over the centuries. Vietnam, in fact, was subjected for a long period to the domination of the Chinese empire, although in remote eras (from the second century BC to 972 AD), and even after that date, Vietnamese legal development continued to be affected by the Chinese cultural influence (with particular regard to Confucian ethics), as emerges from the main Vietnamese legislative codifications, for the most part borrowed from the Chinese models: in modern times too, the code promulgated in 1812 by *Gia Long*, first emperor of the *Nguyen* dynasty, presented several similarities with the Chinese *Tang* and *Qing* codes.

At the turn of the nineteenth and twentieth century, the country endured the French occupation. In fact, Vietnam became part of French Indochina in 1887, freeing itself at the end of the Second World War, in 1945, under the leadership of Ho Chi Minh, the charismatic leader of the independence movement *Viet Minh*, later the prime minister, and finally the Vietnamese head of state. Divided as a result of the 1954 Geneva agreements into the pro-communist North Vietnam, and the pro-Western South Vietnam, supported by the United States, the country reunified just over 20 years later, on 2 July, 1976, at the end of a harsh and painful conflict, which saw the North Vietnamese troops victorious.

Vietnam, as can be noted form its official title, the Socialist Republic of Vietnam, today represents one of the few remaining socialist countries (along with the People's Republic of China, Laos, North Korea and Cuba), following the collapse of the USSR and the Eastern European countries that gravitated around the Soviet power.

This emerges from a certain rhetoric of a communist type that can be seen in its legislation (as will be seen later), as well as from the general establishment of state institutions, based on the principles of democratic centralism and socialist legality.[23]

4.8.2 *The State Powers and the Local Administration*

The current Constitution (adopted in 2013) is the fifth constitutional charter of Vietnam, after those of 1946, 1959, 1980 and 1992, which in a certain way, marked the stages of the evolution of the Communist Party of Vietnam (CPV). The new constitution adopted by Vietnam in 2013 partially innovated the constitutional system, exhibiting a greater emphasis on the protection of fundamental rights, but overall it left the existing equilibria, from a political-institutional point of view, unchanged, not welcoming the call for reform in the democratic-liberal sense raised by many parties, including those included in "Petition 72" formulated by a group of Vietnamese constitutionalists.

It is a rigid constitution (its revision requires a qualified majority of two-thirds of the National Assembly) and consists of 120 articles.

As in the texts that preceded it, the 2013 Constitution includes, in addition to a clear socialist imprint, a certain patriotic "inflection": to cite an example, Article 68 of the Constitution, on the issue of defence of the homeland, establishes the duty of the State to promote the full development of patriotism and "revolutionary heroism".

In light of the institutional structure outlined by the Constitution, the National Assembly (*Quoc Hoi*) is the main legislative body of a unicameral nature, entrusted with fundamental functions such as, the promulgation of the most important laws, the appointment of the highest offices of the State, the supervision on the constitutionality of legal acts of primary and secondary rank, as well as important duties in matters of state

23 *See* P. Nicholson, *Vietnamese Legal Institutions in Comparative Perspective: Constitutions and Courts Considered*, in K. Jayasuriya (Ed.), *Law, Capitalism and Power in Asia: The Rule of Law and Legal Institutions*, London/New York, Routledge, 1999; B. J.M. Quinn, *Legal Reform and Its Context in Vietnam*, in *Columbia Journal of Asian Law*, vol. 15, 2002,, 219-281; M. Sidel, *Law and Society in Vietnam*, New York, Cambridge University Press, 2008; M. Sidel, *The Constitution of Vietnam: A Contextual Analysis*, Oxford, 2009; J. Gillespie, A. Chen (Eds.), *Legal Reforms in China and Vietnam: A Comparison of Asian Communist Regimes*, London/New York, Routledge, 2010; Bui Ngoc Son, *The Law of China and Vietnam in Comparative Law*, in *Fordham International Law Journal*, vol. 41, 2017, 135-206.

finance and political direction (Article 70 of the Constitution). The National Assembly meets in plenary session only twice a year: for this reason it is flanked by a Standing Committee, which carries out most of the ordinary legislative activity, on the model of the homonymous organ envisaged by the Chinese Constitution.

The election of the 500 members of the National Assembly is formally based on the democratic principle of universal, secret, direct and equal suffrage. Nonetheless, the Vietnamese Communist Party benefits from a full control over the electoral system and the institutional apparatus, more generally, in light of the leading role that the Constitution itself attributes to it, as a vanguard and faithful representative of the interests of the working class, people engaged in struggles, and of the whole nation. The ideological base of reference for the CPV is constituted by Marxist-Leninist doctrine and by the thinking of the "father of the fatherland", Ho Chi Minh, expressly referred to by the constitutional text (Art. 4 of the Constitution). The Party is endowed with a sort of structure parallel to the formal institutional structure and exerts its influence on this latter.

The mandate of the deputies elected in the National Assembly has a duration of five years, unless revoked by the very same voters: in Vietnam, in fact, the institute, typical of socialist regulations, of the revocation of the electoral mandate, formally operates in the event that the voters' lose confidence in their representatives (Art. 7 of the Constitution) but de facto, occurs when the single party deems that a deputy deserves to be ousted.

In continuity with the previous constitutional charters, power is exercised jointly (i.e. rejecting the principle of the separation of powers, considered "bourgeois") by the National Assembly, at central level, and by the people's councils, at the local level, as an expression of the sovereignty of the people, being thus, the various functions delegated to other organs. In fact, in a similar way to other socialist countries, Vietnam is based on the principle of democratic centralism, by virtue of which the sovereign people exercise power through the National Assembly and the people's councils that it itself elects.

The executive functions are exercised by the Government, the head of the state administration, which is divided into people's committees located in the provinces and municipalities, in which the national territory is divided: at the head of the government sits the Prime Minister who is a member of the National Assembly and designates the other ministers, who are then nominated officially by the latter. He is responsible for the actions of his Government before the Assembly and may suspend or cancel decisions, directives and circulars of the Government, individual ministers, people's councils or presidents of people's committees (Art. 98 of the Constitution), in order to ensure the full implementation of government initiatives, with a view to better centre-periphery coordination and greater efficiency.

To counterbalance the authority attributed to the Prime Minister, there are the responsibilities of the President of the Republic, a figure already contemplated in the Constitutions of 1946 and 1960, but reduced to a merely ceremonial role at the death of the first Vietnamese president, Ho Chi Minh in 1969, and then replaced by the Council of State, a collegial body, in the 1980 constitution, and finally restored, in the 1992 constitution and confirmed in the current constitution. Chosen by the National Assembly among its members, for a term that lasts the same as that of the Assembly itself, the President represents the Republic, signs international agreements, promulgates the laws, designates candidates for the main institutional offices and can request their removal from office. He is the commander in chief of the armed forces, declares the state of war, and grants pardons (Art. 88 of the Constitution).

The Vietnamese judiciary apparatus is articulated on three levels, district, provincial and central; at its vertex, there is the Supreme Court of the People.

The President of the Supreme Court is appointed by the National Assembly on the recommendation of the President of the Republic. His term of office lasts five years, in a similar manner to that of the Assembly. The other judges of the Supreme Court are appointed directly by the President of the Republic.

The Constitution does not fail to recognize the fundamental principle of independence of the judiciary (but limited to the proceedings: Art. 103, para. 2, of the Constitution) and the right of a defence (Art. 103, para. 7 of the Constitution). Nonetheless, a power of control over the judiciary remains in the hands of the National Assembly and the councils of the judiciary: the judicial bodies respond, in fact, for their actions to the representative bodies of the same level. According to the Law on the judiciary of 2014, the mechanism for appointing judges underwent some changes (some indeed introduced earlier, in 2002): the judges of the Supreme Court are appointed by the National Assembly. The judges of the other courts are appointed by the President, on the recommendation of a special Council for the selection and supervision of judges. If, on the formal level, this "centralized" mechanism seems to offer greater guarantees than in the past, it cannot escape the observer the fact that the appointment remains subject to the approval of the Party: the candidate, in fact, in addition to an adequate legal preparation, honesty and professional experience, must have a "firm political position". In addition, judges are subject to external influences due to the fact that their term of office lasts ten years (the first term lasting five years), after which they can be reconfirmed: reconfirmation by the Council for the selection of judges, could prove to be difficult for judges deemed "inconvenient" or "not very collaborative".[24] In addition, judges are not guaranteed immovability: they can in fact be transferred in order to ensure the functioning of the judicial offices. In the hypothesis of a transfer from one court to another placed in the same district, this is ordered by the President of the People's Court of the province. Vice versa, if the transfer takes place from one district to another, this is arranged by the President of the Supreme Court of the people. It is evident

24 P. Nicholson, *The Vietnamese Judiciary: The Politics of Appointment and Promotion*, in *Pacific Rim Law & Policy Journal*, vol. 14, 2005, 1-33.

that even a transfer can assume a sanctioning capacity towards judges not aligned with the indications of the Party.

The Penal Code and the Code of Criminal Procedure, both dating back to 2015, echo and integrate the constitutional guarantees, incorporating fundamental principles such as the presumption of innocence, the right to a fair trial of a reasonable duration, the prohibition of arrest unless as a result of a ruling of a people's court or a public prosecutor's office, except in cases of *in flagrante delicto*, the prohibition of torture or other treatments that harm human dignity.

The people's public prosecutors are given extensive investigative powers that go beyond the limits of criminal matters in the strict sense, having as their object any activity, carried out by private citizens or public administrations, that could lead to a violation of the law: this has determined the so-called penalization of civil law, a phenomenon that some have traced back to ideological factors, resulting in the private sector being viewed with some suspicion.

Vietnam is a unitary state. Its territory is divided into 58 provinces (*tinh*) and 5 municipalities (*thanh pho*) placed under the direct control of the Government. The provinces are, in turn, divided into districts and the districts into municipalities, cities and constituencies. Local government, according to a system that has many similarities with the Chinese system, is entrusted to local administrative units, organized in people's councils and people's committees in each level (provincial, district, sub-district). Some are elected directly by the people and respond to the people and people's councils of higher level (for example, the district council responds to that of the provincial level, the latter responds to the council of higher level, i.e. the National Assembly); the others represent the executive organ at the local level and are accountable for their operate both towards the hierarchically superior bodies (the people's committees of a higher level) and towards the people's councils of the same level, who nominate them, in accordance with the principle of dual dependency.

The Vietnamese economic constitution, over time, has undergone a series of reform interventions (be it a constitutional revision or a constitutional charter adopted *ex novo*), which have helped to change its aspect with respect to its original connotations. These changes have taken place in a climate of a gradual transition from a planned socialist economy to a mixed market economy.

The first, profound changes are linked to the reform policy adopted by the Communist Party of Vietnam during its VI Congress, initiated in 1986: the so-called *Doi Moi* (Renovation), was inspired by the economic reform desired and promoted a few years earlier by Deng Xiaoping in China.

Thus, following the Chinese example, economic policy is based on "market socialism" (a principle acknowledged in the Constitution itself, Art. 51), a hybrid figure that is based on the market, but does not abandon the leading role played by the state economy; in contrast to previous economic policies, equal importance is explicitly acknowledged to all economic actors, regardless of the sector to which they belong (public or private), where previously public ownership (state and collective) formed the foundation of the system (Art. 15 of the Constitution 1992).

In a similar way to China, the ownership of land belongs to "all the people" (Art. 53 of the Constitution), in the name and on behalf of which the State manages its use, assigning to natural or legal persons, the right to use the land, which can be revoked by the State only for the purposes of national defence, national security, or public interests related to socio-economic development, in exchange for compensation (Art. 54 of the Constitution).

The constitutional foundation for the protection of private property is represented by Article 32 of the Constitution, which, contrary to the dictates of "pure" socialist doctrine, permits private property also for the means of production. The Civil Code of 2015, however, more fully regulates the institution, laying down the legal conditions for the establishment, transfer and termination of this right as well as forms of protection.[25]

Legitimately owned assets cannot be expropriated, except where absolutely necessary for needs related to defence, security, national interest, emergency or natural disasters and on the condition of fair compensation, which takes into account current market prices (Art. 32 of the Constitution).

4.8.3 Fundamental Rights and Freedoms

The position of the catalogue of fundamental rights in the constitutional charter of 2013 has significantly changed compared to the previous texts, having been placed before Chapter III regarding the economy and society.

The constitutional text solemnly sanctions the respect of political, civil, economic, cultural and social human rights (Art. 14 of the Constitution) and the principle of equality, albeit merely formal and with a stringent formulation as per Art. 16 of the constitution; however, positive provisions are envisaged in subsequent provisions to guarantee equal rights and opportunities in the field of gender discrimination and in favour of some disadvantaged groups. It also contemplates the inviolability of the person, together with the protection, in particular, of life, health, honour and dignity (Art. 20 of the Constitution), as well as a long list of individual rights and freedoms: the right to education, private economic initiative, private property, health, work, freedom of movement, opinion, the press, assembly, information, association, demonstration, religion, etc.

However, the exercise of these prerogatives encounters strong limitations on a formal level, as well as in fact: first of all, the rights are declared inseparable from the duties

---

25 On the civil codification process in Vietnam, *cf.* A. Serafino, *Il processo di codificazione in Vietnam (il codice civile e la legge commerciale)*, in *Riv dir. civ.*, 2001, I, 665-702.

established by law and the Constitution. Thus, from a socialist perspective, it is the duty of every citizen to participate in maintaining national security and social order (Art. 46 of the Constitution, toned down in relation to the corresponding provision of the 1992 Constitution that required all citizens "to help protect public property, legitimate rights and interests, maintain national security and social order and organize public life"). With respect to the past, the text of the Constitution is devoid of the ban on the diffusion of anything that can be considered "reactionary culture" (Art. 30 of the Constitution 1992) and restrictions on the freedom to carry out cultural and information activities, if they are deemed contrary to the national interest (Art. 33 of the Constitution of 1992). Nonetheless, some important limitations remain in primary legislation: for example, the 2016 Law on publishing entrusts the media with the main task of spreading the lines and policies of the CPV, being the press considered the "Party voice", even before that of the state agencies, social and professional organizations and "people's forum" (Art. 4). Furthermore, criminal law punishes the "abuse of democratic freedoms in order to harm the interests of the State and the legitimate rights and interests of other citizens or bodies" (Art. 331 penal code).

Added to this, there is a restrictive application practice in relation to the exercise of rights, in particular freedom of association, expression and religion, despite the fact that Vietnam is a member of the International Covenant on Civil and Political Rights: complaints are frequent, raised above all by the NGOs, concerning the arrest of human rights activists, bloggers and political dissidents and campaigns of persecution to the detriment of some ethnic groups, the *Khmer Krom*, in the *An Giang* province, and the *Degar* (known as the *Montagnards*, a name attributed to them stemming from the French colonization of Indochina) on the Central Highlands.

On the other hand, from the point of view of the protection of fundamental rights, some progress has been made in the fight against poverty and following the repeal of the CP-31 decree governing the institution of administrative detention.

4.9 Laos

4.9.1 Brief Constitutional History

The region that today corresponds to Laos was unified under the reign of Lan Xang in the fourteenth century. Part of the kingdom of Siam (current Thailand) from 1778, it was then integrated into French Indochina in the late nineteenth century, achieving independence in 1953, as a constitutional monarchy, with the official name of the Kingdom of Laos.

Although formally neutral under the Geneva Accords, Laos was drawn into the Vietnam War, owing to the fact that along its territory, parallel to the Vietnam border, the Vietminh guerrillas had set up their supply lines, known as the "Ho Chi Minh Path", which from

North Vietnam, along the Annamite mountain chain, carried weapons and other supplies to South Vietnam. Precisely due to the strategic importance of this path, which ran mainly in its territory, Laos suffered repeated and heavy aerial bombardment from the US.

In 1975, the communist movement *Pathet Lao* came to power, forcing the king to abdicate and proclaiming the Lao People's Democratic Republic; in those years and in those that followed, due to the conflict, hardships and the changed political framework, hundreds of thousands of Laotian citizens left the country (approximately a tenth of the population), seeking asylum in neighbouring Thailand.[26]

Laos is still today a single-party socialist republic (the Lao People's Revolutionary Party), in a similar way to Vietnam, in accordance with the model represented by the People's Republic of China. Due to the fact that it is closely aligned with Vietnam's policies, Laos has long been regarded as a puppet state of Vietnam.

4.9.2 The State Powers and the Local Administration

In the Laos Constitution, which was last amended in 2015, one can find the principle of democratic centralism (Art. 5 of the Constitution) and the leading role of the Laos People's Revolutionary Party (Art. 3 of the Constitution) established, in analogy with the Vietnamese and Chinese constitutions.

A cautious process of democratization was undertaken at the end of the 1980s, in parallel with the gradual economic liberalization undertaken, based on the Chinese and Vietnamese model.

The traditional tri-partition of powers is not acknowledged in the Laos Constitution, due to the fact that these powers are all entrusted to the National Assembly, an elected unicameral organ that represents the sovereign people. It directly exercises the legislative function and, indirectly, the executive and judicial functions, through control and appointment mechanisms. The National Assembly, in fact, has the power to appoint, and potentially revoke, the highest offices of the state (the President of the Republic, the Prime Minister, the President of the Supreme People's Court and the President of the Supreme Public Prosecutor's Office). Moreover, it has a specific power of interpellation, which assumes a significant political role, with regard to the Prime Minister, the President of the Republic, individual Ministers, the President of the Supreme People's Court and that of the Supreme Public Prosecutor's Office, who are called to respond for their actions in oral or written form, in accordance with Article 63 of the Constitution.

---

26 For the historical context, *see*, W.C. Robinson, *Laotian Refugees in Thailand: The Thai and US Response, 1975 to 1988*, in J.J. Zasloff, L. Unger, Leonard (Eds.), *Laos: Beyond the Revolution*, London, Macmillan, 1991, 215 ff.

In the exercise of its functions, the Assembly is flanked by a Standing Committee, a body composed of the President and the Vice-President of the Assembly and a smaller number of its members, reproducing, in essence, the paradigm represented by the constitutions of the PRC and Vietnam. The Standing Committee is responsible, among other things, for preparing the sessions of the National Assembly, appointing judges, interpreting the Constitution and laws, monitoring the activities of the executive bodies, popular courts and public prosecutor's office (Art. 56 of the Constitution).

As previously stated, there is no real political debate, as evidenced by the last elections held in 2016, resulting in 144 of the 149 seats of the National Assembly being allocated to the Laos People's Revolutionary Party.

The President of the Republic promulgates the laws, proposes, to the National Assembly, the person to be appointed as Prime Minister, nominates the vice presidents of the Supreme People's Court and the Supreme Public Prosecutor Office on the recommendation of the respective Presidents. Furthermore he is the commander in chief of the Armed Forces and ratifies international treaties.

The Government is mainly entrusted with executive functions. Therefore, its duties include firstly the implementation of the laws and the management of central and local administration. The Government also concludes international treaties, proposes laws, adopts decrees, and organizes the security forces and national defence.

The relationship between the Government and Parliament is peculiar: the latter can pass a vote of no confidence in the former, but the President of the Republic can request the Assembly to reconsider this vote of no confidence. Should the President intervene to this effect, the Government is obliged to resign only if the Assembly confirms for a second time the previously expressed vote of no confidence (Art. 74 of the Constitution). On its actions, the Government reports both to the Assembly and the President of the Republic.

The Supreme People's Court is at the vertex of the judiciary, and is composed of district courts, provincial courts and courts of appeal. Concurrently, the Supreme Public Prosecutor's Office is at the vertex of a structure of public' prosecutor's offices located throughout the territory at various levels. The Supreme Court and the Supreme Prosecutor's Office supervise the work of their subordinated offices.

Around the end of the 1980s the so-called New Economic Mechanism (*Rabop Mai*) was initiated, aimed at reforming the economy, with a gradual opening of the markets. Laos opted, in a similar way to Vietnam and the PRC, for a "oriented" market economy, that is to say, combined with elements of state socialist control (Art. 18 of the Constitution).[27]

---

27 On the evolutionary processes of constitutional identities at the global level and in particular of socialist countries, *see*, recently, Son Ngoc Bui, *Globalization of Constitutional Identity*, in the *Washington International Law Journal*, vol. 26, 2017, 463-533. In this regard, the author finds in the constitutions of Vietnam

Private property is today constitutionally guaranteed together with state and collective property (Art. 16 of the Constitution); all economic sectors benefit from equal protection.

The various constitutional provisions that revoke the importance of international economic cooperation and protection reserved for foreign investment can be related to the interest that the Laos government has shown for the *World Trade Organization*, which it requested to join in 1997. The phase of the necessary negotiations was completed more than fifteen years later and in 2013 Laos became officially a member, after having joined ASEAN in 1997.

The Lao People's Democratic Republic is a unitary state. The local administration is articulated on three levels: provincial (which includes provinces and cities), district (which includes districts and municipalities) and village. In general, each level has the function of implementing laws, orders and decrees coming from the hierarchically superior levels and, at the same time, controls the actions of the administrative authorities placed at the lower level. In particular, the head of the municipality is responsible for urban planning, with village leaders having the responsibility of guaranteeing public order and peace within their territory.

4.9.3 *Fundamental Rights and Freedoms*

The protection of fundamental rights in the legal system of Laos encounters profound contradictions. If on the one hand, the constitution solemnly proclaims these rights, starting with Article 5, recognizing, at least from a formal point of view, the principle of equality, the right to education, work, the vote, freedom of movement, opinion, press, assembly, association and religion; on the other hand, Laos has obtained, in fact, in the international statistics drawn up by international humanitarian organizations, the worst records in terms of effectiveness of protection,[28] due to the strong restrictions on the exercise of civil and political liberties: reference is made here, first of all, the control over the media, but also the repression carried out via arbitrary forms of arrest and detention against those who manifest political dissent.

Moreover, although the Constitution in several passages refers to the multi-ethnic dimension of the country, nonetheless the protection of these minorities is subject to various limitations. In particular, the *Hmong* ethnic group, concentrated in the central and northern areas of the country, is the subject of real persecution campaigns: the ethnic question is intertwined with political problems. Indeed the *Hmong* are considered "collab-

---

and Laos the dynamics of "constitutional globalism", while the People's Republic of China is traced back to the different phenomenon of "exceptionalism", highlighting its "eccentric" scope.

28 For example, the statistics of *Freedom House* or the *reports* of *Human Rights Watch* and *Amnesty International.*

orators", due to the fact that many *Hmong* soldiers were recruited by the United States to fight alongside them during the Vietnam conflict.

A last disturbing fact is represented by the trafficking in human beings, a phenomenon that the Laotian authorities are not able to counter effectively: many Laotian citizens fall victim to labour exploitation and prostitution, often in neighbouring Thailand.

4.10 CAMBODIA

4.10.1 *Brief Constitutional History*

The first among the countries of Southeast Asia to borrow political institutions and religious traditions from India, Cambodia experienced for almost a century French colonial domination, which ended in 1954. Following its proclamation of independence, the history of Cambodia was however tormented, and for a long period long marked by the political instability and the dictatorship of Pol Pot (whose real name was Saloth Sar), prime minister and leader of the "Khmer Rouge" movement, between 1975 and 1979: in those years, hundreds of thousands of people lost their lives as a result of summary executions and internments in labour camps (the most recent estimates, still debated, amount to one million seven hundred thousand people, equal to more than 20% of the Cambodian population).

Cambodia was then invaded by Vietnam and this brought with it a new phase of civil conflict, which ended only 20 years later, in 1998.

In 2001, with the assistance of the United Nations, a special tribunal was established for crimes of war and against humanity committed by the Khmer Rouge between 1975 and 1979, which sentenced several perpetrators to life imprisonment.[29] Some difficulties in the proceedings were encountered in relation to the involvement in the cases *de quo* of some members of the current political-military hierarchy of the country.

The Cambodian legal framework is very varied, inspired by the French legal tradition, but with elements also stemming from customary law, from the *common law*, as well as echoes of the legal system of communist matrix (a legacy of the Vietnamese influence period, in the eighties).

After joining ASEAN in 1999, at the Cancun summit, Cambodia also joined the WTO, in September 2003

29 Regarding the contribution made by the Special Court in ascertaining the responsibilities of the crimes committed during the Khmer Rouge regime and more generally the international criminal justice system, *see* S.M. Meisenberg, I. Stegmiller, *The Extraordinary Chambers in the Courts of Cambodia. Assessing Their Contribution to International Criminal Law*, Berlin, Springer, 2016.

4.10.2 The State Powers and the Local Administration

With the Constitution approved in 1993, still in force, the fifth in the history of the country,[30] the monarchy was restored: therefore, to date, Cambodia is a parliamentary monarchy. Succession to the throne does not take place on an inheritance basis (Art. 10 of the Constitution), but via election. The king is chosen by a special Royal Council of the Throne, consisting of the President and two vice-presidents of the National Assembly, the President and two vice-presidents of the Senate, the Prime Minister and the leaders of the two main monastic orders (*Mahanikaya* and *Dhammayutikanikaya*) of *Theravada* Buddhism. To be elected as ruler of Cambodia, the candidate must be over 30 years of age and belong to the royal family: the king must indeed be a direct descendant of one of the three monarchs who succeeded one another between the end of the nineteenth century and the beginning of the twentieth century. The queen is instead relegated to a mere supporting role, being precluded from any political commitment: as expressly stated in the constitution, she must dedicate herself to social and humanitarian interests and support the king in his diplomatic and protocol duties.

Although he holds the position of Head of State, as well as being a symbol of national unity and guarantor of independence, sovereignty of the country and respect for international treaties on citizens' rights and freedoms, the sovereign does not have autonomous powers of a political nature, but rather is called upon to perform his specific duties, when required, by the Government. Art. 17 of the Constitution reinforces this norm ("the sovereign reigns but does not govern"), establishing its firm and binding nature.

Among the main functions of the king is the appointment of the Prime Minister and Ministers, the promulgation of laws passed to the Parliament, the ratification of international treaties (subject to the prior approval of the two branches of Parliament), and he is the command in chief of the Royal Cambodian Armed Forces.

The Cambodian Constitution, the result of a collaboration with some organizations (such as the *United Nations Transitional Authority of Cambodia*, UNTAC), which was recently subjected to a constitutional revision in 2014, explicitly acknowledges in Article 51, the principle of the separation of powers, entrusting legislative power to Parliament, which is composed of two Chambers, the National Assembly, elected directly by the people, and the Senate, indirectly elected.

---

30 On the constitutional history of Cambodia, a wide panorama is offered by P. Hor, P. Kong, J. Menzel (Eds.), *Cambodian Constitutional Law*, Phnom Penh, Konrad-Adenauer Stiftung, 2016. *See also* J. Menzel, *Cambodia – From Civil War to a Constitution to Constitutionalism?*, in C. Hill, J. Menzel, Jörg (Eds.), *Constitutionalism in Southeast Asia*. Vol. 2: *Reports on National Constitutions*, Singapore, Konrad-Adenauer Stiftung, 2008, 39-68 and S.P. Marks, *The Process of Creating a New Constitution in Cambodia*, in L.E. Miller (Ed.), *Framing the State in Times of Transition: Case Studies in Constitution Making*, Washington (DC), United States Institute of Peace, 2010, 207-244.

Indeed, the political weight of the Cambodian parliament is relatively weak compared to the other institutions, notably the Government. This is evident, in particular, in the legislative process, where the vast majority of legislative proposals are government initiatives and the percentage of approval of bills without amendments or merely marginal amendments, is very high.[31]

The members of the National Assembly (at least 120 in number) are elected every five years with a proportional electoral system. There is no vote for Cambodian citizens living abroad. The members of the Senate, on the other hand, are appointed every six years by the sovereign (two senators) and by the National Assembly by a relative majority (two senators). The remaining senators are elected via "restricted" suffrage (Art. 100 of the Constitution), by members of the municipal councils and the National Assembly. The Cambodian Senate is therefore a hybrid, presenting, at the same time, elements referring to the monarchy, via the senators of royal nomination, elements referring to the parliament, through the senators of parliamentary nomination and local administrations. Originally, the 1993 Constitution envisaged a single-chamber parliament; bicameralism was introduced (*rectius*, reintroduced[32]) with the constitutional revision of 1999 to overcome the stalemate resulting from a political crisis, in which no party had reached the threshold of consensus necessary to govern. The Senate was therefore envisaged as a solution of political-institutional compromise with the aim of achieving a national reconciliation between the opposing political forces.

The National Assembly is entrusted with the approval of laws, including those of the budget, amnesty, proclamation of war, and control over the Government, exercised through a vote of confidence and the proposition of questions, functions shared with the Senate, albeit with some significant differences: the latter, in fact, participates in the legislative procedure with a merely advisory role, being able to express its opinion on the bills or legislative proposals, and with the power to propose amendments in the time limit, indeed short, of one month or, in cases declared urgent, of five days (Art. 113 of the Constitution). The last word in the final approval of the laws lies with the National Assembly: in fact, a rejection by the Senate of a bill in its entirety has the only effect of postponing the final approval to a second reading by the other Chamber, which must approve the project with an open vote by an absolute majority.

Furthermore, underlining the different political weight between the two chambers of the Cambodian parliament is the control function on the Government, due to the fact that

---

31 Reported by Norbert Feige, a German legal advisor to the Cambodian Parliament for several years: N. Feige, *The National Assembly of the Kingdom of Cambodia*, in P. Hor, P. Kong, J. Menzel (Eds.), *Cambodian Constitutional Law*, cit.op., 113.

32 It was a return, due to the fact that there was in fact a second chamber, it was envisaged during the Khmer Republic, before the communist regimes of the democratic Cambodia and the Popular Republic of Cambodia in the seventies and eighties of the twentieth century adopted a unicameral parliament, in line with the socialist tradition.

the Senate is deprived of the fundamental instruments represented by the initial confidence vote and the motion of no confidence, which instead are entrusted to the National Assembly, in Articles. 90 and 98 of the constitution.

Executive power lies with the Cambodian Government, which is formed by the Prime Minister, the Deputy-Prime Ministers, senior ministers, ministers and secretaries of state. The Prime Minister is appointed by the King, among the members of the National Assembly who belong to the party that was victorious in the elections: indeed, since 1998 Cambodia has always had the same Head of Government without interruption, Hun Sen, a prominent figure of the Cambodian People's Party. In addition to the typical functions of the executive, the Government has the power of legislative initiative, guaranteeing public order, conducting national, fiscal and foreign defence policies, enacting regulations, as well as that of promoting national reconciliation, culture and national identity.

The judiciary, with the Supreme Court at its vertex, is an independent power and guarantor of the impartiality and rights and liberties of citizens. The King is delegated with the task of ensuring the independence of the judiciary and individual judges, assisted by the Supreme Council of the Judiciary, a self-governing body with disciplinary powers. Peculiarities in the Cambodian system, however, are represented by the fact that the Minister of Justice is one of the members of the Supreme Council.

The Constitutional Council is entrusted with a control on the constitutionality of laws, to which the King, the Prime Minister, the President of the National Assembly, the President of the Senate, 1/4 of the Senators or 1/10 of the members of the National Assembly and the courts, can file an appeal (Art. 141 of the Constitution). Citizens are entitled to raise a question of constitutionality only through the Presidents or the members of one of the two chambers. The control of constitutionality can be anticipatory (and which has as its subject matter laws not yet promulgated by the King), as well as subsequent. The Constitutional Council is also consulted by the King regarding constitutional revision proposals. A further duty of the Constitutional Council is to judge disputes in electoral matters. In exercising this last function, the Council has been criticized regarding its neutrality and independence, criticisms that have partly affected its prestige.

The Kingdom of Cambodia is a unitary state. At a local level, administration is entrusted to the *Reach Theany* (the capital city of the kingdom), *Khet* (provinces), *Krong* (municipalities), *Srok* (districts), *Khan* (arrondissements), *Khum* (municipalities) and *Sangkat* (neighbourhoods).

4.10.3 *Fundamental Rights and Freedoms*

The Cambodian Constitution presents a broad list of rights, including social rights and the protection of minors and women from economic and sexual exploitation (Arts. 46-48 of the Constitution), which evoke a phenomenon that is unfortunately widely present in the country.[33]

Political rights, first of all, encounter a series of restrictions. For the duration of the electoral campaign (*rectius*, in the 21 days preceding the date set for the elections) non-governmental organizations must maintain a neutral behaviour, refraining from uttering "insults". The references envisaged by the Cambodian Electoral Law adopted in 2015, seem generic and easily usable in an instrumental way by the authorities to silence voices of political dissent.

Furthermore, in November 2017, the Supreme Court ordered the dissolution of the main opposition political party, the Cambodia National Salvation Party, on the basis of reasons considered to be rather vague.[34] This event was condemned by international public opinion as a blow to the multi-party system and the fragile democracy of the country.[35]

Civil rights also have limited protection in Cambodia:[36] although expressly contemplated by the constitutional charter, the fundamental freedoms of peaceful assembly, opinion and press (Art. 41 of the Constitution) are subject to repeated violations by the authorities in the name of public order and security.

On the other hand, in a state that identifies Buddhism as its state religion, freedom of religious belief, acknowledged in Art. 43 of the Constitution, is guaranteed in an effective manner in its various facets, by the freedom to adhere to or renounce a religious faith, freedom of worship, freedom to form or join religious associations, or to proselytize, etc.[37]

---

33 The data provided by various humanitarian organizations present in Cambodia confirm a widespread use of child labour, employed in agriculture, in industry, even in illicit activities such as drug trafficking and sexual exploitation.

34 Previously, the party had boycotted the National Assembly, refusing to take part in parliamentary work for a year. The boycott ended following a compromise with the majority party (the Cambodian People's Party).

35 Among all, *see* the communiqué issued by the UN High Commissioner for Human Rights on 17 November 2017: http://www.ohchr.org/EN/NewsEvents/Pages/DisplayNews.aspx?NewsID=22406&LangID=E (consulted 27 December 2017).

36 Serious deficiencies in the system of protection (including jurisdiction) of fundamental rights had already been reported in the work: Basil, Fernando, *Problems Facing the Cambodian Legal System*, the Asian Human Rights Commission, 1998.

37 P. Kong, *Freedom of Religion in Cambodia*, in P. Hor, P. Kong, J. Menzel (Eds.), *Cambodian Constitutional Law*, op cit., 438.

4.11 Burma-Myanmar

4.11.1 Brief Constitutional History

Burma, whose political-institutional history is still very tormented, was a colony of the British crown dating from 1886, first in conjunction with India, and subsequently, independently, dating from 1937, until 1948, the year of the proclamation of its independence.

Following a coup in 1988, the group headed by the vertexes of the Burmese armed forces, and which paradoxically bears the name of the *State Peace and Development Council* (SPDC), took power, changed the name of the country from *Burma* into *Myanmar*[38] and suspended the 1974 Constitution. The country remained virtually devoid of a fundamental law until 2008, when a new constitutional charter was adopted after being approved in a referendum, which contributed to consolidating the political power of the SDPC.

Although the last elections saw the victory of the *National League for Democracy* (NLD) party led by Aung San Suu Kyi, the role of the military forces in the institutional framework of the country remains very strong, as does a hostile attitude towards the other political forces. This is borne out by the story of the NLD leader, awarded the Nobel Peace Prize in 1991, who, for years had been subjected to house arrest (first from 1989 to 1995, then from 2000 to 2002, and finally from 2003 to 2010, when she was released following international pressure).

On the occasion of the 2012 supplementary elections, Aung San Suu Kyi was elected a member of the Lower House (*Pyithu Hluttaw*) of the Burmese Parliament, and at present she holds the posts of Councillor of State, Foreign Minister and Minister of the Presidential Office.

Nonetheless, she could not accede to the office of president of the country, although she wished to run in the presidential elections of 2015, due to the fact that the current constitutional text (Art. 59(f) of the Constitution) requires full Burmese citizenship not only for the Head of State, but also of their parents, spouse, children and sons and daughters in law. This rule is considered by many to be a solution clearly designed to preclude Aung San Suu Kyi's succession to such an office, given that her children are of British citizenship. As will be seen later, the attempt to reform the Constitution carried forward by the NLD before the presidential elections did not come to a successful conclusion.

The picture is still very uncertain: after 50 years of almost uninterrupted military regime (1962-2011), the country has equipped itself with a parliamentary republic form of government, while still maintaining some peculiar characteristics, typical of a military type regime,

38 In 1989 the military junta chose to change its name to Myanmar (the full name is the Republic of Myanmar), but the name was not universally acceptEd. Both names refer to the majority ethnic group in the country; here they are used interchangeably.

for example: the constitutional provision that establishes that 25% of the members of the two chambers of the Assembly of the Union be appointed by the military (Arts. 74, 109 and 141 of the Constitution).

The Burmese legal system inherited the legal tradition of *common law,* a legacy from its period of British colonization, although little has remained from that tradition, following the subsequent legal and political developments that have affected the country, leading to the introduction of legislation in contrast with the Anglo-Saxon legal heritage and an institutional structure in which the judiciary lacks the necessary independence.[39]

Finally, Burma has been a member country of ASEAN, since 1997, and of the WTO, since 1995.

4.11.2 The State Powers and the Local Administration

Today Burma is undergoing a delicate transition from a military dictatorship to a democracy. The constitution currently in force is that of 2008, desired and "written" by the group of the SPDC and bears, therefore, still traces of the previous military regime,[40] as can be deduced from the incumbent presence of the Armed Forces (*Tatmadaw*) in almost all the institutions.

The party of Aung San Suu Kyi (NLD), which also won an absolute majority in both chambers at the last legislative elections, failed to achieve the democratic reforms it had set itself. Among these, in particular, the proposed constitutional reform proposed in 2015 and aimed at lowering the quorum required for the review of the fundamental charter, from 75% to 70%.

The Burmese Constitution, in fact, is rigid and can be reviewed only with the favourable vote of three quarters of the members of both Chambers (and, in some matters, added to the vote of the Chambers with the same qualified majority, the necessary approval with a popular referendum, is required). This 75% threshold, which has remained unchanged, essentially imposes the consent of the parliamentary component of military nomination, which therefore still benefits from a real power of veto.

In the framework outlined by the 2008 Constitution, the President of the Republic is elected by a constituency that includes members of the Parliament and the personnel of the Armed Forces. He promulgates the laws, with the right to refer these laws back to Parliament with his own observations (albeit the legislative assembly can decide not to

---

39 On the stratification of different legal traditions in Burmese law, refer to the following contribution: M. Crouch, *The Layers of Legal Development in Myanmar*, in M. Crouch, T. Lindsey (Eds.), *Law, Society and Transition in Myanmar*, Oxford/Portland (OR), Hart, 2014, 33-58.

40 On critical positions, *see*, on this point D.C. Williams, *What's So Bad about Burma's 2008 Constitution? A Guide for the Perplexed*, in M. Crouch, T. Lindsey (Eds.), *Law, Society and Transition in Myanmar*, op cit., 117-139.

follow these suggestions). He concludes international agreements, sends messages to the Chambers, appoints ministers in collaboration with the Supreme Commander of the Forces Armies, as well as the judges of the Supreme Court.

Legislative power is entrusted to the Assembly of the Union (*Pyidaungsu Hluttaw*), a bicameral parliament composed of a lower house, the *Pyithu Hluttaw* (the House of Representatives) whose members are elected on a municipal basis, and by the *Myotha Hluttaw* (the House of Nationalities) whose members represent the states and regions. As previously stated, a quarter of the seats in both branches of the Burmese Parliament are reserved for persons belonging to the ranks of the Armed Forces, appointed by the Supreme Commander.

Parliament has residual legislative power over all matters that do not fall within the list of those attributed to the legislative competence of the regions, states and autonomous areas.

The State Counsellor is invested with the same functions as those of a Prime Minister, an office created ad hoc for Aung San Suu Kyi in 2012. Military control extends like a shadow even on the Executive: several ministers (the Minister of Defence, Minister of Internal Affairs and the Minister of Border Affairs) are selected by the Supreme Commander of the Armed Forces and are themselves active military servicemen.

The Supreme Court of the Union (Art. 18 of the Constitution) is at the head of the judiciary, which in line with the Anglo-Saxon tradition can emit *writs* (*habeas corpus, mandamus, certiorari,* etc.). Below are the High Courts, operating at the state or regional level and the municipal or district courts. The judges of the Supreme Court are chosen by the President of the Republic; however, their appointment is subject to the approval of the Assembly of the Union, which may refuse if it considers that the chosen person does not meet the requirements of Article 301 of the Constitution.

The Constitutional Tribunal is entrusted with the task of judging the constitutional legitimacy of the laws of the Republic, regional, state and autonomous areas and the regulations of the executive, as well as deciding disputes between the Union and Region or State or between Regions, etc.

The local administrative levels contemplated by the current Myanmar Constitution are: villages, neighbourhoods, municipalities, districts and finally states or regions, in addition to autonomous administrative areas. Also at the local level, representatives of the Armed Forces sit in the assemblies and governments of the regions and states (Arts. 161 and 262 of the Constitution).

4.11.3 Fundamental Rights and Freedoms

The Burmese Constitution of 2008 envisages a catalogue of duties and rights, which seems to be unbalanced in favour of one another, and, among the latter, social and economic rights with respect to civil and political rights.

Emphasis is attributed to peace and public order, whose maintenance is specifically envisaged as the duty of every citizen (Arts. 21(c) and 387 of the Constitution). Restrictions on the formation of political parties (Art. 407 of the Constitution) are varied.

In matters of religious freedom, it is expressly forbidden to exploit religion for political purposes (Art. 364).

Turning to the plan of effectiveness of protection, the country is in the international limelight also as a result of the obvious violations of rights, especially with regard to certain ethnic minorities, and fundamental freedoms of expression and assembly, violations that have been followed by official sanctions adopted by the United States and the European Union.

Although some timid steps towards the establishment of democracy have been undertaken (for example, the release of 200 political prisoners in 2016 is a positive sign), the situation has plummeted in recent years in the Rakhine state, in the north-western part of the country, where the *Rohingya* ethnic minority of Muslim faith[41] was subjected to violence and rape, which resulted in a mass exodus of the *Rohingya* to Bangladesh. Despite appeals from government organizations (primarily the United Nations High Commissioner for Refugees) and international non-governmental organizations, the migration and humanitarian crisis is still ongoing and far from finding a solution.

41 E. Abdelkader, *Myanmar's Democracy Struggle: The Impact of Communal Violence Upon Rohingya Women and Youth*, in *Pacific Rim Law & Policy Journal*, vol. 23, n. 3, 2014, 511-542.

Comparative Public Law Treatise

Founded and directed by Giuseppe Franco Ferrari

Vincenzo De Falco, Administrative Action and Procedures in Comparative Law, 2018, ISBN 978-94-6236-842-2

Silvio Gambino, Jorge Lozano Miralles, Fernando Puzzo, Juan José Ruiz Ruiz, The Spanish Constitutional System, 2018, ISBN 978-94-6236-843-9

Eloy Garcia, Elisabetta Palici di Suni, Martin Rogoff, Direct Democracy in Comparative Law, 2018, ISBN 978-94-6236-844-6

Mauro Mazza (Ed.), The Constitutional Systems of East Asia, 2019, ISBN 978-94-6236-898-9